Clem Marshall

Being Cheddo

ATROPOS
ATROPOS PRESS
new york • dresden

Clem Marshall

Being Cheddo

**A Pan-Afrikanist Rastafari-Inspired
Melding of the Mind**

ATROPOS

THINK MEDIA SERIES IS SUPPORTED BY THE EUROPEAN
GRADUATE SCHOOL

ATROPOS PRESS
new york | dresden

151 FIRST AVENUE # 14, NEW YORK, N.Y. 10003
MOCKRITZER STR. 6, D-01219, DRESDEN, GERMANY

BOOK INTERIOR DESIGN BY: MILENE NEY
COVER DESIGN BY: DAVID CRIXEL

ISBN: 978-1-7375591-7-7

"I am the Word and you are the Deed; now your destiny begins",

sang the Keeper of Memories, the Gewel, Praise Giver to the founder of the legendary Malian empire (Niane, 1965: 58).

DEDICATION

This work is dedicated to Eshu, who brings energy into the spaces of where our deepest thoughts can freely meet. Eshu, the Yoruba's Divine Messenger of the Crossroads, is the Spirit of Contrast, Contradiction, Change, and Transformation within the human soul. We see red blood and remember that life is present, an ever-flowing, unbroken stream. White ashes remind us that all our past experiences are always alive in us. Blackness, as in the womb, foretells the future and predicts unbroken rebirth (Fatunmbi, 1993).

O Waaqa Gurraachaa, Great Mother/Father Blackness of The Cosmos, may the harmony that reigns above descend upon us here below! Ashay! Ashee! Asé! Ashe!

ACKNOWLEDGEMENTS

This book, is a harvest of rich relationships and precious intimacy shared with many wise souls. I received generous encouragement and unstinting support for this publication from Prof. Wolfgang Schirmacher of the European Graduate School, a freethinker whose spirit opened up to the hidden Cheddo world that I long to share. Only his championing of new ideas makes this offering possible. Thanks are also due Dr. Andrew Spano,

I have been able to work productively because, around me, I have a gathering of supportive souls. I bow to educator and journalist Prof. A. Peter Bailey for sharing both ideas and ideals of his mentor, Br. Malcolm X with me, and I continue to draw strength and inspiration from the insights of Guyanese Elder Sar Ra/Jim Bristol, whose gifted designs and knowledge of Kush-based symbols can turn my thoughts into visible beauty for all the world to see.

My sister, I also rely on and receive guidance from Senegalese psychologist Prof. Aziz Salmone Fall; Indigenous trailblazer Prof. Lila Pine, and Ayitian writer Sr. Chantal Isme. Black Trade Union pioneer, Sr. June Veecock, Br. Arnold Minors and Harlem's Dr. Arthur Lewis all help me to keep body, mind and spirit in balance.

As I remember the words and sacrifices of selfless Ghanaian Ancestor, Bankie Foster Bankie, inspired builder of Pan-Afrikan institutions in South Africa, Namibia and South Sudan, I feel fortified in facing the unknown, while Prof. Kwesi Prah of CASAS in South Africa unfailingly offers me expert advice on language and linguistics. Oromia, a timeless land straddling Ethiopia, has bequeathed me Sr. Kuwee Kumsa and Br. Leenco Lata. They are my sister, brother and mentors in becoming Oromo, guiding me as I reconnect roots to the Black Cradleland of humanity along the River Nile.

Today, I maintain a nourishing exchange with the decorated, Paris-based choreographer and actor, Elsa Wolliaston, as well as the multitalented Emilie M-C Benoit. In addition, I reap benefits from the inter-generational perspective, which Prof. Candace Veecock brings to our shared sense of mission. In the end, I seek out and value uncommon ways of seeing, because of my father, Jim, a Cheddo freethinker to his day of rebirth and my guardian spirit, my mother Clar, whose dreams of selfless self-determination I was born in part to fulfil. To all those whose energies kindle questions in me I say, "Nyu bokk xeet! – We're family" and pour out a Cheddo libation as witness to their blessings in my heart.

LIBATION: THE PROTECTIVE WORD

To prepare myself for this work, I pour a libation as an act of veneration. The act of pouring expresses the gratitude to the Creator existing in my mind (Asante, Abarry, 1996: 92). I reflect, as I begin, on the energy of silenced, hurtful words locked up in the tissues of my flesh. It is through the windows of our ears, eyes, nostrils and mouth as well as the vibrations that flow wordlessly between human bodies that we register insult, a sting that can instantly shatter our peace of mind or lodge inside us for a lifetime, as bitter as regurgitated bile. Therefore, before I undertake this study, experience teaches me to prepare myself for the toll that remembering so much will take on my body and my mind. Preparation sources itself in stillness and distils consciousness. Looking at my elders has taught me to invite and feed a calming spirit through the act of pouring libation.

This is an act of self-preservation. It would not be intelligent, I believe, to run my fingers through sulphuric acid without protective gloves. And one of the ways I have learned to provide a prophylactic for my mind, when I undertake potentially painful activities, is to immerse myself in Afrikan deep thought (Bynum, 1999; Carruthers, 1995: 15). In this study, I am using libation as an activity to invite ancestral Afrikan wisdom into this initially academic process. I consider the study itself a form of libation as thanks for the guidance and insights that are the precious legacy of those thinkers and writers, keepers of freedom for the Afrikan mind, whose destiny, in small part, I fulfil.

In the practice to which I have been initiated, the rite of libation usually takes the form of pouring water on the ground. It may also include chanting sacred words, quiet introspection, eruptions of joy, acts of affirmation and spontaneous praise. I approach this work as a feast of praise and prayer in celebration of my Ancestors.

TO OUR ANCESTORS

I-in-You and You-in-I pour Sacred Water
In thanks to our Ancestors
Who know Sacred Water is without enemy
Never enemy to any woman or any man
Praying through eternal Water for perpetual peace
Woman man man woman
Heart beside heart inside every heart
I-in-you and you-in-The-I pour Sacred Water
Reflecting The First Waters
Pouring forth all Life
Each drop a universe
Every drop indistinguishable
In every cup river or sea
I-in-You and You-in-The-I pour Sacred Water
Keeping time with tides in our veins
Moved by Djuti's myriad rhythms
Of moons and stars from afar
I-in-You and You-in-The-I pour Sacred Water
Over the bones of lives lying broken
Gasping for resurrection under deep-bedded seas
Drops trickling down to soothe aching siblings
Sobbing brutha for sistah lover for lover
Infants whimpering for mothers lost
I-in-You and You-in-The-I pour Sacred Water
For lips parched by our forgetting
Holy tongues stopped from preaching truths
Linguists outliving tombs
To speak wisdom for the worlds to come
Where journeys start anew
I-in-You and You-in-The-I pour Sacred Water
For throats strangled by thirst

Bellies starved to fatten the strangers they never harmed
Drowned promise of lives not lived
I-in-You and You-in-The-I pour Sacred Water
Blessing The Black Watery Womb
First Mother Denquenash Wondrous One
Life breathing into life-giving Water
Renewing every mother's womb
I-in-You and You-in-The-I pour Sacred Water
Water of Black Rivers circling our Globe
Cleansing all beings again yet again
Polishing all into ruby perfection
Crystal red dazzling with light from our Blood
As I-in-You and You-in-The-I pour Sacred Water
Honoring Atmu, Great Mother Of The Waters
Gentle Atmu ruffled by a breeze
Terrible Atmu toppling mountains down
She-Who-Embraces-Every-Shore
Cradling destinies midst hurricanes
Lest the oceans swallow up our world
I-in-You and You-in-The-I pour Sacred Water
Awakening vibrations
Swirls of spirals inside out
Bone flesh hair and skin becoming sea
Sea morphing mist into sky
O Mirror-of-a-Million-Galaxies declaring The All Divine
I-in-You and You-in-The-I pour Sacred Water
Vowing to travel paths learned long ago
Timeless through Space and trackless through Time
Adoring Justice above by reflecting Justice below
Through Ma'at Mother Harmony
I-in-You pray and You-in-I pray
Ashay
(Marshall, 2004)

A note on style: Over the years since the publication of this work, colloquial usage has changed with the social climate inside North America. Today, when I teach, it has become increasingly difficult to write or refer to "the N-word" except in the most narrowly prescriptive form. Although I have always employed it in a serious way which respects its significance for Black readers, I find that using the word today can disrupt discussion or even "trigger" hurt. I have therefore, I sincerely hope, make appropriate adjustments.

A note on the text: The incantation quoted comes from the Proud Story of the Great Sundiata in song. Born severely disabled and unable to walk until he was seven, the embodiment of the spirit of the Mande people inspired an empire that spread across western Afrika (Niane, 1965). What is unique in world history is that this empire grew through the influence of its culture – music, poetry, songs, ritual and dance, but never had to use coercion, force, or arms to dominate peoples who resisted its way of life. Its amazing ability to conquer from the bottom of society rather than impose laws from the top mirrors the spread of Black culture through Spirituals, Jazz, Rock-N-Roll to Hip Hop across the Americas, Europe and Asia today. (Niame, 1965)

The 'kora' is an eighteen stringed instrument made with a gourd. Within Mandinka cultural circles, it is the traditional instrument of 'gewel', 'griots' who tell histories in song (Bebey, 1980). A kora player confessed to me in May 1992 that he broke family tradition by sharing some of his technique with a White musician. That person soon went on to declare himself a "master" of the 'kora', a title that was usually reserved for elders with a lifetime of experience and skill. As irony would have it the kora teacher was unable to make a living from his art while his White student went on to a successful career.

A caution: Many of the men in leadership positions who have described themselves as Pan-Afrikanists in the past did not demonstrate a full understanding of some of its core values. They include female regenerative power as the key symbol and first principle of Afrikan ancestral culture and gender equality as its concomitant. This is an attempted rendition of hieroglyphic script, a form of writing that omitted vowels. Various scholars illustrate this very early script in diverse ways. However it may be written for modern readers, this term gives the original Kemetic name for writing, 'Sacred Word'.

CONTENTS

1
Book

A Discussion with Prof. Baba A. Peter Bailey (APB)

PREFACE

The text of this book unites an Internet interview with Prof. A. Peter Bailey, conducted by Prof. Clem Marshall, between August 2021 and November 2024, with the original text of Talking Cheddo (2009). First, a few words about my interlocutor here:

A. Peter Bailey (b. Alfonzo Peter Baily, 1938) is a member of the Organization of Afro-American Unity. He has lectured extensively at universities and is a significant voice in the discourse space of Pan-Afrikanism. A former colleague of Malcolm-X, serving a pallbearer at his funeral in 1965, he is also an author and journalist. After studying at Howard University, he was associate director at the Black Theatre Alliance and associate editor at Ebony magazine. His involvement with other related publications informs his long career as a scholar and activist. His books include *Seventh Child: A Family Memoir of Malcolm X* with Malcolm X's nephew, Rodnell Collins (1998); *Revelations: The Autobiography of Alvin Ailey* (1995); and the memoir *Witnessing Brother Malcolm X: The Master Teacher.*

I write Cheddo, a Wolof word, with an H for English speakers, like those in Gambia. However, in Senegal, where I first encountered it, it is written "CEDDO." For me, the goal of Cheddo or Thinking for Self is Demystification. Because impressions, ideas and thoughts are streaming non-stop in my head, I find that I need to keep clarifying where they are coming from and how they are making me feel, moment by moment. And, in doing so, I look for the cultural link in everything that resonates in me. That, for me, is the process of Demystification! Throughout our conversation, Prof Bailey and I also use the term "Pan-Afrikanism," although today, personally, I would creatively prefer to use "Kush-Konsciousness" or "Kushtopianism" instead.

In tandem with reclaiming my fullest selfhood, I am weaning myself from the use of "Afrika," a term which Roman Empire colonizers concocted and stamped on a culture and populations that preceded Europe's entry on to the world stage. In place of Africa/Afrika, in future writing, I intend to re-identify our Motherland as "Kushtopia," a word rooted in KUSH, a name that history, both oral and recorded, connects to our very early Ancestors. The populations of that lavishly-watered, fertile, multi-forested landmass with its rich diversity of resources and cultures used Kush, long before random, uninvited strangers from across the desert or over the sea ever crossed their paths.

ON RASTAFARI REASONING

Through reasoning, without overt teaching, generous Rastafari breddren/brothers easily drew me into their circle of plural selfhood. That happened seamlessly through their use of "I-n'-I" instead of "I" and "me." "I-n-I" is an expression which I take to mean both "I and I" and "I in I," where the individual and the group meld into one. And in a Rasta yard/compound, there are many dwellings where inclusive families, not necessarily related by blood, do indeed live as one. In those spaces, a conversation becomes a dancing discourse, like the spontaneously dancing spirits of the Batwa peoples, with one idea leaping from one mind to another and then occurring to everyone as unspoken inspiration, through movement, sounds, chants, songs, and invented words.

Sometimes Rasta-far-eye breddren might start humming, "From the rivers of Babylon," which listeners instinctively knew, and would let the tune hang in the air, rising and falling out of nowhere and giving birth to streams of thoughts that would float around but never really end. And so it was, with my big brother and mentor, A. Peter Bailey. Although we began by taping our discussion, interview-style, on a particular day, our reasoning looped back every time we spoke by phone for the next three years.

As we kept returning to Talking Cheddo, we would dive deeper into each other's mind, probing opaque spaces between definition and meaning, sharpening our understanding and overstanding, distilling our feelings and words. Standing atop the main Carnival stage in Port-of-Spain one year, I had a condor's view of the bands arriving from multiple directions and converging on the stage at the centre where each would perform. The bands each held their own rhythm and marched to their own beat at their own pace. And, marvelously, without any policing or external control, they flowed peacefully and seamlessly through each other, like tides in the river.

Each band remained intact, full of high spirits and making its own way, in its own direction. That was a symbolic moment for me. We can, I felt, come together, guided by the GPS pulsing in our blood, move as one in rhythm, blend our bodies and minds and then move apart again without ever missing a beat. What a gift from our Ancestors! Quote from Canadian anthropologist Dr. Carole Yawney, who spent a lifetime walking alongside Rasta-far-eye: "Reasoning typically produces multi-layered discourse of varying degrees of complexity."

INTERVIEW WITH APB

The following is my interview with A. Peter Bailey, who will be known throughout as APB, and I, GCM. It's hard to reproduce in text, but keep in mind there was plenty of between us throughout this interview, which will give you an idea of the spirit of it. As I say above, it took place at different times over several years, sometimes by video chat, and sometimes by phone. For part of it, he was in Washington, D.C. and I was in Toronto.

GCM: Hayyee, hayyee, hangafa kiyya, my beloved big brother, the one and only Prof. Alfonzo Peter Bailey! In the Spirit of Waka Guracha, The Great Black God and returning to our source, I greet you in the Oromo tongue and put you on notice that I now hold irrevocable, first-class citizenship in the Black Cradleland, all up and down the River Nile – the longest river flowing for the longest time. I would also like it on record that you're my go-to sounding board when I sense my vision getting blurred around significant aspects of Pan-Afrikanism. And so, O grand, rising Sage of Harlem, the Malcolm X capital of the wide, intact-yet-scattered Black World, I humbly beseech you to "ground" or reason with me. And as Rastafari [Rasta-far-eye] elders would say, "Teech, breddren, teech!"

I think sharing our thoughts about my book can open up yet another window on Cheddo, and do so sans pain or strain. And although Cheddo is a term I only acquired by spectacular good fortune, I've refurbished it and made it my own. For me, Cheddo symbolizes a collective legacy of Indigenous and timeless deep-thought, which unites a vibrational field of Free-thinkers around the Black world. Whenever the climate, the times or the crumbling of oppressive systems or human beings in parasitic mode turn into Superman-type Kryptonite and undermine our collective purpose, I feel the Ancestors inside me prescribing Cheddo.

Arguably, as we keep circling around solutions, Cheddo may already be offering Black populations an ancestrally-potent cultural detox for our myriad addictions to self-destructive beliefs and behaviours.

APB: It feels like we've been walking around stoned on Whiteness for a very long time.

GCM: So, like you, I accept the urgency of PanArikanism. It's high time for another Ayitian or, more accurately, Ayitian Revolution to cleanse our mindscape, so Black freethinking can ignite more of humanity to operationalize their individual genius.

When Cheddo consciousness swept me up, back in the day in Dakar, Senegal, I instantly sussed out its potential to rescue highjacked Pan-Afrikanism . Let's tell the truth, baby, like Sister Aretha Franklin sings it! Today's institutions directing Pan-Af-rikanism have been often twisted into tools for soul-dead, self-promoting land-grabbers or degenerated into a playground for red-carpeting academics and peripatetic intellectuals.

APB: Uhm. Uhm. Uhm. I can tell that you've got your fencing mask on. I'd better watch out.

GCM: My biggest gift from living in Dakar was dining out daily on Black-on-Black spirit-food. Once I had escaped Air Afrique into the air my Ancestors breathed from before humans discovered time, I grew more spine.

APB: I think I have a pretty good idea how you felt, but what exactly did you mean by "spirit-food"?

GCM: Simply put, my son said it best, as we were buying mangoes in "Sandaga Market" on our first day in Senegal.

"Dad, it's like we've always lived here," he said. "We have," I answered. ... Out of the mouths of babes, they say...What can I add? It did feel like we were living out Biblical prophecy and fleeing "captivity" like Ancestor Bob Marley sings.

When I say "spirit-food," I'm remembering images that I'd known growing up in the Caribbean. In Dakar, they popped up all around me and fed me enough calm, confidence and self-love to end the hunger for home in my heart. Every new scene was a mirror of time lived before, and each memory said that I'd returned intact.

Peace and certainty washed over me as I strained to see as far as I could see. All that land, a voice inside told me, belonged, by birthright, to me. Here, no one would dare mock me with the question I've heard time and time again, "But where are you really from?" For the first time in my life, once Afrika had fed my spirit her food, I could watch myself growing more secure and steadily becoming totally full.

APB: That's cool! Now let me begin by telling you what I got out of Talking Cheddo and why I think it's a great book. It was Br. Malcolm who, at the age of twenty-four, for the first time, made me start thinking of this whole thing of attacks on the mind. And I have been deeply involved in that since then. There are only three people who had a national platform who I knew who dealt with this subject in any kind of serious way. And that was Br. Malcolm, Dr. C. Delores Tucker, when she went after that whole gangsta-rap thing, talking about attacks on the mind of young Black people, especially young Black males, and Dr. Frances Cress Welsing, the psychiatrist.

But she never had, like a big national platform. She was mainly in the academic world. Every now and then, however, books are beginning to appear that deal with this syndrome. And when your book came along, I really became interested. For me personally, I judge a book by three things.

It's knowledge-expanding: A book has to be knowledge-expanding. I have to learn something I did not know. The second thing, it's got to be thought-provoking: It's got to make you think. And then, the third thing, it has to be challenging: And by "challenging" I mean there are certain things you might believe and then there's something in the book.

If the book has that kind of a grip on you, you find yourself saying "I don't agree with that but blah-blah-blah. Those three things, that's what Talking Cheddo was to me. It was knowledge-expanding. It was thought-provoking and it was challenging. And then, of course, it dealt with the subject of Pan-Afrikanism.

GCM: Thanks again, Br. Peter. As can be expected, my thinking around Cheddo has evolved over the last decade. Where I once saw it as a noun and a description of Black folks from a particular place in global historical time, I now think of Cheddo as a verb. One acts Cheddo in order to be more Cheddo or become Cheddo.

And with that new framework, I'm unmasking the Cheddo spirit in individuals who I embrace as part of an expanding circle of freethinkers across the spectrum of gender, age or length of service to Pan-Afrikanism . What reassures me about receiving your advice, is that I know you to be a tough-love Pan-Afrikanist. So, Professor A. Peter Bailey, I'm relying on you to show no mercy when you think I'm too uncritical of Black folks, and to make sure I don't forget like Spike's movie says, to *Do the Right Thing*. Wearing masks for COVID is nothing new for Black folks. We've been wearing masks to survive for as long as I can remember.

APB: I'm not cutting Black folks any more slack. An intelligent people ought to know better by now. Not after six hundred years? No way! When I talk to young people, I tell them straight up that if they continue to refuse to learn the lessons of the past, they'd better be prepared to deal with the consequences. I'm fed-up hearing about what's wrong and what people who have an unbroken, unparalleled record of harming us. owe us. So, what? To anyone awake enough to listen, I'll say it loud and clear so they get it. You'd better change now, or you ... are ... doomed!

GCM: I'm still trying to figure out what keeps holding us back. Writing Talking Cheddo was my way of first uncluttering my own mind. I was focused on hearing my own unfettered spirit, without the distraction of random, careless, ignorant, arrogant or mostly just out-and-out mean put-downs that folks like you and I, or as the Rastafari say, "I-an'-I," have to deal with every day. And any of us smart enough to have made it through our generations-long "anti-Black pandemic," have had to learn to distance ourselves from the pain of dealing daily with our own harsh reality, from the moment our eyes could focus.

APB: Sure, we've survived. But we're still catching hell. Survival isn't enough.

GCM: Once living in the Motherland taught me about Cheddo, a new, unique way of seeing everything was opened up to me. At that time, I was already wondering how we might learn to think differently in today's anti-Black world. With Cheddo, missing pieces of my own exile-centred ID began to show up and fall into place. Over time, I gradually came to accept being Cheddo, and taking it for granted that we had a philosophy that is 100% ours. In a manner of speaking, my thinking had returned me home.

APB: How does Cheddo relate to the Pan-Afrikan Movement which already has a history and is alive and moving forward? Won't Cheddo just confuse our people?

GCM: By and large, Cheddo thinking remains autodidactic. There is no hierarchy of written knowledge that gives some individuals authority over others. So, all we need to do in opening up Cheddo-thinking is to encourage others to think through the idea of historical Black philosophical independence for themselves. What's to confuse? It just happens to be ancestrally anchored, self-generated and unapologetically Black. And like the diamonds the world lusts after, it has always been under our feet.

APB: Thanks. That answers some of my questions.

GCM: I don't countenance claims that Black populations suffer from a "civilizational vacuum," as a long line of both Brown and White imperialists have pretended, hinted or hoped. What we rarely point out, and leaders of all stripes seem to mostly ignore, are anti-Black strains embedded in other cultures, philosophies and religions.

Remember the hierarchy of the human species pioneered by the Swedish scientist Karl Von Linné? At the very top are brilliant blonds with flowing golden tresses and at the very bottom are nappy-headed Blacks who can't string two thoughts coherently together. Even for the brave few who broach the topic of instinctive, anti-Black bias, doing so can explode academic, professional and political careers.

And yet it's hardly a secret. In a paper passed on to me by my late brother, Bankie Foster Bankie, the tone of even a proudly Arab thinker like Helmi Sharawy of the Cairo Museum demonstrated how normalized that bias has become.

While teaching Anti-racist Education at York University, I even received an unsolicited package, as my colleagues also did, from Canadian psychologist Prof Philippe Rushton of Western University in Ontario. Basically, he argued for a hierarchy of brainpower based on penis-size, with Asians on top, Europeans in the middle and penis-privileged Afrikans way, way down on the bottom.

APB: You've got to be kidding, of course?

GCM: I promise, I kid you not. I think the title of his book was Race, Evolution, and Behaviour...

APB: Later for that! I've a question for you. What makes you feel that Pan-Afrikanists, of all people, would target you for being Cheddo?

GCM: It's more than just my feeling. I'm almost convinced that most Black people, including Pan-Afrikanists, have become so invested in and acclimatised to imported cultures or religions that many often misdiagnose unapologetic Blackness as a kind of reverse racism. After all, this Black-first stuff is now up against beliefs their families embrace.

Let me give you a concrete example. I was one of three panelists at an Afrikan Liberation Day celebration a few years ago, where we'd collectively decided that each of us would describe how we came to Pan-Afrikanism . A stately sister was the first to speak - self-identified as mixed race, Christian and raised with little focus on Black life until her graduate studies under a Caribbean-born thesis supervisor at university. He was the author of Racism and National Consciousness, a pioneer in its time, in the seventies. In fact, our sister openly credited him with her gradual political development and eventual embrace of Pan-Afrikanism.

APB: Are you saying one parent was Black and the other White?

GCM: As far as I know, yes! And until the late seventies, really, Toronto was still home to just a sprinkling of seventh-generation Black Canadian families and a scattering of immigrants from the Caribbean.

Canada, like Australia, had an effectively airtight Whites-only immigration policy until the sixties. So, growing up Whitish, our sister would have had few opportunities to experience Blackness of any kind, much less Pan-Afrikanism. Over the seventies, however, waves of draft-adverse brothers traveling along the Underground Railroad that ran over the Peace Bridge from Buffalo, New York to Niagara Falls, Canada. I suspect that many of those young men escaped unwanted martyrdom in Vietnam by settling in TO instead.

By the sixties, the anti-draft generation could also blend into a rapidly growing Black Caribbean community of farm workers, domestic workers, random professionals and students, who were "darker than blue," as the jazz classic goes. Blackness had arrived in White-on-White British-cloned Toronto.

APB: Vietnam was a big wake-up call for many of us. Br. Malcolm's disciple, Muhammad Ali, influenced by Stokely Carmichael (later Kwame Touré) enraged Whites when he repeated, "No Vietcong ever called me n--" (the N-word.)

GCM: I was telling you about the deep bias against Blackness that can surface even among Pan-Afrikanists. As the Lion says in Black Aesop's fable, "let's get back to eating our sheep!"

The second speaker on our Afrikan Liberation Day panel was an obsidian brother, like me, from Senegal. The real deal, right?

So, on this ALD, our Senegalese speaker, who looked like a young Paul Robeson stepped forward and spoke up. Like most Wolof Muslim-raised boys, he had grown up memorizing sacred Arabic texts without ever learning to read Arabic, just as, in the Caribbean, I had been made to memorize sacred Latin prayers in Catholic school without learning to read Latin.

As he grew up, he said, he also fell under the spell of his village elder Cheikh Anta Diop, pronounced SHER-ANTAH-JOP, the quintessentially Black-conscious nuclear physicist, anthropologist, linguist and historian, who authored The African Origin of Civilization: Myth or Reality. Dr. Diop's name now graces the University of Dakar.

APB: I am willing to admit that our generation, unlike today's teenagers and twenty-somethings, grew up under the shadow of many remarkable giants. Our formative years were crowded with the likes of Ghana's father of Independence, Dr. Kwame Nkrumah and Mary McLeod Bethune. What's a tribute worthy of such a grand soul who, one generation removed from enslavement, not only starts a university but also sits in the US delegation that's key in the founding of the United Nations?

GCM: In suggesting a panel, I had projected that our three stories from Canada, the Continent and the Caribbean would show how Pan-Afrikanism made us all one and the same. So, when my turn came, as the last speaker and pressed for time, I merely gave a snapshot of growing up Christianized, teased as "an English duck" because of imbibing the British influences in my school, and being thoroughly Europeanized and colonized.

GCM: I even confessed to being a "euroholic," like some anxiety-prone clone of White ID that I couldn't ever own. I described my education or "Miseducation" as Carter Woodson put it. It consisted of too much Chaucer, Shakespeare and singing "Rule Britannia." Finally, I was free to let them see how Pan-Afrikanism had rescued me. I told our gathering that after I had soaked up the usual "isms" from my schooling, I landed on anarchism or freethinking in a European way.

However, later on I discovered that, eons ago, our Ancestors had developed Cheddo, a freethinking system that grew out learning from Life that was unique to us. It was the first time that I'd shared my beliefs in such an open forum, and I sighed with satisfaction as I sat down. That didn't last long. There was instant feedback – hostile, swift and searing. Quite literally, my ideas were treated like a stray skunk and cleared from the air.

Whatever brand of Pan-Afrikanism was in that room that day had room for Christians, Muslims, Marxists and even Rastafari, but not Cheddo. My kind of hardcore Black sovereignty over our own minds, it turned out, was more than all those Black progressives around me could swallow.

By daring to privilege ideas of spirituality preserved inside some distant "Black Before," I seemed to have caused the majority, most of them folks I knew, to get intellectual, religious or cultural indigestion. And as I'm speaking now, that incident reminds me of how my mentor, the late jurist Bankie F. Bankie, born in Ghana, described a Pan-Afrikan setback he suffered, while invested in building PACON (the Pan-African Centre of Namibia). Br. Bankie wrote: "Without Identity there can be no people and without a people there can be no Nation or multi-national state."

So, while the stated intention of all those students and activists getting together on a stormy Saturday on Afrikan Liberation Day in Canada was to affirm solidarity as individuals of Afrikan ancestry, for me, it backfired. The folks in that room held stronger personal loyalties to the culture of groups historically invested in dominating Black populations and our Motherland into perpetuity.

GCM: In fact, by the 18th century, White folks had little doubt of where Nature ranked Blackness anywhere in the globe. Swedish scientist Karl Von Linné was explicit is putting blonds on top, Asians next, followed by Indigenous populations from this hemisphere and nappy-haired, luscious-lipped folks like you and me dead last.

APB: In Br. Malcolm's words from long ago, "Give your brain as much attention as you give your hair, and you will be a thousand times better off."

GCM: That ALD revealed a surprising contradiction, eh? Especially when our identity was so solidly in place eons before there were Persians, Arabs, Europeans or West Asians in our midst. However, today, their IDs have become so mixed up with ours, in our Motherland, though not in theirs, that it can make us behave like some kind of willing, spiritual prey. In this brother's humble opinion, for many Black people, their self-image is entwined with peoples and institutions historically and demonstrably intent on Black cultural genocide. Or even worse, in order to dispossess us and own our birthplace forever, they are obsessed with physically annihilating us.

APB: I don't need to tell you that it's deeper than disappointing when our best intentions and efforts fail. But putting things in perspective, it makes Br. Malcolm's visit to the continent even more remarkable. He was warmly received by Heads of State from Left to Right, when he went to Afrika shortly before he was assassinated.

GCM: And here's some more good news! After the earthquake struck Ayiti in 2010, President Abdoulaye Wade of Senegal offered Haitians land for resettlement. His speech hit a high note, I thought, especially when he declared Ayitians/Haitians sons and daughters of Afrika, and wondered aloud whether some of them were descendants of enslaved Senegalese. Unfortunately, President Wade's offer of Repatriation never got off the ground.

Had President Wade seen my documentary, All Eyes On Afrika, he would have seen a clip on Jean-Baptiste Belley/BELL-LAY. Kidnapped as a two-year-old from Gorée Island, made infamous by its "Door of No Return," Ancestor Belley became one of three Ayitian members of the "Convention" (Assembly) which guided the French Revolution.

Senegal's former Chief Information Officer, Prof Abdou Rahman Cissé and I had once shared a Belley moment. Confronted by a huge portrait of the hero on entering Br. Abdou's Dakar office for the first time, I immediately quoted Ancestor Belley's intervention against racism at France's revolutionary Convention, aloud, "Now that we have dethroned the aristocracy of the blood, we must dethrone the aristocracy of the skin."

That quote sealed the bond of brotherhood between Abdou and I forever. On the other hand, according to Oromo author, Leenco/LENN-CHO Lata, His Imperial majesty, Haile Selassie of Ethiopia also gave Jamaican Rastafari a piece of the Oromo population's ancestral land in 1955. That unique repatriation initiative in Shashamannee/SHASH-A-MAN-NAY/Shashamane is still going on.

APB: I don't remember hearing about President Wade's offer at the time. Now, I think it was probably a missed opportunity to promote Pan-Afrikanism within Ayitian and other grassroots Black communities.

GCM: That's why we need Pan Afrikan journalists like you, Br. Peter. We really can't afford to blink, because these opportunities flash by and are forever lost. Anyway, I let everyone at the Afrikan Liberation Day gathering I was just describing know that I had zero desire to convert anyone or prescribe what they should believe.

-In fact, I choose Cheddo because it frees us all to think for ourselves, and treats all beliefs, mainstream or historically hidden like Vodun, Candomblé and Obeah with equal respect. On the other hand, on that day that's seared into my soul, some staunch Pan-Afrikanists ganged up on me to silence my unapologetically Black beliefs. And they did.

APB: Help me understand this! Are you really telling me that they dragged you over the coals at an Afrikan Liberation Day event? Why? They must have been out of their you-know-what minds!

GCM: I can only repeat what Wolof grandmothers would say, "Wax-nge degg [WAAH HUNGAH DUGGAH]– which in Christian Ebonics is, "Preach, brutha, preach!" or "Lawd only knows." They acted like I had offended or hurt them by just affirming my own chosen conversion to an indigenous, ancestral Black faith. Maybe Cheddo felt like it was too Black and too far back for them.

APB: That stuff is deep!

GCM: And that's why I believe that when our time comes to meet the enemy on the beaches, like our Ayitian Ancestors met the French, we should be ready for no-holds-barred psychological warfare. And that's especially true for our youth. However, I'm also sorry to predict that whenever the next assault comes, some of those in the first wave of our attackers might look like us. And they'll probably be coming at us both from the side and from behind. We have to learn how to steel our minds in case we have to take on a brother or a sister or two.

APB: I'm aware of that. Black fingers pulled the trigger to kill Br. Malcolm. We can't wait for every self-denier to be ready for self-determination. That was one of the mistakes we made before. I think we have to stop trying to persuade the ones who are forever wavering to join us. I don't believe you can build anything strong or lasting with ambivalent people. Potential builders have to be Pan-Afrikan – first. Period!

GCM: Sometimes, when Black interests and survival are in direct conflict with one of our other identities, we have to make hard choices. Let me give you a known yet mostly ignored example!

In pictures, Ḥamad ibn Muḥammad ibn Jumʿah ibn Rajab ibn Muḥammad ibn Saʿīd al Murjabī, better known as Tippu Tip, looked a lot like Uganda's dead dictator, Idi Amin. He fits the archetype of an unambiguously Black man. However, despite being blessed with distinctly Bantu DNA from the Dar es Salaam area, in Tanzania, Tippu Tip, or 'the big, bad marauder', as that name broadly translates, identified exclusively with his Omani-Arab roots.

Obsessed with getting instant riches, he headed Arab-centric gangs raiding unprotected Black communities, both in Zanzibar and beyond. His Omani clansmen funded and supplied him with guns way more efficient and deadly than anything the peaceful Black villagers had ever seen, and he became a scourge, abducting any unsuspecting Black body on sight. As Br Bankie Foster Bankie points out: "The Arabs call Africa a cultural vacuum waiting to be filled by Islam. ... It so happens that conservative reactionary Islam, in alliance with Western intelligence agencies, are pushing Arab expansion in Africa."

In our day, the martyred Sudanese leader, John Garang denounced wannabee Tippu Tips, like the "Jellaba." These are blue-Black men who self-identify as Arabs and have continued to incinerate thriving Black communities like Darfur.

Why are so many Black-identified populations, waiting passively for desert killers to pour in from outside their homeland as if they are modern equivalents of legendary dodo birds? The only explanation that makes sense to me is that, in their DNA, they're not used to seeing other human beings as predators. Overwhelmingly, even today, Black folks persist in treating the anti-Black heirs of their Ancestors' enslavers as family and friends.

If we look up "slavery" on the Internet today, we're likely to trip over a significant number of guilt-driven writers endlessly chanting the big lie, "You sold your own," or even more confusing, "We sold our own.."

APB: That story proves A, why identity is key, and B, why it was so easy to target us.

GCM: But what I still haven't figured out is why, having now seen the dangers we failed to foresee, we seem to have learnt very little, and keep trusting those who kill us. In fact, we still over-trust.

Incredibly, in Congo, succeeding governments have trusted foreign companies to tell them how much gold they are shipping out every day. I would argue that Pan-Afrikanists trusted too much and then forgave too easily when the US government, its country's banks and its Red Cross administrators presided over the evaporation of $6 billion dollars of Ayiti's earthquake aid. Black President Obama let all the

White people plus Black collaborators in charge walk away with those vitally needed funds.

Similarly, overnight, it seems, we have also forgotten South Africa's TRC evidence and how apartheid's Dr. Death Masson spread cholera and injected infected AIDS blood into his over-trusting Black victims.

APB: That's sad.

GCM: In fact, I remember how reading your book, The Harlem Hospital Story: 100 Years of Struggle Against Illness, Racism and Genocide, shocked me and shook us awake. Even activists in the Civil Rights Movement didn't fully imagine just how vulnerable we were to medical malpractice with unstated Black extermination in callous minds. Whether we're in places where we're many or just a few, experience proves that we have a long history of being used as guinea-pigs, drugged or disappeared.

And Br Peter, since your boys grew up receiving medical care from our beloved departed Dr Thomas Hyatt, I'm sure, that like me you recall how Dr. Tom's team had to travel to Dimona in Israel to bring healthcare to the small group of Black Hebrew Israelites, who had emigrated to that contested land.

As a result of their visit, those Black medical experts, all Harlem-based and unshakable Pan-Afrikanists, eventually secured Congressional legislation guaranteeing the Hebrews Israelites basic human rights, as US citizens, so they could reside and survive in Israel with dignity.

APB: I knew Tom, but I don't recall the details.

GCM: Similarly, looking through my Ancestors' eyes, I don't swallow the narrative around the unprecedented outbreak of cholera in Ayiti in 2010.

After all, for apartheid, cholera was a ready-made biological gasoline bomb they could toss anywhere, watch it explode and walk away. After all this time, after all, we still have no transparency about apartheid's secret web of global support embedded in Europe, North America, Asia and beyond. So, this over-trusting brother talking to you was shocked when President Nelson Mandela arbitrarily championed Reconciliation, while trampling Justice underfoot.

Thinking of Genocide in the title of your book, and looking back on Ayiti and South Africa, I'm not at all surprised that Harlem Hospital's big guns summarily fired Mama Betty Dopson, the hospital's first Black Director, for letting you tear off the blinders around Harlem Hospital from Black folks' eyes.

APB: Why do we let these things still happen in 2024?

GCM: I must say I believe, because giants like Dr. Clarke helped me to see it, that our approach is linked to Afrika's non-patriarchal, mother-centred ancestral culture. Even today, a mothering spirit, that privileges reciprocal giving and equal exchange is the cultural glue that holds us together. Black women, more than any other group, have raised other people's children with the tenderness others only show their own.

And the Marxist historian, Eugene Genovese, tellingly pointed out that, during the US civil War, there was not a single case recorded of Black men raping or mistreating the White women, children and older folk Southern racists left in their care.

I'm not going to point fingers at any group. But just compare that record to all the civil wars or conflicts going on around the globe today!

APB: If that's where equity is leading us, it sounds a lot like the broken promises of integration.

GCM: My definition of equity is based on a principle that's not the standard fare. I created it in the course of pioneering, comprehensive model of Anti-racist Training, which I developed and delivered for the entire Ministry of Education in Ontario.

In preparing for that work, I had dug deep and come up with a concept that existed but generally had not been applied as it ought – much like the Universal Declaration of Human Rights or principles of the French Revolution. So, my take on equity is time-tested, practical and available to all.

In fact, I stumbled on it while carrying out my research, and realized that it drew on old English law. Equity measures are the sum of measures required in any situation where the application of available law has proved inadequate in producing a visibly fair and acceptable outcome.

APB: I didn't know that.

GCM: But let me tell you what really keeps me up at night. It's how open we are to everyone else's agenda when it comes to our lands, resources or cultural assets, even after all we've already endured. What if that's who we really are - beings who survived through trust and evolved to see trusting as the best way to survive from the first light of earliest Time?

Look around us, Black women are still raising other women's children more than anyone else, and they invariably treat them like their own. Is that same strength now a weakness? How do we remain in the real world, conscious of how it has treated us, and do not remain, interminably, the world's most likely and likable human prey?

APB: You tell me! How would you accommodate our history to the ideals you've described in *Talking Cheddo*?

GCM: For me, Cheddo is about getting as deep as we can inside our Blackest self. It doesn't shut the door on others, but it says, "Black woman, Black man, Know thyself! And do that - first!" To tell the truth, I didn't get to my current convictions based on my talents in research. Proverbially speaking, I stumbled upon Cheddo - both the philosophy and the name. As for that encounter, it was either fate or chance, take your pick. I also credit a few joyfully generous thinkers, all Ancestors now, who seamlessly and effortlessly taught me what I needed to learn and now feel I know.

APB: I see the way you have been guided as a priceless gift

GCM: And don't I know it!

APB: In turn, it's vital that we who have lived inside such pivotal times pass our experiences on to those willing to complete the work.

GCM: Yes, I feel it's our collective ancestral trust. For the priceless gift of opening up the door to my sojourn in Senegal, I must bow to my big sister from another mother, as they say in Dakar, my rock, Sr. Lorraine Isaac, a former head of the Peace Corps in that region.

My reality-school teachers included Mama Una Mulzac, founder of Harlem's legendary Liberation Bookstore and daughter to Hugh Mulzac, Pan-Afrikan pioneer and captain of the Garvey Movement's first ship. Mama Una, a fearless feminist and revolutionary thinker had also lived in Guyana on the invitation of her close friend, Chicago-born President Janet Jagan. And here's something else most folks don't know!

By some twist of cosmic irony, one of the Garvey ships, the SS Shadyside, is still lying at the bottom of the Harlem River around 157th Street, a gentle breeze away from the site where Mama Una ran Liberation Bookstore for all those years.

APB: I didn't remember that.

GCM: Besides her, I am indebted to Martinique's poet cum parliamentarian, "Papa" Aimé Césaire; Rastafari/RASTA-FAR-EYE elder, Mortimo Planno, and jurist, diplomat and Pan-Afrikan institution-builder Br: Bankie Forster Bankie, alongside his mentor Prof. Kwesi Prah, who is to me the authentic, living world-expert on indigenous Afrikan languages.

I also lived and learned Pan-Afrikanism at the feet of Senegalese media pioneer and iconoclast, Prof Abdou Rahman Cissé as well as Harlem's peripatetic, afroholic educator and Broadway artiste, Mama Esther "Queenie" Brown.

Those builders were key in my concretizing my Pan-Afrikan ID. They told me stories that made me see below the surface. They steered me through muddled thinking and made integrity seem inevitable. Last, and most directly, and especially for the word "Cheddo," itself, I credit Senegal's iconic filmmaker, trade unionist and creative guardian of Black spirit, Ousmane Sembène.

That artist recorded for posterity how President Senghor, during a rare meeting, chided him for being too wrapped up in serving their nation's faceless masses, when he could instead be pouring that energy into his own career, growing wealthy and piling up personal awards. Needless to say, good-brother Ousmane Sembène didn't pay any heed to President Senghor.

APB: Talk about a living library! What a special gift to have known such giants!

GCM: I always crack up when I watch that video where Br. Malcolm tells off folks who look like you and me but are silly enough to say aloud, "I'm not Afrikan" or "I didn't leave anything in Afrika."

I never tire repeating our icon's riposte, "You left your mind in Afrika." His words could easily apply to most of scattered Afrika, because overwhelmingly, populations from the Americas and Caribbean have never set foot on the Motherland. To me, that's the only acceptable excuse for our folks who sense no loss of the spiritual, cultural and material treasures that were left behind, when our Ancestors were yanked up and out from our Motherland by their roots.

APB: I think we should make it a priority to create opportunities for every Black child, who so chooses, to get to Gorée Island in Senegal or one of the sixty plus "castles," really "prison camps," along the Ghanaian coast. Children need to see where White financiers and small-scale, mutual-society investors, locked up innocent children as young as two years old. That's something I wish our Black millionaires would help to make come true.

GCM: I feel as if I were granted a special privilege going there. And when I stood by The Door of No Return on Gorée Island, I felt as if I had been flying, like a dove, and just landed back in my nest – home again on Motherland soil. I guess I did go back for some of that Cheddo wisdom that my Ancestors had buried in the soil, in trust for me, for over forty generations.

Best of all, however, for my video, All Eyes On Africa, I actually got to shoot a scene in that very doorway carved into the cliff-face and hanging over the sea, while Sr. Esther Brown soulfully sang the line from a spiritual that says, Sometimes I feel like a motherless child, a long way from home.

APB: In my visit to Cape Coast two years ago, I, too, stood before the 'Door of No Return' in the "Elmina Castle" in Ghana.

GCM: Calling those prison-forts "castles" is just another way mis-educators mess with Black people's minds, hiding their crimes behind exculpatory euphemisms. Every flavour of European, it seems, took part in the rush for fleshy "Black gold," as they branded the families, whose bodies they recruited mercenaries to hunt. Even the impressively blameless Danes, it seems, developed a taste for profits harvested from dehumanizing innocent Black children, women and men.

APB: That's another aspect that many other writers have ignored, how normalized enslavement became for so long.

GCM: The so-called "slave trade" was not restricted to a few rich or ruthless individuals, as many of my Progressive and Leftist friends like to say. It became a part of Europe's everyday culture, like going to the market or to Church.

Trinidad's first Prime Minister, historian Dr. Eric Williams, who wrote his doctoral dissertation on England's enslavement of his Ancestors, lifted the covers off the hidden connections between "Christian" England and its crimes against those it chose to torture for profit. In fact, his findings so went against the grain that his profs kept trying to get him to distort or ignore them. In the end, he did leave out some damning evidence just to get his doctorate and become credentialed. Later on, however, he published everything in his book Capitalism and Slavery.

APB: That's a very important book.

GCM: Dr. William's research revealed that it was not the upper-class in English society that was solely responsible for enslaving innocent Afrikans. Peers of the land shared their peculiar addiction to Black blood-money with ambitious servants and the working-class.

So, tailors and barbers or milliners, who made hats, would morph into enslavers. Those commoners could pool their pennies, outfit a ship and hire and arm willing gangs of killers to man them. Then the ships would sail off, with the Church's blessing, to abduct and torture peaceful villagers who had never done them harm, from far across the sea.

Marxism, from my reading of Capitalism and other texts, identified the foundation of Capital as property or things. Yet, in my humble view, the seed capital of modern capitalism was overwhelmingly accumulated on the backs of millions of unpaid human beings by using up their blood, flesh, bones and brains. Karl Marx did of course write penetratingly about revolutionary France in around 1848. However, he also failed to mention the first French colony to put Abolition of Slavery laws into effect in Martinique in 1848.

Therefore, my question for all my Marxist peers is this: Is it possible to have a full understanding of capitalism without a clear understanding of Black Bondage?

And so, in my old-fashioned view, we still have a collective responsibility, to keep exploring the significance of their being uniquely Black. It was freethinkers like Elders Aimé Césaire and Ousmane Sembène, who finally helped me, emotionally-speaking, to come to terms with the blank spaces and missing faces, if I probed past three (3) generations in my own family tree.

APB: Today, lots of companies seem to be doing a brisk business selling "ancestry kits."

GCM: Popularized by stars like Oprah, White businessmen sell Black folks the means to trace their ancestry, via DNA to specific regions in Afrika. It dawned on me that our folks were now willingly paying some Whites to fill in gaps in Black bloodlines that other Whites had cruelly erased. And once again, Black willingness to trust is on display!

To tell the truth, I feel we're way too gullible in accepting whatever plausible narratives other groups spin for us, even when it's obviously in their interest to feed us lies. Case in point, I met, took and still have a picture with the Elder/Aunt publicly identified as the long-lost direct relative of the author of Roots. However, I was told by unshakable authority of someone who was there when they met that the connection was a spiritual rather than a biological one.

APB: I didn't know that

GCM: While on that topic, I'm also still waiting to be convinced by stories of sudden, mass conversions of Black populations to those major "world religions," whose followers convinced themselves that enslaving us was righteous and just. Why, my heart asks me, would my Ancestors have been so readily seduced by random Arab traders appearing out of the desert or Europe's first missionaries bearing Bibles they could not read from unimagined lands far across the sea?

What would make so many Black folks fall so fast for a few words by nondescript strangers, who peddled no-frills versions of upper-class beliefs and relayed profound, cosmic ideas in tongues their listeners could not speak? And were those first Arabs and Europeans super-polite, unlike today's soccer crowds and cops who just love calling our kids N-?

How come they are made to appear so different from their present-day kith and kin? Surely villagers would have rejected them on sight and refused to "trade" anything with them, especially their own kith and kin? Children are prized across our Motherland and everywhere we survive.

I'm easily persuaded that that was in fact what most likely took place. Apart from the minority of aberrational thieves and scoundrels that populations of all ancestries produce, Black folks, definitively, did not spontaneously sell our own flesh and blood.

APB: What do your findings suggest?

GCM: The Portuguese who made contact with Mutapa/modern Zimbabwe early on left the only written records I know on that period. One of their strange stories is of a ruler sending off his two sons and heirs to "study" or be trained in religion and culture of the Portuguese. I don't buy that. Which ruler sends off his heirs to be indoctrinated by enemies or even allies in lands he has never seen? I believe the Europeans kidnapped them.

I've also never been able to find any record that explains why the marauding wealth-addicts, after presumably converting our Ancestors to their Word, never treated us as politely as they must have done in order to win us over so quickly.

What would make Black fathers and mothers, in generations gone by, abruptly banish the Ancestors who from childhood brought them comfort in the darkness of any sleepless night, and whose bones were in some cultures buried beneath their very beds?

And I found that ancestral tradition still in practice among the Howellites, the original Rastafari family, when I climbed up to their founder's home in Jamaica. As I spoke to Mama Ah-dri, their Matriarch, the graves of previous generations were solidly supporting us, under the rocks and mounds of stone beneath our feet.

APB: Once you put it like that, I find it unlikely.

GCM: For crying out loud! Europeans, in particular, still seem to have a hard time communicating with Black populations - even today. Just think South Africa! That divide in reality jumped out at me wherever I travelled in rural Afrika, where most of our bloodline live.

Time can stand remarkably still in those villages, I found. And it was palpable, even in the odd places where schools in French or English had opened up isolated populations to the outside world. As my eyes swept over vast landscapes, I could sense how our people's ancestry is like an anchor, and how much individuals feel bound to the soil where their grandmothers and grandfathers lie buried.

In fact, when I spoke to the leader of the veterans in Zimbabwe's land reclamation campaign, he said that, apart from general dissatisfaction with the pace of the Mugabe government's land reform, he had made a personal vow to take back the land where his grandfather was buried and on which White squatters and intruders from the UK were illegitimately living, before he died.

APB: That rings true. As a people, we are still very family-oriented.

GCM: To my knowledge, Br. Peter, most Black people, human beings period, feel attached to the way of life they know and to the place they say they are from. Take Northern Nigeria! As we speak, churches are being torched and pastors killed on suspicion that they are trying to convert non-Christians to their own faith. In the case of Tanganyika, during their Independence season, it is reported that bands of missionaries swooped in to compete for vulnerable Black souls. It was as if the retreating colonizers were desperately grabbing everything and everyone before they had to go.

Seen through culturally ancestral eyes, therefore, authorities like PM Julius Nyerere and President Abeid Karume of Zanzibar, one Christian and the other Muslim, appear hostile, or at best ambiguously socialized to the practice of Indigenous Black religious rituals.

Officially, PM Nyerere even banned Black religion. For some targeted communities, the sudden break with their deep-seated psycho-spiritual connections was sometimes more than they could bear. On occasion, from media reports, after the Nyerere ban, mass hysteria would sweep through a school or even engulf a whole village.

APB: That's understandable.

GCM: Mass hysteria might have been a pretty rare occurrence, but the records show it did happen, and some psychologists suspect the cause to be a broken, invisible connection that traumatized and deracinated those affected. - I find it plausible that Nyerere's regime's actions left those students and villagers feeling as if they were drifting in uncharted waters and treacherous seas. But who knows?

We missed a chance for Afrikan-centred scholars, giants of Pan-Afrikan psychology like Drs. Amos Wilson, Frances Cress-Welsing or Asa Hilliard, and those are just a few from the US alone, to examine and evaluate the costs of Afrika's unprecedented cycles of mass conversion before they passed away.

Out of personal experience, I'm willing to argue that any conversion requires a leap of faith and the internalization of a new identity. In our case, those new identities have always subordinated Blackness to a Divine Ideal's Image of a different hue, and that Ideal has been worshipped with rituals from a different culture.

Up to today, I believe that hard yet critical questions about the relationship of ancestral Black religions to other belief systems, especially Christianity, Judaism and Islam, remain unasked. In my childlike way, I wonder if "world religions" fear that, as happened with the World Trade Centre, once key pillars get too tested and stressed, the whole anti-Black edifice in which they have invested their own mental security will come tumbling down?

APB: I'm trying to remember if I've ever heard those questions posed before, in the way you do them.

GCM: Even my beloved mentor, Ancestor Abdou Rahmane Cissé, an open-minded, pioneering Pan-Afrikan journalist in touch with cultures across the continent and the globe, was caught by surprise when I broached the topic. As he enthusiastically told me of his efforts to preserve his, then, disappearing mother tongue, I asked him how he would say "God" in his native "Saafi-Saafi." [SAAH-FEE]

"Yalla," he fired back, without missing a beat. "No," I responded, "I mean what did Saafi-Saafi speaking people say before they learned to say, "Yalla"?

For, even to my untutored ear, "Yalla" sounded like "Allah" the way the dominant religion in Senegal, a generally more acceptable religion worldwide, would say "God."

"That question never crossed my mind," Abdou chuckled, and then warned me, "you'll probably get the same answer no matter who you put it to in Senegal."

Soon after, however, he emailed me. "Yalla" his message said, had replaced "Koog-Seenn," which was the only equivalent expression he found in "Saafi-Saafi." "Koog is God," he explained, "and Seenn means The Only One.." "But even our small band of remaining Saafi-Saafi speakers don't use it now."

It struck me, then, that even as they preserved the rest of their language, they had already lost a core Saafi-Saafi concept. For they had already forgotten how, when or why they had surrendered the sounds that their Ancestors intuited to affirm the presence of Cosmic Mind in their midst.

Instead, those villagers, through no fault of their own, had substituted imported sounds from the philosophy embraced by their dominant, uninvited guests.

Linguistic loss, Abdou had added, as he dared to recall what he knew, had resulted when familiar beliefs, icons and practices were outlawed on the heels of what historians usually call "mass conversion." In fact, near where Saafi-Saafi was spoken, some pre-conversion burial mounds were still visible, he confided. And those structures, he speculated to me, were built in the style of the Great Pyramid in KMT which we know as Ancient Egypt.

And here's a happy update! Under the Foundation guided by Br. Abdou's widow, Prof. Gabriella Meerbach in Amsterdam, there is now a functioning Studio, which offers programs in Saafi-Saafi near Thiès, [CHESS] just outside Dakar.

APB: Was he claiming an Indigenous Saafi-Saafi connection to Ancient Egypt?

GCM: Jackpot! In fact, his research had already led him to a nearby village called, "Thioupie" [CHOO-PEE], which he thought might be derived from "Ethiopie (French for "Ethiopia)." However, because my teacher passed on so prematurely, I am now left to wonder.

As a teacher, however, I'll bet you a trip to the Motherland that if stories like this were in the textbooks Black students get to read around the world, their teachers would absolutely own their interest and attention in class. That's why I'm convinced that in the future successful education for Black populations will depend on having Black designers of curricula and Black teachers in Black-run schools sharing a global Black vision and mission.

And I witnessed how quickly and efficiently the US Peace Corps could teach its volunteers to speak Wolof, Mandinka or any of the indigenous Black languages all over Afrika.

Any of our billionaire celebrities or even a consortium of a few could fund a similar program today and repair the damage of forced linguistic exile in Canada, the US, the Caribbean and all over the Black Diaspora.

APB: That's also the way I see it too. The duty of our generation is to make Pan-Afrikanism dance in the gifted heads of all the young lives we are privileged to touch.

GCM: In Jurassic times, I taught oral French. Those years of learning and practicing how to teach language provided me with first-hand proof that digesting a culture or language only happens when we use them daily and they take on meaning in our routine activities.

For example, Br. Bankie Forster Bankie, seasoned by living in many Black worlds, became a sustainer who nursed and nurtured three Pan-Afrikan organizations - CASAS the (Centre for the Advanced Study of African Society) in Cape Town, South Africa; PACON the (Pan African Centre Of Namibia) and PAISAS the (Pan-African Institute for the Study of African Society) in South Sudan.

Yet Br. Bankie was spectacularly self-effacing, even as he made remarkable sacrifices for the ideals he was determined to serve. He told me that he had taken a personal pledge to do something to advance Pan-Afrikanism every day of his life. Even if it boiled down to just sending out critical information by email, he never broke his promise. And I, for one, am a fortunate beneficiary of his dedicated service and sage advice.

APB: I like that you keep coming back to things we can do in Talking Cheddo.

GCM: Here's what I do to debunk the popular prejudice that Afrikans, had to be taught monotheism, and that before "world religions" replaced their ancestral faiths, they were governed by 'superstition."

That falsity is rampant even though history convincingly documents the fact that Akhenaton/Akhenaten introduced Monotheism into KMT/Ancient Egypt before any of the world religions were born. When that kind of discourse is foisted on me, I wait until "God" gets mentioned. Then, I deliberately inject an Afrikan name for God. For example, I might say.

Oh, you mean "Mwari"? That's a way some folks say "God" in Zimbabwe. And others say "Nyame" in Ghana and Ivory Coast. Then, if asked, I would explain that those names also The nicest response I'm likely to get is, "I didn't know that." More predictably, however, I will overhear, "I thought they had many gods." And, I think unfortunately, those remarks can come just as easily from the mouth of a post-doctoral, home-grown and highly-educated Afrikan.

APB: I'm not surprised. The colonial education system has remained largely unchallenged and unchanged.

GCM: That's so true. But I believe that by deepening and spreading knowledge of our ancestral culture we can counter the zombie stigma hanging around the neck of Black belief systems. Take me, for instance. You're probably exhausted from hearing me declare that I'm a freshly-baked, adopted Oromo from ancient Oromia in modern Ethiopia.

Waka is the Oromo word for God, and it has not only been easy for me to learn it but also to integrate it into my daily discourse. When I started paying attention to the Oromo spoken around me, I quickly picked up a few common expressions and words, because I kept hearing them.

Anyway, I soon realized that Oromos would call on "Waka" if the elevator broke down, the way my grandmother would add "God willing" to any and every decision she made. However, the Oromo sister and brother who adopted me taught me that when your heart and life were a wreck, you'd look up, lift your arms to the sky and call out, "O Waka Guracha (O Great Black God)!."

APB: I have a vivid memory of looking at six Sunday services on TV, when I was in Accra two years ago for a Pan-Afrikan conference. In every church, the preacher was Black, and so was everyone in every congregation. The uniform image of human beings on my screen was Black. Then, without warning, it switched to White. Every angel was White, as was every saint and every statue or portrait of Mary or Jesus – White in White on White!

GCM: Isn't that something? Down the street from where I live in Toronto there's a Catholic Cathedral, which used to house a carving of a White Archangel overpowering a Black demon. I'm here to attest that that tableau is a favourite and frequently-repeated theme in Church iconography. No matter where we're born, Black psyches are moulded around beliefs that God must not ever be made to look like their mothers and fathers.

Oromos, on the other hand, have always sung praises to Waka Guracha. As far as human minds remember, that probably took place even before "Kush," which generally refers to Sudan and surrounding lands, and was also the civilization that founded KMT/ KEH-MET, which the world has been taught to call "Egypt."

Speaking geographically, the Oromo Motherland shelters the most populous Kush-speaking area on the planet. And authorities as diverse as prophet Ezekiel in the Bible and French historian and geographer Dr. Louise Marie Diop Maes, spouse and colleague to Cheikh Anta, also confirm that Kush predates KMT/Egypt.

APB: What a remarkable reversal of fortunes! I know of Hebrew as a world-class language today, but until your book I didn't know about Oromo.

GCM: And yet it's ancient, Afrikan, and still spoken widely around the civilizational and world-civilizing River Nile. In fact, both world-class linguist Prof. Kwesi Prah and psychologist Dr. Amos Wilson have provided sound explanations of the benefits that would accrue if Oromo or some other ancestral language became the lingua franca of global Pan-Afrikan life. I dare to promise you and any doubter anywhere that doing so would be a master-stroke of operationally Black mindfulness.

APB: I agree 100 per cent with making a common language a Pan-Afrikan priority.

GCM: But that strategy won't work unless we have convincing reasons for making it a second language of daily communication for global Afrika.

It's our job to make a global Black nation feel imperative, exciting and imminent. And with access to today's technology, I trust that we can easily universalize a Black language, livestream positive images, re-interpret our history and begin uprooting the ages of zombie stigma which often hobble Black minds.

For a start, here's some good news! Since Oromo is no longer considered a "slave" language or banned by rival, less populous but more dominant ethnic regimes in Ethiopia, it has already streaked around the globe. So, today, Oromo-speaking communities have taken root in Minneapolis, Regina, Copenhagen, Toronto, Sydney (Australia) and beyond.

APB: That's true. I used to think of Ethiopia as really distant, but now I get invitations to Oromo community functions here in Washington, DC.

GCM: Now let me tell you about an experience I had of just teaching "Waka Guracha" to a group of Black teenagers in Nova Scotia.

I'm sure you still remember the delightful meetings you had talking up Pan-Afrikanism with students at Mount St. Vincent University in Halifax. They've all long graduated, but I know they still talk about meeting you. Truth is, our youth are famished for truths about how we, and they, got stuck at this alien address in our journey through time and space.

And I feel that they could really use guidance that would come with seeing through your eyes and hearing Br. Malcolm's voice at this time. Let's face it! Our folks are largely groping their way around in the psychological fog of social media that blinds and entraps multitudes today.

APB: Halifax was a memorable trip for me. Before that, I had had no idea that there was such a historically significant Black community next door in Canada. And I remember being really impressed that they already had a Black Cultural Centre even before one had been built by the Smithsonian in the US capital itself.

GCM: Well, in pre-pandemic times, the Black Educators Association in New Glasgow, another Nova Scotian town where Black refugees from the killing South had settled seven generations ago, invited me to do a workshop on identity with students who were about to graduate from high school.

After getting the generic North American academic warning of, 'Beware-Black-Boys', I won't say from who, I said my polite thanks, closed the door so we were in a safe Black-family space and posed a question. Then, as those eager minds were turning it over, I began telling our children my own Waka Guracha story.

APB: Nova Scotia is a lot like the Black South, isn't it? So, the youth in your audience were probably suckled on Sunday school.

GCM: Wax-nge degg!/WAAH-HUNGAH-DEGGUH! Once again, "Tell it like id tiz!" That's why I wanted to take them with me down the road of another kind of Black history, which I was sure they wouldn't get at school or Sunday school. And it worked.

The question I posed was, "Do you think you know an Afrikan word for "God"?

The class was immediately hooked. I won't soil your Pan-Afrikan ears with all they had been taught and believed about Afrikan religions. I held my nose as, without the slightest hint of embarrassment, they innocently "dissed" their own Black Ancestors. On principle, however, I don't blame anyone, especially younger generations, for being miseducated by popular culture.

The discussion became really charged, however, and I took the opportunity to unpack or disprove some of the misinformation they aired.

APB: That must have created some tension, exploding myths they had internalized about Black beliefs.

GCM: I took time to answer their questions and challenges thoroughly, providing the kind of facts they could google immediately. Tech can really be our friend when we need to engage younger minds today. Backed up by the new info on their screens, I then retraced my own path, step by step. I recalled incidents that were significant in my own journey from "Hail Mary" to "Waka Guracha." In fact, some members of the group, who were Catholic, could immediately relate to my memories of having to learn the Catechism by heart.

Others were intrigued to hear me tell how I was inspired by the thousands of children jailed during the Children's Crusade in Birmingham, Alabama at the height of the Civil Rights Movement, or how students I taught in Toronto became inspired by the children of Soweto later on.

They were all ears when I walked them through my time as secretary of the first Black History Week Committee in TO, and maybe Canada, all the way to my being introduced to "Waka Guracha, the Great Black God."

As I tried to describe how that moment had changed me, they sat still, holding their breath, as if unwilling to miss a word by even breathing out or in.

APB: Just listening to you, I get the feeling of excitement in that room.

GCM: Then I modeled Oromo prayers for them by acting out two different scenarios.

For the first one, we imagined that I was a sure A or at least a B+ student in English or Black Studies, only recently added to the curriculum in Nova Scotia. So, for an A+ I said, I'd pray, "O Waka! Please help me! - Yaa Waka na gargaari!" I made them repeat it with me, together and individually, until everyone got it right.

In the next scenario, I played the kind of student who was turned off school and could only score D in Black Studies. Then I said. What am I to do? I need an A+ to get into Mc Gill, Dalhousie or UofT.

That's a Major League ASK, I said. It's time to call on my Great Grandma as well as my Granma. After all, they've both been Ancestors a long time and would definitely know what to do. If that didn't work – I held centre-stage and paused … If that didn't work, I would throw my arms wide and cry out, "Yaa Waka Guracha!" – "O Big Black God!"

The classroom exploded. As one body, they leapt to their feet pumping their fists and acting like their team had just scored. The rest, as the Spiritual sings, was history – "…Flowing deep and wide"!

In fact, the Regional Director for the Black Educators Association, which had contracted me, reports that, even years later, individual students, included a young man who is now a lawyer, are still referring to that session. They all remember "Waka Guracha."

APB: Now I know it too.

GCM: To repair the fragmented education that most Black students receive in public schools today, we need to create identity-specific, dignity-safe zones focused on sharing positive experiences. I trust that, eventually, young learners will link Black vibes to victory and not failure, as mostly happens in their learning experiences across White-skewed societies they know.

APB: Coming back to the religious question! When I was a member of the Organization of African American Unity, I didn't have to become a Muslim like Br. Malcolm. In fact, Br. Malcom made it clear from the beginning that his Islamic faith was a personal, religious matter. On the other hand, Pan-Afrikanism had brought us together in his new organization, which he defined as secular.

GCM: Once I had grasped my new-found authority based on Cheddo, I had no trouble rebutting claims by colleagues or in popular culture that conversion had benefited Black populations. From my expanded information-base, I've become increasingly convinced that mass conversion was sourced in coercion or brutal force.

In the generations that followed conversion, the new rulers monopolized the social structures for propagandizing their land occupation and racial domination. What was effectively a strategy for brainwashing converts into surrendering their hard assets like land was portrayed as a blessing.

Pan-Afrikan re-education, our experience suggests, would render a significant service by encouraging more research into the intention, goal and psychological costs of mass conversion in Black history. And it would potentially link it to land-loss and generalized penury today.

APB: We need Black leaders who accept responsibility for leading our people.

GCM: An equally pernicious propaganda system stigmatizes Ayiti as the perennial "poorest country" across the globe.

It doesn't mention the six billion in US dollars effectively disappeared under the watch of the USA, the UN and the Red Cross. To date, neither the media nor members of the Congressional Black Caucus seem willing to even suggest that those responsible return such blatantly-misappropriated funds.

Instead, the false hashtag, "poorest country" is perpetrated by even the liberal media. That label also ignores the billions or more, in today's currency, that France extorted as "reparations" from Ayiti. Her crime was facilitated by her colonizing allies around the world. Hashtag "poorest country" also ignores the looting of Ayiti's gold reserves by the USA during its illegal occupation from 1919 to 1934.

In addition, Ayiti lives in an era where Hedge Fund billionaires can enforce pernicious debts. That practice included forcing President Aristide to pay interest on international (World Bank/IMF) loans even before he received the funds that he was to use to boost the economy. Go figure!

There has also been no public accounting, in my research, or compensation for the economic costs and chaos of targeted destruction of Ayiti's pig and rice industries. In total defiance of international legitimacy or moral law, the "poorest country" lie persists, even when, in addition, Venezuela's Petro Caraibe's gift of millions have been disappeared into thin air. That has all happened during this decade, under uninvited "stewardship" and unhelpful and immoral domination of Ayiti's destiny by the USA and the indistinctly identified "international community."

What universal measure would today's world employ, I wonder, to determine whether Asia and Europe have brought Afrika gain or loss through their systems of governance, domination or imposed religious beliefs?

APB: That was not discussed in many social circles I've been in.

GCM: Ironically, Black mothers, largely "invisibilized" in histories of those times, suffered the greatest loss from mass conversion. Until then, they had held, exclusively, the most coveted real estate on earth, under a unique contract of Cosmic trust, passed down from generation to generation from before remembered time.

The record is clear. The wealth-seekers who entered the Black Motherland, always graciously received although uninvited, never took advantage of opportunities to establish fair exchange.

As with the Ogoni people in Nigeria today, while strangers grew rich, the Indigenous people reaped a bitter harvest that destroyed their peaceful, prosperous existence. And those stalwarts who dared to stand up for their kith and kin were cut down by the immoral exploiters from overseas and conniving, local elements.

In the end, however, mother-centred, flexible, Black culture, no doubt reinforced by Nature in all her forms, withstood the Arab and European attempts to erase their identity and take over all of our Black Motherland.

APB: Although, as you say, Asia and Europe did not succeed in replacing Afrika's Indigenous population, they removed and destroyed so many Black bodies, as Walter Rodney documented in How Europe Underdeveloped Africa, that the population practically collapsed between 1450 -1950.

GCM: In Talking Cheddo, because I wanted readers to examine available hard evidence of what had taken place, I included artifacts like the Mani Kongo's 1526 letter to Portugal's rulers. When the Portuguese violated trading agreements and started kidnapping Kongolese families instead, the Mani Kongo fired off a resounding "No!"

His letter is heart-rending. Here is a potentate bending to beg for the lives of his near and dear, his inclusive family, as the perfidious Portuguese Christians fail to respect rank, gender, title, function or class! Disappointingly, the existence and content of that letter, as well as the role of foreign patriarchal ideas in undermining ancestral land rights, still pass under the radar of most writers and educators today.

APB: That's another idea that I haven't seen raised as yet.

GCM: Here's my view! Although ancestrally-anchored Black societies remain in their essence mother-centred, patriarchy proved largely seductive to Black men as well, and has largely been adopted as an operational norm.

The outcome of generations of compromised patriarchal leadership is reflected in the African Union's defence of colonial borders today. Power now rests in cliques of unscrupulous individuals, who impoverish the populations they rule with foreign guns and sanctions and keep them vulnerable in a dangerous world.

Under the ironclad land system our Ancestors had invented, however, foreign wealth-seekers were denied a snowflake's hope in hell of possessing a grain of sand or a blade of grass from our Motherland's sacred soil. Therefore, wannabee land-grabbers faced three choices - convert them, kill them or both.

APB: They certainly killed enough. I did notice that you make "land" a central theme of your work. However, I don't remember you linking land ownership to the Cheddo system as plainly as you're doing now.

GCM: Afrika has long been a magnet for wealth-seekers and land-seekers from afar. Way back, it was the Persians, who were followed by the Greeks. Later the peripatetic Arab gossip or spy, Ibn Battuta recorded the wonders he found in Afrika with awe. By 1798, Napoleon had arrived on the scene with 150 of France's finest minds, its "savants," who were primed to extract Black know-how and artistic genius from the culture they gazed on with admiration. Even today, a scramble of foreign corporations and governments cling to the same exploitative Eurasian tradition.

However, as long as Black mothers remained guarantors and guards of the sacred soil, foreign home invaders could never legitimize land-grabbing, and since they would remain strangers into perpetuity, the culture kept them at bay, while holding the Indigenous Black societies intact.

APB: You are obviously thinking of the land question beyond its economic importance.

GCM: Definitively! I believe land must continue to play a key role in any strategy for total Black liberation. The Maroons in Jamaica understood that, as did the leader Zumbi and other builders of quilombos (freed settlements) in Brazil. There were also sanctuary communities in Surinam as in the US South or anywhere Black freedom has had to exist under threat of attack.

Marcus and Amy Garvey understood that, and today, Rastafari/Rasta-Far-Eye from Jamaica to South Africa do as well. The rules of the colonial relics we call countries today were not conceived for Black Liberation but our degradation under anti-Black domination into perpetuity. However, speaking from personal experience, the potential of adoption of those of us in the Diaspora, as individuals or groups, can re-ignite interest in embracing Pan-Afrikanism within Overseas Black populations.

APB: Doing that would be a salvation for our people.

GCM: To me, the common explanation of Afrika's voluntary and easy surrender of Ancestor-based beliefs, which was/is the Motherland's social glue, has always felt far-fetched. In fact, from my own lived experience, wide reading and research, the bond between land and Ancestors is still tight.

When taking me to meet his family, I remember how a Mandinka brother, Keba, called his home village "mon pays," which in French says, "my country." In All Eyes On Africa, Chief Elizabeth Jibunoh, in Lagos, speaks forcefully about the significance of "where do you come from."

Even today, my research suggests that about ninety percent of rural Afrika populations still enjoy inherited collective land rights. Without any written title, that gives them a kind of social insurance vested in just being who they are. In many states, however, election profiteers of imposed foreign political systems have worked hand-in-glove with putative land-thieves determined to extinguish those legacies.

Perhaps instinctively, female defenders of the land like Kenyan Nobel laureate, Mama Wangari Maathai have passed on its stewardship to daughters, as she did to Sr. Wanjira Maathai, who follows in her footsteps in protecting the land.

To our global shame, however, these keepers of Cosmic Black legacies have usually faced continual, insidious psychological and physical attacks. And, as you never tire reminding me, we should have developed more successful strategies for self-protection by now. If we are to survive as an identity, it's essential that we prioritize defending the defenders of our ancestral lands.

APB: Those folks claiming to lead us need to get real. I don't get it. It isn't as if we don't know that every other race is after our land. If you call yourself a Black leader, your responsibility is to Black people in general.

GCM: After living on the continent, I came to understand how belonging worked over there. No one pays attention to it, because being Black and belonging is as natural as breathing air.

Take my first Dakar to Banjul cross-border trip! Wherever I went, my Black face and Indigenous features were a portable ID. I didn't ever have to show paper anything.

And because border security would assume that I was local, I could pass without suspicion in any crowd. Later, for Toronto or New York! Over here, both the police and an unofficial but unblinking White gaze regard me twenty-four-seven with suspicious eyes. Even random strangers at parties or colleagues in the academy have scolded or questioned me for dressing and generally looking too "Afrikan."

"I know a Nigerian doctor," they'd say, "but he just wears regular clothes."

Within this climate, where Blackness can never be incognito but is always under scrutiny, I wasn't surprised when a book showed up to air the unspoken question, Black Like Who? Somehow, I can't imagine a book that would ask, "Chinese" or "English" or "Jewish" or "French" or "Indian" or "Arab Like Who"? And yet folk wearing all those identities, just like Kush/Afrikans, are scattered around the globe.

APB: I blame us for that ... We compromise about identity too easily. Once I was doing a story on the New York cultural scene, with a focus on Black male actors. When I arrived and opened my notebook to begin my interview, the actor, who is well-known, made a pre-emptive strike.

"I'm an actor," he said, "who just happens to be Black." I stood up, said thanks and shut my notebook.

"I came here to do a story on Black actors," I said. "When I get an assignment to do a story on actors who happen to be Black, I'll give you a call."

With that, I turned on my heel and left. I've never interviewed him. I'm convinced that we should never beg anyone who's reluctant about being seen as Black. It just makes for a more confused Black world.

GCM: On the other hand, in my experience, Black confidence, often racially misread as arrogance, predictably tends to excite unmerited or otherwise negative responses.

Let me tell you what once happened to me at work! I was leading a "Diversity" workshop and conducting an exercise on social identities.

"I'm more Afrikan than you," someone challenged me, and sucked oxygen out of the room.

"I'm Indian but I was born in South Afrika," she continued. "While you, you come from the Caribbean."

Would you believe it, Br. Peter? Big bad, Black-on-Black me? IN MY FACE! This was a dissin' to my face!

I breathed in slowly and softly replied.

"You're right. I was born in the Caribbean, but I'm from Afrika. With my looks, had I been born in Beijing, I doubt that anyone anywhere there or here would call me Chinese."

No doubt, because I look like King Tut's blood brother and can pass for Robert Mugabe's Overseas son swept the room.

For Asians and Europeans, ID generally equates geography. And to me, as an Overseas Afrikan, that acts as a guarantee of social security that, until I became Oromo, had been stripped from and denied to me.

APB: I believe that the question of the Diaspora must be resolved at the level of the African Union.

GCM: I'm not sure that I would endorse that.

Many of those foreign-linked heads of state have usually operated like Judas goats who transferred control of collective lands to foreign entities.

Before elections, they never announce to Indigenous landowners that they intend to develop their land, which would also mean taking it away from them without their consent.

But as soon as they are enthroned in their air-conditioned Mercedes, those "leading Blacks" rush laws through European-cloned parliaments or issue executive orders that overnight impoverish populations they have never served and who owe them nothing.

APB: I'm glad that Talking Cheddo is putting that message out, so our folks can start paying more attention to the process.

GCM: Uniquely in this world, Afrikan ID has become ascribed and tied to birthplace rather than ancestry.

I remember, in Toronto, swapping Afrikan experiences with a Caribbean sister, who had worked on the continent with the UN, while a young brother, fresh out of Sierra Leone, was looking on.

At some point, I remember the sister saying to me, "I am tired of listening to you preaching Blackness. I want to hear from the real Afrikan now." With that, she turned her back to me and faced our younger brother. I lost it.

"Please tell me like I'm a four-year old," I heard myself asking, "just when did I give up my ancestry? Or, at least, please let me know the person you know, that is alive or dead, who ever had the authority to take my ancestry away from me?"

APB: That's why Br. Malcolm called our group the Organization of Afro-American Unity. Putting "Afrikan" in the organization's name distinguished us from others, who claimed descent from the "Asiatic Black man." I hope Talking Cheddo, will prove useful, especially to our young people, as they try to sort out any identity confusion they may be dealing with.

GCM: And that gets us back to the whole question of where essentially Black populations come from. For me, it's obvious and a no-brainer – Black people come from Afrika and Australia.

We come out of Black culture and are Black culture. I make the analogy that the wood is in the fire and the fire is in the wood. We are in Black culture and Black culture is in us.

So, the identity that you call Pan-Afrikanism and I now include in Cheddo comes from the same place – our Black Cradleland.

In fact, some historians, including Australians, also make the case for an early settlement of Black people from Afrika in Australia, some fifty thousand years ago.

Remember that the Lewises, Mary and Arthur, both doctors and an unequivocally committed Black Harlem family who we know, went to Vanuatu at Independence, fit in like a glove and helped set up medical services for our sisters and brothers over there.

Having grown up guessing about where I could say I was from, unlike my Indigenous, Chinese, Indian or European schoolmates, just the certainty of knowing I'm fully Afrikan has reinforced my sense of self-worth. - Increasingly, Black folks in this hemisphere are stepping into this life already steeped in their ancestry and confident of bearing priceless gifts.

APB: Yet, from my point of view, it seems that previous generations, certainly mine, were somehow given a stronger sense of self than the generation growing up or in charge today.

GCM: Yes. Tensions over ID, especially since post WW II "integration," have unfortunately undermined rather than enhanced Black self-esteem.

As I feel it, today our world teeters on the brink of a catastrophe-in-waiting, pregnant with over-watched and over-policed, hyper-vigilant Black males.

Since the situation I'm describing, including the kind of hyper-vigilance it generates is unique to us, it demands both skilled healers and urgent, informed global Pan-Afrikan attention.

APB: I agree, and that's another reason why I think your book is relevant right now. It's amazing to me that so few people who have national platforms, in this country at least, deal with the whole question of psychological warfare.

By telling you, publicly, that she was more Afrikan than you, that Indian woman was making a targeted attack on your mind. And even though you were supposedly in charge of that workshop, she knew she could get away with it, because you are a Black man. Most of our "leading Blacks," as psychologist Mamie Clark calls them, just don't deal with psychological warfare. They channel their energy into electoral politics and civil rights.

GCM: In my Introduction to Talking Cheddo, I encouraged those who already had the skills to mix up a cocktail of cutting-edge neuroscience and ancestral Black deep-thought that would provide a "prophylactic" against the relentless propaganda onslaught that targets Black minds.

APB: I always tell people that the most important thing that attracted me to Br. Malcolm when I heard him speak in 1962 was … (He pauses and reflects)

The first time I heard him speak he spent forty-five minutes of a three-hour speech talking about attacks on the mind.

I was twenty-four years old and had never before heard anyone talk about attacks on the mind.

And I remembered growing up in Tuskegee Alabama. During Jim Crow in Tuskegee, unlike many other places, you didn't have Black people sitting in the balcony at the movies. We had a completely separate theatre side by side with the White theatre. And we would be there every Saturday – ages six to thirteen. I was down there every Saturday from about ten in the morning to about three o'clock in the afternoon, watching movies.

And most of the time we were watching Tarzan movies.

So, here was this theatre full of Black youngsters between say, six and thirteen years, and we'd be there every Saturday cheering Tarzan and Cheetah over the Afrikans.

In fact, we would laugh at the Afrikans, because when they were together, they spoke their own language. To us, that meant they didn't speak English. So, they were ...like ... ignorant.

And when I remember growing up in Tuskegee, and you'd call somebody a SOB or a MF, and that might start a fight. But if you called them an "Afrikan" or "Black" then that was a definite fight.

GCM: I remember that, all through my boyhood, using "Negro" was definitely preferable to "Black." We hadn't yet graduated to "Coloured."

And yet when I stumbled upon the definition of "Negro" in the outdated Encyclopedia Britannica in my High School library, it made me cringe. I dreaded the thought of any of my friends, even Black friends, reading it.

APB: Today I consider myself a strong, total Pan-Afrikanist, to such an extent that my position is, nowadays, that I can't take you seriously if you say you are a Muslim Pan-Afrikanist, or a Christian Pan-Afrikanist or a Nigerian Pan-Afrikanist or a Jamaican Pan-Afrikanist. You must be a Pan-Afrikanist Muslim, a Pan-Afrikanist Christian, a Pan-Afrikanist Nigerian or a Pan-Afrikanist Jamaican. Pan-Afrikanism has got to be your first identity. And I think your book helps to explain the absolute importance of that approach.

GCM: When I wrote Talking Cheddo: Rescuing Pan-Afrikanism , I was already convinced that unprincipled, egocentric pretenders had seized historical Pan-Afrikanism by the throat and were "vampirizing" it.

I chose to call the antidote to present trends, ancestral deepthought, "Cheddo," based on inspiration visited on me the day after my moving to Afrika for a year's sabbatical. I count it ancestral guidance that led me to the doorstep of legendary Pan-Afrikanist Ousmane Sembène, "the father of Afrikan film."

Looking up from his doorstep, I read a sign that said, "Villa Ceddo Wedo." When I asked, our justly celebrated brother told me with pride that it meant, "Home of the Freethinking Tukulor," one of the smaller ethnic groups in Senegal.

APB: Let's stop a moment. One of my problems re Afrikans on the continent is their endless obsession with ethnicity. It divides us.

GCM: I think I know where you're coming from, Br. Peter. You believe we need to combat ethnic conflict, because it destroys our unity. But wherever I went - Morocco, Zimbabwe, Kenya or Senegal, just being Black, made me belong to local Black communitites.

From what I hear these days, however, that feeling might have been destroyed by ANC betrayals and subservience to White Supremacy in South Africa. White South Afrikans are still being treated like the real owners of the land and Black people as landless nomads. Similarly, in Canada, even seventh generation Black Nova Scotians routinely get asked where they're from. Not so anyone with White skin, even if they are unable to communicate in either English or French and only landed in Canada yesterday.

In reality, however, Black ethnicity is much more fluid than the media portray it. I can't cite a scientific study, but I have lived experience of examples that inform my understanding of ethnicity in the Motherland. By way of example, President Robert Mugabe, who was a Shona teacher from Zimbabwe, chose as his life's partner Sally Hayfron, an ethnically Fanti teacher and comrade-in-arms from Ghana.

Even in death, all of Zimbabwe, whether from Ndebele or Shona populations, honour her as "Amai/Mother," for mothering the orphans of their Liberation War. An equally stirring example was President Patrice Lumumba, from a tiny ethnic group, the Batatela, being entrusted with a clear majority win in Congo's first end-of-colonization, open election.

And I remain especially impressed that that visionary, young, Pan-Afrikanist PM would pick a seasoned diplomat, a member of Senegal's Wolof majority to represent the newly-independent Congo as its first ambassador to Cairo. And, incidentally, as to illustrate how fluid ethnicity is in practice, as opposed to how outsiders portray it, Ambassador Fall from Senegal was himself married to Nubian Egyptian scholar at the University of Dakar.

Given such striking examples of inter-ethnic solidarity, it seems to me that playing up "ethnic conflict" is often a race supremacist ruse. As I see it, it serves external forces invested in destabilizing Afrikans to marshal their media power to keep us feeling divided and in disarray. Consider, for the moment, the time-worn trope of "Black-on-Black violence or Black-on-Black crime."

I've never once, in all my long years, heard White-on-White violence – despite WW I and WW II. Nor have I heard any other group spoken of in those explicitly divisive terms.

APB: I didn't know about Mugabe's wife. Was that his first wife?

GCM: Yes. She was. But bear with me! I like to offer my classes a picture of ethnicity in symbolic terms.

For me, an open hand validates our diversity, symbolizing The Many, while a closed fist affirms our unity as one culture sourced from a single ancestral line. If we follow the teachings of Ancestors from up and down the Nile, KMT/Ancient Egypt, they tell us that whether we see ourselves as individuals/the One or one cell of an inter-connected body/the Many – we're always the same.

Divisive colourism or bias against darker skin is a more recent phenomenon, and it's, arguably, fallout from our "Maafa," a Swahili word meaning Great Suffering, as the US writer, Sr. Marimba Ani, names it. And colourism was once so rampant in this hemisphere, in my lifetime, that even Baptist bishops and Muslim imams were overwhelmingly chosen less for their piety than for their pigmentation.

APB: In his film, School Daze, Spike Lee takes on Black fraternities and sororities, where the prevailing culture was - the lighter your skin, the higher your prestige.

GCM: We older heads, especially in the Caribbean and Americas, were all born under the tyranny of the "lighter equals brighter" syndrome. It's hardly news noting that it became so because of the abuse and violation of Black women and girls by White men, over generations.

Under French tyranny in Ayiti, even the slightest hint of Black ancestry, measured by the shade or tint of a person's skin, would tell that society how human they were. So, octoroon, for example, meant a person who was one-eighth Black, and presumably of higher status than a quadroon - someone one-quarter Black.

However, overnight, under Ayiti's revolutionary president, Jean-Jacques Dessalines, and in his nation's 1805 Constitution, it was decreed that every citizen, from that moment on, was Black - No shade, nil ethnicity, nada race!

APB: This is the first time that I've heard of generic Blackness being applied as the standard in any society.

GCM: And no other society has reached that moral height anywhere in the world until today. Now, let's go back to our reasoning about ethnic conflict!

Of course, I believe we should confront the negative fallout, including the violent clashes, caused by ethnic rivalries. We all saw what mayhem it caused in Kenya, during several election campaigns. However, I believe it's counter-productive for us to treat it as if it's the whole story, even at its most destructive.

If people can't get on in Kenya because of ethnicity, how come the population isn't also fighting Europeans and Asians on the basis of ancestry? Why aren't Indigenous Kenyans taking back their best land, which is now still illegitimately occupied by the heirs of European colonizers or immigrant Asian nationals?

Inexplicably, those groups seem to always be left untouched when the country goes up in flames. And they aren't forced to sacrifice anything or lose everything like Kikuyus, Kalenjins or Luos. Here's another example from our immediate lived experience!

What the heroic Paul Rusesabagina did as a Rwandan Hutu married to a Tutsi in rescuing thousands of Tutsis from genocide, was in every way as noble as the rescue of thousands from the persecuted Jewish population by the German, Oskar Schindler, during the Holocaust. And yet our hero, Rusesabagina, was kidnapped from the air by Rwandese agents and jailed for ten years. On that atrocity, The International Court and The African Union have remained largely, and strangely, silent.

APB: It's shameful to see how little pressure world powers have exerted to save him from dying in a Rwandan prison. Fortunately the media reported that he was finally freed in March this year.

GCM: Honestly speaking, I don't buy the media's "innate ethnic hostility" propaganda as the basis of Afrika's ills.

White self-protection insulates their minds from self-doubt. Then they sell Black populations, including many of our public intellectuals or leading Blacks, a deadly mix of plausible deniability.

How often have we not read or heard, "slave raiders didn't go inland," as a kind of definitive argument against European "slave-raiding"? Then, on the other side of the coin, there is an argument of plausible culpability, "you sold your own."

And, in my experience, Liberals, especially Whites, never tire telling us there is no conspiracy against us. They do so despite the obvious conspiracy misnamed the "Berlin Conference," where diverse European nations planned Black demise by dividing up Afrika with no Afrikan present.

In my humble view, the truth about their conspiracy and the evidence of our cohesion is revealed by our lived experience. For starters, let's just cast our minds back to how quickly Ayitians, from anywhere and everywhere in Africa, bonded to overthrow their enslavers!

Why, if ancient ethnic divisions didn't prevent our Ancestors from bonding across ethnicity under those traumatic conditions, do we accept that they are the reason we are so often divided today?

And the history of coming together in Ayiti is not unique.

Black bonding against Bondage is repeated in the 1823 Demerara Rebellion in Guyana. What the pundits too often fail to highlight is that it wasn't ethnicity, but loyalty to Christianity, which defeated our freedom-fighter Ancestors in that instance.

It was indeed their Christian loyalty, which convinced some of those brutally enslaved men and women to betray their own brothers and sisters in order to protect their White persecutors from reaping just retribution.

APB: Those are powerful examples for re-educating present and coming generations.

GCM: It's sobering how easily we tend to accept arguments that are not borne out by history or our lived experience, and allow them to undermine the reality of the unity that has sustained us to this day.

As for this born-again Oromo, I'm ecstatic about the culture! Right now, my brain feels like a sponge, as it tries to absorb so much new learning. What's especially thrilling is that, in processing my thoughts, I'm finding reflections of Oromo rituals and beliefs that I've grown up instinctively knowing, in the culture which raised me – although I was born so distant in time, place and inner space from the beautiful, generous families adopting me today.

There's an Oromo saying from my Borana region that begins, "An Borana arrabi…" Here's my interpretive translation into English verse!

> "I'm a True-Blue Borana from Kush,
>
> With a Blue-Black mark on my tongue
>
> Let the whole world beware,
>
> Don't try me. Don't dare,
>
> My curse brings empires down."

And, as my sainted grandmother would warn any would-be offender, in the tones of her Guyanese gravitas, "Don' mek me put meh mout pon yuh! Or "Don't let me put my mouth on you!"

APB: How common is an experience like yours, do you think?

GCM: I don't know and don't feel the need to guess. What I am sure of is that return to the ancestral womb is possible. If this experience found me, in the vastness of global Blackness, it is sure to find many other eager disciples like me.

Let's be clear! I don't in any way believe that title to a specific region of Motherland soil grants me special ethnic privileges.

The way I take it, the most comforting part of becoming Oromo is being rescued from the anonymity of being seen as an Overseas orphaned Afrikan.

And because adoption is normal in Oromo culture, as in Afrikan societies generally, there are specific, functioning rituals for adopting individuals, families, clans and entire populations.

Speaking personally, adoption is a blessing that solders my spiritual umbilical cord, severed by genocidal abduction and forced exile all those many generations ago.

At some ineffable level of consciousness, it gives me a feeling of being transcendently whole.

APB: I hope you're right about being positive about ethnicity, but that's not what I see when I look around in places like Ethiopia or South Africa today.

GCM: On the specific question of the civil war in Ethiopia, as a Pan-Afrikanist trying to walk in your footsteps, I've been inviting everyone to read my Oromo brother Leenco Lata's book, *The Horn of Africa as Common Homeland*. The title speaks for itself.

APB: What is it that you're seeing that the rest of us don't see yet?

GCM: Just as we've mostly, over here, graduated out of the most backward aspects of colourism, I trust that our sisters and brothers on the continent will soon shed the visibly destructive features of ethnic rivalries that make them easy pickings for passing predators.

Let's take a stab at unpacking Ethnicity 101!

Off the bat, no one can deny that there's always complexity within each and every ethnic group.

Let's look at the Tukulor filmmaker, Ousmane Sembène's people, for example! They are a predominantly Senegalese ethnic group, though they also live in nearby countries, and are affiliated to the Serer and Wolof, two larger ethnic groups in Senegal.

While widely-known as early converts, and therefore pioneers for Islam, that's not their whole story. Those same Tukolor people, while they were tirelessly committed to spreading Islam, simultaneously nursed a strain of indomitable Freethinkers, like Ousmane Sembène in their breast. Both streams, one visibly Muslim and the other invisibly Cheddo, have existed and, arguably, co-existed, until today.

Again, let's make it plain! Although the Cheddo tradition is mostly not pointed out or talked about, it surfaces when a mother pours water on the ground to clear the path for her travelling adult daughter or son and bring them safely back home. In global Afrika, Cheddo, though mostly unspoken or even unknown, thrives everywhere under the radar.

So, whereas the media highlights ethnic conflicts, they seldom chronicle the sacrifices and courage of daily challenges to clerical, political and social conformism. And I believe our sense of shared, unbroken humanity will grow as stories like Baba Sembène's are more commonly told.

APB: But how do we get past all the inter-ethnic killing and kidnapping in Nigeria, Congo, South Africa or even Ethiopia these days? Different communities seem intent on dominating or destroying each other, and only seem able to consider those individuals who look like them.

Are they being deliberately blind? Can't they see that while they fight over crumbs, non-Afrikans are corrupting their governments, destroying their civil institutions, deploying mercenaries or drones and cheerfully trucking away their people's security and wealth?

GCM: Some do. There are circles within circles in Kush/Afrikan society, and, as Br. Bankie taught me, different tasks for each circle to complete. Just as every story is not for every ear, those who get glimpses through a wider lens must sometimes work in isolation in order to get the Ancestors' work done.

APB: Okay, now. You know I'm not big on abstraction. Be more concrete.

GCM: Here is further insight from Bankie Foster Bankie the successful Ghanaian builder of pioneering Pan-Afrikan institutions in South Africa, Namibia and South Sudan. He didn't let ethnicity hold him back.

> "There is no other part of the world, but Africa, where in this so-called 'civil war', the aggressor has the total support of a Nation, the Arab Nation, and due to the split in the AU, Arab/Africa, it is unable to meet the naked aggression of the Arab side. CAR (Central African Republic) is proof that Africa is unable to secure its own interests - peace and security."

GCM: I already mentioned journalist Prof Abdou Rahman Cissé. He lived his life, in his relationships, not only outside ethnic boundaries but as a first-class, world-class citizen. Yet, simultaneously, he also defended the existence and legacies of his small ethnic group, and his mother tongue, "Saafi-Saafi." This Freethinker's vision eventually prevailed, and, today, there's even some Saafi-Saafi TV programs on Senegal's airwaves.

APB: That's the kind of practical approach to culture that I applaud. I'm tired of these endless conferences with a hundred workshops that do nothing to change our people's real lives for the better.

GCM: Across the Afrikan continent, the evolués or foreign-educated elite rule the roost. As Professor Kwesi Prah in Cape Town has pointed out, speaking and living European have become addictions for far too many Afrikan Heads of State. For example, South Africa's President Ramaphosa flaunts his familiarity with fine French wines. Prof Prah has pointed out how some members of the Mercedes mobilisation class are more European than the Europeans, while others out-Arab the Arabs. Instead, we can recharge indigenous languages, as happened so successfully and rapidly with the promotion of Hebrew.

A generation of Black regimes, in my view, have squandered opportunities for developing Yoruba, Swahili, Hausa or Oromo, widely-spoken indigenous languages, into the lingua franca of the Motherland and Global Afrika.

APB: I can hear your admiration for your Senegalese soul brother and gratitude for his Pan-Afrikan presence in your life.

GCM: I wish I could have introduced you to Br. Abdou, who was also Senegal's first Ombudsman.

Like Professor Prah in Cape Town, he questioned why ministers of education had their children schooled in London, DC or Paris, while their constituents lacked adequate primary schools or couldn't afford school fees. Sadly, Br. Abdou's out-of-the-box "African Bamboo Foundation," was stopped on its way to providing schools made from bamboo across Afrika.

In All Eyes on Afrika, he passionately addresses the racist stigma of "lazy" Blacks. In person, he denounced the psychological damage of simple sentences like, "You sold your own" to Black unity and self-esteem, countering disinformation with logic, figures and facts.

APB: I understand his response, but we can't excuse those who looked like us and cooperated with the kidnappers.

GCM: I totally agree. However, I also evaluate that history in broad, panoramic terms of intensity and scale. Just so we don't make the mistake of thinking those days are past, there's a President-Kidnapper in the news even as we speak. We'd better not name him, just in case we have to take a flight and our plane is landed in some unknown East Afrikan destination.

Of course, we know he couldn't do it alone, and gets help from his buddies in "international community" intelligence services. Yes! And Ayiti's oligarchs do seem addicted to playing deadly games of musical chairs. And, in South Africa, activist groups like "Abahlali baseMjondolo," have publicized political murders by ANC operatives, who continue to provide cover and impunity for apartheid-minded Whites.

APB: Since corporate interests wield power globally, so must we. That's why Br. Malcolm put our condition on the table at the OAU (Organization of African Unity) for all the world to see.

GCM: The present AU cannot advance Black Liberation, while it is held hostage by anti-Black interests, as Br. Bankie explained.

And although apartheid presumably fell, so little changed that Br. Bankie concluded that he, myself and other committed Pan-Afrikanists, had been duped. In one of the last exchanges we had, he told me that the Anti-apartheid Movement was really set up to save Whites from prosecution or giving back stolen land, not to secure justice for Blacks.

Today's AU, in my humble opinion, has failed to address or even put the UN-manufactured cholera crisis in Ayiti on the international table for open debate. Similarly, the AU seem paralyzed in the face of the present Kenyan regime's disgraceful sacrifice of its people's human rights to an apartheid heir's corporative interests. Such a dismal display of ineptitude and abandonment of responsibility disqualifies its members, in my ordinary Black man's eyes, from the respect due an organization conceived in sacrifice and invested with the hopes of so many people.

APB: The Civil Rights Movement and flag Independence also failed in the end.

GCM: It's sobering to look back.

Although Ayiti achieved the impossible in simultaneously defeating three empires, the most her population can boast today is, "Ammale jirra" / "We're still here," as Oromo stalwarts say. Way over the continent to the West, Wolof families, too, greet each other, "We're still here!" / "Nyungi fii rekk!," affirming, in my view, the same cultural insistence on survival and resilience.

I also really wish that some academic with privileged access or some brave investigative journalist would publish the full text of all the documents signed by Black leaders with White colonizers at Independence, or with the apartheid regime before they installed President Nelson Mandela!

Why haven't we been able to stop our global caste-oppression, although we've produced a Black Wall St. as well as countless giants like the Garveys, Winnie Madikizela Mandela, Paul Robeson and Robert and Sally Mugabe? Why have we been so slow in learning how to protect our role models, their legacies or the vulnerable populations they served?

APB: What I want to know is, how much longer we're going to settle for just feeling good for surviving? No other populations feel that that's good enough.

GCM: I agree. But that's our reality. Emancipation morphed into Jim Crow and post-apartheid politics have become a horror show.

Why? That's why, in Talking Cheddo, I stepped back, sat down and took a good look at how we got here. I'm still figuring out what's really going on inside our heads that keeps us from breaking out of this dungeon of vulnerability and abuse.

Am I wrong in feeling that the other "caste" can come from anywhere without anything and quickly get rich and famous off Black backs? To clarify? I view the world as having just two castes. One is Kush Folks, which to me means Black Folks with ancestry from along the Nile - any height, shape, hair-texture or hue and living anywhere on earth.

APB: That's one of the reasons I'm against cutting individual checks for Reparations. I promise you, two days after those checks are cashed, most of that money will be deposited in bank accounts of all those other groups we've already made famous, comfortable and rich. We have to change our thinking. Period. I don't blame the rest of the world for walking all over us, because it's our fault if we keep letting them get away with it.

GCM: As early as the year nineteen-twenty, I believe, Pan-Afrikan pioneer, WEB Dubois, in The Souls of Black Folk, sounded the Black genocide alarm. He warned us to pay closer attention to the unique price we had paid in making it through so many "holocausts" that they exhaust our imagination.

Personally speaking, I long to identify the specific blood cells, like we do with antibodies or mitochondrial epigenetics, that had changed their nature and ours over the course of our catastrophic forced exile from our ancestral selfhood and dignity.

How else did our Ancestors become, over generations, such fleshy yet robotic creatures; able to ignore excessive physical pain and the kind of anguish seeded by random rape of their mothers, sisters, wives and daughters or the envious castration of their sons?

And yet, if our foremothers raised the children of the men who raped them and their daughters with tenderness and mothering love, is there anything human beings who happen to be Black would not or could not overcome or live beyond?

How did freethinking Cheddo psyches absorb the agony of forced brutalization that some intellectuals still label labour, over a lifetime, knowing strangers would always reap all the visible rewards? How did we come through all that with our capacity for joy and our humanity intact?

APB: That's why when in our situation people say, "Well, I don't know what you're so upset about. Everybody was enslaved." I say, I agree with you, but what happened to us didn't happen to anyone else. It's frustrating how often I hear "slave labour" used. It's a misnomer.

GCM: The reality is that whenever we hear or use the word "slave," everywhere I've visited or lived, speakers are silently adding the description "Black."

And yet, I've heard discussions of several recent novels where young writers from Nigeria or other regions that lost lots of their kin to enslavement, confess almost tearfully, "my family or my people had slaves."

And I do know readers of every colour, who swallow that stuff whole. I'm now praying they get to read Talking Cheddo, where I offer an alternative perspective on the historical, social and cultural context of Black populations' experience of Bondage.

Let's look again at how knowing our history can help us understand why we do what we do. An Oromo proverb teaches us, "Language is a boat that carries culture" / Afaan doonii aadaa baadhatu." Arriving in Dakar with a head burning up with questions, I quickly learned that the Wolof word "jamm" meant slave.

However, I soon figured out that for my Wolof sisters and brothers jamm carried more layers of meaning. Let me explain! "jamm" and "sangg" are names for two sides of a give-and-take social relationship that can only happen within the context of a culture of inclusive families. There, someone who happens to be born in your village may be treated just like a biological sister or brother.

I remember hearing the doorbell to Sr. Esther Brown's apartment in Harlem one day. A "brother" from Ghana, who we had just met in passing in our travels was standing with his trunk at our door. And we soon understood that because we had exchanged addresses, he figured we were family and could turn up unannounced.

I believe that in the sense he understood it, Black culture is unique. It therefore becomes vital that populations in the Diaspora re-learn the rules that govern our relationships. For example, words like "jamm" and "sangg," in regions like Senegambia, never included the master-over-slave, forced exile, dehumanization and genocide that writers translate as "slavery" today.

Travelling far outside any city one day, a group of sisters, attracted no doubt by Black strangers in a big, fancy car, broke spontaneously into a praise-song about us. At the end of their song, one sister, eyes sparkling like a teasing teenager, challenged us. "We are your slaves, now you have to give us a gift." Can anyone seriously imagine that speech ever passing between the kidnapped and their kidnappers?

Having had that experience, I'm even willing to go out on a limb and declare that Black solidarity depends on deeper kinds of understanding we usually only gain from being soaked in and soaking up a culture. Black folks over here need to reinvent or re-discover appropriate and necessary rituals of rebirth.

APB: I agree. And I tell those willing to hear, all the time, that every group of people on earth were enslaved at some time or other. But most other times they were enslaved, they were captured by a country on the continent. If I'm in this country and you're in the next country and I enslave you, no matter what I do, you're still in an area with which you are familiar. You know what to do in that situation. But when you take people seven or eight thousand miles away, it takes some strong people to survive that. And we need to credit ourselves and our Ancestors. We're a strong people.

GCM: I feel that historians have mostly ignored the deeper truth about enslavement staring us in the face. Without being uniquely resilient, how else would Afrikans have survived and continued, despite enormous odds, to thrive? What I fear more is that we haven't taught ourselves and aren't teaching our children to pay enough attention to how we've become who we are. Some of the significant details we continue to miss might be just what we need to help us find the cosmic purpose in our presence in this hemisphere.

Just the other day, our brother Aziz from Dakar reminded me of sanankuya, another practice built into our ancestral culture. It's a way of breaking down social barriers and neutralizing hierarchy. That's a lot like playin mas in Trinidad or The Dozens, ways of deflating pomposity in Black America.

What if we have always carried the medicine for what ails us in the very Being we've been and have become? Let's not forget the Wolof proverb: Nit nitay garabam! Another human being is the medicine for curing all human beings. And how do we make ourselves whole again? Just imagine! How was it possible for any people to be taken into the unknown, stripped of speech that let them make sense of their world and stay human?

How did our Ancestors communicate in so many different tongues, so quickly, and then become super-productive, mastering the latest machinery of the Industrial Revolution - often within one generation?

APB: To start with … Our minds had to be strong to keep us from going insane.

GCM: While studying Hospital Administration years ago, I volunteered at the main Mental Hospital in TO and had one of those ahah moments we all get from time to time. In a flash, it became clear to me that mental illness occurs on a spectrum, unlike what we generally see in the media or on TV.

That said, I realized that if you don't pay attention, another's sickness can and will eventually suck you in. And since racism is a form of ongoing, long-term cognitive dissonance and mental imbalance, as Black folks, we are always at risk.

APB: Once again, Br. Malcolm said it right. "Give your brain as much attention as you give your hair, and you'll be a thousand times better off."

GCM: Let's step back, so we can take a better look at the whole picture! We were shorn of the comfort of everyday practices and beliefs. We had our psyches battered by random, mindless violence where every orifice could be and was violated by faceless White males or females. And there was no one else to help us repair ourselves. Let's suppose we could enter the minds of refugees from war in the Middle East arriving in Europe and North America today! And then let's imagine the challenges they face in learning how to act German or English or Canadian or Greek! Then, if we dare, let's plumb the experience of those sufferers and the suffering of "Black folks"

APB: I repeat. That's a different kind of slavery than when someone captures you and takes you seven thousand or eight thousand miles away from every kind of scenario that you're familiar with.

GCM: I do understand that some individuals, and maybe some groups, can bear more pain than others. What I'm challenging scientists, psychologists, artists and philosophers to explore is how so much Black pain has given birth to so much beauty and joy which enriches and today enraptures the whole world?

Just how did our Ancestors learn foreign tongues so quickly and so well – learning that were intentionally denied them, except to teach them to fetch, carry and obey like well-trained dogs? On Southern plantations, after fourteen-hour days under whips and the shadeless sun, our sainted Ancestors somehow summoned up reserves of humanizing energy from secret space deep inside. Out of nowhere came the peerless, poetic Spirituals to beguile abusers and continue to tame randomly restless spirits from afar to this hour of this very day.

That's one of the reasons I still go to church. I want to hear that Black sound – it's unique, and never fails to lift me up.

GCM: Lest we forget, those who enslaved our Ancestors also tried to "season" them, which meant turning them into things that didn't think or feel. Plantation bosses feared losing production and profits if the "peace" of the broken-hearted was ever broken. So, White society learned to sniff and snuff out the slightest hint of independent thinking. Warped minds felt they could eventually remake flesh and blood into a kind of pliable wood or malleable concrete However, thanks to Waka Guracha, The Great Black God, we're still flesh, blood, in fit and fighting form!

APB: No disrespect, Br. Clem the Guracha, but I think it took more than prayer and singing to set us free.

GCM: [WAH-HINGAH-DUGGAH] "Wax-nge degg"! / You spoke the truth – Right on! As my Wolof teachers would say.

My bias is that we were saved by the very nature of who we are … For isn't that why organisms thrive or go extinct under stress? We are a seriously adaptable ancestral group. Matthew Henson went from New York to the North Pole, learned the language, handled dog-sleds like a pro, accepted a new Indigenous name, made family and eventually had to fetch Admiral Robert Peary, the White explorer (or so they say) to the spot where they planted the US flag.

Improvisation isn't just about jazz. The evidence of history locates it in our bones. Truth to tell, Jazz exists because we must improvise. Coleman Hawkins took the Saxe brothers' instrument and taught it to moan like a human being in ecstasy or pain. Just stop and listen to the Black soundscape going on around you! When one rhythm gets tired, a new one jumps to the front, and then the whole party starts dancing forward again. What's there to say? Could it be that it's just "a Black thang"?

KRS 1, one of the principled and principal Hip Hop pioneers, says that it was fate and failing White schools, which pushed young "Bloods" (sixties style) from Bed-Stuy in Brooklyn, and Compton in LA and Port-au-Prince in Ayiti and Kingston's "Dungle" in Jamaica together in the streets of big-city USA.

The way he lived it, those young Black men had no fungible assets except self-love and brotherly-love. So, they played their music, then danced for and with each other through sweaty summer nights. And the rest is the history of a many trillion-dollar industry! At first, White media and even the Black mainstream put down Hip Hop as "noise," and only stations like WLIB, Black-conscious Radio in New York City, recognized its worth and treated it with respect.

APB: Our greatest contribution to the music world was Soul music.

GCM: Real Hip Hop for me is also soulful.

When they got bored waiting for LPs to end and their equipment crashed, those young brothers, who teachers didn't want in school, started scratching records, and cutting-and-pasting snatches of R&B, manufacturing Hip Hop out of internalized Black rhythm and polluted urban air.

So, from the belly of Black New York City stepped forth a brand-new, billion-dollar industry that streaked around the teens-to-twenties world, transforming ancient cultures, opening up new careers and making multitudes rich. Economists talk about the dynamism of the Industrial Revolution but cultural dynamism is us. Cheddo is spontaneous spiritual combustion, an endlessly inventive, Freethinking Force always bubbling up inside us. That's what I'm talking about when I say we're a Cheddo people.

And maybe, just maybe, that's why, it was only with Black people, in Ayiti, in 1804, that an uprising of the enslaved was able to overturn caste, definitively, to create a uniquely-free citizen, whatever their ancestry, which the Ayitian Constitution could define as Black.

Culturally speaking, just give a yes or no answer. Talk to me like I'm four years old! Aren't Koreans performing K-Pop, Brits and Germans and Ukrainians and French and every brand of European and Tibetans and Arabs and Israelis – along the spectrum from progressive to deeply evangelical or conservative all living the BLACK experience as if they are Black in their day-to-day today? Weren't the Ayitians just being prescient in 1804?

APB: They do get credit for being the only successful slave rebellion in history.

GCM: That's no longer factually true. Generations later, in 1964, our global Black family had another triumph, this time against Arab enslavers in Zanzibar.

Sadly, Ugandan-born John Okello, who led the uprising, was immediately removed by the ruling Black political class in next-door Tanganyika, who allowed themselves to function as allies of Zanzibari and British colonial authorities. I'm still waiting for some truthtellers who were there to give a view that is not coloured by their anti-Ancestral faiths or Europeanized ideological beliefs.

Without brave new testimony, it means that we don't and probably won't ever know what the revolutionaries might have decided if they were left to work out a new dispensation without Julius Nyerere's anti-Cheddo intervention.

APB: As a Black journalist, I'm shocked that Zanzibar's extraordinary victory has remained so remarkably hidden by academics and the media. Really - from The Left to The Right.

GCM: When we think of how cleverly Global Afrika has been made to forget the grandeur of Ayiti's triumph, isn't it logical that the forces which engineered and have cultivated such flourishing oblivion would not risk letting a second "Black cat" out of their "slavery story" bag?

So, Br. Peter, Black humanity's second victory over Bondage has been mostly washed out of global consciousness. Like a mother guinea-pig that eats her babies to protect them, Tanganyika's forces promptly invaded self-liberating, Black-Conscious Zanzibar, bypassed her freedom fighters, exiled John Okello and buried her Cheddo glory under the safe Black-denying hybrid of "Tanzania."

Had the eloquent President Mandela been around, he might have dubbed "Tanzania" a "neologism," and dismissed it as he did "Azania," the name favoured and promoted by South Africa's Black Consciousness Movement before the patriarch re-appeared on the scene. Isn't it strange how precipitously President Mandela assumed the right to make decisions against the advice of his spouse, Mama Winnie

Madikizela, the main architect and supporter of his eventual assumption of power?

APB: This is the kind of history that should be mandatory in Black colleges and schools.

GCM: The template was set when Patrice Lumumba became Prime Minister on Congo's Independence. It was Black faces in uniform, willing surrogates of White colonial power, who kidnapped and murdered him. In 1964 Zanzibar, John Okello may not have been an acceptable revolutionary image for westernized progressives like Julius "Mwalimu" Nyerere and Abeid Karume.

However, he was the Zanzibari choice to lead their revolution, and mainland politicians owed a much more transparent accounting to the island's women and men, who had risked everything to defend their dignity, and, by extension, our dignity as well. Talking Cheddo challenges Black scholars and journalists to re-examine significant events like Zanzibar's revolution that, if more known and understood, might better equip us to protect the lands and freedoms to which we are still heir.

APB: So, just what do you think it is that keeps tripping us up, and why haven't we learned how to stop it?

GCM: I don't have an answer, and that's why Talking Cheddo invites readers b to focus on broad patterns that have shaped our evolution through time - especially modern time. It was and is my intention that, by pooling the power of our minds, that collectively, we will craft the solutions we need.

The way I see it, Ayiti remains both the beacon and the template. She is a living example of our potential and a guide in navigating pitfalls that lie in our path. For example, Napoleon's kidnapping of Toussaint L'Ouverture and his family (including his 105-year-old godfather) in 1802 is played out, over and over again, like a Blues refrain, in Black liberation history.

Fast forward to 2004, armed White abductors, with their hand-picked Black collaborators, exiled the president overwhelmingly and freely chosen by Ayiti's masses. Over 60% of the electorate voted, and Lavalas/The Flood, President John Bertrand Aristide's party, received 67% of the vote.

Now let's touch down in the Motherland, Nigeria, to be precise! It was other Black men and their anti-Black foreign accomplices who were allegedly behind the poisoning of President-Elect, Chief Moshood Abiola.

APB: I think that it's important that your work helps to focus attention on these stories. There's a lot that passes beneath the radar.

GCM: I found, as I travelled in Afrika, that there were silences about ugly secrets that would often ambush me from time to time.

Here's one! From my first visit to "La Cour Des Maures," the Mauritanian silver market in Dakar, I couldn't help observing, with my Pan-Afrikanist eye, that each stall had a lighter-skinned Moor in charge, with someone who could easily pass for my brother playing servant and seated on the floor. When I asked my Senegalese guide what was going on, he replied without embarrassment, "Ce sont les esclaves des Maures (They're slaves of the Moors)." In fact, he made slavery sound like the most normal practice in the world. "But they look like us," I blurted out, horrified.

APB: I don't remember seeing anything like that on my trips to Afrika. But I'm not shocked.

GCM: I still am. The persistence of Bondage in Mauritania is a glaring example of the failure of the UN and the African Union and Progressives in Senegal.

It also reminds us that if any nation, religion, ideology, belief system or creed could have saved us, or wanted to save us, we would have been saved by now. Here's the deal, Br. Peter. Just tell me like I'm a four-year-old! Why is Zimbabwe still crippled by sanctions of the self-righteous international community, while Mauritania is allowed, since the seventh century, to enslave innocent Black people with impunity?

APB: That's our fault, Clem. We should have made it clear that if anyone touched Zimbabwe, they'd face a boycott by Black people across the globe. We have real power, purchasing power, but we're not using it.

GCM: And I would like us to help to mobilize it. Meantime, getting back to Dakar! When I picked my head up from the ground in disbelief, I discovered that the presence of enslaved Black Mauritanians was indeed a norm across Senegal.

To me, it was incomprehensible that Black folks with authority would allow anyone who looked like their relatives to be enslaved under their watch. What ever happened to "Never Again"? And wasn't the champion of "Negritude," Poet-President Senghor been in charge? Why isn't there a functioning Underground Railroad from Mauritania to Senegal and safe houses to welcome every freedom-seeker?

In fact, au contraire, highly-placed informed sources told me that the hero of Independence, President Senghor, under French tutelage, had transferred Senegalese citizens and their land to Mauritania, without their consultation or consent, to make "peace" during a border dispute. Similar anomalies can pop up unexpectedly across the Motherland. And because I haven't seen them described in other books, I wanted to highlight some of them in Talking Cheddo.

APB: Senghor is another case of a "hero" having feet of clay! Similar political sellouts operate in the US as well.

GCM: President Houphouet-Boigny's "independent" Ivory Coast was another eye-opener for me. In what they call "the Paris of Afrika," French Intelligence, not an Ivoirian brother or sister, vetted me and other Black travellers at their airport. I remember looking over at a Ghanaian brother, who just shrugged. While we were held back and questioned, everyone White was waved through.

APB: That's what I'm talking about. Br. Malcolm was warning folks on the continent about this kind of indignity a generation ago.

GCM: I feel the way others feel free to treat us has always been related to the question of who really owns Afrika? Scenarios like those I've described are calculated, I feel, to announce to the world that Black ancestry has no value, even in our own Motherland.

Here's another of those moments that have shaped my Pan-Af-rikanism ! Checking on a delayed monthly transfer of my pay from Canada at the main Senegalese bank in Dakar, the only person with decision-making authority they would let me see turned out to be a Frenchman. I had to remind myself that this was happening post-Independence and under a president named "Abdou Diouf." The incident, although disappointing, made me recall other information I had been given by an im-peccable source, about Senegalese debt and the French-run banking system.

As the story goes, there was a campaign to pay off the debt France claimed they were owed by Senegal at independence. So, in cities and villages, anti-debt rallies were held, where patriotic Senegalese women would dance and toss their gold bracelets and other jewellery into piles in order to pay off their country's debt. The campaign ended. The money disappeared into French banks and has rarely, if ever, been spoken of again.

APB: Living with those stories must have disappointed you. It's like me looking on as Black people disappear from my neighbour-hood every day. After a while, the Whites moving in treat you like you're the stranger. And, sadly, you eventually begin to feel like you're the stranger.

GCM: But I've got a bigger shock for you. Listen to this! One day, quite by accident I bumped into French troops playing ball in the street behind the presidential palace in Dakar. That's where their barracks were located. Big Brother France was obvious-ly, blatantly even, still in charge of proud Leopold Senghor's and Abdou Diouf's "independent" nation. In fact, as an Afri-kan, you had to travel to Guinea or Ghana in those days, if you wanted to be able to credibly say, "This is mine."

APB: Br. Malcolm had enormous respect for President Sékou Touré of Guinea. And, as a Pan-Afrikanist, it must have pained him to see Senegalese forces, during Senghor's regime, conspire with French race supremacists to undermine Guinea's independence.

GCM: That attempt by some of the Monrovia Group, the more colo-nized members of the OAU (Organization of African Unity) to bring down Sékou Touré in collusion with France, sealed the deal for me. He was so principled and incorruptible, his admirers say, that when he passed, he left no personal fortune to his heirs, not even a house. That was who Senghor conspired to overthrow. Given his poems and the public "persona" Senghor projected around Negritude, I never picked him to play Gunga Din. That was old British Empire propaganda film, where a shoeless Indian foot soldier dies fighting his own people to save British troops.

APB: That's you colonials again! You guys still have to bow to the British Queen, don't you?

GCM: Don't get too uppity, Mr. America, our Motherland is still largely kept underfoot by your President. Afrika's masses are still waiting in line for self-determination, in the tradition of China, India, Algeria or Vietnam. In those countries, unlike anywhere in the Black world, when colonization ended, the colonizers had to go home. In Asia, it didn't matter how long the colonizers had lived there or what they had built. Eventually, they had to get out. Think Goa and Hong Kong!

APB: Br. Malcolm warned us against "house N-." Those sad souls who would say, "Massa, weez sick," whenever their White enslaver fell ill.

GCM: Despite six, seven or eight global Pan-Afrikan Conferences, depending on which ones you include or exclude, consciousness-wise, I don't believe we're there yet, wherever there needs to be. Perhaps that's because consciousness, as I feel it, is slow-cooking and never microwave, and ours has been slowly cooking for generations. In my day-to-day life, self-reflection is a familiar, although sometimes disturbing presence, and consciousness is the companion who monitors my impulses and reactions, moment by moment.

Those gifts from the Ancestors can be invisible guides, questioning new knowledge, absorbing fresh ideas and turning over big moments that map the significant experiences that have shaped how I get to call myself, "Black."

APB: I believe that Br. Malcolm used the time he spent in prison for self-reflection and that was the engine of his growth.

GCM: To be honest, Br. Peter, the growth of my own consciousness has been excruciatingly and, sometimes, frustratingly slow.

In Ayiti, however, society changed at warp speed. Maybe it was because under the influence of the drum, they had conjured up invisible vibrations and magnetic forces that moulded the minds of the population into collective coherence, thus propelling our Ancestors to a higher state of consciousness those many generations ago.

And Ayiti's defenders didn't just do everything Black folks needed to do faster, for their time, for our times and for the generations to come. Simultaneously, somehow, they also managed to reach far higher. What I'm trying to explain is that where the revolution landed, in 1804, was on a much higher plane, a sacred space, which even today, we are still striving to attain again.

APB: You keep coming back to Haiti.

GCM: What I would like our folks to do is focus on the lessons our Ancestors embedded in us in overthrowing forced servitude in Ayiti and Zanzibar. Both of those revolutions were not only successful, but also Pan-Afrikan in practice as well as in spirit.

The inspired and inspiring Dutty Boukman, we don't really know why, was sold to Ayiti by enslavers in Jamaica. Once over there, however, he wasted no time bonding with those Ayitians who were already organizing for freedom.

APB: I think it's important that you continue to stress the Pan-Afrikan aspect of the Ayitian Revolution.

GCM: I found it refreshing to discover parallels between the two revolutions, generations and continents apart, that I had not suspected would be there. For example, Boukman/British-trained to read books, enslaved in Jamaica, found himself suddenly parachuted into the midst of embracing Black faces, ready to die for freedom.

Similarly, John Okello/British-trained policeman to shoot a gun, colonized in Uganda, unexpectedly landed in Zanzibar to find a job and was swept up by embracing Black souls ready to die for freedom. These two Black brothers from another mother were adopted into their new families and placed their skills and spirits on the altar of Black Liberation. Ayiti marched forward first, in 1804, and Zanzibar stepped into her footprints in 1964.

I'm hoping that we can find again that special sanctuary they prepared for us in history and left in our trust. Like Cheddo, it is "Mindspace" and "Sacredspace," where there's always dignity and every soul sister or soul brother is forever free.

APB: I've always heard it repeated, even relatively recently, that there's been only one successful slave rebellion in history. And I'm surprised that we've never really learned about the parallels between Ayiti and Zanzibar.

GCM: The narrative that insists on "the only successful slave rebellion in history" is a conventional and convenient hashtag, but, historically, it doesn't provide context to the events.

One hundred and sixty years after Ayiti, in Zanzibar in 1964, John Okello channeled Dutty Boukman, then challenged the Arab monarchy and hierarchy built on enslaving Blacks and overthrew it. Both victories sent out the message that being enslaved, even being born into Bondage, has never accustomed Black people to accept servitude to foreign despots as destiny.

APB: I agree. And I tell people all the time that most every group of people on earth were enslaved at some time or other. But most other times they were enslaved, you know, they were captured by the country next door. That's a different type of slavery than when someone captures you and takes you seven or eight thousand miles away from home, away from everything you're familiar with. That was our situation. So, when people say to me, "I don't know why you're so upset, everybody was enslaved," I tell them, I agree with you. But if I'm in this country, and you're in the next, and I enslave you, it doesn't matter what I do, you're still in a place that's familiar to you. You're at home and you know what to do. When we're talking about being taken seven or eight thousand miles away, it takes some strong people to survive that. And we need to credit ourselves, our Ancestors, for being a strong people who could triumph over that situation.

GCM: Let's go back and examine the use and destructive use of the word "slave"! I began Talking Cheddo with an analysis of language, because language has been used to trap us. For example, when folks say, "Everybody has been enslaved." The same word "slave" described a different kind of oppression and terror when it was applied to "Slavs" in Europe as opposed to Afrikans in forced, genocidal exile in the Caribbean or Americas.

Like currency, words can change in value depending on their context and location. So, we in Canada carefully observe how our "dollar" appreciates or depreciates in relation to the US "dollar." Same name, different value. During the late nineteen seventies, you needed $2 USD to buy 1 Nigerian Naira. Today we still call those currencies by the same name, but their values are completely different. In my view, it's vital for us to be clear about the unique history that created the conditions we face today.

And our diagnosis must be specific, if we are to develop remedies that can deal, not only with political and economic questions, but also with parallel psychological needs – the memories we carry in our blood.

APB: I remember *Roots* on TV. Especially the scene where they are beating Kunta Kinte to get him to change his name – "Your name is now 'Toby'! Say, "My name is Toby." That scene showed the combination of the psychological and the physical. That enslaver understood very well that he couldn't keep him enslaved with that name. He had to get rid of that name "Kunta Kinte." I don't know if I ever told you this story. Nine years ago, I was vending my books at an Afrikan Cultural Day in Virginia, and the friend who I was expecting to help me didn't turn up. Along the way, I became desperate for a break but didn't want to leave my table unattended. Luckily, a young brother came to my rescue. When I returned, we continued talking and I said to him, "What's your name?"

"Frank," he answered.

"I'm not calling you Frank," I said. "What's your real name?" He'd already said he'd arrived from Nigeria just 7 months before.

"It's Owolayi," he replied.

"Then that's what I'll call you," I said. We're still in touch, and he was so stunned that he tells people that story to this day.

GCM: Now you've got to hear my story about the name I was given when I lived in Senegal. It happened the first time I traveled outside the capital, Dakar, and went down South. I was invited by a Mandinka brother, Keba, who wanted me to meet his family "in his country," as he called the village that he came from in the lush Casamance region of Senegal.

Although we'd set out from Dakar in daylight, by the time we arrived, there was a moon framing the village's conical, thatched homes. And even though his family had already turned in, we were welcomed and fed. They were delighted to have a guest from far away. When hosts can say "Amnaa gan/I have a guest" to other villagers in Senegal, they swell with pride.

APB: Sounds very much like life in Mississippi to me.

GCM: So, it's an even bigger deal when Senegalese families have a visitor from afar. Their stock shoots up – way up. When morning came, my first duty was to meet the elders and be greeted by Keba's folks. I stepped outside, startled by the whiteness of the sun, and was right in the heart of Keba's Mandinka family – a many-layered, multi-generational melange.

A princely, cotton-haired Elder was seated in honor at the centre of a semi-circle standing respectfully around him. By Cosmic coincidence he was wearing a robe of a vest of woven, black-and-white fabric that I had made in Paris and own to this day. Keba introduced me to his grandfather as if he were presenting an ambassador at court, and I could feel the strength in the elder's fingers as he grasped my hand and looked deep into my eyes.

"Sant-waa? / What's your family name?" He asked.

"Mangi-sant Marshall," I triumphantly replied in my non-Indigenous, Canadian-tinged accent.

"Du Marshall le/LAY / You're not a Marshall," he said. "Du tubaab le/You're not a White man.

"Yangi-sant Manga / your family-name is Manga."

Chastened, I bowed without hesitation to his ancestral authority, and have been "Manga" to the initiated ever since. Much, much later, I also learned through a random comment from a stranger that "Manga" meant "the warrior from ancient Mali." I cherish my "Manga" memory.

But, in hindsight, it exposed my comfort, all my life, with someone else's English grand-dad's family name. And here's the clincher! I'd even acted as Eshu, the Deity of Disorder, in Aimé Césaire's play "Une Tempete," a French adaptation of Shakespeare's Tempest, where Césaire's Caliban confronts the magician Prospero with, "Appelez-moi X /Call me X" – modeled after the famous declaration of Br. Malcolm X.

APB: And that shows another thing about the importance of your book. A lot of academics and journalists don't deal with such attacks on the mind. I admit that the passage of time and the new situation of the world have curtailed the physical manifestations of White supremacy. They have. That's obvious. Not eliminated them, but lessened them.

However, one of the things we learn in your book is how this unrelenting attack goes on and on. We have to build up a barrier to protect our young people's minds appropriately also, to keep them from succumbing to psychological warfare.

GCM: While I was teaching, I observed how even first graders, whatever their heritage, race or gender, understood that the little Black boys were the easiest to target and get into trouble with teachers. So, in Talking Cheddo, I take a stab at producing a prophylactic for super-stressed and abused Black minds. It's done in stages. The first step I took was to unpack the psychological impact of words and images in, "The Report of the Kerner Commission" – published after Dr. King's assassination. In fact, it's in the news again today. I'm pretty sure Jelani

Cobb, New Yorker Magazine writer and professor of journalism at Columbia University, just edited a new work about it.

APB: It's remarkable how relevant that report is at this time. As a journalist it made a particular impression on me because it criticized mainstream media for spreading rumors that fueled the unrest of the sixties.

GCM: I remember reading "Kerner" around 1968, while unsmiling, afro-topped students were front page, running rings around university presidents and their protectors. However, looking back, I now consider The Kerner Commission the opening salvo in a series of programs, not really designed for truth or reconciliation, but carefully crafted to distract and pacify Blacks rebelling against systemic White anti-Black racism. The iconoclastic energy of urban uprisings as North America transitioned out of the sixties, sent White society the message of un-negotiable urgency. Something had to be immediately done or big-city America would dissolve under their feet.

So, it was an opportune moment for Talking Cheddo to unpack the language of The Kerner Commission, with its "exculpatory euphemisms" like "the Middle Passage." How could a ship ferrying Black victims to genocidal plantations be any more on a "middle passage" than cattle cars in Europe fetching Jewish victims to concentration camps? Euphemisms can be seductive.

They even ensnared no less an icon than US artist Tom Feelings. That committed Pan-Afrikanist, who lived in Guyana for a while, illustrated a work with haunting evocations of the journey of his Ancestors into Bondage, and then gave it the title, The Middle Passage.

After analyzing Governor Otto Kerner's report, my book jumps ahead 30 years to 1998, when the global icon, Nelson Mandela, had already become president of South Africa. His fellow anti-apartheid celebrity, Archbishop Desmond Tutu, published the "Report of the Truth and Reconciliation Commission" as a map out of the deadly maze called apartheid. Were we to call the Kerner Report "Black Pacification: Part One," then its South African counterpart could be aptly labelled, "Black Pacification: Part Two."

APB: I did get the connection between those two Reports in Talking Cheddo.

GCM: It's not hard to guess why there is such palpable dejection in Black South Africans' eyes these days. I'm mostly reluctant to follow the news, because I can predictably expect it to break my heart – especially after our high hopes for a society that would be equitable, Black-respecting and just.

When two Black sisters from South African now resigned to living in Toronto told me we had been fooled, I took notes and followed the fingers they pointed at the beneficiary class of the ANC and the White-controlled Communist Party.

To me, their sense of betrayal is understandable. After all, bitter experience has already taught me that our folks, Black folks, including myself, have a genius for overlooking realities we prefer not to see.

So, when, by accident, I found out that President Mandela had attached his name to that butcher of Black populations, Cecil Rhodes, and formed the "Mandela-Rhodes Foundation, that sealed the deal for me.

APB: By now, no serious Pan-Afrikanist should have any illusions about the ANC, the South African Communist Party, establishment religion or the AU.

GCM: Our brother, Bankie Bankie, who knew his Karl Marx as well as any progressive, would have agreed with you. Br. Bankie had built strong bridges with Rastafari/RASTA-FAR-EYE elder, Mortimo Planno, in Jamaica.

When he died, he was working closely with key activists around global Afrika, especially South Africa, Namibia and the two Sudans. Before that, this Pan-Afrikanist par excellence had lived in Cape Town and directed Professor Kwesi Prah's Centre for Advanced Studies of African Society.

APB: That's quite a Pan-Afrikan resumé.

GCM: In the end, however, Br. Bankie concluded that the show-trial put on by Ringmaster Archbishop Tutu and the main actors of the TRC had served the purposes of apartheid. As he explained it, the TRC had been made deliberately spectacular, and had also proved psychologically effective and culturally lethal for Black populations. This was confirmed to me by a former friend of Bankie's, who was a member of the TRC. In the end, however, our selfless, departed Ancestor judged the TRC 100% distraction and high-class farce.

APB: How do you see it being a tool of apartheid?

GCM: It seems to me that, as it was crumbling, the apartheid regime desperately needed to provide a pretext for giving immunity to monsters like Dr. "Death" Basson, who is still around, for their crimes. Secondly, Mama Winnie Madikizela Mandela had proved too formidable to assassinate, for killing her would have unleashed such revenge it might have threatened existing White wealth. Therefore, Br. Bankie surmised, Whites hatched a plot to destroy her reputation and cause her loyal following to doubt or desert her.

That was the master-stroke of the TRC. I don't remember a single White male face, like the architects of apartheid, surfacing to directly accuse Mama Winnie of crime. In the end, apartheid's nemesis suffered reputation assassination by Archbishop Tutu's innuendo. And, for the assassins, it worked wonderfully well. Your book The Harlem Hospital Story was an early-warning alarm of the kinds of horror White medical malpractice, as perpetrated by Basson, is still unleashing, with impunity, on often unsuspecting or blindly-trusting Black populations.

And, if you remember, a bold team of politically-seasoned and savvy Harlem doctors, including your family pediatrician and our beloved brother now passed on, Dr. Tom Hyatt, went on a unprecedented fact-finding mission to Israel, presented their findings to the US Congress and got legislation successfully passed protecting a group of Black Hebrew Israelites who had emigrated to Israel from Chicago.

The Israeli government agreed to provide adequate living conditions and humane medical services for the Black Hebrews, who felt persecuted when they migrated to Israel. Based on the TRC, I'm skeptical about the covert and coercive COVID decisions by national and international authorities. Obviously, quite understandably, they have a difference resonance with Black folks.

APB: As Br. Malcolm predicted, those post-apartheid chickens are now coming home to roost.

GCM: To be frank, Br. Peter, I see "The TRC Report" as a plausible scam. It's aim, like the fraudulent mortgage documents used during the 2008 Lehman Bros. financial collapse, was to strip honest Black homeowners in the US and South Africa of their most valuable asset - land.

Like the US banks, The TRC allowed its looters "legally," even if illegitimately and immorally, to enjoy their ill-gotten gains. It remains a monument to mass deception, as well as a warning against patriarchy in the Black Liberation struggle. By operationalizing patriarchy, it was possible to discredit Mama Winnie and legitimize her removal from power. Yet she was visibly the best-equipped to lead, by virtue of experience, charisma and her people's enduring trust.

When Soweto happened, eyewitnesses say that it was Winnie, like a fierce Mama-goose, wings wide open, who shielded the children, after the vanguardist males of the ANC or the Communist Party did not stand up. In Talking Cheddo, I cite "Africa Magazine," in 1976, and Winnie Mandela's autobiography Part of My Soul, which give a detailed account of her heroic actions at Soweto. The media, as usual, misinformed us. I was Chair of the "Anti-Apartheid Coalition" in Toronto, but I also fell for the old okie-dokie and never asked the right questions at the right time. I'm willing to bet my next big check that Black folks are the most trusting souls on earth. Don't hold your breath!

APB: This reminds me of your story about how teachers got upset over an anti-apartheid poster at your school. And they claimed the poster was hurting the feelings of the White children.

GCM: I was stunned when that happened, because the poster wasn't violent. I didn't find it scary at all. And the kids I showed it were intrigued, not upset. What I like about the poster, and it's hanging in my hallway as we speak, is that it's a laid-back, understated attack on White supremacy.

Keith Haring, then a young New York City celebrity, and White, was the artist/cartoonist. On his poster, a tiny, White outline of human figure is stretched out on the ground, clinging to a noose that reaches up around the neck of a giant, Black figure several times its size. And the foot of the big Black figure is on top of the White figure, almost blotting it out. To a simple mind like mine, that poster simply means, "Say no to bullying." And aren't all teachers supposed to be against bullying, anyway?

APB: I would like to think so.

GCM: So, that was the poster they were blaming for traumatizing White students. I thought, "Black students have feelings too." But that didn't come up. Despite my protests, the principal and VP, male and female, both Black, agreed to take it down. Meanwhile, on TV, White soldiers could be seen beating up and shooting at Black people, including children.

APB: I remember what it was like going to a Catholic school in Tuskegee, Alabama.

GCM: Wow! My first school was Catholic too. With Irish priests and nuns. And they taught us, little Black boys, to sing "My bonnie lies over the ocean ..."

APB: My Catholic school, in a school full of Black children in Tuskegee, Alabama, we were not taught anything about Black history. After Christmas and Easter, during the school year, the biggest day was St. Patrick's Day, because all our teachers were Irish-Catholic nuns. Those nuns taught us Irish history, especially when it came to dealing with England, and made Queen Elizabeth I seem like a terrible person. But later on, when I attended an all-Protestant public school, we were taught that same history from an English point of view. In those classes, Queen Elizabeth I came across as a heroine.

GCM: It's now pretty clear that how our children are taught history, especially Black history can shape whether they grow up feeling good about themselves. And the media makes sure there is no shortage of ugliness for them to absorb.

We mustn't forget Time Magazine's deliberate darkening of OJ's image, meant to turn readers, by reflex, against him. No wonder juries, with almost no exception, hand down judgments of "justifiable homicide" after Black men are gunned down by police.

Whether they are beloved Soul-music stars like Sam Cooke or unknown teenagers like Trayvon Martin, relentless propaganda has created an avatar of "sexually bizarre" and dangerous Black men, who deserve to be killed. That image haunts Black men, deprives many of their lives and sullies their memories in death.

APB: I remember that OJ picture and the bizarre story authorities told of Sam Cooke's death as well.

GCM: Once an anti-Black virus infects bloodstreams at an early age, it can cripple your life. I was once asked to debate a Black, Caribbean-born prof in Toronto. In preparation, I was sent a YouTube clip, and in it this reputable academic said he was thankful that his Ancestors had been "slaves."

APB: What?

GCM: You heard me right. It's probably still up on YouTube. I reacted like you did, when he said words to the effect that he was grateful because their enslavement had paved the way for him to become a PhD and a comfortable professor today. To me, he has become the uncontested winner of the gold medal for egregious Black Gratitude.

Opening up the question, I heaped praise on our Ancestors for having the courage and know-how to survive. Then I reminded the audience that "slavery" was merely a deceptive euphemism for "genocidal forced exile" and "genocidal forced labour." We had been uniquely deflowered and defamed, I said, and also robbed of Afrika, the richest real estate in the world. My opponent's opening thrust was to mock me for being too "Afrocentric" and "romanticizing" my Motherland.

APB: That must be another one of those brothers who Br. Malcolm would say had left his mind in Afrika.

GCM: I parried, and challenged him to name any group in recorded history which had not "romanticized" or glorified its own people, land and ancestors. Then I pulled out Mansa Musa, ruler of Mali in the 14th century, widely cited as the richest person who ever lived. On pilgrimage (Haj) to Mecca, the records say, he gave away so much gold that the market crashed. I'm sure my opponent is still coming up with lines to rebut me.

APB: Acting grateful for being over here is what we do in the States also. I write a weekly column that goes out to about a hundred newspapers. And in a recent column, I had reason to refer to Thomas Jefferson High School, one of the elite high schools of this country. To tell the truth, even today, I can't get my head around how we can celebrate the Fourth of July, a date on which twenty-four signers out of the fifty-six people who signed the Declaration of Independence, including Thomas Jefferson, were enslavers? And the other thirty-two owned or were invested in the ships that transported our Ancestors all over the Caribbean and the Americas!

GCM: You grew up celebrating the Fourth of July while I, an ebony-smooth little boy, was learning hymns with lyrics like, "Wash me whiter than snow." Psychologically-speaking, I've got to confess that our folks have been living with domination for so long we've learned to eat insults as if they were cornflakes.

APB: Black folks have no end of excuses for letting White folk get away with abuse.

GCM: I've heard it all. When a less-qualified White woman was given a bilingual school-board post for which I had applied, and she didn't even speak French, a Black female administrator remonstrated with me.

"She's a nice woman."

Other times, when I've taken offence at racial innuendo or insult, some of our leading Blacks have said.

"Chill, man! They don't mean anything."

The compromised and compromising amongst us clutch at straws, and I'm easily convinced that some folks instinct for shame has atrophied over time.

APB: Do you remember how the talk shows blew up when J. Lo used the N-word?

GCM: Folks were going like … Whoa! I don't believe she just said that…? Doesn't she know that a Black boyfriend doesn't make her Black?

APB: Then P. Diddy jumped in and said he gave her a pass …

GCM: Yeah! That once-upon-a-time brother, gave her a pass. Did His Richness ask you for permission? He sure didn't ask me!

APB: Did what? That's our fault for letting her and letting him get away with doing that…

GCM: Our Brother, Bankie Forster Bankie who, by the way, was from Ghana, would definitely have scolded Diddy for "putting personality above principle."

APB: That's exactly what Diddy did.

GCM: And while we're on judges like Br. Bankie, here's what I just heard happened to a retired Black supreme court justice in Vancouver. At a dignified eighty-one, he was handcuffed for strolling while Black through that city's Stanley Park. Unfortunately, Justice Romilly's response to being humiliated was to warn other Black men, not to "escalate" when profiled. That says it all. Period.!

"You dii-ig?

APB: I'm not surprised. It's part of a sickening trend. We've slipped backwards since Br. Malcolm's time.

GCM: That really hurts! You're the smart one. Please tell me what to do with folks like that. I wish I could ascribe that attitude to the conservatism that sometimes comes with age, but it's pervasive. I was at the Apollo/theatre in Harlem, on a Wednesday, "Amateur Night," in the days when audiences were just local and Black. I'm right up front, feeling at home, surrounded by a young crowd dissing each other and cracking up. Suddenly a female in uniform, their generation, full of herself, ordered me, who could have been her father, to take off my kufi. Remember! We're talking New York now, where religious headgear like mine, atop lighter skins, usually gets more respect instead of uninvited insult. While I was caught off guard and speechless, her peers who surrounded me, tore into her.

"Can't you see he's an Afrikan, they said?"

I was relieved that they defended me, but wondered who they thought they were. And wondered even more who she thought she was, and how we had all got to that sorry place.

APB: And yet, we already have a blueprint of what to do. The Pan-Afrikan historian Chancellor Williams, a generation ago, told us what to do.

GCM: O yeah! The Destruction of Black Civilization was one of my first wake-up texts. I think it was on your recommendation I got it for my birthday decades ago.

APB: In that book, chapters 14 and 15, the brother listed concrete ways in which Black people can respond to this history that keeps tripping us up. It's one of the things I noted that you do as well in Talking Cheddo. You make concrete suggestions about what we can do about present conditions, and in your last chapters you give examples of what we need to be doing in terms of this system that is messing around with our children.

GCM: You're right. We've lost community control of the standards that govern our children's education. I thought that working through some case studies would show how we've been able to overcome problems, even complex ones. based on real situations from California to Nova Scotia. I can remember sitting around a table with teachers who I'd never met before. And, to quote my mother, they were "bad-mouthing" the students and their parents. You know the drill. "There's no father at home blah blah blah," echoing paternalistic assumptions of innate Black, female inferiority.

APB: In the US, that idea became popular when, in 1965, Daniel Patrick Moynihan presented his "Report on the Negro Family" to the government on behalf of the Department of Labor. It pathologized Black families as "matriarchal" and being mostly inferior to White families. Then Moynihan went on to hypothesize, "It is probable that at present, a majority of the crimes against the person, such as rape, murder, and aggravated assault are committed by Negroes ..." That could be deduced, Daniel Moynihan argued, from studies on the arrest, conviction and incarceration of young Black males. Today, fifty plus years later, with irrefutable evidence, it's abundantly clear that mass criminalization was driven by anti-Black racism, not a Black propensity for crime. At the same time, one could read story after story about horrific things happening within many White families.

GCM: And, by the way, Br. Peter, the student body those teachers were "dissin," were drawn, in large part, from public housing. Many residents were seventh generation Canadians with Black Nova Scotian roots, and there was a significant Jamaican immigrant and Indigenous population as well. Feeling my stomach knotting up, I tried to shut out the voices of my new colleagues. Eventually, however, I gave up, looked around the table and said,

"I'm guessing that none of us here is an Einstein or Marie Curie, but we got through university anyway."

The temperature plummeted in the room, the discussion ended, and we moved on to the next item on the agenda. In my head I could hear, "Each One Teach One." "Each One Teach One" going around and coming around, alongside a longing for a magic carpet to fly the Black kids home with me to Afrika and teach them myself.

APB: Black community control of our children's schools should be a non-negotiable item. We are the only pilots who can be trusted to guide them mentally home. It's our duty to rescue their minds.

In my view, Thurgood Marshall did posterity immense damage, when he misrepresented Black achievement by describing Black schools as inherently inferior. By coercing the NAACP into demanding "integration" rather than "equality," he bears unique responsibility for Black economic and social decline. Black economic hubs had been bolstered by independent Black thinking, developed under independent Black teachers in independent Black schools.

Once our schools were seen as inferior because they were Black, our hotels, our banks and where we lived, dined, partied or shopped became inferior too. Our communities abandoned whatever we had that was exclusively ours, became infected with White Red-Carped syndrome and developed symptoms of "the-first-Black-to-be-seen-at-a-White-whatever" disease.

With our minds in disarray, we became addicted to spending our money with other communities. Our economic hubs, like 'Black Wall Street" dwindled away, as Black businesses, from florists to funeral homes, began to slide into decline.

GCM: Why do you fault Thurgood Marshall and not the plaintiffs who brought the Brown V Board of Ed suit?

APB: Barbara Johns and her preacher father, from Farmville, Virginia had asked the NAACP to support them in their demand for equal educational resources – arguing that Blacks and Whites were equally taxed. The racist practices of the school board included sending dirty, torn-up textbooks discarded by the White High School to the Black High School that Barbara Johns attended. The Black community never thought for a moment that their school, parents, teachers or students, were inferior. However, they knew they were being shortchanged in funding. It was Farmville-flavoured apartheid, but still as much apartheid the South African brand.

GCM: Thanks for this lesson, Br. P. I never realized that Thurgood Marshall had distorted the intention of the plaintiffs and changed Black American history at such a profound level. Talking over that history with you has convinced me that, collectively, we need to revisit those events. Today's school-age generation needs the significant details we've just discussed in order to make sense of contradictions we are living out today.

APB: The integration question should be on the table in activist circles like Black Lives Matter.

GCM: I remember Sr. Una Mulzac of Liberation Bookstore putting me on guard as big White distributors began to compete with her by hiring needy young men to sell Black books at prices below cost on the streets of Harlem - sometimes even on the sidewalk that ran around her corner store.

She had to sweep that sidewalk every morning, even though she paid taxes, and had begun to feel the toll of the years. She swept the pavement to avoid paying exorbitant fines, sometimes levied several times a day, for the garbage that was not picked up by the city and that the wind blew her way.

Her fans, and we were legion, respected and cherished her, as one of those caring Harlem villagers we instinctively trusted to raise every child.

APB: I remember the Liberation Bookstore as well. Sr. Una was there all day, every day. She would often be caught eating lunch in-between serving customers.

GCM: Over the years Sr. Una made it her mission to get the young people hanging out on the street to dip into the treasures waiting just inside her door. Some of those toddlers she inveigled into browsing grew into students, then academics or writers of poetry and plays, who made Harlem more famous and Harlemites proud.

From watching Sr. Una relate to struggling neighbours around her store, I learned a lot about how Cheddo villages, populated by autodidactic villagers could enhance learning, if Pan-Afrikan educators committed to a plan.

In all her years at Malcolm X Blvd. and 131st St, there was only one break-in, and her stolen radio was back by that noon. There was no need for cops, court and or questions. The Black community took care of its own.

APB: I'm glad Sr. Una had her property returned. But I wouldn't excuse whoever was willing to break into an elder's bookstore. They didn't care or think of the community as theirs, and we shouldn't coddle them. Brother Malcolm would have told them that in behaving that way, they were really worse than the KKK.

GCM: In yesterday's Harlem, where being Black could be so electrically sweet, "Liberation Bookstore" was more like an intelligence stock market than a bookstore.

Freethinking Black minds, like the filmmaker of Sankofa, Haile Gerima, could rendezvous there across distance, ethnicity, religion or class. Liberation Bookstore could only thrive because the community loved it. Professor John Henrik Clarke and all the conscious Black academics across the city filled their reading lists from its shelves.

The store had resources to share and inspire young readers, because celebrities like Mama Camille Cosby bought pricey books on Afrikan art, spreading Black knowledge and wealth around as gifts.

APB: To those of us who were in The Movement in the sixties, Harlem was always the uncrowned capital of our Black world. Isn't that why the Garvey Movement only went global after taking root in Harlem? Its soil had already been watered by both genius and suffering and was already rich. Ready for seeding global Black pride.

GCM: After viewing Sankofa, Haile Gerima's outstanding contribution to Pan-Afrikan and Cheddo consciousness, I recalled that, as an immigrant from Ethiopia in New York, he had, in discovering Harlem, encountered Sr. Una. As she did for many of us, she guided him into the heart of Black America and Global Afrika. As they say, "the rest is his genius."

The motto above Liberation Bookstore read, "Each One Teach One," and Sr. Una wasn't playing. It's my motto too. In spite of reality, even harsh reality, that motto has travelled with Blacks and kept us going. And today, with evolving technology, we can put it into practice – as never before.

APB: I think that with enough consciousness, our super-rich deejays and red-carpet stars could easily fund the kind of education we need.

GCM: By the way, you're right next door to Baltimore, where there is another community builder whose thinking I would describe as being in my Cheddo tradition. Did you know Kurt Schmoke when he was mayor?

APB: I never interviewed him, although I did get to shake hands at a public event where he was present. He was the first Black mayor with enough guts to let a security company associated with the Nation of Islam compete for a contract involving public housing projects with some over-the-top challenges.

GCM: According to all reports, his success in that experiment disappointed many establishment politicians, when, as he had predicted, the "Nation" did turn things around. The sites where they served became safer, cleaner, more like home for the families that lived there, and the drug dealers melted away. From what I've heard, Br. Peter, because that model worked so well, New York City's first Black mayor, David Dinkins, also dared to give it a try.

I had visited folks I knew in one of the designated projects in the Bronx before the Nation was brought in, where every visitor would feel the tension in the air. Enter the Nation of Islam and the climate changed overnight! You could park and not worry about your hubcaps; the elevator worked, the ground was litter-free, and I swear, even the air smelled clean. However, as often happens with our colour, anti-Black envy found fertile ground and grew until Mayor Dinkins caved in and aborted the successful experiment.

APB: In addition, Mayor Dinkins was given a rough time, especially by the New York Police.

GCM: As a Pan-Afrikanist, when Kurt Schmoke became Baltimore's first Black mayor, I sat up, took notice and followed his career from afar. His Honor was ready to get rolling, it seemed, from Day One. Black people were catching hell in Baltimore, ad all the White mayors before him had failed abysmally. Mayor Schmoke rolled up his sleeves, washed his hands, took out his scalpel and got to work. As the first Black mayor of a major big city his election caused more than a ripple across the nation, and definitely inspired Pan-Afrikanists like me.

APB: There is no doubt that he was an improvement over his White predecessor.

GCM: From the news coming my way, he seemed to be operating at fever pitch in every direction at once, doing an octopus administrator thing. But then why not, we have always been a polyrhythmic people! In fact, his modus operandi mirrored the multiple rhythms of Baba Olatunji's Afrikan drums, Sun Ra's interplanetary sounds, or Toto Bissanthe's Haitian invocations. By pulling Black folks together from diverse communities and pooling their strengths, his bold and inventive initiatives rescued Baltimore, transformed its mood of defeat and restored hope.

APB: I remember that his election generated a lot of excitement in the popular imagination.

GCM: Our mayor, for Pan-Afrikanists belong to us all, focused on at-risk Black boys, intuiting that coaching and remaking them into academic stars was a fast way of dismantling the crippling stereotypes of failure that even some well-meaning Black educators had internalized. Mayor Schmoke introduced a program for the gifted with an enriched curriculum and carefully selected and groomed Black boys who showed potential for success. The first graduates became poster-boys whose achievements won public acclaim, made their community proud and renewed their self-esteem.

APB: That's a model that we should be trying to implement wherever we have failing school systems.

GCM: A White colleague told me that it's a model that worked selectively with Appalachian students as well. As he had figured it would, having experienced their children's success up close and in real time parents had reason to hope. Left-behind communities began to re-invest and to take back ownership of their children's academic future.

As strong leaders do, Mayor Schmoke also gave credit to a community mentor, Van Standifer, from a nearby town, whose creation of Midnight Basketball proved to be a stroke of genius.

As a father of Black sons, public administrator Van Standifer had focused on finding creative solutions for the explosive cocktail of stress, frustration, deprivation and drug-use which was destroying young men between seventeen and twenty-two under his watch. Like they say, the rest is history.

Midnight Basketball has spread like Hip Hop. In my Cheddo eyes, out-of-the-box thinkers like Br. Schmoke and Br. Sandifer belong to our autodidactic, self-teaching, ancestral traditions. During bondage, many of our Ancestors actually did teach themselves to read from a scrap of Bible or some random page of print. Then they would immediately begin to spread their new skills, like birds which always teach their new songs to other flocks.

When Mayor Schmoke was presented an opportunity to serve, he stepped forward and took risks in order to transform the unhealthy situation he had inherited. I remember wishing, in vain, that another high-profile Black constitutional lawyer, had also used his unique political "first" to get rid of the "slavery" clause in the US Constitution, once and for all.

We have to make ourselves available to those young people who are already conscious and anxious to do for self. One of our past mistakes was waiting around interminably for those who were reluctant to join us.

Sr. Una would stop little girls and boys passing by with their moms or dads and ask them to read her a line or two from a new picture book she'd just got in. And then she'd give them the book.

Another generous Harlem Spirit, playwright j e Franklin, is today still working in a similar mode. She freely gives away copies of her brilliant invention, which she calls Hip Hop Aesop, a combination of philosophy, storytelling and rhythm to our children at random. Her game and the vibrant illustrations engage them instantly and soon they are reading without stress or tears.

Since Brown vs the Board of Education and desegregation in 1954, Cheddo educators wonder why Black parents, supposedly sound in mind, have been sending their babies into buildings where they are over-punished, over-policed, over-suspended and starved for respect or affection? It boggles the mind.

APB: Thurgood Marshall misrepresented what Black populations wanted for their children.

GCM: As educators and parents, we know, even without academic studies that confirm our instincts, that children learn with love and trust. I remember trying to help an eight-year-old with his math homework. It was new and proving hard for him. So, looking over his shoulder, I said,

"Let me show you!"

"No!" He protested. "Don't do it for me. Just let me sit on your lap."

He did, and soon solved the problem on his own.

APB: I think your book is more accessible to readers because of real life stories like that.

GCM: That young student was family, and whenever I remember that day in Dakar, I'm again convinced that learning happens mostly in the heart. Our children want to please, and when they see approval in our eyes or hear it in our voices, they feel secure. That's when they lose their fear of flying and can take off into the physical or intellectual unknown.

APB: We need to keep spreading those stories of how we teach and learn so parents take up the challenge, whatever their own formal education.

GCM: So, speaking as a Pan-Afrikanist, I would say we have no choice. We've got to find ways of controlling how our kids learn. I've seen Homeschooling work successfully for some families. What's to prevent good friends, or just neighbours, getting together and homeschooling their kids?

APB: I keep coming back to the key to today's dysfunction. Many of us didn't ask for integration into White schools in 1954, but Thurgood Marshall was a total integrationist.

GCM: At the risk of saying too much, here's my truth! It's probably going to be harder to make this system serve us than to rebuild a system of our own. Education can't flourish in hostile environments, just as plants can't flourish under acid rain. The architects of White education systems designed them to throttle opportunities that might enhance Black empowerment.

When a highway is built to go east, veering off for a while won't get drivers to a destination that's due west. Failing Black students is what race supremacist systems are designed to do, and that continues to happen despite heroic efforts to steer them in the opposite direction.

Culturally Black schools with Black principals and teachers nurtured leaders like Martin Luther King and more geniuses of rhythm, poetry, melody and movement than we could ever count. In fact, the affirmation and reaffirmation of Black genius was one of the delightful aspects of reading your biography of Alvin Ailey. And you make that formula for success transparent. What you captured was an experience of Black-on-Black intensity and creativity, which is like rubbing sticks together until they burst into flame.

APB: That's why Alvin thought it was important that a Black writer tell his story. Because, often when outsiders tell our stories, they do so from a different cultural perspective.

GCM: As Pan-Afrikanists inspired by Br. Malcolm X, we have no trouble taking up the space we need to run our own affairs. After all, self-taught Black folks did invent ways for gathering up and passing on the knowledge of herbs we needed for healing constant scabs and scars under the whips and wounds of enslavement. By the way, who do you think taught our Ancestors to find the North Star that guided thousands out of bondage to Canada from the Deep-South? And I personally still marvel at Black genius for hiding messages in spirituals and creating symbols that Whites might look at yet not see, which mapped out paths to set the hunted free.

APB: That legacy is one of the reasons I have admired the way some Black churches helped to make freedom real. Canaan Baptist

Church of Christ in Harlem's pastor, the Rev. Wyatt Tee Walker documented the rich history of spirituals from origins on the killing fields of Southern plantations in his book Somebody's Calling My Name. More than anyone else, he made me see the spiritual and communal importance of our music. If I were working with a mixed group of Black girls and boys today, every meeting would open and end with Nina Simone singing "To be Young, Gifted and Black." And if there were just boys or young men present, every meeting would open and end with Donny Hathaway singing, "He Ain't Heavy, He's My Brother."

GCM: So, leaning into those constant strengths in our history, I can't help feeling confident about what's to come.

After all, given the fortitude our Ancestors summoned to overcome forced bondage, and forced exile, and apartheid and a global anti-Black caste system, we should prove equal to any challenge we're presently facing or likely to bump up against in the future. Since Ayiti, populations invested in equity have been holding their breath, waiting for Black shock troops to lead the way in liberation for all humans again.

Ho Chi Minh, the Asian Toussaint L'Ouverture or "Uncle Ho," is also one of my heroes, who one of my mentors, Prof. KK Prah, quotes as saying, "It is a well-known fact that the Black people are the most oppressed of human-kind."

When he lived in the US, Uncle Ho would attend Marcus Garvey's rallies, and reportedly it was Garvey's "Afrika for the Afrikans" that inspired his slogan, "Vietnam for the Vietnamese."

Besides, Black enslavement is unique. What happened to Black populations hasn't happened to anyone else, and I feel it still bubbles up as memories in our blood. Distant, deeply buried trauma can still make my heart race and turn my legs to water. For me, and many like me, those feelings are demonstrably real.

I won't explain away and don't accept our experience of being universally targeted and treated as a lower caste, but I'm also determined to uphold Cheddo principles that open our windows and hearts to the world.

APB: Getting back to the language of zombie Black stigma that refuses to die! I hate when people say "slave master," and I always immediately say "enslaver" instead.

GCM: In Talking Cheddo, I also call the men who snatched Afrika's daughters and sons at gunpoint, "terrorists," and their innocent captives, "hostages." And in lessons about stigma, we sometimes compete in inventing more accurate terms to describe the nuances of Black captivity, and then we let ourselves feel how they land in our hearts. For example, speaking personally, I began to think of Ayitians differently when I rejected descriptions like "the institution of slavery," and started calling that crime against Black humanity, a crime. The more we've explored the details of Ayiti's history, the larger she looms, and the more heroic she grows in our eyes every day. Our examination of significant detail in class even led one super-sceptical adult learner to ask bluntly why any Black person, in their right mind, would just call brutal, sadistic torturers "men," and not find a more precise way of signalling to the world how dangerous they were.

APB: That sounds like a useful exercise for encouraging independent thinking. I may try it next time I'm working with my young study group.

GCM: Letting outsiders define our experience is one of the ways we have undermined our own worth. I'm convinced that those observing or even studying our experience won't and really can't ever provide a full picture of who we are. As we'd say in the day, "It's a uniquely, indelibly, inescapably, ineffably Black thang, ..."

APB: According to you, "Nobody would understand."

GCM: For me, there's a kind of detail I'm always trying to find amidst the deluge of data in the media or just everywhere in our daily lives. What I want it to do is be specific about Black pain, so we can count the costs. If I had to, I'd label what I look for, significant detail.

For example, it took a Pan-Afrikan historian, C.L.R. James, to make me really grasp the enormity of France's crimes against humanity in Ayiti. Some of the tortures they used, like stuffing human behinds with gunpowder and then blowing the person apart, foreshadowed the Brits testing out bombing civilian populations in Somali. Then I imagined Cecil Rhodes first testing machine-guns against Afrikans with spears in what became Zimbabwe and mowing them down "like wheat."

Ten million plus Belgian murders in Congo to get possession of that population's rubber, diamonds and gold fries my mind. However, it is matched by apartheid's use of cholera, and government agents in the US who dropped bombs on Black neighborhoods, in broad daylight, in Tulsa in 1921, and in Philadelphia in 1985.

APB: Yes. In some ways your book links blatant physical atrocities of the past to documented psychological damage inflicted on our daughters and sons by schools that are too often run like prisons today.

GCM: For example, who would have anticipated that the children of Black middle-class parents in Queens, New York would be registering failure rates of eighty plus per cent in Math and abysmal performances in English today? - Black students in New York are failing Language Arts no less! What irony, when the Black Rap and Hip Hop invented by Black students in New York are revolutionizing and energizing even foreign languages on life support across the globe!

APB: I believe that New York City's schools are suffering from festering old wounds.

GCM: I know you were living in Harlem when the powerful, White-identified teachers' union savaged the Black community. Backed up by the White public and their media, the Teachers Union falsely painted Black parents not only as anti-White but anti-Semitic, and deemed them unqualified to make decisions about what programs would meet their own children's needs. In the end, the Teachers Union won.

Their White privilege and racist power defeated the hopeful Black parents who didn't "know their place" and dared to step out of role. New York's teachers not only successfully blocked

Mayor Lindsay's attempts to heal the wounds of the education system and rescue standards that continued to plummet in all subject areas, they were even paid by the city for going on strike.

Although Black parents were beaten back, in the end, the community left with their heads high, fell back on Cheddo traditions of self-reliance, and founded the independent "Uhuru Sasa Shule," a successful independent Afrikan-centered school.

APB: I was around when leaders like Jitu Weusi and Black college students said, "Enough is enough!"

GCM: Those parents knew instinctively that they should revive tradition. After all, by depending almost entirely on our own kith and kin, half the Black US population could read within ten years after Emancipation.

Similarly, contrary to popular White narratives, the glory of organizing and running The Underground Railroad belongs almost exclusively to Black individuals and communities who risked their fortunes and lives repeatedly to help and hide fleeing freedom-seekers who looked like them.

APB: Those were the Ancestors of Black Nova Scotians, who I met when I lectured there a decade ago.

GCM: I've got a confession to make. I benefited personally from Uhuru Sasa and participated for at least a decade in the Afrikan Street Festival which had grown out of their first graduation celebration. During the period I was flying back and forth to Afrika, I helped to run a family booth selling crafts from the continent at The African Street Festival. Later, when I was making my documentary All Eyes On Africa, I interviewed some of the organizers and participants. At its peak, renamed the "International African Arts Festival," it featured emerging local artists like KRS One and even superstar Fela Kuti with his forty-piece band.

APB: Talking things through with you is a useful exercise because you make me remember and also challenge some my own ideas. I like it, because the more we define what we need to do, the clearer the way forward becomes.

GCM: If you asked me what was the most important lesson our children really need to learn, right now, I'd say that it is that we can thrive on our own when we're left alone. Unfortunately, that vein of self-reliance runs counter to contemporary Hip-Hop Red-Carpet stardom. Many young performers from our community act as if they don't mind being ridden, as long as they can live in a gilded stable, with millions of "likes" for a crown.

APB: I believe they lack Pan-Afrikan role models.

GCM: That's hardly surprising when school systems, perhaps globally, systematically suppress the history of self-determining Black women and men. Those individuals represent the Cheddo spirit, which includes but is not limited to Pan-Afrikanism . There's a Wolof saying, "Lu ren jaan jaan ren jaanko jaan, (For every snake that goes deep down, another snake burrows even deeper still)." As a "long-memoried" people, we must forever carry multiple images of our Ancestors and their understandings of the Cosmos, like portable intelligences, in our heads. That, to me, is the power of legacy and the Cheddo way.

APB: It's significant that despite a hundred years of engineered oblivion, young people worldwide now know the stories of the builders of Tulsa and "Black Wall Street," which was destroyed in 1921. Only a global conspiracy linking White journalists, editors, academics, preachers and politicians could have buried a tragedy of such Biblical proportions for 100 years!

GCM: As educators, both of us know that most groups have a glory-narrative at the heart of their telling of their people's history. Even if there is no concrete, objective or factual evidence behind it, they tell it and insist that the world accept that that's who they are. I propose that we resume the telling of our core stories, and that our task, as we move into the future, is twofold. We have an obvious duty to fill in breaches that divide the stream of our consciousness or bewilder us.

So, concretely, we must retrieve the Benin Bronzes and other looted treasures that define our ancestry. And in order to repair our sense of selfhood, we must rehabilitate our heroes and defenders like Mama Winnie Mandela and the Rev. Adam

Clayton Powell Jr. Where necessary, we must also eliminate or fix the distortions that have kept us from finding the strengths we need and can only find in each other, in order to keep expanding into the fullness of most authentic selves.

APB: And because of the psychological war being waged against us, we need to teach those stories repeatedly and everywhere.

GCM: Speaking personally now, I've found that one of the hardest things to do is to get well-meaning friends to stop interrupting when we start to stand up and speak out against institutions they benefit from or hold dear.

APB: Sounds as if you have a story!

GCM: You bet I do! After a White Toronto cop shot a Black father - in his bedroom, begging for his life on his knees, with his little daughter looking on - a handful of us met at one of our homes, reasoned and decided to form the "Black Action Defence Committee" or (Bad-See) in Toronto. We were all hurting, so we strategized that we had to process our raw, Black experience in a sanitized Black space, by ourselves, and without outside distraction. At the very next meeting of the group, one of the community's leading Blacks turned up, without invitation, with a White friend in tow. Nobody wanted to be the one to say he couldn't join us, but one brave brother finally did.

APB: In Br. Malcolm's OAAU We had one visible Asian supporter, a victim of US Japanese internment, Mary (Yuri) Kochiyama. When her letter of introduction came to me, I passed it on to Br. Malcolm. Like the gentle soul he was, he received her gracefully, and she became an ardent supporter for a little over a year before his assassination. Although Yuri Kochiyama would often attend our public meetings with her children, we only had Black members in the organization. She was a real ally, who understood the significance of brother Malcolm's words, "You were bombed and have physical scars. We too have been bombed and you saw some of the scars in our neighborhood. We are constantly hit by the bombs of racism — which are just as devastating."

GCM: I have my Asian icons too. I admire the leadership of the Chinese Revolution for having had the foresight and fortitude to shut out both friend and foe for forty years. They had to hang tough, but it got them out of their multi-generational cycle of foreign interference and domination.

Now just look at the mess that post-colonial Afrika is in! ECOWAS and the AU have morphed into instruments of personal ambition, foreign subversion and state repression rather than vehicles of popular liberation.

APB: Please explain to me why, with all the evidence of history, we haven't figured out that we should do what the Chinese were able to do?

GCM: I feel frustrated too. Why has Congo stayed a killing field – sixty plus years after multinational mercenaries, missionaries, spies and the Emperor of South Kasai where the diamonds are, Kalonji Mulopwe, conspired to murder the people's Pan-Afrikan hero, Patrice Lumumba?

Why, in Nigeria, when the Pan-Afrikan philanthropist, Moshood Abiola, overcoming ethnic, class and religious divisions, won almost 60% of the vote in the 1993 election, did not the whole Black world rise up and support him for the good of us all? When purportedly democratic governments, like the US, tried to persuade him to step down, he stood tall and refused.

In the tradition of Chief Lobengula, when con-man Cecil Rhodes produced a fake deed to Zimbabwe's land, Chief Abiola responded, "This vote belongs to the Nigerian people. I could not surrender it even if that was what I wanted to do." And so, the Internet says, a prominent Black politician, of Caribbean heritage, was in his prison with a US delegation, when he allegedly drank tea and died.

Off the record, Nigerian officers from Intelligence have been telling a very different story of international collusion in politically-motivated poisonings, including that of President-Elect Abiola. As a result of that thwarting of the Nigerian people's will, oil-spoiled Nigeria was turned into a warren of self-serving, shameless super-robbers, obsessed with pomp, privilege and personal gain.

APB: As a Black journalist, I'm surprised that we heard so little about the Abiola affair. And I certainly would have sat up and paid attention, if someone had said that a Black Secretary of State was so prominently involved.

GCM: My brother, let's be clear. The assassination of President-elect Abiola should have galvanized us like the Black Lives Matter Movement has done today. When we let our giants be cut down before our eyes, we signal the world that we have not suffered enough. Lest we forget, our enslaved grandmothers used to say, "The one who is most easily beaten is most often beaten." Chief Abiola's death, like Br. Malcolm's or a swath of assassinations of committed strategists, broke the momentum of Black Liberation Movements. To me, that is the message these assassinations send to the global Black brain, and why they are carried out.

APB: We need continuity, and at one point I thought that would be the main function of the AU. You don't seem to expect very much from them.

GCM: You're right. When we see how ECOWAS and the AU address the tyrants, in my opinion, like the present regime-heads of Kenya, Uganda, South Africa and Rwanda in Kenya that emerge in their midst, it gives the Black masses little reason for trust.

Why, when a few years ago they refused, en bloc, to have any foreign forces stationed on their soil, have they capitulated and permitted over fifty bases without providing any rationale to their collective constituencies? I suspect that there is not a single viable Black army outside Zimbabwe today, and those brave defenders have been starved for equipment by racist White sanctions.

APB: I don't blame anyone else for that, Clem. I blame us!

GCM: I agree. Progressive and conservative regimes alike do not share the information needed to build trust in their constituencies. It's not unlike the opaque operations workings of some members of the Congressional Black Congress. Where there is no transparency, one cannot validly earn trust.

APB: Our situation is not the same as the continent, where Blacks are the overwhelming majority. Surely, all those millions of educated and wealthy individuals should have worked out how to protect their country's resources and lives by now! Every other continent has done it.

GCM: I can't agree with you 100% on that. Yes, I do decry Black power-brokers in South Africa, as they well deserve, for consenting to be post-apartheid pawns. But did they personally have the power to murder Chris Hani, marginalize Mama Winnie Mandela and manipulate the leadership of the ANC?

Rather, in my view, international money-driven forces, left with no place to hide, cut a deal with Mama Winnie Mandela's patriarchal husband and a club of good old boys, including P.W. Botha, F. W. De Klerk, Joe Slovo and the ANC brass. Once the deal was done, Bishop Tutu and some high-profile Black women were co-opted for cover. The way I see it, Black populations continue to endure persecution unjustly, just as enslavement was not punishment for Black-on-Arab, Black-on-White or Black-on-Black crime.

History records that that when Arabs and Eurasians first strayed across the Black Motherland, not a single explorer, traveller, missionary or stranger reported finding culturally-generated famine, orphans, beggars, homelessness, prisons or poor-houses. In addition, gender-wise, a Scottish "explorer," Mungo Park, who was sheltered and fed by two very independent women at the cusp of the nineteenth century, marveled as they spent the night weaving, chatting and singing songs. Again, no mad-houses shut up sisters or brothers in distress. And everywhere wide-eyed strangers travelled, they could rely on the sound of drums to find dancing, hospitality and a feast.

APB: But, today, some Black people are hurting their own people, and I have no sympathy for them.

GCM: I remember Br. James Baldwin debating that point with Professor Paul Weiss from Yale University a generation ago.

APB: Was that on the Dick Cavett show?

GCM: Careful! We're dating ourselves.

Dr. Weiss tried to scold Br. Jimmy for Black ingratitude, one of the predictable complaints of nice White folks. After all, Weiss pointed out to our Ancestor, he had become a famous Black writer. He chided Baldwin, in Margaret Thatcher tones, for acting as if Whites had a collective responsibility for the crimes committed against Black populations.

Who can forget UK PM Margaret Thatcher's, "There's no society. We are all individuals?" Br. James wasn't having it. "I don't know what most White people in this country feel," he said. "I can only conclude what they feel from the state of their institutions." Professor Weiss was not a happy camper. As he stared the ivy-league academic dead in the eye, Br. James spoke the language of lived Black experience, telling him bluntly that White privilege benefited all White people.

APB: I still won't give us a pass for allowing this mess to go on for such a long time.

GCM: I'll bite. We did make one monumental mistake. Whenever and wherever colonialism ended outside Afrika, colonizers went home. But in Afrika, even President Mugabe, although Ian Smith and his South African killer/collaborators had bombed Black schools and poisoned village wells, as now revealed on the Internet, permitted the colonizers to stay. I sympathize with his thinking, but feel it has proved an unaffordable mistake.

Smith's estate, which I visited long after independence, was still as large as one of our Toronto suburbs. On the other hand, when President Sékou Touré turned down continued French tutelage, they trashed the country before they left, even ripping phones from walls and damming up sewage pipes.

APB: That's what I mean. Our presumably conscious leaders let them stay, so we've only got ourselves to blame.

GCM: I have no logical answer for you. Our leaders were looking on as the Brits had to leave India. No one was allowed to stay in China. The French were driven from Algeria, and the Americans ended up dangling by their fingers from their helicopters, as they got the hell out of Vietnam. Perhaps the more open-hearted Afrikan response to outsiders, generally, is a result of our still unfathomed Cheddo strength rather than a weakness. From time immemorial we had lived at the centre of the earth, where water, light, warmth, food and beauty were plentiful and free, and we had done so without human predators.

No wonder we never cultivated instincts for protecting ourselves from fresh varieties of ourselves, who we tended to greet with scientific interest and expectations of delight. Motherland culture had developed imaginative mechanisms for making peace. For example, if one lost a son in inter-ethnic strife, he could be replaced by adopting the slayer's brother, and making one new family out of two grieving groups.

APB: Are you not just making excuses for folks who don't deserve it? Every Black man isn't a brother, you know. "Brother" is an honorific to me, and a reward for integrity and service.

GCM: I totally agree. I don't believe in excuses, but I'm a firm believer in giving each other as many chances as our spirits can bear.

Just look at Br. Malcolm and his transformation into a political genius over time! I won't pretend to forgive a sister or brother if I don't feel it. However, in honour of the same principle, I won't force myself to be harsh if my heart tells me to forgive. Life doesn't offer us all equal chances. What if it will only let some spirit have one fleeting moment to really shine? Until then, I believe we are learning and preparing. Speaking personally, I can still feel myself growing, and I feel safe, like being mothered, when I can find the space for the whole family to grow with me and through the experiences my Ancestors give me.

APB: You can go down that path, but I'm not accepting excuses - not at this critical stage. If we don't get it together and do so real soon, it might be too late and we might all be doomed.

GCM: You and I both agree that there is no liberation for us without the Motherland and there's no liberation for the Motherland without us.

However, knitting the torn flesh we share back together is as delicate an operation as grafting skin. We've been so long divided from the Motherland that we've got a lot of mending to do.

While I lived in Senegal and would made short trips outside Dakar, villagers would greet me, "Naka Canada (How is Canada)," as if any stranger was related to everyone else where they came from. They expect us to be family to those who live where we're born or reside. And as my mentors from the continent have showed me, they are used to reaching out and treating neighbours, whose languages and religions they've come to know over generations, as family.

Although we Cheddo and other Pan-Afrikanists working for rebirth realize that Indigenous Blacks might define us in English, Arabic, Spanish, Portuguese or French, we know that we can transcend limitations by using body language, like 'skin-to-skin' aka "fist bump" and the drum.

APB: I am encouraged that you see Cheddo as a vehicle of global re-education by us, about us, for us.

GCM: It is my conviction that Cheddo can provide a buffer against death-inspired, suicidal religiosity that has been pushing southwards since the eighth century, encroaching on what Br. Bankie Forster Bankie would describe as the: "Borderlands … that area of Africa running from Mauritania on the Atlantic Ocean, eastwards through the Sahel, to Sudan on the Red Sea." Cheddo-centred thinking, however, is empty of the ambiguity that seems to paralyze so many Heads of State who squander time and resources needed to secure our ancestral legacy.

APB: To me the "Borderlands" are a straight-up political problem. There is no excuse for a resource-rich nation with a population of over 200 plus million like Nigeria to be unable to protect its people from roving bands of random religious or greedy bandits.

GCM: Cheddo challenges individuals to think through and judge decisions that affect their free will regardless of the rank made by authorities of any stripe for themselves. Let me tell you why I feel confident that Cheddo can overcome multi-generational anti-Black indoctrination. With Hip Hop throbbing everywhere, who can deny the spontaneous globalization of Afrikan culture? It was ever thus.

GCM: During bondage, Black music and movement, like "Jungle Music" later on, were initially banned. Left to exercise their free choice in the Cheddo tradition, however, populations that speak every imaginable tongue seem ineluctably drawn to Black-invented ways of infusing joy and even attaining instant ecstasy from the ordinary activities of everyday living.

That approach to labour and production distinguishes the place labour occupies in Black life from its value to other cultures. As the Greeks noted, learning, for instance doing Math or working, as in building pyramids, were never separate activities from generating joy for along the Nile, all of whose populations they called Ethiopians.

Socrates called Black Aesop the greatest philosopher who ever lived for combining, poetry, philosophy, storytelling and rhythm. It's that genius for infinite and inventive combination of the unexpected that provides the transformative spark in all we do.

So, slave labour, as understood today, has never dominated our Ancestors' imaginative world. Our bodies cannot become units of production because their purpose in our heads is to be family, to share delight and to generate joy. That's runs counter to the self-alienating Marxist or Eurasian definition of labour.

My intuition says Black Salvation and Liberation rest on some yet unquantified vibrational force. That just happens, as with other species, to be how we have evolved in becoming who we are today. The phenomenon of Hip Hop immediately comes to my mind. Sans institutions, armies, and in spite of negative media, financial or bureaucratic empires, it has churned Black culture into a kind of global butter for the bare bread of the oppressed, marginalized, dispossessed or despised, wherever humans survive.

Black culture does what the best-funded NGOs would love to claim they can do. Without causing disruption or evoking even a hint of humiliation, Hip Hop has gone into communities of every shape, identity and hue, bringing and freely sharing its

APB: skills and tools, which they can choose to use independently to better their lives from then on. I can't think of any other culture that does that better than our folks, Black folks do.

APB: Are you sure you're not just putting a good spin on a bad situation?

GCM: Here's another plausible idea! Many of the early Afrikan leaders like Sir Abubakar Tafawa Balewa of Nigeria, Dr. Jomo Kenyatta of Kenya and Dr. Kenneth Kaunda of Zambia were scholars or teachers, thought logically and had been trained to adjudicate competing opinions in the classroom.

APB: Did you hear what you just said? You said "they thought logically." That's exactly why we lost our lands to strangers in the first place. Europeans or Asians would never have opened up to Black folks swarming all over Europe or Asia. And do you know why, Clem? Because all those strangers, every last one of them, thought racially. And what frustrates me is that while they still do, and even after all they've put us through, we refuse to learn to think racially too. If we don't learn to, I'm sorry to say it, we are doomed!

GCM: I guess history has proven that Ayiti's liberators were 100% correct in their analysis of the character of their oppressors and in developing appropriate strategies for their self-protection. I've read somewhere that one of the leaders, and I'm betting on Jean-Jacques Dessalines, called "Machan Desalin" in Ayitian Kreyol, predicted, "If we let our oppressors own land in our nation, they'll eventually enslave us again!"

APB: As I was saying, one of the good things about Talking Cheddo is that it says what we can do, based on what our Ancestors have demonstrated that we can do.

GCM: I wonder sometimes how the way things are now compares to what our folks went through in The Depression? We did do for ourselves during those difficult times. We had no choice. Up to the late eighties, in Harlem, there was still a dining room off 125th St. where students could eat home-cooked meals served with mother-love by Father Divine's faithful followers. This was going on a full lifetime after his mission had fed depression-era multitudes, both Black and White. How come Black folks have so dared to shine during some of the world's most challenging times?

APB: I remember Dr. John Henrik Clarke reminding us that, during the Depression, Father Divine's "Heaven" was one place where you could always count on getting a good meal for five cents.

GCM: During the Depression, Marcus Garvey was also big up here in Toronto. In fact, his Movement purchased a building that was mortgage-free and still serving the community well into the eighties. It had space enough to house classes for the volunteer-run Black Education Project, which I was a part of, and hold New Year Eve community Dances. During the second Underground Railroad, when Soul brothers from down South, inspired by Br. Malcolm and Br. Muhammad Ali, came up to Toronto to escape the Vietnam War, the UNIA /United Negro Improvement Association would even serve as a site to crash for a night or two.

APB: I remember being impressed that both the Hon. Marcus Garvey and Br. Malcolm taught themselves to be orators and paid serious attention to words.

GCM: Yes. Garvey was serious about being an orator. He is reputed to have practiced making speeches aloud while with no one around, and trying to out-shout the sea.

APB: On the other hand, there are some Black folks who don't get the power of words. They have already succumbed to psychological warfare and consistently use the N-word in public. Or they use Black as an epithet. Let there be no ambiguity, you can never use the N-word positively in a public way!

GCM: The image of a well-known rapper comes to mind. Here he is, a rich, middle-class, college grad who ought to know better. Yet he publicly indulges young Whites yelling N-. Smiling like a truly enslaved mind, he tells those insulting him and his parents, "I'll give you guys a pass on that."

APB: Jokers like that need to be made to repent in public, or Black folks should boycott them. I'll say it again. There's no way to use the N-word in a positive way.

GCM: Let's not delude ourselves. The powers-that-be are fully aware of the damage N- is doing. In the sixties, when the Black Panther Party was opposing and exposing racist policing in Oakland, White cops made a game of spraying N- like bullets, around. After a while, Huey Newton and Bobby Seale began to return their fire by shouting, "Pig"!

APB: Those two young brothers were serious warriors. They had raw courage.

GCM: Well, as far as the boys in blue were concerned, "N-" was OK, but "PIG" was not. So, the police got City Council to ban anyone from calling cops, "pigs." The fight spilled over into a full-blown constitutional debate over "free speech." Some of the hypocrites promoting the ban argued that N- was mostly used by Blacks, anyway. So, according to their logic, good Whites were saving Blacks from being insulted by other Blacks.

APB: Early rappers like KRS1 and Public Enemy never wrote degrading material. Their lyrics were positive, and if someone used it, the N-word, there would be only Black folks around.

GCM: When Outsiders saw that Rap was strengthening us, and also making a few artists rich, they wasted no time buying their way in. And that changed the music and the movement.

APB: We should know by now that we have an attractive culture. Black culture has always attracted the world.

GCM: What's not to like? It's open, accessible, portable, pleasurable and, above all, FREE! Most Outsiders can't believe their luck and wish they could make us forget that it is ours, in the way that some dispossessed Appalachian Whites now identify quintessentially Black banjo playing as their exclusive musical heritage.

APB: When it comes to Hip Hop, I blame Blacks who betray our culture more than outsiders who treat it as a cash cow.

GCM: So, Br. Peter, we come full circle, back to psychological damage. Are our sons and daughters selling out their heritage because they are terrified of poverty and desperate for fortune and red-carpet fame?

APB: They sell out. Br. Malcolm used to say to these kinds of young people, who were wreaking havoc in their communities that the injury you are doing to our people, you, for all practical purposes, have become an ally of the White supremacists and racists.

GCM: On a question of principle, we should denounce any Black face that sells out Black space.

APB: It's still our fault. And that's another reason why your book is important. You don't just describe what's happening. You look at history in detail and suggest logical reasons for why we do what we do and how we can make real change.

GCM: Br. Peter, for years now, you've talked to me of gathering Pan-Afrikanists together for a couple days and focusing our discussions on finding solutions to the situations holding us back. Your conference idea was to convene a pragmatic Pan-Afrikan gathering on how to use that time for a forensic audit that identifies our strengths.

APB: Like harnessing our music and using our power to boycott those who injure or insult us.

GCM: Thinking music for me means Nina Simone, Marvin Gaye and We Shall Overcome! I bet Ayiti's fighters drummed on the beach, and drove those French, Spanish and English troops to distraction. Why haven't we used our unique strengths as effectively since then?

APB: Tell me what you mean.

GCM: Think! Ayiti's Black victors were able to plan in total secrecy when they met in the "Bwa Kayiman" or "Alligator Swamp." Doesn't that tell us they knew that no White would dare follow them there? I can see it. Growing up in Guyana, we learned that the Cayman was the fiercest animal in the water. For us, it was "Jaws." And, quite literally, it ruled the river.

APB: I guess I would never have learned to swim.

GCM: But seriously, Ayitians, like singer and actor Cayotte Bissanthe have long believed that their Ancestors had a relationship with the caymans in the swamp. So, they could plot their freedom campaign in the "Bwa Cayiman" safe from attack, while their spirits were fortified by the chants on their lips and drumming in their hearts. When I toured Gambia with a team of Black journalists years ago, working on a travel article for a Toronto daily, we visited their Crocodile Shrine. I even got to sit next to the sacred mama crocodile and touch her.

APB: You did ... WHAT...?

GCM: Scared yuh, eh?! I sat down next to this Gambian brother who was the crocodile priest, with a twelve-foot (12-foot) mother croc between us. He said, "Don't be afraid. This is a sacred animal. It won't harm you. It can do no harm."

APB: That's enough of that for me. Let's get back to my "pragmatic Pan-Afrikan" conference. By the way, I like your emphasis on being "pragmatic." I think that we've already had generations of gathering data, and proving again and again that we've been mistreated. It's past time we just got on with doing what we need to do by, with and for ourselves. Nobody else is going to do it for us. And why should we expect them to?

When we meet, I intend to focus on solutions, not on all the wrongs we've suffered or hardships we've come through. Right off the top, I'm going to say: "Good morning. Welcome! White supremacy is evil. It targets us and has no redeeming features. Now I've said it, if there's anyone here who doesn't agree, please leave now, because we can't build anything lasting with ambivalent people." Then, for the next two days, we will only talk about solutions.

GCM: It's taken me a lifetime, literally, to make sense of our history. However, I do feel confident that I can move forward now starting with Ayiti and leaning on Cheddo's past as well as its promise.

Instead of education, which to me is training that pushes my mind wide open, regular schooling raised me on "Whitecraft." That's another of those words I've had to make up to help me make sense of this world. Unblemished Blackness, Waka Guracha, as the Oromo name it, is for me the mirror of Ma'at or Balance, the guiding principle of day-to-day life in Kush along the Nile, the founders of the pyramid culture identified as "Egyptian" today.

In Paris, in another era, singer Toto Bissanthe, a peerless guardian of the Ayitian arts, taught our troupe to sing Ouvri' Bayé (Open the Gates), in Kreyol, and ignite ancestral energies from deep inside. To me, she was so steeped in her culture that she had become a walking, talking, acting, singing history-book on Ayiti. Of course, Toto would also tell this story far more poetically than I ever could.

When asked how the revolutionaries had defeated three imperial armies – the Spanish, the English and the French – as she recounted it, her heroic Ancestors would merely smile cryptically. Then they replied, she said, "When we began to fight on the beaches, thousands of shadows stood up and fought by our side."

APB: With that inspiring story, I guess this is a good place to end.

END

2
Book

Exploring Pan-Afrikanism to
Sustain Self-Determination

INTRODUCTION

This is a book about how we teach hard truths about the Pan-Afrikan experience – Kusthic truths. It illuminates significant patterns of imposed degradation and the way Pan-Afrikanists have responded in count(er)ing the costs of this long 'winter of our disrepair', carving out new spaces for liberatory education. I have divided my work into four parts. In Part 1, *Discourse On Afrika*, readers are invited to enter the conversation through the door of Pan-Afrikan meanings in writing and speech. Part 2, *Degrading Afrika* examines words and social practices used to degrade Afrikans. This exchange allows readers to share information about the lived experience of those who bear the costs of humiliation. In Part 3, *Denying Afrika,* I analyse the reports of two liberal commissions that publicly set out to correct injustices against Pan-Afrikan populations on two continents while denying both the depth of White responsibility and the gravity of Black suffering. Part 4, *Embracing Afrika* looks at the language, material culture and spiritual traditions that remain viable and are sources of indispensable energies for Pan-Afrikan rebirth and for principles of Pan-Afrikan education. In sum, this book takes readers on a journey that traces culturally defeating processes that degrade and deny Afrika, both historically and in our time. It also demonstrates and explores the significance of Pan-Afrikan psychological, material and spiritual principles which, in our contemporary global context offer the best hope for regeneration, not only of embattled Black youth but also for impoverished school curricula.

In most of my operational life, because I am Black and male, I live with and under suspicion. I must repeatedly prove that I am not criminal, immoral or of questionable social worth (Walker, 1980: 32; McIntyre, 1993: ii). That reality makes it vital for me to develop an accurate understanding of the social climate informing my "presentation of self" (Goffman, 1959: 13). Another significant aspect of my identity is the place where I live. Caribbean by birth as well as Afrikan through ancestry and culture, I live in Canada and work across North America carrying out research, writing, speaking and consulting in education and the arts. Through constant communication, I therefore remain closely connected to events in Black communities in the United States and the world. All these experiences shape who I am, what I can do and also construct the bars of the social cage against which I must test and prove myself.

In general, those of us who study or teach still regurgitate, with major or minor adjustments, many of the 'truths' we were taught or imbibed in our youth. In my case, many of those manufactured 'truths' include distortions of Afrikan experience invented by European or Asian intruders into Afrika. While erstwhile colonizers no longer govern today, their words continue to colonize our destiny and our dreams (Wilson, 1998). Whether we are born Afrikan in the Americas or the Caribbean, therefore, our behaviour often mirrors the mistakes of many artificially concocted nation-states in Afrika. On that continent, political leaders far too zealously enforce today the borders Europe carved out to serve her interests when she ruled them with bayonets, whips and guns (Grovogui, 1996). Pan-Afrikanists can ill afford to invest in the sophistry that undermined our Ancestors yesterday and significantly destabilizes Afrikan minds today (Nkrumah, 1970). Those forced divisions of ancestral Afrikan communities in the nineteenth century split apart ancient clans and ethnic groups (Pakenham, 1991). In our times they continue their siege against Afrika's interests, undermine her integrity and allow outsiders to gobble up her wealth and bleed her populations dry (Grovogui, 1996; Duffield, 2001).

The bitter fruit we eat today falls from a tree with roots centuries deep. In the United States, journalist and educator Ida B. Wells named Whites for their defamation of Black freedom fighters on the heels of their hard-won emancipation, pointing out, "The history of this entire period which reflected glory on the race should be known... [Yet only] the white man's misrepresentations are in the public libraries and college textbooks of the land" (Wells, 1970: 5). Today's anti-Kushitic forces continue to poach our stories and reframe our words. Martin

Luther King's inspiring words, "I have a dream" and the powerful Civil Rights' marching song, *We Shall Overcome* have gained popular currency. They have only done so, however, at the expense of a general 'disremembering' of the Civil Rights leader's *Letter From The Birmingham Jail*, a passionate denunciation of liberalism and its collusion with White supremacy (Chambers, 1968).

When he defied an injunction against demonstrating, local forces arrested Martin Luther King together with hundreds of Black children, with or without their parents. His jailors sought to silence him with solitary confinement. However, King still found a way of challenging the four bishops, three preachers and one rabbi who condemned him for "unwise and untimely" actions. Denied writing material, the Black leader penned his fiery rebuttal on the margins of newspapers and other scraps smuggled in by a Black turnkey (King, 1967: 146). King told the godly clergy and erstwhile allies, "Groups tend to be more immoral than individuals". From a fortress of moral authority he thundered:

> We have waited for more than 340 years for our...God-given rights ...[It] is easy for [others] to say, 'Wait.' [Emphasis added] But when you have seen vicious mobs lynch your mothers and fathers...and drown your sisters and brothers... policemen curse, kick and even kill...when your first name becomes 'nigger'... and your wife and mother are... never... respected... then you will understand why we find it difficult to wait (King, 1967: 150-151).

The constant verbal assault of enemies, would-be allies or friends is a debilitating haemorrhage that bleeds our resources and energy. It weakens resolve and threatens Pan-Afrikan resistance by distorting our victories and devaluing the sacrifices our Ancestors have made.

In service to Pan-Afrikanism, therefore, thinkers like Ato Quayson seek to expose the ways in which powerful political lies, such as those the Nazis and European imperialists invented and used, expand or abort the chances Afrikans have in life. Quayson's insightful phrase, "the social life of images" raises the spectre of the debilitating images of Afrika and Afrikans that cut a swath through popular culture, complicating and sometimes crippling our day-to-day lives (Quayson, 2000: 142). For example, when Europeans fabricated the image of the 'negro' and imposed it on the Akan, Shona, Nubian or Kushitic Afrikans they enslaved, they started a process that still casts its long shadow on Black life today (Steele, 2003; Neal, 2002; Powell, 1979). Over generations, the proliferation of pictures of Afrikans held mute in captive spaces, waiting for guidance or rescue by 'good Whites' have made the idea of a 'negro', a Black pawn created by Nature to serve White interests, an operational reality across the globe. Even when as Afrikans we win, therefore, our triumphs are usually communicated to our children in demeaning distortions. P. D. Ouspensky reminds us, "An objective work of art is [like] a book, except that it affects the emotional and not only the intellectual side of man" (Ouspensky, 1977: 27). When we suffer, however, those who feel guilty for causing or witnessing our pain smother our moans under euphemisms that 'condition' succeeding generations of Afrikans to absorb more defeat.

So, in resistance, this work constructs a counter-narrative from Black scholarship, teaching practice and media studies. It also harnesses journalism and accessible archives of race and cultural domination to fuel Pan-Afrikan re-education. This study excavates Afrikan history, archaeology and the arts, including architecture, dance, song, satire and cuisine. It engages insights gained through and from community advocacy to illuminate history. However, this book also casts an unsparing eye on the price we pay when the words we reflexively employ reinforce our subjugation and suppress "radically opposed utterances" whenever they break through unbidden to the surface of our minds (Grovogui, 1996: 5).

I also ground my investigation in conscious, continuous introspection, reflecting on ambivalence, ambiguities and contradictions in my own life. Through all my deliberations, of this I am sure, 'We come into this world crowned with hair like wool but we are not sheep'. Our Ancestors did not produce us, nor do they survive in us to be perpetually burnt as offerings on the altar of any group's self-righteous rationalizations for possessing our bodies, harnessing our energy, milking our spirit and hijacking our lives. Full members of the human race, Afrikans know all human beings are bequeathed the gift of life by Creation and are entitled to experience it to its fullest with our every breath.

Chapter One is a 'negotiation' of the meanings of significant terms. I call this exercise a 'negotiation' because it opens up to readers a selection of concepts for their exploration and reinterpretation. Writer and reader can then together negotiate the exchange that links meaning to definition. The 'negotiation of terms' illuminates familiar words like 'Identity'; explores the operational relationship of 'ancestry' to 'biological race' and demonstrates how the problematic international relationships of Europeans or Asians to populations of Afrikan ancestry shape the way we experience being 'Black' in day-to-day life around the globe.

At the same time, in this discourse, I am deeply conscious of my own evolving understanding of the transformational power of language. I open a space for readers to join me in weighing some terms frequently employed in the media. Old meanings are forced to yield to challenging and sometimes jarring 'new' expressions constructed by retooling familiar words. I deliberately deconstruct and re-combine phrases and words in unfamiliar, unpredictable ways in order to stimulate cognitive dissonance, forcing us to rethink our biases and interrogate our assumptions. Speculatively, I also forge reconnections with ancestral languages and positive expressions from our Afrikan past, sometimes reclaiming foundational beliefs distilled from the knowledge that shepherded us through past adversity into present time.

This work shows how strong emotions evoked by powerful words have often been a shield from the worst ravages of our persecution, from racism and from the pervasive humiliation of social subjugation. On the other hand, it demonstrates the corrosive power of 'exculpatory euphemisms' that rob our language of the passion it requires to express the anguish of unfathomable wounds. I also draw attention to how soothing circumlocutions can deny nobility to Afrikan suffering, hiding or obfuscating the high price exacted by this ongoing "holocaust" as W. E. B. Du Bois named it in *The Souls of Black Folks* in 1903 (Du Bois, 1989).

'Exculpatory euphemism' takes note of disturbing contradictions in the accommodations we make as Black people to survive under the domination of Whites. Constantly socialized for survival under oppression, like Booker T. Washington, an apologist for the Europeans' enslavement of his people, we have often learned to put our persecutors' interests above our own (Du Bois: xx, 1989). Even as generations of our Ancestors were born into bondage, today we are born into apology for the atrocities inflicted on them and their fallout, the anti-Kushitism (see Chapter One) in our own lives. As Black resistance pushes back constraints to our freedom, the White world can choose to attack in response, hold fast to its unjust systems or allow space for change that fosters justice. This book demonstrates how 'White Supremacy' maintains hegemony by employing grammar and vocabulary to hide White investments in Black distress, distance us from our own history and misrepresent our Ancestors, portraying them as if they were not flesh, blood and fully human.

Okot P'Bitek notes that with the coming of 'uhuru' (freedom) and parliamentary independence to Afrika in the nineteen fifties, "white Africanists" felt forced or obliged to monitor, measure and modify their words so that "the plain [racist] language which was once used habitually without question in the days of robust self-confidence [became]…diplomatically taboo" (P'Bitek, 1980: 23). As a product of that era, the concept of euphemistic, comfort words has personal resonance for me, helping me to come to terms with my own desensitization and resulting collusion with aspects of my own degradation. As Afrikans, how we speak of atrocities our race suffered in the past and the violations that still persist has an impact beyond our own group. The failure of the Pan-Afrikan Independence, Human Rights and Civil Rights generations to speak plain truth about the undeserved hurts we have survived robs the world of priceless experience of how all humanity bleeds when societies substitute hypocrisy for human rights. In Ormund McKague's documentation and examination of racist violence in Canada, Whites-in-supremacy had shaped how a confessed young, female racist and the 'village' that raised her regarded Blacks. He lets the young woman's own words explode Canadian self-righteousness:

> One can treat blacks like dirt for years, cease such treatment, and almost immediately they are willing to be your best friends...because blacks do not have the capacity either to tell injustices or to remember them [while] Jews, she stated, are quite a different threat (McKague, 1991: 93).

Her words echo those of General Smuts while on a US tour in 1930. John Cell reports that Smuts, one of the architects of apartheid, "declared that the black man's patience was one of the world's marvels second only to the ass's" (Cell, 1987: 246). It is a sobering thought that sometimes the Afrikan impulse to appease and make peace, like good seed scattered on sour soil has borne such tasteless, toxic fruit.

In Chapter Two, I examine the power of 'wounding words', confronting the painful history and the pervasiveness of the terms 'nigger' and 'slave'. Especially in educational circles, I have found the word 'slave' to be analogous to 'nigger' with reference to the corrosive impact and silencing power it still wields in many areas of Black life. In exploring these words, I analyze diverse anecdotes drawn from written records, oral accounts and popular culture. I also draw insights from my colleagues who create or educate, passing their observations through the prism of parallel experiences in my own learning and life.

This work, therefore, comes to grips with the exceptional persistence of stigma from these two terms and their high cost in frustration, pain and numbed self-negation to generations of Black youth

(Wilson, 1991). En passant, I question the way 'nigger' has been variously transmuted into "the n-word [and] as its defenders insist...a term of endearment [or] neutralized for polite use in 'progressive', integrated venues of conferences and corporate sites" (Kitwana, 2002: 115). I note how, in parallel time, it runs rampant on the street, vulgarized into 'niggah' only to be cannibalized by White-controlled, consumerist culture, as satirized in Spike Lee's film, *Bamboozled* (Kitwana, 2002: 204). Today 'slave' and 'nigger', especially when used in multiracial groups, trail multiple contradictions and send out mixed messages. To count(er) their costs this study holds their operational significance up to the light and offers analysis as well as Pan-Afrikanist strategies for addressing the damage that they do.

I provide an in-depth analysis of the concept of slavery, originally applied to Eastern Europeans who were Slavs, and how that aspect of Slavic identity has migrated across race and now adheres instead to global, scattered Afrikans and to Afrika herself (Patterson, 1991: 357). As a part of my analysis, I recall specific interpretations of some of the distinctions made on the Afrikan continent between service and servitude. My work demonstrates how I came to understand those distinctions from "groundings", as Walter Rodney describes multi-layered, intuitive, ancestrally centred communication, with my cultural mentors or teachers from Senegal and Ghana (Rodney, 1971; Cissé, 1997; Asomansing, 2003). I also illustrate, at some length, a process Europeans employed in developing Afrikan lexicons and in interpreting or translating Afrikan languages for the benefit of European commercial, religious or political interests.

By reviewing relevant features of missionary linguistic history and practice in two West Afrikan communities, I expose some arbitrary methods and idiosyncratic approaches of colonial scholars that have shaped our understanding of ancestral Kushitic concepts today. I challenge orthodox historical pictures of Afrikan servitude in pre-Arabized or pre-Europeanized societies. Those portrayals, usually presented from a European or Arab supremacist perspective, linking shade, hair and culture to caste, foster the inaccurate impression that

Afrikans, in those times, were responsible for their own subjugation. The explanation of choice is that Afrikan leaders were generally in conscious collusion with Arab and European 'slave makers'. Similar assumptions saturate the popular culture and appear in the History and Social Science courses frequently encountered in North American schools (Beason, 1989; Hilliard, 1995). Their cumulative effect is to create a false popular consciousness of Afrikan holocausts (Wilson, 1993). Chapter Two therefore provides an opportunity to assemble a number of alternative historical and contemporary interpretations of 'service' and 'servitude' that run counter to the vitriol of the images White Supremacy never tires of consuming as the generations come and go.

In Chapter Three, I examine the impact of 'wounding deeds' on Pan-Afrikan life through analysis of six scenes selected from myriad experiences in classrooms and schools over a period of twenty years. These scenes demonstrate how linguistic devices can be used to manage and dilute Pan-Afrikan consciousness. They also show how institutions react when we defend our dignity as individuals and how they increase their assault on the vulnerable structures we have constructed to safeguard the assets of our group. The scenes I describe reveal the everyday culture of psychological assault and the ongoing physical threat of racist violence that lurks behind the linguistic violence of insult and denial analyzed in chapters one and two (Yette, 1971; Gwaltney, 1980; Pinkney, 1994). I also use the opportunity to provide analysis of the behavioural responses and direct speech that victimized Blacks use in these situations as they attempt to resist infantilization, domination and the ubiquitous injustice hidden under the pervasive discretionary power of biased institutions.

In Chapter Four, I examine the reports of two liberal commissions set up in response to Black resistance to racism. That examination presents detailed, linguistic and pictorial analysis alongside focused reflection on how supremacist institutions use communication to manage and dilute Pan-Afrikan consciousness, even when they appear to be redressing injustice. To that end, I weigh two official government-generated documents. The first report is an investigation into civil disorder in the United States called *The Report of The National Advisory Commission on Civil Disorders* (The New York Times, 1968). The second chronicles the deliberations of the *Truth and Reconciliation Commission of South Africa* (TRC, 1998).

The Report of the National Advisory Commission on Civil Disorders familiarly called *The Kerner Commission Report* was produced, in 1968, under the White dominant US government, in response to a season of Black rebellions for fundamental Human Rights. White media adopted the term, 'The Civil Rights Movement' and taught the public to use it during those extraordinary eruptions of the human spirit that marked the nineteen sixties. Journalists, politicians and social critics of all races followed suit, instead of labelling the events a Movement for "Human Rights" as an earlier Black petition to the United Nations had done (Patterson, 1971). This study reads the spaces between metaphors. It peers behind the lens journalists and politicians have used to create stills of pathological Black life while omitting significant evidence of a relentless White siege. It is significant that neither commission names, probes or pathologizes the 'White rage' that brings the Black resistance they call 'rage' into being.

The other report analyzed in this chapter comes a generation after Governor Otto Kerner's report. *The Report of The Truth and Reconciliation Commission* is produced across the Atlantic in South Africa under a Black president and his multiracial allies in a "non-racial" government. I sift the language the Commission invented and persuaded the world to use in remembering the horror that was official apartheid. It is critical for Pan-Afrikanists to keep in mind that, while memory shapes experience, language moulds memory and prepares us to act on the choices that frame our lives. My critique of the two reports throws light on a tough question for all Pan-Afrikanists. Why does exemplary Black sacrifice, as in the Ayitian Revolution from 1791 to 1804, the US Civil War from 1863 to 1865, independence struggles that spanned generations across the Caribbean, the Americas or on the Afrikan continent succumb so predictably to subversion from within and without? (James, 1983; Grovogui, 1996; Mandaza, 1999).

In reviewing the report, while not succumbing to seductive anthropomorphisms, I embrace the wisdom of our Ancestors who learned to sing listening to birds and to hunt looking at lions. In so doing, I draw insight from A. Félix Iroko's documentation of how his Ancestors adapted to living beside the pestilential mosquito, using a common natural threat to survival to cement relationships within and between human groups (Iroko, 1994). Conscious of limits in comparisons between human and natural social worlds, I also reflect on scientific observations from other sources, using them to illuminate Afrikan culture and thought.

Over millennia Afrikans certainly noted patterns of animal behaviour. European zoologist David Attenborough describes, "volunteered vulnerability" in the animal world where, "a wolf rolls over and exposes its throat and belly to the teeth of its enemy...[and] a wild male guinea pig...will turn his rump to his conqueror" (Attenborough, 1990: 210). From early-recorded history, Afrikan peoples have studied natural life around them and applied the insights they gained to enhance their understanding of the universe. This book honors every area of Afrikan experience, including animal science, as sacred text that holds lessons in trust for Pan-Afrikan re-education.

In quest of restorative re-education, this study embodies the struggle to understand the cultural implications of our serial seduction, as Afrikans over hundreds of years, into processes that produce self-destruction (Bynum, 1999; Wilson, 1993). By reflection and introspection it invites Pan-Afrikanists to theorize about our automatic, collective responses, learned over thirty generations, to threats involving White social power that can render us tense and afraid. This work demonstrates by analysis how the reactions we learned have sucked us into quagmires of quasi-voluntary subjugation. Evidence of their psychic damage is often expressed in the substitution and acceptance of 'comfort words' for plain talk about Afrikan suffering and its attendant traumas. North American society is also slow to denounce unearned European privilege, racial injustice and white-colour crime. I therefore use these two liberal, 'sympathetic' reports of global significance, issued by commissions summoned to right past wrongs against populations of Afrikan ancestry to reveal how institutions and language can function to anaesthetize society as a whole and numb it to Black achievement, sacrifice or pain. Normalizing euphemisms are employed to keep European psyches in a linguistically safe comfort zone instead. Sometimes I just let riffs lift up my soul or reach down deep inside to play the bass notes on my spiritual scale. Drawing lessons from Chapter Four, I remember that Mohandas 'Mahatma' Ghandi reminded us to "set a limit to our worldly ambition [while] our religious [spiritual] ambition should be illimitable" (Ghandi, 1993: 21).

In Chapter Five, I turn a wider lens on Pan-Afrikanism in popular culture, framed within a multiracial world by offering a visual and linguistic analysis of two documentaries. Both videos are set in contemporary US society and present groups that come together with the express purpose of discussing race. Although that was not their articulated goal, these documentaries illuminate the centrality of the collective Black experience to questions of race in this hemisphere.

Reflecting her work as a self-identified Black/Afrikan woman, Shakti Butler's *The Way Home* is a layered, multiracial, multicultural, all-female reflection on racial identity in a pluralistic society (Butler, 1998). Lee Mun Wah's *Color of Fear* features a multiracial group of male participants meeting in a weekend retreat to focus on enhancing their understanding of racism. The women, grouped in conversation by ethnic, linguistic or religious affinity, geography, culture and race, challenge as well as support each other, providing depth and texture to their conversations. *The Way Home* lends itself to close examination of the participants and their exchange, allowing viewers to concentrate on the places where Asian, Latina, Jewish or European women also report on their experiences of Blackness. Often speakers do so without being aware that what they say has implications for how, as women and men of Afrikan ancestry, we are allowed by the larger society to express the uniqueness of our humanity. Hidden assumptions about Black values and social worth also emerge from what other groups report about 'race talk' within their discrete communities.

In order to show how the costs of Black Maafas (see Chapter One) remain hidden even in intimate spaces and intentionally frank discussions of race, I not only pay attention to the words I hear but also analyze silences between speakers and within the diverse groupings of the two videos. I find significance in the participants' conscious gestures as well as the more spontaneous reactions that their body language betrays. The structure of the discussions also allows viewers to discover the difficulty many Blacks have in conveying the breadth and depth of our experience of race, even to the targets of other kinds of racism.

In the documentaries, these groups of conscious women and men, largely representative of the racial and ethnic diversity of this hemisphere, carry in their collective identities histories of genocide, forced exile, migration and multiple oppressions. The way they talk about race has significant lessons for Afrikans and the world at large. This study demonstrates how people of Afrikan ancestry potentially continue to suffer, directly or indirectly, the fallout from past generations of forced servitude. It examines the clarity, restraint or freedom with which the members of the Afrikan American group express their feelings about that ancestry to each other and to others outside their group. I also look for evidence in the ways they respond to the presence of stigma in their lived experience as well as the way they feel about how other racialized groups relate to Blacks. From my analysis of these videos, I draw out language for assessing how Afrikans might counter the multiple ways in which society uses race to shape the ways we can communicate across the divide of class, colour, culture or race about the Black Maafa.

Like *The Way Home*, Lee Mun Wah's *Color of Fear* presents passionate discussions of diversity. He focuses on race and does so within a single, racially diverse group of men. His video, while approaching similar issues as Shakti Butler's production, does so from the perspective of a self-identified, US-born, Chinese man. In workshops where I have used it, *Color of Fear* has proved to be an unsettling experience at times. Without explicitly doing so, both videos raise questions about the complexities of Black femininity, masculinity and identity within the frame of White supremacy in North America today (Butler, 1998; Mun Wah,

1994). Looking at both documentaries from a Pan-Afrikan perspective, however, the most intense scenes occur in exchanges that explore relationships between Black participants and members of other groups. In *Color of Fear* this is especially true of exchanges between Victor Lewis (Black) and David Christiansen (White). In analyzing the videos, I raise questions about the meanings we attach to centralizing Black experiences of White supremacy in multiethnic, multiracial group conversations on race. I also examine the curious relationship of observer-and-observed that singles out Black participants in multiracial groups.

In Chapter Six, this study demonstrates the importance of orality, art and culture in Pan-Afrikan rebirth by using examples of historical records passed on in oral or written form by witnesses of Afrikan ancestry. It also sifts European accounts of Afrikan history and distils evidence that points to a deeper culture that outsiders often miss or misrepresent. For example, Nigerian dance expert, Omofolabo Ajayi chronicles the dismissive pronouncements of European missionaries against all Afrikan dance as "[leading] to fornication" or in the words of anthropologist E. P. Taylor "imitation fornication" (Ajayi, 1998: 4).

This study also uses analysis and evidence from my lived experience in diverse Afrikan communities that still communicate within their ancestral linguistic framework as well as the expert commentary of Afrikan observers and teachers within localized cultures. Such evidence bolsters the findings of Maurice Vambe, a Zimbabwean researcher who analyzes myth, legend, proverbs, religious ritual, song, poetry and popular culture among Shona populations to argue convincingly that since, "…representation is a social construct…[it] is in itself a source of the production of social knowledge about society and interpretation of society" (Vambe, 2001: ix).

I also bring my personal experience of the riches I rediscovered in our ancestral cultures by learning to express myself in Afrikan tongues, even in a limited way, within an Afrikan context. Living in Senegal taught me much about the difference between definition and meaning in interpreting unfamiliar sounds. As I was progressively exposed to the language and became conscious of embedded cultural meaning in everyday communication, I began to feel more spiritually connected to local Wolof speakers. I then truly experienced greetings as "a way for the Wolof to show respect for every member of the community" (Melching, 1981: 8). I also began to see how easy it would be for European or Asian interpretations of Afrikan reality to miss the richness that adhered to nuances embedded in the words, the context of conversations and the spontaneous generosity that accompanied oral interactions. Again, inspired by my lived experience, this work demonstrates how reconnection with our ancient tongues produces new voices to challenge the confines of the hostile, narcotizing, neutralizing or neutering communication systems we have learned to use.

In Chapter Seven, I examine two tools of Pan-Afrikan re-education generations apart. One is a polemic written in 1830 by a free Black man in the United States. The other is an educational documentary I made in 1993. The first part of the chapter (Part A) analyses David Walker's *Appeal to the Coloured Citizens of the World but in particular, and Very Expressly, to those of the United States of America* that launched a call to consciousness to Afrikans enslaved in the US and to populations of Afrikan ancestry across the globe (Walker, 1993). The report denounces racism from a personal, historical, ancestral, and geographic perspective. The *Appeal...* is the first broadside launched by a liberated Black mind across the bows of the SS America, 'Slave Ship America'. That polemic is a powerful indictment of Whites for unspeakable crimes against Blacks under the unparalleled brutality of a system of forced servitude. Walker uses language like flint on stone to spark the consciousness of his Black sisters and brothers and ignite the conscience of humanity of every shade.

David Walker was an Afrikan born in 1785 into relative freedom in South Carolina, while his father and most members of his race in the US were still enslaved. As one of a small minority of 'free' Black men, Walker was relatively unencumbered by the expectations of allies or colleagues who might oblige him to placate or please them. The clarity and directness of his expression stand in marked contrast to the circumlocution of the two other 'authoritative texts' produced by the United States and South African governments examined in an earlier chapter.

By contrast, in Chapter 7 (Part B) I ask readers to share my experience of making *All Eyes On Africa*. In that video I use art as a vehicle to engage viewers, from a Pan-Afrikanist perspective, in producing a nourishing discourse about contemporary and historical Afrika. I attempt to do this in language that is visual, musical, poetic and emotionally intense (Marshall, 1993). *All Eyes On Africa* is a tool for Pan-Afrikan re-education about the Black Maafas that catapulted innocent millions into forced exile across the Atlantic and produced seed capital for economies around the world (Rodney, 1987; Robinson, 2000; Genovese, 1976). Along the way, by way of reference, I draw examples from a fictional re-creation of enslavement, Ethiopian Haile Gerima's film, *Sankofa* (Davis, 2000). Gerima's work is informed by his lived experience on the Afrikan continent as well as his acquired Black culture from studies in the US. *All Eyes On Africa* approaches its subject matter with fresh eyes for Afrikan realities. In analyzing it I also pay attention to how Spike Lee uses the feature films *Bamboozled* and *Get On The Bus* to hold up a corrective mirror of contemporary Black culture (Kitwana, 2002; Neal, 2002). Lee's two works also open up spaces for the kinds of transformative learning and re-education that can advance Pan-Afrikan self-determination.

In Chapter Eight, I survey the territory covered in previous chapters and I extract key principles that I use as guides for Pan-Afrikan reeducation. I suggest an approach for learners who choose to be healers and change makers in a renewed Pan-Afrikan world. This chapter harnesses insights from my professional formation as a teacher-observer, curriculum-developer and consultant and puts them to the service of reeducation for Pan-Afrikan self-determination. From the wealth of historical and cultural information embedded in architecture and the arts across the Pan-Afrikan world I cull and apply strategies appropriate to our re-education for self-determination. In this chapter I also draw sustenance from proverbs, sayings and guiding principles passed on to me from birth by Pan-Afrikan communities. I take this opportunity to highlight ways of living that hold significance for Pan-Afrikan re-education. Practices anchored in ancestry frequently offer lessons in self-determination. Those lessons flow directly from my experience of the material culture of communities on the continent as well as in the Caribbean, North America and Europe.

This is a chapter to remind us to sing new songs and rekindle the fires that free our minds in preparation for challenging, unpredictable times. I conclude my study by reiterating how critical it is for Pan-Afrikan re-educators to attend to the power that images and euphemisms wield in betraying consciousness. The work ends on a note of spiritual rebirth.

A PROCESS FOR PAN-AFRIKAN RE-EDUCATION

This work interrogates the colonizing and alienating use of language while exploring appropriate methods for Pan-Afrikan re-education. It draws examples from sociolinguistic studies with a focus on ancestral Afrikan languages; oral history; popular culture; official government documents; historical eyewitness accounts of stories that shape Afrikan experience; newspapers and other media; museum studies; library and archival studies; architecture, art, music and dance; selected scenes from student and faculty life; anti-racist and Pan-Afrikan video documentaries; evidence from posters, flyers and other ephemera as well as the witness of my own learning from lived experience during significant periods of residence or travel across Afrika, North America and in the Caribbean. The purpose of this study is to provide a practical, accessible record of Afrikan degradation, denial and regeneration for the use of Pan-Afrikan re-educators. It therefore seeks out healing words and restorative visions for the wounds left by the 'Maafa', the Great Suffering that has scattered Afrikans for four centuries by force across the globe (Ani, 1994). In a spiritual sense, this study addresses the mass graves of that period and fills the void they left by invoking the memory of countless Ancestors whose dust sanctifies the sites where they rest. Through the details of their lives this study also makes a collective reconnection with the principle of female and male equality that is central to Afrikan ancestral practice and Pan-Afrikanism today (Chinweizu, 1987; Schwarz-Bart, 2001).

In the long history of Kushitic Afrikan civilization, certain figures tower above others, celebrated and venerated in both religion and art. Nefertari, Hatshepsut and Tiy of the 18th dynasty wielded significant influence during their time and on subsequent generations (Hilliard, 1991: 222-223). European interpretations of Afrikan governance systems refer to these pre-eminent spiritual leaders as 'Queens'. However, for centuries after the end of her reign, Nefertari was remembered not just as a ruler but also an enduring icon of divine inspiration. Today, an image of Nefertari still stands in impermeable, imperishable Black majesty in the Berlin Museum (Du Bois, 1990: 126). Numerous other examples support the principle of female and male equality in ancestral Afrikan life (Busby, 1992; Bynum, 1999).

In more modern times Abolitionist Frederick Douglass was a prominent advocate of women's equality. In an editorial dedicated to his "coloured sisters in Philadelphia" in 1849, he predicted that, "The greater the obstacles with which they have to contend, the greater will be the victory when it is gained" (Douglass, 1992: 53). In today's Nigeria, Igbo feminist Joseph Thérèse Agbasiere argues, "that the Igbo traditional belief system, especially the aspect of it that deals with the notion of the person, shows that Igbo womanhood is an eloquent testimony to the will to arise" (Agbasiere, 2000: 4). On the other hand, Eugenia Herbert finds connections between spirituality and feminism in traditional Afrikan practices for melting down iron during metallurgy (Herbert, 1993). As it re-centres Women in Afrikan life, this study also centres Afrika in her world.

Using a Pan-Afrikanist approach, this book moves the scholarship of Black educators from the margins to the centre of the knowledge we use to transform our lives. While cognizant of Eugene Genovese's study of Afrikan cultural retentions in the United States, this study revisits the often unacknowledged, pioneering anthropological research of Paul Robeson, whose passion and knowledge of his people's culture influenced his friend Genovese (Robeson, 1978; Newton, 1975; Genovese, 1974). As we learn from Gunnar Myrdal's sociological examination of racism in the US, we also pay attention to how his insights were shaped by the particular framework he was able to borrow because of his contact with sociologist pioneer in the study of Black communities, W.E.B. Du Bois (Myrdal, 1964; Du Bois, 1964). In a significant way this work approaches European documents about Afrika by reading against the text. It uses language to reconfigure the contributions of Afrikan 'informants' to European writers and pays those skilled observers of their societies the respect their expertise is due (Fabian, 2001).

Other aspects of the approach I adopt in this study include the use of personal anecdotes, academically neglected information from popular culture or the fruits of long scholarship. I only use them, however, when their ultimate impact is to uplift Afrikan people as a whole by shedding light on truths that hold significance for the Pan-Afrikan world. This work declares its bias, unlike the undeclared biases of many Eurocentric writers that this study documents at some length (McLuhan & Fiore, 1968: 79; Boahen, 1977; P'Bitek, 1980; Harris, 1987). Therefore, where the examination of past injustice risks causing more immediate pain, I place the rights and interests of sufferers first. This study only explores the source and effect of slurs when doing so enhances potential healing for Afrikan populations that are the targets of those slurs.

In addition, this study illuminates significant autobiographical details in the lives of Kushitic artists, thinkers and community builders that can help the larger community to better measure the human costs of their achievements. For example, while musical genius Louis Armstrong smiled through lips that bled from blowing his trumpet every night, it was White manager Joe Glaser, who was able, because of his social location to build a personal fortune on Armstrong's talent and pain (Armstrong, 1999: 84-86). Although Armstrong, in his role of Black music popularizer knew how it felt to be treated like "some kind of God" by audiences, he also had to face the derogatory name of "Satchmo" or

"Satchelmouth" ungraciously inflicted on him by White journalists over his long career (Armstrong, 1999: 45; Bergreen, 1997: 354).

This work affirms the power of Afrikan music to transform society and its generally uncounted global legacy. Using the musical 'diplomacy' of jazz artists like Louis Armstrong, the West penetrated the propaganda defences of the Axis powers during WW II. Later, with skilful manipulation of Afrikan American musical forms, capitalist ideology also broke through the 'Iron Curtain' during the 'Cold War' (Armstrong, 1999; Panassié, 1944). In spite of unfavourable conditions, Afrikan music has created models of a potential multiracial world by building bridges across colour, caste, class, religion and race in carnivals such as those in New Orleans, Brazil, Trinidad, Brixton (in the U.K.) and Toronto, Canada (Steumpfle, 1995; Liverpool, 2001; Guillermoprieto, 1991; Burns, 2000). My work honours the 'contagious' multiracialism and multiculturalism of Afrikan cultural forms.

Because this study holds pictures of endurance and successful resistance in a protective Pan-Afrikan gaze, it records that Louis Armstrong kept his dignity in spite of social pressure and physical pain. The artist's performance standards never slipped and, in spite of how the critics named him, he would usually refer to himself as "Pops". Armstrong was also often brave, speaking his mind to music critics, complaining to President Eisenhower over mob violence in Little Rock and standing up to racist United States Governor Orville Faubus of Arkansas as well (Armstrong, 1999: 9; Bergreen, 1997: 371). This study therefore provides the necessary details for making Kushitic resistance more visible by bringing informed discussion as well as diverse insights to the subject. Speaking on the subject of Black visibility within White supremacist media, anti-apartheid activist Archbishop Desmond Tutu remarked, "What is unseen does not exist, and to ignore something long enough it will disappear" (Tutu, 1982: 46).

The prospect of finding a pre-fabricated methodology for this project was slim, so I have called upon the spirit of Pan-Afrikanism to provide me the courage to set out for the horizon without guarantees of discovering land. However it proceeds from known territory to the unknown. Commencing with a review of approaches suggested by prior experience and the literature of expanding research, this study reveals and explores unfamiliar avenues for engaging, coding or communicating data in support of Pan-Afrikan self-determination (Drake, 1969: 66; Lynch, 1969: 42). In this book, investigation and analysis treat familiar, euphemistic expressions in Black communications in general, but are particularly focused on illuminating euphemistic discourse within Black populations already familiar with the rhetoric of identity. It weighs its goals and theories against Frank Smith's views on 'intentional discourse' and is also supportive of Smith's theory that, "language manifests itself across the entire range of interests and intentions" (Smith, 1983: 51). After all, as human beings, when we think, and even when we dream, our words inform every act.

This study explores the contradictions we have internalized collectively, as Afrikans, and now translate into accepted conventions or patterns in our everyday speech or body language (Wilson, 1993). Building on Smith's insights, this thesis unpacks processes that can ensnare Black communities, making us convey messages that subvert our conscious intention of defeating White domination and upholding our dignity as individuals or as a group.

My analysis also draws on Dorothy Smith's reflections on the social organization of language and in doing so demonstrates that the 'ambivalent socialization' of Afrikans under White supremacy has birthed beings of hybrid consciousness (Smith, 1999: 137; Du Bois, 1965). Quite often, as Blacks living within White supremacist societies, we are most comfortable expressing ourselves with words whose circuitous ambiguity threatens to bend time, space and mind. That language is designed by the dominant society to facilitate its control. Such communication prescribes how, as Afrikans, we describe our experience when other races trample us underfoot. Like children who suffer parental abuse yet yearn for their parents' approval, our hybrid words usually placate White power. This study hypothesizes that we learned to do so for our survival, trying to distract Whites from wielding unpredictable terror and random persecution against us. It also uses examples, statistical research and anecdotes to demonstrate that there is a collective memory of past Maafas informing the way we talk about our suffering today (Wilson, 1993).

Along the way, I encounter the work of feminists whose experiences of sexism yield insights into anti-Kushitism. For example, Joan Barfoot shares stories of the seductive power of the language of her elders. From deep inside the bosom of extended families or within comfortable, familiar spaces that should have made them feel stronger and free, many women, she notes, learned a vocabulary that ensnared their emotions and mind. Reflecting on her socialization as a girl, Joan Barfoot muses:

> The social information girls absorbed in my youth…was sometimes subtle, sometimes blunt – but always pervasive. Mainly it distilled to the notion that women's prime interest should be in obtaining the support and protection, preferably along with the love, of men (Barfoot, 2001: 5).

Pan-Afrikanism, I argue, demands that we remain vigilant. Not only does our conditioning in ambivalence breed insecurity, but it also promotes rivalries and conflict within our dominated group for the approval or benefit of those who exercise significant control over our fate.

Through reflecting on their relationship to 'discriminant sampling' as a relevant methodology, this work benefits from the observations of a selected group of Black women. As John Cresswell asserts, that method is a useful process within qualitative analysis. In fact he speaks of developing open coding categories after which, "The researcher poses questions that relate the categories and then returns to the data and looks for evidence, incidents and events that support or refute the questions, thereby verifying the data" (Cresswell, 1998: 53). The methodology he discusses is useful in analysing communication within the Black Women's Council in *The Way Home* in order to better understand how anti-Kushitic socialization shapes the language they choose. This study diverges from his process outlined in the statement, "…after the researcher writes the theory, the literature is used for supplemental validation" (Cresswell, 1998: 53). Instead it takes the position that theories, literature and living practice are seamless parts of an apprehended whole and the cumulative evidence they provide about Afrikan experience demonstrates that they happen together so that each is true because the other is true.

Historically, the Black community has learned to survive within an environment designed to erode our sense of group solidarity yet feed on the unique culture that we have been able to create (George, 1999). This study therefore provides readers with snapshots of the complex navigation of Black life. Research shows that Blacks collectively ascribe special significance to building up collective consciousness by sharing significant information through meetings across age, gender, ethnicity and class (Gwaltney, 1981: 12, 13). The unique circumstances that have made and shaped Pan-Afrikan experience, therefore, suggest the need for an approach that expands the common experiential framework of methodologies constructed in and by institutions under White supremacy.

As Blacks and Whites we may live side-by-side, this work demonstrates, while, in terms of our consciousness, we remain cocooned within parallel worlds. In support of that observation this study shows that, as populations, Afrikans and Europeans, as well as peoples of every ancestry, need maps that are specific to the mindscapes we navigate over intergenerational time. Investigations into "cognitive mapping" by Roger Downs and David Stea provide useful data about the sway symbols hold over the organization of our thoughts (Downs & Stea, 1977: 61). In their work, as geographical methods are interwoven with psychological insights, they explore the "purpose", "perspective", "scale" and power of symbols. Those categories prove useful in this study as guides for Pan-Afrikan analysis of the influence of symbols in popular culture (McLuhan & Fiore, 1968: 56). For example, within popular culture there is awe for the Great Wall of China and general indifference to or ignorance of the very existence of equally impressive Afrikan achievements like the Great Dykes of Benin City in Nigeria (Garlake, 1985; Finch, 1999). Downs and Stea also raise significant questions that are valuable clarifiers when applied to Pan-Afrikan experiences of White supremacy. Among other questions they ask, "Does a person possess the spatial information and problem-solving strategies necessary to live successfully in a particular spatial environment?" (Downs & Stea, 1977: 65).

Applying principles gleaned from their work, this study yields useful knowledge about mechanisms that already exist to produce parallel streams of healthy consciousness and so protect Black minds or spirits in hostile social space. By paying close attention to spontaneous responses from Black-conscious speakers in three documentaries (*The Way Home, Color of Fear* and *All Eyes on Africa*) and to lived exchanges in contemporary Afrikan villages, I learned as much from smiles, sighs and silences as from the definitions and meanings I ascribed to words. I shared 'a Black experience' that added up to more than the sum of individual experiences and meant much more than I could convey to those I encountered with words alone.

In order to engage in the spirit of linguistic rebirth, this work marries music and words in ways that Afrika has done from primordial time. This study gains from Kuhn's insights into "paradigm" shifts in scientific thought that occur within contexts of multiple advances or experiments in new ways of thinking. New ways of seeing the world, Kuhn proposed, replace frameworks that had existed before (Kuhn, 1970: 10).

I too seek a new way of seeing. As a Pan-Afrikanist, I search for theories or methodologies that apply to the unique experience of Black people moving towards global self-determination. For example, Malcolm Gladwell marshals arguments to show how broad social changes can result from the cumulative effect of many small actions or minor events (Gladwell, 2000). Some of his ideas reinforce my own conviction that the broad educational work we do, either as individuals or in small groups, can cumulatively transform the circumstances that disadvantage Afrikans across the globe.

Gladwell, however, manages to spread anti-Kushitic, racist notions even as he provides insight into social change. He is apparently in blissful unawareness of the impact of race on the examples he chooses to illustrate his arguments. Describing police capture of a "full catch" of Black youth jumping turnstiles, he applauds the 'efficacy' that produces their public humiliation when they are paraded as part of "a daisy chain" in handcuffs (Gladwell, 2000: 145). For me those images resonate with a history of my Ancestors in shackles and coffles paraded before an indifferent, collective White gaze. Gladwell also justifies the vigilante shooting of Black youths by a White man on a New York subway by citing the conviction of one of the youths two years later. In his words, "It's hard to be surprised when people like this wind up in the middle of a violent incident" (Gladwell, 2000: 147). The writer pays no attention to the fact that the first violent act was carried out on the Black youths by a White man who was later exonerated by White institutions and the larger White public.

Informed by a Pan-Afrikanist's interest in the lives of those young men, I feel alienated by the lack of empathy in the analytical framework Gladwell offers his readers. Drawing insight from the approaches cited above, therefore, it is my intention to present this experience of intellectual, emotional and spiritual investigation as a kind of 'riffin', a magical concoction of sound to incarnate meaning. My language is therefore deliberately enriched by metaphor, adverbs, descriptors that expand the power of fact and argument with an intensity of feeling that aims to convict and convince.

'Riffin' is Black culture's music-based description of a complex way of feeling, playing or singing. For the purposes of this study, a 'riff' is a grouping of words that touches a chord in our soul. It's a way of using an instrument or voice to collapse style into content and content into style, each mirroring images of the other and itself (Bebey, 1980). The Venda people of Namibia, for example, believe that music is like a mother's milk and vital for human growth. Musical ability among them is valued more than formal erudition connected to books (Blacking, 1995: 54). In the vocabulary of Ebonics, the language of Black America, music is indeed an ancestrally 'Black thang'.

Globally recognized thinkers like Mahatma Gandhi, influential Indian revolutionary and disseminator of large ideas, have long recognized the power of music to transform social conflict. "Music means rhythm, order. Its effect is electrical" (Gandhi, 1993: 138). European writer Silvano Arieti's research also links music to creativity in ways that resonate with the centrality of music to Pan-Afrikan experience (Arieti, 1976: 236-241). Today, my research draws on the work of Afrikan-centred musicologists who are expanding our understanding of how the rhythms, instruments and voices of an often dispossessed, despised Afrika exist at the centre of global achievements (Ajayi, 1998; Floyd, 1996: 23).

The records on walls of ancient caves show that our presence on this planet literally begins with how we remember sound. It also links Pan-Afrikan education to how we dance as well as how we talk or sing about events, embedding their messages in our bodies, imagination, intuition and minds (Garlake, 1987: 30). For a description of Afrika at an earlier period of European penetration we have the testimony of Olaudah Equiano, an Afrikan hostage who later escaped bondage. He left a description of his pre-captivity existence in Afrika where his universe wore a garland of celebratory sound (Equiano, 1999: 34). Western trained musicologists like Eileen Southern also identify the pride, confidence and active defence of Black humanity that Pan-Afrikanists understand when we speak of 'Soul' music. (Southern, 1997: 517). Similar convictions come down to us enshrined in phrases like 'Soul Sistah' or 'Soul Brutha' today.

To a significant degree, music is the language of our sacred spaces. It embraces the coded Spirituals born of captivity in the United States as well as messages of rebellion, reparations and repatriation in Jamaican Reggae. Music has been our "Mdw Ntr", our Sacred Word in the scattered Afrikan world. Today, judging by the way we consume music, we are still hungry for the special nourishment of "a Divine conversation ... concerned with the fundamental orientation of a people." And it is that, "...communication between the divinities and the inspired priests or poets [that] may be considered a Divine Conversation" (Carruthers, 1995: 5). In my view, music has also functioned in place of the languages we have been denied by a history of genocide, 'castrated' tongues, exile more bitter than bile, and unending cycles of humiliating physical and psychic torture which challenged our will to survive (Walvin, 1993; Kiple, 1988).

Afrikan survivors have been driven towards the invention of vehicles for private communication in the presence of hostile forces, in order to invent spaces where our humanity can breathe. That imperative of invention continues to inform our music and speech. It answers the "why" of Black music that Afrikan-centred musicologists and cultural analysts continue to ask. Because our sacred music must operate in secular space, where it can be cannibalized and commercialized, we are constantly at risk of losing its protective, spiritual armour. So even our codes and passwords, invented for our survival, live under constant outside pressure for change (Reagon, 1992).

For Pan-Afrikanists, meaningful sounds quickly morph into new hieroglyphics that express emotions engraved on our psyche by time. As jazz trumpeter Archie Shepp eloquently describes his own experience, "The Black instrumentalist, apart from the vocalist and dancer, was able to do his own thing in a world where his words were music, and his language was his own" (Shepp, 1981: xviii). To borrow from the wisdom of self-identified "Hip Hop feminist", Joan Morgan, "We need a voice like our music–one that samples and layers many voices... forcing us to finally confront what we'd all rather hide from" (Morgan, 1996: 62). The riffs I refer to can be long or short, so that some points gather meaning from a classroom scene while others are captured in poetic prose. 'Riffin' creates an amalgam of free verse, free association and freethinking. Linking 'riffin' to methodology, I invoke the power of music, a force increasingly seen as a language of the emotions and recognized in "discrepancy theory" as "...a reaction to unexpected experience" (Jourdan, 1997: 309).

The language of riffs that I explore in this study is like the sudden eruption of a horn section or the scat-language improvisations of a singer in full voice. Although my thinking strives for freshness as a way of breaking the shackles of embedded alienation from self, it is in harmony with previous learning, illuminated by systematic analysis and married to the deep thought of heightened intuition (Sidran, 1981: 90-91). It is a language suited for the goals of Pan-Afrikanism, its principles and educational possibilities.

As I move from redefining the familiar to inventing the iconoclastic, a riff sometimes falls upon my work like a spark from an unbidden spirit. It can conjure up the resonance of songs, shadows of films and inspirational conversations that guide our steps on paths towards the language of our liberation. A riff may be a shout, a verse, a heady chant or the murmur of a prayer in prose that springs from the centre of my heart. The voice I speak with, in poetry or verse, always, unless otherwise identified, remains my own.

PAN-AFRIKANISM: UNITY FOR
RECLAIMING LAND AND MIND

This study questions and counters consistent assertions of geographic and cultural disunity that surface in relation to Afrika in the media or popular culture. Under that convention, most of the continent is labelled 'sub- Saharan Afrika' and covers the places where the most descendants of Afrika's oldest populations survive. V. Y. Mudimbe marshals evidence to show that the name "Africa" itself is a neologism in the history of the continent. For theologian Walter McCray the most credible indigenous name for the whole continent discovered to date is "Alkebulan" (McCray, 1992: 149). However his choice is not the only one. The division of the continent is both of recent vintage and quite arbitrary. It is political, not geographical, while the evidence of a unified culture is compelling. Several scholars have collected evidence to show that the Sahara has been and continues to be a bridge, not a barrier to the unity of ancestral Afrikans (Diop, 1974: 22; Bernal, 1987: 11; Ankh Mi Ra, 1995: 7). Arab historian Helmi Sharawy writes,

"The Sahara has been for more than 1,000 years the meeting point of two cultures always" (Sharawy, 1999). A personal encounter reinforces my conviction of the part language has played in making an artificial division real in the popular mind. Taking stock of her past adventures, an elder relative, grown too ill to travel, confessed that her great regret was never having been to Afrika. Yet, in that same conversation, she described the excitement of seeing the pyramids on her trip to Egypt many years before. With gentle humour, we finally persuaded her to let go of her regret since Kemet (Egypt) had always been, and was, indeed, still in Afrika.

In contradiction to prevailing propaganda, records show a ninth century route from Ghana to Gaogao across the Sahara and Mali to Kemet. The sixteenth century Arab travel writer known as Leo Africanus also recalled the wealthy Black inhabitants he met in oases across the Sahara (Segal, 2001: 93). 'Sub-Saharan' promotes an image of permanent division between a fictitious 'White Afrika' and 'Black Afrika". Under this false dichotomy, Black is 'sub' and inferior while White is superior. Nigerian philosopher, Innocent Onyewuenyi points out that with growing consciousness comes a "...rejection [by Afrikan populations] of imposed nomenclatures like Negro, Bantu, Bushman, Hottentot, Pygmy, Berber, Moor etc., and a request to be called African or black" (Onyewuenyi, 1994: 21). 'Sub-Saharan' exists because forces outside ancestral Afrikan culture, Arab or European, exercise effective control over the formal systems of information that project Afrika to the world (Sharawy, 1999; P'Bitek, 1980; Rotberg, 1973). Misrepresentation is also reinforced in popular culture by a proliferation of White-looking, deceptive images of ruling groups in ancient Kemet. That barrage of misinformation fuels Black misconceptions of our history and feeds into delusions that reinforce White supremacy (Pieterse, 1992; Asante & Mazama, 2002).

The subliminal message is that Whites who looked like the Europeans or 'near-Europeans' from the Mediterranean or West Asia today, built civilizations among 'intellectually inferior' Black populations. Logical minds question why those early achievers would be so generous to Afrikans yet neglect to build with equal grandeur for their own ethnic groups, in the places where their populations were densest (Asante & Mazama, 2002). Logically, such a practice would have allowed more of their own people to enjoy the fruits of their own genius and labour in the sites where their cultures were most intense.

In the case of ancient Berbers, for example, texts often mix race and origin into a potent cocktail of confusion. Today people called 'Berbers' range from Black to White. 'Kemetologist' Cheikh Anta Diop points out, however, that "Berber" has linguistic connections to Afrikan languages like Wolof but not to any European or Asian tongue (Diop, 1991 & 1974). His findings are supported by a stone Berber face from Carthage during Roman times held in Italy's Pardo Museum. Both in hairstyle and looks the image seems indistinguishable from that of a typical Masai male today (Franklin, 1967: 229; Beckwith & Fisher, 1997).

One example of how our unfounded presumptions and prejudices can shape the way we understand race in history is a world-famous, White-looking bust promoted as Queen Nefertiti of ancient Kemet (Arnold, 1997: 66). There is, however, unambiguously Black representation of Queen Nefertiti and her co-ruler Amenhotep in the possession of the Louvre Museum in Paris (David, 2002). A range of prominent academic texts in fact confirms for open-minded readers that the identification of the ubiquitous White-looking bust of Queen Nefertiti is based on speculation or race-affirmative faith (Mertz, 1966: 161; Hobson, 2000; Finch, 1999; Grimal, 1994; Russmann, 1978; Sow, 1990; Smith, 1998).

Even today, however, through the anti-Kemetic writings of academics such as Mary Lefkowitz, similar controversy surrounds the race of Cleopatra, the most famous queen of the Ptolemy dynasty at the time of Rome's foray into Kemet (Moses, 1998: 8). W. E. B. Du Bois had already provided scholarly evidence of Cleopatra's Blackness in 1946, arguing credibly, "[the] earliest Ptolemies were white; but as time went on [through inter-marriage] they changed more and more toward the

Negroid" (Du Bois, 1990: 140). One wonders at the investment of White historians over such a long time in denying that Afrikan achievements accrue to the heritage of Black populations that have always constituted the majority race in Afrika. Because no signed art comes out of Kemet, as is the case of all ancestral Afrikan art, ambiguity of origin surrounds many of the best-known museum pieces. Like much Black music, expropriation of ancient Black art by outsiders has also been made easier because both music and art are collectively created, produced and owned.

Barbara Mertz, an Egyptologist of international repute demonstrates how ambiguity defeats those who seek infallibility in identifying Kemetic portraiture, noting, "The same head has been identified by different scholars as a portrait of Akhenaton, his successor Smenkhkare, and his wife Nefertiti" (Mertz, 1966: 161). Yet Mertz is categorical about the famous, unsigned head of Nefertiti, "Some, though uninscribed, are identified beyond any reasonable doubt" (Mertz, 1966: 161). Following her own logic, Mertz is more accurate when she records that her peers choose not to doubt that the bust is Nefertiti's than when she interprets the evidence left by unknown Afrikan artists in the distant past. My experience leads me to support Afrikan scholars, like Cheikh Anta Diop and Innocent Onyewuenyi who prefer to reserve judgment instead and preserve our right to keep testing European interpretations of our ancestral history (Diop, 1991; Onyewuenyi, 1994; Celenko, 1996).

A number of primary sources show that the popularized Nefertiti image diverges from other representations the Kemites identified as their Queen. In those alternative images, to a twenty-first century, North American eye, she appears unambiguously Black (Russmann, 1978: 211; David, 2002: 174-175). Popular histories, it is seen, can bend research to the service of White supremacy. For example, combining information from a range of disciplines, Charles Pelligrino attempts through elaborate explanation to refute the idea that Kemet was a Black civilization. He frames a funerary representation of a prince and his wife in the following words:

Egypt was a multicultural nation state, a Bronze Age 'melting pot' settled (not always peacefully) by Semitic tribes people, merchants from the Minoan world, and, as demonstrated by this limestone funerary statue depicting an Egyptian prince, immigrants from the interior of the African continent (Pelligrino, 1994: 193-199).

The reason for Pelligrino's tortured description only becomes clear when we see that the "Egyptian prince" is depicted with hair, skin tone and features that render him unambiguously Black, even within the unscientific lens of popular culture today. Pelligrino obviously feels obliged to explain away the evidence of his eyes and rationalize the 'contradiction' of an Afrikan (read 'Black') prince ruling "Semitic tribes people" (read 'Whites'), Pelligrino's real Egyptians, in their own land. Therefore Pelligrino proposes that, counter-intuitively, those ancient White immigrants from Yemen, Arabia or Asia created the culture they found on arrival and then generously permitted Black 'immigrants' from other parts of the continent to be their overlords. In this case, turning 'Black' into 'White' seems to require as much miraculous power as messiahs who turn water into wine.

Other evidence of mummies, sculpture, painting and artefacts points overwhelmingly to a civilization with a strong resemblance to the civilization of Nubian, Nuer, Oromo, Acholi, Baganda, Somali and Shilluk peoples of today (Mair, 1979). Those ancestrally-Afrikan ethnic groups predate all Arabs, West Asians or Europeans and, despite constant Arab racial cleansing as in Darfur in the Sudan, still populate that area in our time (Sharawy, 1999). To use the vernacular, 'eyeball evidence' of some mummies like that of Rameses II and other priestly rulers of the 19th dynasty confirms the presence in that population of six-footers with the slender build, long arms, hairless bodies, clean-shaven faces, long narrow feet, prominent calf muscles, chocolate coloured skin and other physical features that have been predominant in that area of Afrika, from ancient times until today (Grégoire, 1996:

9; Diop, 1974: 74). Those traits are found less readily in the populations of adjacent Mediterranean or West Asian peoples, either in the records of ancient times or in the features of their populations in our day. (El Mahdy, 1989: 87; Diop-Maes, 1996).

To continue, even cursory acquaintance with Afrikan history and geography confirms the prevalence of extensive and frequent communication from one end of the continent to the other from before recorded time and right up to the modern era (Gadalla, 1999; Finch, 1999). It was the relative ease of travel across Afrika that in fact facilitated her penetration by the 'colonizing gang' of outsiders from across the desert or across the sea. Although Arabs had penetrated Afrikan society earlier, European colonialism began to take serious hold after 1870, when "David Livingstone started walking from one end of Africa to the other, drawing maps" (Martin, 1985: 11). Arguably, because of the immeasurable period passed in meeting, marrying, sharing and learning from each other, there is a foundational, cultural and linguistic unity across Afrika that reaches far back before European, Arab or Asian presence on Afrikan soil (Prah, 2002: 51-64).

Evidence of that unity includes the fact that all Afrikan ancestral land was communally owned and in most societies property was passed down from mother to child (Oliver, 1999). The Scotsman Mungo Park, no friend of Afrikans, was so struck by the revered status of Afrika's mothers that he wrote, "Everywhere in Africa, I have noticed that no greater affront can be offered a Negro than insulting his mother [and]… the Herero swears by his mother's tears" (Park, 1945). Afrikan ancestral religions and social relationships on both sides of the Sahara are also matrifocal and inclusive (Eweka, 1989; Amenumey, 1986; Ani, 1994). That is true for the Dinka or Nath, in the northeast (in Sudan) as well as for the Khoisan and Shona at the southernmost tip of Afrika in South Africa and Zimbabwe. After conflicts, male Dinka captives, for example, would often marry the daughters of their captors (Mair, 1979: 126).

Religious conflict appeared as Arab Muslims and European Christians grafted patriarchal, supremacist, exclusionary religious attitudes, uninvited, on to Afrika's ancestral roots. Stable ancient communities were then wrenched apart in cycles of inter-religious conflict between Christians and Muslims, foreigners or their converts, who not only attacked each other but also heaped contempt on Afrikan believers who would not surrender their Ancestral Faiths. Roland Oliver tells us that:

> The effect of the trans-Saharan trade [genocide through enslavement] was in some measure to reduce this harmony... [and] the slave hunter was provided with an ideology of jihad, which encouraged aggression against naked animists wherever these were to be found (Oliver, 1999: 111).

In addition, there is mounting scientific data confirming Afrika's cultural unity (Finch, 1992: ii). Roland Oliver tells of discovering a significant linguistic connection, "There is a puzzling link, presumably very ancient, between these languages [Niger-Congo] and five small groups of languages spoken in the Nuba hills [Sudan]" (Oliver, 1999: 50). Kwesi Prah, Peter Garlake among other scholars have also revealed that other linguistic links, as well as practices of pyramid building and mummification, are also found among ancestral Afrikans in widely separated regions of the continent.

It is perhaps with that invisible cultural thread that survivors began to weave the Pan-Afrikan quilt. Pan-Afrikanism began in the Caribbean among Afrikan Freethinkers of diverse ethnic origin and education. They developed a unified political consciousness as a result of forced exile and persecution liberally stirred with the singular horror of being innocent targets of inexplicable atrocities. Those Afrikans were also bound to each other by a common ancestral culture of hope (Martin, 1985; Blyden, 1994). The Pan-Afrikan spirit took root from Jamaica to Guyana, in Haiti or across the Americas, wherever fortress-like mountains, impenetrable forests, treacherous swamps and plentiful possibilities for food created favourable material conditions for founding liberated sites, fostering resistance and nurturing spiritual escape (Williams, 1984, 66; Beckles, 1989). On the other side, fear of Afrikan uprisings was an active canker gnawing at the hearts of hostage-making White populations in all of those lands (Da Costa, 1994).

The Europeans who terrorized Afrikans fed off their own insecurities and instituted continuous reigns of terror. The captain of one Atlantic 'death-ship' cut up the warm heart and other organs of a murdered captive and then forced horrified Afrikan witnesses to eat their brother-captive's flesh (James, 1989: 9). As resistance multiplied, the European slave-makers unleashed unspeakable orgies of revenge. Their blows fell equally on the timid Afrikans who tried to sit on the fence as well as the committed leaders who inspired others to cast their shackles aside (James, 1989: 12). Historian Vere Daly shares his research on the capture and torture of one such unbending Afrikan spirit inappropriately called "Amsterdam" (after the home port of his Dutch captors) in histories of early Guyana. His story is an epic of personal courage. In the diary of a European doctor who witnessed Amsterdam's fate at the hands of his English captors:

> [They] sentenced him to be burnt alive, first having his flesh torn from his limbs with red-hot pincers… [after] being compelled to…watch thirteen of his comrades broken on the wheel and hanged, and then made to walk over their dead bodies on the way to his own execution (Pinckard in Daly, 1993: 134).

Readers absorb Dr. Pinckard's shock at what he witnessed from the details he chooses to record, highlighting the vengeful nature of the Whites who roasted their victim alive after torturing him.

In similar chronicles from those times, the raw courage of Afrikan prisoners in Europe's undeclared war against their race shines through. To escape bondage, some brave souls leaped into cauldrons of boiling sugar on plantations, while others 'creatively' threw back their heads and choked themselves by swallowing their own tongues.

Facing death without flinching, many would often sing upbeat, hopeful songs of farewell to those left behind, while raising joyful cries to greet the Ancestors they were confident of meeting again very soon (Latimer, 1991: 46-47). Michael Veal demonstrates in his study of Pan-Afrikan musical artist, Fela Ransome Kuti of Nigeria that, in our day, the movement continues to weave Afrikan cultural forms, especially music and words, as a weapon and a shield for self-defence (Veal, 2000: 36-44). Forced to organize in order to survive, Afrika's "scattered" survivors have paused to drink deeply from an underground spring of cultural unity, lying just below surface distinctions in religious practice, traditions of governance, linguistic diversity, cuisine or looks (Martin, 1985; Gadalla, 1999; P'Bitek, 1980). It is a unity that harks back to "the culmination of a long period of development that apparently began in the Nile valley some 12,000 years ago" (Finch, 1992; Martin, 1985). Indeed, it is perhaps Black people's peculiar experience of forced exile above other considerations that makes Pan-Afrikanism so real. In a historical treatment of the way new communities evolved because of forced Black dispersal and exile, Joseph Harris describes 'Diaspora' as, "the emergence of a cultural unity abroad without losing the African base, either physically or spiritually; the psychological or physical return to the homeland, Africa" (Harris, 1982: 5).

Ironically, the regular surplus produced by Afrikan food science provisioned the European ships that transported innocent victims across the Atlantic (Carney, 2001: 69-71). Invisible within the ranks of those shackled captives and encoded in their very ways of being, another civilization crossed the ocean and put down roots in a new hemisphere (Eltis, 1983: 255). Over time, many Afrikan beliefs, practices and technologies proved compatible with the environment as well as with this hemisphere's First Nations' civilization that the Europeans always disturbed and largely destroyed (Mulder, 1991). It is evident from the historical record that, even as they lived through their indelible trauma, Afrikans turned diverse ancestral skills into tools for preserving both their body and mind. For example, Angolans, prisoners of the undeclared war of Europeans against Afrikans, introduced rice cultivation, health foods like okra and ginger, as well as the nutritional and medicinal practices that reflected the advanced agricultural technology their society had long developed into this hemisphere (Carney, 2001).

On the continent, as European imperialism and colonialism replaced the routinized capture of Afrikan civilians, subjugated societies found inspiration in the struggles of severed communities overseas. Whether at home or abroad, survivors hungered for human rights and self-determination (Quaison-Sackey, 1963: 68; Nkrumah, 1985; Biko, 1986). Contemporary pan-Afrikanism therefore continues to evolve in response to a global Afrikan need. In our day, according to political analyst Bankie Foster Bankie, Pan-Afrikanism, "represents a minimal program of survival for all Africans at home [on the continent] and abroad" (Bankie, 1992: 6). Pan-Afrikanism flourishes when nourished on models of ancestral courage that despise fear to remain inexhaustibly hopeful in the face of an uncertain future. Without denying the odds arraigned against us, it remains grounded in the spirit of endurance and rebirth that has informed ancestral Afrikan culture over countless generations (Frankfort, 2000: 19; Gadalla, 1999: 193; Kunz, 1971: 118; Bynum, 1999: 166).

PAN-AFRIKAN REGENERATION

Pan-Afrikanism shapes our contemporary soundscape. Even without benefit of a conclusive survey, popular music culture provides many examples where 'Afrika' is embedded in the title or lyrics of songs. At the height of Black Nationalism in the sixties, Frank Kofsky documents, "All [the] selections with Afro-American and African titles" that bore witness to Pan-Afrikan consciousness and includes *Tanganyika Strut, African Lady* and *Message From Kenya* (Kofsky, 1970: 49). In the eighties, from the Caribbean, Peter Tosh and Bob Marley also raise anthems to Afrika. Tosh's *African* is explicitly Pan-Afrikanist, affirming as it does that our Afrikan ancestry is more significant in our lived experience than the nationality into which we're born (Davies, 2000:

7). Analyzing lived experience, as demonstrated in this work, shows how ancestry commonly trumps nationality, religion and ideology in daily, global social relations.

Archie Shepp, tenor sax virtuoso born in the US, expresses his desire to, "work more with African rhythms" and speaks of his need as an artist to "absorb" the vibrations of Afrikan daily life on both continents. He goes on to state, "The underlying symbolism of jazz has always been Black" (Shepp, 1968: 120). In the proud, hopeful tradition of Pan-Afrikanists, Shepp claims for Afrikan music, "[a] quality of human dignity despite all obstacles, despite the enslavement of the Black man and then his oppression" (Shepp, 1968: 119). While his words ring true, they fail to embrace the feminist principles, as earlier stated, that also inform Pan-Afrikan endurance and spiritual triumph.

Broadly speaking, then, one finds evidence of Pan-Afrikan connections wherever people of Afrikan ancestry survive in the world. It occurs in magazine articles, music, art, dress, culinary preferences or woven into the daily exchange of popular culture (Cunard, 1970; Black Diaspora, 2000: 14; Nantulya & Othieno, 1999: 4; Walters, 1999). In that tradition, US born architect Ginelle Anderson has travelled through Afrika charting how the shadows of temples from Ancient Kemet leave outlines on traditional architecture in Nigeria and the Cameroon. She challenges Afrikans in the Diaspora to reflect on and embrace that rich Kemetic legacy whenever and wherever we build (Anderson, 1988: 5).

Pan-Afrikanism has sometimes found expression, albeit in an understated way, in the academy (Baker, 2001; Kiteme, 1992; Ani, 1994). Scholars such as Louise Spencer-Strachan, however, have begun to speak a more "direct" language. She articulates the need of the Afrikan leadership class in Jamaica to rid itself of "negative feelings" about its heritage. Her bold Pan-Afrikanist goal is to, "correct some of the myths and falsehoods perpetuated over centuries about Africa and its people" (Spencer-Strachan, 1992: 1).

On a spiritual level, the promise of regeneration through our offspring and the presence of our Ancestors as models of integrity in our midst stand as fundamental pillars holding up a Pan-Afrikan world-view (Ephraim-Donkor, 1997). The defence and rebuilding of a coherent, collective sense of self are key elements of any viable society and inform the goals of Pan-Afrikan education. In the context of the Afrikan Diaspora, some psychologists name that process of defending and rebuilding "nigresence", and trace its roots "back to the times of slavery...[when] white slave owners [tried to] deracinate their slaves" (Parham, 2002: 45).

In this study, Pan-Afrikanism is a geographically inclusive concept that shelters self-identified, operationally Black people from the Pacific Islands and Australia under an ancestral Pan-Afrikan umbrella (Barrow, 1979). Based on a global historical perspective, Pan-Afrikanism is open to ancestral Australians whose "dream travel" links them to an Afrikan origin, "approximately 50,000 to 60,000 years ago" (Bynum, 1999: 15). Black peoples from Afrika as well as those born in the Pacific region, in former Spanish colonies like Colombia in Central America or Afrikan Portuguese speakers in Brazil, all share histories as survivors of genocide, displacement, dispossession and colonization by Europeans (Wade, 1995).

In the United States, Samoans or Australians who the society identifies as Black are forced to live an Americanized experience of race (McMullin, 1998; Reed, 1997). From its earliest manifestations, Pan-Afrikanism has therefore put the protection of the most oppressed at the centre of its practice. When Haiti defeated France, her people declared their nation a refuge for all First Nations of the Americas or Black peoples fleeing European enslavement (James, 1989; Farmer, 2003). Today even Afrikans who have been Arabized can find refuge and solidarity under the Pan-Afrikanist umbrella, sharing as they do both stigma and persecution for being Black with the Afrikan world (Tilahun, 1979: 43; Segal, 2001).

Many Black peoples had their identities stolen from them when imperious Britain renamed foreign lands, including that vast area which the world now calls 'Australia' (Stevens, 1984; Cove, 1995). By reading into the evidence of shared ancestral practices, beliefs, the similarities in carved images and physical resemblance of Afrikans and the peoples of the Pacific, Pan-Afrikanism treats Afrika and the Pacific as part of an ancient cultural connection rather than an impassable geographic divide (Barrow, 1979). Pan-Afrikan affirmation therefore counters the bifurcation of identity that has resulted from being robbed of our names and belief systems only to be subjected to the constant threat of incarceration and attack (Baker, 2001: 7 & 89). It faces the historical task of working through a stark, bitter legacy of collective Black insecurity from living under the domination of socially powerful Whites. Pan-Afrikanism consciously responds to a history, which forces us to compete for social space with other marginalized groups. It powerfully addresses populations living with subjugation on account of our identity as immigrants, our race, class, shade, gender or religion and our differences which often unwittingly compound our difficulties by acting as buffers between us and a dominant White society (Farmer, 2003; Fryer, 1984; Scobie, 1972; Berlin, 1998; Litwack, 1979; Walker, 1980: 51; Du Bois, 1964).

There is an ineluctable logic of self-reliance, self-determination and self-defence within Pan-Afrikanist thinking. It surfaces in the words of Hendrik Witbooi, the martyred leader of the Nama people whose progeny live in Namibia today. Witbooi had tried the path of compromise when European military forces invaded South-western Afrika in the late nineteenth century. He even made and kept treaties that required him to serve German interests, sometimes at the expense of resisters from his own cultural group or other neighboring Afrikans (Davis, 1990: 179). In the end, however, the constant pressure and betrayals of his German 'allies' forced Witbooi to conclude, "Peace means my death and the death of my nation, for I know there is no refuge for me under you" (Davis, 1990: 180). So he took up arms and embraced martyrdom.

Black Muslims in the United States have had a similar experience. Their leader, Elijah Muhammad compromised with publicly identified White racists like Mayor Daley of Chicago and advised his followers not to upset Whites unnecessarily. However, historically, that approach has never provided them the protection they sought from targeted assault by the political system (Essien-Udom, 1963: 108-112). One spectacular example of persecution came when the Nation Of Islam tried to start farming in Alabama in 1969. Not only were their herds poisoned, but they also had to flee for their lives (Yette, 1971: 127-129). What NOI farmers faced in the US mirrors the experience of prosperous, British-identified loyalist Afrikans in Shelburne, Nova Scotia in 1784. When jealous Whites torched the homes of this enterprising community, they were forced to abandon their property to save their lives (Walker, 1980: 32). To date, reparations have not been paid.

Pan-Afrikanism is informed by the suffering of Afrikans under White supremacy as well as the six hundred year First Nations' 'encounter' with Europeans, in this hemisphere. Afrikan survivors have internalized the lessons of Christian mistreatment of other Europeans within Europe and the mass murder that ended a millennium of fruitful Jewish integration within German society (Paul, 2000; Strauss, 1997: 315-317; Feuerlicht, 1983). Such examples persuade Pan-Afrikanists to prepare for the worst. Even Paul Robeson, one of the most conscientious coalition-builders that the progressive, global community produced in the twentieth century, was convinced that security for Afrikans meant being prepared to stand alone. "It is no use telling me that I am going to depend on the English, the French, or the Russians. I must depend on myself" (Stuckey, 1984: 22). Like Robeson, Afeni Shakur, a leader of New York's Black Panther Party in the nineteen seventies is unequivocal. To dominant groups she says:

> You do not want us to rule you and we do not
> want you to rule us. We will rule ourselves, make
> our own progress, our own mistakes, our own
> friends, and our own enemies. We will judge our
> own… We will live (Shakur, 1995: 163).

Pan-Afrikanist consciousness brings to light our collective needs and the logic behind the demands of our global community, which exists under threat of annihilation even as it must constantly negotiate the experience of dehumanization (Yette, 1971; Baker, 2001). Another revolutionary, Assata Shakur accuses Eurocentric society of relating to Afrikans through its craving for lies, explaining, "and the thing that keeps it going is that so many people believe the lie" (Shakur, 1987: 158). Pan-Afrikanism speaks out against the insult of being treated like captive witnesses without tongues while others represent us, expropriating our history, culture and even the nobility of our victimhood. Deborah Willis, a curator of Black experience describes how she mediates that expropriation of voice through diligent research that interrupts the parade of stereotypes. In her words, "My search for Black photographers [is] an attempt to respond to the proliferation of negative, derogatory images of black people" (Willis, 1994: 15).

Pan-Afrikanism questions the disrespect inherent in the framework of race supremacist custom that lets others analyze or dissect our intimate lives and leaves us frequently naked before indifferent, contemptuous eyes. Ending such misguided appropriation of a Black gaze is a fundamental and non-negotiable Pan-Afrikanist response to the flood of voices that drown out our own. Where we do not yet own or control adequate means of communication, Pan-Afrikanists may choose temporary silence rather than allowing others to speak in our stead. Perhaps that is why anthropologist Hugh Brody asserts that under certain circumstances some groups might count it a blessing to be neglected.

To parody a popular love song of yesterday, today's racial, cultural world is 'a many-splintered thing'. There are also growing immigrant communities, "diasporas", that are Japanese, Jewish, Indian, Chinese, Pakistani, Arab, Korean or European sub-groups, living in foreign lands (Chaliand & Rageau, 1995; Vaziri, 1992; Takaki, 1993; Pan, 1990; Daly, 1993: 177; Seecharan, 1993). As can be expected, each racial or cultural group has unique needs growing out of its specific experience and defines its interests to suit those needs. The most committed and frank Pan-Afrikan thinkers are therefore attuned to the dangers of inter-group jealousy that may block paths to Afrikan survival and self-determination (Prah, 1997). This is a major challenge for Pan-Afrikan education and practice, which embrace possibilities for alliances in a fractured world. In today's increasingly multi-cultural, multi-racial societies where Afrikans survive, other groups of colour are often open to being used against us in pursuit of their own interests, even when those interests are fleeting and conditional rewards.

Carlos Cooks, Panamanian-born leader of the African Nationalist Pioneer Movement in Harlem from 1940 to 1966 promoted Black unity for self-defence and self-determination, pointing out how other persecuted or marginalized groups had taken effective control of their destiny in the face of their own suffering (Cooks, 1992: 12 & 35-38). Harlem based historian John Henrik Clarke warned Pan-Afrikanists about dangerous alliances. He noted that although Black craftsmen had invited immigrants from Europe to join the Chicago chapter of the 'Knights of Labor', the newcomers teamed up instead with White racists to prevent Black workers from making a living (Clarke, 1991: 39).

To date, European colonizers and other immigrants to the Caribbean, Americas and Afrika have collectively always put their own interests first. That has been to the detriment of the First Nations they encountered and also the Afrikans whose forced labour laid the economic foundations of the societies in which transplanted Europeans now thrive (Cooks, 1992: 67). For example, many Lithuanians fled dire poverty as well as religious, cultural and ethnic persecution in the former Soviet Union to race-based opportunities in apartheid South Africa. Consciously or not, in bettering their life chances they were entering a White supremacist conspiracy to dispossess Afrikans in perpetuity 'by any means necessary' (Mbeki, 1964). Collectively, privileges of skin vaulted the Lithuanian economic or religious refugees over the heads of Black First Nations into the ranks of oppressor Whites. Among others, John Cell describes how race privilege set them on their path to becoming the richest socially, culturally and politically identifiable group in the world (Cell, 1987; Khoisan, 2001).

Indentured Indians form another Diaspora that has profoundly affected Afrikan recovery from genocide and blocked the path to self-determination both in the Caribbean and on the Afrikan continent. Their experience is not the same as persecuted Irish or Jewish immigrants who could eventually become beneficiaries of Whiteness in a White supremacist system (Ignatiev, 1995; Hill, 1997; Mangru, 1993; Ingham, 1967; Mansingh, 2002). On the contrary, in immigrating to ancestrally or displaced majority Black lands, on the continent, in the Pacific or to the Afrikanized Caribbean, most Indians were escaping the vicissitudes of both harsh poverty and/or caste discrimination at home (Carpenter & Barlow, 1970). In the end, however, many impoverished Europeans as well as Indians, as groups, have reaped advantages from unjust structures that hold Black people permanently below them in the economic systems of majority Afrikan societies (Rodney, 1979 & 1982).

I am struck by how often this approach defines the relationship of Afrikans to oppressive power from outside our communities in multiracial settings. For example, there was a remarkable difference between the goals of Martin Luther King's 'passive resistance' campaigns, launched to ensure democracy for all citizens of the United States, and Mohandas Ghandi's 'passive resistance' used to challenge racist oppression by Europeans in South Africa. Ghandi sought "partnership with the white people of the country" which by definition could only mean an alliance against the Black majority. His pro-Indian campaigns did not "threaten the supremacy, let alone the survival, of the white man's country. Afrikans did…" (Cell, 1987: 254-256). In fact, during the "unnecessarily ruthless suppression" of the 1906-1908 Bambata uprising of the Zulu people, Ghandi spoke proudly of his services to the colonizers against the Afrikans fighting to stop British suppression of their religion on top of theft of their labour and land. Seemingly oblivious to the ambivalence of his social location, the Indian liberator later proudly wrote, "…in 1906, at the time of the Zulu revolt, I raised a stretcher-bearer party and served till the end of the rebellion…I received medals and was even mentioned in dispatches" (Ghandi, 1979: 408).

In all of these situations, however, there have been some rare voices from among the "buffer" races or groups who have challenged their brothers and sisters on moral grounds. Although he shares their ancestry and history, historian Clem Seecharan faults Indian leadership in Guyana for "ignoring the feelings of the Afro-Guyanese, and the political, economic and cultural space this group was also demanding" (Seecharan, 1993: 55). Indeed, European records show that, before Indians arrived, Afrikans, even during bondage, had provided proof of business acumen. One historian writes, "In the towns we find slave bakers and butchers. In Georgetown, Demerara [Guyana], in 1823 it was said that the slave stall holders sell the best meat, and are the most punctual in the payment of the stall rents" (Walvin, 1993: 12). With the arrival of other racial groups, however, including people of dark skin, Afrikans were pushed further down the social and economic ladder. Across the imperialist world, opportunities for their upward mobility disappeared under waves of racist legislation yoked to restrictive commercial policies and practices. The White men in power, the primary profiteers, used discriminatory social custom and the law to create a buffer class of Asians or poorer Whites between themselves and subjugated Black populations (Ingham, 1967; Ignatiev, 1995; Williams, 1994: 24).

Even today, despite political independence in the regions mentioned, Afrikans collectively pay the highest costs and reap the least benefits from participation in an exploitative global economy (Grovogui, 1996; Mandaza, 1999). By way of example, economist Selwyn Ryan outlines the process significantly responsible for the economic plight of the Afrikan population of Trinidad (Ryan, 1992: 1-12). Indeed, evidence from a range of sources suggests that those systems that disempowered or dispossessed Blacks long ago have left their imprint on Black life today. Enduring, unfair economic relationships enable today's White society and its surrogates to continue profiteering from Blacks (Robinson, 2000; Stevens, 1984; Cove, 1995; Rodney, 1982; Da Costa, 1994). Ironically for visibly disenfranchised Blacks, however, the structures that shape their dispossession or economic distress today remain largely invisible to the public eye.

For instance, Clem Seecharan's otherwise perceptive work describes Indians as arriving in Guyana in 1838 as indentured workers to compete against Afrikans for jobs and land, conveniently replacing the captive workers who had arrived involuntarily centuries before (Seecharan, 1993). In failing to distinguish the different circumstances of Indian and indigenized Afrikan arrival, however, historians like Seecharan have not given appropriate weight to the disparities in the initial conditions faced by each group. Racism first reared its head in that region when Aboriginal populations were nearly exterminated by Europeans and Afrikans were brought as forced substitute sacrifices. Indentured populations of Indians or Chinese arrived long after Caribbeanized Afrikans in forced exile had already wrested marshy, snake-infested coastlands from the rivers and sea and built the infrastructure of thriving economies at incalculable human cost. Unlike the more recent plantation recruits, however, the Afrikans who preceded them had also been forced to work under the direct threat of guns, shackles, torture and whips (Williams, 1984; Daly, 1993).

In the process of building Caribbean economies, uncounted Afrikan lives were aborted after their bodies had been mangled. Mining pioneers in the bauxite industry had to split rocks with "spades, shovels and pickaxes" and forced Afrikan labor lifted "100 million tons of mud" to build waterways that were the lifeblood of the sugar industry in Guyana (Quamina, 1987: 19; Rodney, 1982: xviii). Yet Blacks were not only left to fend for themselves after emancipation but also taxed to compensate their White exploiters. Unfair levies on Afrikans also paid the transportation costs for the Indian immigrants the White government brought to compete with Afrikans for the plantation jobs (Williams, 1984; Ganns, 1982; Daly, 1993; Tafari, 2001: 33-34).

Indians in the Caribbean, the largest indentured immigrant group, were sufferers too. Yet, for a variety of reasons that we cannot fully explore in this work, they did not make common cause with the Afrikan population, still devastated by the unfathomable trauma of enslavement. Rather, during the Angel Gabriel Riots of 1856 in Guyana, Indian immigrants joined forces with Portuguese shopkeepers and pawnbrokers to suppress Black resistance to both economic exploitation and racist injustice (Ganns, 1982: 21). Next door, in the island of Trinidad, as Mahin Gosine points out, Indians also embraced the slogan, "All ah we is one", despite their internal ethnic and religious differences, thus signaling racial unity of Muslims and Hindus against Black majority power (Gosine, 1986: 52). A similar slogan featured during the fifties in my country of birth, Guyana, where, as an Afrikan and non-Hindi speaker, I learned phonetically to identify the ubiquitous chant, "apaan jaat" or "vote race", used by some sections of the Indian leadership to rally majority support along racial lines. Sadly they were not alone and some leaders of Afrikan, European or mixed ancestry were equally eager to exploit racial divides (Danns, 1982).

The complexities of European domination often dictated the nuances of Afrikan response. By way of illustration, Seecheran's Indian ancestors, though indentured, were guaranteed a continuous connection with their motherland. On the other hand, where my Afrikan Ancestors were concerned, the rulers of the society would deliberately destroy or degrade any apprehensible connection to Afrika (Mangru, 1993: 17). According to Indian historian G. R. Naidoo, European employers also considered Indians racially superior to the Afrikans they displaced and replaced in East Afrika. He writes, "There was a lot of contact between whites and Indians, who wined and dined frequently. Colour restrictions did not apply to Indians, whereas there was a great deal of resistance on the part of whites toward the African" (Naidoo, 1988: 39). In popular culture as well, while European scholarship projected Afrika as a cultural wasteland, it often affirmed and honoured the cultural achievements of ancient Indian civilizations (Seecheran, 1993: 22). Further, Europeans postulated a pseudo-scientific racial link that they shared with Indians, members of the "same common stock - the Aryan family" and therefore a kind of darker cousin. Both groups claimed that they were "[heirs] to the ancient Arya name" (Elvry, 1993: 27).

Records show that the racial link Europeans posited between Britain and India had operational significance. It enhanced the life chances of Guyana's Indian population. Benefits came in the form of health care, land, livestock and later commercial opportunities denied by law, fraud, duplicity or noxious custom to Afrikans (Mangru, 1993; Rodney, 1982; Ryan, 1992; Daly, 1993). Even outside the Caribbean, on an individual yet symbolic level, being perceived as "Aryan" was an advantage to Guyana's first Prime Minister, Cheddi Jagan, of Indian descent. As a student at historically Black Howard University in segregated Washington DC, in the nineteen forties, he was able to get off-campus employment denied his Black colleagues. During summer vacation he was also able to find employment on 125th Street, the most prestigious commercial site in New York City's Harlem. His employability didn't suffer during a time when White businesses still denied Harlem's Blacks, however gifted or qualified, any job whatsoever in the business heart of their own community (Alexander, 1990: 46).

Alongside the Indo-Guyanese leader's experience, Afrikans can learn other valuable lessons from US race history. Between 1900 and 1940, while Arab Muslim immigrants settled and farmed the US Mid-West, Indian newcomers were also able to put down roots in California farmlands where some grew rich and most were assimilated (Singh, 1997: 197-233; Sowell, 1996: 27-35). On the other hand, as late as 1969, when seventh-generation Americans, Black Muslims, paid cash for a 900-acre farm in rural Alabama, jealous Whites torched their property, poisoned their cattle and drove them away (Yette, 1971: 127-129). Over time, South Asian Muslims have also been able to set up businesses inside Black populations in the United States, often selling unhealthy liquor or pork products their faith protected them from consuming. It is significant that they have done so with little or no evidence of rejection or harassment by members of the community they misuse (Rashad, 1991: 3- 5).

Ambivalent treatment of Asians still applies today. On one hand, the dominant culture often holds them up as examples of successful assimilation, role models for some of the core values it faults Blacks for lacking or for just being 'nicer folks to have around' (Singh, 1997). On the other hand Asians are also portrayed as clannish, aggressively competitive and a kind of amorphous threat (Chun, 1995: 105-106). Histories of social hierarchies based on colour, shade and looks dictate the importance of exploring how society treats ancestry if we are to grasp the significance of anti-Kushitism (the range of negative responses to Afrikan ancestry and culture) and its antidote, Pan-Afrikanism (Gubar, 1997; Fredrickson, 1982). The plight of anyone identified as Arab or Muslim in the West since the destruction of New York's World Trade Center, however, graphically exposes how easily any groups not identified as White can lose their preferred status over Afrikans within a climate of White supremacy.

Pan-Afrikanism grew out of the political commitment of Afrikans across the globe to abolition, emancipation, independence, nation building in the Afrikan Diaspora and the creation of federated regions of Afrikan states (Garvey, 1987; Sekou Touré, 1978: 11; Nkrumah, 1985; Nyrere, 2001: 77; Sankara, 1988). On a psychological level, Pan-Afrikanism works invisibly to reverse the ravages of dehumanization, foster independence and dismantle internalized barriers to selfdetermination (Wilson, 1993; Serequeberhan, 1994: 92-93). Politically, Pan-Afrikanism is available for alliance against White racist domination. However, such pacts only prove useful to Afrikans when they start from a base of self-determination and self-reliance as well as a respect for Afrika's history and hopes.

This study imagines Pan-Afrikanism as the engine of Black liberation and it enshrines Pan-Afrikanist education as one of the pillars of that project. The Pan-Afrikan engine revs up to face the legacy of generations of White terrorism that has engendered a culture of fear (Baker, 2001: 42; Tutu, 1994: 4-5). To defeat our internalized terror, therefore, Pan-Afrikanism summons successful models of courageous resistance from Black history (Tutu, 1994: 179). There is Haiti, for example, where ten thousand (10,000) poorly-armed, hastily-drilled Afrikan laborers defeated sixty thousand (60,000) of Napoleon Bonaparte's veteran troops and demonstrated that spiritually fortified Blacks could succeed against the overwhelming military might of French, British and Spanish forces (James, 1989; Farmer, 2003). That universally unique victory exploded European assumptions that Afrikan society was "primitive". Those ideas stood, in all their unreality, on theories and perceptions of White military invincibility. With one symbolic blow from her mighty arm Haiti tore White confidence to shreds. Academics, like anthropologist Lucy Mair, had earlier argued authoritatively for White supremacy within Europe's intellectual circles:

It is a fact of history that it was the European peoples who discovered these others, and in most cases established dominion over them, and not vice versa...The European peoples had ships... and weapons which generally allowed them to win any battles in which they were involved...This is one sense of the word primitive [my emphasis] (Mair,1978: 1-2).

Mair's leap of logic first takes historical evidence of European domination for proof that Europe's technological and cultural superiority was based on its racial essence. Then she uses it to explain away the pervasive brutality and dehumanizing intention of White rule. However that history was engineered and produced by philosophies of conquest married to economies of war, heavy cannon and machine-guns. When Dessalines defeated Napoleon in 1804 it was the equivalent of a filmic stake in the imperialist vampire's heart. Haiti's decisive win ended France's parasitic oppression, genocidal forced labour and raised hopes for an end to forced Afrikan exile. Her victory, both then and now, enshrines the kind of spectacular public refutation of White supremacy that engenders cognitive dissonance in the popular mind. Pan-Afrikanist education understands that dissonance feeds doubt and that that doubt gives birth to desires for new ways of seeing.

In the United States of the nineteen sixties, Martin Luther King's confrontational leadership of the Black population also exposed the limits of White power. King demonstrated that even an aroused middle-class schooled in accommodation and composed mainly of Christian pacifists could paralyze the vicious White, supremacist, Eurocentric state armed to its teeth (Abernathy, 1990). Let us return to our imagery of change as an engine. In second gear, Pan-Afrikanism teaches racial pride. Pioneering scholars like Margaret Just Butcher, Arturo Schomburg, Cheikh Anta Diop and Ivan Van Sertima have already prepared that ground (Asante & Abarry, 1996). As Black populations we can therefore now use those earlier discoveries as the basis of ongoing Pan-Afrikanist popular education in sites under our control. Douglas

Mack describes how conscious messengers who travel back and forth linking major Afrikan populations make Pan-Afrikanist unity as real today as during the eras of Marcus Garvey and Martin Delany (Mack, 1999: 117-151; Tafari, 2001).

Our history of myriad connections remains unbroken. Carlos Cooks raised volunteers in Harlem for the defence of Ethiopia from Italian invasion in 1935 (Harris, 1992: xiii). Amy Jacques Garvey, Dudley and Margaret Thompson of Jamaica as well as Paul and Eslanda Robeson of the US studied Afrikan culture, travelled widely in the Afrikan Diaspora and inspired audiences with their lived message of collective Afrikan ancestry and destiny (Thompson, 1993). Robeson's commitment to Pan-Afrikanism was unequivocal:

> I think a good deal in terms of the power of Black people in the world... I'm proud of Africa as one of those West Coast Chinese is proud of China... Look at Jamaica... Although I may stay here the rest of my life, spiritually I'll always be part of the world where the Black man can say to these crackers, 'Get the hell out of here by morning.' If I could get a passport, I'd like to go Ghana or Jamaica, just to sit there for a few days and observe black power (Robeson, 1957: 41).

The Robesons and other Pan-Afrikanists also formed close personal ties with leaders like Ghana's first president, Kwame Nkrumah and steeped themselves in both the politics and cultural diversity of the Afrikan Diaspora (Garvey, 1987; Robeson, 1981; Thompson, 1993).

Today's Rastafari form the latest link in the cycle of forced exile and return. Documentation by scholar Carole Yawney states, "we now find communities of Rastafari not only throughout the Caribbean, North America, the United Kingdom, South America, Japan and the Pacific but in many African states as well" (Yawney, 2003). These modern ambassadors preserve the tradition of Afrikans confidently cementing links across the bridge of ancestry, overcoming divisions of language, ethnicity, water or land. In this hemisphere, Afrikans collectively exercise marginal influence on educational sites like museums or galleries. However, there is room for generating Pan-Afrikanist connections in our centres of worship, places of recreation, reflection or work. In those sites, we can share information and introduce symbols that reinforce positive feelings about Afrikan achievement in the present and past (Marshall, 2003). These messages are also important for all populations, especially in our schools.

Pan-Afrikanism as an engine at full throttle manufactures and spreads hope. It counters situations where, to public eyes, Afrikan populations are under such constant siege their situation should only inspire despair (Pedicelli, 1998; Patterson, 1971; Porter, 1997, Pinkney, 1994). Pan-Afrikanism, however, sources its hope outside predictable boundaries of daily experience. Aimé Césaire called the forces he summoned in Afrika's defence, "les armes miraculeuses -miraculous weapons [my translation]" (Césaire, 1991). Grounding himself outside material reality, Houston Baker also attests to occupying a "haunted place" (Baker, 2001: 31). Based on ancestral spirituality, Pan-Afrikanism accesses parallel dimensions of past glory to project a future of success (Awolalu, 1996). In the tradition of Fanon and Césaire the Pan-Afrikanist world-view imagines an Afrikan personality of expansive humanity and rejects the image of Blacks as the ineluctably infantilized subjects of any other race (Césaire, 1971; Myers, 1988: v; Fanon, 1967). Instead Pan-Afrikanism speaks to a world dominantly shaped by ancestral Afrikan values of generosity and egalitarianism.

Pan-Afrikanism is based on sound psychological principles that anchor the self in ancestry and community, while Pan-Afrikan education relies on "experience, learning and practice [for] enlightenment" (Myers, 1988: 37). Pan-Afrikanist hope is not blind. Rather, there is an Afrikan religious continuity, captured in syncretic movements like 'Vodun' in Haiti, 'Candomble' in Brazil, 'Santeria' in Cuba, 'Garifuna' in Belize, 'Obeah' in Guyana, 'Hoodoo' in North America or 'Rastafari' in Jamaica at the root of Pan-Afrikanist confidence in the future (Davis, 1997; Foster, 1986; Genovese, 1976; Tafari, 2001; Christoph & Oberlander, 1996).

The significance of ancestral belief in Pan-Afrikanist liberation and certain aspects of self-determination particular to Pan-Afrikan education flow out of the special context of Afrika's bruising experience of cultural imperialism. Because she has suffered historic persecution rooted in European or Asian superstitions about her race, Afrika faces a concomitant demand for equal investment in her own belief systems as a form of psychic protection. Amy Garvey noted how Marcus Garvey recognized that need and filled it by "[returning] millions to Afrika spiritually" (Garvey, 1960: 59). To do so, Garvey presumptively declared God 'Black'. Many scattered Afrikan communities have used ancestral faiths, including an enduring belief in the presence of Ancestors among us, to create parallel realities to the suffering we often experience in daily life. As Byron Foster argues, "the Garifuna trance-dance can be interpreted as signifying...the primordial power of the dead to reconstitute Garifuna society" (Foster, 1986: 47). The rituals the Garifuna consciously employ have their parallels in daily Afrikan life. Sometimes they appear as libations wordlessly poured, and at other times they are embodied in songs, chants and dances that refresh the spirit within secular spaces.

Afrikan spirituality is practical. It is a way of both escaping and facing the challenges of otherwise unbearable suffering. As Afrikans we find support for our survival within the shared experience and culture of people of like ancestry and experience. Today, through music, Afrikan spiritual retentions respond to the needs of the Black Hip Hop generation. Anthony Neal identifies "feelings of exile [which] are real [for young Blacks who need] to ward off attacks...on their intelligence, culture, and identities" (Neal, 2002: 178). The strategy of musical escape he describes might well parallel other strategies of cultural immersion practiced by minority groups within societies that deny and devalue, attack or dismiss their ancestral beliefs.

Although he was not religiously Jewish, the philosopher Karl Marx understood the importance of religion in Jewish life. While Marx notes that the pressure for Jewish integration into Christian society was a response to persecution and a need for refuge, he also argues, "[Civil] society could not convince the Jew of the unreality of his religious essence" (Marx, 1992: 241). Black lived experience also shows that although, for centuries, White supremacist society has programmed us to deny our ancestry, breaking bonds to Afrikans in quest of acceptance by others, it has failed to sever our connection to our spiritual past.

2
Book

Part I:

Discourse on Afrika

1

Chapter

When Words are Deeds

· ▬ · ● ▬ · ● ● ● ▬ ● ● ▬ ▬ · ● ● ● ▬ ● ▬ · ● ● ●

HATSHEPSUT'S SACRED COMMAND

In French literature as well as dictionary definitions, "le mot juste" embraces layers of meaning. It is the "correct" word as well as the "right" word, both in terms of content and style. It's a word that looks, feels and sounds, as it ought to be, so that, long after it has been spoken, it lingers like good taste on the tongue. In this case, I am also inscribing it with meanings such as 'just', 'reasonable', 'logical' and 'fair'. For words that would tilt at the towers of inequity and injustice of a multigenerational war of Europeans and their surrogates against Afrikans must be, by definition, harbingers of justice long denied.

The task I've set myself is a monumental challenge and I am not seduced by delusions of easy success. In Canada and the United States, where I work with teachers, artists, and students to enhance equity in the curriculum, that work convinces me that "le mot juste", the right word for Afrikan experiences of discrimination, disinheritance and legacies of suffering because of genocide are still mostly in embryo in popular and academic discourse.

"Injuste", by way of contrast, is used to represent any communication whether it is written, oral or implied which is unjust, unclear, inappropriate, ugly, unfair, unhealthy, inhuman and causes such cognitive dissonance it feels wrong. Conscious of my heritage and ancestry in every area of my life, especially my work, I search constantly for 'le mot juste', the word that does honour to the ashes of those indomitable Ancestors who suffered and endured so that we could be here. I also look for ways of naming events that fit the crimes that Afrikans have resisted and lived through. It is an ongoing challenge, and I confront it in this study by using current language in innovative ways or by creating 'new' words in response to righteous psychic demands.

Let me also begin with a caution. Because we must speak often in generalizations in order to avoid endless subordinate clauses, I use 'Black' or 'White' with the implicit understanding that I am not essentializing every member of either race. That understanding should be obvious in an exchange of ideas. However, this declaration has become necessary because of the frequency with which that issue gets raised in personal conversations, as well as in my professional practice. Within this chapter I will explain in some depth terms that are central to my arguments. My intention is to distinguish their use as 'mots justes' and 'mots injustes' while locating them within Pan-Afrikan philosophies and a Pan-Afrikanist frame. Ashay! So let it be!

AFRIKAN AND BLACK

For the purposes of this book the terms 'Black' and 'Afrikan' are conscripted to serve the goal of Pan-Afrikanist, Black self-determination. They are used to describe persons of Afrikan ancestry and 'lived experience', in an anthropological sense, who choose to identify themselves as 'Black'. Some scholars contend that the Roman Empire first used the name 'Afrika' in reference to a specific area of the continent where a small number of its citizens were permitted to settle. Pioneer Pan-Afrikanist, W. E. B. Du Bois states, "[the] Romans called the district around Carthage, Africa" (Du Bois, 1990: 141). That part of today's Afrika is in the eastern portion of what some of its First Nations referred to at one point in history as 'Alkebulan'. To translate this ancestral name, biblical scholar Walter McCray suggests phrases equivalent to 'the lands where Black people live' (McCray, 1992: 149).

Our identities, like the human rights we claim as inviolable, are both constructed and assumed. According to considerable scholarship from an Afrikan-centred perspective, the earliest writing retrieved shows that the people of 'Kemet' and 'Kush' generally referred to as 'Egypt' by European oriented historians, described themselves as "Black" (Hilliard, 1995; Carruthers, 1995). "KM" is both the root of Kemet (Egypt) and our word for 'chemistry'. By its very meaning, therefore, it enshrines recognition of the fact that ancient Arabs and Greeks learned their science and medicine from Black scientific communities (Afrika, 1989: 122; Finch, 1999). Whiteness, as a way of defining ancestry, must have arisen later than Kemetic identity and done so in the context of already existing Black identities. By way of example and analysis, this thesis explores how White identity has been assumed and constructed to expand and rationalize European plunder of Afrika's cultural and material resources as well as the resources of other groups.

This study also shows that Europeans have usually attempted to define themselves and Afrikan people with an eye to what benefits or advantages them. In one stunningly counter-intuitive example, *Holiday*, a glossy mainstream US magazine of the fifties and sixties, turned a seven foot, obsidian-Black member of the Tutsi ruling class into a White man. The editors did so with the disarming aplomb of the captain of some virtual 'Titanic' approaching an iceberg of Black identity in the midst of a sea of frozen ideas. In its 1959 special on Afrika, timed to signal the 'coming of age' of a continent bristling with European-trained mercenaries and cultural or ideological missionaries hiding behind independence flags, *Holiday* introduced its readers to a full page picture of "Charles Mutara III Rudahigwa, Mwami of Ruanda" in living colour. The rubric beneath his picture reads, "[The Mwami of Ruanda] in the hill pastures of Ruanda-Urundi, where he rules the Watusi nomads, a giant people of Hamitic (Caucasian) blood" (Holiday, 1959: 64-65). This is in marked contrast to the arguments made by a German writer earlier in the century. "Is a North American negro-a man, that is, speaking American English, a Germanic tongue, as his own-is he a German...? No, for a German is tall, fair and light-eyed" (Gunther, 1992: 2).

Even a cursory glance at the picture invites our suspicion that the "Mwami" makes an unlikely "Caucasian", which after all is only a pseudo-scientific substitute for 'European' or 'White'. In fact I feel safe in asserting that no mainstream North American magazine today would go to print choosing "Caucasian" to describe any of the First Nations of Rwanda or Burundi. The record shows that Europeans have a long history of 'Whitening' important and impressive Afrikans, and the 'Whitening' of Kemet (ancient Egypt) is one of the most egregious and persistent examples of that practice (Asante and Mazama, 2002). Pan-Afrikanist scholars argue another truth, "There is ample evidence…that the Egyptians…were Black people…(and) that the kingdom of Egypt itself was founded by Africans of Nubia, Sudan and Ethiopia" (Onyewuenyi, 1994: 58). Throughout modern times, right up to today, however, Kemet is relentlessly, if not religiously, projected as a White, or at least non- Black civilization, both by the academy and in popular culture (Bernal, 1988; Celenko, 1996; Grégoire, 1996; Cunard, 1970).

Although colour is significant, my argument does not base identity on skin colour alone. The examples and analysis provided often make it illogical to count individuals as Black when their looks give them access to privileges generally denied Black people and they enjoy social perks at the expense of most Blacks. Operationally, I consider them members of the racial group they choose to serve and identify with most of the time, although such a definition usually requires explanation. Nor does Black identity in this work describe those people who have some connection through parentage to Black communities yet are not Afrikan-identified, live in a peripheral relationship to Black life and assert the right to represent themselves as Black only when there are material or psychological benefits to be gained.

Historically, as a category, people ambivalent about their identity who have access to the cultural capital of the Black community have often played the role of buffers. They deflect collective Black criticism of White supremacy, diffuse and dilute Black resistance and, by fomenting internal conflicts, distract those most affected by anti-Kemetism (Garvey, 1987; James, 1989). In the end, buffers use up the energy we need in order to transform the calamitous conditions Afrikans face under White supremacy. They trap us into engaging in endless, inconclusive attempts to convince them and the world of the justice of our cause. It is self-evident that reluctant recruits must make, at best, unstable partners. They do not enhance our difficult, protracted Pan-Afrikan defence of our dignity or affirmation of our right to first-class citizenship anywhere we find ourselves in the world.

Mostly, those who choose to opt in and out of Black identity have faithfully served White supremacy at the expense of other Blacks who, operationally, can only be Black (Chideya, 1999: 53). In his memoirs, Louis Armstrong writes of a time when pianist Jelly Roll Morton claimed that he "was from an Indian or Spanish race...with no 'cullud' ancestry" (Armstrong, 1999: 4). In his unique spelling style, Armstrong comments wittily on the irony of Morton's internalized anti-Kemetism and unrewarded pretensions, "No matter how much his Diamond Sparkled he still had to eat in the Kitchen, the same as we Blacks", Armstrong wrote (Armstrong, 1999: 4). The biology of racial mixing makes it impossible to predict accurately how a child with mixed Afrikan ancestry will look. Any trace of Blackness, however, generally functions as a barrier in achieving high status among Whites. By way of example, I cite the case of a St. Patrick's Day Parade Queen, "Tara Heckster, who is half-Irish, half-black-Nigerian, was the target of a number of racist epithets" (Heinrich, 2004).

A significant problem, in operational terms, has been White-looking and acting leadership of Black communities. Historically, a disproportionate number of Blacks with lighter skin and 'non-stereotypic Afrikan looks' has aspired to be leaders or been facilitated in occupying visible, high-status offices through White supremacist systems. Pan-Afrikanist thinkers like Amy and Marcus Garvey also pointed out that Blacks raised within a European, Christian cultural framework also generally internalized White images of Jesus Christ, the apostles, saints and popes (Garvey, 1987; Wessels, 1990). In the seventies, US theologian James Cone challenged that toxic orthodoxy with his ringing declaration, "Christ is black, baby, with all of the features which are so detestable to white society" (Cone, 1975: 5).

Demonstrably, the dominant society prefers Blacks who look more like it imagines itself to be, White (Mun Wah, 1994). Trying to become one of the 'chosen Blacks' has created a conflict in the psyche of many women and men. Feminist thinker bell hooks reflects on the self-destructive nature of such internalizations, calling our attention to an "image of conflicted longings, [of] the black female who sees herself as most desirable when she has a look of whiteness" (hooks, 1995: 15). White supremacy routinely exploits that conflict to create buffers within dominated populations. In the context of an exhaustive study of Black activism and the frustrations attending it, US educator Jake Patton Beason states his case bluntly, "Now if you don't feel you belong to the African race, by all means, that's your right. But you should not be the leaders and the representatives of those who identify with Africa and the Black race" (Beason, 1989: 113).

It's a question of power. Power is a scarce resource, a jewel, especially for those, like Blacks, at the bottom of political and social hierarchies all over the world. Moral power is like a rare black pearl paid for from a treasury of unfathomable pain. It grows when authorities throw grandmothers like Winnie Madikizela Mandela in jail, harass and torture her to the point of causing a heart attack (Mandela, 1985). It gains lustre from a host of brilliant unrecognized young Soweto martyrs who will never be allowed to shine. It is the miraculous courage of the children who stood up for Khoisan, Xhosa and Zulu language rights against forced education in Afrikaans under apartheid (IDAF, 1983: 99-102). It is over two thousand student marchers, singing *"We Shall Overcome"*, some as young as eight years old, defending their parents' voting rights only to be tossed like broken toys into Birmingham's jails by vicious Alabama judges during the Civil Rights Movement (Abernathy, 1990; Morris, 1984; Marable, 1984). Leadership is the highest return on a collectivity's investment and it smells of patent immorality when those who don't invest in the Black community conspire to live off its dividends by garnering status, privilege, prestige or wealth.

It bears repeating that identity is understood as operational in this study. Blacks can have only illusionary or imaginary experiences of being White in a White supremacist society, where the structures and institutions operate daily to confirm the domination of Whites and the subjugation of Blacks. By employing a system of linguistic alchemy, still inadequately explained by Black scholars, it appears that we have generally convinced ourselves, as Afrikans, to assume the burden of sustaining Whites in their delusions. In the words of Victor Lewis, a Black participant in the documentary, *Color of Fear,* "You pretend we're White. And we pretend we're White" (Mun Wah, 1994). The lived reality of specific, oppositional racial experiences, however, does not negate another equal reality, which affirms that, as humans, we also share many hybrid identities.

We who are descendants of Afrikan survivors historically scattered by forced exile across this hemisphere are especially marked by the legacy of the first Afrikan prisoners-of-war exiled on these shores. The prisoners-of-war whose spirits I now conjure are those captives taken in the course of ongoing, undeclared wars against Afrikans by Europeans, by europeanized West Asians and by arabized societies. For example, statistical information tells us that:

> [O]n one day in 1993, 98 per cent of the inmates confined in the supermax prison in Baltimore, Maryland, were African Americans. [In fact] the overwhelming numbers of black men imprisoned in the United States makes them by far the most threatened members of our society when it comes to the new form of enslavement being implemented through the prison system (Davis, 2001: 43).

Since the first surviving Afrikan exiles were all male, they sought refuge and found sustenance for their race through partnerships with women from the First Nations of the Americas. Leo Strauss speaks of a similar strategy of group preservation among Jews facing anti-Semitism in Europe (Strauss, 1997: 315). Similarities in biological identity, as suffering humans, however, have not necessarily translated into equality of lived experience. If the sum of our identities is a flower, as Caribbean Canadian educator Enid Lee imagines it, then each petal of identity plays a role in how we experience the world (Lee & Marshall, 1993: 28). North American society and, arguably, global society as well, force Afrikans to invest more heavily than most other groups in our ancestry today. That occurs because, as Philip Harper argues, "African heritage specifically has constituted …the justificatory trigger for Blacks systematic oppression in U.S. society" (Harper, 1996: 71). It is reasonable that those petals of our identity we must defend the most are the ones that society demands we deny, dilute and disown or insists that we leave behind.

Examples of the unequal impact of our layered identities on our lived experience leap out at us from popular culture. Famed US golfer Tiger Woods, whose mother was born Korean and whose father is an Afrikan born in the United States, spoke jokingly on TV about coining the term "Caublasian", a combination of Caucasian, Black and Asian, to describe his heritage when he was a child (Wright, 2000: 236). For many Blacks, however, his joke had a hollow ring.

In my experience, our public use of humour to distance our selves from Afrikan identity is often illustrative of unspoken tensions that gather like storm clouds whenever a Black person appears to be acting 'out-of-role'. At whatever cost to our dignity, White supremacy needs to feel secure and the shadows of genocide or enslavement must be chased away. Woods, after all is a young, Black man of working class parentage who has bested experienced and rich White men at their own game, on their own operationally segregated turf – their golf courses. Evidently, he doesn't know his place.

Tiger Woods' success has elicited mixed responses from the White media and golfing community. In 1997, Fuzzy Zoeller, the 1979 Masters Tournament champion, crystallized contempt for his young rival by evoking the racially charged image of Tiger Woods introducing "collard greens" into the hallowed precincts of their country club (Zoeller, 1997). Assata Shakur, from the other side of the fence, recalls how her mother would speak Spanish and would avoid collard greens in order to avoid being seen as Black (Shakur, 1987: 28). Through a long-internalized protective reflex, both the player, Tiger Woods, and the political activist, Assata Shakur, cannot help but be aware that images of 'niggers' eating 'soul food' evoke negative stereotypes of Black people in the popular North American mind. No individual achievement serves to erase the collective stereotype.

In Canada, when Ontario Provincial Police were recorded making racist remarks about Mohawk protesters and speculating about baiting traps for Aboriginals with beer, listeners heard one officer contemptuously remark, "Works in the South with watermelon" (CBC, 2004). Unexplained, this taped conversation was later played by the media. The speakers were obviously making the unspoken assumption that their audience would be familiar with the hidden history behind the image of eating watermelon as an anti-Kemetic slur and grasp its deeper meaning. No journalist commented on it.

Food rears a mocking head again when, in the summer of 1989, a gang of Italian Americans murdered an Americanized Afrikan (African American) teenager. Those young Whites gave a highly successful, spontaneous performance of modern day lynching in Bensonhurst, New York. Later, in a counter demonstration against a protest march by members of New York's Black community, members of a jeering mob of Italian Americans raised watermelons aloft. Presumably they had purchased the watermelons as props for what they identified as a Black event (Pinkney, 1994: 192).

In workshops or mixed gatherings that discuss identity, participants who visibly might appear to be of Afrikan ancestry often deny being Black. As I facilitate diverse groups, "Don't call me Black" or, "I'm not Afrikan, I'm Jamaican" and "I'm Canadian or West Indian" have become familiar refrains. Similar sentiments have also surfaced in other research within communities of Caribbean-born Afrikans in the United States. One interviewee cited in a United States study proudly proclaims, "black business is not in my book…I never knew I was black until I left Jamaica…when I was 22" (Waters, 1999: 55).

Indeed I have heard equivalent statements in settings as different as a gathering of imprisoned Black men and a university class where there were very few Blacks. This study listens to and accepts statements that deny Blackness at face value. In my experience, the same individuals who reject Black identity publicly have often confessed in private that they were 'profiled' by police, 'stalked' by security guards in stores, falsely arrested or mistreated because they were Black. Sometimes others who continue to deny the centrality of Black identity to their experience have also admitted accepting the benefits of 'affirmative action' from institutions that identified them as 'Black'. Nevertheless, in spite of the inherent contradictions of such situations, this study does not challenge anyone, whatever that individual's biological history, for choosing not to identify as Black or Afrikan.

As a conscious Pan-Afrikanist, I view Black identity as a tool for defending and rebuilding those social structures that are the bulwarks of self-determination for all groups. A. Peter Bailey, a distinguished Pan-Afrikan elder and writer has recommended the following approach. While commenting on the pitfalls of certain interracial debates that glamorize public rejections of Black identity, he advised against struggling to win over any individual who was a potential but reluctant 'Sister' or 'Brother'. "Those terms are honorific," he counselled. "Don't try to convert anyone who prefers not to be part of the Black/Afrikan family... We can't build a strong, liberated community with ambivalent people" (Bailey, 1993). As a Pan-Afrikanist I do not regard Black identity as equivalent to a profession, a social goal, or a creed. Rather, for me, it means recognizing our ancestry and collective experience as vital tools that can rebuild communal strength. A strong Black identity is a prophylactic for individuals facing psychic attack as well as an antidote to serial genocide and cycles of cultural, economic and political domination by other races.

This study also intentionally attends to the diversity within Blackness (Gilroy, 2000: 15; Shoat, Stam, 1997: 1-5, 178-241; Degler, 1971: 102-103). It acknowledges that there are individuals and groups of Afrikan ancestry who base their identity on religion or class. It recognizes others who prefer to trace their heritage through the cultural heroes of the groups they embrace. Such groups include Christianized Blacks who cope with the cognitive dissonance of invoking the presence of White saints (Ancestors), worshipping under the symbolic wings of White angels, singing hymns about being washed 'whiter than snow' and trusting their deliverance from the earthly, immediate atrocities of White supremacy to the eternal, heavenly ambiguity of a Saviour in the image of those who have done so much harm to their race (Stowell, 1922). In fact, many Black Christians count it their special burden to "help civilize" and to "missionize" those they regard as "real" Afrikans, the 'misguided idolaters' who continue to worship through icons that resemble them and their Ancestors (Hare, 1991: 88). There are parallel streams of believers who feel the same among Afrikans who follow Islam, Bhuddism, Hinduism or Judaism (Rashidi, 1999).

There are other Blacks who sociologists have identified as members in good standing of an exclusive cultural club of like-minded "exiles" from their operational racial experience. Those Blacks would come under Nathan Hare's banner of *The Black Anglo-Saxons* (Hare, 1991: ii). Generally, they espouse the outlook expressed in the opening lines of the first published, self-identified Black conservative intellectual in the United States. In George Schuyler's words:

> A Black person learns very early that his color is a disadvantage in a world of white folk. This being an unalterable circumstance, one also learns very early to make the best of it. So the lifetime endeavor of the intelligent Negro is how to be reasonably happy though colored (Schuyler, 1966: 1).

Without invoking the ravages of the falsification of consciousness, it is difficult to explain Schuyler's baffling logic. His statement unequivocally equates being "intelligent" with learning how to adjust to the impositions of a White supremacist society and become conditioned to a status of permanent subjugation within that society. This phenomenon is more widespread than I believed before undertaking this study. Even such prominent Black leaders as Ralph Abernathy, deputy to Martin Luther King and boxing icon, Muhammad Ali have taken politically ambiguous stands, in terms of Black community interests, and rallied Black voters for the openly anti-Kemetic (anti-Black) policies and positions of United States politicians like President Ronald Reagan (Marable, 1984: 194; Obadele, 1991).

Also in the United States, Ralph Wiley identifies a current strain of conservative men and women of Afrikan ancestry, deeply integrated and implicated in White culture who assign themselves roles as interpreters of Blackness for the benefit of movers and shakers within the artistic and academic circles of the dominant society (Wiley, 1996). In Canada, Rinaldo Walcott explores similar territory (Walcott, 2003). Luminaries whose reputations Wiley topples with his pen include academic Albert Murray and writer Stanley Crouch as well as the famed composer and trumpeter, Wynton Marsalis. Wiley notes, with some bemusement, that Marsalis and Crouch still use 'Negro' rather than 'Black' (Wiley, 1996). A direct rebuttal of their defence of the use of "Negro" comes from Raphael Powell, a Black theologian in New York:

> Negro does not exist because history deals with man [humans] and the record of his [their] doings, and no ancient history has given an account of negro. That is because negro has never existed…it is an evil word which is being spread like a communicative disease in the body of your race (Powell, 1979: 4).

Marsalis, in his own defence, explains, "I didn't say 'black', I said the United States Negro culture… because 'white' is part of Negro" (Marsalis, 1996: 202). The gifted musician's linguistic sleight of tongue leaves him vulnerable to harsh critique. Harold Cruse was less than kind to an earlier group of conservatives. Of those prominent members of Harlem's leadership class in the nineteen fifties and sixties, Cruse writes, "Taken as a whole, the black bourgeoisie in the United States is the most politically backward of all the colored bourgeois classes in the non-Western world" (Cruse, 1967: 327).

Marsalis, like many of those who confuse assimilation with Black salvation, ignores the history of how Whites became a "part" of "Negro culture". He also neglects to add up the costs that we collectively and individually continue to pay for a 'partnership' we collectively resisted and never sought nor sold. The price tag on this spurious, forced partnership includes lost opportunity for artistic expression and growth as well as purloined cultural capital. Robert Staples, on the other hand, reminds us "although Black entertainers often have unique skills and American society highlights all Black entry into elite positions, they have a visibility difficult for Euro-American entertainers to attain" (Staples, 1994: 235).

In plainer words, there is a kind of perverse 'affirmative action' program in permanent operation. It favours White entertainers or athletes of minor talent who receive major rewards when they invade historically Black cultural spaces or multiracial spaces where Black creators and achievers hold sway. Olympic coach Harry Edwards cites the example of Binga Dismond, "The original Negro track sensation" and the Ben Johnson figure of the 1916-1917 US sprint season (Benjamin, 1988: 62; Edwards, 1969: 78). Charley Paddock, one of the White men who benefited at Binga's expense testified that Binga "could beat any man alive at 440 yards. But he was required to run on the outside of the pack, all the way around…[until] eventually, discouraged, he disappeared" (Paddock, 1969: 78). So too did countless Black musical innovators such as Little Richard.

As Pan-Afrikanists we free up our imagination, daring to dream of a world where the unique musical genius that flows from Etta James, Little Richard, Bo Diddley or Ike Turner, pioneer composers and musical innovators, returns with fabulous financial and social rewards for the Black communities that gave it substance and form (James & Ritz, 1995; Turner & Cawthorne, 1999). Hazel Carby points out how even renowned White 'liberals', John and Alan Lomax, contrived to rob famed Blues pioneer "Leadbelly" and his impoverished family of two-thirds of the royalties generated from the compositions that genius bequeathed to posterity to enrich the whole artistic world (Carby, 2001: 106). It is through attention to the lived experience of many famed artists that this study fills out the canvas of manufactured Black loss that transmutes invisibly into White gain. Richard Penniman, iconized as 'Little Richard', says of Ike Turner, "It makes black history. He stood behind his craft but he never got the recognition" (Little Richard, 1999: xv). In his turn, Ike Turner commented on 'Elvis' (Presley), at the time of his speaking, a yet uncrowned king of Rock-N-Roll:

> A white guy who drove a gravel truck [and]… would sneak in the side door and hide behind the piano while I was playing and doing my stuff, all that crazy shit with my legs and all…[and so] that's where he [Elvis Presley] got all that shit [performing style] from (Turner, 1999: 47).

New York Black society magazine *Ebony* editor Phyl Garland attributed elements of Presley's style to pioneer Chuck Berry whose song title *Rock-'n'-Roll,* in 1957, launched an era, a genre and named a revolution in global culture (Garland, 1971: 16). It is difficult to imagine authoritative voices today crediting White musicians with originating the popular music of the United States or 'World' music (Ward & Burns, 2000). What if the stupendous fortunes and significant employment generated by such music had flowed back into the communities that sourced Rock Music instead of their being siphoned off to create an enormous pool of 'proxy' wealth for White imitators like Elvis Presley, The Beatles, Mick Jagger and Eminem? All of the stars named above were extra-cultural transients with undeveloped musical skills when they made forays into the lives of exceptionally proficient, gifted and superlatively generous Black talents (Garland, 1971; Kitwana, 2002). None has adequately compensated or acknowledged the Afrikans from whom they learned.

What if the compound interest from Black cultural capital had enriched Blacks inside their communities rather that Whites on the outside and been available to nurture coming generations groomed to inherit the crowns of our artistic giants as they passed on (Cashmore, 1997)? The greatest beneficiaries of Black culture, across the bitter encounter that generations of Whites have forced on the Black race, have remained outsiders who returned little of the riches and respect they garnered to the communal culture from which their blessings flow (Dates & Barlow, 1990: 25-54; Rogin, 1998; Rivelli & Levin, 1979; Hutchinson, 1997; Chambers, 1998; Anderson, 1994).

It was its "legally pilfered" wealth from Black artists that provided capital for Columbia Records to "purchase the patents necessary to introduce electric recording techniques into the record industry" (Dates & Barlow, 1990: 40). In words that transmit an irony beyond their literal meaning William Barlow also writes, "Paramount Records was the first label fully to take advantage of [emphasis added] the wealth of talented Black performers popular in the South" (Dates & Barlow, 1990: 40). In similar vein the ancestors of Paramount's owners had taken advantage of generations of strong, skilled Afrikans to build capitalism for their own people to enjoy.

Across the board, Whites in the record industry acted like 'Equal Opportunity' plunderers. They stole the compositions of rural artists with disabilities like Blind Blake and Blind Lemon Jefferson. They stole copyrights from artists denied educational opportunities like Sylvester Weaver, many of whom signed agreements they could not read. When the White 'Texas Playboys' recorded Weaver's groundbreaking and bestselling *Guitar Rag* as *Steel Guitar Rag* they erased both his name and ownership and they did not pay him a penny of the royalties that were his legal and moral right. Similarly, White businesses also fleeced hardworking, talented, independent women like Bessie Smith, who earned over a million dollars in royalties for Columbia without receiving a single cent (Dates & Barlow, 1990: 38-39).

In the light of such evidence, Wynton Marsalis' description of Whites as a "part" of "Negro culture" is a painfully insulting euphemism at best. To counter the impact of Whites making themselves "part" of Black culture, Black communities have had no choice but to pick up the broken pieces and to heal the spirits of Black artists whose chances for material survival were aborted, whose rhythmic inventions were expropriated and whose spirits were crushed. In the name of pluralism, multiculturalism and cross-cultural unity, Pan-Afrikan communities often pay a high, hidden price for the fictitious equality of some nebulous 'panHuman' exchange.

When Wynton Marsalis' presumes to configure the violent White exploitation and subjugation of Blacks in terms of 'partnership', therefore, his argument begs comparison to the logic of a rapist who falsifies a victim's experience of assault. 'Look at the beautiful child we've produced together!' the imaginary rapist says, as if the child conceived in violence is the fulfilment of mutual choice and benign providence. Falling into a similar trap of self-deceiving illogic, Wynton Marsalis forgets to compute the divide between the creation of "Negro" culture by Blacks and the exploitation or enjoyment of its benefits through manipulation, pressure, or institutional force by Whites. Tenor sax innovator Archie Shepp, a precursor of Marsalis, avoided the pitfall of euphemism, saying bluntly and accurately, "You (Whites) own the music and we make it" (Shepp, 1988, 26).

Pioneer Black educator Carter Woodson and psychologist Amos Wilson are among those Black scholars who have documented and analyzed the rationalization of subordination by oppressed groups and its specific manifestation among Blacks (Woodson, 1969; Wilson, 1993). On a more artistic even if ironic note, Ralph Wiley refers to Stanley Crouch's defence of the cultural status quo as Crouch's *"I'm Reconciled* [emphasis added] riffs" (Wiley, 1996: 207). White society, not surprisingly, showers rewards on prominent Blacks who can be used as symbolic promoters of Black reconciliation within a context of unchallenged White exploitation.

There are also significant numbers of Afrikans on the continent who, like Schuyler and other North American conservatives have learned to devalue the legacies of their Afrikan ancestry. Many Afrikan converts to Islam and Christianity on ancestral soil adopt mechanisms for religious or cultural accommodation through assumed amnesia. Within the public arena, they project their identity as only Arabized Muslim or Europeanized Christian. In so doing, many also tend to trace their ancestry through Arab, Berber, Hebrew, Asiatic or European, as opposed to Afrikan, roots (Nyaba, 2002: 27-50).

Previous discussion in this study has demonstrated that, as Afrikans, we have a prior, precious, demonstrably enduring and inclusive identity. When I describe myself as a 'Caribbeanized', 'Canadianized', 'Latinized' or 'Europeanized' Afrikan it is by way of respecting the multiple layers of identity that have been grafted onto my fundamental Afrikan self. Among the pioneering works in Pan-Afrikanist education from which I have drawn invaluable information are Evelyn Dandy's illuminating analysis of Black communications in the United States; Richard Allsopp's commentated dictionary for the English-speaking Caribbean; Ian Smart's work in reconnecting Spanish speakers in this hemisphere to Kemet; J. J. Thomas' ground-breaking investigation of French-influenced Creole a century and a half ago and Kwesi Prah's exhaustive, revolutionary survey of ancestral Afrikan languages from his base at CASAS (The Centre for the Advanced Study of African Society) in Cape Town, South Africa today (Dandy, 1991; Allsopp, 1996; Nehusi & Smart, 2001; Thomas, 1969; Prah, 1997).

These innovative thinkers and researchers assure us that our original Afrikan tongues, markers of ancestral personality, remain active across oceans and over generations. Such retentions suggest that our collective memory is able to leap over a formidable social, transgenerational and geographical divide. Indeed Afrikan continuities may one day prove to be strong evidence for the theories of scientist Richard Sheldrake. This pioneer investigator of human consciousness continues research into possibilities of expanded and uncharted human spiritual ability which might potentially grow out of new (to modern society) scientific discoveries in areas of unexplained phenomena within this vibrationary universe. Sheldrake, in fact, cites colonial European records of "local chiefs and spirit mediums [who provide baffling information] about events in distant places" (Sheldrake, 2003: 217).

How we define and present ourselves to the world must remain a matter of individual choice that flows from assumptions about our individual human rights. At the same time, I remain aware that our operational identity has an impact that goes beyond us and shapes our collective, global Afrikan identity as well. There are often tensions within sites of collective identity where some individuals are strong while the group remains generally vulnerable. That observation is as true for Afrikans as for Women and other groups that resist social domination. For example, some Dalit, the 'Black' people of India, affirm an ancient common ancestry with Afrikans while others vehemently deny any such connections (Rashidi, 1999; Rajshekar, V.T., 1987: 43). This work, however, does not explore the Dalit relation to Pan-Afrikan, 'Black' identity. Rather it examines the societies in which my awareness and information base benefit from lived experience as well as active research.

In 1894, Matthew Jacobson, a United States professor of law argued for immigration rules that would let all those who "contrasted with Africans - Japanese for instance - qualify as white" [emphasis added], deeming, "contrast with Africans" the decisive factor in determining which groups should be let into the country (Jacobson, 2000: 76). Culling the archives of United States law and custom, Jacobson mounted evidence to show that groups such as "swarthy Europeans... pure Hindus and other minor Asian stocks...Semitic peoples...especially the Hebrews...were rendered indelibly white by the presence of [Afrikan or other] populations even more problematic than themselves" (Jacobson, 2000: 76). The criteria he used to define those other populations remain unclear.

To bolster his case, Jacobson also quoted an unnamed United States senator who argued, "the Chinaman...is infinitely above the African in intelligence, in manhood, and in every respect" (Jacobson,

2000: 74). In an earlier generation Gerald Morton Stanley, a penniless adventurer magically morphed into an expert on all things Afrikan, had written breathless dispatches to the Herald in New York from the racist frontlines he helped to open up in Afrika. For example, Stanley regaled and titillated his White readers with scurrilous lies of "becoming black man's meat" (Jacobson, 2000: 150). Indeed some well-informed readers might have credibly argued that Stanley's unprovoked crimes of murder, mayhem and defamation against Afrikans merited the fantasy he described. On the other hand his admirers no doubt found comfort in knowing that Afrikans had evidently developed finer tastes than 'roasted Gerald Morton Stanley' could ever satisfy. On the other side of the debate about the worth of Black women and men in the United States, "…[the] National Association For the Advancement of Colored Peoples (NAACP) took the case of African-Americans' [basic human freedoms and rights] before the United Nations" as did a coalition of leaders charging genocide in Paris in 1951 (Jacobson, 2000: 115; Patterson, 1971).

Recent research now confirms a growing pool of women and men of mixed parentage who prefer to identify themselves as 'biracial' or 'multiracial' (Brown, 1995: 125). As earlier argued, it would be both disrespectful and futile to try to impose an unwanted 'Black' identity on them. While a public language to describe mixed race keeps evolving, it is worth noting that, within Black communities, parallel mechanisms have long existed to identify those from our group who see themselves as being 'on a cusp' as well as others who identify unequivocally as 'Black'. A Toronto writer with a White mother and Black father put his feelings this way:

> Unless you are so light-skinned and devoid of Black facial features that you can pass for white you don't get to be white in this society if you have black parents … This is one of the reasons why I self-identify as black (Hill, 2001: 41).

Black identity is therefore the considered choice of most persons of mixed racial heritage, not because they don't care about their White parent, but in order to avoid the potential stress of living moment by moment under threat of humiliating rejection by other Whites because of their Black ancestry.

In the video *The Way Home* (see Chapter Five) two Biracial speakers with White mothers, are of one voice. One young woman says, "I wanted to have this happy Brady Bunch [White TV family] kind of life...[but] eventually I came to terms with the fact that I'm never going to be White" (Butler, 1998). In turn, another speaker recalls, "realizing all the differences [between Black and White] and having people say [I'm] adopted and saying 'no, I'm not adopted this is my mother' [and] realizing that I could never be White [emphasis added]" (Butler, 1998). In the southern US slavocracy, some states could legally prescribe White identity and denied it to anyone with one Black ancestor in the previous two generations. In addition to that stricture, if an individual showed any recognizable trace of Black ancestry that was reason enough to override prevailing social convention and deny them the privilege of being treated like someone 'White' (Berlin, 1981: 161).

It is ironic that in today's popular culture charges of 'reverse racism' by Blacks seem to be increasing. Even within some progressive academic circles the 'who-is-racist-and-who-can-be-racist' debate rages on, largely unresolved. Blacks are often criticized for putting pressure on those who are of mixed ancestry to identify with their group. Such behaviour is then characterized as 'racist', as if strategies for daily survival that demand Black unity have the same impact as customs and institutions that punish and oppress Blacks on the grounds of race.

Issues of multiracial identity trouble Black life and I am convinced that a more thorough study of this phenomenon would probably yield us valuable insights. With little fear of contradiction, we can say that, in general, it is anti-Kushitic (anti-Black) prejudice that has been at the source of resistance to treating Blacks as well as other peoples of color as equal to Whites. Since in the operational hierarchy of race 'Black' means 'lowest and base', it is not surprising to learn that in nineteenth century South Carolina, "free Negroes wriggled out of the free Negro caste by claiming Indian ancestry" (Berlin, 1981: 164). In the testimonies of most groups in *The Way Home* it also appears harder for non-Afrikan groups to recognize and accept Aboriginals, Arabs, Asians or Jews who share Black ancestry than for them to accept individuals with other combinations of mixed ancestry (Butler, 1998).

In my view, Blacks have never had the power or controlled the social mechanisms, in this hemisphere, to successfully police entry into any group, including our own. Far from imposing our standards on others, dominant groups have found it relatively easy to penetrate Black gatherings and force their desires or dictates on us. In the United States, which to this day remains operationally a largely segregated society, the self-determinist Black leader, Malcolm X, was accused of being a 'racist in reverse' (Carson, 1991; Wolfenstein, 1993; Collins & Bailey, 1998). I remember hearing those accusations among university students and in public spaces when news of his assassination reached Canada in 1965. Of course, as an uncompromising Black nationalist and a Pan-Afrikanist, the influential leader did not promote any integration that reconciled itself with subordination to another race (Malcolm X, 1965: 5). Malcolm X's refusal to be infantilized or to accept second-class status, I submit, makes a rather thin case for anyone labelling him racist.

As people of Afrikan ancestry we have long faced a globalized, seemingly indelible prejudice against our kind. Those who point out that, in the course of world history, most groups have served time both on the discrimination bench as victims or in the penalty box as perpetrators, do us no service. Such descents into generalization fail to acknowledge the way in which our Pan-Afrikan experience remains unique. Universalizing our experience can dilute it to the point of denial. It obscures the impact of distant injustice on our present life chances and the concrete disadvantages we face in today's world. Denial can feel like disrespect. It reinforces the feeling that where Europeans are concerned, "The association of blackness with all things evil, ugly and

CLEM MARSHALL

satanic and whiteness with all things pure, beautiful and godly [is] fundamental to their (European) psychology" (Cell, 1987: 3-4). The range of examples cited above strongly suggest that a similar code of colour-coded supremacy, in a hierarchy that privileges lighter, if not White, skin operates among East, West and South Asians as well as within some populations of the Pacific region. Given these realities, against what race can Blacks collectively take racist action?

Operational 'shadism' and anti-Kushitism are neither a Black invention nor under Black control. In fact, the phenomenon raises so many significant social, historical and political questions that it deserves and demands a separate forum for adequate exploration. I cite the following example merely to illuminate the particular relationship of Blackness to all other shades of the racial spectrum. Comments from informed witnesses of the Black Freedom Movement, during which tensions sometimes soared between Blacks and other racial groups in New York City, are recorded in a chronicle of those times. Sometimes writers would put the particular events they chronicled into a wider historical context. The text of one such occasion reads:

> From the Black man's point of view, they wrote, "he is always chasing what other Americans-who came later and have given less-always seem to have, or always get before he does… The Jew qua Jew is not the adversary…[rather] whosoever stands in the way of their [Black people's] recovery…is the enemy, whatever his race, color or religion. He [a Black individual] was vaguely [emphasis added] aware that "Polacks" and "Jews" and "Italians" and "Irishmen" and poor whites were against him. But then, weren't all whites? (Weisbord & Stein, 1972: xiv).

It is significant that the generic "Black man" of the quote is only "vaguely" aware of the sources of his discomfort and pain. Many forces, including the subtle interplay of language and image, competing theories of social construction and attribution of outcome as well as the distraction of constant stress with its concomitant desire for the relief of simple explanations, all contribute to the vagueness of the awareness that he feels. One of the goals of a Pan-Afrikanist education and this work is to provide Afrikans with clearer anti-racist and equity lenses. These lenses should sharpen our vision and enhance our understanding of the extreme marginalization we still experience within the context of post-colonial, post-segregation, post-apartheid multiracial and multicultural societies.

From another angle, I find the phenomenon of blaming racial exclusion on Black people untenable. During our long history of bondage, the evidence shows that Black mothers did not reject the biological children of White rapists but embraced them as fully credited members of inclusive communities. In contrast, Asian communities generally rejected children of mixed parentage born during the Vietnam War (Obadele, 1991; Tani & Sera, 1985). What special spirit prepared Black mothers and wrapped them in its arms so they could survive beside White rapists whose very presence spoke humiliation and still raise vulnerable daughters and sons with pride? Unlike women in many other communities, Black women, victimized by rape were accepted and supported within enslaved populations. In step with inclusion, records disclose no caste system or general discrimination operating in Black communities against those with White blood. In fact, given the facts, it is reasonable to infer that the opposite is true. Black people of mixed ancestry, in many Black communities, have historically enjoyed privileges associated with how White they appeared to be (Gwaltney, 1980; Spencer-Strachan, 1992; Walters, 1999; Hill, 2001). Charles Johnson's investigation of the mores of plantation society, however, offers a different perspective. He said, "[since] mulatto men [had] a reputation for being poor providers for dark women, [most women] wanted a husband [who was] good and dark [emphasis added]" (Johnson, 1969: 57).

While accepting that identity embraces an element of choice, I also feel that some of us, because of how we look, our social location and other tangible or intangible factors, have only one racial identity available to us. And when that identity is Black it trails burdens of stigma and imprisoning social status in its wake. Operationally, the evidence marshalled here shows that Black populations do not generally force an unwanted Black identity or claim of consanguinity upon the vulnerable. Rather, most people of mixed ancestry have found their Black identity a refuge of last resort. That tradition finds voice in the folk saying among Afrikan populations in the US South, 'home is the place where, when you have to go there, they have to take you in.'

Since Black is synonymous with Afrikan, when naming us as a people, I use the upper case. I also spell 'Afrikan' with a 'k' following a number of Afrikan-centred scholars such as Kamuti Kiteme, born in Kenya; Amos Wilson, born in the United States and Kimani Nehusi, born in the Caribbean (Kiteme, 1992,1; Wilson, 1988: 2; Nehusi & Smart, 2000: 85). 'Afrika' is the spelling commonly encountered in earlier Europeanized versions of ancestral Afrikan languages. In this study, using 'Afrika' and 'Afrikan' also connotes a global identity. It is intended to advance self-determination through reclaiming our right as human beings to choose our names and define who we are in ways that we decide. I also use 'Afrika' in recognition of the symbolic meaning ascribed that name by a growing body of musical composers, poets, performance artists and contemporary Pan-Afrikan scholars. No other continent lives so gloriously in the titles of the music of its daughters and sons (Davies, 2000; Veal, 2000; Floyd, 1996; Pongweni, 1982).

It is not an unreasonable assumption that when 'Black' is used to designate people of Afrikan ancestry, as a conscious and popularly accepted replacement for 'Negro', it would be written with an upper case 'B'.

I find this reasonable because 'Negro', although fast disappearing is, where it exists, usually written with an upper case 'N' (Houghton Mifflin, 1992: 195). An upper case "B" is hardly revolutionary since, "in its issue of 6 May 6 1893" a London periodical *Society* covered the visit of feminist Ida B. Wells to England with the "hope of arousing sympathy for the Blacks" (Wells, 1970: 90). Surprisingly, however, mainstream media in Canada, including *The Globe and Mail* and *Toronto*

Star, continue to use a lower case 'B', up to the present time (Mackie, 2003; Mallan, 2003). One might presume that their sense of their readership tells them that they will be rewarded for continuing to deny Black people the simple respect of a grown-up 'B'.

Hatshepsut's Sacred Command

Yet doubts disturb my dreams

No pillow brings me peace

Nights I must ponder

Days to come still unlived and far away

O Bloods of my blood what will you then say

Left with these pillars standing in stone

To show your world

How we were what we'd done

Do not then claim

You could not know

As if we died

Nameless and nondescript

Do not then view

Sacred Kemet's past

Framed by envy of foreign eyes

Slave and victim of hostile myth

(Marshall, 2004)

Note: The lines above represent my own liberal adaptation of a translated inscription found on a pillar in the royal ruins of Saqquara in Ancient Kemet (Busby, 1992: 13).

ANCESTORS

In sum, Black identity, in this study, assumes shared genetic ancestry that affects appearance and the effect of such appearance on experience and collective memory (Harris, 1998). Ancestry also assumes shared culture, history and geography from distant, beginning times. Wolof speakers in West Afrika celebrate ancestry in a saying, "Lu reen jan jan reen gen koo jan: However deep the root another root runs deeper still [my translation]" (Samb, 1983: 31). Even more significantly, however, ancestry also stands for the transmission across generations of coded, collective Afrikan memories of invasion, displacement, replacement, dilution of culture with erasure in mind, forced exile or labour and genocide as well as the generalized denial of the impact of those histories on Afrikans in the modern world. I also pluralize 'Ancestors' since it is Afrika's collective heritage and not the glory of individuals from an elite that I cite, and I capitalize "Ancestors" out of personal reverence for the sacrifices they made. It is my way of celebrating those saints and stalwarts whose victimhood has been rendered historically nameless although they suffered one of humanity's most unspeakable seasons of disgrace.

ANTI-KEMETIC & ANTI-KUSHITIC

Today, in the popular culture of North America, young men of Afrikan ancestry often refer affectionately to each other as "my Nubian brother". They are, without knowing it, rehabilitating the taunt "Tenth Nubian [emphasis added] Light Foot" (Eppinga, 1996). It was hurled contemptuously at the first Black graduate of prestigious West Point Military Academy, Ossian Flipper and members of the "all-black Tenth Calvary in Georgia in 1877" (Eppinga, 1996). Somehow, the idea of the proud Nubia of history, spread between today's Sudan, Ethiopia, Somalia and Egypt, as the world's foundational civilization has escaped the ravages of anti-Kushitic defamation to become a refurbished icon of unconscious, embedded Black continuity and pride among our youth. In today's Nubia, the opposite is unfortunately true. The Arabized class in control consciously tries to erase evidence of past Nubian achievements and denies their Black roots (Sharawy, 1999; Nyaba, 2002). However, recent scholarship does confirm the centrality of Nubia in Afrikan and world history (Aubin, 2002: xvi). Nubia therefore continues to hold promise as an image of pride that could be useful in rebuilding eroded Afrikan identities.

I've also often felt the need to be more precise in identifying the specific hatred or discrimination directed at Afrikans because of our ancestry. So in seeking out a term of broad scope that signified a general latent or active bias against all Black people and Afrikan-identified culture, I experimented with the term 'anti-Nubian'. However, at the suggestion of Ugandan popular educator, Paulo Wangoola of Mpambo Multiversity, I later settled on "anti-Kemetic" to describe the range of discriminatory practices inflicted on women and men of Afrikan ancestry (Wangoola, 2002). Continued research that deepened my understanding of the linguistic and cultural history of the earliest Afrikan settlements, however, has led me to see the ovarian and seminal qualities of the name "Kush", made familiar to most Afrikans because it appears frequently in the religions of The Book. Anti-Kushitic, therefore, not only resonates with Pan-Afrikan history, it has the linguistic advantage of rolling easily off the tongue.

EXCULPATORY EUPHEMISM

Following the progression from insult that assaults the Black psyche to euphemism that assuages White guilt, in both popular and formal discourse, this study examines some striking examples of the ubiquitous use of euphemisms as well as narcotizing 'comfort words'. It begins to unpack the working of this dehumanizing process, calling to mind the term, 'comfort women', a euphemism coined to describe Korean and Filipina women abused and exploited by Japanese military men during WW II. The study of euphemism, therefore, looks at how, historically and operationally, White male communicators have fashioned a wrestler's cage, barred on top, on the bottom and on every side, in which Women, Aboriginals, Afrikans, Asians and other groups that the social institutions dominate and devalue are conditioned to assault and injure each other. Like captive gladiators, subjugated peoples cannot escape pressures of inter-group conflict because the promoters of their manufactured carnage hold the keys to the arena in which they must survive.

This book, therefore, pays attention to the phenomenon of exculpatory euphemisms that have been rendered so 'banal' they pass for 'neutral' or 'normal' speech (Arendt, 2000). The anti-Kushitic tradition of sanitizing defamation is a hoary one. It goes back to Christian and Islamic scriptural texts such as the notorious "Curse of Ham", already debunked by Timbuktu's Islamic scholar Ahmad Baba in the seventeenth century. It persists despite the lack of textual evidence for its defamation of Afrikans said to be based on the book of Genesis in the Bible (Alford, 1986: 81; Diop, 1990: 44-45). One might expect that, in modern times, scholarship would have buried the Hamitic myth, justly and intelligently, under generations of rebuttal and mountains of learned research. However, as Bradford Chambers demonstrates, this lie lingers on, invisible but deadly, like carbon monoxide in the air. He writes, "The old belief identified Ham so closely with the black race that blacks are often called *Hamitic*" (Chambers, 1968: 20). In North American society, people of Afrikan ancestry still live under constant bombardment of verbal and visual racism from sitcom TV's Kramer to Radio's Imus and CNN's biased coverage of Hurricane Katrina in 2005. As Afrikans we are enveloped in toxic clouds or caught in a net of symbols and sounds of disaster that weave feelings of catastrophe into the fabric of our daily lives. Small wonder that filmmaker Spike Lee calls his (Black) community *Bamboozled* in his film of the same name (Neal, 2002: 124).

The noxious attacks of powerful communications systems under White supremacy reinforce the daily assaults of major elements of popular culture and fuel disrespect for Black women while demonizing

Black men (Dates & Barlow, 1990; Naficy & Teshome, 1993; Newkirk, 2000; Nichols, 1981). Modern society fairly crackles with the static of a kind of electric, noxious noise. Afrikans face constant stares of careless knowing, uncomprehending pity or pitiless contempt. Those looks create a psychic glare that suffuses the air, blinding many to reality, distorting our experience and constantly distracting us from the pursuits that lead towards the fullness of our human destiny. The ineluctable, global, anti-Kushitic seizure of body, mind and spirit, under which we have lived for so long, is unique in the annals of human history. A healing response therefore calls for both new combinations of ancient skills and inventive strategies that can transmute subjugation into liberation.

To unpack exculpatory euphemisms is to examine how Black people make meanings we can live with out of codes of communication created or crafted to conceal our pain and cauterize our senses against a constantly emerging consciousness of White culpability for much of our suffering. By delving deeper into understanding the social construction of our experience, I therefore expose some of the ways that learning to communicate in the language of our domination has often seduced me as it does other speakers of Europe's tongues into being unwitting apologists for crimes committed against us. Transgenerational legacies of corrosive memory inevitably lead us to a reservoir of poisoned experience although we desire to resist the forces misshaping our lives.

In daily Afrikan life we breathe in familiar terms and recycle them again. Like friendly snakes with hidden fangs, these words shoot venom into our veins. For example, an influential Black activist in the United States used the term "Aids in Blackface" as the title for a forum he helped to organize. Warren Hedges comments, "The fact that an African American activist [conscious of racist stereotypes of Black women and men] like Harlon Dalton could wander into this metaphor so blithely only underscores how deeply such imagery often operates" (Hedges, 1997: 241, 247). And to this observation, a bruised Afrikan spirit buried deep inside my ancestral memory breathes, "Amen!"

HOLOCAUSTS

Choosing this term and pluralizing it does not disrespect usage by Jewish scholars and members of the wider community who refer to the Nazi genocide as "The Holocaust". However, I follow the usage of Bruno Bettelheim, a Holocaust survivor, who pluralizes the term in reflecting its history. "When the holocausts of past times were viewed as God's will, they had to be accepted as such" (Bettelheim, 1980: 9). As early as 1903, the eminent sociologist W.E. B. Du Bois, whose rich scholarship has illuminated race theory from a Black perspective, used the term "holocaust" to describe the horrors of the anti-slavery war, called the Civil War, in the USA. However other interpretations of the term are well taken. "In fact, it was the Nazi holocaust that discredited the scientific racism that was so pervasive a feature of American intellectual life before World War II" (Finkelstein, 2000: 148). In using that word I also take into account the diversity within Jewish culture and populations. In that vein, my own reading and personal contacts within the Jewish community have introduced me to the term "Shoah", "The Destruction" as well (Gilman, 1996: 87). A parallel exists within the Afrikan community where the term "Maafa", "The Great Suffering" is gaining currency. It is a name unique to the serial genocide perpetrated by Europeans against Afrikans since the fifteenth century (Ani, 1994: xxi). In part because it carries the resonance of an ancestral tongue, referring to "The Maafa" has already become the choice of a growing number of Pan-Afrikanist scholars, whether based on the continent, the Americas, Europe or the Caribbean.

There are other considerations that illuminate the term "holocaust". For example, historian Ali Mazrui contends, "The Greek word "holocaust" should remain a generic metaphor... American children need to know that genocide was part of the birth of this nation. The holocaust began at home" (Mazrui, 1995: viii). Indeed, as we struggle to tell and retell our own stories, it is impossible to escape constant parallels across cultures and communities around human tales of celebration or suffering. Parallels between 'The Shoah', 'The Maafa' and other 'holocausts' are inexact but they exist. Rabbi Henry Cohen points to similarities such as the Nazi separation of Jewish family members and the dismemberment of Afrikan families throughout bondage. He also evokes pictures of deported Jewish populations crammed into airless boxcars on trains beside images of Afrikans forced into exile stuffed in the suffocating holds of death ships where, according to Eric Williams, they were allotted a space only five feet six inches by sixteen inches for crossing the Atlantic (Cohen, 1968: 48; Williams, 2007). Observing 'similarity' does not necessarily convey 'disrespect'.

I do not gloss over the fact that Afrikans have a unique and un-enviable relationship to enslavement in the history of this planet. At the same time I accept the reality that 'slave', as a concept, is not exclusive Afrikan property. Those veterans who survived Japanese prisoner-of-war camps, Nazi concentration camps or Soviet Union labour camps for political prisoners also describe their ordeal as 'slave' labour. There is however no evidence that in so doing they intend to disrespect the Afrikan experience of enslavement, its accompanying horrors of lynching and its blood brother, Black male genital mutilation (Ginsburg, 1988; Raper, 1970; Allen, 2000).

Globally, Black people continue to suffer from historical dispossession of our ancestral lands to enrich Europeans or Asians in Kenya, southern Afrika or Australia (Horne, 2001; Grovogui, 1996; Ingham, 1967; Stevens, 1984; Le Vine & Luke, 1979). Afrikans also suffer ongoing genocidal wars funded from outside to impose foreign control of their resources (Melvern, 2000; Jennings, 2001, Nkrumah, 1985). Mark Duffield writes that in Liberia, "foreign firms were essential in consolidating [Charles aka warlord] Taylor's social position. Firestone Tyre and Rubber Corporation and French commercial interests were involved... [during] the early 1990s" (Duffield, 2001: 176). Women and men are still subjected to ongoing capture and enslavement in Mali, Mauritania and the Sudan. It follows that as a race we are made to bear all the attendant scars of unfathomable trauma caused by thirty generations of global dehumanization. It is also significant that we are trying to do so without the respect or opportunity for healing that apology and reparations might generate (Maduno, 1994; Segal, 2001).

Increasingly, in North America today, state persecution makes Black people fodder for prisons as well as guinea pigs for surveillance technologies, experimental drugs and risky medical practices (Monmonier, 2002; Roberts, 1997; Hornblum, 1998; Kiple, 1988; Jones, 1982; Mauer & Chesney-Lind, 2002). A look at history shows us how much remains unchanged. Before Emancipation in 1830, in his famous anti-slavery *"Appeal..."* (see Chapter Seven) David Walker notes, "... all the inhabitants of the earth (except, however, the sons of Africa) are called *men*" (Walker, 1993: 27). His words are a sobering reminder that in trying to replace Afrika's First Nations as owners of the continent Asians and Europeans continue to force Afrikans to walk over burning paths no other race has been forced to tread so relentlessly for so long, (Williams, 1976).

IDENTITY

In this study the most important aspect of 'identity', like all other intellectual concepts, is its operational impact on our lives. I therefore explore identity to demonstrate how we harness it, as Pan-Afrikanists, in defence of our collective personality or use it to enhance self-determination. As Afrikans, identity plays a major role in every sphere in which we create or express meaning. It often shapes the moral choices we must make and, as defined within White supremacist society, dictates the boundaries of the actions and activities in which we participate. Identity also shapes our lived humanity, and Claudia von Werlhof argues that, in capitalist, operationally global society today, capital constructs that identity for or against us. "The extent to which someone is defined...as 'human'...the degree of their social identity – is not determined by the simple fact of their existence, but through their relationship to capital...the scale of their property or ownership of goods" (Mies, Bennholdt-Thomson & Von Werlhof, 1991: 107). There is a special irony for Afrikans in von Werlhof's words. Since we were defined at the dawn of capitalism as 'property', we are still to define the peculiar kind of relationship property that owns the richest property on earth can have with other races in manifest control of property in the world (Williams, 1994).

Pan-Afrikan historian Imari Obadele collects evidence of the dehumanization of Afrikans in the United States and provides learners with significant detail. "In Paragraph 3 of Section 2, Article 1 of the enduring [US] constitution the Founders wrote: Representation and direct taxes shall be apportioned...according to the whole Number of free Persons...and excluding Indians not taxed, three-fifths of all other persons [Afrikans]" (Obadele, 1991: 13, 14). Even in the US constitution, therefore, the unique relationship of Afrikans, irrespective of gender to capital and humanity was set down in terms of unambiguous, arrogant, racist contempt. Each Afrikan, from the cradle to the grave, whatever (s)he had accomplished along the way, was defined as three-fifths of a 'human being'. No other humans in history have had their humanity negatively measured with such exactitude. As social beings, we construct or inherit identities that weave patterns through our daily activities, affecting our life chances both as individuals and groups. In our society gender and race identity are generally imposed by custom and reinforced in the ritual of everyday living. Still, it is possible for individuals to negotiate their relationship to the groups they have inherited by biology, ancestry or geography. For members of groups that have been historically marginalized, however, the cost of distancing themselves from the protection and nurture of their roots often increases their vulnerability in the larger society.

Over generations, communities of sufferers can also store up 'resistance capital' in a collective bank and make it available to individuals from their group in crisis situations. This is of critical importance, for example, to Gay or Lesbian Black women and men. They need their communities to survive the daily stress of anti-Kushitic, racist oppression in North America. Yet 'coming out' often puts enormous pressure on them to disconnect themselves from the very networks they need when they suffer 'profiling' by police or experience discrimination in recreation, at school and at work.

In this study I use fire as a generative metaphor for identity. We can reasonably predict how our own identity operates at different levels of intensity depending on context and our social location. Flames at the centre burn with the greatest intensity. For me, individuals who share an identity are the wood or coals that fuel the same fire. Those who are Pan-Afrikan and for self-determination, as I identify myself, may by interest, inclination and investment become more involved in areas that bear on our racialized social identity on an ongoing basis. We could therefore be accurately described as operating at a high level of intensity, or as it were, ablaze at the melting point of the fire.

On the other hand, members of our group who are less invested might move in and out of the fire's centre but still remain connected most of the time. At an even further remove from the centre, some individuals of shared ancestry may choose to live as if their racial identity has no bearing on their 'life choices' or 'life chances'. In this work, therefore, I do not attribute Black identity to those who can and do pass for White. I acknowledge, however, that when some social upheaval occurs that sharply divides society on the basis of Black and White, such as the widely televised beating of Rodney King by Los Angeles police or O.J. Simpson's infamous trial in the nineties, then those Afrikans on the margins have often found themselves catapulted into the centre despite their best efforts to remain 'safely' on the fringe (Nelson, 2000; Simpson, 1995; Cochran, 1996).

Learning from the paths blazed by two Black women pioneers helped to deepen my understanding of how 'identity' operates in shaping our 'life chances', influencing the risks we take and the choices we make. Both accomplished women were born into times of tumult and transformation inside their local Black community, the nation of their birth and the wider Afrikan world. This is a cautionary tale and I've named it, "A Tale of Two Sistahs", attempting in the spelling 'sistahs' to capture the sound and feeling of 'sisters' in Ebonics (Dandy, 1991).

The first sistah, Ida B. Wells was a child of post-Emancipation US, born into bondage, in 1862, three years before formal freedom was proclaimed. Her social location, talents, guts and the politics of her era vaulted her into positions of leadership. She embraced service to her bruised, dispossessed yet spiritually inexhaustible people. Wells was uniquely gifted. She worked as a journalist, community builder and educator at a time when gender and race opened up chasms, daily, under her feet. Her fearlessness and sacrifice earned her the loyalty of a race hungry for knowledge. Her readers devoured any information that could give them a clearer sense of their social space and how they came to be located where they were (Wells, 1970).

In those days, Black learners anxiously salvaged scraps of books, using them to practice reading or to teach each other to read (Stowell, 1922: 18). Wells came to know her community intimately as she bravely traveled across the South documenting the ubiquitous outrage of lynching (Wells, 1970). She fought discrimination in public transportation and won important victories in court. Ida B. Wells challenged the most influential Black conventions for being composed almost entirely of men and forced them to change. Her example of female courage brought hope to vulnerable groups of desperate women and men, anxious about the violence from vengeful racist Whites that hovered like an executioner's axe over their necks. As an adult educator, she shared her knowledge in enough detail for her community to make informed decisions about its welfare. And she could proudly report that a grateful race, "treated [her] like a queen" (Wells, 1970: 42).

Ida B. Wells owed her status and social power to the people she served rather than the dominant society that persecuted them. Her fame and influence were organic, not cosmetic. We have the rich legacy of her careful record of those tumultuous times and how they transformed Black life. She chronicles the achievements and unique energy of a people newly free, bursting forth in education, science, music, dance and transforming the whole world by its touch (Wells, 1970; Burt, 1969; Haskins, 1977; Wilson & Wallace, 1992). Her many legacies bear witness to her sense of duty. Wells was about paying back the community and commitment to her collective self. She refused to leave the dispossessed members of her race behind. Instead, she left posterity and all humanity a testimony to the grandeur, glory and spiritual rewards of learning how best to serve (Wells, 1970).

At the other end of the spectrum of Black collective identity, Oprah Winfrey was born in 1954, the year before Rosa Parks famously refused, as she had done many times before, to move to the back of a bus (King, 1987: Morris, 1984: 51). Oprah was nine years old when dynamite was thrown into a Black church in Birmingham, Alabama, killing four other little girls and exploding the myth of a civilized White America before the whole world (Marable, 1984; Morris, 1984). By the time Oprah was sixteen, Black leaders Medgar Evers, Martin Luther King and Malcolm X had also been murdered and resurrected, as martyrs, in the safe keeping of Black folks' souls (Billingsley, 1992).

When racist institutions felled Martin Luther king, Black rage erupted from the belly of over a hundred cities in the United States. The unending examples of persecution and callous indifference by the dominant society finally ignited a powder keg of righteous anger across the land. Fire-tipped words accompanied the uprisings. They evoked ancient symbols in the Afrikan psyche in which our communities would rise again like the phoenix from their own ashes. Chants spoke cleansing fire and rebirth, spreading like untamed sparks from lip to lip. Slogans like, 'Burn, baby, burn!' fulfilled the ambiguous promise of the old spiritual, *God gave Noah the rainbow sign, No more water, the fire next time* (Lester, 1969 & 1969; Carmichael & Hamilton, 1967; Cleaver & Katsaficas, 2001). As Oprah was growing up, teenagers and twenty year olds in local chapters of the 'Black Panther Party for Self-Defence' were feeding children before school or checking adults for high blood pressure and sickle cell anemia. Carrying their raw courage for a shield, they also monitored armed and dangerous White officers in an effort to stop the police brutality that engulfed Black life (Foner, 1995).

Revolution was in the air in Chicago, Milwaukee and down South, all the places that informed Oprah's formative years (King, 1987; Marable, 1984; Morris, 1984). Yet accounts of her growing up Black in the very crucible of Black liberation describe her as if she were looking on from the outside. "... I just never had any of those angry black feelings... Truth is I've never felt prevented from doing anything because I was either black or a woman... I wasn't a dashiki kind of woman" (Winfrey, 1987:75). That biographer also makes a point of communicating a sense of distance between her and the Black community in which she grew. That includes its activists like Olympians John Carlos and Tommy Smith who suffered and sacrificed to open up unprecedented opportunities for a few gifted and ready individuals of Afrikan ancestry to enjoy (Edwards, 1969). In her words, "They [other Black students] all hated me, no resented me...[but] I refused to conform [emphasis added] to the militant thinking of the time" (Winfrey, 1987: 75).

Understanding the climate surrounding Oprah's boasted refusal to "conform" to "thinking" that challenged the 'Jim Crow' status quo requires deeper analysis (Woodward, 1966: 7). We must remember that this was a time when thousands of elderly, deeply conservative Black churchgoers were also willing to march with Martin Luther King to ensure equal facilities and educational opportunities for future generations (Abernathy, 1990; Morris, 1984). By rejecting even "militant thinking", Oprah would have effectively had to shut down some of her own critical faculties and to accept the existing frame of 'racist status quo thinking' by default. Biographer Norman King implicitly connects her meteoric rise to stardom to her silence on the human rights issues that inspired Black militancy. From a Pan-Afrikan perspective, in packaging themselves for mainstream, corporate success, the silence of some Black stars, male or female, counted as much as or more than their talents. Keen attention to the prescribed codes of dress, looks, hairstyles, speech and the presentation of an ingratiating, edible, public persona was required (King, 1987; Goffman, 1959). Indeed, Oprah's resumé reads like an anti-discrimination survey of appointments and opportunities that were routinely denied to her community and White women at large. Denied, that is, before the Civil Rights 'Sacrifice' Movement of torched Black churches, bombed homes, Black dreams and bodies blown to bits blew open those doors, long bolted shut, for her and others to walk through (Morris, 1984; Abernathy, 1990; Billingsley, 1992).

Tokenism, the mainstream's selection of accommodating, 'alibi' Blacks for highly visible rewards, usually operates, at the level of symbol, to convince Whites that they have adequately compensated all Blacks for long histories of collective harm (Hacker, 1992). Norman King's cautious biography of Oprah leaves it up to readers to figure out how much her promotion by powerful media forces in the dominant culture dictated her attitude to her people's plight. Some readers no doubt will speculate about whether her willingness to "conform" garnered support for her career or shaped its success. There is no doubt that while the globe's most famous talk show host was blazing a path to unparalleled fortune, other young women and men her age were putting scholarships on the line, sacrificing their only chance for college, mortgaging potential careers or quietly, without fanfare, laying down their lives (Marable, 1984; Cleaver and Katsaficas, 2001; Morris, 1984).

By their acts of courage, they not only refused to "conform" to racist norms, they also paid for our right, as their collective heirs and survivors, to create a world where all people of Afrikan ancestry can potentially thrive. Oprah's use of "conform" turns reality upside down. Her 'exculpatory euphemisms' lift her magically above the clubs bloodying unbowed grey heads or Black grandmothers crying teargas tears. They license her to ignore fire hose blasting marchers full in the face and 'nigger-hungry hounds' ripping children's flesh. Taylor Branch reminds us of pictures in those turbulent times that appeared on a front page of *Muhammad Speaks* and in the *New York Times*. Reportedly, they made President Kennedy "sick".

The Black Muslim weekly carried "the photograph of a police dog biting the midriff of a Birmingham youth, paired with…a white policeman holding a shotgun over the prostrate, handcuffed corpse of Ronald Stokes in Los Angeles" (Branch, 1998: 87). Unfortunately, we have never been allowed to hear whether those photographs made Oprah as "sick" as they did the White president, although knowing would have given several generations an unforgettable lesson on "race". Instead what we do hear, the bubble around Oprah, seems to transport her into another dimension, almost as if she were free to float outside time and beyond space, a bemused visitor from a planet where hierarchies of race have never held the central place they do in Black lives, up to and including the most gifted, famous and rich.

I asserted earlier that this was a cautionary tale. For me, as a Pan-Afrikanist, it rings a warning bell in the middle of moonless, treacherous seas. It sounds an alarm about the seductive power of attractive Black messengers. They can promote social ambivalence about our human rights, constantly under siege because of our race. As Wilson Key reminds his readers, in the mass media [and popular culture]:

> [C]onscious data are always superficial and illusionary and it is necessary to go beyond consciousness to gain a perspective into meaning–it appears there is much more going on in newspapers [and popular culture] than merely all the news that's fit to print (Key, 1981: 65).

Oprah's colour, size, gender, education, daily presence, disproportionate visibility and enormous public wealth all serve to reinforce the dangerously deceptive message that we are all playing on a 'level if (slightly bumpy) playing field', where Blacks can achieve as much as Whites. To the 'chosen few', picked to reap the rewards of the sacrificed many, the promise of extraordinary personal fame, wealth, political status or artistic freedom instead of work, shelter, dignity and human rights for all members of their group can be a seductive one. Louis de Jong, writing about the fragmentation of Jewish solidarity in Nazi-occupied Holland, sounds a similar warning. "It was a general practice to allow certain exceptions in order to be able maintain the general rule all the more easily" (De Jong, 2000: 360). Hannah Arendt, who quotes De Jong for the edification of posterity, advises us to pursue an "inner dialogue", to use deep thought as a counter measure to the moral confusion that stalks and can so easily trip us up when we are forced by circumstances to survive in pressure-cooker times (Arendt, 2000).

When we dialogue with ourselves, the words we choose take on particular weight. Peter Baehr reminds us, from his own insights into Arendt's writings, that words reveal identity. Arendt argues that through identity we make meaning, by weaving the many strands of our experience into a coherent history (Baehr, 2000: 409). My own observations in my work confirm this. The words we select for use, directly or indirectly, are intentional. I'm certainly not alone in asserting that historical biases are embedded in sexist and racist definitions such as 'fireman' or 'welfare queen'. Such terms, once treated as neutral by the dominant society are now held up to scrutiny and often denounced for reinforcing institutional bias. 'Fireman' fathers the ludicrous assumption that only men can fight fires, while 'welfare Queen' fills the air with toxic suggestions that impoverished Black women are this society's preeminent parasites (Lee, 1985: 39; Rainwater & Yancey, 1967).

Language often spreads like a bloodstain around Black pain in this society, from the slur 'nigger' to the taunt 'Aunt Jemima'. Those words have weight because of the historical baggage they drag behind them (Commission on Systemic Racism, 1994: 16). Hurtful words like those are metaphorical bullwhips that fall, in the societies where they have resonance, more severely on raw, vulnerable and exposed Black backs. In addition to slurs, there is a language that governments often use to deceive their populations. In an analysis of the officialese used to justify or hide the horrors of war, John Collins and Ross Glover offered this observation, "[Every] act of political violence…is intimately linked with the use of language" (Collins & Glover, 2002: 7). George Orwell, cited by the same writers, also affirms that the deliberate use of "euphemisms" makes violence more "palatable" (Orwell, 2002: 7). Marshall McLuhan throws further light on how euphemism works, pointing out, "immediate and overt honesty can be camouflage for ultimate exploitation" (McLuhan, 1981: ix). Moreover, McLuhan asserts that exploited populations generally invest in their own subversion, providing the very lubricant that makes euphemisms glide smoothly by in day-to-day exchange. He writes, "[women and] men are united only in their eagerness to be deceived by appearances" (McLuhan, 1981: ix).

Let us turn our attention to the specific experience of Afrikan men in North America. As an advocate for Black men, I contend that when we use the framework of class or patriarchy to analyze the behaviour of Black males in North America we must, to be fair, also take certain unique factors of the Black male experience into account. I use 'unique' because White patriarchy targets Black men as a group for public scorn, forced obsolescence, assassination and institutional violence more than any other group in this society (Davis, 2001; Serpico, 2000: 50). Houston Baker laments, "black male death is everywhere, everywhere around us" (Baker, 2001: 33). The collective memory of those who have been so brutally assassinated, exterminated or 'disposed of' in earlier times hangs, in mute witness, like a pall over Black communities today. Imari Obadele reminds us that, from Emancipation in 1865 until 1957, in the United States, over 100 (one hundred) Afrikans:

> [M]ostly but not exclusively male were roasted in barn fires, by Whites, or riddled with bullets or drowned or hung from trees...usually on suspicion of having lusted after...some White woman, or for having the courage...to organize... labor... [pursue] human rights or [standing] in defense of family... (Obadele, 1991: 254).

Since, as Wilson Key demonstrates, human behaviour usually follows the logic of our unexamined assumptions, it is important for us to explore the logic behind White society's atrocious treatment of Black men (Key, 1981). Observations of male domination and age-old biases concerning innate gender differences have tended to associate high levels of energy with males and by extension with male aggression around the globe. Feminist Maria Mies argues:

CLEM MARSHALL

[T]he emergence of male dominance over women is due to the historical fact that some men or groups of men were able to establish a monopoly over arms…[and that the] 'extraeconomic violence' against women and colonies has remained the basis for the establishment of the wage labour relation… (Mies, 1991: 8)

Child psychologist Marguerite Wright's observations address the concerns raised by Mies' analysis through the focus of a Pan-Afrikan lens, "Black males are more likely than males of any other race to be viewed as troublemakers and to be harassed by police" (Wright, 2000: 232).

Black men have been disproportionately portrayed and misused by Whites as sources of raw energy. Dominican monks seeking to alleviate the suffering of Brazil's First Nations, in 1511, offered up Afrikan men as substitute sacrifices and 'surplus' Afrikan energy as a rationale. They argued, "as the labour of one Negro was more valuable than that of four Indians, every effort should be made to bring to Hispaniola many Negroes from Guinea" (Williams, 1984: 37). In Jamaica, in 1832, a 'plantation owner' gave Afrikan physical superiority rather than mental or moral inferiority as a rationalization for Europe's crimes, noting, "[the] white man cannot labour under a burning sun, without certain death, though the negro can in all climates with impunity" (Walvin, 1993: 98).

With remarkable ease Black men slide from 'hardest worker' to 'ominous threat'. Hazel Carby recalls the persecution of Paul Robeson. Progressive Whites first treated him like a Black pet and then as a threat when he "rejected the terms and conditions on which his acclaim depended". Carby warns that contemporary icons such as golf champion Tiger Woods and basketball star Michael Jordan could easily suffer the same fate (Carby, 2001: 3). In fact, she tellingly draws our attention to the contradiction between corporate marketing strategies and social policies today. It allows "the multimillion-dollar international trade in black male bodies [in sports and advertisement to take place while] … hundreds of thousands of black male bodies [are] languishing out of sight of the media in the North American penal system" (Carby, 2001: 1).

A salutary example of the pervasive degradation of Black men by Whites in the United States comes from an unexpected source. Governor Lawrence Douglas Wilder of Virginia was the first elected Black governor in US history. A conservative and a Republican. Wilder looked almost White, had straight hair and in the style of his dress fit popular stereotypes of a rich White man. He was also the product of elite schooling and spoke with an upper class accent as a result.

On his own radio program, a fact that showed how privileged he was in contrast to most Black males in the United States, the governor recounted how a White guard choked him at a security checkpoint. In the course of doing so, he described how humiliated he felt during and after the guard's assault. Despite his harrowing experience, the 'almost-White' governor claimed not to know whether racism influenced the attack. Grace Carroll argues that the confusion and ambivalent reaction of Afrikans in similar situations are no surprise, given the absence of clear language identifying racism, sexism and other "micro-aggressions against our humanity" (Carroll, 1998: 20). On that fateful day, the privileged cocoon in which the governor chose to exist most of the time exploded on contact with the rabidly racist world in which Blacks with less choice must constantly live. Although intellectual debate today tends to see the concept of race as fluid, Black males continue to live within a granite hard, persistent tradition of gratuitous, White institutional violence that first forced exile upon our Ancestors and then stranded them on hostile foreign shores.

KUSHITISM, KEMETISM OR AFRIKAN SOUL

The use of the term 'animist', attached to Afrikan religious and spiritual rituals or practices, demeans Afrikans, ascribing inferior status to our ancestral faiths in comparison with the beliefs of Asians or Europeans (P'Bitek, 1980: 57, 59; Mbiti, 1970: 10; Woolson, 1977; Bhaktivedanta, 1981). It makes an arbitrary and ambiguous distinction between monotheism and polytheism since the Bible itself begins with a plural description of the Creative Force, "Then God said, Let Us make man in Our [emphasis added] image, according to Our likeness" (Nelson, 1985: 1). Historically, the misrepresentation of Afrikan religions has proved costly to the race since spiritual force is often an essential component in the survival of oppressed peoples. However, generations of Afrikans have deserted our spiritual heritage because of violence, coercion or because of the defamation spread by "the religions of The Book' (Williams, 1976).

The inner spiritual force invoked above is collective, ancestral, memory-based and so outside easy human reach or manipulation. Even the arch materialist Karl Marx links Jewish religious faith and spirituality to the group's success in material affairs:

> Since the real essence of the Jew is universally realized and secularized in civil society, civil society could not convince the Jew of the unreality of his religious essence, which is nothing more than the ideal expression of practical need (Marx, 1992: 241).

On the other hand, significant teachings of Muslims, Jews and Christians, popularly known as the peoples of 'The Book', and their surrogates, propagate embedded slurs against Afrikans (Blyden, 1994; Chinwezu, 1987: 135). During the fifteenth century European pillage of Afrikan populations, Christian authority lowered the bar to the point of defining Afrikans as people without souls while essentializing 'soul' as the defining attribute of human beings. As late as 1860, Irish immigrants living in New York City weaned on Christian beliefs thought of Afrikans as a "soulless race" (Pinkney, 1994: 263). That powerfully pernicious idea still resonates in dominant European and Asian circles through the language of texts on "world religions" and ancient spiritual "mysteries" (Woolson, 1977; Casson, 1977). For example, a publication called *Great Religions of The World* by the National Geographic Society covers a range of contributions ranging through Hinduism, Buddhism, Judaism and Islam to Christianity (National Geographic Society, 1971). In over four hundred pages, there is not one religious entry whose origin is associated with Black or Afrikan peoples in the popular mind - not Vodun, Yoruba, Shona or Gikuyu. By contrast, Jomo Kenyatta, Kenya's first president wrote that his people the Gikuyu worship "One High God, Ngai...on important traditional occasions [and at the same time] constantly commune with the spirits of their Ancestors" (Kenyatta, 1965: 222).

Hymn to Aton

We know

The One The Creator Aton

Chosen by the Sun we wed the Sun

And know The One from within The One

Freed from this foliage of flesh and dust

We root where Being is born

Scattering our seeds like exploding stars

We mount spiral stairways

Open doors into new beginnings

Hug Time flirt with Forever

Buried yet breathing again with spring

Bounding beyond our globe

Breaking through our eggshell skin

To incubate each secret part

Of every sacred art

We transcend science

In flashes lighting up our minds

All the Vastness beyond Vastness feels to us like home

CLEM MARSHALL

We float above heights of high

Plunge beneath depths of deep

Forge right into left fit up into down

Ashes by day we are fires at night

Our bones are flint hard as Nile water

Our hair is wool soft as Sakkara stone

Our backs bend to form new horizons

We are the black spores of our Mother the Earth

We are her rivers oceans and streams

Our sighs and tears spawn mists for every age

We color all that comes into Being

Shadow every womb on its way to the tomb

Cradle our own corpse as it awaits rebirth

Shuffle off the shroud of old crinkled skin

Guided by Time to leave the grave behind

We dance across Space

Soul bouncing soul

One Drum One Word One Unwinding Mind

We are Aton Endless Aton

Before Time is Time and Space is Space

Color is Color or Form is Form

One With The One from inside The One

Eye-seeing-into-Eye

Creator to Creator We know The Creator

The One Who Is The Many

Aton

(Marshall, 2004)

Monotheism is no stranger to Afrika. Rediscovered graven texts, such as the one at the source of the preceding adaptation in verse, can be found in many structures in Saqquara, in ancient Kemet – now within modern Egypt and Sudan (Simpson, 1998: vi). Those impressive architectural achievements were dedicated to the development of advanced technology as well as the sciences of the spirit and mind (Finch, 1999). Such awareness contradicts anti-Kushitic assertions that Afrikans lacked the monotheistic sophistication of Asian or European-based cultures. I find it useful to put the literary and philosophical accomplishments of my Ancestors into a contemporary context using our modern vocabulary. Those ancient Afrikan texts over 5000 years old have the authority of moral insight that speaks to us today (Freke & Gandy, 1999: 133). They therefore bear treatment as Afrikan scriptures as socially valuable as the more recent sacred texts that govern the Jew's Talmud, Christian's Bible, Muslim's Koran or the Hindu's Bhavagad Gita.

RACE AND RACEPROOFING

Today, definitions of race often provoke contention. It appears fashionable, I've observed, for pundits like Stanley Crouch to point out the biological imprecision of race with the smug air of scientists on the cutting edge of some momentous discovery (Crouch, 1995: 49). Often the tone of expertise also suggests more, implying that people who insist on speaking about race are either willfully backward or surreptitiously promoting racist ideas.

This study underscores the significance of race as an operational, as opposed to a biological category. In fact, looks are often an unreliable marker of race. In the video *The Way Home* (see Chapter Five) a speaker in the multiracial council with one Asian and one European parent says, "our race becomes our face" (Butler, 1998). Therefore, in a racist society, those who are marked for attack or undermined through race are obliged to pay attention to race, even if only as a strategy for self-protection. As Farai Chideya notes, "even advocates of a 'multiracial' category realize that issues of community and equality far transcend the language we use to describe each other" (Chideya, 1999: 55). However, there is also evidence of a competing compulsion among those at risk to dilute or forget experiences related to their gender, race, sexuality or other 'disturbing' identities (Reed, 1997; Archer, 1999).

At times I feel like a spectator at a race towards 'racelessness' in a relentlessly racist world. Constance Backhouse discovered this pervasive feature of Canadian history in her research on racist laws. "Some racialized cases are simply irretrievable", she tells us, "lost in the racelessness of the Canadian legal records" (Backhouse, 1999: 14). And she returns to this theme when she identifies "colour-blindness" as a part of the "false mythology of racelessness that has plagued the Canadian legal system for so long" (Backhouse, 1999: 274). As this professor of law points out, race cannot be ignored, if those targeted by racism in the society are to develop methods for dismantling racism. I call this identification strategy, 'raceproofing'. At its best it can provide a prophylactic, an invisible shield for both body and mind from accidental, gratuitous or deliberately abusive attacks.

Recently, in Canada, two professors of psychology and their researcher subjects who identify themselves as Jewish undertook a study, "to see how stressed they get when reading about the Palestinian-Israeli conflict" (Goldenberg, 2003: A5). The purpose of their study was to find out "the effects of perceived media biases [by measuring] the level of cortizol in...saliva [to] reveal how strung out the media coverage makes the participant" (Goldenberg, 2003: A5). A similar strategy is long overdue by psychiatrists and psychologists equipped, not only with tools of their discipline originally designed to address White needs, but also with appropriate instruments for addressing the diverse needs of selected Black populations. Vital work in that direction is already ongoing. Some Pan-Afrikanist healers, such as Joy De Gruy-Leary in the US are already committed to finding appropriate treatment for the traumas suffered by people of Afrikan ancestry. This study takes note of her concept, "post traumatic slave syndrome" in Chapter Two.

Alexander Thomas and Samuel Sillen cite a US survey that reveals, "[the] reluctance of white psychiatrists to recognize or to point out to patients that racial prejudice is an unhealthy symptom" (Thomas & Sillen, 1993: 152). Such research holds a potential yield of useful information for use in training counsellors for and from the Black community. This work opens a door on that discussion. Given the ubiquity of 'profiling' by police, discriminatory surveillance and defamation in the media faced by people of Afrikan ancestry in many societies, research on the health costs of racism by Pan-Afrikanists could someday be usefully applied to measuring and alleviating the impact of racism on day-to-day Black existence. In Canada, in 1993, the Ontario Court of Appeal concluded, "racism, and in particular, anti-black racism is a part of our [Ontario] community's psyche" (Commission On Systemic Racism, 1994: 43). What might be no more than a moral challenge to trouble the minds of a minority of non-Afrikans, however, remains a running sore of physical and mental anguish that can infect and diminish Black lives.

During a ceremony re-naming 'Lenox Avenue' as 'Malcolm X Boulevard' in Harlem, New York, in April 1987, I listened attentively when Gil Noble, the prominent host of TV's *Like It Is*, described himself as "a race man". For Afrikans living in the United States, particularly those belonging to the Civil Rights generation, the word man used publicly and with pride, carries a particular healing power. Until the nineteen sixties, within the dominant society, Black adult males remained publicly boys for life. Charlie Sifford, the first Black professional golfer to play at the famed Greensboro, North Carolina course tells how a gang of racists dogged his tracks and taunted him, "Hey, boy, [emphasis added] carry my bag" (Sifford, 1996: 602). So 'race man' is a title whose significance is widely understood in the older Black community in the United States, as is the term 'race woman', when applied to human rights pioneers like Ida B. Wells (Wells, 1970). Black communities tend to treat both terms as honorific forms of address that would normally foster positive reactions (Wells, 1970). Hazel Carby used the concept as the title of a book, by way of demonstrating that it incorporates notions of strength, self-determination, adulthood, unbowed, unfettered personhood and communal self-defence (Carby, 1998).

Within certain specified contexts, therefore, an otherwise macho term holds special meaning for Americanized Afrikans. As over-policed, over-incarcerated Black men, our masculinity in North American society often rests on shifting sands (Sabo, Kupers, London, 2001). Most Blacks are only marginally associated with common markers of male status and power, such as substantial private capital, property ownership, social mobility, highly regarded offices or occupations, being crowned 'kings' of popular music (including our own), freedom of movement in public spaces, the inviolability of one's body and a secure family life.

The institutions or systems where those experiences occur are consistently outside of our control. White males usually police the roles they permit Black males to fill and can treat us as 'males' only as long as doing so serves their interests and does not challenge White supremacy. It is their will that decides when and where Black men can function as surrogate patriarchal, sexist, macho or powerful White men. Unfortunately, although Black males are excluded from significant areas of White patriarchal privilege, they have been frequently incorporated into its misogynist agenda. Under that influence we have our roles as father, husband, family member or friend, our relationships to Black women and each other subverted, aborted, dismissed, devalued or detrimentally compromised, either by White supremacist power or our own internalization of it (Carby, 1998; Wells, 1970; Genovese, 1976: 484).

Adam Clayton Powell Jr., a 'race man', was arguably the most influential, elected Black politician in US history. Using his political clout, he shaped a range of projects that supported Black liberation, including scholarships to provide educational opportunities for a significant number of nationalist leaders in Afrika and Asia (Alexander, 1990: 135,123). Congressman Powell represented Harlem, New York, from 1945-1966 and was Chairman of the 'House Committee on Education and Labour', a budgetary body, in the 87th US Congress (Powell

Jr., 1994). Adam Clayton Powell Jr. is credited with injecting the phrase "Black Power" into US politics and popularizing the notion of Black resilience with the slogan, "Keep the faith, baby" (Alexander, 1990). Like Gil Noble, Adam Clayton Powell Jr. proudly defined himself as a 'race man'. Today, that term still wears connotations the 'ba-ad nigger' of yesteryear. 'Bad nigger' was the racist label Whites gave those Black people, like freedom fighter Harriet Tubman who refused to accept subjugation (McGovern, 1965). Other courageous Blacks like Malcolm X were also ready to stand up against frontal White attack by being 'ba-ad'. The spelling represents a Black tonal variation on the White slur, indicating a speaker's will to defy White power with actions that declare like Malcolm X, "We care nothing about the odds" (Malcolm X, 1981: 8).

In North America, we can chronicle changes in Black fortunes and evolving White notions of Black acceptability by tracing the use of 'race' as an adjective or noun. In this hemisphere 'race' as an adjective was once synonymous with 'Black' (or 'Negro'), while today the noun 'race' has expanded to embrace all people of colour in questions of bias or discrimination.

For example, from 1921 until 1949, all Black music was marketed as "Race Music" by the White cultural establishment in the United States (Haskins, 1987: 70; Garland 1971: 67). This title distinguished it from White music, which presumably was 'raceless'. Popular lore says, in fact, that the sound of Black music was inseparable from the prejudices against Blacks in White minds of the day. In radio interviews, pop star Elvis Presley was instructed to say where he went to school. Since segregation was still custom or law in the land, giving the name of his school would convince listeners that he was a White artist with exceptional skills in mimicking Blacks.

It is an unsettling irony that a mere decade or so later Presley, and not Chuck Berry or other originators of the sound, style and performance art he purloined, was illegitimately crowned the (White) "king of (Black) Rock-N-Roll' (Garland, 1971: 16-18). As long as Black music remained 'Race' music its social capital and the deed of its ownership remained mostly in Black hands. The change in name aggravated a contradiction in Black life under White control. It is the usual attribution of many if not most Black achievements to Whites. While it is by singing and playing together that Black artists have produced and created their innovative sound, popular culture and the media have named their inventions, "American music", "urban music" or "global music" (Kitwana, 2002; Kofsky, 1970). On the other hand, when Black men on a city's deadly streets or imprisoned in institutions destroy each other, the media label the phenomenon, "Black-on-Black violence" not the very American violence that it is (Wilson, 1991).

Race evolves in parallel spheres today even as Blacks and Whites live side-by-side and feed from the same cultural source. For Blacks, the term 'Race Music', in spite of its original negative intent, can provide a certain level of cultural security by telling the world that this was our music. In its time, the term also served to reinforce solidarity, instil pride in our collective creativity and provide a rare opportunity for Black folks to establish exclusive group ownership of valuable social capital. Samuel Floyd notes, "*Billboard* magazine introduced the term 'Rhythm & Blues' to replace 'Race' as a marketing label, but the term did not embrace jazz, traditional blues, and other folk genres as had the earlier designation" (Floyd, 1996: 176).

Generally, for Whites, 'race music' meant them (Blacks) and not us (Whites). It also symbolized Black emotions and passions that were out of White control. 'Racism' identifies polyrhythmic music as poachable territory like other Black possession such as our land, inventions, children or even our sexual performance, for 'needy' or 'greedy' Whites. Jerry Wexler, a White music magazine writer for *Billboard* from the North, dropped the "Race" title in order to slip under the racist radar that kept Whites, especially in the South, from buying Black music. In doing so, however, he made it easier for those same bigots to steal the cultural capital they had refused to buy. Indeed, even up North, there was widespread ambivalence in White attitudes to Black music. Great jazz artists like "Billie Holiday and Thelonious Monk had their [union] cards taken away...and spent years trying to get their cards back, while some [Black musicians] were refused cards outright" (Carby, 2001: 147). One ludicrous outcome was that, until 1990, there was a cabaret law in New York City designed "to control the supposedly degrading abandon of Black music" (Carby, 2001: 147). Yet, long before 1990 rolled around, Harlem's Black syncopation had travelled to Europe with American troops during WW II and blazed a trail for the successful marketing of 'American' culture around the world (Panassié, 1944).

If the uncomfortable truth were told, 'Race music' was, broadly speaking, a more accurate description of the Afrikan traditions that created Black music across the United States. It was race, more precisely racism that forced Afrikans to develop in a culturally separate space. It was 'race' that robbed Afrikans of the rich tradition and range of instrumentation they had been forced to leave behind and 'race' that forced pioneers like John Coltrane to re-invent ancestral ways of playing. It was 'race' that propelled exile and the nostalgia for a distant home into the centre of Black consciousness. It was 'race' that stripped Afrikans of shared healing spaces and turned us inward to dig for comfort inside our own souls. It was 'race' that made music the only socially possible expression of ancestral Afrikan rites to celebrate The Divine. I could easily recognize the logic of 'race music' in my travels across rural Afrika from the nineteen eighties and on. In villages where I stayed, I joined in ceremonies much like those I had known in the Caribbean, where major events were combinations of instrumental music, song, dance and feasting, all those expressions of our humanity that make us move and feel like one.

WHITE

I find it a challenge, and in some ways a presumption, to define any 'identity' I have never inhabited. And so I rely here on the work of White scholars who have brought their experience of Whiteness to the insights they share. At one end of the spectrum Whiteness is the Texas statute of 1906 that states, "All persons not included in the definition of "Negro" shall be deemed a white person within the meaning of this article" (McIntyre, 1993: 31). On occasion, when I encounter the anti-Kushitism of some 'persons of colour', from Asia or the Americas, I am tempted to credit White racists with having got their definition right when they named all "non-Negro" persons as "white" (Singh, 1997; Reed, 1997). Beyond definitions, however, undifferentiated 'Whiteness' has empowered all Whites and continues to give even the most marginalized among them potential caste-power over all Black people across a White defined world (Kivel, 1996). Even some groups universally recognized as persecuted have been afforded the umbrella of 'Whiteness' in relation to Blacks. Matthew Jacobson, among others, observes that, "Jews in the former slaveholding states of the [US] South were the first Jews in North America to see themselves as white [emphasis added] (Jacobson, 2000: 62).

The inherent power of White skin was established in, "The US law empowering the "Posse Comitatus" in 1793 that gave "any white person the right to seize an alleged fugitive" (McIntyre, 1993: 31). 'Whiteness' at that time became the property of "…the European peoples and their colonial progeny" (Jacobson, 2000: 75). In today's North American society it operates in the legal world. As contemporary social scientists like Alphonso Pinkney have documented, when mainstream institutions like universities, hospitals, political parties and schools make accusations against Blacks, those accusations are usually immediately treated like received truth (Pinkney, 1994: 120). Whiteness meant 'entitlement' for those Italians who invoked Affirmative Action to institute Italian American courses at City University of New York and also gain promotion for Italian professors on the back of the Black struggle for equality in education (Gioseffi, 1997: 162).

The concept can also be stretched to include the consciousness of members of 'Caucasians United for Reparations and Emancipation', a group of Whites who declared themselves followers of Elijah Muhammed's 'exclusively Black' Nation of Islam in the United States (Reed, 1997: 11). There is also room in Whiteness for progressives like the academic Robert Elliot Fox, who characterizes himself as "post-white [and] pan-human", and sees his peers also as, "can(n)on fodder" (Reed, 1997: xi-13). While some Whites are claiming the luxury of being post-White, however, Blacks are stuck, like the proverbial Tar Baby, with the unrelenting fallout of the ruin Whites have collectively introduced into uncounted Afrikan lives. It is against that consistent marginalizing experience of Blackness that Whiteness best defines itself.

In a world where 'equal' slides easily into 'same', it is understandably hard for many Whites to define Whiteness in terms of its fixed privilege or its role in oppressing Blacks. On the other hand, since Afrikans, in recorded history, have no collective or significant experience of persecuting Whites because of their race, Black populations find it a challenge to imagine Whites, whatever their ethnicity, as equal sufferers under the caste system they have imposed on us. It therefore becomes difficult for both races to find agreement in a common interpretation of what it means to be White. In his exploration of the subject Noel Ignatiev "asks how the Catholic Irish, an oppressed race in Ireland, became part of an oppressing race in America" (Ignatiev, 1995: 1).

The beleaguered Irish poor who escaped to North America in the nineteenth century quickly became 'White', holders of certificates of privileged humanity when thrown into competition with Blacks for housing, jobs or positions of social status. In fact, two groups, Irish and Jewish Europeans, both negatively racialized in Europe up to the twentieth century, achieved "Whiteness" once they came into the proximity of Black populations in the Americas (Gunther, 1992; Reich, 1991; Degler, 1971; Ignatiev, 1995). Similarly, in South Africa, even the most marginalized White immigrants from other parts of the world were stamped preferred under apartheid over all classes of Blacks (Cell, 1987; La Guma, 1978).

I accept Andrew Hacker's observation, "America is inherently a 'white' country: in character, in structure, in culture" and concur when he describes the state of American society as "America's version of apartheid" (Hacker, 1992: 4). Although that assessment may seem harsh, there's data to support it. After a White mob shot teenager Yusuf Hawkins in Bensonhurst, New York City, in August 1989, Black protesters marched in the neighbourhood where his killers lived. Residents wrapped themselves in American and Italian flags to jeer the marchers. Even as one White held up a sign saying, "We are not racists", however, another asserted when interviewed, "This is Bensonhurst. It is all Italian. We don't need these niggers [here]" (Pinkney, 1994: 185-200). Whiteness, in a race supremacist world, is as often blind to its contradictions it would appear, as men are generally blind to sexism in a patriarchal world. To quote Ralph Wiley's blunt words, "In the most dependably absurd American sense, 'White' means privileged, and 'Black' means unprivileged" (Wiley, 1996: ix). For my own usage I extend Hacker's remarks to include all of North America, Europe and countries like South Africa, Namibia, Senegal, Ivory Coast, Uganda, Zimbabwe and Kenya where Whites have imposed themselves, remain in significant numbers, and retain sufficient economic or political influence to dominate Afrikan daily life. In this work, therefore, I pay particular attention to debates around the "universalization of whiteness". For instance, Montag asks readers to consider how race theorists like Buffon imagine that "… to be white is to be human, and to be human is to be white" (Montag, 1997: 285). That insight might be one way of understanding why many people of color, when opportunity presents itself, prefer to identify as White. Carl Degler in fact reminds us that, in Brazil, the remarkably elastic category of White identity could be stretched to include even a "Negro who is wealthy" (Degler, 1971: 105).

In apartheid South Africa, all Japanese were accredited the status of 'honorary Whites' (Cell, 1987). One of my acquaintances from Mauritius, of mixed Afrikan racial parentage, told me that for business purposes he too was afforded 'honorary White' status. So too were selected Black dignitaries from adjacent Afrikan nations who the apartheid regime found politically useful. As a child in the Caribbean, I learned early to differentiate between 'real Whites' and 'local Whites'. Members of my family, I remember, would hold some of the 'local Whites' in contempt for denying their Afrikan roots. Often we would know the grandmother of the clan who in her private life was comfortably Afrikan but also notice that the 'Whitened' family would generally keep her conveniently out of the public light.

Among people with White skin there are also those who desire to separate their identity from Whiteness because they feel outside its circle of privilege through gender, religion, culture, sexuality or class (Allison, 1994: 13). Again because White professor, Robert Elliot Fox teaches Black Studies and is intentional about opposing racism, he describes his experience as moving from being White to "post-White". He writes that his "whiteness became porous as a result of living engagedly for seven years and living emotionally and intellectually in the world of black writing and black art for a much longer period" (Fox, 1997: 13).

Fox's argument presents difficulties for me, given the experience of Jews who lived as Germans in Germany for a thousand years before The Jewish Holocaust (Kivel, 1996). In their case cultural competence and lived experience did not transcend racialization. Does living in close proximity to women and studying women's writing and art also make some men, 'post-male'? The theory falls down in my analysis because Whiteness as identity is 'operational' and not 'intentional'. Viewed from that perspective, Fox cannot be "post-White" unless he operates in a social space which offers him the possibility for exercising his "post-White" sensibilities and for mediating the impact of patriarchal Whiteness on those who cannot be 'post-Black', 'post-Red' or 'post-Female'.

At a human level, it is tempting to move past those tensions that often seem to create impenetrable walls and prevent the meeting of progressive spirits across the race divide. However, I find value in leaving space for deeper learning to take place. For, sometimes, our very identity and social location have been integral in protecting us from those specific hardships that are critical to our understanding yet invisibly woven into the fabric of the daily lives we cannot share, the lives of members of those very groups we desire most to support. A generation ago the writer James Baldwin nipped false liberalism, and its offspring post-Whiteness, in the bud. He pointed out that we don't "cease playing a role simply because [we have] begun to understand it" (Baldwin, 1985: 291). Understanding is merely the beginning of consciousness, not its culmination.

My experience of making alliances with individuals and groups working for social justice has yielded some important lessons. Even where great need exists within our community, I've discovered, help from those with more social power can still taste of domination. As progressive individuals or organizations of all stripes, we can be allies and useful as witnesses for each other, without needing to exert influence over another's decisions, put our presence on display or take control of joint ventures. The famous anti-slavery raid at Harper's Ferry that unleashed the US Civil War in 1859 is a striking example of misguided, paternalistic zeal. The White revolutionary, the Rev. John Brown acted without the approval of Harriet Tubman, Mary Ellen Pleasant and other Black leaders who had made and funded comprehensive plans for a wider, national revolt (Wheeler, 1993: 101). John Brown's pre-emptive actions did not respect the process that his allies expected him to follow. He seemed to forget in taking the decisions he did, that Black liberation was about their freedom and rights and not his own.

Anxious to 'free' Afrikans from bondage, John Brown expropriated their right to choose the manner and time of setting themselves free. Yet informed choice, freely exercised, is fundamental to human dignity. In responding to an immediate impulse to take personal leadership in attacking the American government, Brown robbed abused Afrikans of a unique opportunity. For they were poised to reclaim the right to self-determination Europeans had wrested from their Ancestors and forcibly withheld from them all their lives. Brown, evidently with the best intentions, stepped into an apparent breach in Black leadership. However, he failed to take into account that artificial gaps in Black leadership have been a constant of Black experience since the disastrous intrusion of foreign forces including Arabs and Europeans into Afrikan life generations ago (Beshir, 1974: 10; Delany, 1993; Ani, 1994).

Chancellor Williams marshals records over thousands of years to support his theory that whenever Afrikans relaxed their vigilance and admitted outsiders from Asia or Europe catastrophe befell their First Nations (Williams, 1976: 255). On closer scrutiny, we discover that the continuous need for new leadership has been engineered by a historical disfigurement of Black society. There has been ongoing, relentless decapitation of Black resistance through assassination, defamation and marginalization of its chosen leaders in politics, culture or faith. Indeed, martyrdom and marginalization of leaders in the Black community have become predictable outcomes of our struggle and occur in every generation. Among the names that spring to mind are such icons as Malcolm X and Winnie Madikizela Mandela in liberations struggles and Paul Robeson in the arts (Carson, 1991; Wolfenstein, 1993; Robeson, 1981; Stuckey, 1984; Mandela, 1985; Somerville, 2003). Music critic Frank Kofsky sounds a warning note on the subject of White 'leaders' in Black causes. He writes, "the Negro 'cause' will always attract a scattering of white adherents; but these adherents do not in and off themselves suffice to alter the character of the movement which they penetrate" (Kofsky, 1970: 132). Through my Pan-Afrikanist lens, his observation rings true, not just for music but other areas of Afrikan life as well.

Today's media frequently reinforce paternalistic attitudes by airing infantilizing images of Black adults or leaders from around the globe. TV features a proliferation of aid groups with European or Asian faces in charge of rescuing Afrikans from Afrikan violence. Alternatively we watch innocent Afrikan civilians falling prey to 'generic Afrikan incompetence', cleverly implied by an absence of images of Afrikans doing for self (Pieterse, 1996). In fact, even at home or in schools where progressive administrators or teachers have influence, we often teach Black self-determination framed within texts written by Whites and frozen in the past (Rotberg, 1973). At the same time, progressive Black educators may also feel obliged to display our own pluralistic credentials by retaining progressive Whites in leadership roles, even in the spaces where we are gathered to learn more about ourselves. The contradictions at the heart of our experience create a dichotomy in our practice. 'Whitefaces-in-charge' too often remain the dominant, operational model even when we say we intend to provide leadership experiences for Black youth. Such situations inevitably send out mixed messages to those younger eyes trying to reconcile what we say with what we do.

Of course, White leadership is no more natural for Blacks than male leadership is for women. As Pan-Afrikanist educators it is therefore important for us to explain why Whites are so often at the head of Black projects. To begin, generally speaking, Black populations are dispossessed and under constant stress, a situation that usually translates into cycles of need. Secondly, when a group is inordinately stressed, its members naturally welcome help from every credible source. Such realities set up their own dynamic and create situations in which Whites with money or social power get invited into needy Black spaces. None of the arguments above, however, explains why so many Whites then agree to lead. Experience and logic tell me that the explanation lies elsewhere. Even progressives, it appears, can be tempted to relieve fears of being called 'racist' by making themselves visible champions of the racially oppressed. Such situations are so seductive and hard to see that both Blacks and their White allies need to practice self-criticism as a matter of course.

For example, in the foreword to *Bittersweet Encounter*, C. Eric Lincoln mapped out some of the contradictory ways in which the two groups saw each other during the US Civil Rights era:

> [T]here is evidence that Jewishness is not a high priority for some contemporary youth from Jewish families. But to Black people it often seemed that the Jew has had it both ways. He could be "white" when it was convenient, and he could be "Jewish" when he pleased. But he was never Black, so whatever vulnerabilities he suffered were in a sense (1) voluntary, (2) relative (Weisbord, Stein, 1972: xii).

Similarly, some White feminists acknowledge Black feminist bell hook's caution that, "identifying oneself as oppressed [does not free] one from being an oppressor" (hooks, 1981: 6-9). Again, looking at the unequal relationships between women from a global perspective, Angela Miles argues that, "[while] we are not responsible for having established these [exploitative] relations, we are responsible for acknowledging and opposing them" (Miles, 1996: 103). Ann Bishop shares Miles' activist approach. While arguing for a panHuman, "interdependent" movement, "toward a society based on co-operation", her position is clear, "I am not saying...we should just learn to get along; [that] denies a long, complicated history and all the terrible scars that need healing, collectively, before we can live together in peace" (Bishop, 1996: 11). There are also other models of what self-critical allies can do. During apartheid, an eighty-year-old White activist, Gladys Emma Lee, was often a lonely picketer in Cape Town, South Africa. Frequently, her principled and critically conscious positions would expose hypocritical attitudes within the racist government and liberal White opposition circles alike (Caccia, 1977: 23).

From a Black feminist perspective, bell hooks does some book-keeping on social change. In North America, she notes that, "without...assassination of...leaders...[or] police brutality...white women" benefited from the Black human rights movement, its parade of martyrs and incalculable, invisible costs in lives destroyed (hooks, 1995: 54). Yet Patricia Hill Collins also points out that inside US trade unions and political parties, two of the places where Black men have acquired institutional power, they have marginalized women while monopolizing leadership positions, like their counterparts in White skin (Collins, 1991: 141). As a Black man, I am conscious that our collective oppression does not free us from being sexist oppressors of Black women. As a Pan-Afrikanist I am still trying to find out how women and men related to each other in societies predating the intrusion of foreign beliefs. I also acknowledge that globally, as men, we have historically oppressed women. It was in direct response to his desire to interrupt ongoing gender inequity that Derrick Bell left his job as a Black law professor at Harvard to make way for Harvard to hire a Black female in his stead. It was a, "noble sacrifice" and a model for other Black men. Clearly, however, his action could not alone transform the culture of Harvard or other universities (Wiley, 1996, 139). On the other hand, it shows Whites who claim to be and are progressive that they can make similar choices.

In this society, Whiteness also frames the gender and political relationships between Black women and men although most of our interactions usually take place on a more private stage. Musical and cultural critic Tricia Rose's research reveals:

> [W]omen rappers cannot be situated in total opposition to male rappers [and that] they critique and support male rappers' sexual discourse in a number of contradictory ways. [However] "in the mainstream press…female rappers felt that they were being used as a political baton to beat male rappers over the head, rather than being affirmed as women…[and the White press ignores] male rappers' works [that] take an explicit stand against sexual violence against women (Rose, 1994: 150).

Calvin Hernton's work accurately identifies the, "primary subject matter of the film, *The Color Purple*…(as) black-on-black (male against female) oppression" (Hernton, 1987: 5). I am not unaware of other potential forces, at work in the film, bent on transferring primary guilt and blame for Black female oppression from the shoulders of White men to the 'whip-friendly' backs of Black men. However, I am persuaded by a Black feminist critique that reminds us that Hernton's voice has few echoes among Black men. Society, it argues, will therefore lose an important perspective if his courage is not respected and he is silenced, Since only Black men can stop Black male oppression of Black women, Calvin Hernton reminds us that that burden and challenge remains ours alone.

In North America, living within the orbit of White supremacy, Black men are unjustly projected as the primary predators of White women. As a consequence, White patriarchal society, directly or indirectly, targets us for torture, humiliation, mutilation and death (Ginsburg, 1988; Patterson, 1971; Raper, 1970; Baker, 2001). Whether in pre-Emancipation or post Civil Rights North America, Black men have an ambivalent relationship with White women. That's because, within certain contexts, they are allowed to wield patriarchal power over Blacks. The words of a young Black man born into bondage generations ago illustrate the conundrum, "I thought slavery wuz right. ... My young missus loved me, and I loved her. She whupped me sometimes-I think, just for fun, sometimes" (High, 1988: 456). As this anecdote reveals, even when the White female hand falls less heavily on a Black male or female's head, or is even considered a sometime caress, it remains an oppressor's dangerous hand.

In the video *The Way Home*, a White woman describes herself, "as a Lesbian...[and] as a woman who grew up in poverty", admits that she "...can frequently find ways to distance [herself] from privilege". The speaker then goes on to outline a process of rationalization that allows her to remain 'unsoiled' even when there is 'dirt' all around. "Part of the way I distance myself from a racist culture that is built on economics in part is that I say that I'm not really a part of it because I don't have that privilege..." (Butler, 1998). In pluralistic North American society, groups identified by ethnicity, sexuality or another identity and targeted for oppression experience progressive levels of marginalization from the centre of White patriarchal power.

However, like victims of aerial bombardment in a war, some populations have access to shelters while others do not. Whiteness, even for White women who are vulnerable to multiple types of oppression, operates as a shelter into which they can sometimes retreat to avoid social annihilation. In North American society today, there are few if any comparable shelters for Black women and men.

A contemporary example of the attitude of Black males towards threats posed by faceless White women, even in ultra-sophisticated New York City, illustrates how vulnerable we generally feel. Over a period of months in 1984, White male transit officers randomly charged Black men with fictitious sexual abuse of White women. The officers lied deliberately and calculated that none of the women would ever be called to testify. Yet, already convinced of the way the legal system would work against them, seventy percent of the innocent Black men they charged entered guilty pleas to crimes they did not commit (Pinkney, 1994: 120). White women and Black men are both trapped in a web of patriarchal White supremacy. While White women, and indeed the general society, have been taught to view Black men inside a frame of assault and rape, many Black men have learned to see White women as a dangerous presence with the potential to derail our lives. However, other Black men inhabit a parallel mindscape, in which they seek out White women as protectors whose partnership makes them more palatable to White patriarchy. The writer Houston Baker ironically notes that, as interracial relationships proliferate, how "progressively 'lighter and lighter' the 'race' is becoming" (Baker, 2001: 33).

At the same time, my experience suggests to me that in White supremacist, patriarchal space, Black men are defined in polar opposition to White power and so denied independent male power. When they appear powerful, therefore, it is as 'pretend clones' or willing surrogates of White male power. Historically, Whites, both male and female, can treat Black men like women by silencing them, stripping them of social power and reducing them to sexual objects or sexual caricatures. James Baldwin offers us a snapshot of the way society dehumanizes Black men, "As if you're nothing but a walking phallus... no head, no arms, no nothing" (Baldwin, 1983: 113).

That was the literal image Robert Mapplethorpe, a Gay White photographer offered his viewers. Other 'progressive' designers of advertising campaigns have featured naked-like Black men selling everything from milk to exotic wars in far-off foreign lands (Gubar, 1997: 173; Smith, 1983). I use the upper case when referring to 'White' identity, although most writers, whatever their race, do not, to correspond with 'Black'. An individual who identifies as 'White', many observers cogently argue, does not suffer the same disadvantages as Blacks in this society. There is no verbal equivalent to 'Negro' or 'nigger' in English for those seen as 'White'. An upper case "B" for Black makes a statement about rehabilitation for Afrikans who have faced generations of defamation and stigma, burdens Whites do not bear. Nevertheless, I have found that although uniform use of the upper case ignores differences that Whites and Blacks experience in their daily living, doing so protects serious discussions of racism from descending into a dispute over linguistics, grammar or technicalities of font and size.

WHITE SUPREMACY

From observation, the terms 'racism' and 'anti-racism' appear to be firmly anchored in the ongoing discourse of discrete academic disciplines such as 'Administration', 'Governance' or 'Education' (Yeboah, 1988; Dei, 1996). However, 'White supremacy' has less currency, although, as a concept, it is often used by Pan-Afrikanists interchangeably with racism. This is in no way intended to dismiss the work of those academics that have explored White supremacy at length in their areas of expertise. (Oates, 1983). Other writers have devoted whole books to grappling with teaching the complexities of the concept (Cell, 1987). For the purposes of this examination of how language is used to subvert liberation, however, I am primarily interested in what I experience as banal, avuncular and paternalistic 'White supremacy', the infinite detail of the degradation and subordination that limit Black life in White societies.

Philosopher Hannah Arendt eloquently identifies the quality of such "banality" in the context of the extreme evil of Nazism (Baehr, 2000: 113). Arendt's thoughtful observations on the relationship of Nazis and Jews contain insights about Black and White relationships in today's consciously 'global' world. I feel particularly compelled to understand a strain of White Supremacy that operates so unobtrusively it may even appear benign. Far too often, it jumps out at me when I least expect it, like the vengeful shark in the film *Jaws*. In the way that story unfolds, the shark repeatedly leaps up from the calmest of waters to crunch off limbs or swallow its victims whole. Then, as it digests them, calm descends on the world once more. In the film, the seascape returns to 'normal' so quickly that we are left wondering if the bloody events witnessed a moment before were nothing more than a dream. In my experience, White supremacy can feel like a dangerous whale swimming through Black life, chewing off life chances at random or, more often than not, swallowing up all of our physical energy, our culture, our dreams and, deep below a deceptively surface of daily routines, devouring our souls.

As we negotiate our way through society, most of us automatically put up our guard against rudeness, slurs or the threat of violent attack. Some female writers, for example, note that they live with a heightened perception of sites that signal danger for them but are safe for males (Lees, 1996: 73). I find that I am most vulnerable to White supremacy when paternalism, as invisible and odourless as carbon monoxide, is in the air. In a society where to 'support' more powerful individuals, social groups, politicians and their ideas often means 'obeying' them, it is easy to slip into cycles of subordination and then rationalize them away (Arendt, 2000: 375).

By way of illustrating benign White supremacy, I've drawn an example from a sociological study, *Drylongso*, carried out by John Gwaltney inside Black northeastern urban communities in the US in the nineteen seventies (Gwaltney, 1980). Its findings reflect the wisdom gained by lived experience and in-depth research. John Gwaltney, with the heightened hearing of the blind, listens as participants in his study describe everyday encounters with Whites. The interview I refer to here took place decades ago, but its insights reflect such emotional intelligence they still ring true about how Blacks and Whites measure each other across racial divides.

Porter Millington is in his seventies at the time of his interview with the sociologist. This elder not only distils the wisdom of his years but also makes links to what he had learned at his father's knee. He recalls an incident connected to cooking as part of celebrations for the New Year. One item on his special good luck menu is his specialty, a fruit-based drink he calls, "my jackie", which he decides to share with his White employers, who can't get enough of it. Then, it seems, after he had entertained his guests over several visits, race supremacy kicked in. Instead of thanking him and asking for his special recipe so they could try it themselves, they suddenly became the experts. As Porter Millington told John Gwaltney, "[They] told me how to make my Jackie. They argued with me about how to make my own drink" (Millington, 1981: 103).

His story feels immediately like received truth to Black folks because we have been inundated with images of successive White 'kings' and 'queens' of our music. Somehow icons materialize out of thin air, often with minimal cultural contact with Black communities, generation after generation, to dominate the charts and walk away with the prize money from Gospel to Rap, wherever our music is performed (Kofsky, 1970; Foster, 2000). In Canada, there is even a self-defined White 'master kora player'. After a chance meeting, he exchanged a few favors with a wandering kora artist for a lifetime career. Although his teacher could never make a living from his art in North America, this White disciple is now marketed as a global authority in kora playing. He performs in a field that most Afrikan musicians would accept as the exclusive territory of certain families or clans who raise their children from birth to function as the musicians and historians, 'gewel' (in the Wolof language) of their communities. In Afrikan society, Kora2 playing is in fact not seen as a skill to be picked up by strangers after a few months or years, but is honored instead as a culturally intense and secret ancestral tradition, passed down from parent to child and vital to the survival of the society from which it comes (Stagliano, 1984; Suso, 1993).

As a Black person, it sometimes feels as if Whites, as a group, are determined to out-Afrikan Afrikans and beat us at being ourselves. In a bizarre tilt at reality, US President Bill Clinton was named to the

Black Hall of Fame in Little Rock, Arkansas in 2002. Black politician Rodney Slater claimed, "It is not about the skin. It is about the spirit and soul of this soul brother" (Slater, 2002: 21) Because Slater probably felt obliged, out of personal gratitude for his own appointment to high office, to prove his loyalty to Bill Clinton, his words are understandable. Randall Robinson argues that, in fact, there is little to convince a careful student of political reality of Clinton's generosity or concern for Blacks in a collective sense (Robinson, 2000: 99-106). However, what is harder to grasp, is why President Clinton would allow himself to be placed in such an ambiguous public position. It strains the imagination to think of him being offered and then accepting a place in a "Woman's Hall of Fame' because of his laudable appointments of women to previously 'male' offices in his administration. This incident and others of a similar nature seem to suggest that race supremacy strikes its victims with a particularly virulent strain of blindness to reality.

Our images of "the beat generation", for example, are not of the Black jazz artists whose rhythmic inventions formed the base of "the beat". Rather we have been taught to invest their capital in White writers, poets and other artists who fed their own art from the innovative techniques of Black living, music and speech (Jones, 1963: 233). The irony deepens, however, when Whites appoint themselves guardians of the standards that define excellence in Black music (Jones, 1963: 235). Nick La Rocca, a clarinetist from the disingenuously named, Original *Dixieland Jazz Band*, a White group that slavishly copied Black artists, even made the startling claim, "The Negro did not play any kind of music equal to White men at any time…Even the poorest band of white men played better than Negroes" (LaRocca, 1997: 165). Even Louis "Pops" Armstrong did not escape the paternalism of one studio engineer who felt compelled to teach him how to swing. On the modern behind-the-scenes version of a 1954 Columbia Records recording of W.C. Handy's *St. Louis Blues* we hear someone with a distinctly European immigrant accent telling "Pops" and the peerless vocalist Velma Middleton how to put more swing into their own 'Black thang'.

Parallels to his attitude appear wherever Whites have gained en-trée into formerly closed Afrikan spaces. In an autobiographical text, James Hall, a White man, "from conservative Winnetka, Illinois, a for-mer Eagle Scout and a Catholic" is aware of the inherent contradiction in his role as pretender to the traditions and powers of an Afrikan spir-itual leader. Rhetorically he wonders how he "[becomes] a candidate to be an African shaman?" (Hall, 1994: 3). In the end, however, he con-vinces himself that he can become an instant-mix 'sangoma' in South Africa. In addition, by some counter-intuitive, telescopic computation of racial supremacy, he also believes that he can instantly embody the lived, collective experiences of countless millennia that qualified his Black teachers to become spiritual leaders of their own communities in sacred, ancestral Afrikan ceremonies and religious rites.

Such examples are convincing evidence that, when Blacks and Whites get caught up in bubbles of interracial warmth, their emotional high often makes them vulnerable to mutual cultural delusions. Of-ten their good feeling feeds into historical miseducation and inveigles White apprentices into treating their guides into unknown Black cul-tural territory like 'informants', children, acolytes or pets (Rotberg, 1973: 8). Merely naming 'White Supremacy' or 'racism', however, does not necessarily produce deep thought, cognitive dissonance, trauma or a change in White attitudes. On the other hand there are two words that inscribe and promote Black subjugation even as they describe it. That is why I explore the misuse of language and its role in degrading Afrika, in Part Two and demonstrate how excavating corrosive words and reframing them within an Afrikan-centred historical context can enhance consciousness and advance Pan-Afrikan re-education. The following chapter offers an analysis of those two words, slave and ni—er as a strategy for count(er)ing their costs.

2
Book

Part II:
Degrading Afrika

2
Chapter

WOUNDING WORDS

● ■ ● ● ● ■ ● ● ● ■ ● ● ● ■ ● ● ● ● ■ ● ● ● ■ ● ●

A Songbird's Last Song
Snakes swallow
Songbirds
Down
When songbirds
Forget how to fly
Slowly
The songbird
Slides down a throat
Screaming terror
Crying hell
From its eye
First
Snakes
Freeze a songbird's blood
With pricks
From a poisoned quiver
Shooting a dart
Straight to the heart
With a whispered hiss
Shush ni—er

(Marshall, 2004)

NI−ER: EXPLORING THE POWER OF A TOXIC NOUN

Words that wound not only corrode but also annihilate the very self that is the substance of self-determination. My early exposure to the Bible, in school and at home, left my head ringing with curses that Old Testament prophets launched against kings, potentates and populations steeped in sin. Subsequent experiences, and especially those linked to my sojourn in Afrika, have reinforced my sense that there exists a popular, unspoken yet widespread culture of respect for defiant words. Vulnerable, marginalized, oppressed groups or individuals, I've discovered, often use coded utterances both as weapons of offence and self-defence. In present time, I follow with bemusement the passion that incites unapologetically ethnocentric and supremacist politicians from "settler" and "colonizing" nations, such as White leaders in the US and South Africa, who object to being labelled "racist" (Cell, 1987). Their feeling often finds resonance even within academic circles and workshops on equity offered today. Across the color spectrum, I continue to witness exchanges that betray a deep vein of resistance to the use of 'anti-racist' in describing any part of my personal research or educational practice. There is resistance, as often from Blacks as well as from Whites, to recognizing the deep emotions that accompany the naming of racism as well as a corresponding refusal to treat those feelings with commensurate respect.

As the most overt practices and markers of imperialism, colonialism and segregation learn to hide behind a language of equality, it has become increasingly difficult to specify or identify the agents of the racist hegemonies that influence our daily lives. Noticing race is often taboo to many individuals who would confidently describe themselves as advocates of social justice. For example, editorial opinion by a writer identified as, "a Vice President of the Center for Equal Opportunity" in the United States contends, "tracking race polarizes the nation" (Miller, 1997: 14A). His statement suggests that it is the response to racism rather than the injustice of racism that constitutes a social danger and creates racial conflict between groups. His thinking parallels statements made by South Africa's first Black president, Nelson Mandela and echoed by the nation's leading educators, "Non...racialism recognizes South Africans as citizens of a single rainbow nation, acknowledging and appreciating difference and diversity" (Mandela, 1997: 6; Turner, 1997). How, one wonders, can the divisions of many generations and the stain of apartheid be so easily wiped away?

Words can and do hurt. That hurting potential takes shape by conferring security, comfort and self-definition and determination, on some, while prescribing domination, stress and subjugation for others. For example, feminist thinkers like Bernice Webb in Britain and pro feminist artists like the dramatist Bernard Shaw have explored terms like 'slut' and 'whore', to expose how popular discourse routinely treats them as both 'understood' and synonymous with female immorality. Even France's famed realist novelist, Emile Zola, was not above putting pen to prejudice. He bequeathed to posterity a misogynist image of a "whore", prescribing that, "The rage of debasing things was inborn in her" (Kistainy, 1982: 23). What, fairness demands, is the male equivalent of "whore"?

My Pan-Afrikanist approach defines our destiny as an equal partnership between women and men, linked to ancestral Kushitic cultural values. In order to establish our immediate priorities, we would study each situation and pass it through the prism of collective, collaborative visions for the future. It follows that today's Pan-Afrikanism demands vigilance against the deep current of sexism that has devalued female leadership, created conditions that encourage gendered strife, undermined respectful collaboration and destroyed nascent liberation movements. Nor can Pan-Afrikanists ignore the misogyny on continuous display in the language of our youth and how it is spread by the commercialized popular culture. Deborah Root notes, "the apparent seamlessness between culture and the marketplace means that anything can come under the purview of capital" (Root, 1996: 86). Her words take on added significance when we link them to Nelson George's commentary on student attitudes on the campus of historically Black Morehouse

College in Atlanta. The writer describes how young Afrikans, both female and male, were ready to justify, "defend and party to the sexist chants [and misogynist lyrics] of 2 Live Crew" because singer Luther Campbell's, "getting paid [getting super rich] justified everything" (George, 1999: 180-181).

Whether the slur used is "whore", "ho" or "chickenhead", a Hip Hop term that brands some young women as only capable of being mercenary and shallow, the expressions are not mere definitions that describe or predict behavior (George, 1999: 184). They form part of an arsenal of sounds and sights, words and pictures that concretize the domination and devaluation of women of Afrikan ancestry. The hurting words cited above are designed and used to strip Black women of their power and keep them in their place (Rose, 1994). They stand in the path of Pan-Afrikanist education and the enhancement of liberatory consciousness. In the examples we've reviewed, language serves as a central 'seminal' as opposed to 'ovular' instrument with which men verbally assault women in our society and, within Hip Hop culture, single out young Black women for particular abuse.

Keeping those thoughts in mind, I pay attention to a comment made, en passant, by an English linguist in 1836. It reveals in part how hurting words have been deliberately invested with noxious meanings that give them the power to destabilize Black psyches. Godfrey Higgins demonstrates that Europeans often hid the truths they believed about Afrikans while publicly embracing convenient, self-serving lies. By way of buttressing his argument that all humanity descended from "one pair" and that that couple was "black", the writer takes his readers into his confidence. He however admits that "[he would] find as few persons [in England] to agree with [him], as the African negroes do when they tell Europeans that the devil is *white.*" In a confessional tone rarely recorded by Europeans of his day he continues between parentheses, "(And yet no one, except a West-India planter, will deny that the poor Africans have reason on their side)" (Higgins, 1992: 51).

What most strikes me about Godfrey Higgins' statements, however, is how differently Afrikans value blackness and whiteness in the mid-nineteenth century from today. That the original observation quoted puts 'white' in italics indicates to me, as a reader, that Higgins was aware that it would be difficult for his contemporaries to admit that any culture would consider 'whiteness' a sign of moral depravity. Does he then assume that the fantasies of White supremacy were so deeply embedded in the popular psyche of his day that even informed Whites would see no 'truths' but their own? How significant, therefore, that Blacks were able to override the conditioning of White society and embrace the popular anthem of anti-racism in the US Civil Rights Movement during the sixties, James Brown's, "*Say it loud, I'm Black and I'm Proud.*" Brown's popular culture hymn heralded Afrikan reinvestment in the value of Blackness generally and especially in Black dignity, against all odds. This rebirth took place even though, between Higgins's time and Brown's, global Afrika had been so successfully indoctrinated that many of her children, our parents and peers, had learned to attach and internalize debilitating ideas of mental and moral inadequacy to both Black culture and skin (Moore, 2002: 166).

WHEN WHO WE ARE SEEMS WHAT THEY SAY

Through O.J. in blackface on the cover of Time

We are violence against women screaming helpless in their homes

Through Sistahs policing police in that jury of White peers

We are courts coddling criminals in a system soft on crime

Through the jungle of White science with its Green Monkey myths

We are tales of tangled sex and scary carriers of AIDS

Through Hollywood reruns of Birth of a Nation lies

We play thugs invading homes for fixes of crack cocaine

Through campaigns
Against circumcision and Gangsta Rap
We are mutilating sexual brutes and mutant sexist pigs
Arrogantly endangering every woman's right to be
Through BET's booty bottoms
Below pumped-up breasts
We are in-your-face lust light years beyond disgust
Cold-blooded corruptors of innocent teens
Time bombs ticking with world damnation
Dangling from our damaged genes
Through Jerry Springer deadheads
We are the best argument for sterilization by any state
Through reconciliation a la Rodney King
We are reparations as waste
Cash flushed down the drain
Through Willie Horton campaign ads
We are revolving prison doors
Dark rapist shadows lurking beneath beds
Legions of lazy Black males
Phantoms of fleeing fatherhood
A mockery of mothering and welfare queens
Through The Bell Curve
We are affirmative action forced fed to better folk
Firing of the best
Hiring the undeserving and unqualified
Through Rwanda
We were always genocide
Exterminating our own
Like President Mbeki of South Africa
We are ignorance breeding AIDS
Like President Mugabe of Zimbabwe
We are Idi Amin clones
Robbing industrious settlers

Peacefully farming our wasted empty lands
Brainless bullies of innocent Gays
Through sound bites on radio
Clips on CNN
We are metaphors for suffering
Owners of famine
Poverty engrained in the bone
Exotic deaths by mystery disease
Vanishing Nature
Ethnic hates
Landscapes of garbage humans stalked by vultures
Carelessly posed around
Through Oprah
We are proof that those who don't make it
Have them selves to blame
Through infinite confirmations of every blemish or fault
Our only good fortune lies in this
That sacrificing Saviors
White Jedi knights
Daily risk both life and limb
To rescue Us, Earth's foolish Black Folks from ourselves
(Marshall, 2004)

Word and deed function often as one in the history of Afrikans in this hemisphere and both are embedded in the layers of persecution that have shaped our lives. At presentations on teaching the Maafa to mostly White teachers and administrators, I am regularly asked about the appropriateness of books that use what teachers call the "n-word". Educators often cite, *To Kill a Mockingbird* or *Huckleberry Finn*, novels that most participants and the academy generally consider interracial 'classics'. Uniformly, White teachers, and less predictably Black ones, defend those books on literary merit or on the grounds that students like stories that promote positive relations across race.

I am not persuaded by their argument. My own experience, from observation and participation in classroom work covering Social Studies or Sociology, from primary school to university, refutes it. Firstly, when we have clear evidence of White atrocity, as in the Los Angeles police beating of Rodney King that an onlooker captured on video, teachers generally try to move past any discussion as fast as they can. Secondly, to date, no teacher at any level has offered to use photographs of Whites lynching Blacks as a teaching tool. Some have argued that their students, colleagues, and especially the parents they served, were unprepared for such strong fare and would see showing such pictures as promoting hatred against White people. A third example confirms the reluctance of teachers to deal with negative images or words about Whites. A famous anti-apartheid poster by the late US artist Keith Haring shows a giant, black cartoon figure with its foot on a small, white figure holding a noose around the black one's neck. When I shared it during anti-apartheid educational activities, some teachers complained that it would frighten the children and demanded that their administration take it down.

On the other hand, judging by the frequent presence of texts such as *To Kill A Mockingbird* and *Huckleberry Finn* in curricula for racially mixed student populations, educators seem generally comfortable with asking Black students to work through whatever discomfort or distress they feel about racist stereotypes 'for their own good'. That good is defined as an opportunity to benefit from the literary or moral learning conveyed by the text. Yet, as Joy De Gruy-Leary argues, terms like 'nigger' and certain situations that may not adversely affect all students can trigger feelings of deep humiliation for Blacks. She compares such feelings to flashbacks similar to those brought on by post-traumatic stress caused by war or rape (DeGruy-Leary, 2001). As a social worker she conducted research and created a psychological scale for measuring the affliction she names, "post traumatic slave syndrome." She argues that although it may not put every Afrikan individual at risk it can expose significant numbers of vulnerable Blacks to severe adverse effects. We have no system for assessing the state of mind of students who fall into that category when they enter the classroom. However, we can logically assume that they would experience severe stress when the word 'nigger' is read or said, especially in mixed company.

In the case of negative portrayals of Whiteness, however, teachers, in my experience, are apt to respect the feelings of White students. Their sensitivity to that community then influences the curriculum they choose and guides how they teach it. Speaking candidly, a White male, Paul Kivel observes, "When the subject is racism nobody wants to be white, because being white is 'bad' and brings up feelings of guilt, shame, embarrassment and hopelessness" (Kivel, 1996: 147). White faculty, students and community members frequently challenge speakers who use the term 'racist', on the grounds that it is unfair, makes them feel guilty and stifles the free expression of opinion. Yet, as I noted earlier, 'racist' is still a relatively new word in public discourse. In my experience, at conferences and in seminars, speakers sometimes scale the heights of circumlocution in order to avoid saying 'White' and 'racist' or put 'male' (meaning White male) and 'violence' in the same phrase.

In my view it is important to explore how individuals, to whom 'ni—er' does not usually apply, appropriate the right to use it as they see fit. When, as Black identified individuals, we use 'nigger' in race-specific Black gatherings, tensions rarely emerge. Unless a Black-identified person within the group 'ni—erizes' or mocks another individual's lips, colour or hair, the word floats freely around. In fact, 'nigger' often functions as a kind of mild glue that binds a group of friends or even strangers closer together. It bears witness to their shared ancestry and collective vulnerability. Once outsiders enter the circle, however, the dynamics are bound to change.

In the fall of 2002, the Canadian Broadcasting Corporation held a forum on police 'profiling' (discriminatory surveillance, arrest and charges against Blacks) at Lord Dufferin PS in Regent Park, an inner city Toronto area with a significant Black population that reports a history of police harassment (Pedicelli, 1998; Marshall, 2002). The moderator Andy Barrie did not challenge a high-ranking police officer for repeating the word ni—er in response to a Black mother who used it, as she explained, in an effort to convey the painful reality she lived. Instead Barrie needled another Black woman, disrespectfully in my view, with the question, "What is your community going to do about your thugs?" (Marshall, 2002) Although police officers, adults entrusted with protecting our youth, beat up Black teenagers, as has been documented in Ontario courts, Barrie and other media personalities have never called them thugs.

That incident prompts me to speculate that Barrie would not have permitted a Black person to refer to the police as 'pigs' to their face during that same forum. Yet 'pig' used to be innocuous and in common usage, until supporters of Black resistance to police brutality in California and young Whites in the anti-Vietnam War movement invested it with negative potency (Tani & Sera, 1985). The word surfaced again with telling force after a four-day rebellion by prisoners who were disproportionately Black at the 'Attica Correctional Facility' in upstate New York in September 1971. When the state's police forces had finished their grim task, there were one hundred and twenty inmates as well as some hostages wounded or killed in their wake. Within the prison graffiti appeared that said, "32 Dead Niggers". Other graffiti later countered, "Fuck you Pig" (NY State Special Commission on Attica, 1972)! In fact, even before those events, the Black Panther Party newspaper, and on occasion even its seasonal greeting cards, would regularly depict the police in caricature as pigs in uniform. Its defenders have argued that that was the community's way of teaching fearlessness through contempt for police violence (Tani & Sera, 1985: 188).

It is significant that today, in Canada and the United States, some academics, entertainers and artists, of all colours, argue that 'ni—er' and its most recent variation 'niggah' are harmless terms. They make the startling claim that its prevalence in popular speech today neutralizes centuries of institutionalized and popularized defamation of Afrikans (Marshall, 2000; Neal, 2002: 9). By a clever feat of invisible sleight of hand opinion-makers extract value from the historical Black suffering invested in 'ni—er' and transfer its power to dehumanize or humiliate, by inference, to the society at large, including White police. If everyone is a "ni—er", no one is. Yet only during the sixties to eighties, and in a very limited way, have police forces been insulted as 'pigs'. In its posters and papers the Black Panther Party, from the sixties on would run regular cartoons with caricatures labelled, "pig cops". Their publications were unique to their time and space, severely limited in scope, and have never been replicated by any other organization or group (Cleaver & Katsiaficas, 2001: 185). Mainstream efforts at aborting the use of 'pig' as a verbal equalizer for 'ni—er' were immediate and appear to have been so successful that the term has effectively disappeared from police protester confrontations. It is even absent in much-maligned Gangsta Rap or Hip Hop culture and songs.

'Ni—er', however, despite rationalizations to the contrary, has retained its power to wound Afrikans whenever it is still hurled, missile-like, in confrontations from prison to playground. When the popular US sitcom actor, Michael Richards, used it against Black males in his audience in 2006, its venom remained patently potent. That incident also demonstrated the differential treatment that the media and society accord Whites and Blacks who verbally transgress. Although Richards is of Jewish ancestry, there was no charge equivalent to the media's conviction of Louis Farrakhan and Jessie Jackson for "Black anti-Semitism' when they used hurtful language about Jews. In fact no equivalent vocabulary exists. As we retool our language for liberation, anti-Kushitism becomes available to fill that void.

Of thirty-six (36) common slurs identified by inmates in research on racism in Ontario's prisons, twenty-one (21) are listed as directed against Blacks with 'ni—er' topping the list (Commission on Systemic Racism, 1994: 16; James, 1995: 37). Even in a Black-positive space, my observation has been that once an outsider says, 'ni—er' Afrikan self-esteem begins to evaporate. Sometimes silence descends on the group, while on other occasions the tone of the gathering perceptibly changes. This expression does not appear to be losing ambiguity in the treacherous territory where Blackness and Whiteness usually meet. In fact its influence continues to grow, as American English increasingly becomes the language of a globalizing experience. Throwing 'ni—er' around robs Blacks of the safe space some individuals have carved out to keep their dignity intact. Having to confront Whites about our hurt, on the other hand, always means risking our pride. Such situations are fertile ground for the kind of paternalistic, avuncular, carelessness reserved for the racially vulnerable. These ambiguous scenarios recall stereotypes of the 'harmless old man' who touches a young woman inappropriately and then defends his actions with a look of hurt 'innocence', excusing himself with, 'I meant no harm'.

Teacher culture in North America, as I have illustrated anecdotally, is conscious of White feelings, respects them and strives to be gentle with them. When the same group thinks 'nigger', however, it anxiously tries to avoid or control the expression of strong emotion by Black students or their community. In fact teachers often hold any meaningful discussion hostage by framing their exchange in a style that does not permit emotion to come through. On several occasions where they were forced to listen to Whites saying 'ni—er', as if it was like any other word in a written text, I noticed that Black teachers, students or community participants would leave the gathering as soon as they could.

My position on using 'ni—er' has evolved over time. For me it has never been a comfortable word for mixed company. When those who are not vulnerable to its hurt have claimed that they are using it to rob it of its power, I have found their argument potentially pernicious and tenuous at best. In informing my judgment about how this word is used, human feeling trumps dictionary definition or style. That seems logical since we use words with purpose, to stimulate or motivate, to get action or a reaction. We accept generally that great speeches can move society to accomplish great deeds, and in every culture a mother's lullaby acts as medication in sound. The words we choose to communicate ideas about who we are, therefore, become significant forces in shaping our space to be human. What I have discovered from my personal experience, as well as in discussions with a range of educators, whatever their identity, is how little society at large seems inclined to know about the history of this word that we hear so often and that so many individuals or groups feel empowered to define and redefine.

'Ni—er', like other degrading stereotypes, has been laundered, like drug money, passed through public institutions, like drug dollars, and normalized as solid currency for use in day-to-day life. The complexities surrounding the abusive use of 'ni—er' get compounded when the person using it is from another persecuted group, like Canada's First Nations playwright, Ian Ross. His play *farWel* takes place on a reserve and has a cast of six Aboriginal characters. The first five names are inoffensive. However, in the dramatist's directorial notes, the sixth character's, "body is full of scars which are mostly hidden by clothes. He's dressed in dirty jeans, very old oxfords and an old sweater... Nigger's face is rough and his complexion is dark, very dark[my emphasis]" (Ross, 1997: 13).

To talk intelligently about the character, "Nigger", we have to talk about much more. Indigenouus and Afrikans share a special history in this hemisphere. The record shows that the first Afrikan survivors were all male and the mothers of their children were all, by necessity, opportunity or love members of Aboriginal Nations (Obadele, 1991). Like so much of early Afrikan history on this continent that story has become 'lost, stolen or strayed', except for a few elders who keep it alive. At the Million Youth March called in Harlem, New York, in September 1997, a Native elder, Longwalker, told the marchers of the obstacles he had overcome in order to be present at that event (Kitwana, 2002: 170). He said that many people from both inside and outside his own community had warned him not to support the march. "How could I not be here?" He asked. "When the first Afrikans escaped from the Whites my people took them in...I am here to support Dr. Khalid Muhammad ". The man he referred to was a now deceased Black leader then under intense institutional and media attack, as well as being a regular target of elements within the Black leadership class (Kitwana, 2002: 167; Cleaver & Katsiaficas, 2001: 50).

Longwalker's comments recall an early settlement of a non- Aboriginal group that probably took place around the Peedee River, South Carolina, as early as 1526 (Ernst & Hugg, 1976: 9).

Those settlers, the record tells us, were Afrikan hostages escaped from murderous Spanish hands and their only allies, in those terror-driven times, were the First Peoples of the land. I believe that the memories of that union, and countless other alliances over thirty generations, hold meaning for Afrikans in the Americas and the world today. They explain relentless White pressure to split Afrikan and Aboriginal alliances for self-determination apart. For Aboriginals and Afrikans, when they unite to tell their truths, become a moral powerhouse that none of the myth-machines - the media, universities, schools, TV, theatre or film can defeat (Deagan & MacMahon, 1995: 12-13).

However, since ambiguity must inevitably surround its use, 'Nigger' steps off Ian Ross' stage and into the multiracial audience it attracts. Its use in this play does nothing to enhance the images of either Black people or Red people, while leaving White supremacy intact. It also undermines the solidarity that helped both Afrikans and the First Nations survive in this hemisphere, side-by-side, over generations, by resisting the mercenaries of White genocide together (Mulder, 1991: 28-31). The difference between Afrikans and all other non-Aboriginal residents of Turtle Island (the Americas) is that Afrikans did not arrive on these shores as invaders or immigrants. We never helped ourselves to another people's land, nor tried to displace them. Afrikans did not come here as seekers of fortune or to escape debt, disgrace and prison. The first Black people to settle here about four centuries ago also faced genocidal forced exile at the hands of European strangers they had never harmed. In parallel time, like the Mayan people in Mexico and the Mohawks of Canada, our sisters and brothers on the Afrikan continent are still suffering fallout from Asian or European invasions. When the slur "ni—er" comes from an unexpected source, such as a member of the First nations who we learned and long to trust, it doubles the hurt we feel.

Black people didn't have their land taken away from them in this place. Instead we were taken from our land. 'Ni—er' is a measure, in this part of the world, of how Whites have tried to strip us of our personhood as well. After taking away our children, religion, names, songs and drums, Europeans cut off our penises, breasts, thoughts and tongues. They so harmed a harmless people that guilty conscience drove their writers, with terrorist pens, to create fictitious 'ni—ers', alien-like things whose humanity bore no resemblance to their own. For if Afrikans were not 'ni—ers', deserving treatment as 'things', what name could there be to define those who repeatedly perpetrated such moral obscenities against them?

Once their publics had internalized the delusion that Afrikans were 'ni—ers', Europeans went on to ni—erize the world. The Indigenous have been called 'prairie ni—ers'. During the Vietnam War, Arabs were mocked as 'sand ni—ers'. One Quebecois intellectual interpreted his group's subordination to English-speaking Canadians as analogous to being "White niggers" (Masse, 1999). And the list multiplies. After all, no group volunteers to be treated like appendages to the human family. However, as Afrikans, when outsiders, even those members of other groups who also suffer at the hands of our oppressors, appropriate the moral power of our pain and treat our suffering as our shame, it can only feel like betrayal and gratuitous insult.

There is another danger for us in the ambiguous use of terms that mark our identity. Ambiguity increases the difficulty of identifying those enemies who not only set out through genocide to destroy us, but disguise our demise by clothing themselves in our ancestry and name. For example, modern Egyptians generally express pride in a glorious heritage thousands of years old, although it is common knowledge the present population descended from Arab invaders in the 8th century. Logically, their ancestors could not be the builders of the pyramids their descendants claim, but generally European and Asian academics do not seem to challenge them on that account. The population that presently dominates the land has in fact engaged in a relentless campaign of extinction against the last remnants of groups still carrying the Coptic tongue. Yet that is, historically, the only language that does reach back to pharaohnic times. Similarly there are White and Black Berber and Moorish populations on the continent today (Bovill, 1999). Elements in both White groups have engaged in enslaving and defaming those they identify as Black. However, both Berber and Moor refer to populations that were originally identified as Black. For ancestral Afrikans this poses an existential dilemma. If my enemy kills my parents and adopts our ways and name can he in time legitimately and morally displace me as their heir? That question suggests another. Is there an unsavoury and hidden history behind the mystery that surrounds the very origins of the name Blackamoor? It's sound and meaning both suggest that there may have been a time when it simply meant a Blacker Moor, in other words, a Moor of ancient Afrikan ancestry, and not a descendant of those who crossed the desert to usurp both title or land.

It is true that other groups, because of their language, culture, religion, class, gender or genitalia, have been treated, in discrete time and space, like Aboriginals and Afrikans. Usually, however, when they stand beside a Black person their stock shoots up on the 'Status Exchange'. This means that even those who feel vulnerable because they suffer some form of oppression and episodically claim the right to call themselves 'niggah', in songs or on the street, are likely, eventually, to fare better than Blacks. That phenomenon occurs even in prison. Demonstrably, it happens wherever there are Black bodies around (Parsell, 2006). In an English newspaper, the 'Social Democrat', a commentator tried to come to grips with the nuances of the term as early as 1897, writing, "Niggers remain niggers whatever color they are, but the archetype is found in Africa" (Social Democrat, 1897).

Cognitive dissonance does not prevent, 'to work like a nigger' and 'as lazy as a nigger' from sharing the same page or mind. Although 'Nigger' is inextricably bound up with backbreaking 'forced labor' in the collective psyche, it still manages to remain tied to images of infantilizing dependence. Seduced by the temptation of avoiding confusion, memory does not recall that it was to avoid working the First Nations of this hemisphere into oblivion that Catholic clerics from sixteenth century Spain eventually made substitute sacrifices of Afrikan men, women and children in their place. The noble intention of rescuing the First Nations, however, was a sentence of genocide for us. In my view, that unique history shared by our peoples is betrayed when any writer, but especially an Aboriginal man, like Ian Ross, puts cleverness before his responsibility to care for our shared humanity. One can only wonder what internalized images of his own race supremacy convinced him to create a degraded character and name him, 'nigger' in the tradition of White supremacist minds.

My Drum Talks Us
My drum talks Carib
Like the angels sistering me
For we only lived where angels
Lent us their tongues
Devoured our songs
Praise The Ancestors for hurricanes to snap our bonds
And toss us like coconuts
Free
Upon Carib shores
My drum speaks Seminole
Whispers Creek
To Red Warriors ready to die
For Min
The Black Passion within me
Stalking the Hunters
Of my flesh
Slipping past their hounds panting
For my sweat
To tear off my breasts
Chew into my sex
Growling and bickering over my blood
My drum talks Ho, Ho, Ho Chi Minh

Pawning his people's dreams

Pausing in battle to set me free

Honoring Harlem

Remembering Garvey and Howard U

Echoing Afrika for Afrikans

Asia for Asians

Europe for the Europeans

Meaning Vietnam for the Vietnamese

My drum talks Sista Brutha Ally Truthteller Friend

Winging me up

When hatreds dash me down

My drum talks One Mother One Tongue

Beating

One Heart One Navel String

One Journey Without End

Ka Kamit Kush

Nubia Ethiopia Punt

Al-f-ru-i-ka Afri-ka

Alkebulan Sudan

Denquenash O Beautiful One

Mother Of Mothers

Ashay

(Marshall, 2004)

Although the play *fareWel* is written by an Aboriginal about Aboriginals, naming its main character "Nigger" and unleashing stereotypes on the public stage has direct impact on the lives of Afrikans in Canada. The playwright's use of "Nigger" illustrates how even some individuals marginalized by class or race feel entitled to use a word that singles out Blacks for contempt. Contradictions festoon the lives of sufferers from discrimination. I was told the story of an Afrikan man in a suit and tie crossing a busy Toronto intersection when an Aboriginal man, seeming the worse for wear, asked him for change. When the Black man didn't produce the coins fast enough, *"Nigger!"* suddenly rose above the traffic's roar. He was startled because the verbal assault came from the erstwhile beggar that he was about to help. Sometimes we find the truth about the way others see us too brutal for our ears. However, most Blacks learn sooner or later that we are branded 'ni—ers' at birth and remain vulnerable to its venom whatever the lips that let it slip.

Black individuals who become wealthy or achieve high office, like Lincoln Alexander, a former Lieutenant Governor of Ontario in Canada and the first Black Governor General Michaelle Jean do not shed the hurtful stigma of this term. It sticks to them even when, like Michael Jackson, they lighten the color of their skin. Never permitted to escape the costs of their ancestry, they are merely allowed to become a sports star 'Michael-Jordan-ni—er', a TV superstar 'Oprah-Winfrey-ni—er' or a UN Secretary General 'Kofi-Annan-ni—er'. In the US, sports celebrity Jim Brown was both a physical giant and the hero of the Cleveland Browns football team. However, he confessed that he never stopped feeling physically unsafe and as if he didn't belong in his own city's Little Italy (Pinkney, 1994: 267). David Walker, a pioneer defender of Afrikan human rights in the United States, quotes an explicit statement of White supremacists in North Carolina in 1830, "A Nigar ought not to have any more sense than enough to work for his master" (Walker, 1993: 72). From the evidence, in the subterranean channels of many human minds, that pernicious idea still endures.

The wounds we wear from long history seem loathe to wear out their scars. While Afrikans are called 'ni—ers' in North America, Whites in Zimbabwe and South Africa refer to the First Peoples of those lands mockingly as "munts', "a derogatory corruption" of a word meaning 'person' or 'kaffir' from an Arab word for 'unbeliever' (Frederickse, 1982; Magubane, 1982: 13). Similarly Blacks are labelled 'abed' across the Arab world or called 'sale nègre' in circles that use

French (Depestre, 1967; Sharawy, 1999. Slurs against Afrikans seem to exist in every tongue but our own and are designed to hurt our feelings wherever we end up on the globe. A Rhythm & Blues song from the sixties says, *Ain't nuthin' lik' duh real thang,* baby. In the real world, we are the real niggers, whether the role we play is chief, queen or commoner. In fact, all peoples of portable Afrikan ancestry are members of the Black race. Afrikans in Canada have not escaped the global plague. In the report on racism in the Ontario justice system cited earlier four of the most common slurs are against Aboriginals while a full twenty-one are against Afrikans. 'Ni—er', as usual, heard everywhere and on every lip, sprints away with the gold (Commission on Systemic Racism, 1994: 17).

Until the mounting of *Without Sanctuary,* a photographic exhibition of lynching by the Historical Society of New York City at the turn of the twenty-first century, popular North American culture seemed to have successfully taught itself to ignore the history of White atrocities against Blacks. There were few reproductions of the evidence of widespread hanging, castration and roasting of live bodies that Whites inflicted on Blacks between the advent of Emancipation and The Civil Rights Movement. They often lynched for the entertainment of cheering crowds, in scenes reminiscent of the bloody circuses of ancient Rome. The surprise of a Black Congressman, John Lewis, confirms the public's ignorance of even relatively recent historical information on lynching. Lewis writes in the Foreword of the publication accompanying the display, "Despite all I witnessed during the height of the Civil Rights Movement, and all I experienced of bigotry during my lifetime, these photographs shocked me" (Allen et al, 2000: 7). Given the history of depravity that accompanied enslavement, one wonders why?

As the Nazis discovered so effectively, where there are no pictures, survivor stories or eyewitness accounts, the past can easily descend into a blur. From where we sit in history, we cannot meaningfully appreciate the human costs Afrikans bear or the heroism that distinguishes Afrikan survivors. That is why James Cameron's story of his own escape from lynching, with its sensual, emotional evidence, has been so important for my own education. Founder of America's 'Black Holocaust Museum' in Milwaukee, Wisconsin, he was until his death the only known US survivor of a lynching. When I met James Cameron in the nineties, he told me how he was rescued after being strung up to be hanged from the branch of a tree. Remembering, his eyes still filled with tears, although that extraordinary event took place in Ohio in 1930, when he was only sixteen years old (Cameron, 1982).

As he tells history, 'ni—er' figures prominently in his near-death experience. His book records such shouts as "Get those goddamn ni—ers out here!" from the mob outside his cell. His teenage ears heard the implicit threat to his life in the words, "We know how to treat Black-ass ni—ers!" He also told me that he could never forget how the mob kept howling, chanting, "We want those ni—ers-now" (Cameron, 1982: 55)! Forced to run through a gauntlet of screaming faces, his teenage psyche is scarred by the horror of little White boys and girls scratching him and biting him on the leg. In his own words, "And over the thunderous din rose the shout: 'Ni—er! Ni—er! Ni—er!' Again and again the word rang out until it seemed that it was the only word in English that held any meaning in their lives" (Cameron, 1982: 72).

In my view, that last observation captures the unique texture of 'ni—er' in Black and White relationships. The word was never designed for any purpose but Black dehumanization. It was never developed as a lethal psychological weapon against any other people. It is race-specific, like a biologically discrete germ, and it is targeted against our ancestry in order to destabilize and destroy Black spirits that dare to resist domination. Once a White attacks or a surrogate White launches 'ni—er' at its target, the slur closes in like a heat-seeking nuclear device. Robert Parker, the proud Southerner who was President Johnson's personal chauffeur recalls the humiliation of being called "ni—er" by the President himself (Parker, 1986: v). When Lyndon Johnson gave Robert Parker a laisser-passer so he could escape harassment as a Black man driving an expensive car in the US

South, it read, *"To Whom It May Concern, This ni—er drives for me"* (Parker, 1986: 52). Because of the poisonous authority vested in 'ni—er' from internalized stereotypes over thirty or more generations and the corrosive power of attendant external forces with sway over our lives, that single word can often reduce Black folks to incoherence or render us dumb.

The English language holds no other slur of equal power. No other word combines such universal threat of annihilation and guarantee of immediate humiliation. 'Ni—er' is like a poisoned dagger hidden in the folds of institutional robes. Our Ancestors were alternately branded "sugar mules" when forced to labor in Caribbean cane fields and "cotton ni—ers" when their fingers were worked raw in the US from picking the cotton they would never get to wear (Williams, 1994: 9). In Canada and the United States today, 'Ni—er' means 'profiling' in every area of Afrikan life. 'Ni—er' justifies unjustly designed and administered drug laws for Black possession of "crack" and White possession of "cocaine". 'Ni—er' sanctifies unequal sentencing by biased judges (Jackson, 1970; Carter, 1975). 'Nigger' ensures more suspensions and expulsions of Black students from school (Porter, 1997; Dei, 1995 & 1996). 'Ni—er' in the workplace signifies "last hired, first fired" (Marshall, 1992). 'Nigger' has also guaranteed, over the years, that hundreds or thousands of innocent Black men and women have been silently marched behind concrete walls from death row to a lethal injection, a hangman's noose or the electric chair (Carter, 1975).

Moreover, because English is now the language of imposed and engineered globalization, Afrikans have become portable hostages shackled to this word like an iron ball and chain. 'Ni—er' carries inside it memories of innumerable, incurable horrors and wounds. As James Cameron recalled, "A crowbar glanced against my chest. A pick handle crashed down against the side of my head" (Cameron, 1982: 72). 'Ni—erwords' are inseparable from blows to body, spirit and mind. As we navigate the societies we live in today, clothed in our Afrikan ancestry, color, culture and flesh, words have morphed into the ubiquitous terror of 'ni—erdeeds'.

Ni—er

Ni—er?

Never again!

Ni—er's not a word

It's the crack of a cracker's whip

Sting of a cracker's lip

Though fools act like it's hip

To spit ni—er poison into corneas crying pain

Blinding the Innocent

Insensitive Insane

For the enemy's gain

Pleeze Brutha pleeze Sistah

Don't you make it profane

(Marshall, 2004)

Attracted by the notoriety of another horrific incident involving a Black teenager, in 1987, I began to follow the legal proceedings around the rape of a churchgoing, honor roll student named Tawana Brawley in upstate New York. Local TV and press coverage, in March 1988, had gratuitously, illegally and scandalously included images of her body, nude to the waist. Tawana had publicly accused a gang of influential Whites of rape, giving detailed descriptions of six of the men present during her ordeal in what Afrikan residents described as "historically racist" Dutchess County. A transcript of the medical records published in the New York City Black press at the time confirmed that she had been sexually attacked and physically violated (McIntosh, 1998).

Interviewed by a Black journalist, her mother, Glenda, described Tawana's appearance when she was in the hospital. "I almost fainted", she said. "I saw 'KKK' [Ku Klux Klan] written across her chest and "ni—er" written twice across her stomach" (Leid, 1988: 22). In an editorial, voices from the wider Black world developed the theme of collective hurt and connected the way the rapists used 'ni—er' with the history of racist rapes of teenagers by White men both in the United States and across the Pan-Afrikan world. For example, in his memoirs, President Lyndon Johnson's chauffeur has also told the story of how his sister was raped and his father proved helpless in preventing it (Parker, 1986: 4,5). The interconnections of word and deed have underscored the unique coercive power of 'ni—er' whether it is written or said. An editorial in New York's Black *City Sun*, stated, "[This] is *the Black* community's ordeal…[and] we must insist that Tawana Brawley is entitled, because her people have fought and died for it, to the right of personhood" (Leid, 1988: 22).

Given the history of race in this hemisphere, and especially the US, Tawana Brawley's case was hardly a surprise. Among similar stories, I recall what a former Toronto student told me about being called 'ni—er' when he was around ten years old. It was, he whispered, like a kick in the gut, and his humiliation was compounded because his unknown White attacker also spit in his face. Although he was with an Asian friend as well as several European friends at the time, none of the others was attacked. At the level of collective memory, his anguish bears the stamp of generations of racist custom that have targeted innocent Black children, women and men.

In this society, this work argues, the psychic pain that student described has become a by-product of Black genetic heritage. Psychologist, Judith Rich Harris, exploring the 'nature or nurture' dilemma, touches on the relationship between our genetic inheritance and social legacies. She explains the phenomenon this way, "Direct genetic effects have consequences of their own, which I call *indirect* genetic effects -- the effects of the effects of the genes" (Harris, 1998: 30). As Evelyn Fox Keller, a philosopher of science cautions, we still have much to learn about what genes are and how they really work (Keller, 2002). It is a logical supposition that when that Black child heard "nigger", he was a stranger to its long, tortured history. However, it still touched chords and fibres in his being. Years later, when the student confided in me, he said, "I felt like I was going to faint…like something had sucked all my breath out of me". His language is telling. When the breath goes out of us, we die. Was his, perhaps, a near-death experience, comparable to people rescued from drowning or those whose hearts stop beating under a surgeon's knife? The trauma he survived that day is not exceptional. It fits a pattern that conforms to Black experience across North America and occurs wherever White supremacy controls us or hijacks our ability to control our own lives.

A socially charged word, packed with defamation and contempt can explode innocent lives. Perhaps 'nigger's' potency resides in the earlier suggestion that, like shell-shocked victims of war, Blacks are vulnerable to words, smell, sounds or images that trigger trans-generational flashbacks to our collective experience of genocidal forced servitude (De Gruy-Leary, 2005). Such considerations are relevant in examining the public use of 'ni—er' today. I look, in particular, at its implications for teaching a history of Black experience that can move us beyond euphemism in the classroom. As a Pan-Afrikanist I feel it is important for educators to figure out how what we learn from this exercise might inform teaching of the Maafa, the Great Suffering and breaking the cycles of silence that have attended it up to today. My special targets are the young people steeped in expressions of popular Black culture, who mostly view the world and organize their lives without benefit of a Pan-Afrikanist perspective (Kitwana, 2002: 203).

'Ni—er' was never designed to uplift people of Afrikan ancestry and, by all available evidence, it never has. To counter the argument that today's Hip Hop entertainers are merely reflecting the harshness of Black underclass reality, I would refer them to the songs produced by our Ancestors a few generations ago, in the teeth of some of the most violent and dehumanizing regimes on record. Whether in spirituals or other liberation music, Afrikans in bondage produced uplifting songs. That music did not just inspire Afrikans but was so powerful that these songs have proved a boon to all humanity (Reagon, 1992; Allen, 1995; Pongweni, 1982). On the other hand, 'Ni—er' has fulfilled its function, with horrendous psychological and genocidal costs, in degrading Black people. We require key questions, therefore, in order to measure whether and how Black resistance has transformed the 'ni—erized' world and to calculate the costs we still bear when it is used today.

From the examples and arguments outlined above, it is evident that 'nigger' can and does fall prey to manipulation by hostile or unsympathetic forces. It can also fall under the control of careless, indifferent or misdirected hands from our own community or be used to hurt individuals and groups. Our emotions are still too raw for us to treat this expression with distance and make literary distinctions about its use. It is even possible that this word, on its own, wields the potential of turning some Black students off schooling for good.

The Black community is still portrayed as ambivalent, however, about outsiders using 'ni—er'. For some young people, ambivalence suggests that they are invisible or that their feelings don't matter. Often, when little boys and girls explode in anger at classmates who use the term, adults in charge would punish them more severely than their detractors. Far too frequently, I've observed, they end up being sent home to calm down. Those responsible for the verbal attacks are usually allowed to remain in school where they can render the space unsafe for their Black peers. Anecdotal evidence collected by The Black Secretariat, a Toronto community advocacy group confirms the differential treatment Black students receive when 'ni—er' is used (Johnson, 2003). Students, parents and teachers have provided firsthand evidence of how the discretionary use of 'Safe School' or 'Zero Tolerance' legislation by school boards disproportionately targets Black students by suspending or expelling them when they respond to taunts of "ni—er" by defending themselves (Porter, 1997; Brathwaite, 1998: 255-280; Hilliard, 1995; Dei, 1995).

In some schools I've visited, teachers have approached this treacherous terrain by agreeing on two broad principles rather than insisting on many narrow prescriptions. Experience has taught them to avoid listing the ways or times 'ni—er' can be used. Rather, they pay attention to how the slur affects a student's life chances, ranging from feelings of social discomfort to experiences of mental or physical trauma. Because pain and suffering are not evenly distributed or evenly felt in the world, responsible educators often employ a system of 'moral triage'. They direct their resources and energy towards those students most gravely injured by the wounds of this treacherous slur. Morally responsible educators should logically aim to affirm the humanity of every individual they teach. There can therefore be no reason to use 'nigger' unless it somehow contributes to building up the self-esteem of Afrikans students as well as the Afrikan community at large. Those who bear and have borne the 'ni—er-burden' should be the only ones who derive any potential 'benefit' from its use. It is morally unacceptable to defend using 'ni—er' at the expense of the psychic wellbeing of students of Afrikan ancestry in order to educate other students.

Another possible reason for training our radar on 'ni—er' is its usefulness in jolting hearers awake. It alerts Afrikans who are then better prepared to protect our group from those who have harmed us in the past and might do so again. Pursuing that logical line, sometimes using euphemisms such as 'the n-word' obscures the evidence of history and elevates smooth social relations above the need for self-defence. Euphemisms also carry the risk of lulling communities into a false sense of security. They can narcotize us and even put us into a kind of permanent sleep, increasing our vulnerability in a treacherous, dangerous world. Amidst seductive invitations that promise reconciliation for forgiveness, 'nigger' reminds its targets of insults and humiliation. Memories of castration are predictably repulsive but they can also stiffen Black spines. For example, the famous singer, Ike Turner, never got over witnessing the castration of a young Afrikan man like himself (Turner, 1999: 45). It shows disrespect for the sacrifices of our Ancestors when our community fritters reconciliation away without demanding reparations or even evidence of sincere remorse. Therefore even the harsh sound of 'ni—er' with its echoes of barbarity and pain can prove a useful tool in keeping our eyes open and be a blessing in disguise.

It costs other groups nothing to refrain from using 'ni—er' in public. However, logic tells us that there can be exceptions for educational purposes. Outsiders committed to enhancing their knowledge of

Black holocausts and expanding their empathy for Black populations should not be prevented from using 'ni—er' in closed circles without Blacks present or with Black individuals who give informed consent to its use. The 'ni—er' dilemma poses practical problems for today's multiracial societies rather than resting on moral absolutes. It demands an explanation every time 'ni—er' slips through non-Afrikan lips. Therefore, teachers reading a novel that uses 'ni—er' would probably avoid conflict by directing students to say 'the n-word' instead. Doing so not only avoids the risk of giving offence but also signals concern and respect for the dignity of all those present. Educators who see themselves as allies will logically welcome Black leadership around issues of identity. They will probably also understand when Afrikans demand private space for healing and recovering their strength. Allies understand that sometimes stepping aside and 'butting out' may be the most useful contributions to justice that they can make. As moral beings, we do not need to enter or occupy every space in order to "do good" or "be good".

Beware

Shun the ni—erword

Soul Sistah

When you hear the ni—erword

Soul Brutha beware

Ni—er means nuthin'

Makes our suffrin' a nuthin' thing

As if Baad Fannie Lou wasn't left for dead

By crackers bustin' heads down South

Ni—er betrays Nani high in Jamaica's hills

Forgin' freedom fighting fierce

Washing courage red with her blood

Willin' her heartbeat into defendin' Maroons

Ni—er scorns Sistah Ida's pen

Writin' their lynch mobs down

Ni—er washes

Killer king Lucius Clay white

For branding LC

On nursin' mother breasts

Don't nice up ni—er now

As if yesterday's ni—erhunters

Don't suck our blood today

As if Dr. Death and his biothugs

Stopped shakin' cocktails

Of anthrax with AIDS

As if conspiracies of schools

Won't blunt our babies' minds

Fakin' cures for false ADD

As if torturers with barbwire brains

Didn't dig out Emmet Till's teenage eyes

As if motherlynchers and fatherlynchers

Never pickled Nat Turner's dick

Or strip the flesh from Amsterdam's chest

With fire-red tongs

To melt him down

Eyeballs runnin' down into breathin' balls

I-an-I need Soulwords

Bruthaman

Let's choose Soulsounds

Sistahwoman

An' soothe our Soul

For Soul keeps old cures in suffererinwords

Soul wears new innocence washed bright in blood

Soul ignites flames that will always burn

Soul fills promises we were born to keep

Soul makes us soar

Ni—er pretends this hell's over

While predators still howl and dance around

Soul spirits us far

Beyond their fangs

To higher sacred ground

(Marshall, 2004)

In many ways, it is easy to demonstrate to the world that 'ni—er' is spiritually, emotionally and socially destructive to Black life. In discussions both in and out of the classroom, I find it more challenging to explain, not only to Europeans or Asians but also to many Afrikans that the term 'slave' is dangerous too. Generally, in both academic and popular culture 'slave' is not only acceptable but also regarded as 'neutral', 'objective' and 'universal'. It is often used to describe analogous conditions, across cultures, both in the present and the past. In my view it is also a word that our society has invested with its own addictive innocence. Questioning the word 'slave,' therefore, on the basis of its racist and anti-Kushitic connotations implies questioning the integrity of this society at large. In the next section, I examine the ubiquitous misrepresentation of the word 'slave' and its pernicious association with Afrika's ancestral heritage.

SLAVE: HAITI'S SPIRIT NEVER BENDS

Mahatma Gandhi observed that, "...if we obey laws repugnant to our conscience...[then we are submitting to] slavery" (Gandhi, 1993: 48). Slavery, in the understanding Gandhi's wisdom gives us, is what takes place inside our heads when we forget that we are free human beings and begin to think like slaves. In 1804, Afrikans in Haiti, daringly conscious of their own humanity, humbled Napoleon, Europe's conquering hero of the day. Theirs was a quintessential victory of that "the curse of Ham" sentenced Afrikans from birth to a mythical, eternal servitude under peoples of lighter skin and straighter hair (Davis, 1990: 21; Diop- Maes, 1996).

It is noteworthy that, even today, there is an absence of popular recognition or official acknowledgement of the grandeur achieved by Afrika's survivors in the field of Human Rights. On the contrary, while movements in Finland, the Americas and Australia have raised hopes for official government apologies for Europe's genocidal atrocities against First Nations on those continents, Pan-Afrikanists have waited in vain for parallel initiatives that signalled equal recognition or remorse in connection with The Maafa and other Afrikan holocausts, anywhere in the world. History indelibly records, however, that Belgians murdered ten million of the Congo's approximately twenty million population between 1898 and 1908. Genocide on such a biblical scale deserves attention and restorative justice comparable to the reparations paid Nazi victims of WW II (Bettelheim, 1980; Strom & Parsons, 1982, Bittker, 1973).

Documenting the horror of Belgian terrorism, a European historian, Adam Hochschild writes, "When a village or a district failed to supply its quota of rubber or fought back against the Belgian regime, Force Publique soldiers or the rubber company 'sentries' often killed everyone they could find" (Hochschild, 1998: 226). In a current Toronto Black community weekly, publicity for 'The Campaign to End Holocaust and Genocide' lists eighteen groups that suffered genocide in the twentieth century. Surprisingly the list omits the Belgian genocide of ten million Congolese as well as the German genocide of the Nama and Herero people of South West Africa (Davis, 1990; Nkrumah, 1969; World Federalist Assn., 2004: 7). The advertisement demonstrates the power that denial exerts on Whites for crimes they collectively commit against Blacks.

Abolitionist Samuel J. May confessed to similar collective emotions of US Whites in 1831, "We are prejudiced against the blacks; and our prejudices are indurated...by the secret, vague consciousness of the wrong we are doing them. Men are apt to dislike those most, whom they have injured most [emphasis added]" (May, 1969: 304). Instructively, in the example cited, it is a Black paper, *The Jamaican Xpress* that distils the publicity that 'disinforms' the public about Black holocausts. Today's Western society publicly accepts its obligation to remember the six million Jews slaughtered by the Nazis. It is therefore a spectacular educational failure that the same popular culture keeps the public so woefully ignorant of the slaughter of ten million Congolese by Belgians, another European nation, just a generation before (Nkrumah, 1969; Lindqvist, 1996).

Across the continent, carrying out extermination campaigns against the Herero and Nama peoples of South West Africa, now Namibia, German troops practiced the genocide they later expanded in WW II (Pakenham, 1991; Boahen, 1985). The record shows that in 1904, Germany's Lieutenant General Von Trotha gave orders that "Within the German boundaries every Herero, whether found with or without a rifle, with or without cattle, shall be shot" (Von Trotha, 1998: 282). Equally significant is the fact that the campaign that almost succeeded in exterminating the Herero and Nama populations of South West Afrika was hatched in the minds of grandfathers of some of the very Nazis who would later target many other innocent groups in Europe and cause havoc in populations around the globe (Davis, 1990; Lindqvist, 1996: 149). The European cycle of death remained unbroken when their agents conspired to overthrow Patrice Lumumba's elected government in January 1961. Kwame Nkrumah was president of Ghana, with troops serving as UN peacekeepers on the ground, and wrote:

Recruiting offices have been opened in [apartheid] South Africa, in France and elsewhere, and wages of over [$1000 US] a month are being offered to former German fascist officers and former collaborators of Hitler and Mussolini in other countries to persuade them to enlist [as mercenaries] (Nkrumah, 1969: 131).

Apart from the Belgians, Europeans carried out other deliberate extermination campaigns in Afrika, while attempting to excise the memory of those atrocities from the public mind. On the heels of WW II, in 1944, French troops, in defence of whose nation Senegalese soldiers had fought valiantly at tremendous human cost, surrounded and wiped out a camp of veterans in a Wolof village called Thiaroye. The veterans had dared to demand the pensions they were legally due in 1944 (Cissé, 1997). The French army's bloody act, *"sharper than a serpent's tooth"* reads like a Shakespearean tragedy of ingratitude and beggars our human imagination. Since then, at dawn on the anniversary of the massacre, according to renowned Senegalese journalist, Abdou Rahman Cissé, French troops stationed permanently on Senegalese soil cordon off the area to prevent pilgrimages by the survivors of the veterans they machine gunned in cold blood (Cissé, 2004).

Cumulative evidence leads to the conclusion that there is an ethos of extermination informing Europe's relations with Afrika. Boris Bittker's description of anti-Kushitism in the United States serves as a template for measuring the impact Europeans had on Afrikan life. The experience he outlines is beyond "official misconduct". In his words, "racial discrimination against blacks was systematic, unrelenting, authorized at the highest governmental levels, and practiced by large segments of the population" (Bittker, 1973: 21). Edward Blyden's research also exposes the European mindset that predicted a time when "Young ladies on camp stools, under palm-trees, will read with tears -- *The Last of the Negroes*" (Reade, 1994: 273). Sven Lindqvist shreds the mask of innocence that Europe's governments and populations have hidden behind for so long. Speaking of the silence that surrounds these crimes, he says bluntly, "It is not knowledge that is lacking" (Lindqvist, 1996: 171). When French troops rampaged and massacred innocent villagers in Central Afrika on the cusp of the twentieth century Lindqvist writes, "[the] French left wing…had little interest in digging…into the affair…[although] educated Frenchmen knew roughly, or even precisely, by what means their colonies were captured or administered" (Lindqvist, 1996: 170). The lack of remorse that runs through the genocide and economic exploitation Europe forced on Afrikans infects contemporary relationships with its culture of contempt (Lindqvist, 1996). Summing up the impact of European destructiveness on Afrika, another historian, John Cell writes, "Over the last quarter of the nineteenth century... the demands of the expanding labour market, and the last push of pacification had resulted in a decline of twenty-five percent or even more of the African population. ... Indeed, until after World War 1, the concern with Africanists was with underpopulation " (Cell, 1987: 197).

Within my experience, as it was for Holocaust survivor Bruno Bettelheim, members of the wider public, whatever their religious background, filter out talk about genocide where those sharing their ancestry are to blame. Some educators even become upset when questions about European culpability are raised. Bettleheim puts it simply. "From the beginning of time, those who have borne witness have been an embarrassment" (Bettelheim, 1980: 313). Marshall McLuhan also argues that the public has generally shown itself wilfully partial to official explanations (McLuhan, 1981). For Pan-Afrikanists, that means Europeans not only accept their own interpretations of world history but also provide and believe European interpretations of how Afrikans feel about that history. Even Bettelheim, with his Eurocentric eye, selects the picture of a Black protester in Birmingham, Alabama being dragged away by a policeman to symbolize the suffering Afrikan masses endured during their Human Rights struggle in the United States (Bettelheim, 1980: 270). From a Pan-Afrikan perspective, his choice misrepresents the gravity of the situation Blacks endured. Marching and being dragged away does not capture the severity of the police beating that crippled Fannie Lou Hamer. It bears little resemblance to the bombing that blew four little girls in Birmingham, Alabama apart in Sunday school (Branch, 1998; Morris, 1984). That was a time of crucifixion in the community's collective experience when Blacks in uncounted millions were willing to risk their livelihood or even lay down their lives (Marable, 1984). More significantly, the common 'politeness' that banishes the gory reality of anti-Kushitism to the periphery of our consciousness betrays the intensity of Afrikan feeling about the enormity of European crimes. As a result, most classrooms or venues where racism is examined exist as spaces censored, not only through silence, but also by the saturation of a language that hides painful truths behind a distancing discourse. Under those conditions, censorship does not have to be imposed. It is part of a package and already coded into classroom discussions before they unfold.

This is an appropriate moment for us to examine differences between European concepts of 'slave' and how they were translated into two ancestral Afrikan languages. The deep impact of religion on the meaning of 'slave' goes back to biblical times. Historian David Davis reminds us, "The Hebrew word for slave, '*ebed*', was used in one sense to refer to a righteous punishment sanctioned by the Lord" (Davis, 1970: 63). That sense of divine sanction of forced servitude still infects Muslim and Christian uses of the term as well. Notions of color and caste often run through major Asian and European religions with Black permanently anchored to evil and servitude in the sacred imagination (Bhakitvedanta, 1981; Woolson, 1977). On the contrary, Afrikan experiences of service generally occurred within non-judgmental, affirming communities. My research suggests that both Asians and Europeans twisted a historical experience that was qualitatively different from their own and then misused it to justify the genocidal servitude they imposed on generations of Black populations (Blyden, 1993; Sharawy, 1999).

Let us turn to West Afrika, where European historical tradition claims that 'traders' (enslavers) purchased most of the women, children and men who were subsequently forced into brutal exile in the Americas and Caribbean. Historian Robert Rotberg, after a significant quantitative study of descriptions of Afrika in accounts of White invaders (explorers) admits, "much of the travel literature of the nineteenth century thus contains only perfunctory descriptions of African life" (Rotberg, 1973: 6). What then, is the basis of the common claim that "slavery" was one of the norms of Afrikan life? Primary research is a logical antidote to the prevailing biases in the academic information base on the enslavement of Afrikans. My first examination of 'slave' comes from my limited exposure to Twi, one of the Akan group's languages in Ghana. The other comes from my study of Wolof, today the majority language of the

Senegambia region of West Afrika. Because I have taught and translated French and English and study Afrikan ancestry, I cherish my lived experience, though brief, with the languages I cite. In the following discussion I examine the words used to translate 'slave' in both of these ancestral Afrikan tongues, as exposed in current lexicons and dictionaries, in order to measure translations both in terms of their linguistic accuracy and for the spirit they eventually convey.

None of us, including Europeans, can escape the bias of our own tongues when we attempt to speak another language. For example, the Wolof name spelt 'Jallow' in ex-English colony, Gambia, is rendered as 'Diallo' in ex-French colony, Senegal. On both sides of the artificial European-drawn border, the name sounds the same on the Wolof tongues that speak it. This is why I have chosen to spell "Cheddo" in a way that respects its sound as opposed to its more common spelling "Ceddo" in French-speaking Senegal. The Europeanized spelling of Wolof words is also a relatively new science. It has sometimes caused conflict in Senegal during the reign of its first president and French language expert, Léopold Senghor. Addicted to Eurocentric formalities, the president passed laws that were so absolute they threatened some nonconformist Senegalese with jail terms for 'mis-spelling' their own family names (Cissé, 1997, Kesteloot, 1991).

My treatment of these languages, however, is confined to the insights they can offer about how our thinking has been shaped by colonizers who have often forbidden us to think. Nothing I write is intended to impugn defenders of orthographic purity in either tongue. However, close analysis suggests that ancestral languages may also prove reservoirs of vital information for rebuilding Black self-esteem and clarifying the truth about the use of noxious terms like 'slave' and 'slavery'.

The following is an example of hidden information about Afrikan achievement that might be retrieved from ancestral retentions. On the trail of Afrikan grammatical retentions in North American English, I even found evidence to suggest that early Afrikan advances in preventive medicine were brought to this hemisphere by our Ancestors. In the records left by a Bostonian historian, Cotton Mather, he writes, "These Africans all agree on One Story [about inoculation methods]…People take Juice of Smallpox; and *Cutty-skin*, and Putt in a Drop" (Mather, 1987: 199). In providing posterity a lesson in linguistics, Mather inadvertently offers Afrikans information about the medical and scientific advances our Ancestors shared so generously with their enslavers. Indeed, the courage to reinterpret 'slave' rescues significant cultural information on Afrikan history from its generally accepted hegemonic Eurasian definition and defamation. Bruno Bettelheim ascribes the alienation of youth to inter-generational failure in connecting youth to the realities of survivor history and rescuing them from a discourse of humiliation in the vocabulary of their oppressors (Bettelheim, 1980: 351). As Pan-Afrikanists free their history and education from centuries of bias, we too become better prepared to again inspire our youth.

Serer (a Senegalese First Nation) by birth and Wolof speaker all his life, Abdou Rahman Cissé, a former Director of Information in Senegal, often advised me on linguistic history and meaning in Afrikan tongues. He was trained both as a linguist and a journalist and has carried out extensive field research into indigenous Wolof and other Afrikan cultures. Cissé pointed out that, when 'jaam', translated as 'slave', is slightly altered tonally, it becomes 'jamm', meaning 'peace'. He therefore theorized that the original relationship communicated by those sounds did not rest on subjugation and domination but was a prescription for fostering social peace (Cissé, 1997). It stands to reason that, if there is a conflict between two clans who exchange and raise each other's children as their own, as the customs surrounding the experience of "jaam" suggest, those children become a kind of breathing insurance in human flesh against further dispute.

This idea gets support from the fact that, in ancestral Senegal, except for a tiny minority who formed the castes of artists, musical historians, jewellers or labourers (albeit with full human rights) working on royal land, the members of all families bore the status of 'geer', meaning 'landowners' (Malherbe & Sall, 1989: 100). A social commentator who lived and studied in Senegal, Molly Melchin, also bears witness to an egalitarian Wolof sense of individualism and pride in their humanity irrespective of caste, office or wealth that is portrayed in their greetings. She writes that "...[their] greetings are a way for the Wolof to show respect for every member of the community...[and] Wolofs often express anger...by refusing to greet the person" (Melching, 1981: 8). Guided only by the dictates of their Ancestors, ancestral Africans proudly held themselves beyond the control of any designated caste of artisans or external political control. They call the spiritual-cultural system they inherited 'Cheddo', a word that can be loosely rendered as 'Freethinker' in modern English usage. Even today, from my experience, most declared Christians and Muslims in Senegal still carry on some of their ancestral Cheddo practices. For example, before important journeys, some villagers pour libations on the ground to their Ancestors, without identifying the origin of that rite.

I am aware there are other less benign interpretations of West Afrikan society at the time of European intrusion. Two such accounts are observations by foreigners, Cadamosto from Portugal in 1455 and Englishman Francis Moore in the eighteenth century (Mahoney, 1995: 21). Their accounts cover a time when institutional slavery of White men and women was very much a part of the European imagination and experience. Evidence of this is captured by Michelangelo's genius in his life size statue *The Dying Slave*, sculpted between 1513-1515. In Paris' museum of world renown, 'Le Louvre' and in gleaming marble it lives for posterity, speaking of a time when enslavement was not yet synonymous with Blackness alone in the European mind (Quoniam, 1977: 86). Michelangelo was carving servitude in White face and form even as Europeans were beginning to make meaning out of their contact with Afrikan peoples who were wealthy, civilized and generous beyond their imagination (Rotberg, 1973). How ironic that within the same generation Europeans invented a role of perpetual servitude for the rich, free, dancing spirits they encountered. They infused Afrika's veins with their own brutal fantasies that few Afrikans outside the orbit of Arab influence or control had ever known. Robert Rotberg's evidence of Europeans' generally scant knowledge of Afrikan life helps to explain, but not excuse, why they fell so massively, so quickly and for such a long time into such deep error.

With some understanding of the context of Europeanized interpretations of culturally based Afrikan relationships of 'service' as 'servitude', we can now examine the term jaam, adopted by lexicographers to translate slave. Those interpretations still carry the odour of the generations of captive Europeans of 'Slav' ancestry that eventually gave the practice its name (Patterson, 1991: 357). On the other hand, in a Senegalese context, 'jaam' has more resonance and broader meanings than the European hatched 'Slav(e) relationship implies. To begin with, "jaam" is the title given the children of your father's sister. Secondly, it exists in opposition to 'sangg', the children of your mother's brother. Europeans, however, imposed a narrower meaning of 'master' or 'mistress' on 'sangg' (Malherbe & Sall, 1989: 100). I logically expect that most Afrikans, then or now, would find it difficult to imagine having a 'master', 'mistress' and 'slave' relationship with our siblings, relatives or peers. There is a qualitative difference between the consciousness reflected in the European and Afrikan words. While the Wolof evokes 'voluntary service' through family obligation, English and French impose notions of 'forced servitude' in interpreting those original Wolof terms.

Based on the observations above, it would appear that European translations of Afrikan terms often come to us intellectually and emotionally charged with distortions of meaning. In the Wolof world of multiple marriages and complex inter-relationships of families and clans, individuals often combine oppositional roles. When individuals fill the role of 'jaam' they perform errands and light household tasks. On the other hand, as 'sangg' the same individuals must give up any garment, even favourite clothes to any 'jaam' that asks, in return for services rendered, because custom demands that they do (Malherbe & Sall, 1989: 91). The human transactions that characterize these free gifts of goods and services are a far cry from popular ideas of the 'vampiristic' relationship of forcibly feeding European or Arab strangers off Black labour, talent and emotion that can arbitrarily and forcibly transform any free, disconnected human being into someone else's designated 'slave' for life. In even cursory research, I discovered that similarities exist in the history of how Europeans have also translated 'slave' into the Akan language, 'Twi'.

My Twi-speaking advisor is a former teacher of Twi to advanced students in his birthplace, Ghana. The dictionary word commonly suggested for 'slave' in Twi is 'odonko'. I say "commonly" because depending on the context, there are other words also translated as 'slave'. In other contexts, 'odonko' can also mean 'stranger'. When I asked my advisor whether it was significant, as I had heard from other Ghanaians, that 'odo' means love and 'nko' 'don't leave me', a combination that says in effect, 'I love you, don't go', he did not give me a definitive answer (Asomansing, 2003). At this time I have only been able to verify that multiple explanations of the original meanings of these terms do co-exist and I believe they merit future investigation in more depth. To sum up, there is enough evidence to throw into doubt the commonly circulated European and Arab claims of indigenous 'slavery' in Afrika.

The definitions or terms we have examined appear designed to create confusion about how Afrikans treated each other in earlier times, before our Ancestors experienced foreign intervention and Arab or European control. On the other hand, Western ideas of slavery run deep. We know, for example, that in ancient Greece Spartan slavery was so brutal and cold that the Spartans declared a year round open season on all 'Helots' or 'slaves'. In like vein, English invaders would hunt down the First Nations of Australia in the eighteenth century and murder them, either for pleasure or at the slightest hint of resistance and revolt (Bury, 1956: 132; Stevens, 1984; Cove, 1995).

That pattern also repeats itself generations later in the way the Dutch Boer invaders in South Africa go hunting after the pacifist San people, shooting them down like tethered game in the confines of their homes (Lindqvist, 1996; Davis, 1990). It stands out again in the churlish cruelty of those British exiles celebrating their new lease on life in the Pacific by wiping out the gentle Indigenous peoples that helped them survive (Stevens, 1984; Cove, 1995). The 'slave' pattern is discernible in the way SS guards treat Jewish prisoners in Nazi concentration camps (Bettelheim, 1980; Wiesel, 1995). The information we receive in popular culture on the ongoing caste system in India tells us that it, too, is rigid, colour-driven and deeply degrading. For example, a Dalit activist writes that despite formal, political recognition of Dalit rights, some 'Untouchables' have been lynched in modern times merely for drawing water from a proscribed well (Rajshekar, 1987: 60).

On the other hand, we have relatively few easily accessible, graphic images of the European enslavement of Afrikans, although these crimes against humanity took place in the hemisphere in which we live. Both historically and in the contemporary era, Black suffering has often taken place offstage or behind closed doors. Pictures of the kind of brutality Black men and women face and fear, like the beating of Rodney King, create the public consternation they do precisely because they are so rarely publicly shown. A journalist describing that event captures the mood of his community to behavior that should logically excite the passions of any injured group, "[The] Black community is inured to police violence. Abusive behavior... has become commonplace" (Nelson, 2000: 13). When innocent Afrikans suffer today, we frequently do so behind tinted windows in patrol cars, in underground prison cells, in security rooms at the back of shopping centres, in alleyways leading off main streets, in worksites secured from public view, under private procedures in public clinics and laboratories or hidden away behind locked doors in addiction and mental health institutions. In the hearts and heads of a public shielded from ever seeing these sites of our persecution, there is little consciousness and less empathy for what we endure.

As I made my way through school, the history and present reality of Afrikan pain generally remained a closed book. Yet European enslavement of Afrikans in the Caribbean had matched or surpassed all other atrocities in recorded human history, both in terms of its relentless ferocity and its mind-destroying depravity. Some demons carelessly taught engineering skills invented the "speculum oris" and then taught their kith and kin to use it for force-feeding captive Afrikans who chose to starve themselves to death. The device worked by applying hot coals to tender lips with jaw breaking power. It can only be described, in recounting the history of technology, as a moral obscenity in steel (Dow, 1980: 66-68). Not to be outdone, Thomas Thistlewood, an Englishman grown wealthy from the terror he wielded over innocent Afrikans in Jamaica, forced one hapless man to defecate into an Afrikan brother's mouth and to hold it shut until he swallowed the excrement (Walvin, 1992: 239). Some of our ancestry were torn limb from limb by horses, wolfed down by dogs raised on human flesh, set aloft in trees for vultures to eat, blown apart with gunpowder stuffed into their anus, boiled or roasted alive and sexually mutilated to a degree unparalleled in any recorded history anywhere on the face of the globe (Ginsburg, 1988; James, 1989: 12). Thousands more innocent individuals have been roasted, castrated and barbecued since formal Emancipation, right up to even relatively recent times (Marable, 1984; Turner, 1999: 45). Because our language of holocausts is wanting, we have lost our sense of their costs.

It is therefore logical to examine the processes by which European missionaries, academics and fortune-seekers usually created Afrikan language dictionaries. Doing so offers a way of understanding why, as a group, we have generally remained so woefully ignorant of many horrendous events that should logically be branded into our collective memory. We have also remained equally uninformed about the intact and humane Afrikan societies, which preceded the onslaught we have come through. In Switzerland around 1884, the very season of the Berlin conspiracy to pillage Afrika, a Basel missionary, Rev. J. G. Christaller developed the first English lexicon in Twi, an indigenous lingua franca in Ghana. The European had no prior knowledge of Afrikan culture or speech and so relied heavily on the twenty-two year old son of a christianized Jamaican-Ghanaian couple, Nicholas Timothy Clerk. This "expert informant's" Jamaican-born father was a Christian convert repatriated to his ancestral land to serve the interests of Basel missionaries. Together with the young man's Ewe, Ghanaian-born mother he had raised Nicholas Timothy Clerk, according to Christaller's biographical note, "in a strictly Christian expatriate Afro-American household in pagan surroundings" (Debrunner, 1979: 359).

His statement demonstrates how his ethnocentric, race supremacist bias had already led him into the error of calling the deeply religious Afrikan society he encountered a "pagan" or godless one. To this day "Gye Nyame", "Only by God's Will" is arguably the most common phrase to pass through Ghanaian lips.

Okot P'Bitek, a historian who has advised UNESCO on Afrikan history, tells us that the foreign 'experts' were usually tangential and often spiritually hostile to the Afrikan community whose language they transcribed. Those were the realities shaping their approach as they compiled many foundational European vocabularies for interpreting what to them were foreign tongues (P'Bitek, 1980). In Clerk's case, his parents and missionary mentors raised him consciously to worship Europeans as ideals and to bow down to images that were uniformly white. At the same time they devalued or demonized the ancestral Afrikan icons and rituals of the people around them that they claimed to serve. The processes that Clerk internalized, it follows, while encouraging him to embrace Europe and its Christian traditions turned him against Afrikan practices and beliefs (P'Bitek, 1980; Mbiti, 1970).

In time, therefore, Nicholas Timothy Clerk came to judge all Afrikan ancestral faiths as inferior, backward and, in the teachings of his European handlers, based on 'superstitions' that intelligent individuals could justifiably dismiss (Wessels, 1990; Tsomondo, 1976: 7). That attitude leads inevitably into error since, for Afrikans, as all peoples, ancestral religious practices grow out of lived experience. For example, some anthropologists and missionaries negatively associate "Ibeji" carvings in Nigeria and the rituals surrounding them to 'cults'. However, the name merely combines Yoruba words for "firstborn (ibi)" and "eji (two), while the rituals that surround the birth and the raising of twins make meaning of a unique feature of Yoruba reality. As an ethnic group, they have the highest incidence of twins in the world (Segy, 1985: 193). Indeed, while Clerk's early education was geographically inside Afrika, like many "mis-educated" Afrikans of our own day, he was emotionally and intellectually shackled to Europe (Woodson, 1969). In an unnaturally natural progression, he deliberately cut himself off from the cultural and religious roots of the local population. Taken as a whole, therefore, Nicholas Timothy Clerk's upbringing raises questions not only about his qualifications for the job that Europeans selected and trained him to do but also about his integrity in accepting to do their bidding.

At the far southern tip of Afrika, in the ancient Mutapa court located within today's Zimbabwe, Portuguese missionaries, carrying out the mandate of their crown, were sent to convert the ruler, the Munhumutapa. Conversion was merely a calculated European strategy to "supplant the Moslem traders" and get their hands on Zimbabwe's gold (Mudenge, 1986: 3; Nhubu, 2001). Through such early deceptions, the European dominant world has inherited religious, political and academic language about Afrika that was created, from its earliest intrusions, to disinherit our motherland and facilitate her subjugation.

In Ontario's governmental circles in today's Canada it is accepted that translators or interpreters bring the power of their own biases to the work they do. That conditions how we accept what they write and say (Cairncross, 1989). Always ready to expose hidden bias, George Orwell also identified the power of the translator in his novel, *1984*, "[The] person who did the translation…would have the power to decide what was the real meaning of what was being said," he wrote (Orwell, 210: 12). Clerk's work embodies the cultural biases that eventually produced the exculpatory euphemisms so embedded today in the global discourse on Afrikan holocausts. Consciously or unconsciously, he created a language that would not only please his European mentors, but also help his overlords to undermine the cultural beliefs of the Afrikan community that sustained him.

Nicholas Timothy Clerk's role therefore becomes, by definition and design, a duplicitous one. To other Afrikans, he presents himself as a son of the soil with a right to know the secret strengths or vulnerabilities of their culture and group. At the same time, however, he is continuously monitoring, grooming and censoring himself so that he can become as European as possible under the camouflage of his Afrikan skin. As a proud Christian, Clerk would have also absorbed European prejudices against inclusive Afrikan families, where rights and rites of inclusion turn 'tenth cousins' into immediate siblings. Christian doctrine, on the other hand, has generally considered polygamy or inter-clan adoptions as primitive or sinful (P'Bitek, 1980; Kenyatta, 1965; Mbiti, 1970). Such internalized biases would explain why Clerk, in good conscience, given his lack of grounding in his mother's ancestral customs, would interpret and inaccurately translate specific Afrikan practices or concepts into terms shaped by the way Europeans have seen and been in the world.

Since words are about meaning and are attached to human experience, words like 'odonko', from Twi and 'jaam', from Wolof, within the cultural mindscape of indigenous speakers, describe customs that foster social interdependence. At the same time, especially when viewed with a miseducated outsider's eyes, they appear to reproduce master-servant relationships commonly found in European societies. On the contrary, in their Afrikan context, the same words occur in a social space where rights and privileges outweigh obligations to serve. Today European interpretations of those indigenous Afrikan relationships have become enshrined in our culture, their meanings invested with the trappings of centuries of Afrika's suffering from inhumane European or Arab domination and terror.

The methods of Arab and European enslavement of Afrikans combined dehumanizing brute force with mind-altering religious doctrine. On the one hand, some Arab scriptural interpretations and traditional practices treated Afrikans as 'uncivilized unbelievers' (kaffir), cursed by God (Rotberg, 1973: 7). On the other hand, generation upon generation, Christianized Europeans were persuaded to accept the lie that Afrikans were born without souls, thus effectively separating them as a species from the rest of the human race (Blyden, 1994). Since souls are by definition invisible this strategy worked like a charm, for no one could disprove its assumptions. Yet a library search of authoritative texts for this study reveals no record of equivalent 'slave' treatment of Afrikans in pre-Arabized or pre-Europeanized communities on the continent (Ki- Zerbo, 1990; Williams, 1976; Kunene, 1976). The question of dividing humanity by the presence or absence of souls seemed foreign to the preceding generations of Afrikans across the continent from the beginning of recorded time. I have found no European philosopher who has asked what experience or mindset moved his cultural world to first invent that concept and then find it so difficult to discard.

Perhaps, because captives or those who served never lost their value as human beings, there is no parallel historical pattern of 'masters' inflicting the kinds of routine atrocities Afrikans suffered, either from Europeans in the Caribbean and Americas or from the castrations they commonly suffered at the hands of both European and Arab captors. On June 24, 1924, a British official, Lord Raglan's records show that the Egyptian government, "in the Sudan, condoned participation of its own soldiers and officials in the Slave Trade…[reducing the indigenous Afrikan population to a minority among] settler-Arabs [my emphasis]" (Tilahun, 1979: 42). Even in our time, an unwritten and even unspoken collision of interests seems to unite the West and the beneficiaries of minority Arab rule who perpetrate atrocities against Sudan's indigenous Afrikan majority.

Oral or written records that passed between 'jaam' and 'sangg' or recorded events in families where 'odonko' lived paint a very different picture than that left us by European historians (Malherbe & Sall, 1989; Ki-Zerbo, 1990). Generally, Afrikan relationships of service, and even many relationships of servitude, then and now, appear to maintain a fluid, mutual, anti-caste bias and a pro-equality, Cheddo, Freethinker, tradition.

Through the preceding analysis of the words 'nigger' and 'slave' it becomes evident that forcing Afrikan cultural history to wear the dress of misdeeds perpetrated against Afrikan populations by terrorist European or Arab enslavers leads ineluctably to condoning injustice on the basis of intellectual error.

WHERE TERRORISTS ARE "SLAVEMASTERS," THEY MAKE HOSTAGES "SLAVES"

The language of captivity is ubiquitous in the media today. Groups that kidnap innocent civilians, even in fighting oppression, are routinely referred to as 'terrorists' and their victims are ascribed status as 'hostages'. On the other hand, innocent Afrikans, who were similarly kidnapped in undeclared wars by duplicitous Europeans or their agents are branded 'slaves'. In addition their brutish captors and enslavers are given socially acceptable names like 'slave master', 'sailor', 'captain', 'middleman', 'planter' or 'slave trader' (Walvin, 1992; Da Costa, 1994). In linguistic terms, it is significant that writers routinely use terms that describe the agents of Afrikan persecution by their professional function rather than by their immoral crimes. For example, historian Emilia Da Costa takes a clinical approach to the economics of inhumanity when she writes, "the supply of slaves was dwindling as a consequence of the interruption of the slave trade" and describes, "Dutch planters [emphasis added]...who started with nothing and through perseverance, industry, and frugality...built...a fortune" (Da Costa, 1994: 40-42). With similar euphemistic restraint James Walvin describes the catastrophe of Arab invasion. "With the coming [my emphasis] of Islam...Arab merchants recruited [emphasis added] Africans in abundance, shipping them across the Sahara, the Red Sea and from the East African coast" (Walvin, 1992: 26). These writers and others generally ignore the criminal nature of the horrors they describe, and their words remain mostly passionless and neutral. This occurs even when authors refer to the branding of captives with hot irons, or describe how their tormentors strip them naked and rape them, or tell how captors bind them and lock them down in the filthy holds of cold, leaky ships. Nor are there tears shed when strangers routinely tear nursing infants from their mother's arms and throw them overboard (Dow, 1980; Mannix, 1969; Litwack, 1979; Berlin, 1998).

Even the everyday conversations we share show us how deeply the language of our dehumanization has penetrated our Afrikan psyches. In an interview during Black History Month, a Toronto student from Sierra Leone informed his radio audience that his Ancestors, the nation's founders were "returning slaves from Jamaica". Logically, if free Afrikans, kidnapped and taken to the Caribbean were later able to return, they were Afrikans going home. However, the language we unconsciously employ suggests, as the history books teach us, that "slaves" were brought to the Caribbean plantations. It is therefore logical to believe that those who managed to return are also "slaves". However, as if to prove the unbroken continuity of their ancestry, Afrikans born in Jamaica use and appropriately name Afrikan foods like "fufu" (pounded) yams and "sensey" (ruffled) chickens in their original Akan tongue, to this very day (Williams, 1999: 13; Allsopp, 1996). The mere process of being taken hostage and targeted for abuse does not and cannot organically transform an Afrikan into a 'Jamaican' or a 'slave'. We can draw instructive analogies from the social oppression of other groups. A woman who suffers rape remains a woman and does not become a qualitatively inferior, raped human being for the rest of her life. Even if the culture she lives in misuses her victimization and attempts to devalue her, her deep personality, her 'womanhood' remains viable and valuable in her relationship to the world outside.

In French as in English, in Afrika or off her shores, our speech often reflects the teaching of our oppressors. While making *All Eyes On Africa* on Gorée Island in Senegal, I filmed a young Wolof guide to the airless, windowless caverns in the ground called, *"La maison des esclaves (The Slave House)"*, where Europeans had held Afrikans as prisoners-of-an-undeclared-war. The teenager made several attempts to describe the shackles he held up for the camera to view. However, I was not comfortable with a description, which presumed that Europeans, "had to" heap chains on their Afrikan victims because, as he explained in seemingly endless takes, "they kept escaping." Despite my urging, the young guide proved incapable of revising the French script that he had learned by heart. As history books usually do, it used a vocabulary that blamed Afrikans for trying to escape. I tried, unsuccessfully, to get him to say that the Afrikans escaped because they loved freedom. Within the meaning of my Pan-Afrikanist interpretation, the shackles he held up were evidence, not of Afrikan 'recalcitrance', as the sign above one cell branded its innocent inhabitants, but rather markers of European depravity.

In Nigeria, I had a similar experience with a mature and sophisticated businessman of considerable erudition and expertise. By way of demonstration, he attached shackles to his feet in one of the former 'forts' (local prisoner-of-war camps) where Europeans and their agents kept innocent captives. The prisoner-of-war camp was beside a river with easy access to the sea. However, my cultural advisor would break into strange, high-pitched laughter every time he tried to explain how the instruments of torture had been employed. It was as if our nameless, invisible Ancestors were interrupting him, having decreed speech inadequate for the horror they had been through. As it was he never finished what he wanted to say, for they made it impossible for him to speak their pain in that sacred place. It was a graphic illustration of the ultimate failure of even such charged words as "Maafa" and "Holocaust", which we find in the work of cultural historians like Marimba Ani and Bruno Bettelheim who struggle to describe horrors too deep for words (Ani, 1994; Bettelheim, 1980).

Present convention still names the floating concentration camps that ploughed the seas with desperate Afrikans on board, 'slave ships', as if they were built to take a willing, designated workforce on a Caribbean bound cruise. Cumulatively, a subliminal message also seeps through the language used to chronicle such cataclysmic events, for it treats Afrikan suffering as less significant than the suffering of other populations. That subterranean message reminds readers and listeners that Afrikans are not 'human' in the same way that other peoples are human. By accepting the devaluation of Afrikan life in the past, it can prepare those educated within modern Eurocentric or Arabocentric systems to ignore the devaluation of Afrikan life today. Given that Belgians murdered ten million Congolese at the beginning of the twentieth century, why has Germany's Adolph Hitler stood so alone as evil incarnate? Why was not Belgian's King Leopold allowed to enter the Olympiad for the title of "Greatest Monster of Modern Times" (Hochschild, 1998; Lindqvist, 1996)?

In my workshops, I've found that the experimental substitution of 'terrorists' or 'hostage keepers' for 'slave masters' and 'plantation owners' jars listeners grown used to euphemism. Some participants have tried to justify Eurocentric terms on technical grounds. For example, I have been told, 'Hostage doesn't fit because there was no demand for ransom.' That statement is historically untrue. There was instead a widespread practice among Portuguese enslavers, and also to a lesser degree among all the Europeans involved, of allowing skilled Afrikans to sell their expertise on the open market and then use some of the profit they made to buy freedom for themselves or their loved ones, usually over considerable time (Genovese; Berlin, 1998 & Litwack, 1979). That argument reveals how little factual detail on the history of Afrikan bondage circulates in the marketplace of ideas. Because the Afrikan experience remains largely absent from the popular imagination, the feelings of those who express their sense of distance, discomfort or guilt when enslavement is discussed, usually take center stage. When they do, they stifle opportunities for descendants of Afrikan survivors to process the anguish they might be allowing to surface in a mixed racial environment for the first time. Learning that over generations Afrikans have routinely lived in silence with discomfort, through coercion, necessity or design, can be a humanizing lesson for those who have never had to face such realities before.

The idea of ransom, paid in, "guineas", Afrikan gold, has currency even within the early history of Afrikan enslavement. Historians such as Jay Hinsbrunner have chronicled the ambiguous existence of "free people of color" who existed during the time of European slavocracy. Many of them worked and saved for years in order to 'buy' and in fact 'rescue' family members, lovers and friends (Hinsbruner, 1996; Berlin, 1981). Unfortunately those acts of sacrifice are subject to misinterpretation and sometimes cited as evidence of a class of 'Black slaveholders' who lived in European-style criminal comfort off the genocidal forced labor of their kith and kin. The records also show, however, that holding women or children hostage was one of the devices Europeans used to force Afrikan men to submit to forced labour (Lindqvist, 1996; Nkrumah, 1969; Berlin, 1998). Holding hostages also guaranteed less resistance to forced exile, because fathers and husbands could be coerced into laying down their arms in order to save their familiy's lives. Even in captivity, fear of losing touch with relatives or feelings of guilt for deserting them kept many Afrikans from seizing their first opportunities for escape (Bradford & Blume, 1992; Hochschild, 1998).

'Missionaries' in the context of forced servitude also played an ambiguous role, influencing Afrikan accommodation to European interests. The way they conducted their affairs gave them analogous influence to European diplomats, tourists and NGO workers in our day who provide 'intelligence' for their nation's companies or organs of state. Hans Debrunner writes, "Right from the beginning of the Portuguese discoveries in West Afrika, it was the policy of Prince Henry the Navigator to gain information about their lands, their language, their trade, their religion" (Debrunner, 1979: 34, 40). As Grand Master of the Order of Christ, a semi-military religious organization, Portugal's Prince Henry funded "missionaries" because he was "moved by the desire to know the strength of his enemy [emphasis added] (Debrunner, 1979: 34, 40). Ironically or cynically, the Portuguese missionaries who first arrived convinced those same Afrikans that, far from being enemies, all those who accepted the Christian faith were brothers and sisters in Christ. As a Pan-Afrikanist educator, I encourage young learners to place innocent before 'Afrikan' when describing those prisoners-of-undeclared-wars. I also encourage them to search primary sources for details that would give them a more accurate picture of how survivors had lived before they were kidnapped. When students put themselves in the Afrikans' skin they are able to imagine how they would defend their families, farm, build homes, heal and comfort their siblings or how, as mothers, they would be willing to sacrifice everything in order to protect the babies at their breasts. Rather than humanizing the predators (captors) by describing them as 'sailors', 'captains' or 'investors', we can instead rehabilitate the images of those humans they treat like prey. It is discomfiting but necessary to remind learners that the presence of Afrikans in this hemisphere reflects a history of forced exile and forced servitude. As descendants of Afrikan survivors we exist to bear witness to the endurance of our ancestry and in doing so to provide the groundwork for feeling pride rather than shame for having survived.

Revisiting the translations of some of the languages Afrikans were forced to leave behind furnishes missing information for settling contentious disputes over the nature of learning, governance, material conditions and the arts in pre-European and pre-Arab Afrika. On the continent, linguists Kwesi Prah and Helmi Sharawy assign a central place to mother tongues in reconstructing Afrikan history, "The presence or absence of this factor [linguistics] in the analysis of the interaction [of Arabs or Europeans] with the African countries is not an accident" (Prah, 1998; Sharawy, 1996). A consciously pro-Afrikan lexicon culled from the experience of learner-survivors in this hemisphere holds potential for promoting a very different understanding of the interminable nightmare of our 'Maafa' or 'Great Suffering', which has been mislabelled the slave trade (Ani, 1994).

Details of the 'Maafa' reveal the faces of the Afrikans behind the confusion of cold statistics we have usually learned in school. For example, writing in his diary during his voyages in the fifteenth century, the English pirate and kidnapper, John Hawkins, notes how he prepared to capture Afrikans living in the Cape Verde area because he found them "of a nature very gentle and loving" (Du Bois, 1990: 50). Presumably, their very gentleness made them more trusting towards strangers and an easy prey. The Europeans arrived with nothing of value to teach and much to learn. During that same era, engineering genius was flourishing in southern Afrika in the opulent communities of Great Zimbabwe. There the Karanga people had already constructed a wall of a million granite blocks weighing 15000 tonnes whose ruins strike onlookers with awe even today (Garlake, 1985). While the English criminal Hawkins, with royal backing, was plotting to take his terror into

Afrikan communities, other Afrikans were carrying on with their rich social lives. In Benin City in Nigeria, walled moats as formidable and extensive as any wall ever built, displayed an ingenuity equal to the Kemetic pyramid-building societies who the City's Bini people count as kin (Eweka, 1989; Egharevba, 1968). In the east of the continent, Kushites in Ethiopia were carving elaborate cathedrals out of solid rock in Lalibela, while societies in Uganda and Kilwa were building palaces, with indoor pools, surrounded by walls five miles long (Garlake). Those ongoing achievements, and there were many more in spirituality, medicine, cuisine, dance and the plastic arts, made nonsense of the lies of gangs of bloodthirsty, thieving Europeans and roving, murderous Arabs who claimed to be capturing Afrikans in order to civilize them (Garlake, 1985: 13-14; Du Bois, 1990; P'Bitek, 1980; Bebey, 1980).

As late as the nineteen eighties, I witnessed a mother-in-law in a village in Senegal pass on the art and science of making palm oil to the young wife of her son. To my untrained eyes, the process seemed full of ritual, intricacy and mystery. In the end it took the women two nights and three days of focused attention to complete. Such enduring customs that preserve ancient expertise also serve as witnesses to the stable societies to which those who followed them belonged. They demonstrate how even women and men who were neither wealthy nor associated to any leadership class could dispose of their own time. These customs are also evidence of populations with an efficient system of education, organized to pass on all the skills they needed to lead full and enriched lives. Historians Joseph Harris and Babacar Samb also demonstrate that Afrikan populations enshrined many common practices and ancestral customs that demanded a significant degree of personal freedom as well as independent thinking. It is arguable that since many of these ways of living have survived the constraints, violence and tensions of European or Arab tyranny through enslavement, they are probably inspired by the kind of life that Afrikans enjoyed before (Harris, 1987: 29-77; Samb, 1990: 281-294).

The presence of that uncommon generosity of spirit that can foster civil harmony is usually a reliable marker of a successful civilization.

While living or travelling in Senegal in the eighties and nineties, I witnessed such generosity and the high status accorded families with guests. "Amnaa gan - I have a guest" was the proudest boast any villager could make. Neighbours would spontaneously shower gifts on hosts who had the honor of receiving visitors. The retention of such a cultural practice makes 'trade' an unlikely Afrikan concept, when the word describes capturing either one's neighbours or taking strangers by surprise and then selling them into bondage in foreign lands (Chinweizu, 1987; Somé, 1995; Finch, 1999). While the logic that prizes the accumulation of 'things' is foundational to capitalism and converting human relationships into the slave trade, I have already shown that ancestral Afrikan societies placed the highest value on relationships between individuals and within groups (Williams, 1994; Marx, 1999; Bynum, 1999; Ani, 1994). Data collected by Kenya's first president, anthropologist Jomo Kenyatta illustrates how even divisions of labour and trade in everyday items like pottery were integrated into a philosophy of mutual service and respect (Kenyatta, 1965: 84-94). Trading in the lives of the sisters and brothers, daughters and sons or other members of their inclusive families does not conform to the norms of an embracing, reciprocal and giving cultural environment, where adopting strangers confers greater status than getting rich off of their goods.

Therefore, for the sensibilities of conscious Afrikans, that father of all euphemisms, the slave trade, packs the power of a semantic kick in the gut. Firstly, the use of the definite article confers particularity of meaning. Significantly the Atlantic genocide of Afrikans has become a veritable benchmark in the popular subconscious for atrocity that cripples the imagination. What makes this Afrikan experience so unique? After all, forms of servitude have been recorded in many societies, and, across the globe, loss of personal freedom was often a compromise that saved a local transgressor's life or spared captive enemies from death (Patterson, 1991: 10). No such contractual association ever existed, however, within the parameters of the slave trade, which Europeans made specific to Afrikans, by anchoring genocidal servitude to ancestry and colour. Recalling his experience on board a death-ship kidnapping innocent Afrikans, an Englishman, Dr. Alexander Falconbridge wrote:

> Previous to being in this employ I entertained a belief… that the kings and principal men bred Negroes for sale as we do cattle…All the information I could procure, confirmed me in the belief that to kidnapping and to crimes (and many of these were fabricated as a pretext) the slave trade owes its chief support (Falconbridge, 1980: 139).

His eyewitness' account is persuasive evidence that the slave trade was an atavistic attack by predators from outside on unsuspecting, vulnerable prey. The use of the slave trade also inscribes a deceptive, universalizing quality, a kind of inevitability that normalizes targeting Afrikans for atrocity and accepts heinous practices in perpetuity. Numerous examples in this study show how the terms 'African', 'Negro', 'colored' or 'Black' have in diverse contexts, been made synonymous with 'slave' for popular consumption. According to anecdotal accounts, the term 'abid' or 'abed' (slave), although considered rude, is still applied indiscriminately to people of Afrikan ancestry by many contemporary Arab populations (Sharawy, 1999; Abdulhamid, 2003; Samb, 1990: 281). Because kidnapping and enslavement of Afrikans by Arabs still occur today in Sudan, Mauritania, Chad and Mali, the term retains its immediate sting. In those sites, social commentators observe, the less Afrikan-identified you are, the more respect you get (Sharawy, 1999; Abdulhamid, 2003). One observable effect of the phrase the slave trade, therefore, has been to mask Afrikan suffering and give it the appearance of a fixed, socially acceptable identity rather than the result of a syndrome of injuries and atrocities inflicted by human agents. It launders genocide and hangs it out to dry as if it were no more than an occupational hazard incurred in the development of legitimate human industry.

Historically the role of 'slave' was first attributed to the experience of captive "Slavs" from Eastern Europe (Patterson, 1991: 357). Even though traces of those earlier identities remain embedded in European names, such as Greek names that end in '…slavos', it is self-evident that the stigma linked to them has migrated and has been grafted onto peoples of Afrikan ancestry instead. 'Slave' has therefore functioned as an engine of social transformation, denuding Afrika and scattering her children across the globe. It has therefore successfully recast ancient free peoples in the image of perpetual servants, obliging them to resist the constant expectations or demands of predatory outsiders. Understanding that history helps explain why, today, outsiders from other races and cultures generally feel free to intrude into private spaces, copy our music or other creations, use the fruits of our genius to grow rich and give little or nothing in return (Wilson, 1998; Kitwana, 2002; Beason, 1989; Allen, 1990). The false consciousness of 'slave' has helped to deform our history and trap an ancestrally free people of irrepressible, spontaneous laughter who spread joy over pain into a limiting social space. Francis Bebey's study and Jomo Kenyatta's culturally rich autobiography document for posterity how their people's educational system socialized children for harmonious living through rhythm, dance and song (Bebey, 1980; Kenyatta, 1965: 95-124). My research suggests that the most popular instruments in global, musical culture originated in Afrika, and J. H. Kwabena Nketia traces 'the piano' to Uganda by way of the Congo (Nketia, 1977: 25). 'Slave', on the other hand, creates the false impression that innocent Afrikan hostages were 'willing' or 'natural' participants in slavocracies or dehumanizing systems of governance even before Europeans began to prey on them. That popular misconception is culturally at variance with a considerable body of evidence from the study of ancestral Afrikan practices that continue to structure social relationships in contemporary life, across global Afrika (Veal, 2000).

The last word in the noxious phrase is trade. There is considerable irony in using a word that evokes commerce for the serial genocide that Europeans and Arabs inflicted and in some instances continue to inflict on Afrikan populations. Logically, our sense of discord can only escalate when we compare the economic systems of Europe, Asia and Afrika before the intrusions into Afrika began. Among the continents, Afrika's economic system was the least dependent on outside goods for her population's lifestyle. Overwhelmingly Afrikans lived in a land of plenty and general social harmony. Left to their own devices, they did not engage in the dehumanizing, depersonalized, commercial relationships that Europeans and Arabs called 'trade' in their dealings with Afrikans (Boahen, 1977; Mahoney, 1995: 3-27). Afrikans continuously resisted the labor that was disconnected from their individual or collective needs that outsiders tried to impose on them (Sonko-Godwin, 1995: 23). The record is rife with the atrocities visited on them to snuff out that resistance. Sven Lindqvist writes, "[Belgian King] Leopold's representatives simply requisitioned labor, rubber and ivory from the natives [of the Congo], without payment. Those who refused had their villages burned down, their children murdered and their hands cut off" (Lindqvist, 1996: 24).

Indeed, when Europeans began their "slave trade" around 1550, most Afrikans still lived and prospered without standardized currency. For example, well into the twentieth century, rural Afrikans would leave goods for exchange at the side of major routes with a number of stones beside them. The stones would represent the value of the goods in cowry shell and iron bar currency. Traditionally, goods would be taken and cowries left without any expectation of fraud or theft. Commerce built on such consensual trust was only possible because Afrikan culture, much like First Nations culture in this hemisphere, elevated person-to-person relationships above material wealth. Afrikan society valued entertaining strangers and giving frequent, lavish gifts above the accumulation of property, land or things (Blyden, 131-149; Green & Fernandez, 1999: 122). Besides, across Afrika, in the prosperous societies like the one that built Great Zimbabwe:

> Land was freely available. It was people who represented power ...There was [peace and] neither the desire, technology or weaponry to undertake a siege...There was no market place for there was no market economy... Gold...occurs...almost throughout the country...[and] villagers who found gold...could trade it freely (Garlake, 1985: 13-14).

John Henrik Clarke, a Pan-Afrikanist historian, is explicit about whose 'trade' it was "The germ, the motive, the rationale for the Afrikan slave trade started in the minds of Europeans in the fifteenth and sixteenth centuries...the market was created by Europeans for European reasons" (Clarke, 1994: 62). Examples of cultural retentions such as complex dances and the prolific expression of individual creativity in the arts confirm Afrika's high regard for personhood (Brain, 1979; Simpson, 1998: 189; Torgovnick, 1990: 85-135; Vogel, 1986: 25). Across the spectrum of Afrikan culture there is also a high level of investment in elaborate personal grooming (Anokye, 1980; Mandella, 2002; Sagay, 1983). Attention and care in beautifying one's person are evident from the myriad styles and intricate detail of finely grooved carvings representing the ways both women and men styled their hair. Other evidence of a deep cultural commitment to individual aesthetics exists in patterns woven into fibres or with beads to depict hair, in works that span the continent (Vogel, 1986; Bleakley, 1978; Duerden, 1974; Baldwin, 1987).

A scene engraved on a wall of ancient Kemet shows a female hairdresser meticulously using her fingertips to twist "Lady Kawit's" hair into Rastafari type locks (Simpson, 1998: 189). The process the stylist uses, its attention to detail and the demands on time the portrait demonstrates speak to the centrality of caring for hair that informs Pan-Afrikan culture. Throughout the ages, the form and texture of Afrikans' hair, distinct from that of most outsiders from Europe and Asia who settled among them, shaped the development of a unique culture around its care. Indeed pursuing his research in science and technology, Ron Eglash confirms the geometric precision of 'fractals' that remain present in Pan-Afrikan hair design even today (Eglash, 1999). From the evidence amassed, cultural practices that invested so heavily in personal care, individuality in the arts and inclusive communalism in receiving strangers run counter to the culture of an indigenous 'slave' society. In such societies personal time is compressed into units of labour and turned into currency by overlords who use it to acquire surplus material goods. However, Afrikans in their overwhelming majority disposed of too much dance-learning time, bead-making time, community-building time, celebrating and self-adorning time for us to equate their life chances with the forced, genocidal labor of sixteen-hour days imposed by the Europeans and Arabs who enslaved them (Berlin, 1998; Nyaba, 2002; Tilahun, 1979: 42). Women who can afford to spend up to six hours braiding each other's hair are unlikely to be reporting to "masters" intent on measuring their productivity by the hour or day.

Time and again, Europeans hungry to mine Afrikan resources resorted to forced labor. These interlopers could not induce the Afrikans they encountered in the Kongo or Southern Afrika, in Kenya or Sudan to work for goods or money they did not need, since the peoples they targeted had already realized all their material and social desires within the context of their cooperative communities (Bradford, 1992; Nkrumah, 170; Rotberg, 1973). The Arab or European 'slave' mentality was foreign to Afrika's lived experience or social imagination. 'Slaves' own nothing. Afrikans, whatever their station in life, were by tradition collective owners of all the land, even today the seat of personal or collective economic wealth and social security all over the globe. They also reaped the rewards of their creative talents such as songs and art. West Afrikan audiences still shower kora players with large bills. Indeed, logic argues that a population must be invested in the acquisition of things in order to sustain the urge to develop a capitalist society founded on surplus, redundancy and culture commodifying trade (Marx, 1999; Williams, 1994).

Written evidence exists to reinforce that argument. However it is largely ignored in the history books used in our academies and schools. For example, the following excerpt is taken from correspondence sent by the Mani Kongo, title of the spiritual and ancestral leader of a vast empire in the area generally known as the Congo today, to King Manoel of Portugal in 1526. The Portuguese called the Afrikan leader, Nzenga Meremba, "Dom Affonso". In his ancestral tradition, simultaneously monotheistic and polytheist, "Dom Affonso" saw no contradiction in adding a 'Christian' (in practice a 'Portuguese' or 'European') name to his other spiritual titles. The Afrikan leader's words represent an urgent request for respectful co-existence based on principles and traditions of interracial, intercultural and international diplomacy. The Congolese defender of his people's Human Rights dictated these lines during the early days of European intrusion on Afrikan soil. Europe's machinations had not yet begun to poison Afrikan society by undermining stable communities and "fomenting civil wars in which Portuguese subjects served on both sides" (Nkrumah, 1969: 4). Dr. Kwame Nkrumah felt it important to render the following text in full, in his anatomy of the overthrow of President Patrice Lumumba of the Congo by a global European and EuroAmerican, colonialist conspiracy in 1960:

> We cannot reckon how great the damage is since the above-mentioned merchants [Europeans] daily seize our subjects, sons of the land and sons of our noblemen and vassals and our relatives...They grab them and cause them to be sold: and so great, sir, is their corruption and licentiousness that our country is being utterly depopulated... That is why we beg of Your Highness to help [us] to avoid [them]... We need from [your] kingdoms no other than priests and people to teach in our schools, and no other goods but wine and flour for the holy ...[Please] assist us in this matter commanding your factors that they should send here neither merchants nor wares, because it is our will that in these kingdoms there should not be any trade in slaves or market for slaves [emphasis added] (Mani Kongo, 1969: 3).

Given the sentiments expressed in this document, the slave trade is unmasked as a convenient euphemism for a system where Europeans reap huge profits from brutal exploitation of forced Afrikan labor. Nzenga Meremba of the Kongo, Queen Nzinga of Angola in Southern Afrika as well as King Agaga of Dahomey, who sent armies to destroy slavemaking centres such as Andra (Allada) in 1724, are but a few of the Afrikan leaders whose actions counter the pervasive myths of their complicity in genocide against those they were raised and sworn to serve (Harris, 1987: 88; Kunene, 1977: 18-20). The noxious practice of forced genocidal labour has continued to exist after the Emancipation Movement in its various reincarnations. It flourished as a sharecropping system in the United States, and conscripted work units during French and British colonization. It scooped up displaced farmers under apartheid, and as the records show, was inextricably tied into Belgium's wealth-extraction campaign that meant genocide for the peoples of the Congo:

> We got no pay. We got nothing…We were always in the forest, and when we were late we were killed…Our women had to give up cultivating the fields and gardens…[We] begged the white man to leave us alone…some had their ears cut off…We fled because we could not endure the things done to us (Afrikan Survivor, 1969: 9).

Using the term slave trade also functions to disarm Afrikan minds and arm our oppressors against us. Its presumption is that innocent Afrikans, made prisoners by Europeans in undeclared, unprovoked wars are somehow guilty of unnamed crimes, while predatory Europeans remain unsullied by their heinous deeds. In fact, this analysis and excavation of enslavement yield hidden data and insights on the deceptive machine that inveigles even the well-meaning into devaluing Afrikan life. It does so by silently convicting Afrikans for being forced into suffering and degradation. As is the case with South Africa's Truth and Reconciliation Commission, verbal alchemy is used to transfer the absolution of Black innocence to provide salvation for their unrepentant persecutors instead (TRC, 1998).

MURDER PASSAGE

Given the reality of how Europeans carted Afrikans across the Atlantic, 'Murder Passage' is much more accurate than the euphemistic 'Middle Passage', which is the name most commonly applied by historians, writers and artists, from all racial groups to this superlatively tragic ordeal in human history, "the cruel and terrifying journey of enslaved Africans across the Atlantic Ocean" (Feelings, 1995). 'Middle Passage' describes, inadequately and inappropriately, the forced transportation of Afrikans from the Continent to the Americas and Caribbean by Europeans in vessels so designed they guaranteed genocide. For hapless captives there was inadequate food, water, exercise or even space to move. By European testimony, on an average, Afrikans were taller and more robust. So profiteering Whites, mindless of the difference in size of the human beings they kidnapped, squashed them into floating shrinking-machines. Men and women, wounded from branding with hot irons, were packed, spoon-like, into the darkness, wet, cold and squalor of leaky vessels. While the "ideal" height of the captives Europeans sought was six feet, captors allotted them, "less room than [a corpse] in a coffin", about five-and-a-half feet by sixteen inches (Williams, 1994: 35).

This exploration of texts, concepts and contexts shows that as Afrikans, we have been too often persuaded, over too many generations, to make our enemy's interests and rationalizations our own. Language that distances us from our own reality has also contributed to this counterintuitive phenomenon. In the media, it is not unusual to hear voices from among the recently decolonized praising the 'good old days' of colonialism (Jones, 1993; Lee & Solomon, 1991; Ellul, 1973). In similar vein, those whose race has been defamed and then criminalized by their detractors, often save their strongest condemnation for vulnerable members of their own group (McIntyre, 1993). Such social and psychological deformity is generally one of the significant but uncalculated costs of Black holocausts.

FREEDOM-SEEKERS ARE FREETHINKERS TOO

Those intelligent Afrikans who would naturally try to escape inhuman conditions are generally demonized and defamed as 'runaways' in the anti-Kushitic European fabrications that replace lived Afrikan history (Jones, 1993; Hill, 1981; Berlin, 1998). In contrast, textbooks and popular culture communication have usually invested neutrality and a kind of respectability to the vigilantes and lynch mobs that hunt freedom-seekers down by naming them 'slave patrols' (Litwack, 1979; Berlin, 1981; Pennington, 1970: 81-90). It is usual for police officers or soldiers to patrol to keep the peace and defend a community from wrongdoers. In this scenario, however, the wrongdoers are the patrol, which imposes unjust laws against innocent people. Earlier Euro American medical history, with consummate irony, records how delusional Whites, those who had kidnapped or held innocent Black families hostage, heaping cruelties on their head, slandered all Afrikans shrewd and skilled enough to escape. Doctors invented a disease called, "drapetomania", and, unconsciously demonstrating their own mental deformity, described it as the 'madness' of running away (Gould, 1981).

Escaping always posed enormous risks, and the costs of daring to be free were heavy for all involved. It took extraordinary feats of courage, uncommon energy and inventive genius to outwit the armed, vigilant, ubiquitous and pitiless agents of the slavocracies that held innocent Afrikans in bondage. While abolitionist writers made "white conductors" the heroes of those epic times, hiding Blacks "under a mass of literature written by [them], their descendants, and admirers". However, Larry Gara points out, "[much] of the escape drama was a self-help affair" (Gara, 1969: 335).

William Still, a son of escaped survivors documented the heroism "that required the manhood of a man and the unflinching fortitude of a woman" (Gara, 1969: 327). Women and men walked hundreds of miles with bloodied feet through swamps and snow (Drew, 1981; Ripley, 1986). They hid, for years sometimes, under the very eyes of their enslavers (Jacobs, 2000). They built boats out of reeds, and also concocted potions that hid their scent so that the hounds pursuing them went astray (Litwack, 1979; Drew, 1981). An Afrikan of superhuman fortitude, misnamed "Theophilus Collins" by his persecutors, carried his entrails in his hands as he eluded and outdistanced baying hounds to reclaim the freedom stolen from him (Gara, 1969: 334). Daniel Hill, a Canadianized Afrikan describes the extraordinary exploits of his immediate Ancestors with consummate reserve, "The heroic work of the Black freedom-seekers and their abolitionist helpers did not go unopposed" (Hill, 1981: 39; Drew, 1981).

Names like 'Maroon' honor those Afrikans who were resourceful and courageous enough to set up independent communities and maintain them in the face of relentless pursuit. Maroons existed wherever captives were found in this hemisphere, far to the north, in Ontario, and deep in the south from Florida to Brazil (Deagan & MacMahon, 1995; Mulder, 1991). 'Maroon', was made famous by Jamaican resisters and is still used today by their descendants living on the freed land they inherited (Gottlieb, 2000). As opposed to 'runaway', which suggests illegitimate activity, 'maroon' and 'freedom-seeker' convey a sense of righteous resistance and pride. An educator and historian, Asa Hilliard defines "maroonage" as "...freedom for the purpose of survival and cultural unity" (Hilliard, 1995: 54).

Context is also a critical element in understanding the why of so much misunderstanding that adheres to significant events in Pan-Afrikan history. The following notes suggest a limited frame for viewing the chronology of European activities that undermined Afrikan society and accompanied their predatory raids across the continent. In 1440, the European inventor, Gutenberg, establishes a printing press based on 11th century Chinese technology. In 1454, Afrikan leaders request printing press technology in exchange for European access to Afrikan resources. Two German printers arrive in the Kongo in 1492, the same year that Columbus sets foot on Caribbean soil (Nkrumah, 1969: 1).

In 1518, Dom Henrique, son of the Mani Kongo, visits the Pope in Rome. He is 18 years old at the time and already an accomplished linguist able to address the Pope in fluent Latin. In this same period Antonio Manuel Varda, the adopted European name of a son of the Congo, is the ambassador from the "King of the Congo" to the Vatican. His bust, with a vest of leather "gri gri" (protective spiritual amulets worn in ancestral Afrikan religious practice) still stands in the Vatican today (IPAM, 1970: 77).

In 1526, correspondence denouncing kidnapping and enslavement (cited above) is sent by the Mani Kongo, title of the spiritual, ancestral leader of a vast empire in the area generally known as 'Congo' today, to King Manoel of Portugal. In the next chapter we turn from wounding words to wounding youth and teachers today. They also show the destructive power of language in inflicting that violence and demonstrate the necessity of a Pan-Afrikan educational frame to equip Black students for survival, resistance and academic success.

3
Chapter

WOUNDING DEEDS

- - - ● - ● - ● ● - ● ● - ● - - ● - - ● - - ● ● ●

SIX INSTRUCTIVE SCENES FROM
PAN-AFRIKAN LEARNING LIFE

Education is key for all survivors of Pan-Afrikan hostages who want to know why we are here and how we have been trapped into a global system of forced exile and domination that permits White supremacists to feed and grow fat off our strengths (Wells, 1970; Hilliard, 1995). I have culled and constructed the following stories from my observations in classrooms and studies in contemporary education from a Pan-Afrikanist perspective. They reveal that the invisible fallout from genocidal forced servitude still fuels prejudice in today's daily life. Further, they show how that history distorts learning experiences, cripples academic achievements and strews snares and barriers in the path of Afrikan students and teachers. In these scenes, we peer behind walls and observe confrontations between Black self-determination and race supremacy. Where names have not been previously published, pseudonyms are used.

Since I view education as an applied science of expanding consciousness, I use four questions aimed at finding practical Pan-Afrikanist responses to the conflicts described:

What are the aspect(s) of this situation that than can potentially erode or enhance Pan-Afrikan dignity?

What are the forces in this situation that can potentially impede or improve Pan-Afrikan self-determination?

What are the potential costs of this situation? Who bears them and who benefits?

Where and how are spaces and personal support provided for recuperation and potential redress of injustices against Afrikans?

The stories are presented in two groups. The first three stories lend insight into how students and teachers deal with threats to their dignity. The latter group is aimed at helping readers chart the labyrinth of denial that often runs parallel to the exercise of racist institutional power against students and teachers of Afrikan ancestry.

THREAT

Scene 1: 'Slave' Has Not Lost its Sting

Black teenage learners in a Toronto classroom reject their Black teacher's attempts to engage them in discussions of "slavery". "That couldn't happen to me and my boys," boasts Kai. "We'd know how to take care of those Whites. We're not punks." [The last term is a common slur used by Black males in the United States and translates roughly as 'sissies and cowards'] (Hutchinson, 2000: 2).

These words from a Black youth in the growing, a young man clutching wildly at straws of verbal power tossed his way by a homophobic, macho, mean-spirited and anti-Kushitic world, can be quoted to confirm stereotypes of an aggressive, bombastic, homophobic Black male culture. That information is not illogical based on the hurtful slurs he employs. There may well be, however, another truth beneath the surface of this scene. Kai may be feeling the terror of being vulnerable and rudderless in the rough seas of classroom degradation. Words like 'slavery' convey layered diverse meanings to their student audiences. What a White student hears is not the same as what a Black student feels.

Similar statements that challenge teachers, including Black teachers, surface regularly in the work I do in schools. Kai's bigoted, threatening and boastful words may be no more than a symbolic beating of the male breast. His words send out a warning to the world that serves as a substitute for physical aggression (Attenborough, 1990). This mechanism for mediating injury during conflict is common in the non-human world. My observations suggest that Kai's peers would understand and probably treat his words as mere incantation. They too have learned to use disfigured words like their Ancestors used disfiguring masks to ward off invisible spirits of humiliation and looming despair. For without words to stir the blood when terror clutches the heart, many young Black men shrivel up inside and lose their will to live fully human lives. Zoologist David Attenborough tells us that when some rats yield to stronger rivals in the open they crawl into a hidden place to die, presumably of a crushed and shrivelled heart (Attenborough, 1990).

Young Black men often respond to similar threats with outward bravado, but their eyes and body language often betray the unbearable anxiety they are feeling inside.

It's my view that the trigger to Kai's reaction was the word, 'slavery'. I have discussed its unique resonance for Afrikans in North American society, and pointed out that 'slave' comes from 'Slav'. It was originally applied by Western Europeans to the Eastern Europeans they held in captive servitude (Houghton Miflin, 1992: 1695). Historically, then, slavery has occurred among all racial groups. However, in today's world, it is associated, almost exclusively, with Afrikans. I have worked with educators who report how classroom tension escalates when they teach about White subjugation of Blacks in concrete terms, especially in racially mixed classes. A similar response occurs when they use texts that present an even mildly realistic picture of the European enslavement of innocent Afrikans.

Other educators also report distancing laughter and self-mockery by Afrikan students when enslavement is taught. It's far easier, they say, to deal with contemporary conflicts in Rwanda or other nations where the media show Blacks viciously hurting other Blacks. From these anecdotal accounts, there also appears to be less discomfort when discussions turn to gender, ability, sexuality, anti-Semitism, linguistic diversity, refugee issues, religious persecution or ethnic discrimination. The more Afrikan-identified the sufferers, it appears, the harder it is for those who run classrooms to speak unambiguously about our powerful truths.

Hopefully, significant changes in the discourse on race will occur when the language that Black students learn about hurtful images linked to their identity is a closer reflection of their real feelings. Committed, Pan-Afrikanist, anti-racist educators are challenged to help students like Kai develop that fluency. Listeners whose palms don't become sweaty and whose hearts don't beat faster at the sound of 'slave' would then be offered more authentic glimpses of the experience of being young and Black (Bing, 1991; Alexander, 1970; Gunst, 1995; McCall, 1995; Jackson, 1990). Such opportunities are key for teachers interested in expanding their information base, becoming more skilled in assessments of what they hear or see and enhancing empathy for students like Kai. There are added benefits to crafting language that fosters empathy, breaks silences, interrupts macho denial and corrects miscommunication across the chasm of White security and Black vulnerability. As teachers learn to speak unspoken truths about the genocide and enslavement of Afrikans, we will by, by necessity, create new tools and practice using them in ways that enhance our work in all anti-bias education.

Scene 2: Affirming 'Afrikan' Identity Derails White Supremacy

Black females form the majority of Black educators, and they often pay a high price for defending Black students and upholding their truths (Henry, 1998). To begin with, Black professionals are sitting ducks when institutional power is combined with anti-Kushitic sexism. This story of an exceptional Black teacher takes place in Brooklyn, New York City. In terms of size and density of its representation, this borough is reputedly home to the largest Black population after Lagos, Nigeria, a legend of runaway urban growth. The conflict in this story involves a seasoned, successful, Black drama teacher, Nani Hatshepsut, and a Black female colleague who supports her. At the time it occurs the incident is widely publicized in Black media in New York and is picked up in Toronto.

Ms. Hatshepsut is fired for telling her Black students in a majority Black community school, in classes that are almost 100% Black that they are 'Afrikan'. This name is new for many students accustomed to wearing identities like, 'African American' or 'Jamaican' instead. Their teacher, however, makes sure that she has their parents' prior support for using 'Afrikan' alone. Ms. Hatshepsut also advises her students not to let anyone, and that anyone includes other members of the staff, persuade them to play roles that are demeaning stereotypes, such as pimps and prostitutes, in the plays they perform in class. She reasons with them, saying that since in grade seven and eight they are at an impressionable age, it would be a better use of their class time if they explored positive aspects of their heritage and community.

When she is away one day, a White substitute teacher asks a student to play the role of a criminal. The student balks, and his classmates back him up, repeating what Ms. Hatshepsut had taught them. The substitute teacher complains angrily to the administration. He goes even further, accusing Ms. Hatshepsut of teaching her Black students to be racist by calling them 'Afrikan'. She defends her pedagogical approach and a colleague supports her. The administration, in the persons of a Black male principal and superintendent, fire both Black women.

We can extract useful lessons on the working of institutional anti- Kushitism from this story. I find it instructive that while a White man makes the complaint, two Black faces, the principal and superintendent, preside over the punishment that remove committed teachers from their community. Those Blacks in office serve, in fact, as surrogates for the power Whites often exercise by remote control. White supremacy has refined its techniques for finding Blacks to do its dirty jobs against their own group. Historically, a similar strategy was used in concentration camps, in forced labour 'plantations' and by both European and Arab colonizers (Williams, 1976; Pérez, 1992). Sven Lindqvist records how, in 1899 a French army officer ordered Senegalese troops to massacre 150 innocent Malian villagers, confident that "…Senegalese soldiers…would [not] bring themselves to shoot at a [White] superior officer" (Lindqvist, 1996: 168).

The success of this approach provides a way for Whites who wield institutional power to fire, discipline or deselect Afrikan resisters while keeping their agency out of sight. Surrogates for White supremacy make it harder for individuals and communities to identify the sources of the injustices and hurts inflicted on them. By pitting factions in the community against each other, the forces that desire to control them divide groups and weaken them (Cleaver & Katsiaficas, 2001; Mudenge, 1986).

Black language and how Whites interpret it are also at the heart of this situation. It is instructive that a White man can label a Black woman "racist" for accurately naming students according to their visible Afrikan ancestry. Working as he does in a formally integrated but operationally segregated school system, that White teacher can see that all Afrikan students face challenges unique to their ancestry and skin. His accusation therefore denies their realty and so lacks integrity. In addition, he chooses to exercise his social privilege as a White man against vulnerable Black women.

Reportedly, the supply teacher also invokes the name of Martin Luther King while condemning Ms. Hatshepsut for being "racist" and "separatist". His actions provoke speculation. Would he react in the same way if a teacher were to encourage students from Indian, Chinese, Jewish, Arab or First Nations (Aboriginal) communities to connect themselves to their ancestry? Usually society permits groups to self-identify. South Africans of Dutch European ancestry who call themselves 'Afrikaner' do not seem to provoke similar controversy. The conflation of Afrikan identity and activism runs deep in North American society. In my work, I have also found that 'racist' is often a hard word for Whites to hear. When Black students or faculty accuse Whites of racist behaviour, they are usually required to present irrefutable proof such as an admission of racist intention and have their charge substantiated by White witnesses as well. In this instance, the school's Black administrators readily accept the analysis and accusation of a transient White member of school board's staff.

In order to respond logically to the threats they face, however, groups are obliged to organize their self-defence in accordance with the categories under which they are oppressed. If Women are oppressed as Women, then organizing by class, profession or appearance will always leave the women who fall outside those categories still vulnerable. So it is superb good sense for Afrikan people, captured by race, enslaved by race and dominated by race to organize by ancestry, the most reliable instrument for recognizing and including all those targeted by race supremacy. Therefore a Pan-Afrikanist approach to education identifies our children by ancestry so they can learn to protect themselves as a group and build successful academic careers founded on collective Afrikan strengths.

Scene 3: Break 'Em Down to Break 'Em In

Omar is a successful, Canadian born, Afrikan student who has prepared studiously for his Ontario Academic Certificate, the provincial high school final exams. When he is absent from a crucial final exam his White guidance counsellor is so disappointed that he criticizes Omar for losing his nerve and deliberately staying away. Stung by the criticism, Omar blurts out a story that he had kept to himself until then.

As he tells it, after studying late at school the day before that exam he was walking home when a police cruiser drove by and two officers stopped him. They made him take off his jacket and shoes and stand in the snow in weather that was freezing cold. Then they left him standing unprotected in the open for such a long time that he began to shiver. Chilled to the bone, Omar fell ill, missed his exam and with it lost a year of school and a possible scholarship. In this story, White supremacist policing becomes an instrument for preventing Black academic success.

Scene 4: Black Males are Always in the White Bull's Eye

Michael Porter, a US family therapist living in Savannah, Georgia provides both analysis and up-to-date data confirming a historical pattern of White male authority that targets Black males from an early age. He affirms, "African boys have become public education's monster---feared, mistrusted, and hated, mere animals to be confined to cages (special education classes)" (Porter, 1997: 5). The educator went on to analyze data in Georgia schools and show conclusively that "Black children who outscored White classmates on standardized tests were steered into the low track anyway" (Porter, 1997: 6). Therefore, he argued, the circle that cuts off and strangles educational opportunity for Black students, especially males, becomes hermetically sealed from an early age.

Even students, who are successful, like Omar in this case study, are not safe from the manufactured failure controlled by forces both inside and outside the classroom. Faced with those certainties, Omar needs to learn the language of self-protection in and out of school and prepare himself to respond appropriately to the forces arraigned against his success. I find it instructive that Omar has no words for dealing effectively with the police. He submits in silence. In fact his behaviour mirrors the subjugation of generations of Afrikan men who have had little choice besides lowering their eyes and eating their anger as armed White men violated their persons and their rights (Parker, 1986: 4).

Young men like Omar are often forced to respond to racist slurs, including homophobic ones from police. Unless they do so with extreme politeness, they face assault or aggravated abuse (Marshall, 2003). Omar needs powerful words that can persuade the police not to persecute him. As educators, we are not usually permitted to hear the words that run through his head. One can speculate, however, that he is forced to referee two conflicting scripts. The first script is probably full of passion, anger and self-righteous outrage based on his injured humanity and pride. However, a rival voice, the voice of generations of Afrikans who have swallowed pride to stay alive, is also counseling subservience, throttling spontaneous emotion and urging him to ignore the fact that he is starving for respect.

Psychologist Na'im Akbar identifies this internal tug-o-war as a source of the ambivalence that often causes Afrikans to sink into dysfunction as children or even in their adult lives. Akbar writes, "… the loss of the ability… to shield oneself from a blow began to teach the slave that he should have no self-respect" (Akbar, 1984: 24). Omar cannot protect himself physically or verbally from abuse. We can assume, however, that he must store the displaced energy that it excites somewhere deep in his being. What he needs at the moment of trauma is language that can conserve and transform his energy so that it becomes available for preserving his self-esteem and arming him against possible, future assault.

It is reasonable to expect that young Black men who grow up subjected to similar experiences eventually devise ways of defending themselves. Yet academic institutions, the policing system and popular media, in my observation, by identifying such behaviour as aggression, disproportionately single out Black males for forcible control when they assume a necessarily defensive stance. Black students generally assume a defensive stance during lessons or discussions of the many holocausts that have plagued Afrikan history. For students like Omar, what goes on outside school is rarely brought into their learning world. That leaves significant forces that affect them as Afrikans in a White supremacist society out of sight. Education that aims to prepare students adequately for the challenges of that deeper, hidden world should logically create safe, welcoming spaces in school for them to tell fuller stories about external reasons that might indirectly or directly affect their academic achievements (Steele, 2003: 109).

DENIAL

Scene 5: White Supremacy Sees Green When Black Succeeds.

A Harlem journalist documents the story of a successful Black educator, at the highest levels of the academy, who still remained vulnerable to punitive, White power exercised by remote control. As James McIntosh tells it, Dr. Abdulalim Shabazz is a gifted professor of mathematics. He has the enviable reputation of taking students who are inadequately prepared by earlier schooling and turning them into successful graduates and doctoral scholars. Even President Clinton cites him for his outstanding contributions in his field (McIntosh, 1997). At the university in Atlanta, Georgia where he has spent highly productive years, he is named Chair of his department as a result of his exemplary success. Across the nation he has no peer. Yet a mere month after his presidential citation, Dr. Shabazz is axed from his position as Chair.

Scene 6: Providing For Posterity Prescribes Contingency Plans

One of the charges against Dr. Shabazz is that he raised the issue of "racial injustices against African Americans." A further charge states, "Relevant literature on these issues [read 'racism'] was distributed." This evidence seems to confirm psychologist Bruno Bettelheim's observation that survivors challenge oppressors by their very existence and presence on any scene (Bettelheim, 1980). Dr. Shabazz makes similar arguments in statements to the press, contending that the ability of some Afrikans to reach a state approaching self-determination creates anxiety within the Eurocentric status quo.

This gifted educator is credited with producing, in recent times, directly or indirectly, "half the Black PhDs in mathematics and mathematics education in the US", although there are few Blacks teaching mathematics at the university level (McIntosh, 1997: 17). His biographer states that, "the notion that a mainly Black mathematics faculty, by definition, implies discrimination still persists [my emphasis]" (McIntosh, 1997: 17). Observed from outside, the details of the case show that Dr. Shabazz and the successful faculty team he built up seem to have reasonably anticipated and prepared themselves for institutional White supremacist assault. Recent US history and race history of that particular state, including a bloody, protracted struggle of Blacks for Human Rights, had offered them valuable lessons about potential White reaction to Black social gains. They knew their Pan-Afrikanist approach had to develop tools for self-protection in order to preserve the small space they had won for practicing self-determination. Their experience also taught them to take accurate readings of their environment. They faced the situation at hand by providing for careful scrutiny of all records committed to paper, video or audiotape. In terms of the global Afrikan community, intelligent self-determination makes caution an axiom in the face of the dangers around.

The meaning of this story is woven from many threads. As a convert to the Nation of Islam, Dr. Shabazz chose a more satisfying name than the one he inherited under the shadow of enslavement. From his story readers learn that the name "Shabazz", like the martyred Malcolm X, means, "That which cannot be destroyed" (McIntosh, 1997: 42). His choice of name signals his attention to language and its meaning in his life. It is also significant that, although he teaches Math, the charges against Dr. Shabazz are not framed in terms of his competence in his discipline, but directed against his bureaucratic writing and speech. His criticisms of racist faculty behaviour and unwavering faith in the intellectual potential of his Afrikan students appear to disturb the fragile sensibilities of race supremacy. White institutions, as several studies have demonstrated, often rely on politely ambiguous language and euphemism to oil the wheels of their racist indifference to the failure of Black students in their charge (Porter, 1997; Hilliard, 1995; Dei 1996; James, 1995). The response to Dr Shabazz's breach of unwritten anti-Kushitic norms is predictably swift. Floods of retribution rush in. He is punished for restoring the language of confidence and achievement to his Black students or colleagues.

With rare exception, in my experience, educators, especially when they are Black, pay a steep price for standing up to White supremacy. It might seem advisable for Afrikans in educational institutions to learn to monitor their speech and develop exculpatory euphemisms in order not to cause distress among European, Asian or anti-Kushitic faculty. However, such learned behaviour defeats a primary goal of Pan-Afrikanist education, defined by its commitment to preparing future generations for thriving in any environment, without having to barter away their self-respect.

Humanity is hard currency and respect a billion dollar bill. Let us peer through a window into another Ontario classroom! A Black student is responding to a teacher who tells the class that knowing how many Afrikans were murdered during the slave trade is not important (Newman, 2000). The student balks. After all she has been schooled in the numbers of Europeans killed in two great wars and as a result of the Nazi genocide. In addition, in earlier classes, teachers have insisted that the scale of those atrocities multiplied their significance for the whole human race.

WHEN WE VALUE OUR ANCESTORS,
SOCIETY VALUES US

Differential approaches to the histories of European and Afrikan holocausts do not escape notice by students of Afrikan ancestry. Students have instead frequently revealed evidence of both a personal and collective investment in the subtleties of communication surrounding all aspects of our ancestry. They monitor language, behaviour and the images used in class and note when they imply that Afrikans submit to subjugation more naturally than other racial groups. Fundamental ideological confrontations regularly turn Eurocentric classrooms into sites that can aggravate risks for students of Afrikan descent or, conversely, reinforce their will to resist and succeed (Perry, 2003).

Pan-Afrikanist historian John Henrik Clarke chronicles patterns of thinking and practices that rationalize away the serial European onslaught on Afrika that scattered her children far and wide. As Dr. Clarke demonstrates, both the control of technology for keeping records and the language of record have been tools for controlling how we can inform our deepest emotions. Clarke writes, "Most people, especially Europeans who created most of the documents on the slave trade, write about that subject with the intent to make the victim of slavery feel guilty and to vindicate the perpetrators of the slave trade" (Clarke, 1994: 59).

As Pan-Afrikanist educators, we must stretch, crush, knead, cook again and recreate vocabulary to tide learners over this period of extended forced exile in order to help students reinterpret, rewrite and transform the record of past crimes against us. In fact, even the words 'forced exile' are a challenge to those who commonly describe Afrikans in this hemisphere as 'immigrants', implying that we are marginalized because we failed to integrate or be assimilated like other immigrants. Logic demands that Pan-Afrikan educators melt the frozen language of our degradation and fashion tools for excavating spaces where new forms pf discourse can take root and grow. In so doing we pay due respect to the dignity of those Afrikans martyred in past holocausts and free our minds to harvest strengths from the sacrifices they have made.

White Approval or Black Pride: Kara and Colin are siblings whose mother is a successful, well-known Black professional and whose father is a White educator. By the accident of genetic destiny, Kara looks White, with grey eyes and straight, blondish hair. On the other hand, popular culture stereotypes would classify Colin as un-ambiguously Black, because of the texture of his hair, his features and the shade of his skin.

The children grow up in middle-class comfort in urban North America, within a city that still conducts itself officially as if it were uniformly White. Their mother, however, is an active promoter of Black culture through the arts. Although there are occasional articles in the local media on racism against members of Hispanic or Aborig-inal communities, the siblings never question the racism Black people face in either the community at large or at school. On the surface all seems serene. However, one day the mother overhears a tearful Colin earnestly asking his sister why she does not stand up for him when oth-er kids at school beat him up and call him "nigger". With the honesty of that innocence we usually lose with our youth, Kara replies, "Because I don't want them to treat me the way they treat you." *We Can Always Come 'Black' Home.*

One of the consequences of racial integration is the uneven dis-tribution of risk among those of Afrikan ancestry. The vagaries of for-tune and shade often prescribe our operational identity and how the public treats us. Since "your face becomes your race", those who 'look most Afrikan' to the undiscerning, unkind and race supremacist eye are usually treated as prime targets for discrimination or abuse (Butler, 1998). It is a difficult area for caring adults to confront. Some White mothers of Black children have been unable to hold back their tears in the workshops I facilitate when they describe the way shade or Afrikan features warped the life of one sibling while a lighter skinned sister or brother sailed through school and life. Parents find it hard to hold regret at bay when they witness the painful experiences they unwittingly bequeath their multiracial or biracial daughters and sons. Whatever parents may wish or racial genetics might promise, society generally does not permit those of mixed Black heritage to belong to any race but Black. Ironically, our children are like fish programmed to swim in 'schools'. However, forced to survive in rough seas that are toxic with prejudice, like swimmers in sulphuric acid, they frequently find themselves randomly ambushed by sharp, unexpected pain.

It is my observation that we have paid inadequate attention to the needs of siblings who share genes, upbringing and culture, yet, because of how they look, have discordant experiences in the wider world. Pan-Afrikanism asserts that it is a young person's fundamental human right to be protected from anti-Kushitism, or other forms of identity abuse, by those of us who, as educators, hold the vulnerable psyches of our children in protective trust. The Colins and Karas in our homes need 'raceproofing' before they are sent out into an anti-Kushitic world. 'Raceproofing' includes frank discussion of how 'shadism' works to debase and humiliate those with the physically Blackest skin and most stereotypically Afrikan features. Young people need a roadmap that points out the dangers of distractions like 'One Love' theories, which pretend that questions of a racial divide are simply evidence of inadequate trust and insufficient love between individuals from different racial groups (TRC, 1998). Pan-Afrikanist education provides a realistic analysis of historical betrayals of Black trust in the service of immoral, colour-ranked hierarchies of power. In 1899, Chief Kourtey of the Sansan-Hausa people of West Afrika lamented, "I had done nothing to them [Europeans]. I gave them everything they asked for. They ordered me to hand over six horses and thirty head of cattle within three days. I did so. And yet…[a] hundred and one men, women and children were massacred" (Lindqvist, 1996: 166). In the face of events that defy our collective moral imagination, our daughters and sons deserve an effective, skilled and informed support system to help them navigate racist hostility outside and to soothe their hurt psyches when they are forced to come back home.

Kara and Colin have learned to be silent within their school system, where they have observed Black students regularly punished for speaking up against injustice (Foster, 1997: 35). Pan-Afrikanist and feminist Ida B. Wells is a model for how we can open up safer learning spaces within anti-Kushitic societies. Although born into bondage, she became a teacher and journalist bonded to the liberation of all her people. At a time when those she valued most were most vulnerable, she put their survival before her personal safety or professional gain. She was fired from a precious teaching position for speaking her mind, but refused to back down. In another battle for Human and Civil Rights, Ida B. Wells successfully sued the Chesapeake and Ohio Railroad for its discriminatory seating policies in 1884. She did so many decades before the bus boycott to support a defiant Rosa Parks.

Besides dauntless courage, Ida B. Wells demonstrated superlative skill in negotiating inter-racial relationships within the violently racist society in which she lived. She understood that self-determination demands constant vigilance. She led a campaign against the unjust hanging of returning Black veterans and soldiers in uniform with the slogan, "black boys sacrificed to race hatred". When White intelligence agents tried playing 'good cop, bad cop' to make her back down, she stood her ground. In frustration an agent scolded her. "The rest of your people do not agree with you." She replied, "They don't know any better or they are afraid of losing their whole skins" (Wells, 1970: 370). Her answer bore echoes of pioneer abolitionist, Harriet Tubman, who reportedly said, "I could have freed thousands more if they knew they were slaves." Pan-Afrikanism challenges us to educate each other in proportion to our knowledge, consciousness and gifts.

Young women and men like Kara and Colin need the stories of unbowed, accomplished Black women like Ida B. Wells and Charlotte Forten, unapologetic feminists who always upheld collective Black dignity (Wells, 1970: 370; Burchard, 1995). Pan-Afrikanist education fosters courage in young Afrikans by celebrating such exemplary lives as those of South African freedom fighter Winnie Madikizela-Mandela and Canadian educator, Annette Henry. In an insightful study, Henry lifts up confident Black female voices full of spirit and self-determination (Mandela, 1985; Henry, 1998). Educators Enid Lee, Michelle Foster and bell hooks, thinkers with wide experience and practical ideas, also courageously negotiate the quicksand dividing Black femaleness from equal partnerships with Black males. Working in the United States, Michelle Foster has developed daily strategies for strengthening children through connecting community and school. Simultaneously, her strategies enrich communities by teaching all students to use the power of their own voices for change (Foster, 1997: 34-35). Feminist bell hooks reminds readers, "As an expression of self-esteem we have to promote the value of living consciously in a society where everyone is encouraged to remain unconscious" (hooks, 2003: 79). As we work in multiracial settings, Enid Lee constantly challenges all educators to hold students of Afrikan ancestry 'in our gaze'.

One of the pitfalls of North American Hip Hop culture is its capacity for miseducating, young Black men. Unexamined images often portray an invented, seamlessly multiculturalized, multiracialized, multicomfortable population, living beyond the reality of profiling, poor housing or racialized economic divides. Even Minister Ben Chavis Muhammad, a former Civil Rights Movement activist and head of the National Association for the Advancement of Colored People in the United States publicly makes the misleading statement, "Hip Hop has transcended race" (Chavis, 2003). Mistakenly reading multiracial Hip Hop images to mean that 'we're all the same', young Black men often ignore the power of stigma that singles them out for humiliation and harassment, especially in eurocentric societies. When they are exuberant or adventurous, like young men of all races, they run a gauntlet of discriminatory practices waiting in ambush along their path. That generalization also describes how they experience school, which consumes most of their early lives. As Pan-Afrikanist psychologist Michael Porter states, "[measured] against the conditions of African American boys, public schools should be viewed as toxic" (Porter, 1997: vi).

In the present situation under examination, Colin needs support, information and tools to help him confront the choices before him, as a Black male in this society. Fate makes him a defender of his Afrikan identity and a target of society's unwarranted attack. Pan-Afrikanist education, conscious of his social location, celebrates that part of his being society vilifies most rather than teaching him to avoid the special challenges it brings. Colin might gain considerable insight comparing and contrasting the dreams, choices and lived experience of revolutionaries like Robert Williams and Assata Shakur against the desperate actions of a Mark Essex. Williams and Shakur both escaped into exile to avoid the probability of death at the hands of armed agents of an oppressive government. Mark Essex, on the other hand, had returned as a hero from Vietnam. Feeling betrayed by the race supremacist society he faced, he armed himself and committed suicide by openly attacking a local police building (Tyson, 1999; Shakur, 1987; Leyton; 1986). Males who choose to identify as Black, be principled and still survive, need fine judgment and the intense discipline enshrined in ancient Kushitic codes in order to lead, successful enlightened lives (Carruthers, 1995).

Pan-Afrikan educators are summoned by our own humanity to provide prophylactic protection for younger Black men who have no choice but to live in the world we bequeath them by 'commission, omission or design'. The free flow of interracial encounters and personal attachments often prevent young Afrikans from recognizing or acknowledging betrayals of their dignity. In an atmosphere that feeds on ambiguity, many of our youth strive instead to achieve neutrality. They usually hope desperately that the differential impact of race on their lives will never have to be explored or exposed. Living under the stresses most Afrikans face, predictable ignorance can seem like a solution or an easy way out to them. When the media, academy and popular culture raise burning issues such as 'profiling', most mainstream reporters and pundits generally skate by the historical specifics like the "Maafa" or the obscene details of the persecution that has been visited on the Black race. Rushing toward 'reconciliation' and the comforting embrace of 'raceless' interpretations of world history, North American society generally glosses over or ignores the unique moral and social choices it made in sacrificing so much Afrikan humanity to build the global, modern economy as well as an accompanying culture of comfort for other groups beside Blacks (Rodney, 1981; Grovogui, 1996; Onyewuenyi, 1994).

By definition, Pan-Afrikan educators are morally bound to expose nominally liberal forces when they wield the power of page, screen and distribution networks against Afrikans while paying lip service to human equality. In Part I and Part II, I tried to expose gaping holes in the 'comforting' logic that the dominant society offers in self-defence or as an explanation of its failure, over generations, to make the ideals it preaches real. As this society fails to turn its promises of justice into deeds, it empties them of meaning and they morph instead into moral parachutes for beneficiaries of the status quo.

In Part III, I will demonstrate how good intentions alone are not enough to transform the discourse of denial that generally shapes popular attitudes to Black holocausts. Chapter Four examines the official reports of two commissions created as liberal responses to crises caused by the legacies of racial domination, while Chapter Five explores the limits of two insightful anti-racist documentaries which still fall short in articulating Pan-Afrikan experiences.

2
Book

Part III:

Denying Afrika

4

Chapter

A TALE OF TWO COMMISSIONS

● ●

As I continue this study, I explore the impact of two seminal (male oriented) documents on Pan-Afrikan events that gripped the imagination of the world. The two reports I address are not only historically significant but also illustrate the subtle seductive power of White words that shape Black reality through an inclusive, yet euphemistic discourse. *The Report on the National Advisory Commission on Civil Disorders,* also called *The Kerner Commission Report* after its chair, Governor Otto Kerner of Illinois, was written in 1968 under a White US government (The New York Times, 1968). *The Report of The Truth and Reconciliation Commission,* on the other hand, was written in 1998 under a Black South African government (TRC, 1998). Not only do these reports bridge continents, they link generations, spanning a period of thirty tumultuous years.

21ST CENTURY AUTOPSY OF THE KERNER COMMISSION REPORT

The Commission's members investigated, deliberated and made recommendations, after the hurricane season of uprisings and rebellions by long-suffering Americanized Afrikans in the United States, during the nineteen sixties. These Commissioners also successfully demonstrated that those cumulative events threatened, at a particular moment, to overwhelm the institutions of the United States and tear the fabric of society apart (The New York Times, 1968: 1). This is a wealthy panel, all male, except for one White woman and all White, except for two carefully selected Blacks anointed with the oil of "inter-racial moderation". It is this group that sits, investigates and eventually passes judgment on a Black population, whose members in its overwhelming majority would never have been nominated as representatives of interracial moderation. For they, like Samson in the Bible, had taken hold of two pillars of White supremacy, fear and accommodation, and almost toppled the whole edifice to the ground. This study has a limited focus, lending itself to the examination of patterns of speech in what was arguably the most important official document of its era, in order to better understand how they were used to relieve White responsibility for injustices against Blacks.

Nowhere in *The Report* is there recognition of Afrikan leaders who stood up with their race to create a more just society where we could enjoy genuine inter-racial peace. There was no place on the commission for giants of the stature of Martin Luther and Coretta Scott King or Eslanda and Paul Robeson (Russell, 1999: 115,421). In the annals of White liberalism, leaders chosen by Black communities are generally excluded from decision-making intended to redesign the daily experiences of our race. Given the history of White decapitation of organic Black leadership through conspiracies and assassination, therefore, an objective observer might reasonably conclude that Black leaders constitute an endangered species strangely attracted to martyrdom for our cause (Wolfenstein, 1993).

During more than two hundred years of U.S. "democracy", merely accessing the full potential of their voting power and exercising it in their own interests have remained "impossible dreams" for its Black citizens (Parker, 1986: 184; Palast, 2004). The language Governor Kerner employs in his introduction to the report is very instructive. It reads, "Our nation is moving toward two societies, one black, one white, separate and unequal." Governor Kerner continues, "The alternative is not blind repression or capitulation to lawlessness. It is the realization of common opportunities for all within a single society" (The New York Times, 1968: 1). Yet other words in the report, "What white Americans have never fully understood-but what the Negro can never forget…" immediately betray a difference in the status of "white Americans" who are identified with the nation from that of "the Negro", who is obviously still unattached to American citizenship in official eyes (The New York Times, 1968: 2). No "single society" exists.

The Commission begins its presentation with a summary in which the Chair implicitly validates the composition of the investigating group. To what group does the Commissioner's use of "our nation" really apply? Overwhelmingly, Afrikans in the United States are descendants of survivors of genocide and forced exile stripped of their right to choose many inherent legacies of Afrikan ancestry. Readers can be excused for speculating about the nature of the invisible, nameless forces that were, in the Governor's words, "moving" the Black and White communities of his "nation" apart. When were they ever together? Who separated them? Agency is here made distant or invisible when racism against Black people finally takes on color, flesh and form.

The graphic illustration of this reality, in my opinion, is the New York Times' choice of photographs to give the report its human face (The New York Times, 1968: 282). It is significant that this report is mandated by President Lyndon Baines Johnson in order to find ways "to achieve a decent and orderly society in America". Yet, in the pictures chosen, most of America is consistently absent. The focus is turned disproportionately on the Black underclass. My analysis suggests that the cumulative effect of the pictures selected by the New York Times is intended to frighten or repel its overwhelmingly White readership by presenting a Black population, dangerously wounded like a wild animal hunted down and temporarily contained inside its "jungle" of squalor and rubble in Detroit, Harlem or Watts. In those sites of degradation, the Black population stands in the dock of public opinion, awaiting White judgment like its Ancestors unloaded from ships, beyond the sympathy of kith and kin, stripped naked of historical context and in wanton, disorganized rebellion against its own best interests as defined by wise White men.

Both people and places chosen for these photographs hold lessons for us. There are (51) fifty-one images of Whites, all male, with one possible teenager among them. Among the fifty-one (51) portraits, there are only seven (7) civilians, three (3) of whom are guarding a store. Of the four (4) others, two are standing beside the guards, one is a reporter and the other (possibly a Black man who looks White) is in custody at the head of a long coffle of Black men being herded to jail. The forty-five (45) White men in uniform are unsmiling, alert, ominous and armed to the teeth. We never see where they come from or where they live. They become, in viewers' eyes, disembodied, dispassionate protectors of the property and security of the innocently absent White race.

In contrast to its presentation of minimal White connections to the uprisings, the New York Times shows us one hundred and twenty-six (126) Blacks, again, overwhelmingly male. However, this time, there are also eighteen (18) Black females involved. The only four (4) fully visible women facing the camera are caught sitting in the midst of the rubble and devastation of their homes. One woman holds a tiny boy on her hip. Another, a well-groomed woman sits smiling between two (2) of three (3) White men guarding the store where they all apparently work. In the midst of a crowd of Black men under siege by armed forces during the uprisings, we see two (2) Black women who are being held up from falling by three (3) Black men. In another picture, backs to the viewer, two (2) girls play in a decrepit neighbourhood in Brooklyn, New York. In yet another photograph there are three (3) more women, one carrying a girl, standing with their backs to the camera behind White guards facing the ambiguous figure of a Black man.

The overall effect is that Black women are shown as vulnerable, safe with White men and inadequately protected by Black men. In a gendered, White supremacist society, those are powerful messages about possibilities for changing the racist status quo. Compared to the disciplined ranks of militarized White men, the New York Times depicts the one hundred and eight (108) Black males it selected as looters; as routed packs scattering as they are hunted by the troops; as captives, face down on the ground, as prisoners caged behind bars or mobs out of control, held like wild animals at bay by fire hoses, bayonets and clubs. Even where Black men are not clearly identified, we are still aware of their presence as menacing hulks lurking in the shadows of each frame.

In my opinion, to understand how the situation that called forth the Commission developed, readers would need to see a fuller picture of American life. We need pictures of the wealth of the cities within which blighted Black neighbourhoods languished, ignored. We also need images of the beauty, wealth and prosperity that Black labour had created, and from which most Blacks are excluded, in order to understand our pain as spectators who could see others, all those men, all those mostly White men enjoying the fruits of our people's creativity and hard, unpaid work. Had we first been permitted to see a picture of the President and the Commissioners, it might have shed some needed light on the realities of gender and race, which produce White male rulers of resistant Blacks and cause generations of the marginalized to internalize despair. To understand the events *The Report* describes and attempts to analyze at a feeling level, we need pictures of the White male faces that called forth the ongoing war against dispossessed Blacks. We also need family and community snapshots of the Black leaders, female and male, that shaped our people's resistance (Billingsley, 1992: 22; Morris, 1984). Within the frame of the truncated vision of Black life and erasure of any evidence of White domination that readers were given by the New York Times photo essay, there appears to be no integrating Black vision. Without deep historical insight, however, there is little space for understanding and repairing the rupture racism causes inside Black psyches, within Black communities and between White and Black.

The solution that the Kerner Commission offers for the problem of a bruising racial divide is providing "common opportunities" for all. That response skates over the uncommon nature of the experience of genocide, forced exile and servitude that brought the divide into being in the first place. To paraphrase an insightful comment on 'capitalism', the Commission ignores the harsh truth that the serial genocide against Afrikans in this hemisphere has a White 'address and name'. Instead of daring to unearth more and more truths, the Commission

CLEM MARSHALL

absolves the authors and owners of that genocide by drawing a blanket of secrecy and omission over their names. It is as if we attempted to serve ideals of justice and reconciliation after a rape by concentrating most of our energy on concealing the identity of the rapist.

There are other useful lessons that seem to flow from this report. In justifying the need for action, the Commission begins by defining and devaluing the resistance of the Black community against generations of institutionalized White violence. It then goes on to imply threats against that same community for daring to further resist and sets processes in motion by offloading responsibility for any future White repression onto the backs of beleaguered Blacks.

The Report reads, "Violence [read Black violence] cannot build a better society. Disruption and disorder nourish repression, not justice. The community [read White Community] cannot – it will not – tolerate coercion and mob rule" (The New York Times, 1968: 1). Next, the report provides its exculpatory *coup de grace*, "What White Americans have never fully understood – but what the Negro can never forget – is that White society is deeply implicated in the ghetto" (The New York Times, 1968: 1).

For me, this statement is a revealing example of mea culpa, a symbolic beating of the breast without any operational consequence. By admitting a vague, White connection with the condition of Black peoples' lives, without providing concrete evidence of how that connection works, it serves to absolve Whites from blame in reasonable eyes. There are echoes here of the popular White excuse for racism, or male excuse for sexism. 'It wasn't me somebody else did it. I just inherited their mistakes.' In the context of human oppression what is the measure of responsibility that connects the lives of the implicated to the deaths of the exterminated? What and whom do beneficiaries of crime owe?

It is reasonable to argue that some kinds of "violence", such as that accompanying the American Revolutionary War, the U.S. Civil War, the Russian and Chinese Revolutions and WWII, have been instrumental in building broadly 'better' societies in North America, Europe and Asia. At least there appears to be a prima facie argument for calling the societies better than the ones they replaced. Those nations had languished under forms of British colonialism, Czarist, imperialist, feudal, Nazi or Fascist rule (Obadele, 1991). On the other hand, there is another kind of invisible violence that is embedded in the harsh inequalities of Black life within the richest society in the world. *The Report* deplores living conditions that are also experienced as violation. They signal the ongoing abuse of the nation's Afrikan population that must endure intolerable discrimination, attempt flight from a general blight or face the nation's armed forces which enforce their inferior status from the cradle to the grave.

To continue, the language of the passage quoted above does not assume Whites are innocent because of cognitive inadequacy. It would certainly be against the norm in U.S. society to consider Whites less mentally able than Blacks (Gould, 1981; Block & Dworkin, 1976; Chinyelu, 1996). So, even as Whites are excused, they must be shown to be intelligent, reflective beings. There is, therefore, a subtle change in the weight of the verbs used when referring to Whites as opposed to Blacks. For example, the piece implies that Whites think about their society but have not "understood". It is logical to accept that Blacks in the U.S.A. also think about the society they live in, but *The Report* does not credit them with reflecting on their experience or understanding it. There is no thinking verb applied to Blacks. Had the text treated both groups with equal respect, it may have inspired readers to compare the differential weight of the investment Blacks or Whites bring to the table when they consider issues vital to Black survival and liberation.

Instead, the Commission chose not to explore that idea but rather move silently on. As we read further, *The Report* leaves us dangling and forces readers to speculate about the ways in which Whites are "implicated" in the "ghetto" (Oliver & Shapiro, 1997). Centuries of labour theft, land theft, banking and other economic fraud, job discrimination in terms of pay and promotion, housing discrimination in terms of exorbitant rents for run-down accommodation, with accompanying judicial and police persecution to keep the system in place, are certainly inadequately described in the term "implicated".

An Afrikan-centred documentation of the conditions leading to the protests and reforms of the sixties noted that: Between 1882 and 1903, two thousand and sixty (2,060) blacks were lynched in the United States. Some of the Black victims were children and pregnant women; many were burned alive at the stake; others were castrated with axes or knives, blinded with hot pokers, or decapitated (Marable, 1984: 8).

Those were some of the conditions that drove Black folks, in huge numbers, from the South to the North (Myrdal, 1964: 182-204; Alkali-mat, 1986: 100). In the North, Black refugees faced relentless and piti-less housing and job discrimination. White people were indeed "im-plicated" in the "ghetto". In 1965, on the heels of Black resistance in the streets of the Black Los Angeles community, the President of the Soviet Academy of Science and other prominent intellectuals wrote an open letter to the President of the U.S.A. The letter is direct. It refers to the "monstrous massacre of the Negro ghetto in Los Angeles" (Sobel, 1967: 310). What were they able to see that White Americans could not? Had it employed such uncompromising language, the Commission's responses to Black people's resistance could not have appeared, as they were made to appear, generous and deeply humane.

Let us move on to examine the rest of the recommendations made at the time. With the hindsight of a whole generation, they are upbeat, concrete and market illusory promises of hope:

> [The] creation of two million new jobs over the next three years... [and] efforts to improve dramatically, schools serving disadvantaged [read Black] children through substantial Federal funding for year-round compensa-tory education programmes (The New York Times, 1968: 1).

Those recommendations still awaited implementation thirty-five years later. The more hysterically the media trumpet the palatably vague refrain, "I have a dream", Martin Luther King's humble plea for

White acceptance, the more discordant it sounds against the cacophony of "disparities in education, housing, healthcare, employment opportunities, wages, mortgage loan approval" and all the other systems that spell "America's unfulfilled promise of equality and inclusion [today]" (Kitwana, 2002: xx). In the end, the US Civil Rights Movement, replete with martyrs who incarnated the mood of fearless, conscious determination afire in the Black population at large, settled for desegregation and illusory inclusion instead of competing revolutionary demands for reparations, separation and self-determination (Marable, 1984; Branch, 1998).

Writers like Bakari Kitwana, represent the first generation born after desegregation and nurtured on false expectations of first class citizenship. Kitwana explores and then exposes the feelings that fuel the cynicism, materialism and nihilism plaguing the young Blacks featured in popular culture. He also demonstrates convincingly that this disproportionately male culture of self-destruction comes from a generation that has been 'ambivalently socialized'. While Kitwana and his peers have been weaned on noble words, they are daily forced to swallow the bitter truth that "the civil rights gains …of [their] parents' generation …haven't secured [them their] inalienable rights" (Kitwana, 2002: 133).

Rising above historical White betrayals of promises of equality made during Reconstruction and the two great wars, Blacks who had taken a stand for social transformation placed their destiny in White hands yet once again, only to be again betrayed (Anderson, 1994: 25). That part of the Black population that judged itself middle class made a particularly heavy investment in the liberal promises of President Johnson's "Great Society" (Commager, 1967). Without first getting mechanisms or measures for evaluation of Black social progress in place, civil rights veterans passed on their optimism to their daughters and sons (Parker, 1986; Marable, 1984; Branch, 1998). Those children, by and large, still live in 'segregated' Black communities. Disastrously for their life chances, calculated from data that cover school, work, personal security, protection from imprisonment or longevity, overall conditions for Blacks a generation later are not better but worse (Porter,

1997: 19). With a kind of poetic irony, the Commission's recommendations read like many of the demands for reparations that groups of Afrikan ancestry, from the continent to the Caribbean, are again making today (Robinson, 2000).

EXHUMING THE REPORT OF THE TRUTH AND RECONCILIATION COMMISSION

Were *The Kerner Commission Report* the only one available, we might see patterns revealed by linguistic analysis as particular to place and time – a post-Emancipation U.S.A. However, a document, similar in its national and international scope, completed under Archbishop Desmond Tutu and issued by the Truth and Reconciliation Commission (TRC) in South Africa was presented to President Nelson Mandela in 1998 (TRC, 1998: Vol.1 Ch. 1). *The TRC Report* was intentional and purposeful in dealing with the most transparent example of social and political systems driven by biases of color and culture within a White supremacist superstructure in the modern world.

Apartheid classified people with a refinement based on subtle distinctions of hair texture and shade that would probably have left many Nazis speechless with envy and open-mouthed in awe. In Kwesi Prah's words the "pigmentalists" or "pigmentocrats" are "fantastically sensitive about colour" (Prah, 1997: 125). Racist apartheid measured culture, education and style so that all features attributed to the makeup of the Whitest White were elevated to the highest status and whatever was perceived, presumed or associated with the Blackest Black was relentlessly devalued, pushed down to the bottom and ground into the dust. The apartheid system, like the US Jim Crow system fabricated criteria for judging individual worth based on proximity or distance from Afrikan identity (Myrdal, 1964; Katz, 1995).

The language of *The TRC Report*, like that of *The Kerner Commission Report*, was also forged inside a cauldron of turmoil during a time of heightened Black consciousness, unsettling political confrontation, increasing global attention to White persecution of Blacks and within the context of an increasingly repressive destabilized state. It therefore affords an opportunity for useful comparison with *The Kerner Commission Report,* allowing insights into the way both reports use exculpatory euphemism in recording chronicles of Black courage, ancestral transcendence and transformative political organization.

Composed during the mandate of a majority Black government, the TRC included women as well as a representative of each of South Africa's identified racial groups, drawn from a wide cross-section of the society. One of the investigators, Zenzile Khoisan, has published a record of his service on the TRC. His insights give human shape and form to events that loom large in the moral landscape of a world inspired by the possibility of lofty ideals of 'Truth' and 'Reconciliation'. The process Khoisan describes, from behind the scenes, reflects the fundamental racial tensions within South African society, then and now. In that society White supremacy still values "Asian" above "Coloured" and "Coloured" above "African and Black" (Khoisan, 2001: 12-16). During apartheid, the regime arbitrarily assumed hegemonic power to name, measure, promote, demote, elevate or devalue racial groups by developing micro-social hierarchies in every area of life, including the intensity of its genocidal attacks. June Veecock, as Ontario Federation of Labour's Human Rights Officer, was an official Observer of the 1994 transitional elections that brought Blacks into political office. She describes observing how Asian and Coloured personnel in charge of polling stations in certain areas left elderly Afrikans standing for hours, some from dawn to midday, under a pitiless, tropical sun while allowing members of other racial groups to wait or vote inside (Veecock, 1994).

Testimonies to the TRC disclosed that apartheid directed its most deadly weapons, its systems and plots against the Black majority population.

[The] bulk of victims have been black...Can we [Whites and 'reconciled' Blacks] imagine the anger that has been caused by the disclosures that the previous government had a Chemical and Biological Warfare Programme with projects that allegedly targeted only black people... and allegedly sought to reduce the fertility of black women? (TRC, Vol. 1 Ch.1).

From a Pan-Afrikanist point of view the TRC opened a rare window into global White supremacy, exposing its conspiracy against Black health and our very existence as a race. The Commission's work therefore lends weight to an analysis and approach informed by watchfulness or wariness as opposed to unsuspecting naiveté. In words from Zenzile Khoisan's poignant, poetic tribute to anti-apartheid martyrs:

Now we know who bombed Tiro, shot Rasta... Took blood from an AIDS-infected askari (Khoisan, 2001: 129; Khoisan, 2003; TRC, 1998: Vol. 2 Ch. 6; Gisselquist, 2003).

The unspoken fear lurking behind his words and in the many unanswered questions surrounding the origins and spread of AIDS is that, in hidden spaces and secret ways, 'askari' blood plays a part in the ongoing AIDS crisis in southern Afrika (Maggiore, 2004; "Gisselquist, 2002; Chirimuuta, 1989: 93; Hooper, 2000: 105; Horowitz, 1997: 181; Duesberg, 1996: 163). ''Askari' is one of the derogatory names given generations of Blacks who acted as mercenaries for invading or colonizing Europeans or Arabs in Afrika.

Khoisan's very personal journal reveals how, even inside the sanitized, 'non-racial' walls of the Commission, some Whites who were "good solid, salt of the earth types" continued to devalue and undermine the credibility of Blacks newly-invested with the power to challenge the status quo. Khoisan gives details of how he "wrote a detailed memo about racism in the Commission, clandestine meetings between white investigators...[and a] programme from which most of the black investigators were excluded" (Khoisan, 2001: 116). The Commission's own report also shed some light, although veiled, on a global network of "countries, which may have assisted the programme [of racist biological warfare]..." The "[White] countries" named included the US, UK, Israel, West Germany and most powerful White governments. Since in 1994, "the British and Americans [let it be known] they did not want the programme to fall into the hands of the ANC government", one can infer that they had knowingly let their health institutions use biological and chemical resources to support apartheid's attacks against the Black race (TRC, 1998: Vol. 2 Ch. 6).

What is most significant, from a Pan-Afrikanist perspective, is the hard evidence of how, within self-proclaimed democracies, White supremacy trumps commitment to global justice and inclusive humanity. The 'democracies' exposed by the TRC were willing to co-operate with White apartheid's anti-Kushitic, "chemical and biological warfare programme" but reacted anxiously against the same weapons falling into pro-liberation, Black South African hands. Even the limited data the Commission gleaned within a strictly circumscribed timeframe and then shared with the public strongly suggests that the major world powers as well as global mainstream institutions had turned a blind eye on 'crimes against Afrikan humanity'. For Pan-Afrikanists this information provides a rare opportunity to raise the hood and examine the gears that turn the engine of anti-Kushitic conspiracies. Usually, that engine invisibly yet relentlessly grinds up our rights and dreams in the places where we live, work and play. In the words of the commission:

> The image of white-coated scientists, professors, doctors, dentists, veterinarians, laboratories, universities and front companies, propping up apartheid with the support of an extensive international network, was a particularly cynical and chilling one. Here was evidence of science being subverted to cause disease and undermine the health of communities (TRC, 1998: Vol. 2 Ch. 6).

Specifically the TRC provided evidence of "projects...that had as their purpose the murder of individuals, and the undermining of the health, if not the elimination, of entire communities (for example, projects involving cholera, fertility drugs, botulinum, mandrax and ecstasy)" (TRC, 1998: Vol. 2 Ch. 6).

In voicing his dismay at the Commission's findings, the Chairperson admitted his fear that the news of their conspiracy could unleash "orgies of revenge". Strangely, although born Black, targeted by the apartheid regime and intimately acquainted with its atrocities, Archbishop Desmond Tutu did not voice equal fear for the safety of his own group, one of those "entire communities" that the sworn evidence of his commission had identified with probable "elimination". Yet, given that his commission permitted the main agents and putative conspirators in the extermination programme he had uncovered to remain free, they were potentially at liberty to continue their nefarious, clandestine work. Instead of warning vulnerable Blacks to protect themselves, the Chairperson trivialized the danger they faced by appealing for some token White officials to come forward and say, "We had an evil system with awful consequences. Please forgive us" (TRC, 1998: Vol. 1 Ch.1). It is difficult to imagine a Jewish leader making a similar plea to supporters of the Nazi regime. The Commission's differential concern for its Black and White constituents exposed the contradictions and moral ambivalence at the heart of its vision of a new "Rainbow People" (Tutu, 1994). Without the moral framework of an alternative, transformative information base, accessible to the White population through a mandated programme of popular education, there appeared to be little basis for the highly moral expectations embedded in Archbishop Tutu's appeal. Predictably, his 'desperate' pleas drifted listlessly like dead, autumn leaves in the wind.

In the tradition of *The Kerner Commission Report*, the impact of the *TRC Report* is, in the end, exculpatory for Whites and, at best, ambiguous for Blacks. The interplay of words and images evoked by these reports transform them into vehicles of seduction for some and exculpation for others. The Black population always pays the higher price. Its burdens include the loss of ancestral property or reparations for unpaid labor. In the case of South Africa, the new government assumed the crippling public debt accumulated by a regime that funded the murder of its daughters and sons. On an emotional and spiritual level, however, anguished Blacks were also forced to suffer the immeasurable indignity of reliving their private trauma as public spectacle for the titillation or education of indifferent, uninvested spectators of other races. In exchange, South Afrika's First Nations were railroaded into an illusory world of racial peace and reconciliation where Justice stood silenced and blind (Khoisan, 2003).

The TRC also created a false mindscape where the apartheid system was already relegated to the past. In fact, overwhelmingly, government officials, including judges who sent innocent Black women and men to their death in prison or unidentified killers in the army and police force, were allowed to remain at their posts (Khoisan, 2001: 154; TRC Vol. 1 Ch. 1). The Commission's Chair, now a Nobel Prize winner, sums up its achievement in the following words:

> Thus, we have trodden the path urged on our people by the preamble to our founding act, which called on the need for understanding, but not for vengeance, a need for reparation but not retaliation, a need for 'ubuntu' but not victimization [Italics added] (TRC, 1998: Vol. 1 Ch. 5).

The principles behind 'Ubuntu' are not new and may prove at best a double-edged sword. The Black writer James Baldwin had identified them a generation earlier, even before the events that precipitated the Kerner Commission, "It is a terrible, an inexorable law that one cannot deny the humanity of another without diminishing one's own" (Baldwin, 1964). Yet, it is difficult to imagine how South Africa, after generations of racial inequity and wounding divisions could, in four years, become "one people" by merely switching some of the faces in charge from White to Black, giving official sanction to interracial intimacy and abolishing laws that enshrined segregation. By what moral authority were those who had dispossessed and tyrannized the Black population now permitted, by the stroke of a pen, to assume innocence, Afrikan property, culture and ancestral rights (Davis, 1990: 23, 179-180; Ransford, 1974)?

Pan-Afrikanists encourage self-determination and promote transparency around the political decisions that govern our lives. Who set the TRC's on its path? The ANC government never held a referendum or convened a consultative assembly of the Black population before stripping the First Nations of their ancestral inheritance for all time.

> No other piece of legislation in South African history [the 1913 land Act] more dramatically and drastically reshaped the social map of this country...[It] destroyed, at a stroke, a thriving African landowning and peasant agricultural sector...The Land Act set in motion a massive forced removal of African people that led... to the deaths of many hundreds of people who found themselves suddenly landless (TRC, 1998: Vol. 1 Ch. 2).

Even a brief examination of the opening paragraphs of the Chairperson's preamble gives its readers a sense of the linguistic and psychological devices used to shift the burden of responsibility for Black suffering and the tense racial climate in South Africa from White to Black backs. It is instructive to read the first paragraph and absorb its impact before analyzing it. Foreword by Chairperson:

> All South Africans know that our recent history is littered with some horrendous occurrences – the Sharpeville and Langa killings, the Soweto uprising, the Church Street bombings, Magoo's Bar, the Amanzimoti Wimpy bar bombing, the St. James Church killings, Boipatong and Se-

bokeng. We also knew about the deaths in detention of people such as Steve Biko, Neil Aggett and others' necklacings, and the so called "black-on-black" violence on the East Rand and inKwazulu Natal which arose from the rivalries between IFP and first, the UDF and later the ANC. Our country is soaked in the blood of her children of all races and of all political persuasions (TRC, 1998: Vol. 1 Ch.1).

Nowhere in these opening remarks is there an appeal to the central ideal of any judicial process. Justice does not once appear in Archbishop Tutu's text. Nowhere in it does he make a righteous religious demand for compensation or compassion for the wronged. There is little attention to the rights of populations that were singled out as targets of the monstrous, cannibalistic apartheid machine. Some plaintive appeals do come later, but they are buried under thousands of pages of mind-numbing detail and legalistic facts. In fact, by urging "ubuntu" for all Whites, including apartheid criminals, and using a Xhosa word, the Chairperson sets up 'forgiveness' in apposition to "victimization" of Whites as a group. His framework implies that when Blacks call for justice, urge full accountability for the hurts they endure or embrace self-defence 'by any means necessary', they are guilty of seeking a kind of shameful revenge.

On the level of symbol, juxtaposing the Xhosa word for forgiveness and the English word "victimization" subliminally suggests that Blacks and Whites suffered equally from apartheid's crimes. It also blurs the distinction between the innocent Black population and the overwhelming majority of the White population that repeatedly voted for and still benefits from the system apartheid set up. The Commission's overtly optimistic archbishop mixes two mutually antagonistic cultural traditions attached to interests that are diametrically opposed. He shakes together Kushitic "ubuntu" with Christian 'original sin' to create a potion that the Afrikan majority finds bitter on the tongue and harsh in the throat to this day (Dalamba, 2004). On the other side, the sound of 'ubuntu', translated by the Commission as "restorative justice" also conjures up, within popular culture, a vague spectre of mysterious, pagan Afrikan rites. This Christian 'prophet' in flowing robes summons the ancestrally Afrikan majority and admonishes it to honour the moral obligations that flow from its abandoned, ancient beliefs. In exchange for being collectively dispossessed of their land and accepting the misappropriation of all their valuable collective assets, including their ancestral philosophy, he offers South Afrika's First Nations a nebulous belief in individualized spiritual redemption that effectively negates all present or future demands for restitution.

While he skillfully navigates the unfamiliar waters of 'ubuntu', Archbishop Tutu fails to pay survivors due respect by making equal room for their mother tongues at the head table. Instead, the Archbishop lectures them in tones of Christian religiosity in the foreign tongue of their persecutors and oppressors. However, through 'ubuntu' he asserts his authority to speak for them while in reality silencing them in the name of a shared and sacred ancestry. Mostly, however, his words fly above their heads as a plea for recognition and respect to imperious, impervious Whites. In response the leaders of the apartheid regime studiously ignored his performance by boycotting the sessions. They also ignored his pleas for even a token apology, although the bulk of the Commission's funds end up going in their direction (Khoisan, 2001). South Africa's politically and economically powerful White citizens maintain a stance of careless ingratitude, even as the prelate performs a kind of 'Whitewashing' magic that transmutes their gargantuan crimes against humanity into mere "horrendous occurrences [my emphasis]." The TRC ceremony spirits away their guilt and shame with sacrificial, public offerings of Black women's shrieks, sobs, fits, fainting spells and the deracialized, iconic Archbishop's flowing, abundant tears (TRC, 1998: Vol. 1 Ch. 5).

While living in Afrika, I experienced morality as reciprocity, symbolized by a continuous giving and receiving of gifts. Wolof people express that principle in Senegal as 'teranga', and it is the greatest compliment to be told 'am-nge teranga', meaning 'you are a generous soul [my translation]' (Malherbe & Sall, 1989). This is implicitly understood whether practiced through spontaneous giving to strangers and friends or forgiving when one has been wronged. The TRC therefore betrays the true spirit of 'ubuntu' because the groups that milked benefits from apartheid gave nothing in return. The heirs of European invaders met the uncommon generosity of the Afrikans their people had wronged with "reluctance, indeed...hostility [that] has been like spitting in the face of the victims" (TRC, Vol. 1 Ch. 1). Where there is no reciprocity for generosity, those who receive gifts of the spirit betray the human hunger for nobility and the dignity of all those who trust.

In keeping with his mandate, the Chairperson examines only the more recent atrocities that scar the history of that country, ignoring generations of genocide, pillage, mayhem and rape. In keeping with the euphemistic tones of the report, he names the tragic events that rocked Black Soweto in 1976, "uprisings" rather than calling them a 'massacre'. During that soul-numbing catastrophe, apartheid troops with machine guns mowed down a peaceful gathering of brave, unarmed children in all the shiny innocence of their 'neat-and-clean' school uniforms. Interviewed about the tragic event, Winnie Madikizela-Mandela, leader of the resistance movement at the level of its people and the street, where her presence provided inspiration, said:

> I was on the scene. About 10,000 children were marching...the police let loose a dog on a child...and...the dog bit the child...The dog was killed and the police immediately opened fire; the first shots landed on a ten year old who died on the spot (Mandela, 1976: 16).

Her language is graphic and direct. Instead of the Latinized circumlocutions of Archbishop Tutu, who was not with the courageous children, freedom fighter Madikizela Mandela uses short Anglo-Saxon words that pierce the ear and stir the gut. They are meant for her people rather than their oppressors to hear. On the other hand, the

Chairperson selects, "killings" to describe the butchery of civilians at Sharpeville on March 21, 1960, where White troops shot from helicopters and armoured cars at unarmed Afrikans protesting unjust Pass Laws. When the carnage ended there were sixty-seven (67) broken Black bodies, most of them shot in the back, strewn like debris on the streets or cut down as they tried to flee (Fatton, 1986: 23). "Killings" individualizes and minimizes the massacre of the innocent majority by that powerful minority state and the international race supremacist machine that backed it. Such euphemisms depersonalize slaughter and divert attention from the pervasive, structural nature of the contempt for the people's humanity that was endemic to a political regime that routinely planned and sanctioned a range of atrocities. In his trenchant study, Khoisan notes that, "those attitudes have persisted in the post-apartheid society" (Khoisan, 2001: 52).

The Chairperson uses only one descriptive word, "horrendous", that implies emotion, to convey the devastation and psychological distress of apartheid's Afrikan victims. Even the word, "horrendous", is modified and mollified by the use of "some" before it. Yet apartheid was, by any yardstick, a running sore of human degradation and a political system of monstrous depravity. Its main targets did not, by any reports, experience it as a series of random, episodic hurts caused by bad judgment or bad luck. It was not for them a landscape dotted by "some horrendous" acts. For most Blacks it was a universe peopled by demons in White skin with soul-strangling control, where to wear one's skin was to suffer as well as inhale both indignity and deprivation from the womb to the tomb (Mandela, 1985: 77; Biko, 1986: 87; Fredrickson, 1982).

On the other hand, in the very next paragraph of the TRC report, there is an unmodified, unequivocal celebration of the "wonderful inauguration" of Nelson Mandela. It bursts into the midst of faceless mourners of vanished mothers, fathers, daughters and sons as a vaguely disturbing distraction. 'Mandela euphoria' barges into Black life like a delirious drunk crashing a wake. The most visible gains of Black resistance are written down side-by-side with the good deeds of a few outstanding Whites, However, at the same time, the physical and psychological attacks mounted by the apartheid society on its captive prey are airbrushed away, while ceremonies of sanctification, stripped of any uncomfortable memories, are served up to homogenize the troubled racial histories of the land. Readers are encouraged to compose a portrait that disguises the centrality of color by painting sufferers and their persecutors a neutralizing grey. Archbishop Tutu never admits that the only dignified choice Blacks ever had was to resist. Since the population he describes is composed of human beings, it is a reasonable expectation that they would fight against the continual plunder of their resources, murder of their families and the seizure of their ancestral lands when Whites invaded them. Instead Tutu minimizes any evidence that highlights how Europeans tried to force First Nations into homeless exile or exterminate them in their place of origin (Davis, 1990: 180).

Logically and predictably, for the Black population, an aching sense of dispossession is the real legacy of the TRC. The South African constitution inscribes property rights founded on the violent dispossession of the state's First Nations. For Basutos, their cattle wealth was stolen. For Vendas and Zulus, their natural resources were continually raped from the earth with little concern for the ravages to the land. In addition, for Xhosas, Khoisan and all the First Nations, their culture and family life were devastated. They faced the continuous murder of their children and daily humiliation before their eyes. Not to resist meant surrendering their destiny to bloodstained hands. Whites, whatever their class, gender or other social location, were never faced with a choice between embracing their identity as a part of humanity or death. That eventual dilemma was shackled at birth to the feet of every infant born Black (Davis, 1990: 19- 27, 136; Cell, 1987; Boahen, 1985). Some former TRC commissioners were among civic leaders who sponsored an initiative encouraging Whites as a group to make peace with their past. Called the Home for All Campaign it challenged Whites to acknowledge "that [they] all benefited from the discrimination against blacks in the apartheid system" (Hawthorne, 2000). Instructively, that unique and morally ambitious campaign shrivelled up in its shell.

En passant, it is not without significance that even at the level of a commission mandated to expose the underbelly of apartheid, there is little discussion of how those who apartheid classified as Asians, Coloureds or Honorary Whites may have also benefited from the dispossession of the Black majority (Davis, 1990: 125; Cell, 1987). While operating from his South African base, the Indian patriot, Mahatma Ghandi concentrated on winning immigration and other rights for his own people. Ghandi, who moved to South Africa for career opportunities not available in India or England at that time, apparently did so without any particular feeling for the people of his adopted land. His observations give no sign that he understood that a transplanted Indian population would inevitably place added burdens on the backs of long-suffering First Nations, increasingly pushed off ancestral lands and down the social ladder to make room for uninvited strangers from across the sea (IDAF, 1983: 16-20; Davis, 1990; Mukherjee, 1993: xi; Powell, 1979: 405-408).

It was only in relatively recent times that Indians in significant numbers decided to organize against their own co-optation by apartheid, although they too had long suffered gross violations of their human rights at the hands of Whites (Prah, 1997: 134). To date, the European, Indian and Coloured populations have still to define their interests in ways that do not compete with Pan-Afrikan self-determination. Black folks in this hemisphere know the words of an old song that describes this situation only too well - Everybody wants to go to heaven but nobody wants to die.

The TRC Report creates a sensation of sliding swiftly by Black pain, homogenizing the horrors of apartheid and ignoring its impact on daily life in SA today. The Commission's magic wave of the 'ubuntu' wand has tried to equalize Black people's eternity of terror and White people's carnival of hate, fusing them into a collective memory that speaks equally and inclusively about the wounds of "our country" and spilling of "our children'(s)" blood. The truth is that Blacks did not target White children even when apartheid targeted their own daughters and sons. On the contrary, White children led lives of security, privilege and ease. Their enhanced life chances in recreation, education or the arts were directly related to the misery imposed on Black families by the regime their parents overwhelmingly consented to live inside, either through an "abdication of responsibility" or by deliberate, considered choice (Cell, 1987; TRC, 1998: Vol. 1 Ch. 5).

Although a few highly publicized White anti-racist allies were murdered by the apartheid regime, most White lives were lost in clandestine or overt acts in the service of apartheid tyranny (TRC, 1998: Vol. 1 Ch. 4 & 7). The twisted logic of the TRC's condemnation of Afrikan self-defence against such a indefensible system would, from the evidence mounted in this study, equate the suffering of youthful German conscripts under the Nazis in Europe with acts of selfless resistance by heroes among the Roma, Danes, French and Jews who stood up to the tyranny they served (Bettelheim, 1980; Strom & Parsons, 1982).

No wonder the Commission vacillates when it comes to Black self-defence. In fact, it glosses over generations of struggle and ignores the millions of Black women, children and men raped, tortured, crippled and killed to find a few Black faces to fill the role of poster racists. With startling irony, the TRC picks "instances when white settlers or farmers were killed by [black] supporters of the PAC or ANC [my emphasis]" to teach the world about racism under apartheid (TRC, 1998: Vol. 1 Ch. 4). In the Pan-Afrikanist understanding that guides this study, 'racism' means using race as the organizing principle in promoting domination, subjugation and oppression of another race that is neither threatening nor harming you. It does not mean using race as an organizing tool to defend your group's resources, ancestral lands or culture, the assets on which your survival as full human beings depends. Admonishing suffering Blacks to give up the right to self-defence is tantamount to prescribing that Afrikans commit race-suicide in order to permit other races to thrive. In the South African situation, such a prescription infers that race supremacy is moral and valid, that other ethnicities are more human and their lives more valuable than the lives of Afrikans, whose life chances the forces of European ancestry continue to abort or steal.

William Stringfellow, a White writer, took a different approach to the issue of racism. He found it "profoundly threatening to black and white men [in the United States] in the present [nineteen sixties] time" (Stringfellow, 1966: 151). He asserted, "their reconciliation [emphasis added] one to another first requires that they be reconciled to themselves; to love another means first freedom to love yourself" (Stringfellow, 1966: 151). Cleverly, the TRC marshals its words in a combination of selective scientific theories, Eurocentric legal arguments, Eurocentric academic discourse and decontextualized Afrikan spiritual traditions to immunize White culprits and transfer the costs of their impunity to the "victims" of their abuse (TRC Vol. 1 Ch. 5 & 6). As a Black man well aware of the deliberate and disastrous divisions sown between Xhosas and Zulus by the apartheid regime, Bishop Tutu promotes reconciliation between White and Black while ignoring the need for prior reconciliation between Black and Black.

The Act whose preamble the Chairperson cites was not a creation from the grassroots. Instead it was negotiated by a multiracial command structure in the name of the majority First Nations population that has suffered most, lost most and remains the group most at risk from fallout from the TRC. While Europeans and Asians can and do still keep ties to their ancestral homes, Afrikans on the continent are on the only soil in the world where we have been historically welcome without reserve. To surrender full title to Afrika is to mortgage the future of our descendants to the historical hostility of other lands. Strangely *The TRC Report* boasts that the idea for the Commission grew out of the inaugural address of a high-ranking Asian academic in Cape Town on May 25, 1992, two years before the nation's first democratic elections (TRC, 1998: Vol. 1 Ch. 4). Others contradict that interpretation of events. They insist instead that the TRC was the brainchild of the racist National Party, father of apartheid. That party, bolstered by the racial solidarity of its international allies, plotted to control the ANC, fearing that, under an independent Black government, unpredictable tides of justice would swell up, sweep them away and force them to pay for their crimes.

As late as 1998 when I participated in an educational conference in Cape Town, I was surprised to find myself treated differentially with suspicion and general disrespect by both Europeans and Asians in authority as well as by Blacks occupying service positions. I conjectured that, to them, I was an out-of-place, out-of-role Black male moving within neo-apartheid circles where Black faces were still very rare. My personal experience was not unlike that of Pan-Afrikanist Kwesi Prah's in post-apartheid Namibia. "[There] are areas in choice neighbourhoods …where…the whites who overwhelmingly dominate in these areas look at you in amazement and surprise, like "you don't belong" (Prah, 1997: 45). Those stories suggest that in South Africa's dominant society few members of the dispossessed majority Black population would have been afforded opportunities to participate in the formative stages of the TRC which took shape under White institutions and inside White space.

The record shows that the decision to strike a commission was made in 1992 in negotiations between representatives of the African National Congress and the National Party apartheid government. It took place before the election of South Africa's first Afrikan-led government. The negotiating parties were by definition unequally matched. For generations, the National Party had exercised effective control of the structures of state. It could rely on the loyalty or acquiescence of a generally anti-Afrikan electorate as well as generations of custom that trained Whites to lead and Blacks to follow. It ran the civil service and police as well as the secret service, and it also chose the commanders of the state's nuclear-armed and dangerous military forces. The party also benefited from the support of the most economically and militarily powerful nations of the world. Above all other considerations, the National Party was totally committed to White supremacy, at whatever cost. For generations, it had pursued its goal with singular passion and harnessed the vast wealth it extracted from Black land and labour for the defence of the interests of its own constituency (Khoisan, 2001).

On the other hand, overburdened, with few resources, forced to cope with infiltration, decapitation of its nationalist leadership (including the assassination of Mandela's putative heir, Chris Hani), media onslaughts at home and abroad, the ANC chose to spread its meagre resources thin, neglecting the enormous needs of the Black majority to satisfy a nebulous 'rainbow' constituency that has never supported it at the ballot box. Official international observer, June Veecock asserts that voting patterns of the 1994 election exposed the illusion of significant support for the ANC among Asians, Coloureds or Whites (Veecock, 1994). Yet, faithful to its 'Rainbow Nation' ideals, the ANC bent over backwards to be racially inclusive when distributing the positions, privileges and benefits that came with being in office (Mandela, 1997). While Whites, Asians and those Blacks closest to Whites through alliance, education or a demonstrated belief in assimilation were drawn into the circle of decision-making power, the majority Black population remained "victims" or "the wretched of the earth", relegated to the periphery of events as other-worldly "wounded healers" of the new nation, whose only "right [was] to tell their stories of suffering" (TRC, Vol. 1 Ch. 1 & 4).

One of the hidden costs of the global struggle for Black liberation has been the price paid for the privilege of having allies. Pan-Afrikanists do not deny the possibility of alliance but are vigilant in monitoring the impact of alliances on self-determination. It is always tempting to let down one's guard and sink into the warm, fuzzy embrace of allies who share our humanitarian ideals. Experience teaches that when we do so, however, there is a tendency to shift focus, incrementally, quite often without taking conscious note that we are doing so. The frequency with which non-Afrikans assume leadership positions within Black liberation movements is a mute witness to the pitfalls of alliances that subvert our goal of self-determination. In South Africa, during the final years of apartheid, the head of the armed wing of the African National Congress was Joe Slovo, a White lawyer and "one of the major theorists" of the party (Fatton, 1986: 141; Stengel, 1995). It is a phenomenon without parallel in the freedom struggles of other oppressed peoples - Aboriginals, Arabs, Asians or Jews - and it beggars history, intuition and common sense. There were similar patterns of Whites in controlling leadership positions of the Black struggle in the United States, the other major segregationist state examined in this study.

Marcus Garvey, the head of the most successful Pan-Afrikan mass movement on record warned long ago that, "[the] Negro needs to be saved from his friends" (Garvey, 1973: 59-60). He decried the fact that the pre-eminent mainstream Black organization in the United States, the National Association for the Advancement of Colored People, was dominated by wealthy Whites who presided over it for more than a generation (Cooks, 1992: 38; Alkalimat, 1986: 269-272). During that time, its longest serving president, Joel Spingarn, also spied on his Black NAACP 'allies' for the US Army's Military Intelligence Department (Commercial Appeal, 1993). His spying took place while, across the nation, Black communities were under virtual siege from White supremacist forces. For example, "Seventy-six blacks were lynched in 1919 alone" and the US government later launched "a massive surveillance campaign to counter the influence of black leaders", including trade unionist A. Philip Randolph, anthropologist and artist Paul Robeson, Nation of Islam's Elijah Muhammad and Christian activist Dr. Martin Luther King (Churchill & Vander Wall, 1990: 93, 67; Branch, 1998: 89). Inexplicably, in spite of the revelation of Spingarn's clandestine activities, the 'Spingarn Medal' still remains the highest honour the NAACP can bestow.

Even prominent intellectuals such as Maya Angelou and W. E. B. Du Bois seem to have accepted it without reservation or comment (Martin, 1983: 106-107). Within ambivalent spaces where 'good' or 'progressive' Whites are seen to offer 'palatable' Blacks a hand up, friendship has often become a distraction that shifts Pan-Afrikan focus from its primary goals of self-determination and liberation. Seduced by comforting relationships, we have often exhausted our energies and resources building interracial coalitions or creating circles of self-indulgent, integrationist or assimilationist activity. Sociologist E.U. Essien-Udom observes that thinkers working towards change are often caught up in the coils of "a liberal society where social facts are often glossed over by endless verbiage" (Essien-Udom, 1963: 94). When that happens, as is true to a significant degree of the situation created by the

TRC, the transformative force that flows from Black sacrifice as well as the passion that sustains Black hope are siphoned off, to be drained away in thousands of pages of text describing unrealistic expectations based on vaporous promises of admirable intentions. Black communities often remain trapped and duped in unproductive alliances because those in control of communication inflate those relationships with verbiage. Eventually such partnerships may even begin to take on the feelings of satisfaction and achievement, usually associated with liberation or social transformation, and quell the community's real hunger for the immediate transfer of legal title to resources, services or land.

The TRC compromise follows the pattern of other forums or conferences that purported to negotiate transitions from colonization in Afrika or the Caribbean behind closed doors. Usually such meetings would take place under threat of civil strife and subject to intense pressure from the most powerful political or economic forces of an anti- Kushitic, race supremacist world. Those were the conditions that shaped the TRC so that it predictably:

> [Adopted] Western jurisprudence and cultural idioms...espoused the Western [White] evolutionist view of post-colonial state formation... based on the constitutional protection of select liberties and rights... legitimized the liberal state, proscribed any form of ownership other than capitalist, and recognized colonial structures and boundaries (Grovogui, 1996: 197).

In its report, the TRC evokes the threat of potential White retaliation in order to rationalize its double standard for judging 'crimes' committed by Whites or Blacks. Overwhelmingly, Whites were the perpetrators of theft, fraud, rape, torture, murder and crimes against humanity in the name of the apartheid regime. The very state was founded on policies that generated genocide and buttressed by theft of Black people's labor, resources and land (Davis, 1990; Fatton, 1986).

Under the reign of unrelenting state terror Black political acts were punished as antisocial 'crimes', while White group repression was not accounted 'political' or a 'crime'. Under the terms of the TRC, however, only the perpetrators of "political" crimes could apply for amnesty and only do so on an individual basis. So White repression was redefined as "political".

On the other hand, the majority of South Africa's prison population of Blacks, politically convicted of 'crimes' against the criminal White state and its complicit electorate, were disqualified from applying for amnesty. The result is that, in general, the beneficiaries of the apartheid regime, from jailors to judges, covered by de facto amnesty, have not faced judgment for their part in the atrocities committed against those the system branded "kaffirs", South Africa's long-suffering First Nations (Davis, 1990). Since the TRC offers no clear moral argument for making the same crime punishable for one group, Blacks, but not the other, Whites, 'expediency', 'conspiracy' or 'self-interest' appear to be the only logical explanations for its blatantly unjust decisions.

The language the TRC uses to outline the amnesty process makes apartheid appear nebulous and accidental, although the system was forged with weapons of iron and rooted in hearts of stone. On the contrary, in terms of its structures and impact, apartheid was as concrete and deliberate a tyranny as the Nazi regime (Cell, 1987). It is reasonable to wonder what motivates the members of the Commission to ignore natural justice and justify a political deal that leaves the infrastructure of apartheid – including the economy, secret services, armed forces, judges, police and foreign policy largely in place.

Agency for apartheid's inhumanity is increasingly removed, euphemistically, from the human realm to the realm of the intangible and unseen. Indeed, in buttressing its case for amnesty as insurance against repercussions from Whites, the Commission ignores the heroic record of the children of Soweto and leaders like Winnie Madikizela-Mandela who defied the military might of apartheid's armed forces with nothing but raised fists and fearless souls. Remembering Madikizela Mandela, the record of one eyewitness radiates awe. In her words, "She would stand before police captains with machine guns and tell them to go and get stuffed" (Motlana, 1985: 116). Another witness also recounts how, when Major Visser of the Protea police accused the freedom fighter of starting riots, "she threw a book at him, her shoe, anything she could lay her hands on…You bloody murderer…stop those bastards killing our children in the street! (Motlana, 1985: 116).

Instead of putting its focus on celebrating such heroic resistance, the Commission projected the spectre of apartheid's "human rights criminals…living beside everyone else…who may [emphasis added] be very powerful and dangerous [emphasis added]" (TRC, Vol.1 Ch.1).

One effective result of the TRC's historically incorrect 'compromise' is that the "Dealer in Mass Murder' Dr. Basson, nicknamed "Dr. Death" in the media, was permitted to continue practicing medicine in South Africa, even after his nefarious deeds were publicly aired (Khoisan, 2003). Had the new government of South Africa chosen instead to challenge the United Nations and the conscience of the world, it might have discovered resources for setting up structures that were both more just and also protective of its Black population. It is equally conceivable that those most culpable for preserving apartheid might have embraced exile instead of fruitless acts of revenge and an uncertain future. In reality, many Whites were already fleeing the country. Black resistance made it increasingly ungovernable through open defiance of state institutions at every turn (Fatton, 1986: 34-35).

A curious oxymoron, "wounded healers" betrays the questionable assumptions and ambiguous results of the TRC. Those words bare the raw anguish of Black "victims" in hopes of eliciting empathy from their erstwhile White persecutors. Yet no evidence has existed before or since within collective White history of their treating Blacks fairly or as full human beings. What logical analysis also reveals, but what is left unspoken in the phrase, "wounded healers" elucidates both gender and race. Those on whose backs the Commission erects the enormously burdensome edifice of reconciliation, those most "wounded" and those it commands to heal others before they heal themselves are overwhelmingly, if not exclusively, female and Black.

Within the Black South African and global population, patriarchal traditions have long assigned women the role of absorbers of community pain. Even if all the Whites in South African society were disposed to reconciliation, which the Commissions admits they are not, they could not alone bring about the ANC government's promise of healing. The Commission itself cannot credibly escape naming Whites for being more 'injurers' than 'injured', more "culprits...intoxicated, seduced or bought with personal advantages [than] victims" (TRC, Vol.1 Ch.5).

So it conjures up a special term to imprison Black "victims" in a process that, on spuriously moral, 'crypto-Christian-ubuntu' grounds, requires them, while still "wounded", to donate blood to the very enemy that keeps on turning knives in the rawness of their wounds. To the sacrificial victim, it seems, only belongs more pain.

In *The TRC Report*, as in *The Kerner Commission Report* Black women who have always been the engines of economic, cultural and intellectual transformation in Afrika and "[in] the forefront of the [South African] struggle" are ambivalently cast (Hafkin & Bay, 1976; Weinberg, 1981: 66). The image of resistance on my TV screen throughout the nineteen eighties was Winnie Madikizela-Mandela defending the most vulnerable, like a lioness using her body to shield her cubs (Marshall, 2001). Yet in the TRC proceedings, chocolate-skinned women remain curiously backstage or offstage, rarely portrayed as warriors, key decision makers, thinkers or administrators. When they do enter the popular lens at tension-drenched points in the unfolding tragedy, they are mostly paraded on screen as generic, aged females with media-defined, serving-class faces that weep and crack. Keeping class and patriarchy in place, these mothers-to-us-all perform on cue, as they are prompted to by the dominant presiding male, Archbishop Desmond Tutu, during the televised deliberations on the staged state massacre of their *Guguletu Seven* sons (Khoisan, 2001: 24).

In the Guguletu example of cold-blooded terrorism, an askari, freedom fighter twisted inside out and turned into a traitor against those he loved, led the unsuspecting, young brothers confided to his care to their certain death. He played his part flawlessly so that their stage-managed 'terrorist activities' could be filmed for propaganda purposes and used to manufacture the deceptive images that greased the gears of apartheid's war machine.

Black women's pain, in the TRC proceedings, is framed within the benign gaze of a presiding countenance of patriarchal authority. The cumulative effect of diverse procedural elements and discretionary decisions that shape the Commission's path is a morality play blurring and blending White self-interest, Black self-hatred, expediency and multiracial greed. The combination makes a lethal neo-apartheid cocktail. On the stage of the TRC, by cleverly lighting some aspects of history while keeping others in the shadows or off-stage, White supremacist terror masquerades as a tragedy of betrayals played out Black on Black, while White self-interest struts as an epic of impartiality that sponsors reconciliation to bridge the divide between Black and White.

Throughout the TRC process, Black mothers are as powerful a presence as the Hor-em-ahket that Greeks renamed the Sphinx, which rises majestically above the sands that frame the nourishing Nile. It is a soothing and enduring presence. In their ample bosoms, these women absorb the pain of their butchered sons while reassuring a world that justly fears the looming anger of legions of unreconciled, faceless, menacing Black men, who await their moment in the shadows of revenge. The women's own needs for space to grieve or time to reflect and repossess their own violated humanity remain unmet. In fulfilling the traditional, Black female role as "wounded healers", they are coerced into breastfeeding the world and then turned out to forage like a dairy cow milked dry.

A gendered analysis and interpretation of *The TRC Report* also opens a window on the unique role the Commission assigns to Winnie Madikizela-Mandela. As the designated Black woman, leader, mother and grandmother, she stands for all Black women when she is ordered to the stand. Her voice is presumed to be their voice, her pain for the loss of husband, children and peace of mind, a reflection of all the anguish they feel. For the unpublished purposes of the TRC, Winnie Madikizela- Mandela plays a role larger than the political one for which it tries her and under whose wheels it tries to grind her into inert dust. She is punished for being an assertive woman who not only demands equality with the most powerful White men, defending herself and her cause against their power on public screens, but is also seen, by the world, to win. Her real life role is the antithesis of the 'Mammy' figure of "calm and compassion" that is required for the TRC philosophy to take root and confirm Black dispossession within a patriarchal framework that grants absolution to guilty Whites (Pieterse, 1992: 154; Null, 1975: 123, 159; Rogin, 1998: 120; hooks, 1996: 201).

Winnie Madikizela-Mandela is therefore recast as the Black Jezebel, a woman scorned who can then be sacrificed without remorse for the sins and shameful betrayals of powerful, forgetful men (Guerrero, 1993; Kisch and Mapp, 1992; hooks, 1996). It is significant that the empathetic Archbishop Tutu who, during the TRC wept openly for sufferers, White or Black, never sheds a tear for this woman who suffered so publicly, so much and on behalf of so many for so long. Guilty conscience finally forces Archbishop Tutu to acknowledge his differential treatment of Winnie Madikizela-Mandela. He confesses that she was made a symbol, read scapegoat, to demonstrate his own impartiality and give credibility to the TRC. With shame-driven frustration, the Chairperson finally blurts out, "Can you imagine the outcry if the Commission had put a National Party member through the kind of nine-day grueling hearing to which Ms. Madikizela-Mandela was subjected?" (TRC, 1998: Vol. 1 Ch.1).

Instead of understanding and honor, the TRC offers us the intensely ironic spectacle of its grilling of Winnie Madikizela-Mandela about events she had already explained in courts presided over by some of the same apartheid-era judges who refused en masse to appear or pay it any respect. Cognitive dissonance rises to a cacophony when we learn that the judges trying her had served at the pleasure of ex-president Botha who also refused to appear before the Commission and was never pursued (TRC, 1998: Vol. 1 Ch. 4). As the TRC drama unfolded before the cameras, it inadvertently exposed the injustice in the corrupt underbelly of the Commission. In their lens, a Black woman, survivor of the Soweto massacre of 1976, most visible defender of the defenseless during apartheid, stands wounded in the dock, hunted down by prosecutors and judges seasoned within a legal system that "international human rights organizations condemned…for [the] uncritical application of [unjust laws by its] judiciary" (TRC, 1998: Vol. 1 Ch. 4).

The Afrikaner-led, racist apartheid government, and through it the architects of the TRC, counted on sexism and opportunism within the ANC hierarchy and anti-Kushitic apathy around the globe when it pushed aside Winnie Madikizela Mandela and the visions of justice sourced by her continuous, unflinching leadership on the frontlines of Pan-Afrikan liberation. Not only was she a leader of the Women's wing of the ANC, she was also the only one able "to bridge the gap between the youth and the adults and the different ideological factions" in the country (Motlana, 1985: 116). Madikizela-Mandela experienced the unique challenges that apartheid prepared for Black women. She was banned, imprisoned, tortured and separated from her children. Snipers made numerous attempts on her life, and like all Black women in South Africa during apartheid she lived under the constant threat that the racist regime would use sexual violence to humiliate her (Mandela, 1985).

Given the Commission's own assertion, "the Minister of Justice made it clear that the 'journey' itself must be a conciliatory one", we cannot help but observe that the differential, "gruelling" treatment of Winnie Madikizela-Mandela is a violation of that very principle. Indeed the harsh treatment meted out to her only makes sense as a warning that said, 'Those who dare to value Black humanity over White interests and to serve Afrikan needs with morality by ignoring liberal White assumptions or constraints, have no rights that the ANC office-holders or their manipulators backstage will respect.'

So, this Commission, by accident or design, either undermines or exploits the Black women who take the stand. Their 'ample bosoms', supply the milk of human kindness that purges guilt. Their sighs collapse the moral distance between the Black targets of apartheid, the powerful Whites who structured it and the millions who made it function day by day. In one gripping scene from a documentary about the TRC, *The Guguletu Seven*, a mother reacts with deeply human bewilderment. In a whisper, she asks her son's askari betrayer, why...? We can readily recognize the particular intensity of her confusion and sense of loss. For we know, from personal experience or projection, how 'sharper than a serpent's tooth' betrayal can feel when it comes from faces we have been socialized to trust. (Khoisan, 2001: 120). Even that poignant confrontation of Black on Black betrayal, however, serves the interests of White supremacy, by confirming the presence of deep divisions within the Black community.

Because of the way the Commission positions players in its epic drama, Black women give flesh and blood to the ideal of "wounded healers". Time after time, even as his actions betray the most visible defender of Black rights and healer of Black pain during the last two decades of apartheid, Winnie Madikizela-Mandela, that phrase flows like a soothing balm from the Chairperson's lips. Another discontinuity in logic arises in the Commission's attitude to remembering painful events, "exposing old lies and illuminating new truths" (TRC, Vol.1 Ch.1). In close proximity, it evokes the Jewish Holocaust through the inscription at Dachau with," Those who forget the past are doomed to repeat it". In the same breath, however, it scolds Afrikans, the main targets of apartheid and says, "However painful the experience, the wounds of the past must not be allowed to fester" (TRC, Vol.1 Ch.1). Given the religious credentials of the Chairperson, some may even view the Commission's work here as taking on vague connotations of prophetic inspiration under some invisible divine force. In plainer words, Bishop Tutu assumes the authority to tell Black South Afrikans how they ought to feel.

Using the mechanism of the TRC, opportunistic sexism and religious manipulation snatched defeat from what loomed as certain victory. The TRC created confusion, spread cognitive dissonance and derailed Black consciousness, leaving the Pan-Afrikan population, wherever we reside, eating the ashes of betrayal by our own yet again.

Had Pan-Afrikanists paid appropriate attention to history, they would not have been caught by surprise. There already existed a history of Christianized White supremacy that even opposed Black Christianity in South Africa (Fatton, 1986: 66). Linguist Kwesi Prah tells us that imperialism made missionaries so powerful in Afrikan life that they often arrogantly made up languages and invented "tribes" that did not exist (Prah, 1997: 127). Another historian's prophetic Afrikan eye from the nineteen eighties saw how:

> The missionaries had created an African class of evangelists, teachers, journalists, business-men, lawyers and clerks who often seemed to accept the supposed cultural inferiority of Africans, to accept settler colonialism as a fact of life and who admired the white man for his power, wealth and technology (Boahen, 1985: 197).

Pre-TRC critiques have more to say about the members of the Christianized leadership class occupying high political office in South Africa today, "[t]hey generally acquiesced in colonial expansion and conquest...because...they associated colonialism with Christianity and civilization" (Boahen, 1985: 197; Markovitz, 1977). It logically follows that the authority of 'The Word' in *The TRC Report* is overwhelming based on authorities schooled within European standards of literature, academia, law or political affairs. The way that the report scatters names and credentials of 'the wise' and 'the famous', providing scant biographical background, suggests that its intended readers are familiar with the culture they represent. There are luminaries from the White South African world such as "writer and poet, Antjie Krog... Oxford University historian, Timothy Garton Ash...Judge Albie Sachs [and] American political scientist Harry Eckstein " (TRC, 1998: Vol. 1

Ch. 2). This Report is therefore an unlikely document for South Africa's Black people but much more about them. It defines their pain and delineates boundaries for their passions, love of their people, their family, the self and the land.

Reading *The Report* with the benefit of such insights helps us to understand that it fits into a tradition that has successfully deployed reformist members of the Black leadership class against Pan-Afrikanist consciousness. In particular, the TRC appeals to the class that controls learning and language, inviting it to subvert revolutionary, Pan-Afrikanist change and substitute attitudes that can live comfortably inside exculpation, spreading layers of equal-opportunity blame, they multiply the distance the beneficiaries of apartheid can claim from their monstrous deeds.

It is instructive that no name exists in this report for the men and women who created, sustained and benefited from apartheid at the cost of uncounted numbers of innocent Black lives, not just in South Africa, but across southern Afrika (TRC, 1998: Vol. 2 Ch. 6). Under such a dispensation it is no surprise that "ordinary South Africans [read 'White'] do not see themselves as represented by those the Commission defines as perpetrators, failing to recognize the 'little perpetrator' in each of us [read 'Blacks as well as Whites]" (TRC, 1998: Vol. 1 Ch. 5). Those observations, in my view, are further evidence of how the TRC conflates White responsibility for voting apartheid or sharing in the benefits of apartheid with Black survivalist participation in the robber-settler system under occupation and threat of the gun. A system of subjugation imposed by invaders from outside one's group poses the choice of collaboration at some level, going into exile or embracing death. The similarity of this experience with the slave trade waged against Afrika is not accidental (Williams, 1976; Walvin, 1993; Perez, 1992).

It beggars moral logic to equate the choices Blacks and White could exercise. Whites could refuse to participate in apartheid by regularly defying its customs and rules. On the level of practical, popular education, *The TRC Report* also fails to describe or identify the authors

CLEM MARSHALL

of its preamble by interest, ethnicity, gender, class, caste or race. In over a thousand pages, readers learn little of the forces that might have constrained or influenced the architects of a process that has proffered itself as a model of portable humanity for the world. In the whole affair, in terms of word and image, the most compelling image is that of a Black Christian Archbishop, in European sacred dress, invoking the spiritual guidance of ancestral Afrika through the concept of 'ubuntu'. Wearing flowing robes that placed European religious doctrine at the center of his beliefs, Archbishop Tutu then went on to dispense absolution from an overflowing chalice of ancestral Afrikan cultural and spiritual generosity.

One can only speculate on the extent to which his presence legitimized the misappropriation, disconnection and displacement of moral capital born of the measureless suffering of innocent Afrikans, under conditions designed for despair. In the end, the Commission manages to hand over collective Black moral capital to the collectively guilty White perpetrators as well as the beneficiaries of apartheid's crimes. In so doing, it also shelters them from moral or legal challenges behind its Chairperson's beaming, charming, irresistible, sanctifying, and guilt-obliterating Black face that the media taught viewers to hold beyond reproach. It is inspiration enough for a cautionary poetic tale.

> Black Pearls
> Nature grants innocence special gifts
> As balm for our souls on fire
> Every suffering summons a seed
> Bearing cures within its flower
> Take care not to give
> When others desire
> What we need who need to live
> In the rhythms we know
> Yet don't remember

Ancestor Sister Ancestor Brother

Hurt by hatreds of an unkind world

Honed their anguish

Into pearls

Bequeathing trails of hope in stars

Fashioned from living beyond lifetime's scars

(Marshall, 2004)

The presiding prelate can offer the world no precedent in European religious history to justify asking innocent victims to disown justice and adopt reconciliation. In fact, the Commission's report skilfully evades a crucial question. It fails to ask if or how it is possible to reconcile with enemies before one establishes reconciliation among one's own people and with one's ancestral culture. It makes no attempt to unpack or address the righteous rage in many breasts or seek healing for the undigested grievances which fester at the core of one's fully human self.

For the Christian archbishop does not model his exculpatory exercise on the Christ figure or the Messiah of the New Testament or the Old. His icon is not Mahatma Ghandi, who practiced passive resistance in South Africa before he took it to India and forced the British to leave (Mukherjee, 1993: 96). Nor is the Archbishop's Nobel Peace Prize predecessor, Martin Luther King, who led a non-violent Black campaign for Human Rights in the United States. Indeed, the Civil Rights leader made it very clear that justice was a prerequisite to reconciliation in his stirring, *Letter from a Birmingham Jail* (Asante & Abarry, 1996:740). In the case of South Africa, however, persuading innocent sufferers to practice reconciliation with the 'Other' and alienation from the 'Self' demands a massive demobilization of instinct through powerful images and words. That process can only succeed if Afrikans deny the truths etched into their own souls, and if, in loving others beyond reason or nature they reap such betrayal, they learn at last to always hate who they are.

In South Africa, the schemes of dominant Whites seem to have carried the day. During the apartheid era, as the TRC found out, the State Security Council often targeted resisters for assassination and buried its deeds in its own tongue, Afrikaans. The report says, "Of course, the word murder was never used but euphemisms like *'elimi-nasie'*, *'verwyder'* *'neutraliseer'* and *'uitwis'* [were used]" (TRC, 1998: Vol. 1 Ch. 2). Not only does the TRC employ the face of Afrika to mask crimes against Afrika, however, it also claims, "ubuntu", using Afrika's mother tongue to silence those who demand justice on her behalf. The minefield Afrikans walk through in South Africa today has been seed-ed over many generations. Afrikans and other colonized populations around the world have been carefully miseducated and groomed by media, church, mosque and school to distrust or invalidate evidence of guilt for crimes against our own kind (Woodson, 1969: xxxii). There-fore, it is reasonable to surmise that most, if not all of us, consciously or unconsciously, have learned to routinely bite back words of censure from our lips and finally to excise them from our hearts.

In fact, nowhere within the thousands of pages of the *TRC Report* is 'justice' given equal weight with 'reconciliation'. Although reparations are mentioned, as in the case of the American Kerner Commission, they remain undefined and abstract, naked except for a thin cover of good intentions. For Blacks, dispossessed and persecuted under apartheid, the reality they live has meant the opposite of reparations. The world is still a complicit witness to the transfer of billions of dollars of debt, incurred by the racist regime in its campaigns of mayhem and murder, into the debit column of its Black victims, who, against all odds, had endured and survived apartheid's costly crimes (Khoisan, 2001: 50.104).

Highly placed and educated apologists with Black faces, like many Afrikans world over, have also been carefully curried and groomed to invalidate claims for reparations and hired to sit by the door guarding Whites from the hounds of blame and guilt. Kwesi Prah identifies this local elite by the roles they play in the North (Sudan), West (Senegal), East (Uganda) or South (Zimbabwe). In one sobering example of elite group behaviour in contemporary Senegal, all of the government ministers observed sent their children to schools in France. Prah also reminds us, not without irony, that when members of elites were called, "Obroni [White]" in Ghana, many received it as a form of praise (Prah, 1998: 3). Hannah Arendt points out that, "for those who want to close their eyes" a cycle of exceptions, such as the exceptional appointment of the first Black archbishop under apartheid, Desmond Tutu, can serve as a distraction and keep them blind to evidence of their oppressor's guilt (Arendt, 2000: 360).

Across generations, educators Carter G. Woodson and Kwesi Prah both argue that alienation from self and the suppression of authentic feeling first overtook Afrikan peoples when enemies forced us to substitute their languages and thinking for our own (Prah, 1997: 68). Inevitably, since language is born of cultural experience, Afrikans began to internalize the language of more dominant castes. In practical terms, it means that we could generally be held at the margins of publishing, theatres, halls, TV and other centres that disseminate the science and fruit of our intelligence, all the learning that we cull from our daily collective experience or distill from our relationships with other groups (Gordon, 1994: 60). However, when, eventually, like the Nazi, Adolf Eichmann, our community's preferred language becomes the "officialese" taught us for work or school, or the babyish babble of moralizing talk show 'popularese' we too "[can] become incapable of uttering a single sentence that [is] not a cliché" (Arendt, 2000: 325).

In the societies that have shaped us, some learn cliché-ridden speech through sacred texts that model a celestial piety too lofty for ordinary humans to incarnate. Intellectuals who escape that trap may still internalize other types of clichés as they compete to prove their familiarity with esoteric footnotes and clone-regurgitated literature reviews. Academic prescription, the seductive embrace of arbiters of social taste and the cumulative power of media on ubiquitous talk shows, also spread color-blinding clichés like, 'politically correct', 'reverse racism' and 'there's only one race, the human race'. As educators can generally appreciate, unlearning clichés, like all unlearning, requires hard intellectual and emotional work.

Dissecting two educational documentaries will now help us to see how, even able, anti-racist educators, one a woman of Afrikan ancestry and the other a man of Asian descent, boldly confronting interracial taboos in multiracial discussion groups, still have steep hills to climb. As Pan-Afrikanist educators, we are constantly challenged to remain vigilant against stereotypes that diminish Afrika's achievements or devalue her cultural riches. Diminishing ancestral Afrika in our thoughts can lead to eventual disconnection with our origins. In turn it becomes easier for those who covet our inheritance to separate us from prized ancestral real estate (Horne, 2001; Nyaba, 2002). A part of remaining vigilant is remembering that cultural or religious supremacy as well as colonialism and imperialism have conspired, through language, to convince significant populations within every race to think in ways that degrade Afrika.

5
Chapter

A TALE OF TWO DOCUMENTARIES
THE WAY HOME

● ━ ━ ● ━ ● ━ ● ━ ━ ● ━ ● ● ━ ━ ━ ━ ━ ━ ● ━ ● ━ ━ ● ● ●

In 1997, eight groups of women representing a span of three generations, diverse in their ethnic, racial and social identities met as Aboriginal, Black, Latina, Jewish, Arab, Asian and Multiracial, "councils". They did so separately, and then engaged in dialogue across groups. Black director, Shakti Butler takes a layered approach in creating this female-inspired vehicle for enhancing multiracial educational exchange (Butler, 1998). Director Butler respects the complexities that we must address, as educators, if we are to talk across racial boundaries with authenticity in our pluralistic society. The structure of her research is intended to create a space safe enough for participants to take risks that permit them to experience how we, in the words of writer Patricia Williams, "see things – even the most concrete things – simultaneously yet differently" (Williams, 1991: 150).

I suspect that Butler's study of the differential impact of racial identities on everyday life also makes her aware that Black people are doubly blinded because both our achievements and suffering are buried under dominant historical myths created to justify and sustain patriarchal White supremacy (Bynum, 1999). Out of a similar awareness of the need for popular education on issues of race, feminist thinker Patricia Williams suggests that it takes "listening at a very deep level" to unpack and share the truths from lived experience residing inside our collective memory. Those truths are often cocooned by our desire for social peace and the linguistic bondage that peace-without-justice demands. Even among Blacks, truisms that deny our unspoken or repressed needs or desires often become so commonplace they pass without question into popular discourse. Again as Patricia Williams points out, there is a ready supply of "They don't want to..." phrases available to dismiss the needs of Afrikans and blame us for our own unexplored inadequacies (Williams, 1991: 150, 151).

Butler's skilful construction of the video creates an opportunity for Pan-Afrikanist educators to observe the same Afrikan women discussing identity and racism in a race-specific group as well as in a racially diverse group. Viewers get to see how members of this group support or challenge each other, while simultaneously carving out enough space to grow emotionally and intellectually as well. It also presents a rare opportunity for viewers to compare how Black women situate their identities when relating privately to each other and to also observe some of the ways in which their relationships are mediated by the presence of women of diverse racial ancestry in their midst. The spectrum that Shakti Butler offers viewers is wide, including women who self-identify as Aboriginal, East Asian (Chinese, Japanese or Vietnamese), Filipina, Latina (Cuban, Mexican), South Asian (Indian or Pakistani), West Asian (Arab or Jewish) European (British, Scandinavian, Jewish), Biracial or Multiracially Mixed.

In *The Way Home*, viewers can also note both similarities and differences between the histories and survival strategies, as well as contemporary concerns, of Aboriginal, Afrikan, Jewish and Latina groups. All of those groups have suffered forms of transgenerational genocide or persecution. Carefully following these histories through a Pan-Afrikan lens, viewers may also discover a connecting strand running through them. As different women speak about themselves, that thread seems, almost casually, to link Afrika and things Afrikan into a universal benchmark of degradation. Comparisons to Afrikan experiences surface in oblique references or decontextualized asides. For instance, a Latina confirms that everything that was "despreciado", 'despised' within her community as well as the dominant culture, was related to the "Indian [Aboriginal]" or "Afrikan [emphasis added]" parts of their identities. One woman of Black and White parentage admits, "I wanted to be so White" [emphasis added] and another biracial woman says, "I came to terms with [the reality that] I'm just never going to be White".

When alone, the Black women focus on constant struggles to overcome having, "the nappiest hair" or to mediate the ambiguity of having "the lightest skin". Those internal conflicts over color and Black features, however, are not without resonance in a larger Black-conscious world. A Jewish woman from Iraq speaks with pain of being told, "All you Blacks [emphasis added] are the same..." by Europeans from her own cultural community. Her hand and facial gestures indicate the contempt that accompanied the dismissal of her presumed Black ancestry.

A common anxiety to disown the Sephardic parts of Jewish culture reveals, inadvertently, a hidden cultural anxiety over Afrikan associations. Another woman speaks of "the desperation to detach from anything Sephardic...[that is anything that is] Afrikan [emphasis added]". Eventually, the multiracial richness of the discussion and its emphasis on embracing diversity within all of the groups moves a young Jewish speaker to note that there are "no Afrikan Jews...[that is no] Ethiopian [emphasis added] Jews with [them]". Although Ethiopian Jews are missed, the speaker appears not to know of home-based Jews, such as New York's Harlem-based community of US born Blacks (Higgins, 1998: 20). Without delving into historical or social reasons behind the omission of Jewish Blacks, the speaker then goes on to outline a history of her people including, "[their time] in Egypt as slaves".

Her view of Afrikan history fits popular culture but raises fundamental questions for Pan-Afrikanists. We will return to issues of Hebrew Afrikans and enslavement in Kemet (Egypt) as well the color of ancient Kemites later in this study. However, the Black women present give no indication of feeling that the history of Egypt is also their history, and so they raise no questions about what they hear. Nor do they offer to broaden the European-centred, Jewish or Arab centred infor-

mation base from which Afrikan history is being told. For Pan-Afrikanists, this means that Afrikan reality is reconstructed in the presence of Afrikans, as if there were no Afrikans there. The documentary
therefore misses an opportunity for discussing Afrikan history from
an Afrikan-centered point of view. In failing to raise uncomfortable
questions or to offer alternative explanations of their ancestral history, the Afrikan women present suggest that they may be unaware how
popular culture, as well as European and Asian academic versions of
Kemetic (Egyptian) history, conflict with the careful records or primary sources of information that the Kemites, who were Black peoples,
left behind (Diop, 1991; Hilliard, 1995; Hobson, 2000).

The unspoken, microwave Hollywood interpretation of more
than ten thousand years of Nubia-Kemet-Kush history condensed into
a capsule of Whitened 'Egyptian history' is that White or Whitish men
of nebulous origin built a great civilization in ancient Afrika (Clarke,
1991; Diop, 1991). In the traditions of European and North American
history, those ancient Whites from a mysterious source were also color
conscious or racist and so exploited the unpaid labor of Blacks they
had enslaved (Pieterse, 1992: 128). In contrast to the recycled misinformation the speaker was sharing so confidently, however, the absence
of 'slavery' in ancient Kemet is widely accepted by both contemporary
Pan-Afrikanist and Jewish scholars. One of the latter, Rabbi David
Cahn-Lipman asserts, "Historically, there is no Egyptian record of
such [Hebrew] enslavement" (Cahn-Lipman, 1991: 94).

In *The Way Home*, then, even when physically absent, Blacks seem
continuously present in the imagination and words of all other groups.
For example, several Latina speakers allude to connecting the standard for what is "American [to] lighter skin...[and] certain features".
The complex ways in which culture and race intersect come out in one
Latina's observation that she learned to "get rid of her accent...[and
embrace] rock-'n-roll instead of salsa" (Rose, 1994). There is some irony
in the fact that both of those musical forms are Afrikan-sourced. However records of their ownership and value as cultural or community
capital have been so laundered that their assets have been transferred

to European-identified Spanish or English speakers over time (Guiller-moprieto, 1991; Neal, 2002; Jones, 1963).

Another Latina describes growing up and the sexual implications of her kissing a "Black boy [emphasis added]". She recalls her surprise when her liberal mother showed discomfort with her innocent kiss. Still another admits, "We get...messages [from the adults around]... you don't go out with a Black [emphasis added]." A Chinese woman describes inter-ethnic biases of her family against Vietnamese. She recounts how, when she told her brother she planned to attend her school prom with a Vietnamese escort, he let her know that doing so would be such an unpardonable stain on family honour that he would prefer her to go to the prom "with a Black [emphasis added] boy [instead]."

Arab speakers, on the other hand, talk about the effects of recent wars in West Asia, 'the Middle East', and about the prejudicial treatment they face daily. What is again notable, from a Pan-Afrikanist standpoint, is the coding of their persecution with color, "Anything that is derogatory...or nasty...or evil or bad...is attributed to the evil, dark Arab (emphasis added)". Surprisingly, considering the media's focus on the divide between Arabs and Jews, a Jewish woman's experience mirrors that of her Arab sisters. She describes her mother's fears. "The whole question of being dark and having a dark child was very dangerous... she felt that it was a threat to her survival [emphasis added]".

When a Filipina describes the rejection she faced from her mother's ethnic group at college, she recounts that they waved her away and sent her to the Afrikan American group because of her color and looks. "They would not accept me", she said. "The group that did accept me was the Afrikan American [emphasis added] community...and that's where I felt most love and where I felt accepted." Similar experiences, in which faceless Black men are demonized within everyday family conversations, slip through their language, obliquely, from time to time. Neither the members of the Black 'Council' nor members of other 'Councils' appear to notice or question the fact that the Jewish Council does not talk about Latinas, the European Council makes no

comments about Arabs, the Asian Council does not discuss Aboriginals but that, with the exception of the Aboriginal Council, all groups
refer to incidents involving Blacks or Blackness – Black features, Black
history, Black attitudes, Black culture or Black skin. We can imagine,
however, that their conversations might focus more on Arab identity in
the post 9/11 world.

Cumulatively, in these anecdotes, the base line of degradation
is established as those humans beyond 'the De Gobineau line' where
darker is coded as lesser and so darkest, people or culture that are seen
as most Afrikan, become synonymous with least. Indeed, for French
scientist Arthur De Gobineau, "The Negroid [emphasis added] variety
is the lowest, and stands at the foot of the [human] ladder..." De Gobineau, 1853: 205, 206).

Afrikans are therefore consigned by anti-Kemetic racists to a
place at the bottom of the human hierarchy that is so degraded no other human group could ever fall below it. Hans Gunther attacks "French
policy [which granted colonized Blacks civil rights in the 1920s] for in-
tensifying the 'Black Peril' for the whole world" (Gunther, 1992: 64,65;
Block & Dworkin, 1976: 105, 158).

Fortunately, as the Filipina's moving story demonstrates, Afrikans as a group with relatively strong women who continue to reflect
the enduring inclusiveness of our ancestral cultures have developed an
expandable frame for their collective identity. Based on our common
ancestry, it allows women and men of every shade or texture of hair to
be full members of our communities. Several speakers of mixed ancestry provide evidence for the analysis just made. They tell stories of
finding acceptance among Blacks when no one else would give them
a home. One says, "When I look at myself and society looks at me I'm
Black...No one looks at me and says, 'I bet her mother's White'. I can't
be anything but Black [emphasis added]".

As Afrikans, in a general sense, we can and do collectively provide
a haven where humans of every hue, texture of hair or facial features
have the right to full membership when they choose to identify with us,

serve the interests of Afrikan humanity, respect the dignity of all people of Afrikan ancestry and treat us all as equals. In the documentary, with 'deep listening', we experience the clarity with which Aboriginal women have learned to speak about their long history as targets of racist oppression. One woman says, "To accept that Christopher Columbus discovered America…and it's the same for everybody…that's a lie." Members of the group pile up detail upon detail about their lives that convict their White oppressors of monstrous violations of Aboriginal Human Rights. Another speaker dramatically holds up her ID card as proof of the discriminatory legislation that circumscribes her life. A third boldly asserts, "We are the coal, we are the copper, we are the gold, we are the water, we are the uranium, we are the land herself".

The speaker quoted, an elder of her nation, takes the opportunity to list acts of aggression against her people. Her list of weapons the White government used against them is exhaustive and includes, "tanks, dogs, guns [and] helicopters…It was a war", she says. If we apply the measures of war - unprovoked military aggression, theft of national assets, cultural destruction, depopulation by siege, Blacks, like Aboriginals, are also survivors of devastating holocausts. While the Aboriginal women in the documentary name their reality, however, the Black women present fail to name the transgenerational, undeclared wars by Europe and its sons against Afrika and her children around the world.

By comparing the tone of the language the Aboriginal and Afrikan councils use to describe their history and present reality, differences in European attitudes to each group begin to emerge. Both groups suffered the degradation of enslavement, although numerically more Afrikans were enslaved and also suffered for centuries as well. Whites have therefore lived as oppressors in closer proximity to more Afrikans over a longer time. In addition, the historians also recorded how White fears of Black retribution became especially acute after the Ayitian revolution defeated the French slavocracy in 1804 (Paul, 2000; James, 1989). It is significant, therefore, that while the Aboriginal Council is up-front and often renders a stark indictment of the collective responsibility Whites bear for their suffering, the women of the Black council focus more on internal community conflicts and personal trauma. They cite such personal unresolved challenges as internalized home-grown church-bought homophobia and a White mother's inability to comb her Black daughter's hair. Logically, these internal problems are all by-products of the White anti-Kushitic oppression we experience. At the same time, however, they are influenced and exacerbated by the social oppression Black folks also generally face because of our ancestry in the world at large (Wilson, 1993).

Within the stories viewers see and hear, White and Black meet as equal individuals longing to bridge the divide between them. One Black woman speaks in sad tones of being "cut off from [her] Black family for twelve years" because her White mother chose to raise her. Another woman remembers that, "there were no White people that loved [her]" and shares her guilt at not "wanting [her] White mother to show up [in public areas of her Black life]". Adding her experience to the litany of rejection another speaker admits knowing that her light skin and straight hair were assets in attracting some Black men, and then confesses to her deep hurt on finding out that the nephew she loves only dates White women. Beside her a younger Biracial woman says, "I knew my mom loved me and I knew my father loved me, but they didn't mirror me…I feel like I'm grieving for all that time of feeling so alone".

Ironically, the most passionate scenes the film shows of Blackness defended and racism exposed are presented by White mothers of Black children and the White wife of a Black man. Visibly, they seem more outraged by the injustices Black communities face than the Black women we do hear and see. Even more importantly, they offer an analysis that is grounded in group dynamics rather than individualized experiences. While Black speakers collectively in this video display ambivalent feelings towards other Blacks, confess to internalized prejudices, reveal their sense of guilt, hold back details of how we suffer as a group or of the humiliation and persecution we face because of ancestry, we are shown White women with Black family connections attacking systemic racism without ambivalence or ambiguity. Their language is concrete, unequivocal and courageous. For instance, a White woman describes her life, with "a man as dark as the man [she] married", recalling the "brutal" reality of the racism they face day-to-day. She tells of one ugly confrontation with a White sailor where their unknown attacker sneers, "Pretty White girl. Too bad she's with a nigger [emphasis added]!"

In another example, a White mother tells how her fifteen year-old daughter is "followed around because people suspect she is going to steal something." With frank honesty she openly admits, "We all live in the same house...and [yet] they [family members with Black skin] go into a whole different world". She also recognizes that she has the privilege of ignoring what they must face because of her White skin. "I hardly ever think of that", she says, offering no explanation or excuse. We know that Black women can live in their children's world more than White mothers of Black children can do. However, in *The Way Home* they are not the mothers who bear principal witness against White supremacy for their daughters and sons.

There are a few rare moments in the video when White people, as individuals, do enter the picture identified as potential sources of Black pain. One of them occurs when a self-identified Black speaker tells of being forced to live with her White grandparents and of feeling that they were ashamed of her. She remembers thinking, "I hate these White people" and confesses, "I wanted to be with White people so I could just shove my Blackness ...and my pain in their face". Significantly, her words almost equate 'Blackness' and 'pain'. However, the hate she articulates is born of the hurt in a teenager's heart. She is after all a child. There is no picture of mature, studied rage that can be potentially dangerous to White domination. Her expression of hatred leaves the global racist hierarchy intact and the White world safe to enjoy its addictive innocence. In this rare instance where righteous Black anger against Whites, as a group, threatens to break through the thick layers of participants' longing to reconcile or remain in comfortable space, the video immediately makes an emotional detour. What becomes the speaker's focus is the feeling of hurt she experienced as a child.

On another occasion, the Black elder in the group, a silent presence for most of her time on screen, is deliberately drawn into the conversation by one of the other women. She studiedly resists the encouragement to criticize White society or even Jim Crow segregation and the crippling institutions of her early life. "I didn't feel that bad", she answers, "because that's the way it was...I couldn't change it...I had to [accept things the way they were] what else could I do?" Then she delivers the coup de grace, "Things have got better and I'm grateful [emphasis added]." Her words are spoken with such unqualified gratitude to Whites for their generosity in letting her survive, that they leave their resonance like a soundtrack running behind all the other images and words of every race. For just as Blackness, named or unnamed, flows like a subterranean stream through every conversation, so does the hierarchy of race, although it is subsumed within words of sympathy, empathy, righteous consternation and liberal concern. Shakti Butler's thoughtful, well-meaning film demonstrates just how challenging it can be, in a raceshaped world, to redress our damaged information systems of imbalances, caste structures or hidden inequities. Yet that is the task of educators if we are to create spaces where we can gather and disseminate Pan-Afrikanist truths.

It is surprising to the exploring mind how often within popular culture, images of Black women and men, their silent suffering and their relentless toil function like metaphors for other groups. White authors like Norman Mailer have courted controversy by describing "White Negroes" (Rogin, 1998: 254). One famous Québécois writer, Pierre Vallières, a leader in the province's 'indépendiste' struggle, labelled his book *"Nègres blancs d'Amérique* [White Niggers of America]" (Masse, 1999: 2). Vallières accurately reflected a generalized cultural attitude. Embedded prejudices named the period of authoritarian rule, from 1946 to 1960 under Québéc Premier Maurice Duplessis "La Grande Noirceur" or 'The Big Blackness' (CSN, 1979: 167). Indeed, 'to work like a nigger' passed into the speech of global popular culture long ago. Because we have endured, it appears that the world continues to see Afrikans as a race of gladiatorial warriors or faceless legions of heavyweight champions who entertain in the tradition of Muhammad Ali. Because we are portrayed as super tough and slow to feel for having absorbed such blows for so long, like the proverbial Black 'Mammy' who raised White men who abused her, we are judged undeserving of tears (Pieterse, 1992: 154,155).

A tall, big-boned, dark-skinned Black woman wearing locks, in *The Way Home*, describes her experience with blinding honesty (Butler, 1998). She says, "Because I look like this, I am not allowed to feel stuff that I feel… [People tell me] I'm a goddess, an Amazon…I'm not…I'm a goddamn human being." She then goes on to speak of her unfulfilled expectation that her former spouse, a White man, would provide her access to, "[White] privilege". Her words offer an useful benchmark for measuring how paternalism serves as an instrument of dehumanization in racist social space.

The euphemisms that most Afrikans must accept and internalize in order to please the wider community and keep jobs, status, opportunity, colleagues, lovers or friends usually impose a crippling tax on the communities from which we come and to which most of us must eventually return in order to survive and thrive. This Black woman rejects the ambiguous, paternalistic approval that liberal groups or individual outsiders often invest in us. While being chosen by members of a dominant social group can offer opportunities to elevate us above our peers, it can simultaneously rob us of our full humanity and betray the deep need for self-love at the center of our Pan-Afrikan soul. In such a destructively symbiotic relationship of psychological and social denial shared by both Blacks and Whites, a strange dance often unfolds. In our quest for deeper insight let us turn to *Color of Fear* and an examination of the way Black men in the same society as the women of *The Way Home*, talk about race and what useful lessons they offer for rebuilding a Pan-Afrikan world.

COLOR OF FEAR

Lee Mun Wah, an American therapist of Chinese ancestry, is the self-styled "big connection" in the second documentary analyzed in this chapter. Mun Wah selects and brings together a racially and culturally diverse group of eight middle-class men born in the United States to talk about race and racism in their society. Filming takes place over a weekend in a small-town setting in Ukiah, California. *Color of Fear* was first aired in the United States in 1994. By appearance the nine men possibly range in age between thirty and forty years. Mun Wah opens the conversation with an explanation of how and why he selected them. "I actually know each of you in a special way" he tells the group, "each of you was picked for your honesty...directness...sincerity and the work you do too on yourself."

When the moderator invites each participant to state his ethnicity, they speak in the following order. David Christiansen says, "I am American. Generations back we came from England and Denmark... [I'm] White American, I guess." Hugh Vasquez responds, "My father is Mexican. My mother is Irish." Victor Lewis describes himself as "Afrikan. And some ways back, [of] Cherokee descent." Yutaka Matsumoto says, "I am a third generation Japanese man." Gordon Clay tells the group, "I'm seventh...at least seventh generation Euro- American. My family is...on both sides [it] is Scot...and on my father's side is also English and German." Roberto Almanza declares, "I'm...ah... Mexican...I'm Latino...I'm Mexican...I'm Mexican- American...I'm Chicano." In Lee Mun Wah's words, "I am such as Chinese...uhm... and...I'm...I'm Chinese American..." David Lee speaks both reflectively and emphatically. "I am an American...also...I'm an...all-American [emphasis added] man." Loren Moye insists, "But I do always want to be identified as Afrikan-American or Black, not just an American..."

Human, predator-prey politics can sometimes be illuminated by behavior in the animal world where it is common for the one being stalked to mask its fear lest it precipitate attack (Attenborough, 1990: 210). In the words of Victor Lewis in *Color of Fear* to David Chrstiansen, this is a game in which "You [a White man] pretend that I'm White, and I [a Black man] pretend that I'm White [too]". Race protocol, his words imply, far too often, is coercive and forces Afrikans to ignore the immediate pain of racist indignities while there are Europeans or

Asians in our midst. On the other hand, the members of those groups often learn early on to cultivate a kind of wilful blindness in order to avoid feeling guilty, when they enjoy benefits from being preferred at Afrikan expense. By way of illustration, Loren Moye in the documentary *Color of Fear* describes his working life as a Black man in corporate America this way, "It's a nineties' shuffle but a shuffle nonetheless" (Mun Wah, 1994).

Color of Fear opens with the shadowy figure of a Black man moving panther-like across a shadow-drenched screen against a barbed wire fence. In the background, a soundtrack of unidentified metal rubbing against discordant metal, muffled drumbeats and other unsettling noises suggests those prisons that live in the popular imagination to contain potentially dangerous, roving 'gangs' of Black men. Image and sound frame the ominous, unidentified Black male figure, hair twisted into tiny, pointed 'baby dreds', with foreboding. Just before the camera pulls back to show the opening credits and close-ups of individuals in the group, disembodied voices play in our heads and we are startled by the loud clang of a metal door. That sound recreates the tension and anxiety of banging prison doors that TV has made familiar. Although this documentary is presented as a multiracial, multicultural, balanced examination of racism from many perspectives, the unexamined assumptions behind its initial moments load the dice against its Black participants even before it begins. Wordlessly it has already fixed their presence within the framework of intense terror that this society uses to rationalize persecuting Black men. The video therefore reserves a unique role for the Black male to play in exploring interracial anxiety and fear.

This work by a 'progressive' filmmaker and educator of Chinese ancestry is significant. While progressives and conservatives alike often remind Black males that we are merely a minority among minorities and should not consider our social situation or pain unique, this film and the analysis that follows demonstrate that groups, across the ideological spectrum, reserve special roles for an archetypal, mythical 'Blackman' of their own imagining. Mun Wah's perspective is also in-

CLEM MARSHALL

structive because critics and commentators of every colour have also enjoined 'Blackmen' not to 'play the race card' or create a 'hierarchy of oppression'. Even as society at large cautions 'Blackmen' to act out the myth of the level playing field, however, it assigns them a place at the lowest end of its scale of humanity. That reserved space is not readily negotiated, but fixed instead in the mortar and stone of millennia of misconceptions and fears (Gates, 2001: XIV; Crouch, 1995; Archer, 1999; Allison, 1994).

Cultural critic bell hooks points out the inherent contradiction in the politics of Whites who preach class-consciousness to Blacks when we talk race but ignore the class of a Black offender if that person blames them because they enjoy privileges and incarnate power based on Whiteness (hooks, 1995: 24). Instead of dismantling Black male stereotypes, *Color of Fear* confirms the particularity and centrality of Black male experiences in the thinking of diverse racial groups. At the documentary's end, after the super-angry 'Blackmale' has vented his "misplaced rage", a term repeatedly used by White teachers and students when I've shown this video as a teaching tool, Victor is thrown back into center stage to lead the healing process with a rousing Afrikan spiritual that liberally dispenses microwave, 'feel good' vibes of racial reconciliation.

As in *The Way Home*, participants who identify as Asians, Europeans and Latinos focus on questions of Black influence or power and challenge Blacks for victimizing individuals from their groups. The speakers invest incidents that demonstrate Black culpability with social weight. Latino Hugh Vasquez describes his confrontation with an unknown Black man. Turning to Victor and Loren Moye he says, "You people are powerful [emphasis added]". In the documentary, despite the defence of individual innocence that David Christiansen, David Lee and both Latino men offer against the status they enjoy compared to Black men, the words they choose bear witness to the contradiction they live. They do in reality see the two Black participants as members of a race and representatives of their group. Yet there is no obvious reason for those assumptions. Loren Moye is of a dark complexion, while

Victor Lewis'is light. They don't resemble. Their voices – in terms of tone, vocabubulary and patterns of speech - mark the different experiences in their background and upbringing. However, on screen, when the men of other races speak, their pictures of crude, menacing Black men tumble out into an emotionally charged space. Their listeners either lean visibly forward or sit back with satisfied eyes. Through their body language they generally send out signals that they share the assumptions made.

Significantly, neither Victor Lewis nor Loren Moye manages to expand the lens through which the group sees Black men. They miss the opportunity to help the gathering better understand how the uniquely overwhelming vulnerability of Black men in North America deforms even those men they presumed to be macho bullies from lower class, working class homes. As a Black male viewer, I logically assume that even as they listen, both Victor Lewis and Loren Moye are aware that despite Black voting power, buying power and the power of Black culture to generate wealth, we collectively exercise derisively little control over the institutions or legal systems that prey on our sons. Loren Moye and Victor Lewis are university-educated and skilled in negotiating the middle-class, corporate or academic White world. Yet, they too walk a minefield of daily humiliation with its threat of random ambush by police. Lee Mun Wah's *Color of Fear*, despite its sincerity and good intentions only tells the partial story he knows and does so from the outside Black experience. His documentary reminds Pan-Afrikanists to work for control of our own images and words. In this documentary, as it is generally, those outside our lived experience and less invested in our fate continue to miscalculate and misrepresent the costs we bear as targets of choice of racial supremacy. All that we are, including the intensity of our suffering seems constantly subjected to a dilution and diminution tax, and this occurs even in spaces carved out by the most progressive, liberal forces within multiracial societies.

Across the spectrum of racial diversity, the other men in the room seem oblivious to the trauma betrayed by both Black men's eyes. The tone of the conversation is unexpected because it takes place in California, where the brutal, videotaped police assault on a Black motorist, Rodney King, had already passed into popular culture via TV. In the face of such proven vulnerability, the documentary, in outcome if not intent, inadequately interrogates the costly, ubiquitous myths about menacing, Black male power the society has learned to believe. *Color of Fear* was also made after widely circulated Amnesty International reports condemning the prison and police systems in California for racist bias against Black and Latino men (Porter, 1997). Framed by silence, Victor Lewis and Loren Moye risk the appearance of colluding with yet another depiction of those who wear their gender and skin as dangerous to innocent human beings. By their very presence they confirm an unconscious appeal to caricatures and stereotypes of Afrikan men.

When David Christiansen alleges, "[Black men are] frightening when [they] become very animated", Loren Moye and Victor Lewis, say nothing. So David Christiansen's misleading, racist, depiction of faceless, macho, threatening Black men floats unchallenged in the air around them. In the real world where most Black folks live, we can only wield discriminatory power in the fevered or guilt-ridden imaginations of other populations. Those who have historically arranged to exist beside us often do so while continuing to remain sealed inside protective cocoons of their own anti-Kushitic myths, customs, institutions and hierarchies of skin. Demonstrably, people of Asian, Latino or European identity exercise far more military, economic and social power than Afrikans, both in North America and in the larger world (Akyeampong, 1980; Scammell, 1975; Oliver & Shapiro, 1997). When the only Black men present remain silent in the face of defamatory judgments of their group, Pan-Afrikanists logically ask, 'Are Victor Lewis and Loren Moye playing tricks or allowing others to play tricks on their minds'?

During this well-crafted, probing documentary, I listened in vain for a single voice that dared to detail the unique history of public castrations, White genital mutilation, of Black men or a speaker who exposed the institutionalized rape of Black women. Yet dehumanizing experiences have been central to the servitude Europeans forced on our beleaguered race. Thinker and author bell hooks also points out that many other groups made gains in Human Rights based on the martyr-dom of Black leaders and the sacrifice of Black lives (hooks, 1995: 54).

In *Color of Fear*, there is also no effective response made from a Black perspective when Hugh Vasquez complains, "[Blacks make me feel that] my issues as a Brown person are not as important or as bad as a Black person's". In turn Roberto Almanza tells his story of a confrontation and accuses an unknown Black man of abusing him because of "displaced rage". Yutaka Matsumoto also feels compelled to tell these two men, "I get frightened [of Blacks]." In the end, all these faces of the society's cultural diversity, although speaking to a spectrum of racialized experiences, add fuel to prejudices the media daily ignites against Black men, Victor Lewis takes up the burden of explaining Blackness so that all other races might learn. He is alter-nately cast as 'angry intellectual' and 'super-sweet Blackmale' so that he can deal with the group's need to feel comforted after it had parad-ed its guilty fears. Myths routinely mask Black racial history in this hemisphere and permit society to devalue the personal achievements of survivors of our holocausts such as Victor Lewis and Loren Moye by disguising the enormity of our collective pain. It is telling that when Loren, soft-spoken and darker-skinned tries to articulate some of his aching encounters with White immigrants and other people of color, he speaks haltingly, almost apologetically, and seems reluctant to de-scribe how, "Immigrants come to [this] country [the USA and]...can't speak a word of [the official] language except [knowing how to say] one thing...Nigger! [Emphasis added]."

The anecdotal information in this documentary made in 1994, con-firms in-depth research carried out a generation earlier by the United States based Brink and Harris Poll in 1966. That poll found that "...some 70% of all whites think the Negro is trying to move too fast. And their message to the black man is, Cool it" (Brink & Harris, 1967: 21). As if time had politely stood still, the more expressive White speaker in the documentary, David Christiansen, goes largely unchallenged when he accuses Black people in general of "going in the wrong direction", asking rhetorically, "Why don't you people look for something within yourself that can make you feel equal to us?" David's views may be his own, but he is not alone in holding them. The society that formed him generally acts as if it is oblivious of the history of Afrikan civilization and the confident humanity that Pan-Afrikanist education provides (Hilliard, 1993; Gadalla, 1999). It was no accident that Plato, the Greek philosopher, apprenticed in Kemet or that Europe's famous son and quintessential statesman, Napoleon Bonaparte, took hundreds of artists, scientists and architects with him so that they could absorb Afrika's genius at the feet of Horus-Rising-in-the-Morning, the representation of divine forces renamed "Sphinx" (Onyewuenyi, 1994; Tompkins, 1978).

Even as the outsiders in this documentary misrepresent the lived experience of Afrikan communities and accuse Black men of being 'powerful' in a negative, frightening way, those same men they describe continuously struggle against a wilfully deaf world that ignores our screams of anguish and despair (Wilson, 1993). Yet, in *Color of Fear,* when speakers stereotype Black men they do not seem to be doing so with intent. Instead, they generally appear to be trying to find ways of describing the power Black males have developed to cope with complex challenges to their manhood and survival in a patriarchal, White supremacist world. Educationally, however, the fact that they want to be nice is not good enough.

When indeed, as Black men, we recount the details of our daily experiences, public response usually tells us that the harshness we read so clearly is written in invisible ink where the rest of the world is concerned. Historically, our stories really begin to take public shape when fate and hate soak them in our own fresh blood. For Rodney King, the motorist whose beating by the Los Angeles police scandalized the world, to get access to even a contested kind of 'justice', dozens of innocent Black men had to die. To varying degrees, depending on history, location, class, culture and sexual identity our energies, dreams, bodies and brains become food for other men. Like oaks hosting orchids, many Black lives are finally sucked dry. At the present season of historical time, as the 'designated demons' of the rest of the world, the Black male has no rival or peer (Akbar, 1992; Carter, 1975; NYC State

Special Commission on Attica, 1972; Cleaver, 2001 & 1969; Jackson, 1990; Bing, 1991; Pickney, 1994).

Part Four of this study illustrates some of the ways that Pan-Afrikan culture and traditions, within a broad Pan-Afrikanist approach to education, offer students opportunities to discover antidotes to degrading words and situations. Since educational institutions are sites that students enter to learn both how to survive and what society expects of them, I now examine linguistic retentions as well the rich learning we can glean from the hidden curricula of history and everyday Pan-Afrikan life.

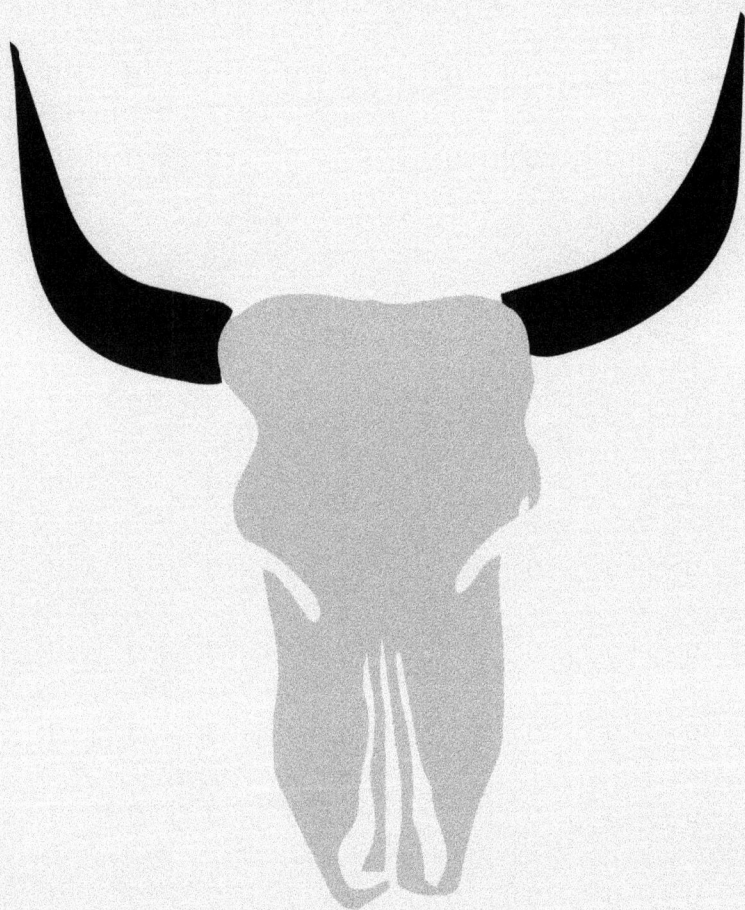

2
Book

Part IV:

Embracing Afrika

6

Chapter

IN ANCESTRAL SPACE AND TIME
CIRCLES AND SOURCES OF REBIRTH

● ▬ ▬ ● ● ▬ ▬ ● ● ▬ ● ● ▬ ▬ ▬ ● ● ▬ ● ● ▬ ▬ ● ▬ ● ● ●

As Pan-Afrikanists, we face the challenge of creating opportunities where a people long denied can recover the strengths of
the culture taken from them. As knowledge grows, we can expect more Afrikans to see how cultural assets they now take for
granted and lose by default might help victims of serial genocide,
forced exile and brutal servitude to survive (Kitwana, 2002; Neal,
2002; Robeson, 1978). Students of Afrikan ancestry deserve safer,
healthier spaces that reward the trust they place in their teachers
and schools. To date, however, few such spaces seem to exist. In
their stead, 'soundscapes' that leave imprints on minds in and out
of classrooms expose the unprotected psyches of vulnerable Black
youth on the frontlines of racist risk.

When educators put Black learners back in the center of their history, the axes of the language we use must necessarily shift as well.
Fundamental transformations, both in the way students think of and
experience learning are then more likely to occur. Logically, then,
Pan-Afrikanist educators must also address the legacy of European
and Arab atrocities against Afrikans and do so without euphemism,
apology or averting our eyes. However, most educators appear largely
unprepared to do so, because how we have learned to speak, write and
think does not equip us to challenge misconceptions about Afrikans
or their history in racialized societies where we live and must survive.

CLEM MARSHALL

Some personal reflections can illustrate that view. As Caribbean-ized Afrikans recovering or rediscovering our right to self-determination, we sometimes still feel trapped by the context of our birth. Historically, we come into the world already ensnared. For we inherit the language and emotional logic of groups that subjugated and degraded us over centuries. Up to the present time, we have always lived as subordinate populations within those cultures, even when our group holds political office, while they continue to threaten our survival and dignity, by 'commission or omission, accident or design'.

WHEN NO OTHER VOICE WILL DO

In North America, Aboriginal peoples have confronted many challenges that parallel our own. They, too, have had to rescue their truths from the hegemonic histories of European invaders. On June 17, 1744 representatives of the Six Nations Confederacy declined a White offer to enroll their children in William and Mary College, Pennsylvania. From that meeting, an eloquent plea for space and mutuality has come down to us, "But you, who are wise must know that different nations have different conceptions of things and you will therefore not take it amiss, if our ideas of this kind of education happens not to be the same as yours" (McLuhan, 1971: 57).

A contemporary Mi'kmaq historian, Daniel Paul, also calls our attention to the misrepresentation of Aboriginal history. Paul attributes the compulsion to tell lies to a linguistic phobia that cripples European writers in describing the atrocities their own ancestors perpetrated against the First Nations of this hemisphere. He writes that:

> Colonial English politicians and military personnel used means of terror against First Nations peoples...Thus the reluctance of most White male scribes to discuss and put to paper the details of such behaviour is understandable.

To do so is to question the very civility of those
who perpetrated the atrocities (Paul, 2000: 9).

His insight can be usefully applied to the way historians treat Afrikan experience in the Americas as well. Outside of such exceptions as
Gullah in South Carolina, Garifuna in Central America and Creole in
Haiti, Guadeloupe or Martinique, we have mostly accessed the legacy
of our immediate Ancestors in our oppressors' tongues, the languages
we have been erroneously taught to call mother tongues (Prah, 2002).
For those who suffer its loss, a lost tongue is like a phantom limb. We
continue to feel its invisible presence as pain. Now that generations
of students in the Caribbean, Afrika, and the Americas have passed
through the postcolonial, post-Emancipation and post-Civil Rights
movements, we can cull from them those experiences that advance
our liberation and suggest strategies for repairing the ravages of Afrikan enslavement. As Afrikans, we incarnate a unique experience of
endurance. We are seeds of survivors, who bequeathed us the skills
they honed within the bowels of White supremacy, which racialized religion, language, law and popular culture (Clarke, 1994; Wilson, 1993).

To preserve a false social peace, both persecutors and the captives
educated to please them processed generations of Afrikans for "compelled
social amnesia" (Wilson, 1993: 122). Yet, judged by the residual richness
and depth of Afrikan connections to ancestral culture, we preserve significant memories, both as individuals and in groups. Indeed, although forced
amnesia has left many psychic gaps, Pan-Afrikanist scholars continue to
gather evidence that unfathomable trauma did not succeed in severing our
conceptual and spiritual umbilical cord. One of those special memories
rests, for me, in texts about ancient Sumer, modern Iraq (Beason, 1989).
They inspire the rhythms of the following words.

Reconnection
Where are the Woolen-headed Priests of Sumer
Asked seekers of truth from afar

CLEM MARSHALL

Sentries in stone now guard the sand

While grief-stricken mourners wander far from
their land

The sage looked up

Her locks streamed down

In strands of tight curls like grey tears

Ah Great Sumer she sighed

Surrendered her past

Hiding truths too deep for her heirs

And when they forgot they wore wool as a sign

They weakened and sickened then died

(Marshall, 2004)

I wrote that reflection on Sumer and adapted verses from a speech by Queen Hatshepsut recorded in the early fifteenth century BCE, as a way of clarifying for myself the contradictory and often confusing information that various European historians present on ancient Kemet (Busby, 1992: 12). The flourishing Sumerian civilization was among the first to set down its achievements and history in writing. By a process of triangulation, we can be reasonably assured that it did so around 4000 years ago (Agar, 1985). Sumerian writing is known as "cuneiform" and composed of wedge-shaped picture-figures cut into tablets of clay. The tablets with this verse were found in an area that is Southern Iraq today. The name "Sumer", according to those records, can be translated as, "Black Heads or Black Faces".

Whether the name is figurative or literal has been subject to interpretation and has frequently sparked academic debate. Some concrete evidence, however, does exist. A Black population calling itself, 'Sumr' still lives in Palestine today. Unlike the Babylonians who succeeded them, monuments also show that the Sumerians resembled contemporary Kemites. They represent themselves as beardless, sometimes with features and hair like Kenyan Masai or as often with shaven heads like the Nuba, Shilluk and other ancestral peoples of Sudan today (Jackson, 1970: 71; Mair, 1979).

SOUNDS THAT UNBIDDEN CLING TO OUR TONGUE

An Afrikan shaman who White Jesuits kidnapped as a boy wrote, "The things I talk about here did not happen in English" (Somé, 1998: 2). In similar vein, a Kenyan poet and writer in his mother tongue also identified the process of devaluation of Afrika's linguistic heritage. Kenyan author Thiong'o Ngugi writes, "The colonial education system denies that the colonized have real human languages. These are described as vernaculars meaning the language of slaves or merely barbaric tongues" (Ngugi, 1983: 94). For scattered Afrikans, the trauma of being ripped from our place of birth happened to a people whose rhythms, tones and style still remain distinct among those who have held us captive for over thirty generations. Clearly the traumas we live and have lived happened to us in different tongues and the part of that tongue we perhaps know and use the least may hold the secret legacy of our Ancestors in it (Dandy, 1991). Today, linguists like Kwesi Prah who offer us greater access to our ancestral languages have become keepers of ancient promises of eventual Afrikan rebirth.

Travelling in Senegal gave me the chance to observe firsthand the cultural power of the ancestral languages I had lost. Greetings in Wolof, the common tongue, are circular, cyclical and resist exact rendition in either English or French. The usual reply to the question, "Nanga def?" "How are you", is "Mangi fi rekk" (Kane & Sembène, 1978: 18). Literal French translates this response as, "Je suis là, seulement", while literal English says, "I am here only" (Kane & Sembène, 1978; Samb, 1983). When I lived among Wolof speakers, both translations proved palpably inadequate, however, because they failed to transmit the feeling in greetings packed with reverence and deeper, ancestral meanings. Those greetings were offered in the Wolof spirit of 'teranga' meaning 'generosity', and as a tribute to the dignity of free-standing, free-thinking human beings. They also carried a sense of The Divine in every woman and man. It seemed to me that when greeters spoke to each other they were also conscious of their Ancestors listening in.

Cultural expert and former Chief of Information in Senegal, Abdou Rahman Cissé, helped me understand more about day-to-day greetings in Wolof. When Wolof speakers meet and converse, he offered, they repeat each other's "sant" their mother's family name to invoke the living presence of their Ancestors. A greeting also binds communities together by stressing the inter-connectedness of diverse last names. "Sant nekkul fenn", the Wolof saying goes. It means that family names are like nomads. They never settle down." The list of the illustrious dead who became Ancestors includes all clan members who were credits to the clan while alive. For the greeters, then, the time they spend together has both sacred and secular meaning. I learned to respect the investment speakers made in formal greetings. Introductions and salutations, especially at the village level, would usually go on for several minutes. Quite often, after a reprise that interrupted the conversation, the repetition of family names and greetings would start all over again.

I was perhaps even more struck by the way speakers said, "rekk", literally translated by outsiders as "only". Judging by their delivery, speakers would use it to mean "right", "exactly" or even "right on", in the style Black Panthers made famous during the Civil Rights era in the US. It certainly did not seem to express in any way the apologetic self-effacement implied in the sterile translation, "I am here only" or the more common response, "I'm fine!" that is suggested by some Wolof-to-English lexicons (Kane & Carrie-Sembène, 1978: 18; Gaye, 1980: 5). "Rekk" was usually spoken with a confidence that conveyed a powerful sense of self. What I would regularly hear and see in faces or gestures of those exchanging greetings would be better translated as, "I am right here", or, "I have a right to be here". It seemed like a powerful ritual for grounding speakers in the occupation and possession of their land. Participating in it I became conscious of the depth of the traumatic rupture that tore my Ancestors by the root from our sacred soil.

In sum, the tilt of the head, the confident smile and the fire in the eyes that would usually accompany the words conveyed sentiments akin to, 'As an independent human being with a free, immortal soul, I need no one's permission or consent to be here'.

There is other evidence that supports the thesis of undisclosed and potentially deeper meaning in the everyday utterances of Afrikan life. By and large, when White travellers and observers described Afrikans living in the US North and Afrika outside the orbit of those apartheid societies, they marvelled at the naturally proud and graceful carriage of the ordinary Black people they saw, especially those living in rural communities beyond direct White contact or control. That is in marked contrast to the shuffling feet and bowed Afrikan heads that historians described in cities under apartheid or in the US South (Parker, 1986; Fredrickson, 1982; Frederikse, 1982). The contrast suggests that those people who stood tall, without White persecutors forcing servility upon them daily, were also people used to being free.

In my view, there is a practical application for what we may learn from the present investigation of linguistic forms and how they function to either enhance our social power or surreptitiously seduce us with palatable euphemisms. As we identify and remove expressions with negative impact, we can replace them with words that are more true to our experience. Reintroducing rituals of affirmation in everyday social interactions in school, college, university or in communal gatherings and popular culture could also provide opportunities for re-building Afrikan self-esteem. As educators, many of us have experienced the power of mutual affirmation within groups of learners. Afrikan populations often used words as psychic massage therapy in pre-Europeanized or pre- Arabized societies. Wolof greetings or the honorific, 'brother' and 'sister' of Black popular speech during the nineteen sixties' Black Power Movement remind us that there was a technology of social harmony that the foreigners violently destroyed when they scattered our Ancestors across the earth (Obadele, 1991).

Since the brutal uprooting of uncounted millions of Afrikans, we have had to use English or other European languages to communicate experiences we felt in our silenced Mother Tongue. I say, 'silenced' because the ghosts of those languages still survive unrecognized in our every day speech. Dandy speaks of "mythaphonics, a combination of speech, music, dance, and nonverbal communication, which they [Afrikans] brought to the new land" (Dandy, 1991: 21). Growing up, I learned to convey, 'yes', 'no', 'maybe', 'definitely not', and a score of nuances in-between, by the same nasal, tonal sound, 'uh' or 'uhm', in different tones and to give it contextual specificity by adding the appropriate body language.

Afrikans in certain areas of the Caribbean also retain an even older form of speech, which is perhaps a remnant of the 'click' sounds in certain Afrikan languages (Prah, 1988; Allsopp. 1996). Traveling in Senegal, Kenya and Mauritania as well as in southern Afrika, I would keep hearing a familiar sound that belonged to the 'soundscape', which had surrounded my earliest years. Rendered as, "steups", the sound is described by Allsopp as, "an ideophone representing sucking the teeth". However, in my estimation, that definition does not adequately convey the passion, contempt or flirtatious humour that can be conveyed by a toss of the head and a "steups" (Allsopp, 1996: 530). It does not require a great leap of imagination for me to see a connection between that sound and the sound I learned first from listening to Miriam Makeba's Click Song in Xhosa (Makeba, 1987). Although I have been a student of language all my academic life, I am still only slowly discovering the richness of Afrikan retentions in the speech patterns of the English Caribbean and Americas.

Indeed, despite pioneering work by such researchers as Maureen Warner and Velma Pollard, information on our Afrikan linguistic legacy is slow in re-entering popular consciousness in both Caribbean and North America (Warner, 1996: 7). Warner points out that there is still a considerable vocabulary attached to the cultural and spiritual practices that have survived forced exile. According to Winifred Vass and Joseph Holloway, who collect evidence of the legacy of Afrika in US speech, the word "jazz", from a Bantu root word, "jaja" meaning, "music that makes you dance" is a part of that legacy (Holloway & Vass, 1997: xvi). Because of the relative newness of studies in the linguistic connections of scattered Afrika, this is only one of many explanations of the origins of words like 'jazz' (Bergreen, 1997). As we rebuild language for our liberation, therefore, it is vital for us to triangulate so that we develop accuracy in measuring the depth of the linguistic foundation on which we stand, build and continue to dance.

Joseph Holloway and Winifred Vass also tell us that Afrikans retained naming practices in the United States well into the nineteenth century, despite considerable pressure to give them up. Furthermore, those authors tell us that Wolof, Fulbe and Mande were often the lingua franca on both sides of the Atlantic before 1730 (Holloway & Vass, 1997: xxiii). There is a need, therefore, for popular education to make our communities more aware of the Afrikan languages our Ancestors once used widely, even in this hemisphere, and the extent of their invisible presence in our speech today. Because of the recent hardships Afrikan societies have faced, a number of refugee and immigrant communities have now established themselves across North America (Wilson, 1998). These newly transplanted sisters and brothers are natural links to the languages lost to Afrikans born overseas, and through them Pan-Afrikanists can perhaps begin to re-attach our severed ancestral tongues.

When I met Ghanaian university students during my studies in Paris, we found we had the words, "fufu", a type of food staple that my grandmother regularly prepared, and "nyam", meaning, "eat", in common. Today, "nyam" lives in the lyrics of Antiguan calypsonian Lord Short Shirt, *"meh mumah mus' nyam, meh wuman mus' nyam* [my mother must eat, my woman must eat]". Kwesi Prah's ongoing investigations at the Centre for Advanced Study of African Society in Cape Town, South Africa, confirm that a form of "nyam" occurs across ancestral Afrikan languages (Prah, 2002). Somehow our bruised and bereaved Ancestors passed those words on to us across a bloody divide of time, space and genocide. As Pan-Afrikanists we can retrace the paths those stalwarts carved out of stony adversity today. For we bear witness, by our very presence, that holocausts set in motion by non-Afrikans long ago still influence the way we speak, think and dream in this time. The ghosts of cauterized, mutilated tongues haunt our reclaimed, reconstructed psyche, striving to give form to the messages whispered to us from inside the marrow of our bones or the platelets in our blood. This study draws on evidence that confirms our passion for the living ancestral word echoing in the poetry, prose, songs, sayings or plays that encircle the triangle of trauma from Europe to Afrika and the Caribbean or the Americas (Ani, 1994; Smart & Nehusi, 2000; Chinwezu, 1988).

We have much to tell each other before our incalculable anguish gets talked away. Those whose present domination over our lives reminds us of past hurt seem in no hurry to say sorry or make amends. In the Congo, as we saw earlier, Belgian occupiers reportedly murdered ten million of its twenty million population between 1898 and 1908 in a genocide that should invite similar attention and restorative justice to that paid the Jewish Holocaust. Apart from the Belgians in West Afrika, there are other parallels of deliberate extermination campaigns across Afrika. In South West Africa, now Namibia, German troops honed their genocidal skills against the Herero and Nama peoples (Pakenham, 1991; Boahen, 1985). In 1904, Germany's Lieutenant General Von Trotha's orders were explicit, decreeing that "Within the German boundaries every Herero, whether found with or without a rifle, with or without cattle, shall be shot" (Hochschild, 1998: 282). There are charges of an ongoing genocide in Darfur. A journalist and translator from that region, Daoud Hari, bears personal witness to atrocities carried out by those serving Arab interests to extinguish the First Nations of the Sudan. Ironically, although Bilad Al Sudan is of Arabic origin and means "Black People's Land", the Arab League maps Sudan into the Arab World.

Such cumulative evidence leads to the conclusion that there is a historical ethos of extermination that has informed the way outsiders relate to Afrikans. Europe's campaigns seem to answer the question,

'How can we render these First Nations of the earth inert so they behave like the property we desire them to be'? It reveals the mindset that predicts a time when:

> [Young] ladies on camp stools, under palm-
> trees, will read with tears – The Last of the Ne-
> groes. (Reade, 1994: 273).

Summing up the impact of European destructiveness on Afrika, another historian writes:

> Over the last quarter of the nineteenth centu
> ry... the rapid spread across Africa of animal
> and human diseases, the demands of the ex
> panding labor market, and the last push of paci
> fication had resulted in a decline of twenty-five
> percent or even more of the African population
> (Cell, 1987:197).

REHEARSING A REFURBISHED TONGUE:

> The present political chaos is connected with the
> decay of language, and...one can probably bring
> about some improvement by starting at the ver
> bal end (Reznikov, 2001: 101).

All languages, like the peoples who speak them, come from somewhere. The history of the English language preserves evidence of its political evolution in the vocabulary we use today. Frederick Bodmer points out that we keep the memory of the Norman-French conquest of the Saxons in the dual list we maintain for animals raised for food. An Anglo-Saxon, 'cow' became Norman, 'boeuf' and is our, 'beef' today. Once separated from the labour of the conquered villagers who raised, slaughtered and served, meat took on airs, graces and anonymity for the nourishment, pleasure and comfort of a foreign upper class (Hogben & Bodmer, 1944: 218).

As Pan-Afrikanists, we face a daunting linguistic challenge. This language we now use to defeat degradation is the very weapon of our subjugation. It leaves a film of defamation lingering on everything we name and it troubles our vision, reflecting fractured images in the mirrors through which we come to know ourselves (Du Bois, 1965). Logic demands that Pan-Afrikanists remain as intentional about rehabilitating the language with which we write, speak and think as the cultures that kidnapped, colonized and debased us have been about controlling it.

Amos Wilson established a psychological connection between racism, language and power:

> There's a connection between the capacity to have other people speak your language and to call things by the names you give them, and power. If we wish to assume power then we must assume the capacity to name and define things (Wilson, 1993: 23).

The historical record clearly shows that those who enslaved and colonized Afrikans also used their languages as weapons to undermine Afrikan resistance (Chinwezu, 1987). In order to effect a transformation in the way we relate to each other and the world, we Pan-Afrikanists must necessarily change the patterns of negative thinking fostered by the languages we've been forced to absorb. The Nigerian writer, Chinweizu, has called attention to the alienation that can occur when Afrikan writers and performers speak an invader and aggressor's tongue to each other. He notes that "in calculating to please alien masters, ... [they] become stylistically strange or unintelligible to [their] African audience" (Chinweizu, 1988: xxxiii). Our first audience must be our sisters and brothers, sufferers of the blood and keepers of our myriad paths to a fuller truth. Human life is not sustainable outside of group experience. From the evidence we've gathered, we can see that when communication does not affirm and sustain life, it risks descending into sound and fury whose ultimate meaning is death.

After the trauma of forced discontinuity and miscommunication of ancestral Afrikan ideas over generations, there is much healing and rebuilding to do. There are groups whose deeds and attitudes over long history mark their desire to dominate us into perpetuity and they have trapped us into denying ourselves over many seasons (Wilson, 1993). There is useful insight on this phenomenon from a writer who employed psychoanalytic-Marxism and Fanon's theories on racism to analyze world revolutionary Malcolm X. Wolfenstein puts the problem bluntly, "He (Malcolm X) has been taught that to be white is human, and he wishes to be human. The consequence is self-hatred" (Wolfenstein, 1993: 33). Based on that learning, in order for us to understand ourselves, our people and the ways we have learned to think, we must rediscover or invent tools, like Malcolm X, that allow us to communicate as clearly and deeply as our present necessities demand.

The investigation of exculpatory language is one such tool. I have used it to clarify the processes that English-speaking Europeans employ, with mystifying 'innocence', while living amidst the havoc they have unleashed on Afrikans across the globe (Nelson, 2002: 15). For the evidence shows, overwhelmingly, that the dominant group has carried on its life wearing blinders to its crimes against our humanity. Yet, as early as 1587, a White cleric Tomas Mercado denounced his compatriots for profiting from a system that used, "deceit, robbery and force" (Williams, 1984: 44). What internal mechanism has permitted White supremacy to block out so thoroughly the thoughts that might lead its children to end their cycles of crime?

On the other hand, even today, Afrikans work within as framework that threatens us with annihilation (Roberts, 1997; Paul, 2000; Yeboah, 1988). This accommodation with systems that would ultimately destroy us may have been essential at strategic points in our history. However, its hidden costs include generations of influential Blacks who confuse our communities by embracing compromises that sacrifice community assets and also betray our human rights (Mandela, 1997; TRC, 1998; Tutu, 1982). Stanley Crouch, a prominent New York journalist of Afrikan ancestry but, in his own judgment, indeterminate racial identity, dismisses Black anger when police have killed an innocent, unarmed Afrikan immigrant like Amadou Diallo or any number of unarmed, young Black men in his city as, "Pavlovian recitations" (Crouch 2002: 165). In similar vein, this popular 'authority' on Black experience trivializes the brutal sodomizing of Abner Louima with a broomstick. Louima, of Ayitian roots, won a lawsuit and received compensation for his ordeal at the hands of New York City's police. Callously, Crouch comments, "That's a very hard way to make a buck…" (Crouch, 2000: 163). Rather atypically, for most mainstream writers today, Crouch also refers to all Afrikans as, "Negroes", calls himself, "Negro", ridiculing the use of 'Black' or 'Afrikan' instead. Indeed, his statements on painful issues are often distanced, dispassionate and empty of human feeling for victimized Black youth, women or men. In the case of Stanley Crouch, it is evident that Black skin doth not a Black brother make.

Popular discourse often confounds Blackness with social pathology (Barrett, 1999: 29). Yet, although Afrikans chafe, protest and even erupt spontaneously, we continuously make enormous efforts to fit into White supremacist society. For instance, both Afrikan men in Lee Mun Wah's *Color of Fear* speak with a combination of hurt and anger about the rejection they experienced in the European-dominant corporate world as well as the educational system, despite conforming to its demands (Mun Wah, 1993). One of the burdens of my study, therefore, is to lend transparency to the social system that rules our lives in ways that consign us, because of our Afrikan ancestry, to existing as a dominated race. Generally, we recognize that this society also remains wilfully blind to the fallout from enslavement, colonialism and the bias of its customs that circumscribe our ability to live with dignity or to enjoy the chances life brings in equal measure to Whites (Grovogui, 1996; Mun Wah, 1994; Butler, 1994). For instance, we were able to see that even as the Kerner Commission addressed Black discontent it failed to confront the legacy of 'slave patrols' or lynching. It also avoided draw-ing conclusions about the shootings of Black men and women by White police forces during the period the commission surveyed (New York Times, 1968; Barrett, 1999: 29).

When dramatic events occur, however, even the most numbed members of North American society cannot escape expanding their consciousness in the glare of the contradictions they live. The Repa-rations Movement today, for instance, brings the collusion of banking and other major institutions with Afrikan bondage into living rooms across Canada and the United States (Robinson, 2000; Bittker, 1973). What often proves most disturbing to viewers and readers of stories in the media, however, is that the capture and forced labor of innocent Afrikans for profit, generations ago, mirror the privatized incarcera-tion of young Afrikans forced to work for corporate profit in prisons today (Davis, 2001). As we witness how these injustices cross time, the language of righteous anger may even become fused with other human rights (Fanon, 1068). Indeed, activist Donald Braman describes, "anger and indignation" as forms of healing when "[they] are voiced in politi-cal terms that help [sufferers such as persecuted Black men and women in prison to] cope" (Braman, 2002: 132).

Every holy book of the 'Peoples of the Book' – Hebrews, Chris-tians and Muslims - in chronological order, has been misused as a tool for enabling color-biased supremacists and disabling color-blind Af-rikans (Blyden, 1994; P'Bitek, 1980, Kiteme, 1994; Mudimbe, 1988). Somewhere in the place where unpalatable truths are secreted away, this society knows that the enslavement, degradation, lynching, rape, cultural theft and castration of Afrikans are without parallel on three continents. My research demonstrates that language, the omission of significant images and suppression of information all work together to make this society speak dispassionately and with distance about bitter events in Black history. When we embrace the religions and Word of those who destroy us, we must, logically, also embrace their versions of our own destruction.

Orwell, a twentieth century pioneer in interrogating the function of the English language in politics, wrote, "[L]anguages would not be able to serve their respective societies if they were deprived of euphemistic ways to refer to the less pleasant aspects of life" (Reznikov, 2110: 50). What the majority society may regard explicitly or implicitly as, "the less pleasant aspects of life" it has, by custom or decree, made the very shape and substance of our lives. Orwell reasons that euphemism oils the wheels of a communication of comfort within and between groups. His insights help Pan-Afrikanists to understand the system that lubricates Black co-existence with other races while living within a White supremacist space. In research that explores the language of today's invasions, genocides and wars, John Collins and Ross Glover also illustrate that "...acts of violence can easily be made more palatable through the use of euphemisms such as pacification [my emphasis]" (Collins & Glover, 2002: 7). From evidence in this study, word power ascribes respectability to groups that commit genocide against Afrikans by erasing their crimes. Demonstrably, that power also has as real and enduring an impact on societies as armies, germ warfare or guns. Conscious of the enduring power of humans to create meaning and how that influences our lived experience, the next chapter presents examples of inventive language that enhance Pan-Afrikan re-education and fosters self-determination.

Chapter Seven analyzes two instruments of popular Pan-Afrikanist education that illustrate some of the linguistic insights outlined above. They are, *David Walker's Appeal to the Colored Citizens of the World But in Particular, and Very Expressly to Those of the United States of America,* and my own documentary, *All Eyes On Africa.*

7

Chapter

WHEN TRUTHS EXPLODE IN BLACK

- - - • - • - • - • • - • • • - • - • - • - • - • • - •

DAVID WALKER'S APPEAL: TALKING LOUD,
WALKING PROUD

David Walker was born into the forced exile of his Afrikan parents, in 1785, in the US South. His birth takes place almost a century before Emancipation, and although his father is in bondage, his mother is nominally free. Under White supremacist law, in which the status of the mother falls upon the child, David Walter is therefore free. (Walker, 1993: 12). He grows up to educate himself, create a prosperous family business and wed a woman who has escaped bondage. David Walker gives her the protection of his name and station, as well as taking care to keep her out of glare of the spotlight that his unusual achievements attract. They both know only too well that the danger of recapture always lurks nearby. Walker practices gender equality. By way of testimony to his trailblazing efforts, Mary W. Stewart, "the first African woman political writer to lecture in defence of women's rights…" credits him with having "[a] profound and enduring" influence on her career (Turner, 1993: 18).

In the absence of any equal among his peers, David Walker becomes the voice of all silenced Afrikans, meaning the majority of his people, in his time. Witness to the insufferable burdens they bear, he gives tongue to their distress, which finds resonance within his heart writes, "They [Whites] think that we do not feel for our brethren [Blacks still in bondage], who they are murdering by inches, but they are dreadfully deceived" (Walker, 1993: 88). Walker also provides support for many of the thousands of successful freedom-seekers who each year try to escape via The Underground Railroad. Bradford Chambers points out that it was natural for him to do so, explaining that, "the majority of conductors were black men, …since white Northerners were easily identifiable…and could not know the details of geography and the hideout locations in swamps and other places, as did the black men who lived there" (Chambers, 1968: 81). Finally, when he is forty-five, and after years of preparation and study, Walker publicly launches the first polemic by an Afrikan against the heinous system of genocidal bondage that had enriched White society (Walker, 1993: 11).

David Walker writes with all the passion of a captive in exile on hostile soil. Like the Biblical David who slew the giant Goliath, Walker aims his verbal missiles at the pupil of his enemy's eye. In the dangerous pre-emancipation US world, his fiery denunciation was in itself a deed of superlative courage. Boldly he declares, "I write without the fear of man…they may put me to death if they choose" (Walker, 1993: 74; 13). He does not speak idly, since a group of White 'terrorists', that history books generally absolve as 'planters', puts a ten thousand dollar price on his head, "dead or alive". The Georgia legislature also makes distribution of his pamphlet a crime. Naturally, when he is found dead within a year of the publication of his *Appeal* suspicions abound within Black circles (Walker, 1993: 17). Yet, through the vagaries of communication that beset Pan-Afrikanist liberation in the belly of the White supremacist whale, even Walker's revolutionary speech, ironically, often uses the cadences of his Christian upbringing and sexist environment. In chastising his oppressors, for example, he quotes from *The Book of Common Prayer*, "Vain and deceitful is their speech/With curses fill'd, and lies". (Walker, 1993: 95). In transition toward self-determination, today's Pan-Afrikanists are also challenged to use aspects of popular culture as stepping-stones for reaching our goals.

Logically, it was necessary that Walker launch his *Appeal* to Afrikan women and men, not Whites, since only those who suffer domination can liberate themselves.

However, there is a parallel message to Whites, although it remains implicit, embedded in the text of his appeal. He launches a challenge for them to change their ways, accept Afrikans as "Americans" and "…treat us [Afrikans] like men [and women]…" (Walker, 1993: 89). Ultimately the Afrikan desire and hope for acceptance remains alive, despite the chronicle of hurts and atrocities that the writer has already exposed. Although a Pan-Afrikanist can admire Walker's courage today, his faith in changing White attitudes and beliefs reminds us how often we continue to hold on to old fallacies that make us trust unwisely. Yet, there are explicit lessons we somehow fail to learn. For example, a Jewish historian points out that," Jewish people lived in Germany for over a thousand years, were financially and socially successful, but were still subject to mass murder during the Holocaust" (Kivel, 1996: 149). Pan-Afrikanism struggles to promote realistic expectations in the arena of racial solidarity and racial justice.

Faith and human trust in groups, in the light of Jewish experience covering a thousand years, are evidently no guarantee of group safety. The evidence provided here shows why, as Afrikans we do well to learn the lessons that histories of global race relations offer to us. Despite his radicalism, Walker leaves a door open for White individuals who can put aside their prejudices and walk through that door to a welcoming Black embrace. However, that concept of the open door holds Black humanity perpetually hostage to potential White change. Since we can never measure the human capacity for change, waiting for the right changes to occur in human hearts becomes a gamble against an infinity of variables. As Pan-Afrikanists we recognize that this strategy has not served and is unlikely to serve Afrikan liberation.

Walker's erstwhile White allies roundly criticized him for affirming that Afrikans, like all other humans, have the right of self-defence. A pro emancipation Quaker, Benjamin Lundy, condemns Walker for "inflammatory" language. While, "granting that the colored race have … much cause for complaint", in suspiciously paternalistic tones, Lundy warns Walker against provoking "the extermination of the colored people" (Lundy, 1968: 60). The frequent assumption of liberal Whites that they not only know what is best for Black people but also care more for our survival than the leaders we have chosen who sacrifice most for our liberation, is an ongoing challenge in alliances between Blacks and Whites. Like Lundy, William Lloyd Garrison, the pre-eminent White abolitionist of his day was ambivalent and discouraging at best in his review of Walker's *Appeal*. In his paper, *The Liberator* he writes, "We do not preach rebellion-no, but submission and peace" (Garrison, 1968: 61). Pan-Afrikanism abhors submission.

We Blacks, collectively, have historically made ourselves vulnerable to well-armed, aggressive Whites. Perhaps we learned from our observations of lions long ago. When defeat seems inevitable, exposing your underbelly saves lives in the animal world (Attenborough, 1990: 210). Prince Abd al-Rahman, an Afrikan enslaved in the United States, recalled how his life was spared in battle by other Afrikans, after he surrendered, as was their custom before foreign social practices wrecked their way of life (Alford, 1986: 22). 'Whites', be they Arab, Asian or European, have never treated Blacks as equals (Kiteme, 1992, 93-120; Prah, 1997: 16-20; Serequeberhan, 1994: 55-85).

The history of betrayals is long. Afrikans in the United States swallowed soothing words from Abraham Lincoln at Emancipation only to have his pious phrases turn sour in their gut (Litwack, 1979). For a decade after Ghana's flag went up in 1957, both in the Caribbean and on the continent, Afrikan leaders lapped up the glamour of rubbing shoulders with European queens, princes and kings at 'virtual Independence' balls (Grovogui, 1996). Right up to the present day real independence, for colonizer designed Afrikan states, remains a dream deferred. Often betrayals have also come from within. Martin Luther King's deputy, Ralph Abernathy pointed out that the class of conservative Black preachers who were fearful of losing status and opposed change heaved a collective sigh of relief on the assassination of Martin

Luther King (Abernathy, 1990: 174); Lincoln, 1974; Branch, 1998). Many of the Black church's reluctant revolutionaries also believed King's premature death released them from the obligation to protest, march and stand up against the White images they worshipped equally, whether they were on church walls or engraved in their hearts (Branch, 1998).

From declarations of emancipation to the compromise that ended official apartheid in South Africa, Europeans holding the reins of military, economic and political power have failed, abysmally, to deliver on promises of change (Grovogui, 1996). When Afrikans united to confront White oppression or seemed poised to break their bonds, Whites would make lofty promises of equality yet honour them mostly in their breach. Most Afrikans have not sought revenge, forgiving predatory Asians or Europeans instead. This practice has prevailed right up to our dealing with the wounds of apartheid and the Mandela regime offering up 'ubuntu' – blanket forgiveness – in response to the reign of sustained White terror and mass murder (TRC, 1998). Such behaviour goes against the evidence of our lived historical experience and can only be interpreted as testimony to an enduring culture of uncommon, counterintuitive, overly elastic humanity. As demonstrated throughout previous chapters, in the global context of our present lives, the story of such lavish gifts of self sounds like a tale of costly unrequited love.

I carry one special memory of the US school desegregation movement burned into my mind. It is a picture of the bravest of little Black girls walking in her prettiest dress through a gauntlet of rabid faces spitting racist insults and raw, sewage-type hate. A fifteen year-old, recruited by Mrs. Daisy Bates, chair of the NAACP in Little Rock, Arkansas in 1957, just wanted to go to school. Her parents dared to desire a well-funded school in exchange for their community's taxes (Duberman, 1965: 76). It took the army, bayonets fixed, to get her through the White mob. Putting this precious child at risk in order to test the limits of the White population's humanity was an act of faith, unparalleled in other inter-ethnic or inter-racial conflicts, by the Black 'village' that raised her and valued her life. A special humanity lights up this moment when we contrast it with human rights disputes between Irish

CLEM MARSHALL

Protestants and Catholics, Arabs and Jews in West Asia or Hindus and Moslems in India. Offered a unique gift in the unfolding saga of US Human Rights, and challenged by their moral history to shine, the White community dropped the ball. It failed to reciprocate Black trust in kind, although Afrikans were willing to put the very lives of their children on the line. Instead, until today, both in popular culture and institutional practice, White North Americans continue to resist and frustrate the repeated efforts of the Black population to create equality in school or the society at large (Porter, 1997; Nelson, 2000; Dei, 1996; James, 1995; Henry, 1998).

This society has still to demonstrate that it understands or values the costs of these acts of large humanity that Black folks have quietly absorbed. In the sixteen hundreds, Bishop Las Casas and the Catholic Church arbitrarily targeted Afrikans to be substitute sacrifices for the First nations of Brazil and the Americas. On many occasions where we have chosen to make sacrifices in order to convince others of our commitment to working out a common human destiny, we have put our own human rights or needs on hold. That costly tendency is evident even in David Walker's *Appeal*. In that stirring call to moral accountablilty, the gifted polemicist also missed an opportunity to put the needs of his beleaguered sisters and brothers first. He could have stated unequivocally that, with or without a transformation of European attitudes or behaviour, his people would never again willingly compromise its right to live out its full humanity.

David Walker may have seized that historical moment to make it clear to all his readers that no race, including his own, should be treated as a stand-in and expected to sacrifice its own life chances in order to offer others fuller lives. For Pan-Afrikanists, that is the task he left for our generation to accomplish. To his credit, Walker also provided us a model for using language for self-defence like unarmed warriors use martial arts. He took his enemy's words and used them to counter their attacks, turning back their own wounding power against them. "Do you understand your own language?" he thunders into a moral void bursting with Christian platitudes and continues:

> Compare your own language …extracted from your Declaration of Independence, with your cruelties and murders inflicted by your cruel and unmerciful fathers and yourselves on our fathers and on us-men who have never given your fathers or you the least provocation!!!!!!
> (Walker, 1993: 95)

David Walker also documents evidence showing both the innocence of his people and the suffering Afrikans faced. He is therefore able to write with the authority of a self-educated member of the race who had taken the time to listen to its stories and research as much relevant history as he finds available, for over ten years. Speaking to the powerful with conviction, he can then say, "The Christians [my emphasis] of Europe and America go to Africa, bring us away, and throw us into the seas, and in other ways murder us, as they would wild beasts. The Antediluvians and heathens never dreamed of such barbarities" (Walker, 1993: 78).

The writer goes on to compare the differential treatment Asians receive and speculates on why they were not the race enslaved. Tellingly, David Walker attributes this to the fact that wronged Afrikans show greater forbearance and a willingness to forgive (Walker, 1993: 82). Although the polemicist does not make the connection explicit, he implies that our long-suffering is connected to our ancestral culture. That culture is still centred, albeit unconsciously, on the immediacy of a parallel spiritual world, its beneficent Creator and the presence of comforting Ancestors. It also rests on our ability to access that other world when we feel most oppressed or stressed through rituals of song, dance and chant that climax in ecstasy (Walker, 1993: 23; Ephraim-Donkor, 1997: 73; Christoph & Oberlander, 1996).

Right up to our day, as evidenced by *The TRC Report,* most Black preachers and politicians, unlike David Walker, still accept the seductive rationalizations our oppressors use to explain away genocidal Afrikan bondage (TRC, 1998). In the US South of David Walker's birth, a generation before he wrote his *Appeal* a senator made the following defence of lynching. He said, "We took them as barbarians, fresh from Africa… We taught them that there was a God. We taught them to tell the truth. We taught them not to steal" (Tillman, 1907). Was Senator Tillman seriously arguing that Afrikans only learned about God after Europeans murdered their daughters and sons? His sense of moral infallibility, even as he lived out a blatant racist double standard, characterizes White Law in our day as well. For example, in the US, there are more severe penalties for crack cocaine, which targets Blacks, and cocaine powder, whose users are mostly White. Paul Kivel points out, "it takes possession of 500 grams of powder (worth $40,000 in 1994) [for Whites] to equal the five-year sentence that someone [Black] possessing five grams (worth only $250) would receive" (Kivel, 1996: 195).

Because David Walker's *Appeal* is also based on field study, it rings with the authentic voice of lived experience. He absorbs all he can about his people's condition from accounts by both Blacks and Whites. Doing so allows him to say without fear of contradiction, "I have travelled and observed nearly the whole of those things [his account] myself…" (Walker, 1993: 96). He is therefore aware of international connections linking Afrika's scattered children in the Americas or the Caribbean to Europe or continental Afrika. Today, a Pan-Afrikan journalist, A. Peter Bailey also points out the critical importance of researching and establishing an independent information base. "It's not just that we don't have information," he told a gathering of Black educators and community builders in Toronto, "Black people lack correct [my emphasis] information" (Bailey, 2001).

In the spirit of the South African and US documents cited above, *David Walker's Appeal* sells hope to global Afrika. It is hope, however, built solidly on layers of consciousness. The first layer demands concrete knowledge of our holocausts. That includes the details of atrocities in the past as well as dangers of extermination menacing us in the present (Berlin, 1998; TRC, 1998). The second level of consciousness consists of a psychological appraisal of our enemies and our own psychological preparation for facing the worst that they can do. Clear-headed assessment of the behaviour of the forces arraigned against us can also disabuse Afrikans of our habit of putting faith in false alliances. As an eminent US social historian puts it, "Large social groups do not have love affairs" (Bennett, 1966: 40). Finally, survival depends on a realistic appraisal of our enemies as well as taking inventory of both our material and spiritual assets. There is little wonder, then, that *Walker's Appeal* fuelled resistance and shored up the spirits of his people for generations after his death. The record shows that Afrikans across the US South would gather secretly when situations were dangerous, or publicly, where they felt safer, to read his words to each other for both comfort and strength (Walker, 1993).

Finally, Walker was interested in creating a world where there was justice for everyone, and, of course, that included his own people. His practice became a model for a long line of leaders like Ida B. Wells, Marcus Garvey and Martin Luther King who roused politically dormant or cautious Afrikans and taught them not to fear. The earliest records of societies in Afrika also show that the Kemites (Ancient Egyptians) did not build empires by imposing their rule on adjacent or distant peoples through fear. Rather, Hebrews, Arabs, Greeks and later groups that chose to enter Kemet did so uninvited for the food, wealth, peace and justice they could find. Historical records also outline their strategies for undermining Afrikan societies by infiltrating circles of power within congregations of Kemet's scholarly priests (Onyewuenyi, 1994). David Walker's appeal to conscience therefore echoes a long Afrikan history of championing the freedom of human minds, the essence of Cheddo's freethinking religious system. That pattern of thought is anchored upon the society's general adherence to deeply held spiritual beliefs and is a part of the enduring language of respect through which Afrikans addressed their own humanity (Cissé, 1997). Let us now continue to explore Afrikan ancestral beliefs through film and my experience of making the documentary *All Eyes On Africa* (Marshall, 1993).

ALL EYES ON AFRICA: HOLDING AFRIKA
PRECIOUS IN OUR GAZE

In my documentary *All Eyes On Africa*, I frame Afrika for the gaze of diverse races through a positive, Afrikan-specific lens. This perspective, one that is complex, self-deterministic and proud, is largely missing in the visual language and descriptions of Afrika in popular global culture (Chinweizu, 1987). What we see, read, hear and eventually learn to repeat about Afrikan culture, on the continent and abroad, is still largely fixed in a frame of dispossession, dependence, defeat and despair. The most glorious of our victories over race tyranny, such as Haiti's decisive defeat of Europe and Napoleon's Empire, or the overthrow of the Arab enslavers of Zanzibar by a rank-and-file Pan-Afrikanist Ugandan soldier, John Okello, in January 1964, are generally hidden from view (Farmer, 2003, Bailey, 1988: 132). To fill the information void that discounts Afrikan heroism, *All Eyes On Africa* provides images of endurance, including an inspired painting of Queen Amina of Zaria from Nigeria's National Gallery of Modern Art (FDC, 1981: 63). From Kenya's National Museum, the video showcases a painting of scattered bodies of unarmed martyrs massacred by British troops in their brutal anti-liberation war against Kenyans. During that onslaught, the foreign invaders spilled the blood of twenty thousand innocent Afrikan women, children and men (Rake, 1988: 57).

As stated earlier, one of the glaring omissions of schooling in this hemisphere is factual, accurate information or images that bring to life the supreme holocaust of genocidal forced exile and forced labour in recorded history. It lasted for four centuries and aborted the lives of over one hundred million Afrikans (Rodney, 1982; Clarke, 1994). *All Eyes On Africa* becomes its viewers' eyes, entering dank holes cut into underground rock where uncounted numbers of our Ancestors were shackled, beaten, branded, raped and killed. The visible evidence of those monstrous prisons created by predators for free human beings belies the White lie that Afrikans had systems of slavery that Europeans merely copied for their use. Before Europeans or Arabs imposed their callous domination on Afrikan soil, no Black rulers or populations built such concentration-camp monstrosities as this documentary reveals. In *All Eyes On Africa*, the camera zooms in on a cell marked, "RECALCITRANTS", where those who dared to resist were singled out for solitary confinement and special tortures even before they were carted off across the sea. Viewers also see the picture of an older Afrikan man wearing an elegant, woven robe like a toga with an incongruous spiked iron collar fixed to his neck. 'In another time and place', this image says, 'he would be a senator lending his people the wisdom of his years'. His calm, accusing gaze looks out at the mind-destroying world that so many generations of Afrikans have unjustly inherited but which Afrikans did not create.

Oppositional images of innocent dignity forced to wear false trappings of guilt and shame are captured in that single video frame, producing a disquieting dissonance that is frozen in space and time. Even more telling, they transport viewers backwards into the interior of the captive's experience, where some are jolted by his resemblance to their own kith and kin. For the perceptive, the mixture of dignity and hurt in his eyes vindicates his violated humanity. It tears away the veil of anonymity that generally keeps the world from getting a clear picture of victimized Afrikans in Arab or European accounts of those tragic and catastrophic times. The power of the elder's mute, 'Why?' to the Universe is amplified in Haile Gerima's film *Sankofa*. Through a breach in Time, captive Ancestors stare back at us and into the eyes of a modern, young woman, a Black model from the United States. When her ghostly European kidnappers strip and try to brand her, she screams out, "I'm not an Afrikan…I'm an American…can't you see…I'm not an Afrikan" (Gerima, 1993). The sound of burning flesh off-screen silences her futile, wailing cry. Although many men and women of Afrikan ancestry in this hemisphere repudiate that connection, they remain targets for the hatred and contempt that a world largely structured around race supremacist power reserves for people of their ancient origins and darker skin.

To counter distortions of Afrikan history, Pan-Afrikanists search out other truths about Afrika in the sites where our Ancestors have secreted them – our cuisine, music, proverbs, prayers, sculpture, architecture and art (Moses, 1998; Masolo, 1994; Chideya, 1995; Kiteme, 1992; Serequeberhan, 1994; Bebey, 1980; Bleakley, 1978). Today, that also means unearthing the spirit-filled Afrikan art imprisoned in European museums and dissecting our community conversations or customs to extract deeper meanings, which remain locked inside (Kecskési, 1987; Gwaltney, 1980). In *All Eyes On Africa, Part II,* narrator Djanet Sears quotes an Akan proverb from Ghana that challenges all their oppressors and affirms their ability to endure, "Ashanti kotoko wokum apem, apem beba". "Even if you kill thousands", the proverb boasts, "thousands more will come" (Cobbinah, 1990).

All Eyes On Africa, therefore, uses works of art to broaden the viewer's understanding of lived Afrikan religious experiences. The US Christian scholar Raphael Powell reminds us that, "Sociologists [Eurocentric sociologists] regard religion as a means used to produce order in society" (Powell, 1979:73). He then goes on to cite accepted icons in the field like Talcott Parsons, Emile Durkeim, Max Weber and Bronislaw Malinowski to support his theory. According to Powell's argument, therefore, Europeans were well aware that the loss and destruction of ancestral Afrikan religious art, as well as the rites attached to them, would serve a disordering function in Afrikan life and the continent's unfolding history. When Nigerian gallery owner Elizabeth Jibunoh reconnects the works of art she preserves to the ancestral religions that Eurocentrism or Arabcentrism displaced, she presents a living refutation of the socially destructive superstitions that Islamic and Christian missionaries grafted onto Afrika's multitude of sacred objects. She calls viewers' attention to the fact that her family had lived with these objects for "over twenty years…and none of [them] had died" but had prospered instead. Similarly, Yoruba artist Lamidi Fakeye speaks matter-of-factly about the way his carvings inform his dreams and predict events in his life. Through these images and witnesses, the documentary therefore becomes an exercise in rehabilitating Afrikan religious experience and a tool for countering the disordering legacy of the invaders who introduced new interpretations of The Divine.

Negative markers of Afrika abound in our visual language. They proliferate on daily North American TV as infomercials for White Non- Governmental Organizations working on the continent. Some of the recurring images are messy, thatched shacks and emaciated, dirty, starving bodies, transmitted in endless frozen frames of sad-eyed children with flies hovering around their heads. There are often also vaguely menacing Black males who vent their aggression in misogynist speeches against their sisters or spew their bombastic, egotistic hatred of their brothers. Another enduring constant is a horizon peopled by incompetent, passive populations of beggars waiting with open palms for the highly visible, predictable mercy of White saviors, women or men. Those images are precisely the ones that *All Eyes On Africa* sets out to refute and invalidate. It does so by refurbishing Afrikan pride with equally available pictures of vibrant, beautiful, confident, caring populations that are spiritually, culturally, intellectually and economically endowed.

Despite the proliferation of items of Afrikan art in museums in Canada and around the non-Afrikan world, there is a dearth of material by or about Afrikans who know those art forms, from the inside, and integrate them into their daily lives. In *All Eyes On Africa*, Winsom, a visual artist recalls her discovery of the Afrikan inspiration behind Picasso's art and many of Western society's famous modernist images. It is therefore ironic that, among others, Picasso denied the Afrikan genesis of the artistic ideas in works such as his painting *Les demoiselles d'Avignon* (Picasso, 1997). Even to the untutored eye, Afrika's artistic influences appear so obvious as to be impervious to denial. Therefore *All Eyes On Africa* functions as a re-educational tool that enhances Pan-Afrikan understandings of our centrality to universal movements in music, dance, theatre and the plastic arts.

In today's art world, the museum-going, gallery-going public remains largely unaware of Afrikan insights into Afrikan art forms (Jibunoh, 1993; Kofsky, 1970; hooks, 1995). Understanding our art forms has proved difficult for most non-Afrikans, since miseducation has generally persuaded them to dismiss and devalue the spiritual and cultural sources of those expressions of the Afrikan imagination. *All Eyes On Africa*, however, obliges viewers to pay attention to the Afrikan religious practices that inscribe meaning in our art. It also demands a Pan-Afrikanist lens that ranges far afield, taking in the scattered Afrikan world from the Atlantic to the Pacific, from the Americas and Caribbean to Europe and Asia and covering every site where traces of Afrikan ancestry survive (Davis, 2000; Arnold, 1997; Simpson, 1998: 71; Shiveley, 1983; Foster, 1986; Christoph, 1996; Bynum, 1999). The kind of re-education proposed is evident in *All Eyes On Africa*. From its very opening frames, the curator and owner of The Didi Museum in Lagos, Elizabeth Jibunoh, describes starting her art collection in her home in order to fill gaps in popular understanding and to correct colonizing misconceptions of Afrika's spiritual and cultural heritage, both at home and abroad (Jibunoh, 1990).

Inevitably, in order to foster change, *All Eyes On Africa* also addresses Eurocentric approaches that influence teaching about Afrika. For Pan-Afrikanists, the documentary is therefore a potential tool for redirecting the Black gaze through a transformative experience of our art. Interviews that include significant combinations of rhythm, reasoning and image provide an expanded, Afrikan-centred information base that enhances analysis of Afrikan art by exploring the diverse views of experts on ancestral or contemporary forms. Significantly, the video's analysis is also woman-positive and ethnically diverse. These Pan-Afrikan educators use *All Eyes On Africa* to triangulate information in a novel way. They show learners how to access and weigh the experiences of Afrikans on the continent, in the Caribbean, across the Americas and around Europe in order to create a holistic picture of Afrikan life by engaging and explaining ancestral symbols that can reconnect them to enduring religious ideas and practices. Denied opportunities and resources for resistance, Afrikans scattered around the world have had recourse to our most portable asset, the cultural capital generated through our creative artistry. It is on that strength that we have especially relied in order to sustain our spirits and fuel our resistance to oppression in the anti- Kemetic world. (Du Bois, 1964; Genovese, 1976; Thompson, 1984; Stuckey, 1984).

Even limited scholarship confirms the extended presence of Afrikans at the lower end of most scales that measure social success, whether they live in North America or the world at large (Wilson, 1998; Grovogui, 1996). Afrikan interests are routinely sacrificed or undermined within the World Bank, the IMF, or the major economic engines of today's world (Payer, 1974; Scammell, 1975). Writing decades apart, political and economic analysts Siba Grovogui and Cheryl Payer demonstrate that, in spite of tokenistic Blacks in alibi positions, Afrikan rights are relegated to the margins of powerful institutions by European or Asian nations and within the United Nations (Payer, 1974; Grovogui, 1996). Indeed the evidence they mount shows that, in terms of Afrikan interests, the international community as represented by its world bodies, seems impervious or resistant to change.

All Eyes On Africa challenges the viewer's imagination by offering uncommon images of successful Afrikans running their own businesses, being inventive and creative in the arts, sharing expertise within their communities and proudly conscious of their place in the world. The video visits Dora Gordon, a batik expert who invents new designs, produces fabric for local and foreign consumption and trains the local workers she employs. Other leaders that we see in the video are also framed at moments of significant success. For example, international statesman, Dr. Kwame Nkrumah is shown at the triumphant celebration of Ghana's transition from a British colony to a politically independent nation in 1957.

Speaking directly to the camera, traditional leaders, Benin City's Prince Ena Basimi Eweka and Alhaji Prince Arulogun of the Yoruba people demonstrate knowledge, care and concern for their people and provide specialized information on their cultural heritage. Prince Eweka, as an official keeper of his people's history, introduces us to a sculpted ancestral figure from the fifteenth century, "Emotan", a child-less "ordinary market-woman" who achieved the status of an Ancestor and became an icon through serving the mothers and children of her state. The prince employs an effective tool of Pan-Afrikanist re-education by describing ancient practices with modern vocabulary and so making their significance accessible to the popular mind. He speaks of Emotan, the female hero of Benin City as creator of "the first day-care centre" in that area, in the fifteenth century. En passant, his works evoke the depth and breadth of Afrika's civilization demonstrated in the prominence of women in civic and economic life and the striking beauty of its bronze sculpture. With quiet authority he reminds viewers that the civilization that produced Emotan, the Benin Bronzes, the exquisitely carved ivory pieces that the British had stolen and other works of art were hard proof of a population that were already mature "six thousand (6000) years" ago.

His is the testimony of oral history that academic conventions are slowly beginning to make more available in universities today. In addition, the tales of the two 'princes' present direct experience of the rape of Afrika by colonial plunderers, and both point out how descendants of those pillaging Europeans continue to keep the sacred icons their nations stole in art prisons (museums) around the White world. Indeed, successive British governments, whether on the right or left, conservative or progressive, have refused to return Afrika's icons to their rightful owners. Prince Arologun, resplendent in an 'agbada' (voluminous wide-skirted robe) of pink 'asoke' lace, a prized ceremonial weave, names a number of stolen objects, including a royal breastplate that was the symbol for *FESTAC*, a Pan-Afrikan festival held in the seventies in Nigeria (IFC, 1977). The national treasures languishing in foreign captivity are so much a part of his people's lived cultural experience that their names trip familiarly off his tongue.

As the camera fills the screen with Afrikan women, diverse in looks and social location, speaking for themselves, the video also interrupts the White media's often incestuous dialogue that speculates negatively on relationships between Black women and men. That discourse routinely pathologizes and misrepresents gender based relationships and casts long shadows over Black communities at large (Chideya, 1995; Morrison, 1992). Film critic Ed Guerrero comments on *The Color Purple* where, "... a chain of fleeting images and gestures occurs that subtly shifts the historical onus for the crime of slavery from the white planter class onto one of dominant society's most popular scapegoats, the black male" (Guerrero, 1993: 53). Guerrero's observations are valid and stand beside alternative analyses by other Black social commentators that argue that, where Black men are elitist or sexist, they should not be spared because of the collective burdens of stigma and persecution we bear (Hernton, 1987; Crouch, 1995). Calvin Hernton and Stanley Crouch's critiques of Black males on gender issues, echo debates within progressive political circles over engaging in public criticism of racism in Cuba. While some political commentators such as Black nationalist Carlos Cooks speak openly of Cuba's failure to eradicate colorism and everyday discrimination by its security forces against Black skin, others praise Cuba's principled intervention against apartheid and her extraordinary contributions to the global health care of populations that have been dispossessed (Cooks, 1992; Brizan, 1998; Horne, 2001).

A Black revolutionary of the Civil Rights era, Robert F. Williams outlined the ambivalent response Black maleness encounters and must navigate in this society. One of the hidden costs of the legacy of enslavement is a climate of popular and official suspicion that envelops Black men from 'the cradle to the grave'. In addition, where Black men, such as Martin Luther King, Medgar Evers, George Jackson, Al Sharpton or Marcus Garvey have taken a stand for human rights in the US they risked death and most were eventually assassinated (Branch, 1998; Collins & Bailey, 1998; Jackson, 1990; Klein, 1991; Lewis, 1988). Simultaneously, however, popular, sexist interpretations of manhood, internalized generally by both Black women and men, demand that to be men they must be seen to resist. The socialized compulsion to resist multiplies Black male experiences of random aggression and intensifies those experiences when they occur (Porter, 1997; Akbar, 1984). Robert F. Williams also noted that young Afrikan males in this hemisphere generally receive mixed messages from the women who are central in raising them (Tyson, 1999: 306-307). On one hand, to protect their sons from an anti-Kushitic legal system, mothers might urge the pacifism of Martin Luther King. On the other hand, they share the Black public's contempt for passivity in its men. Robert Williams enshrined that contradiction when he described how he wrote his memoirs in the shadow of a rifle his Southern grandmother had given him for self-defence (Tyson, 1999: 308).

All Eyes On Africa also challenges a common public perception that the social concern for Afrikan women's rights flows mainly from White women or men in academia, the media and popular culture. It shows instead that there are many Afrikan women and men who are articulate, committed and mutually engaged in facing the challenge of eradicating sexism and rediscovering ancestral practices that foster gender equality. While involved in the pre-independence movement of the nineteen fifties, Angola's poet president, Antonio Neto wrote these words to his mother, "Oh black mothers whose children have departed, you taught me to wait and to hope...I wait no more...it is I who am awaited" (Caccia, 1988: 46). Outside Afrika, however, the commentary and reports of experts or NGOs mostly ignore the range of experiences and attitudes that Pan-Afrikanist men also bring to this key area of our lives. The documentary opens up its lens to include voices and male faces with political or cultural connections that demonstrate both understanding and care for the women who are their mothers, daughters, family, colleagues and friends.

Committed Pan-Afrikanists like Kamuti Kiteme see women as central to Afrikan rebirth. In his philosophical assessment of the state of Pan-Afrikanism today, his only identity-specific chapters are the four he dedicates to articulating and re-establishing the balance between women and men in Afrikan life (Kiteme, 1992). Fannie Lou Hamer, the activist who organized sharecroppers and helped to revolutionize race relations in the US South was astounded on a trip to Guinea when its president, Sekou Touré paid a visit to her hotel an wrapped her in a brotherly embrace. This was not the behavior that she had been socialized to expect of a powerful Black male figure. By and large, mainstream cultural commentators have ignored the fact that progressive leaders like Sekou Touré's consistently promoted feminist principles, practices and policies (Diawara, 2000: 80).

Other Afrikan presidents like Bourkina Faso's Thomas Sankara whose theme for International Women's Day, 1987 was *The Revolution Cannot Triumph Without the Emancipation of Women* have embrace the logical imperative of feminism in building Pan-Afrikanism. Beyond mere words, for the brief time that he headed his nation before foreign-backed askaris (home-grown mercenaries) killed him, Sankara made significant pro-feminist changes in the structure of the state (Sankara, 1988: 201). The regimes of President Samora Machel in Mozambique and the leadership of post-independence Guinea Bissau also reflected attention and commitment to gender equality (Fanon, 1967). Across the Atlantic, St. Clair Drake reminds us that when W. E. B. Du Bois brought together the Fourth Pan-African Congress in New York, in 1927, that "Most of the 220 delegates represented American Negro women's organizations" (Drake, 1969: 82). In eighteenth century Senegal, it was female entrepreneurs, "signares" who drove the economy and "market women" who were the backbone of President Kwame Nkrumah's rise to power (Brooks, 1976: 19). *All Eyes On Africa*, in pursuing Afrikan self-determination, presents Afrikan women and men framed in a wider, more culturally accurate and inclusive historical lens.

Black thinkers and artists have inevitably become increasingly concerned with the power that negative images wield in our lives. It is that concern that draws cultural critic, bell hooks to turn her attention to film and art as tools for extracting meaning from the events and routines that frame Black life (hooks, 1995 & 1996).

In his 2000 film *Bamboozled*, director Spike Lee satirizes White society's consumption of Black culture, including its hunger for markers of our collective suffering like the word "nigger", which it packages for globalized consumerism and profit (Neal, 2002: 124). Parallel to the visual language of Afrikan women as sexual machines gyrating in music videos in the popular culture, a language that demeans Black women also invades our TV screens from the media and even sectors of the academy (hooks, 1996; Kiwana, 2002; Neal, 2002; George, 1999). Where images of social ostracism and subjugation proliferate, Afrikan women seem to outdistance females of other races. As those noxious images accumulate, the Black woman's identity becomes that of a beast of burden or a mute victim of dehumanizing traditional religious or cultural beliefs. Jeannette Dates and William Barlow show how pervasive the practice can be, and that "... all viewers, black and white, [are] raised on black images burdened with meanings linked to sexuality and bestiality ..." (Dates & Barlow, 1990: 135).

Yet there has never been a time in recorded human history when Afrikan women on Afrikan soil have not been at the forefront of the human story as shapers of global destiny (Busby, 1992; Mandela, 1985; Herbert, 1993: 57). Afrikan women from early Nubia led their societies even before the brilliant rule of ancient Kemet's Queen Hatshepsut (Busby, 1992). In contemporary times, Winnie Madikizela Mandela represents for her people and Afrikans everywhere the face of victory and the incarnation of their will to resist. Her physical presence and readiness to stand firm, daily, inspired them during the costly war that eventually brought sexist, racist apartheid, albeit for a brief moment, to its patriarchal knees (Mandela, 1985 & 1976).

While *All Eyes On Africa* features confident women in the arts who run their own businesses and are experts in their fields, it also attempts to inform and change the common vision of Afrikan men as being uniquely unaware of the modern discourse around gender, female emancipation or of the global movement for women's liberation. As he describes his life and profession, illustrating them with his carvings, Ghanaian carver, George Obeng, speaks of the strength and struggle of his mother with obvious respect, explaining the symbolism of his carving of a woman carrying a tower of baskets on her head and holding a child by the hand. He also displays a bust of his daughter, committing himself to work towards a transformed, more equal world on her behalf. In fact, the documentary brings back excluded continental Afrikan faces into the internal discourse on gender taking place between female and male thinkers in contemporary Black society.

When, from a Pan-Afrikanist perspective, we tell a fuller story, feminist writers like Kathleen Cleaver, bell hooks and Patricia Williams find echoes for their ideas in male voices like Calvin Hernton, Ismael Reed and Cornel West. Together they struggle as a community to re-invent and recapture gender-positive, integrative, Pan-Afrikanist space (Cleaver, 2001; hooks, 2003; Williams, 1991; Hernton, 1987; Reed, 1997; West, 1993).

Arguably, a great deal of the power of the symbols which influence Afrikan life today has been passed down through representations of thoughts, religious ideas and images of our Ancestors in carving and sculpture. Today, however, that iconic power often resides in the popular culture, in sports, entertainment or in the images of stars promoted through newspapers, magazines, films, music videos and TV talk shows. Critic Natalie Zenon Davis today looks to films in the belief that they "can make confident observations" (Davis, 2000: 5). Because of all the barriers modern society erects against Afrikan progress, Black collective achievement has frequently been measured and portrayed through the success of outstanding individuals instead (King, 1987). The more that global Afrika tries to climb back to full, independent humanity from the degradations and depredations of generations of genocidal subjugation, the more important are the images of achievers with which we can nourish our imaginations. When images reinforce our confidence and build up our morale, this thesis demonstrates, they not only become healing metaphors of self-determination but also satisfy a deep hunger within people of Afrikan ancestry for a personhood long denied by dehumanizing global forces. *All Eyes On Africa* sources itself in Afrika's long love affair with drawings, portraits, shapes and forms. Those images that remind us of who we are and can be on screens and billboards today are like the pictograms of yesterday, codes that reveal how we have best lived with each other inside a richer ancestral time.

Let's now turn to ancestral Afrikan languages, to the sounds chiselled into words and images and explore them as treasure troves of liberating experiences. Ancestral languages enrich the principles that flow from Pan-Afrikan understanding of our material culture and the lessons from our art embedded in *All Eyes On Africa*. Despite the centuries of pillage and loss she has come through, today's Afrika still houses the most significant archives of all we need to rebuild a liberated, secure Pan-Afrikan world.

8

Chapter

PRACTICING PAN-AFRIKAN RE-EDUCATION

The Pan-Afrikan approach outlined so far applies principles of ancestral spiritual practice where Word and Deed, Nature and Humanity, peoples and groups, women and men function in reciprocity, achieve harmony and in so doing become one with The One (Finch, 1999; Bynum, 1999). Some key concepts and strategies have emerged from that analysis, which has examined and drawn guiding insights from wounding words as well as voices that can lead to cooptation from two liberal commissions on race. We have explored scenes depicting the painful and destabilizing impact of everyday anti-Kushitism as well as two anti-racist documentaries made by an Afrikan woman and an Asian man. By way of widening our lens, this study has also highlighted strategies of Pan-Afrikan resistance and re-education in the liberation polemic, *David Walker's Appeal* and a documentary, *All Eyes On Africa,* that decodes significant features of the art that is omnipresent in Afrikan life.

Assisting Pan-Afrikan populations so we retrieve and reconfigure missing, misplaced or misrepresented pieces of Afrikan realities, present or past, is one of the central goals of re-education (Marshall, 1993). As I explained the popular Rand McNally map of the world to a seven-year old on his first trip to Europe, we both wondered at the distortion that made 9,420,000 square miles of North America appear larger than Afrika's 11,685,000 square miles (Rand McNally, 1968: 2). Similarly, only my careful attention to the text exposed a similar inconsistency in another work, this one by a respected Egyptologist. Early in the work

I refer to, its author Christine Hobson develops a timeline for ancient world civilization that begins with the people of Ur in the Chaldea in 3500 BCE while she speculates that the earliest Kemetic (Egyptian) civilization started around 3200 BCE (Hobson, 2000: 10-11). However, on another page in the same book, the writer invites her readers to marvel with her at statues of Kemetic nobility, noting that "Prince Rahotep is a son of King Snofru, and Princess Nofret, his wife...[whose] wonderful state of preservation make it hard to believe that these statues are over 5,600 years old" (Hobson, 2000: 150). Prince Rahotep is decisively and visibly as much a Black man as Toussaint L'Ouverture, Steve Biko or Martin Luther King. If the Kemetic civilization only began 5,200 years ago, how does this respected expert explain the existence of such an example of artistic genius 5,600 years old? The two preceding examples are representative of the contradictions and uncertainties that often accompany Eurocentric interpretations of Afrika's history and its ancestral cultures. Pan-Afrikan re-education counters those gaps by building up areas of knowledge depleted or disfigured under the onslaught of forced, genocidal alienation of Afrikans from our ancestry, labour, language, culture and land. Introducing *FESTAC* the festival of Afrikan arts hosted by Nigeria in 1977, Committee chair O. P. Fingesi called for [this writer's translation from French], "a periodic return to the Afrikan source by artists, writers and actors who had been uprooted and forced to live on other continents" (IFC, 1977: 8). Pan-Afrikan education promotes regular contact between our homeland and all parts of the Afrikan world.

As we pass on the stories of moral courage, scientific genius and creative power handed down to us, they will help us repair broken intergenerational ties. Frequent gatherings are spaces where we also strengthen the bonds within and between Afrikan populations, providing opportunities for us to create and share collective ecstatic experiences (Thompson, 1984; Bynum, 1999). Wherever Afrikans gather for ceremony or celebration, we usually weave together strands of dance, drumming, cuisine and a wide range of musical sounds. On the continent, sparks that illuminate our ancestry continue to shine through the rites of Dogon and Yoruba populations (Masolo, 1994: 143-184; Awola-lu, 1996). Observers have also recorded how similar practices reappear in the syncretic religious rites of the Garifuna or Rastafari as well as Vodun (sometimes called Voodoo, Vaudou) followers in the Caribbean and Americas (Foster, 1986; Mack, 1999; Thompson, 1984).

Through the recreation of such rites, accompanied by Afri-kan-centred reflection, we continue to anchor ourselves in our liberat-ed past and rekindle confidence in a destiny that promises us that the unfettered freedom our Ancestors enjoyed will dwell with us again. In order to establish accurate measurements of our successes or failures, therefore, we must think intentionally outside the confines outsiders designed to contain our spirit, and in the words of Pan-Afrikanist edu-cator Eva Lee, "measure our corn in our own sacks". We cannot know how far we've come and how much we've accomplished despite the odds if we measure our progress in the sacks of those whose life chances and experiences are significantly different from our own. Knowing that has led me to reflect more carefully on the way that words like "chief", "queen", "king", "pharaoh" or "slave" and the images they conjure up can distort Afrikan realities. Those words, although widely used to de-scribe Afrikan realities related to politics, power and social class, are in fact based on European or Asian experiences culled from the history of their societies. For author Walter Mosley, it is the Afrikan ability to see beyond the constraints of Arab or European domination; to recognize our oppressors as human even as they attempt to dehumanize us and to grow hope in the soil of despair that is the truest marker of our human genius (Mosley Et Al., 1999: 12).

Pan-Afrikan re-education must be both deep and comprehensive. It therefore demands an ongoing commitment to seeking out scholar-ship that bridges the past and future by connecting remote events in our history to the challenges we must face today. Re-education there-fore sources itself on ancient sites where pictures record dancers play-ing the sistrum, a prototype of today's tambourine, used by Kushitic healers to relieve the pains of childbirth (Mertz, 1978: 136; Almond & Seddon, 1999: 37). Other scenes depict adolescent female musicians keeping time with hand clappers in the style of castanets (Mertz, 1978: 134-135). Today adolescent Jolla girls in the Gambia call similar instruments that accompany their rhythmic feet "kaleomak" and use them to keep time when they dance. Mertz's documentation, then, becomes evidence of the ancient springs of common, contemporary cultural practices within Afrikan communities. It is significant that, across the globe, Afrikan populations continue to make dance a central element of their emotional healing and use it reflexively to provide release from the tension of constant pressure within anti-Kushitic societies (White, 1984; Reagon, 1992; Haskins, 1990).

Another Egyptologist of note, Henri Frankfort, points out that written records of early human civilization demonstrate that temporal power devolved from spiritual power (Frankfort, 2000). In keeping with those findings, historian Charles Siefert cites the depiction of a colossal female figure of a ruler-priest on walls of ancient Meroe. Many times larger than the 'deities' paying tribute to her, she is seated on a carved lion as the diminutive images of 'gods' (spiritual forces), women and men offer her gifts (Siefert, 1938: 17). In Kemetic philosophy, the symbol of the transmutation of spiritual or moral power to temporal power is Aset, The Divine Mother of Kemet's first ruler (Frankfort, 2000: 6). She incarnates the "Suten", which is variously rendered as "Throne", "Seat" or "Pharaoh", in keeping with a tradition that is probably manifested today in the Sacred Golden Stool of West Afrika's Akan peoples or the Holy See of the Catholic Church. (Sarpong, 1971; Finch, 1999: 97; Simpson, 1978: 147).

Throughout Kemet's thousands of years of spiritually based leadership, however, invaders, immigrants, or missionizers from far and near have repeatedly challenged the society's reverence for female principles (Diop, 1991; Williams, 1976). They have also sought to replace women and motherhood as supreme symbols of the Creative Principle of the Universe with counter-experiential generative male icons (Eliade Et Al, 2000). Yet today women still retain their central regenerative role in Pan-Afrikan spiritual, public and private space (Ani, 1994; Harris, 1987; Mandela, 1985). The power of a "Sacred Stool", a kind of Soul

Throne, still confers spiritual legitimacy to leaders among Black populations scattered across the world. 'Stools' retain the 'Souls' of nations, as in the example of the Akan, conferring temporal and necessarily temporary power on mortal leaders. Evidence of 'enstoolment' beliefs exists in Zimbabwe in Southern Afrika and persists as well among Ashantis from West Afrika even when they reside in Europe and North America (IFC, 1977: 78; Sarpong, 1971; Wilson, 1998; Marshall, 1993). Far from Afrika a royal "Stool's" symbolic authority is also recognized in sites like Tahiti in the South Pacific where Black peoples live (Barrow, 1979: 30).

To date, psychologists, sociologists or educators have not demonstrated that there is a universally accepted measure for assessing how deeply imposed, alien, sexist patriarchy has wounded Afrikan societies. However, there is evidence of women filling widely diverse roles and functions within pre-Arab or European influenced populations. Tendai Mutunhu reminds us that during Zimbabwe's, "Mwenemutapa Empire...some of the best combat units were made up only of women soldiers [and in more recent times] the greatest military leader and freedomfighter in recent history was [a woman named] Nehanda" (Mutunhu, 1976). Mogwuko Okoye presents further evidence that Afrikan women have always shared equal rights to be both priests and healers. Generally the latter were also chosen as the moral and temporal authorities of ancient Afrikan societies (Okoye, 1977: 32). Such customs are in direct opposition to the gender based practices of exclusion which existed in many other ancient cultures. In spite of the unfathomable damage that colonization and genocidal racism have done to the fabric of Pan-Afrikan lives, women continue to be the guarantors of our continuity and keepers of our ancestral culture. A Pan-Afrikan approach count(er)s the losses we have collectively sustained by recognising and making women's equality again operational in all aspects of our lives. For Pan-Afrikanism is centred in culture, and without the keepers of our culture assuming their role at the 'Seat' of Afrikan life, Pan-Afrikanism cannot fulfil its mission of cultural, political and economic rebirth.

As forces line up on different sides of debates over global Afrikan unity, Pan-Afrikanists enhance that dialogue by finding and introducing accurate information about the spread of Nilotic cultures across the continent and the world (IFC, 1977). It is vital to sustain new ways of seeing by constantly connecting our present experiences to our memories. and knowledge of the journey we have made. Educator Joseph Williams, for example, points the way to potentially rich linguistic sources for rediscovering links between West Afrikan and Nilotic Hebrew history (Williams, 1999). Paul Farmer's comprehensive interpretation and recording of Haiti's story is especially timely for they remind us of the sacrifices that brought Afrikans born in the Caribbean and Americas through Europe's genocidal forced servitude (Farmer, 2003). The costs have been staggering for millions of Afrikan spirits waiting for justice in unmarked graves stretching across the bed of the sea as well as well as for those uncounted survivors who lived out their aborted lives. Our Ancestors were carelessly butchered by Europeans or Arabs and tossed like burnt offerings on the altar of their racist fantasies. In count(er)ing such catastrophe, it becomes especially important for Pan-Afrikanists to absorb lessons from Haiti and Zimbabwe, two sites where Afrikans, in spite of extreme hardship have recovered title to the land (Farmer, 2003; Horne, 2001).

The two hundredth anniversary of Haiti's victory in 1804 offered a unique opportunity for enhancing the work of positive, popular education in Pan-Afrikan hands. It is in the interests of Pan-Afrikan self-determination to rescue the glory of Haiti's heroic people and leaders from the infamy heaped upon them by their detractors. Doing so requires that we counter a popular language of defamation that usually features a debilitating description of Afrikan resistance against European domination coupled with a prescription of inevitable defeat. By and large, the women and men whose determination, organizational skills and military genius destroyed Napoleon's ambitions for world domination remain shrouded today in deliberate, studied obscurity. Anti-Kushitic, Eurocentric historians, biased manipulators of the mainstream media, a wilfully indifferent or suspiciously innocent approach by the popular culture as well as race-denying, polemicized academic institutions have now imprisoned the memories of Haiti's heroes in a virtual dungeon of oblivion for over two hundred years (Farmer, 2003; Schmidt, 1971; Frederickse, 1982; Key, 1981; Lee & Solomon, 1991).

Our Ayitian Ancestors were more than pioneers in the modern culture of Universal Human Rights when they defeated the three major imperialist and racist nations - France, Great Britain and Spain - at the beginning of the nineteenth century. They were also a major international influence, taking active part in the military forces that made it possible for Spanish colonies in the Americas to break free (Farmer, 2003). The symbolic significance of the stunning Olympic upset of Hitler's super race aspirations by US born Afrikan sprinter, Jesse Owens, in 1936 parallels Haiti's defeat of supremacist European delusions, in a series of spectacular, public, military upsets between 1791 and 1804 (James, 1989; Edwards, 1969: 78). It also shows that it is possible for Afrikan and other oppressed peoples to reverse arrogant, apparently invincible historical tyrannies. Haitians spawned a tradition that expressed itself one hundred and sixty years later when a Ugandan soldier from the ranks, John Okello, led a revolution that overthrew the anachronistic and morally obscene Arab slavocracy of Zanzibar in 1964 (Bailey, 1988: 132). Victory for Pan-Afrikanists is never so memorable, instructive or sweet as when the dispossessed, and the most despised, topple the arrogant despots whose boots press down on our heads.

Like Toussaint L'Ouverture's defeat of Napoleon Bonaparte, Owens' feat of winning four Olympic gold medals in rapid succession in the sprints electrified a breathlessly watching world. To date, its political or psychological implications have not received the serious investigations that they deserve. Yet, logically, Owens' victory must continue, even with the passage of time to create cognitive dissonance in the minds of those who hunger after confirmation of their supremacy for just being White. With nary a rude gesture or word, the Black sprinter publicly humiliated Hitler, the champion of delusional racist bigotry at the zenith of his power. While Owens' victories, by force of logic, sowed consternation and destabilizing doubt in the minds of racists, he

CLEM MARSHALL

brought relief to his own people and lovers of human dignity in every corner of his attentive, grateful world.

Today, however, it is sobering to realize that while the tyrant Bonaparte's ashes lie at the heart of Paris inside a mausoleum called 'Les Invalides', displayed in monumental splendour and unsullied glory under gold and glass, European histories of omission have absolved the tyrannical French emperor for kidnapping Toussaint L'Ouverture, the heroic defender of Human Rights, and dumping his dead body, unceremoniously, in an unknown grave (Du Bois, 1982: 1411). His memory has been so thoroughly erased from most historical studies that today few people outside Haiti speak Toussaint L'Ouverture's name. As Pan-Afrikan re-educators continue to restore champions of liberation to their just place in a potential 'Pan-Afrikan Hall of Fame' and disseminate their hidden histories across our world, we provide a psychological antidote against the poisonous amnesia that so predictably attacks Afrikan minds. The treasury of their people's glorious past is especially important for those members of our youth mired today in self-destruction or despair (Akbar, 1992; Wilson, 1993).

Another key activity in counting and countering the costs of Black holocausts, is the dissemination of information about the stolen artistic, spiritual and cultural treasures now in the British Museum, the Berlin Museum, the Royal Ontario Museum and major museums across the non- Afrikan world (Arulogun, 1993; Marshall, 1993). The mask that organizers chose to be the symbol of *FESTAC '77* in Nigeria was stolen, along with two thousand (2000) priceless art bronzes, during the rape of Benin City by the British in 1897 (De Villiers & Hirtle, 1997: 227). While physically recovering stolen items of Afrikan heritage is key, self-determination also requires an accompanying effort to take back the good name of Afrikan genius that created them. Some influential academics of European or Asian ancestry have continued into the modern era to misname or misrepresent the Afrikan originators of many world-class achievements and to dismiss or devalue the contribution of the Black communities that generated them (Segy, 1985; Asante & Mazama, 2002). Often, even as those historians and cultural experts devalue Afrika, they inflate the copies of Afrikan culture or science that members of their own racial group turn out (Rubin, 1984; Williams, 1999; Onyewuenyi, 1994; Hilliard, 1991; Asante & Abarry, 1996).

For example, influential scientists and thinkers from diverse cultural experiences extol the virtues of musical genius and connect it to the higher functions of the human spirit or brain (Ouspensky, 1977: 297; Jourdan, 1997). The philosopher, P. D. Ouspensky makes the observation that intervals in music parallel the patterns in our own thinking and prepare us to understand "why there are no straight lines in nature...why everything with us is *thought*, why everything *happens* with us and happens usually in a way opposed to what we want or expect" (Ouspensky, 1977: 127). Notably, however, scholars do not appear to have produced a body of work exploring and connecting Afrikan music to the high cultivation of Afrikan minds. Yet evidence of Afrikan music's extraordinary appeal as well as its power to generate energy or bring a measure of healing to unhealthy social situations seems self-evident, because our music is so embedded in global daily life (Reagon, 1992). In addition, as Eric Williams points out, Europeans were well aware of the special value of Afrikan energy in terms of our potential labor. They not only deemed Afrikans more productive than the workers of their own race and all others in the world, but Europe also exploited Black endurance in laying the foundations of global capital and the capitalist economy through which her nations have grown powerful and rich (Williams, 1994).

Therefore, another reason for exposing the costs of Black holocausts is to counter the serial assaults that this society regularly inflicts on the Afrikan mind. In 1957, British psychiatrist William Sargant addressed the question of skilful psychological manipulation and its power to alter belief systems of individuals and groups in the following words, "Various types of belief can be implanted in many people, after brain function has been sufficiently disturbed by accidentally or deliberately induced fear, anger or excitement" (Sargant, 1997: 84). The relentless, transgenerational assault on the Afrikan psyche described in preceding chapters is convincing evidence that Afrikans across the globe are prime candidates for the implantation of "various types of belief". This study has demonstrated that, from the scriptural 'Curse of Ham', used by 'slavemakers' as doctrinal 'proof' that Blacks could be justly enslaved, to specious arguments mounted to devalue Afrikan intelligence in *The Bell Curve,* the beliefs imposed on us by West Asians or Europeans have been inimical to our wellbeing and indifferent to the tax they exacted from our humanity (Chinyelu, 1996: 2; Mudimbe, 1988: 46; Russell, 1999: 2).

In addition to our physical vulnerability, however, Afrikans inhabit a world where the very process that might shield our minds is also prey to the seduction of ubiquitous euphemisms and our internalization of racist definitions of our selves. The author Raphael Powell points out that even outstanding US educator Carter Woodson, pioneer of Black History Week, called his discipline "Negro History". With a touch of irony Powell writes, "Born December 19, 1875 he died April 3rd, 1950; not knowing that negro [emphasis added] does not exist" (Powell, 1979: 451). One might make the same comment about Dr. Martin Luther King. Pan-Afrikan self-determination pays attention to language that revictimizes the resister and remains intentionally conscious of the narcotizing effect of familiar vocabularies. For Pan-Afrikanists know from collective memory the literal, lived reality behind the words of influential Russian thinker, George Gurdjieff, who stated that, "Modern civilization is based on violence and slavery and fine words" (Gurdjieff, 1999: 3).

A Pan-Afrikan approach encourages learners to use dramatic public events to stimulate and heighten awareness of threats to our dignity and to pierce through the deceptive camouflage of disabling words. Pan-Afrikanism demands unflagging watchfulness in a toxic environment where many apparently 'innocent' activities mask their potential for causing unpredictable pain. For example, significant numbers of Blacks and Whites considered the O. J. Simpson trial a divisive, race relations' disaster for Afrikans (Morrison, 1992). However, author Toni Morrison brought her keen insight to bear on the event. She used the tragedy to demonstrate how White supremacy organizes its forces across gender, ethnicity and class to crush 'transgressive' Blacks.

Morrison then did more. She harnessed the energies of the intense consciousness that the trial generated across the Afrikan world and turned them against the anti-Kushitic currents rushing through the air on the wings of racist jokes, media misinformation and a White supremacist sense of siege. Riding the intense passions the trial generated past contradictions of gender, diverse identity or class, the author constructed a unifying vision for liberated, post-plantation Afrikan minds. Her writing therefore became an instrument for not only resisting the ravages of the historic 'OJ moment' but also preparing her Black readers for psychic assaults to come (Morrison, 1992). As discussed earlier, nearly two centuries before O. J. Simpson stood on the dock of White public opinion, David Walker, another Black role model, educated and successful in business far beyond the achievements of most Black men of his time, turned his consciously critical eye on the surrounding society. Unlike O. J. Simpson who wrote a book about his ordeal titled *I want to tell you: My Response to Your Letters, Your Messages, Your Questions.* David Walker did not go on bended knee to Whites who had rejected him. Instead, in the spirit of the Old Testament prophets and the rhythms of early Ebonics David Walker 'had White folks told' (Simpson, 1995; Major, 1994: 468).

> Survive
>
> Chisel each sound
>
> Carve it into stone
>
> Make codes where secrets
>
> Hide
>
> Conceal our culture
>
> Lest they hunt us down
>
> Until our race has
>
> Died
>
> (Marshall, 2004)

TELLING OUR TRUTHS

Telling our truths is key to self-determination. For over thirty generations in the West, political and religious leaders, as well as some members of an academic elite, have fabricated and spread toxic lies, attempting to justify genocide against Afrikans (Chinweizu, 1987; Chirimuuta, 1989; Pieterse, 1992). In South Africa, East Afrika and the United States, Europeans have also provided opportunities for other races to serve as their surrogates in exploiting Black material and cultural wealth (Chinwezu, 1987; Powell, 1979; Wilson, 1998). When East Asians (Chinese, Koreans or Japanese) West Asians (Arabs, Jews, Iranians or Middle Easterners) or South Asians (Indians or Pakistanis) invest in White supremacist states that dispossess Aboriginal Afrikan populations, they permit themselves to serve as buffers between White supremacy and Black Human Rights (Ingham, 1967: 275; Cell, 1987; Kivel, 1996).

The papal pronouncement, in the fifteenth century, that Afrikans were a people without a soul, placed us, within imperialist and racist global systems, outside the pale of human consideration. I find comfort in the observation that that defamation, over centuries, sparked an intuitive response that manifested itself in our language centuries later. We not only renamed ourselves 'Soul Sisters and Soul Brothers', but also influenced the world to use our honorific names. Today, popular culture knows our food as "Soul Food". As we return to our source, The Divine Word, the MDW NCHR, we find both our own tongue and our "Ka" or "Soul" again. In Afrika's most ancient ancestral tongues, our scholars tell us, the phoneme (distinct sound) 'K' that sits at the root of KMT or Kemet (Ancient Egypt and Nubia) is illustrated by the rays of the sun appearing over a hill and literally means "Soul" (Ra, 1995: 40). The act of Pan-Afrikan self-determination begins with an affirmation of that ancestral collective Soul.

Affirmation

I believe

In One Great Mother

Breasts feeding

Our whole human race

I believe

In Afrika's time

Where the dead keep faith

With the living

Chanting our chants

Drumming our drums

Guiding our feet

When we dance

I believe Her

Mortal yet immortal

Enduring as the Sphinx

Rising from rest to soar

I believe in Kush

Cradle of all before

Ashay May It Be Ashay

(Marshall, 2004)

RE-BALANCING OUR WORLD

As a Pan-Afrikanist, I have also learned to embrace other meanings of Afrika in this study, as in my teaching. The arguments and evidence that I have presented demonstrate that Afrika, for me, must include "scattered" Afrika (Martin, 1985: vii). To ignore the large body of Afrikans in Europe, in the Caribbean and Americas would mire us in analytical error as we confront the catastrophes in our present or past (Chaliand & Rageau, 1995: 113). It takes a Pan-Afrikanist vision to overcome ubiquitous, consistent anti-Kushitic propaganda which turns our global experience into a *"pointilliste* canvas – a thousand details [that] make a thousand points", drowning us under an infinitude of individual responses to a transgenerational, collective trauma (Ellul, 1973). Communications specialist Jacques Ellul's arguments convince me that if we are to respond effectively, as targeted populations, to propaganda from the dominant society, we cannot take an episodic approach but must "stand back and get a panoramic view" (Ellul, 1973: 145).

An approach that is both historical and global is especially critical for vulnerable, marginalized Afrikans. We must perforce learn from each other since the forces that shape or distort our existence, global capital, propaganda and racism are so effectively intertwined. For example, the deceptions of 'liberal' Whites in revolutionary Black circles are both legion and global. In the United States, the liberal Kennedy administration did not spare moral icons of the Civil Rights Movement such as Martin Luther King from Secret Service harassment (Wolfenstein, 1993; Cleaver, 1969). The anti-apartheid movement was replete with scandals of its own, and a decade after the fall of apartheid, four years after the formal conclusion of the public truths and hidden truths of the 'Truth and Reconciliation' Commission, a White ANC member and former civil or human rights lawyer, Vanessa Brereton, came forward to confess to being a spy for apartheid. The media reported her appearance as follows:

> In the interview Brereton says she began to doubt her involvement with the apartheid state's security forces some time before her misgivings reached a climax in 1989 with the killing of three black security policemen and an askari -- the name given to an African National Congress operative who turned to work for the apartheid State (Sapa, 2003).

The lack of democratic justice or security of human rights where people of Afrikan ancestry are concerned whether they live in Canada, Europe, Australia and the United States logically raises doubts about the consciousness of Whites from abroad who choose to champion Human Rights in Afrika. When the world sees liberal White faces defending Blacks who are then rendered even more invisible or made to appear incapable of defending themselves, it infantilizes the race and serves to reinforce myths of innate Black dependency on Whites (Grovogui, 1996; Duffield, 2001).

Pre-1965 Voting Rights Act absurdities used to disqualify Blacks under US style democracy included a voter-qualifying question that asked, "How many bubbles in a bar of soap" (Parker & Rashke, 1986: 184)? Senator Bilbo of Mississippi was explicit in his opposition to Black voting and human rights, "I'm calling on every red-blooded American who believes in the supremacy and integrity of the white race to get out and see that no nigger votes. And the best time to do it is the night before" (Parker & Rashke, 1986: 24). Intellectual rigor therefore requires us to examine obstacles placed in the path of Black voters across the United States, which publicly champions democracy in Afrikan countries today. It is logical to begin that exercise by examining the peculiar disenfranchisement of the majority Black electorate living in the US capital itself. To this day, the Black population in Washington D. C. is crippled by a double standard that robs it of the 'one person, one vote' ideal its government preaches to Afrikans abroad (Yette, 1971: 266; Bailey, 2001). Investigative journalist Greg Palast also raises questions around the more recent disenfranchisement of Afrikan voters in Florida in the United States presidential election of November 2000 (Palast, 2004).

Equally incongruous or distressing for those who value integrity in interracial exchange is the banality with which the public responds to agencies that assault Black men, and increasingly Black women in North America, Europe or Australia. Evidence points to widespread acceptance of the violation of collective Black Human Rights within the society at large (Pinkney, 1994; Churchill & Vander Wall, 1990: 303). A sociological study that projected the hypothetical case of a Nazi-like governmental round-up of Blacks in the United States found that the majority of citizens, including targeted Blacks, would respond like, 'good Germans' are reputed to have done during Adolf Hitler's regime (Yette, 1971: 259). In Detroit, Judge George Crockett assessed the moral state of the society from his vantage point of being both a jurist and Black, "We have all the laws we need but we have too many police and government officials who do not live by the laws we have (Crockett, 1995: xxii). His statement reads like an indictment of the system from inside, underscoring the contradiction between its words and deeds that sends a warning to Blacks around the globe. Whatever the external forces such as class, education, shade, gender, religion or ideology that divide us, the uniqueness of our vulnerability will continue to unite us under the banner of those who are treated as global prey.

The Afrikan will to fight back has not only sustained Black people but also inspired other justice-loving people in societies all over the world. Garveyism was a model for Vietnam's liberator Ho Chi Minh (Obadele, 1991; Tani & Sera, 1985). Toussaint L'Ouverture's victory in Haiti was a beacon for Simon Bolivar who threw off the Spanish yoke in the Americas with Ayitian support (Farmer, 2003; Martin, 1985). Popular culture, however, has projected solidarity with marginalized groups, across the spectrum of identity, as predominantly a virtue of White, Western societies, ignoring the contributions of Black struggles against oppression. Over the last six hundred years Black culture has profoundly transformed Western society as Black resistance has been constantly on the boil (Genovese, 1976). The Black Civil Rights Movement's *We Shall Overcome* was sung with equal passion in Wenceslas Square by striking Polish miners, by children protesting working conditions in India and by Chinese students affirming their human rights in Tiananmen Square in 1989 (Katz, 1995: 560). In practice, this cry of freedom from countless, nameless Black throats has metamorphosed into the anthem of liberation around today's world. Just as our shared vulnerability mandates the unity of Black and Black, our contribution to human freedom unites us to the rest of humankind.

Beyond inspirational spirituals and freedom songs, Black liberators brought benefits to:

> [C]ountless thousands of women, Hispanics, Asian Americans, disabled persons, Native Americans, and working people" (Cisneros, 1995: 560). [And] Brave and resourceful women such as Rosa Parks, Fannie Lou Hamer and Coretta Scott King inspired generations of women of all colors (Katz, 1995: 560).

Historian E. Curtis Alexander writes:

> [Due] to [the] legislative ability of [Black] Congressman Adam Clayton Powell, Jr. [a powerful Committee Chair in the 87th US Congress 1961-1962]…some of the most important legislation in the history of [the United States] was passed – Increasing the Minimum Wage; The War on Poverty; Aid to Elementary and   Secondary Education; Barring Discrimination in salaries paid to Women for the same work performed by Men…Providing for the training of teachers of the deaf and handicapped children…Education of the Blind… [and] The Older Americans Act of 1965 (Alexander, 1990: 62-67).

When the ground moves, every edifice that stands on it must shift, crumble or readjust. By deliberately holding Afrikan populations at ground zero of its social grid, global society guarantees us pivotal roles as arbiters of the length, breadth and depth of its Human Rights. History shows that when Afrikans insist on full respect for our humanity, societies generally feel logically compelled to also extend full respect to any groups whose interests they have placed above ours (Cleaver & Katsaficas, 2001; Foner, 1995).

Lived experience, historical data as well as analysis, loudly proclaim that, in Afrika, there has always existed a deeply rooted cultural conviction of humanity on fire for liberation. Like the bountiful Nile, however, this deep expression of Afrika's culture has sometimes had to run underground. At other times it has been met by granite-like force, split into different streams and then fused powerfully again. The power of Afrika's culture has also risen above mountains of adversity and expanded the boundaries of the space for expressing humanity across the world.

Black culture was the inspiration for Harlem Renaissance poet, Langston Hughes' poem *In Explanation of Our Times* (Hughes, 1974: 281). My reflection on resistance, alliances, influences and liberation follows in tribute to the poetry and spirit of Langston Hughes.

We May Lose Yet We Will Win

Folks without Honourable in front their names,

From Brooklyn to Baghdad

Are chantin' Reggae droppin' Rap

Fightin' the Sirs of this world

We can't all be Sirs Natty Dred

That requires a rich father with good hair

Sirs call others

Homeless Jobless Dropout Deranged

Gangbangers on the street ADD in school!

Welfare Queens Repeat Offenders

Illegal Aliens Model Minorities

I-an'-I dub deh I

Primitive Native Slant Gook

Queue Jumper Cripple Helpless Unfit

Nigger Fag Spick Spade

Speak White

You're in Canada now

Whiners shut the f-word up

Until fight back time

When Time says it's time

Media and The Web have had their say

Don' mean too much

Same flick same flash

Comes a time for fighting back

For air time

Party time

Just-Us time

Overtime for Peace

Though TV pundits twist our thoughts

Folks like us

Take their words and toss them back

At Judges Generals Governors Lords

Presidents Prime Ministers Premiers Popes,

Finance Fraud Ministers looting by stock exchange

Thugs upon thrones

Ayatollahs Moderators Rabbis Gurus Priests

Thought Patrollers in bunkered minds

World Bankers dispossessing the world

International Money-laundering Fronts

Underdeveloping Nations

Billionaires hawking baby-blow-up bombs

Pushers pushing drugstore drugs

Pin- striped Wall Street Bay Street Money Street Bully-boys

Top grossing-out CEOs

Demonic dealers in diamonds and death

Class deep as caste

Fixers of fashion image or fine taste

Bouncers blocking doorways for choice

Rounding up the riches of the world

While folks with no fancy I.D.

Crouch to work

Bare backs burning under the sun

Eyes glued to the ground

Black to Brown Red Yellow Beige to White

Every tone shade in-between

Back bending

Earning riches around the world

No sirmadam behind any name

Except a whispered Sistah maybe Brutha

Our folks say no more shutting up

So of course that means licks in these times

Nuff trouble Nuff- nuff trouble

In these our times

Because of Us

Refusing to shut up run off bow down

Refusing to fade away

Putting respect behind our names

Thinker

Liberator

Free

(Marshall, 2004)

UNPACKING CODES,
REPACKAGING CONSCIOUSNESS

Psychologist and Jewish Holocaust survivor, Bruno Bettelheim found that the non-Jewish public had difficulty coming to terms with Jewish survivors (Bettelheim, 1980). As survivors of our holocausts, Pan-Afrikanists also find that often those who have seen themselves as our teachers, political leaders and moral models generally resist calling us survivors and honoring us for our survival. Paul Kennedy, in an overview of social trends that he ambitiously prescribes for "the twenty-first century" purports to take the pulse of discrimination against "immigrant communities" and people of color in the White world. Kennedy recognizes that prejudicial acts occur in:

> Britain against Indians and Pakistanis, in France against Algerians and Moroccans, in Germany against Turks, and in parts of the United States against Latin Americans and Asians. [And he notes that] the root of these tensions lies in foreignness, or, to use another word, race (Kennedy, 1993: 43).

In each of the sites the author mentions, Afrikan populations have also been significant or even central targets of the society's racist attitudes. Yet Paul Kennedy, the popular host of a Canadian Broadcasting Corporation program called "Ideas", deletes the Black experience with a touch of his keyboard, like some intellectual death squad commander disappearing its victims secretly in the dark. When Afrikans surrender their independence of mind in exchange for interracial friendship or to facilitate smooth interracial relations, such erasures of their reality from public discourse must logically weigh against confidence in Human Rights or their self-esteem.

Bruno Bettelheim exposes the human potential for self-denial when he describes Jewish collaborators inside concentration camps who dressed in copies of Nazi uniforms (Bettelheim, 1980: 79). Not unlike those innocent prisoners, many prominent Afrikans have tried to blend with the forces dominating or decimating us. The public record and personas of those Blacks who appear frequently in the media packaged as White, like O. J. Simpson, Christopher Darden, Clarence Thomas, Michael Jackson and Oprah Winfrey, have provoked considerable debate within Black communities (Johnson & Roediger, 1997: 197-198; Simpson, 1995: 97; Morrison, 1992: xxix; Darden & Walter, 1996: Andersen, 1994: King, 1987: 76-79). Some stars have bleached their skin, altered their noses, straightened or conked their hair and most political, academic or cultural leaders of Afrikan ancestry in today's world have adopted the faiths of our historical oppressors, praying to Europe's or Asia's Ancestors as 'Saints', rather than to their own. Elie Wiesel, another Jewish survivor, calculates the price of conversion in hope of survival. He does not miss the irony when such conversion fails to provide protection to the persecuted. Similar to those Jews who tried desperately to assimilate and deny their Jewishness, many Afrikan men in the US proudly donned the nation's uniform and fought in its wars. With cruel irony, some veterans who wore the uniform on their return reaped the reward of their misguided loyalty. They were lynched by White mobs for their 'arrogance'.

Pan-Afrikanism works intentionally to restore the knowing why to Afrikan experiences of persecution. It also legitimizes expression of those intense normal emotions evoked by learning more details of the enormity of Europe's and Arabia's crimes against our Ancestors. Most classrooms and popular spaces in this hemisphere, however, are today censored through silence. Generally, they entomb uncomfortable truths inside walls rendered impenetrable by euphemism and the cosmetics of multicultural discourse. Those groups that continue to be socially dominant in our lives, whose very presence constantly, albeit unconsciously, connects contemporary racial hierarchies to our wounded past, no longer need to censor Afrikan speech. Today we are already programmed for their comfort through denial, self-delusion and an eagerness to forget which are already coded into patterns of our speech. So we sanitize our discussions even as they unfold.

On the other hand the potential for developing a new language around Afrikan interests is also real. We can use startling combinations of words to create the feeling of fearlessness Malcolm X evokes when he says, "We care nothing about odds" (Malcolm X, 1981: 8). Raw speech spoken by forceful individuals like Malcolm X and offered within the context of significant events, can break new ground. They also allow us to weigh the odds and opt for living the fullness of our defiant humanity rather than settling for a more secure but under-explored life. From the moment I heard it spoken, the term Black Power was like a wake-up-call. At the time, it came as a frontal, 'in-your-face' affirmation of Blackness from Harlem's congressman and peerless lawmaker, Adam Clayton Powell and blew like a cleansing wind through the Pan-Afrikan world (Alexander, 1990).

Soul-strengthening or revolutionary phrases like "Black is beautiful", "Burn baby burn", "The ballot or the bullet", "Black and proud" and later "God is Black", transformed neutered Black speech during the US sixties (Osahon, 1993). Just registering the conjunction of 'beautiful' and 'Black' triggered aftershocks like an earthquake in countless minds. It was an antidote to the poisonous encyclopedia I had been taught to accept as the ultimate authority on all things in school, up to and including information on my people and myself. Those learned volumes never suggested that Black could be anything other than negative, ugly or depraved.

Over the years, other significant images have reshaped my mindscape. The first post-independence "Miss Ghana" shown on a BBC newsreel was also the first Black woman I had ever seen publicly, in White space, connected to the words like beautiful or beauty. She was a full size woman dressed in rainbow coloured kente robes. Radiantly, magnificently comfortable she inhabited all of her ample being (Yankah, 1987). The honour paid her was like a salve to my fragile, boyish heart. For now mother's Afrikanness could be beautiful; my 'Mammy', my grandmother whose soft brown eyes enveloped my world could be beautiful too. Now the faces of teachers, neighbours and female members of my inclusive family who picked me up when I fell and kissed my bruises away, who adorned and uplifted my life could be admired without ambivalence, confusion or secreted shame. For me, those unexpected combinations of words freed me to love those I needed to love without reservation, so that I could also begin to fully love myself. Magical words, they connected my brain and my soul to my gut.

What would our world be like, I wonder, if the words burned into every Black son's and Black mother's mind in North America, over the last thirty-five years, in school assemblies and ad nauseam on TV, were not the otherworldly, "I have a dream" of Dr. Martin Luther King but Muhammad Ali's gutsy truth, "No Viet Cong ever called me nigger" instead (Jones, 1993; Obadele, 1991; Tani & Sera, 1985)? The iconic Black Panther leader Eldridge Cleaver also used direct speech stripped of circumlocution when he pointed out that, "The assassin's bullet not only killed Dr. King. It killed a period of history. It killed a hope and it killed [his] dream" (Cleaver, 1969: 74).

Black militancy in the United States military during the Vietnam war was the Achilles heel of the nation's ruling class. Since Blacks have been generally disproportionately represented alive or dead in US wars, this most vulnerable of communities can still throw a wrench in the engine of the US military machine (Obadele, 1991; Tani & Sera, 1985). Some political analysts argue that it was the potential of Black disruptive power, which sparked the government's attack on the 'Nation of Islam's' founder, Elijah Muhammad in 1942. It jailed him for four years for counselling Black men to resist the draft (Essien-Udom, 1963: 67). However, Adib Rashad also identifies the Nation of Islam's Wallace D. Fard's, "language that was highly esoteric and appealing to lost causes" as a prime factor in the group's popular appeal and its ability to influence the broader society. Rashad says that Fard's, "Expressions such as... 'The white man is the devil' found literal meaning in [many Black] hearts and minds" (Rashad, 1991: 70). Affirmations of Afrikan experience and humanity and the identification of the race of those suppressing us generally heighten Black consciousness. Logically, the right words in the right place at the right time can alter the shape of the world to which we are heir (Essien-Udom, 1963; Tani & Sera, 1985; Obadele, 1991).

The novelist George Orwell's character, Winston, may have been written to describe the dilemma of Pan-Afrikan Freethinkers in a White worded world. In Orwell's novel *1984*, Winston says:

> The key word here is blackwhite. [It] means loyal willingness to say that black is white when Party discipline demands this. But it means also the ability to believe that black is white, and more, to know that black is white, and to forget that one has ever believed the contrary (Reznikov, 2001: 47).

Winston's words expose one of the hidden costs of the silenced, erased holocausts that Afrikans have borne. If we follow his reasoning it can help explain the confused psychic space that so many Black women and men in this society inhabit today. Memories of those holocausts as well as images, words and thoughts that promise eventual healing have remained with us. I invoke them both as I bring this reflection on the Pan-Afrikanist potential in the world to a kind of ending where new journeys of the mind, gut and soul begin.

WEAVING OUR THEN INTO OUR NOW

Building this work proceeded from a feeling of general unease with my own thoughts around Black experience. However, it soon became evident that what developed has been an exercise in exploring language, culture and history with liberation in mind. This study has attended to how, as Pan-Afrikanists, the language fed to us and the systems on which we often feel forced to feed inculcate habits of dependence; encourage us to internalize practices that devalue our ancestral cultural capital and foster the subordination of Afrikan interests. This study has gathered evidence by sometimes peering past walls into classrooms. At other times new insights and information have come from analysing conversations between groups of Afrikans or discussions of race involving Afrikans and members of other groups. Significant learning came from absorbing the visual impact of images of ancient Afrika in books as well as museums and finding their reflection in our lives today. Unpacking the process of creating positive images through video exposed some of the powerful anti-Kemetic practices that have rewarded those who disrespect Afrikans while denying the injustice we endure.

Mapping Pan-Afrikan culture anew in our minds, this study has shown how, through anti-Kemetic images and language, we are routinely led to 'mis-locate' Afrikan events, customs, rituals and ceremonies, often banishing them from central, public spaces in our lives. This work has also revealed that repeated misinterpretations of the Afrikan origins of world-class achievements have proved costly, robbing Black populations of the wealth of symbolic meanings coded into ancestral Afrikan culture. The meanings we misplace, in their turn, are significant repositories of collective, ancestral knowledge and often transfer essential skills for successful Pan-Afrikan living.

In addition, this study has demonstrated how the language we use can automatically prescribe narrow and degrading interpretations of Black humanity. Such interpretations are often passed on when that language is taught to us and encouraged by Eurocentric or Arabized 'experts' from inside or outside our group. Through a widened lens I have examined the Western secularization of sacred Afrikan rites and how that has shaped our understanding of Afrikan religion. The 'rhumba' was a religious Afrikan dance in preparation for birth that lost its practical application when others stripped it of spiritual connotation (Genovese, 1976; Butcher, 1957; Haskins, 1990; Thorpe, 1990). Lamia Radi's obituary on the death of "the Arab World's most famous belly dancer", in 1999, provided striking evidence that 'expropriation' of Afrikan spiritual capital is also a global practice.

He writes, "[…] Abla Mohammed Karim [of] a middle-class Cairo family took her stage name [Taheya Carioca] from the Brazilian samba [ancestral, spirit-based Afrikan dance]" (Radi, 1999; Guillermoprieto, 1991: 46-49). Today the samba has been reduced to sexed-up 'world' entertainment fit for ballrooms, salons and clubs. Pan-Afrikan education deems it instructive and important to connect religious conversion, the loss of cultural cohesion and the erosion of confidence in a collective Pan-Afrikan self. Because religion and culture are so interwoven in the popular mind, this study has shown how influences flowing from Christianity or Islam still persuade significant numbers of Afrikans to treat Arab or European culture as superior to our own (Osahon, 1993; McCray, 1992; Rashad, 1991).

Pan-Afrikan education searches out the sources and forces of disintegration in Afrikan communities (Jennings, 2000; Mandaza, 1999; Decalo, 1976). Early in the period of Arab and European penetration into Afrika a witness who European records call 'Venture Smith' recorded how:

> [T]he place [his home] had been invaded by a nation not far distant…[and] furnished with all kinds of arms then in use; that they were instigated by some white nation who equipped them and sent them to subdue and possess the country; that his nation had made no preparation for war, having been for a long time in profound peace… (Smith, 1970: 8).

Pan-Afrikan education is corrective, noting that European or Arab histories rarely replay stories of principled Afrikan resistance to incursions by their own group. History shows that dreams of mutuality and interracial harmony that inspired strong Afrikan leaders like King Nzinga Kuwu of the Kongo to welcome Portuguese 'economic immigrants' as 'family' in 1488, exploded under pressure of their treachery when the Europeans began kidnapping his country's daughters and sons (Obadele, 1991: 145). We have also seen how both the academy and popular culture have generally emphasized contradiction and conflict between Afrikans while neglecting to chronicle Black resistance to enslavement or explain intra-group upheavals within the context of the oppressive times or manipulation by Outsiders from inside.

Quite often, and extensively, this study has drawn on available but largely invisible records to reveal White agency behind Black destruction (Churchill & Vander Wall, 1990; Carson, 1991). Mazisi Kunene records the treachery of the Rev. Charles Helm of the London Missionary society who colluded with Cecil Rhodes during his barbarous rampage across southern Africa (Kunene, 1976: 60). Doing so exposes and redefines the roles European, Asian or Arab merchants, missionaries, diplomats or NGOs have filled in the service of imperialism, colonialism and all accompanying acts of serial genocide (Powell, 1979; Nhubu, 2001; Ani, 1994; Duffield, 2001). Conversely, Pan-Afrikan education calls attention to the ongoing, untold story of Black generosity with Black. Over the centuries, countless individuals, ripped from their family roots have grafted themselves through service and loyalty to the Afrikans they met under duress, creating new operational family trees. The practice of transforming strangers into immediate kin has functioned as a Ministry of Self-defence for vulnerable Afrikans in hostile lands. It has also been a safety net for a people constantly over-taxed, over-burdened by competing demands on their energy and resources and denied reasonable hope of ever receiving adequate rewards in return.

This research has also been an exercise in self-determination. I regard this 'in-gathering' of knowledge and the many Pan-Afrikanist, educational projects cited in this work as intrinsic to the process of redressing the reductive, popular approach to Black achievement in the sciences or the arts. In thanks to our Ancestors, this work pays tribute to the grandeur of their sacrifice and does not genuflect to White power as this society usually commands (Parker, 1986). Paul Barrett writes, "Many whites...perceive...in the black middle class, a tendency to embrace victim hood, a lack of gratitude for what they have" (Barrett,

2000: 282). From a Pan-Afrikanist perspective, on the other hand, Andrew Billingsley points out authoritatively that there is overwhelming evidence to show that Black self-determination and self-help continue to live at the core of Black survival. His research reveals how:

> The resourceful black grandmother, the vital black church, the effective black school, the successful black business enterprise, the authentic black scholar, the hard-working, long-suffering black masses, the upwardly mobile sectors: all hold important keys to the regeneration of our families, our communities, and our society (Billingsley, 1994: 23).

In this exercise of Pan-Afrikan re-education, I define myself, think and create for myself as well as celebrate the ancestry that mirrors The Divine in all human blood.

This work has shown that Pan-Afrikan education necessitates transparency to counter the fog-making, myth-making linguistic machine that holds many Afrikans in its thrall and frequently buries Black trauma deeper than the reach of conscious analysis by even willing and ready minds. The anti-Kushitic machine of plausible myths I have described curdles self-love and seduces unwary Afrikan women and men into prostituting our selves. Pan-Afrikan learning, within the boundaries of this reflection, provides a shield against the commodification of Black identity by members of any other race.

This Pan-Afrikanist work is planted as an indigestible, ancestral stone in the guts of all annihilating anti-Kushitic machines. As the machines grind to a halt and silence returns, Pan-Afrikanists listen keenly for the voices of those who passed this way before. In the 1780s our Ancestor, Ottobah Cugoano spoke an enduring truth, "But our lives are accounted of no value, we are hunted as prey in the desert, and doomed to destruction as the beasts that perish" (Walvin, 1993: 20). In the sixties, Pan-Afrikanist Malcolm X promised us a renewed world,

"The world of tomorrow will be Black–and righteous…[and] there will be true freedom, justice and equality for all" (Malcolm X, 1963). We who have survived hear our Ancestors' words across time and space. We bear their truths in the fibres of our flesh and vow through our work to value their lives by never devaluing our own.

> When Who We Are Is What Our Story Says
> By right of ancestry
> Memories of rhythms
> Promises of final victory
> Dancing in Afrika's heart
> We endure despite adversity
> Downtrodden we rise to thrive
> Arms fit to enfold all tender shades
> Pleasure in Her pulse and Her blood
> Washed with flame reborn from dung
> Singing justice in Ma'at's sweet tongue
> Are we not still the spark Ptah made us to be
> With riches growing from our soil and soul
> Scattering harvests of faith like jewels over our globe
> Humanity's mirror for endless Humanities to Come
> We kindle futures without pain for sufferers of the earth
> Our energies feeding energies coursing through our veins
> We are Creation's prize and survive to honour Her still
> Our prayers to Ma'at hold pyramids up and humble human time
> Beyond avalanches dumped in atrocities around our head
> We keep our will
> (Marshall, 2004)

THANKS TO MIN WHO COMES AGAIN

Monarch butterflies cross the oceans as one generation and return as another to their grandparents' place of birth. Those tiny butterflies also retain memories of their Atlantic crossings over several generations. As survivors we too remember what we must remember to bridge generations, like they do. To mark this step on my journey, therefore, I summon the Sacred Word inside my blood. I conjure up "Le mot juste." The right word for the right memories holds keys for liberating our captured minds. Pan-Afrikan psychologists, like Edward Bynum are even now investigating how, as humans and Afrikans, we live inside "the family unconscious, the shared field of experience that each member of the family participates in, [which] is seen to unfold like a wave over at least three or four levels or generations" (Bynum, 1999: 98). I give praise and thanks to Min, the Kemetic, Kushitic evocation of the presence of duality and the potency of transformation that spins life into death into decay and into life again (Frankfort, 2000: 25).

In our ancestral Wolof tongue, which Pan-Afrikanist Cheikh Anta Diop connects so convincingly to ancient Kemet, we trace the collective memories that have guided this work towards spiritual reunification of the Afrikan world. It is the Word of Anubis the Jackal, wise in subtle distinctions between flesh that sustains life and flesh putrified by death, "Luy deg? La nep wax – What makes truths true? Only when we speak truth do we make it so [My translation]" (Samb, 1983: 31; Diop, 1974). To Min, Sprouting Eternal and Ever Upright, Sower of a Trillion Seeds, I dedicate this offering in rhythm for a song (Almond & Seddon, 1999:103-4)

Rebirth

Where do the butterflies go?

Ask the children

Searching for truths with their eyes

Hungering to know

How seas morph to skies

Quivering with shiverings of butterflies

Grandmother looks down

Her words lift their hearts

Email from a distant star

They glide she sighs on wings whisper-soft

Past lands tumbling into the sea

Piercing right through space

Powered only by grace

Beyond time to forever-will-be

Yet faithful as the first flake of winter

Or returning spring summer or fall

Kind Souls and butterflies

Will find their way home

Their Souls shall be reborn

ASHAY

(Marshall, 2004)

BIBLIOGRAPHY

A

Abdulhamid, Waleed [Personal Communication]. 2003.

Abernathy, Ralph David. *And the Walls Came Tumbling Down.* 1990. Harper Collins.

Abubakari, Imari. 1991. *America the Nation-State: The Politics of the United States from a State-Building Perspective.* 1st rev. ed. ed. House of Songhay.

ACIJ (African–Caribbean Institute of Jamaica) ACIJ Research Review. 1984. (1).

Ackan, C. A. 1988. *Akan Ethics.* Ghana Universities Press.

"P'Bitek, Okot." *African Religions in Western Scholarship.* Uganda Literature Bureau. 1980.

"Ani, Marimba, Yurugu." *An African-Centered Critique of European Cultural Thought & Behaviour.* Africa World Press. 1994.

Afrika, Llaila O. "African Holistic Health." *Beltsville, MD: Adesegun.* Johnson and Koram Publishers. 1989.

Agar, Michael H. 1985. *Speaking of Ethnography.* Sage Publications.

Agbasiere, Joseph Thérèse. 2000. *Women in Igbo Life and Thought.* Routledge.

Agee, Philip. 1975. *Inside the Company: CIA Diary.* Penguin Books.

Aiken, Hugh G. J. 1971. *Did Slavery Pay: Readings in the Economics of Black Slavery in the United States.* Houghton Mifflin.

Ailey, Alvin, and A. Peter Bailey. 1995. *Revelations: The Autobiography of Alvin Ailey.* Carol Publishing Group.

hooks, bell. 1981. *Ain't I a Woman?* South End Press.

Ajayi, Omofolabo S., and Yoruba Dance. 1998. *The Semiotics of Movement and Body Attitude in a Nigerian Culture.* Africa World Press.

Akagha, Fidelis S. E. 1985. *Strategies for Economic Development in Africa: Theory and Policies.* Vantage Press.

Akbar, Na'im. 1984. *Chains and Images of Psychological Slavery.* New Mind Productions.

———. *Visions for Black Men.* Visions For Black Men: Mind Productions & Associates. 1992a.

Akyeampong, Yaw A. 1980. *African Development: A Positive Direction.* Ghana Publishing Corporation.

Alexander, E. Curtis, and Adam Clayton Powell Jr. 1990. *A Black Power Political Educator.* ECA Associates.

Alford, Terry. 1986. *Prince Among Slaves: The True Story of an African Prince Sold into Slavery in the American South.* Oxford University Press.

Ali, Muhammad. 1991. "Quoted in Obadele, Imari Abubakari." In *America the Nation-State: The Politics of the United States from a State-Building Perspective.* Louisiana. 1st rev. ed., House of Songhay.

Alkalimat, Abdul & associates, eds. 1986. *Introduction to Afro-American Studies.* Twenty-First Century Books Publications.

Allen, James et al. 2000. *Without Sanctuary: Lynching Photography in America.* Twin Palms Publishers.

Allen, Norm R. Jr., ed. 1991. *African-American Humanism: An Anthology*, edited by N. Y. Buffalo. Prometheus Books.

Allen, Robert L. 1990. *Black Awakening in Capitalist America.* Africa World Press.

Allen, William Francis et al. 1995. *Slave Songs of the United States.* Dover Publications.

Allison, Dorothy. 1994. *Skin: Talking About Sex, Class and Literature.* Firebrand Books.

Allsopp, Richard, ed. 1996. *Dictionary of Caribbean English Usage.* Oxford University Press.

Al-Mansour, Khalid Abdullah Tariq. "Laws Without Justice: Do You Still Want to Be a Lawyer". SF, CA. First African Arabian Press, edited by Rae Pace *Young and Black in America.* New York: Random house. 1970.

Almond, Jocelyn, and Keith Seddon. 1999. *An Egyptian Book of Shadows: Eight Seasonal Rites of Egyptian Paganism.* HarperCollins Publishers.

Amenumey, D. E. K. 1986. *The Ewe in Precolonial Times.* Sedco Publishing Limited.

Amin, Samir. 1973. *Neo-colonialism in West Africa*, translated by Francis McDonagh. Penguin Books.

Andersen, Christopher. 1994. *Michael Jackson: Unauthorized.* Simon & Schuster.

Anderson, Claud. "Black Labor, White Wealth: The Search for Power and Economic Justice." *Edgewood, MD: Duncan & Duncan.* 1994.

Anderson, Genell. 1988. *The Call to the Ancestors.* Amar Publications.

———. 2002. *D.W. The British Museum.* London. British Museum Press.

———. 1995. *The Black Holocaust for Beginners.* Writers and Readers Publishing Inc.

Anokye, Akua-Adiki. 1980. *African Hairstyles.* Self-published.

Aptheker, Herbert. 1987. *American Slave Revolts.* Columbia University Press.

Archer, Bert. 1999. *The End of Gay (and the Death of Heterosexuality).* Doubleday Publishing.

Arendt, Hannah. 2000. "The Origins of Totalitarianism." In *The Portable Hannah Arendt,* edited by Peter B. Baeher. Penguin.

Arhin, Kwame. 1985. "Traditional Rule in Ghana." *Past & Present.* Sedco Publishing.

Arieti, Silvano. 1976. *Creativity: The Magic Synthesis.* Basic Books.

Armah, Ayi Kwei. 1979. *The Healers.* Heinemann Educational Publishers.

Armstrong, Louis. 1999. "Personal Letters." In *His Own Words, Selected Writings,* edited by Thomas Brothers *Louis Armstrong.* In Oxford University Press.

Arnason, H. H. "History of Modern Art: Painting." *Sculpture. Architecture.* Prentice Hall. 1968.

Arnold, Dorothea. 1997. *The Royal Women of Amarna: Images of Beauty from Ancient Egypt.* Metropolitan Museum of Art.

Arulogun, Alhaji Prince [Personal Communication]. 1993.

Asante, Molefe Kete. 1996. *Afrocentricity.* Africa World Press Inc.

———, Abu S. Abarry. *African Intellectual Heritage: A.*

———, Ama Mazama. 2002. *Egypt vs. Greece and the American Academy: The Debate over the Birth of Civilization.* African American Images.

Asomansing, M. Kwame [Personal Communication]. Mar. 10 2003.

Attenborough, David. 1990. "A Natural History of Animal Behaviour." *The Trials of Life.* Little, Brown & Company.

Aubin, Henry T. 2002. *The Rescue of Jerusalem: The Alliance Between Hebrews and Africans in 701 BC.* Soho Press.

Awolalu, J. "Omosade." *Yoruba Beliefs & Sacrificial Rites.* Athelia Henrietta Press Inc. Publishing In The Name Of Orunmila. 1996.

B

Backhouse, Constance. 1999. *Colour-Coded: A Legal History of Racism in Canada, 1900–1950.* University of Toronto Press.

Baehr, Peter B. 2000. *The Portable Hannah Arendt.* Penguin.

Bailey, A. Peter [Personal Communication]. Febr. 5 1993.

Bakari, Kitwana. 2002. *The Hip Hop Generation: Young Blacks and the Crisis in African-American Culture.* Basic Civitas Books.

Baker Jr., Houston A. 2001. *Turning South Again: Rethinking Modernism /Rereading Booker T. Durham.* Duke University Press.

Baldwin, James et al. 1987. *Perspectives: Angles on African Art*. The Center for African Art and Harry Abrams Inc.

Baldwin, James. 1985. *Price of the Ticket: Collected Nonfiction 1948–1985*. St. Martin's Press.

Bankie, Bankie F. 1992. *An Intra-African Diplomatic and Foreign Policy Projection for the New Situation*. HARP Publications.

———. 1995a. *Pan Africanism or Continentalism*. HARP Publications.

Barfoot, Joan. "Starch, Salt, Chocolate, Wine. 2001. In *Dropped Threads: What We Aren't Told*, edited by Carol Shields and Marjorie Anderson. Vintage Canada Edition.

Barrett, Lindon. 1999. *Blackness and Value: Seeing Double*. Cambridge University Press.

Barrett, Paul M. 2000. *The Good Black: A True Story of Race in America*. Plume Books.

Barrett, Stanley R. 1979. *Is God a Racist? The Right Wing in Canada*. Toronto University of Toronto Press, Terence. *The Art of Tahiti and the Neighbouring Society, Austral and Cook Islands*. London: Thames And Hudson.

Battiste, Marie, and James (Sa'ke'j) Youngblood Henderson. 2000. *Protecting Indigenous Knowledge and Heritage: A Global Challenge*. Purich Publishing. https://doi.org/10.59962/9781895830439.

BBC News. "South Africa's Violent Farms." UK. 2003.

Beason, Jake Patton. "Why We Lose – Why the Black Man/Woman Rests Firmly on the Bottom in America, Africa and Elsewhere: An Anthology for Black People's Cultural Survival." *Milwaukee: Col D'Var Graphics*. 1989.

Bebey, Francis. 1980. *African Music: A People's Art*, translated by Josephine Bennett. Vol. 1. Lawrence Hill and Company.

Beckles, Hilary McD. 1989. *Natural Rebels: A Social History of Enslaved Black Women in Barbados*. Rutgers University Press.

Beckwith, Carol, and Angela Fisher. 1997. *"Men of the African Ark*. Rohnert Park, CA." *Pomegranate*.

Bell, Derrick. 1992. *Faces at the Bottom of the Well: The Permanence of Racism*. Basic Books.

Ben Elvry. "Quoted in Seecharan, Clem." *India and the Shaping of the Indo-Guyanese Imagination 1890s-1920s*. Peepal Tree Press. 1993.

Ben Okri. 1992. *The Famished Road*. Vintage Books.

Ben Sidran. 1981. *Black Talk: How the Music of Black America Created a Radical Alternative to the Values of Western Literary Tradition*. Da Capo Press.

Benjamin, Daniel. Oct. 10 1988. "Shame of the Games: Ben Johnson Is Stripped of His Gold in the Olympics' Worst Drug Scandal." *Time, Toronto*.

———. Mar. 1960. "The Ghost of Marcus Garvey: Inteview with the Crusaders' Two Wives." *Ebony* 1960.

———. 1966a. "White Hopes and Other Coalitions." *Ebony Magazine.*

Bennett Jr., Lerone. 1985. *Before the Mayflower: A History of Black America.* Penguin Books.

Bergreen, Laurence. 1997. *Louis Armstrong: An Extravagant Life.* Doubleday Publishing.

———. 1981a. *Slaves Without Masters: The Free Negro in the Ante Bellum South.* Oxford University Press.

———. 1998. *Many Thousands Gone: The First Two Centuries of Slavery in North America.* Harvard University Press. https://doi.org/10.4159/9780674020825.

Bernal, Martin. "Black Athena: The AfroAsiatic Roots of Classical Civilization" Vol. 1. *The Fabrication of Ancient Greece 1788–1985.* Free Association Books. 1988.

Beshir, Mohamed Omer. 1974. *Revolution and Nationalism in the Sudan.* Rex Collings.

Bettelheim, Bruno. 1980. *Surviving and Other Essays.* Random House.

Bhebe, Nwabi. 1977. *Lobengula.* Educational Books.

Biko, Steve. 1986. *I Write What I Like.* Harper & Row.

Billard, Jules B., ed. 1978. *Ancient Egypt: Discovering Its Splendours.* National Geographic Society.

Billingsley, Andrew. 1992. *Climbing Jacob's Ladder: The Enduring Legacy of African-American Families.* Simon & Schuster.

Bing, Léon. 1991. *Do or Die.* HarperCollins Publishers.

Bingen, James. 1972. "Myth of Population Assistance in Africa." *Ufahamu.* African Activist Association III, *no. 2, Walter Rodney On Problems Of Third World Development.*

Bird, John, Lorraine Land, and Murray Macadam, eds. 2002. *Nation to Nation: Aboriginal Sovereignty and the Future of Canada.* Irwin Publishing.

Bishop, Anne. 1996. *Becoming an Ally: Breaking the Cycle of Oppression.* Fernwood Publishing.

Bittker, Boris I. 1973. *The Case for Black Reparations.* Random House.

"Mannix Daniel P. with Cowley, Malcolm." *Black Cargoes: A History of the Atlantic Slave Trade.* Viking Press. 1969.

'Black Diaspora.' *A Global Black Magazine.* Jun. 2000.

Blacking, John. 1995. *How Musical Is Man?* University of Washington Press.

Blassingame, John W. 1979. *The Slave Community: Plantation Life in the Antebellum South.* Oxford University Press.

Bleakley, Robert. 1978. *African Masks.* Thames & Hudson.

Block, N. J., and Gerald Dworkin, eds. 1976. *The IQ Controversy.* Random House.

Blyden, Edward W. 1994. *Christianity, Islam and the Negro Race.* Black Classic Press.

―――. 1966b. *Topics in West African History.* Longman Group.

―――. 1977. "Adu". "The Effects of the Atlantic Slave Trade on West Africa: A Rejoiner." *Ufahamu.* African Activist Association VII, *no. 2, African Philosophical Thoughts.*

―――, ed. "Africa Under Colonial Domination 1880–1935" Vol. VII. *General History of Africa.* Heinemann, United Nations Educational, Scientific and Cultural Organization. 1985a.

Bohannan, Paul, and Philip Curtin. 1971. *Africa and Africans.* Natural History Press.

Bois, Du, and W. E. B. 1964. *Black Reconstruction in America 1860–1880: An Essay Toward a History of the Part Which Black Folk Played in the Attempt to Reconstruct Democracy in America 1860–1880.* World Publishing company.

―――. 1990a. *The World and Africa: An Inquiry into the Part Which Africa Has Played in World History.* International Publishers.

―――. 1965. "The Souls of Black Folk." In *Three Negro Classics.* Avon Books.

Book of Sources. 1996. Temple University Press.

Bouillon, Antoine. 1998. *New African Immigration to South Africa.* The Centre for the Advanced Studies of African Society.

Boyd, Herb, and Robert L. Allen, eds. 1996. *Brotherman: The Odyssey of Black Men in America-An Anthology.* Ballantine Books.

Boykin, Keith. 1996. *One More River to Cross: Black and Gay in America.* Doubleday Publishing.

Bradford, Phillips Verner, and Harvey Blume. 1992. *Ota Benga: The Pygmy in the Zoo.* Bantam Doubleday dell Publishing.

Brain, Robert. 1979. *The Decorated Body.* Harper & Row Publishers.

Braman, Donald. 2002. "Families and Incarceration." In *Invisible Punishment: The Collateral Consequences of Mass Imprisonment,* edited by Marc Mauer and Meda Chesney-Lind. The New Press.

Branch, Taylor. 1998. *Pillar of Fire: America in the King Years 1963–65.* Simon & Schuster.

Brathwaite, Kamau. 1993. *Roots.* University of Michigan Press.

Brathwaite, Keren. 1998. "Keeping Watch over Our Children." In *Making Schools Matter: Good Teachers at Work,* edited by Satu Repo. James Publishing Lorimer & Co.

Breitman, George et al. 1988. *The Assassination of Malcolm X. Toronto.* Pathfinder Press.

Breytenbach, Breyten. 1984. *The True Confessions of an Albino Terrorist.* Faber & Faber.

Brink, William, and Louis Harris. 1967. *Black and White: A Study of U.S. Racial Attitudes Today.* Simon & Schuster.

Brizan, George. 1998. *Grenada: Island of Conflict.* Macmillan Publications.

"Broadcast on Slavery in Quebec." 2003. *Radio.* CBC.

Brodber, Erna. "Afro-Jamaican Religious and Medical Thought (with Specific Reference to the De Laurence Books)." *ACIJ (African- Caribbean Institute of Jamaica), ACIJ Research Review*, no. 1. 1984.

Bronowski, J. 1976. *The Ascent of Man*. Little Brown and Company.

Brooks, George E. 1976. "The Signatories of Saint-Louis and Gorée: Women Entrepreneurs in Eighteenth-Century. Senegal." In *Women in Africa: Studies in Social and Economic Change*, edited by Nancy J. Hafkin and Edna G. Bay. Stanford University Press.

Brown, Ursula M. "Black. 1995. "Quest for Racial Identity." *American Journal of Orthopsychiatry*. Interracial Young Adults 1: 65.

Brownlie, Ian. 1971. *Basic Documents on African Affairs*. Oxford University Press.

Burchard, Peter. 1995. *Charlotte Forten: A Black Teacher in the Civil War*. Crown Publishing Group Publishers.

Burns, Ken, and Geoffrey C. Ward. 2000. *Jazz: A History of America's Music*. Alfred A. Knopf.

Burt, Mckinley Jr. 1969. *Black Inventors of America*. National Book Company.

Bury, J. B. 1956. *A History of Greece to the Death of Alexander the Great*. Macmillan.

Busby, Margaret. 1992. *Daughters of Africa*. Jonathan Cape.

Butcher, Margaret Just. 1957. *The Negro in American Culture Based on Materials Left by Alain Locke*. Mentor Books.

Butler, Shakti. 1998. *The Way Home*. World Trust.

Bynum, Edward Bruce. 1999. *The African Unconscious: Roots of Ancient Mysticism and Modern Psychology*. Teacher's College Press, Columbia University.

C

Cabral, Amilcar. 1972. "A Brief Report on the Situation of the Struggle (January–August 1971)." *Ufahamu, no. 3* 2 (3). https://doi.org/10.5070/F723016601.

Caccia, Angela, ed. "Thirty Years of Drum: Extracts and Images – As Told by Drum's Publisher, Editors." *Contributors and Photographers, the Beat of Drum: The Story of a Magazine That Documented the Rise of Africa*. Drum Magazine. 1988.

Cahn-Lipman, Rabbi David E. 1991. *The Book of Jewish Knowledge: 613 Basic Facts About Judaism*. Jason Aronson Incorporated.

Cairncross, Larissa. 1989. *Cultural Interpreter: Training Manual*. Ministry of Citizenship.

Cameron, James. 1982. *A Time of Terror: A Survivor's Story*. Black Classic Press.

Campbell, Mavis C. 1993. *Back to Africa: George Ross and the Maroons: From Nova Scotia to Sierra Leone*. Africa World Press.

Canadian Broadcasting Corporation. Jan. 21, 2004. *News Broadcast.*

Cannizzo, Jeanne. 1989. *Into the Heart of Africa.* Royal Ontario Museum.

Carby, Hazel V. 2001. *Race Men.* Harvard University Press.

Carey, Margret. 1991. *Beads and Beadwork of West and Central Africa.* Shire Publications.

Carmichael, Stokely, and Charles V. Hamilton. 1967. *Black Power: The Politics of Liberation in America.* Random House.

Carney, Judith A. 2001. *Black Rice: The African Origins of Rice Cultivation in the Americas.* Harvard University Press.

Carpenter, Allan, and Tom Barlow. 1970. *Guyana: Enchantment of South America.* Children's Press.

Carroll, Grace. 1998. *Environmental Stress and African Americans: The Other Side of the Moon.* Praeger Publishers.

Carruthers, Jacob H. "Mdw Ntr." *Divine Speech: A Historiographical Reflection of African Deep Thought from the Time of the Pharaohs to the Present.* Karnak House. 1995.

Carson, Clayborne. 1991. *Malcolm X: The FBI File.* Ballantine Books, Random House.

Carter, Rubin. 1975. *'Hurricane', the Sixteenth Round.* Warner Communications.

Cashmore, Ellis. 1997. *The Black Culture Industry.* Routledge.

Casson, Lionel, Claiborne, Robert et al. 1977. Mysteries of the Past. American Heritage Publishing.

Celenko, Theodor, ed. 1996. Egypt in Africa. Indiana University Press.

Cell, John W. 1987. The Highest Stage of White Supremacy: The Origins of Segregation in South Africa and the American South. Cambridge University Press.

Césaire, Aimé. 1967. "Discours sur le Colonialisme." In A Dying Colonialism, edited by Franz Fanon. Grove Press.

———. 1971a. Discours sur le Colonialisme / Return to My Native Land. Présence africaine.

———. 1991a. "Les Armes Miraculeuses." In Black Writers in French: A Literary History of Negritude, edited by Lilyan Kesteloot. Howard University Press.

Chaliand, Gerard, and Jean-Pierre Rageau. The Penguin Atlas of.

"Afrikan Survivor, Quoted in Nkrumah, Kwame." Challenge of the Congo. Panaf Books. 1969.

Chamberlain, J. Edward. 1993. Come Back to Me My Language: Poetry and the West Indies. University of Illinois Press.

Chambers, Bradford, ed. 1968. Chronicles of Protest. New American Library.

Chambers, Jack. "Milestones." The Music & Times of Miles Davis. Da Capo Press. 1998.

Chapelle, Tony. Jan. 1998. "Slaves of Fashion: Black Culture Sells." Emerge Magazine.

Chase, Allan. 1980. The Legacy of Malthus: The Social Costs of the New Scientific Racism. University of Illinois Press.

Chase, Frederick Ivor. "Racism and National Consciousness." Toronto, ON: Other Eyes. 2002.

Chavis, Benjamin Interviewed in as It Happens. 2003. CBC.

Cheatwood, Kairri. 1991. "The Race: Matters Concerning Pan Afrikan History, Culture and Genocide." Sun. Native.

Cherryholmes. "Power and Criticism: Poststructural Investigations in Education." Columbia U. Teacher's College Press. 1988.

Chevannes, Barry. 1995. Rastafari: Roots and Ideology. Syracuse U Press.

———. 1995b. Don't Believe the Hype: Fighting Cultural Misinformation About African-Americans. Penguin.

———. 1999. The Color of the Future. William Morrow.

Chinweizu. 1987. Decolonising the African Mind. Pero Press.

———. 1988. Voices from Twentieth-Century Africa: Griots and Towncriers. Faber & Faber.

Chinyelu, Mamadou. 1996. Debunking the Bell Curve and Scientific Racism. Mustard Seed Press.

———, Ain Harlem't Nothin' but a Third World Country: The Global Economy. 1999. Empowerment Zones and the Colonial Status of Afrikans in America. Mustard Seed Press.

Chirimuuta, Richard, and Rosalind. 1989. Aids, Africa and Racism. Free Association Books.

Christoph, Henning, and Hans Oberlander. "Voodoo." Secret Power in Africa, translated by Anthony Wood: Taschen. 1996.

Chun, Ki-Taek. 1995. "The Myth of Asian American Success and Its Educational Ramifications." In The Asian American Educational Experience: A Source Book for Teachers and Students, edited by Don T. Nishida and Tina Yamano Nakanishi. Routledge.

Churchill, Ward, and Jim Vander Wall. 1990. The Cointelpro Papers: Documents from the FBI's Secret Wars Against Dissent in the United States. South End Press.

Cisneros, Henry, quoted in Katz, Wlliam Loren. 1995. Eyewitness: A Living Documentary of the African American Contribution to American History. Simon & Schuster.

Cissé, Abdou Rahman [Personal Communication]. Nov. 1997.

———. Febr. 2004a. Email.

Clarke, John, and Henrik. 1991. African World Revolution: Africans at the Crossroads. Africa World Press.

———. "Christopher Columbus and the Afrikan Holocaust: Slavery and the Rise of European Capitalism." New York: A & B Publishers Group. 1994a.

Cleaver, Eldridge. 1969. *Postprison Writings and Speeches*. Random House.

Cleaver, Kathleen, and George Katsiaficas, eds. 2001. *Liberation, Imagination and the Black Panther Party: A New Look at the Panthers and Their Legacy*. Routledge.

Close, Ellis. 1997. *Color-Blind: Seeing Beyond Race in a Race-Obsessed World*. HarperCollins.

Cobbinah, Jojo. 1990. *Schriesheim, Germany: Books on African Studies*. A Traveller's [Guide].

Cochran, Johnnie L. Jr. 1996. *Journey to Justice*. Ballantine Books.

Cohen, Rabbi Henry. 1968. *Justice: A Jewish View of the Black Revolution*. Union of American Hebrew Congregations.

Cole, Herbert M. I. 1985. *Am Not Myself: The Art of African Masquerade*. Museum of Cultural History.

Collins, John, and Ross Glover. 2002. *Collateral Language: A User's Guide to America's New War*. New York University Press.

Collins, Patricia Hill. 1991. *Black Feminist Thought – Knowledge, Consciousness and the Politics of Empowerment*. Routledge.

Collins, Rodnell P., and A. Peter Bailey. 1998. *The Seventh Child: A Family Memoir of Malcolm X*. Canadian Manda Group.

Colvin, Roy. 1998. *South Africa: The Essence: Who We Are & How We Got Here*. Roy Colvin.

Commager, Henry Steele. 1967. *The Struggle for Racial Equality: A Documentaty Record*. Harper & Row.

Cone, James. 1975. *God of the Oppressed*. Seabury.

Constantine-Simms, Delroy. 2000. *The Greatest Taboo: Homosexuality in the Black Community*. Alyson Books.

Cooks, Carlos. 1992. "'Strange, Isn't It?' and 'Harlem-Citadel of the Caste.'" In Harris, Robert et al. *Carlos Cooks & Black Nationalism: From Garvey to Malcolm*. The Majority Press.

Cooper, Carolyn. *Noises in the Blood: Orality, Gender and the 'Vulgar' Body of Jamaican Popular Culture*. Caribbean: Macmillan. 1993.

Costa, E. V., and Emilia Viotti. 1994. *Crowns of Glory, Tears of Blood: The Demerara Slave Rebellion of 1823*. Oxford University Press. https://doi.org/10.1093/oso/9780195082982.001.0001.

Costello, Mark, and David Foster Wallace. 1990. *Signifying Rappers*. Ecco Press.

Cougle, R. J. "Not by Choice: The True Story of the French–English Struggle." *Self-Published, P.O. Box 4808, Station A*. NB. 1989.

Courtney-Clarke, Margaret. Ndebele. 1986. *The Art of an African Tribe*. Rizzoli International Publications.

Cove, John J. 1995. *What the Bones Say: Tasmanian Aborigines, Science, and Domination.* Carleton University Press. https://doi.org/10.1515/9780773581456.

Cowan, L. Gray et al. 1966. *Education and Nation-Building in Africa.* Praeger.

Cox, Oliver C. 1970. *Caste, Class & Race: A Study in Social Dynamics.* Monthly Review Press.

Cresswell, John W. 1998. *Qualitative Inquiry and Research Design: Choosing Among Five Traditions.* Sage Publications.

Crockett, George. "Quoted in Foner, Philip S." *The Black Panthers Speak.* Da Capo Press. 1995.

Crouch, Stanley. 1995. *The All-American Skin Game, or the Decoy of Race: The Long and the Short of It 1990–1994.* Pantheon Books.

———. 2000a. "What's New? The Truth, as Usual." In *Police Brutality: An Anthology,* edited by Jill Nelson. W. W. Norton and Company.

Cruse, Harold. 1967. *The Crisis of the Negro Intellectual.* William Morrow and Company Incorporated.

Cunard, Nancy. 1970. *Negro: An Anthology.* Frederick Ungar Publishing.

D

Dalamba, Yolisa. 2004. *'Roundtable Discussion on TRC and South Africa.' Counterspin.* Toronto: CBC TV Program.

Daly, Vere T. 1993. *A Short History of the Guyanese People.* Macmillan Press.

Dandy, Evelyn. 1991. *Black Communications: Breaking Down the Barriers.* African American Images.

Daniels, Douglas Henry. "Pioneer Urbanites: A Social and Cultural History of Black San Francisco." *Los Angelos.* University of California Press. 1990.

Danns, George K. 1982. *Domination and Power in Guyana: A Study in a Third World Context.* Transaction Books.

Darden, Christopher, with Walter, Jess. 1996. In *Contempt.* HarperCollins Publishers.

Dates, Jeannette, and William Howard Barlow, eds. 1990. *Split Image: African Americans in Mass Media.* Howard University Press.

David, Evans, Peter Holmes, and Ibbo Mandaza. 1999. *SADC: The Cost of Non- Integration.* SAPES Books.

David, Rosalie. 2002. *Religion and Magic in Ancient Egypt.* Penguin Books.

Davies, Omar. "Reggae and Our National Identity: The Forgotten Contribution of Peter Tosh." *Mona, JA.* University of the West Indies. 2000, et al., eds. *The Struggle for South Africa: A Reference Guide to Movements, Organizations and Institutions Volume Two.* London: Zed Books, 1984.

Davis, Angela Y. 1999. "Prison Abolition." In *Black Genius: African American Solutions to African American Problems*, edited by Walter Mosley et al. W. W. Norton and Company.

———. *Race, Gender, and Prison History: From the Convict Lease.*

———. 1970. *The Problem of Slavery in Western Culture.* Cornell University Press.

Davis, N. E. 1990. *A History of Southern Africa.* Longman.

Davis, Natalie Zemon. 2000. *Slaves on Screen: Film and Historical Vision.* Random House.

Davis, Wade. 1997. *The Serpent and the Rainbow.* Simon & Schuster.

De Jong, Louis. 2000. "Jews and Non-Jews in Nazi-Occupied Holland." In Baehr, Peter B. *The Portable Hannah Arendt.* Penguin.

De Negri, Eve. 1976. "Nigerian Body Adornment." *Nigeria Magazine.* Lagos.

De Villiers, Marq, and Sheila Hirtle. 1997. Into Africa: A Journey Through the Ancient Empires. Key Porter Books.

Deagan, Kathleen, and Darcie MacMahon. 1995. Fort Mose: Colonial America's Black Fortress of Freedom. University Press of Florida.

Debrunner, Hans Werner. 1979. Presence and Prestige: Afrikans in Europe – A History of Africans in Europe Before 1918. Basler Afrika Bibliographien.

Decalo, Samuel. 1976. Coups and Army Rule in Africa: Studies in Military Style. Yale University Press.

Degler, Carl N. 1971. Neither Black nor White: Slavery and Race Relations in Brazil and the United States. Collier-Macmillan Limited.

DeGruy-Leary, Joy. "Quoted in Parks, Brian." Headin' South. The Village Voice: Theater. New York. 2001.

———. 1995c. Drop Out or Push Out? The Dynamics of Black Students Disengagement from School. Ministry of Education.

———. "Sefa." Anti-Racism Education. Fernwood Publishing. 1996.

Dekenu-Ariantch. 2002. "Facing the Challenges of Black Manhood." African Business & Culture 2 (17).

Del Jones. 1993. Culture Bandits, II. (Annihilation of Afrikan Images). Hikeka Press.

Delany, Martin R. 1993. The Condition Elevation Emigration and Destiny of the Colored People of the United States. Black Classic Press.

Depestre, René. 1967. Un Arc-En-Ciel pour l'Occident Chrétien: Poème – Mystère Vaudou. Présence africaine.

Des Origines, À. 1800; Tome II: De 1800 À Nos Jours. "Deschamps." Histoire Générale de L'Afrique Noire: De Madagascar et des Archipels, edited by Hubert. Tome I. Presses Universitaires de France, 1970.

Diasporas. 1995. Penguin.

Diawara, and Manthia. 2000. In Search of Africa. Harvard University Press.

Diederich, Bernard & Burt, Ala. Papa Doc: The Truth About Haiti Today. 1970. Avon Books.

Diop, Babacar. 1990. Le Thème de la Malédiction Des Noirs [the Theme of the Black Curse] in Méditerranéen l'Antiquité. Terebi.

Diop, Cheikh Anta. 1974. The African Origin of Civilization: Myth or Reality. Lawrence Hill and Company.

———. 1991b. Civilization or Barbarism. Lawrence Hill Books.

———. 1991c. L'Importance de L'egypte dans les Civilisations Africaines, Diaspora africaine. Hiver.

Diop-Maes, Louise Marie. 1996. Afrique Noire: Démographie, Sol et Histoire; une Analyse Pluridisciplinaire et Critique. Présence africaine.

Dooms, Patrick. 2001. "Uniting Africa Through Using Super-Languages: Can African Unity Be Encouraged by Harmonizing Languages?" City Press. Johannesburg.

Douglass, Frederick. 1992. "Our Coloured Sisters, the North Star, November 16, 1849." In Frederick Douglass on Women's Rights, edited by Philip S. Foner. Da Capo Press.

Dover, Cedric. 1969. American Negro Art. New York Graphic Society.

Dow, George Francis. 1980. Slave Ships & Slaving. Coles Publishing Co.

Downs, Roger M., and David Stea. 1977. Maps in Minds: Reflections on Cognitive Mapping. Harper & Row.

Drake, St. 1969. "Clair". "Hide My Face? On Pan-Africanism and Negritude". In The Making of Black America. Vol. 1 - the Origins of Black Americans. TE: Kingsport Press, edited by August Meier and Elliot Rudwick.

Drew, Benjamin. 1981. The Refugee: Or the Narratives of Fugitive Slaves in Canada Related by Themselves, with an Account of the History and Condition of the Coloured Population of Upper Canada. Coles Publishing Co.

Du Bois, Claude, ed. 1982. Petit Larousse Illustré. Paris.

Duberman, Martin. 1964. In White America: From Slave Ship to Ghetto Riots – What It Has Meant, for Two Centuries, to Be Black. Signet.

Duchet-Suchaux, G., and M. Guide Chronologique. 1993. De l'Histoire du Monde. Hachette.

Duerden, Dennis. 1974. African Art: An Introduction. Hamlyn Publishing.

Duesberg, Peter H. 1996. Inventing the Aids Virus. Regnery Publishing Incorporated.

Duffield, Mark. 2001. Global Governance and the New Wars. St. Martin's Press.

Dungia, Emmanuel. 1993. Mobutu et l'Argent du Zaire: Révélations d'un Diplomate, Ex-Agent des Services Secrets. L'Harmattan.

E

Edwards, Harry. 1969. *The Revolt of the Black Athlete*. The Free Press.

Egharevba, Jacob. 1968. *A Short History of Benin*. Ibadan University Press.

Eglash, Ron. 1999. *African Fractals: Modern Computing and Indigenous Design*. Rutgers University Press.

Ejeckam, Gershon C. 1977. "African Medical Theory and Practices." *Ufahamu, no. 2, The Interdisciplinary Issue* 7 (3). https://doi.org/10.5070/F773017409.

El Mahdy, Christine. 1989. *Mummies, Myth and Magic*. Thames & Hudson.

El Mallakh, Kamal, and Arnold C. Brackman. 1978. *The Gold of Tutankhamen*. Newsweek Books.

Eliade, Mircea, P. Couliano Ioan, and Hilary Wiesner. 2000. *The HarperCollins Concise Guide to World Religions*. HarperCollins Publishers.

Elkins, Stanley M. 1976. *Slavery: A Problem in American Institutional and Intellectual Life*. University of Chicago Press.

Ellert, H. 1986. "The Material Culture of Zimbabwe." *Zimbabwe*. Longman.

Ellul, Jacques. 1973. *Propaganda: The Formation of Men's Attitudes*. Alfred A. Knoph.

Eltis, D. 1983. "Free and Coerced Migrations: Some Comparisons". Bloomington, IN. *American Historical Review* 88.

Emerson, Rupert. 1963. "Pan-Africanism." In *Africa and World Order*, edited by Norman J. Padelford and Rupert Emerson. Praeger.

"Green, Rayna with Fernandez, Melanie." 1999. In *The Encyclopaedia of the First Peoples of North America*. Toronto: Douglas & McIntyre.

Ephraim-Donkor, Anthony. 1997. *African Spirituality: On Becoming Ancestors*. African World Press.

Eppinga, Jane. 1996. *Henry Ossian Flipper: West Point's First Black Graduate*. Republic of Texas Press.

Equiano, Olaudah. 1999. *The Interesting Narrative and Other Writings*. Penguin Books.

Ernst, Robert T., and Lawrence Hugg. 1976. "Black America." *Geographical Perspectives*. Doubleday Publishing.

Essien-Udom, E. U. 1962. *Black Nationalism: A Search for an Identity in America*. University of Chicago Press.

Eweka, Prince Ena Basimi. 1989. *The Benin Monarchy: Origin and Development*. Bendel Newspapers Company.

Eze, Chukwudi, ed. 2001. *African Philosophy: An Anthology*. Blackwell Publishing.

F

Fabian, Johannes. 2001. *Anthropology with an Attitude: Critical Essays (Cultural Memory in the Present)*. Stanford University Press.

Fafunwa, A. Babs, and J. U. Aisiku, eds. 1982. *Education in Africa: A Comparative Survey*. George Allen & Unwin Publishers.

Falconbridge, Dr. Alexander. "Quoted in Dow, George Francis." *Slave Ships & Slaving*. Coles Publishing Co. 1980.

Fanon, Franz. 1967. *Black Skin, White Masks*. Grove Press.

———. 1967. *A Dying Colonialism*. Grove Press.

———. 1968a. *The Wretched of the Earth*. Random House.

Farmer, Paul. 2003. *The Uses of Haiti*. Common Courage Press.

Fatton, Robert Jr. 1986. *Black Consciousness in South Africa: The Dialectics of Ideological Resistance to White Supremacy*. State University of New York Press.

Fatunmbi, Awo Falokun. 1993. *Esu-Elegba, Ifa and the Divine Messenger*. Self-published.

FDC. 1981. *The Nucleus: Maiden Catalogue of Works in Nigeria's National Gallery of Modern Art*. Federal Department of Culture.

Feinstein, Elaine. 1985. *Bessie Smith: Empress of the Blues*. Penguin Books.

Feuerlicht, Roberta Strauss. 1983. *The Fate of the Jews: A People Torn Between Israeli Power and Jewish Ethics*. Times Books.

Fields, Mamie Garvin, and Karen Fields. 1985. *Lemon Swamp and Other Places: A Carolina Memoir*. Collier-Macmillan Publishers.

FT. 1980. "Nigeria: Twenty Years of Independence." Spectrum Books.

Finch, Charles S., 3rd, and M. D. 1992. *Africa and the Birth of Science and Technology: A Brief Overview*. Khenti Publications.

———. 1999. *Echoes of the Old Darkland: Themes from the African Eden*. Khenti Inc.

Finkelstein, Norman G. 2000. *The Holocaust Industry: Reflections on the Exploitation of Jewish Suffering*. Verso.

Finkenstaedt, Rose L. H. 1994. *Face to Face, Blacks in America: White Perceptions and Black Realities*. William Morrow and Company.

Floyd, Samuel A. Jr. 1996. *The Power of Black Music: Interpreting Its History from Africa to the United States*. Oxford University Press.

Fluehr-Lobban, Carolyn et al. "Tribe: A Sociopolitical Analysis." *Ufahamu* VII (1), In *Memoriam, Henry B. Masauko Chipembere1930-1975: Tributes and Articles by Mtewa & Phillips*. 1976. African Activist Association.

———, ed. "Paul Robeson Speaks." *Writings Speeches Interviews 1918–1974*. Secausus. Citadel Press. 1978.

———. 1992. *Frederick Douglass on Women's Rights*. Da Capo Press.

———, ed. 1986. *The Black Panthers Speak*. Da Capo Press. *Heart Drum: Spirit Possession in the Garifuna Communities of Belize*. Belize: Cubola Productions.

Foster, Michelle. 1997. *Black Teachers on Teaching*. W.W. Norton & Company.

Foster, Pamela E. "My Country, Too: The Other Black Music." *Nashville, TN: Publishers Graphics*. 2000.

Fosu, Kojo. 1993. *20th Century Art of Africa*. rev. ed. ed. Accra, Ghana: Artists Alliance.

Foucault, Michel. 1986. *The History of Sexuality: An Introduction*, translated by Robert Hurley. Vol. 1. Random House.

Fox, Robert Elliot. 1997. "Becoming Post White." In *Multicultural America: Essays on Cultural Wars and Cultural Peace*, edited by Ismael Reed. Penguin.

"Guerrero, Ed." *Framing Blackness: The African American Image on Film*. Temple U Press. 1993.

Frankfort, Henri. 2000. *Ancient Egyptian Religion: An Interpretation*. Dover Publications.

Franklin, Harold. 1967. *The Illustrated Library of the World and Its Peoples: Africa North and East*. Vol. 2. Greystone Press.

Franklin, John. 1968. *Hope, Color and Race*. Houghton Mifflin Company.

Frazier, E. Franklin. 1974. *The Negro Church in America*. Schocken Books.

Frazier, Thomas R., ed. 1970. *Afro-American History: Primary Sources*. Harcourt, Brace & World.

Frederikse, Julie. "None but Ourselves: Masses vs Media in the Making of Zimbabwe." *Johannesburg, SA*. Ravan Press. 1982.

Fredrickson, George M. 1971. *The Black Image in the White Mind*. Wesleyan University Press.

———. 1982a. *White Supremacy: A Comparative Study in American & South African History*. Oxford University Press.

Freire, Paolo. 1968. *Pedagogy of the Oppressed*, translated by Myra Bergman Ramos. Herder & Herder.

Freke, Timothy, and Peter Gandy. "The Hermetica: The Lost Wisdom of the Pharaohs." *New York: P.* Tarcher. 1999.

Fryer, Peter. 1984. *Staying Power: The History of Black People in Britain*. Pluto Press.

Fuller, Neely Jr. 2002. "Quoted in Dekenu-Ariantch." *Afrikan Business & Culture* 2 (17).

Furlong, David. 1997. *The Keys to the Temple: Unravel the Mysteries of the Ancient World*. Piatkus Publishers.

Futrell, Jon. 1982. *The Illustrated Encyclopedia of Black Music*. Harmony Books.

G

Gadalla, Moustafa. 1999. *Exiled Egyptians: The Heart of Africa*. Tehuti Research Foundation.

Galembo, Phyllis. 1993. *Divine Inspiration: From Benin to Bahia*. University of New Mexico Press.

Gandhi, M. K. 1993. "Quoted." In *Reader*, edited by Rudrangshu Mukherjee *The Penguin Gandhi*. Penguin Books.

Gandhi, Mohandas. "Quoted in Powell, Rev. Raphael P." *The Invisible Image Uprooted: A Mystery Revealed*. Philemon Co. 1979.

Ganns, George K. 1982. *Domination and Power in Guyana: A Study of the Police in a Third World Context*. Transaction Books.

Gara, Larry. 1969. "Quoted." In *The Making of Black America*. Vol. 1 - the Origins of Black Americans*. TE: Kingsport Press, edited by August Meier and Elliot Rudwick.

Garlake, Peter. 1985. *Great Zimbabwe Described and Explained*. Zimbabwe Publishing House.

———. 1987a. *The Painted Caves: An Introduction to the Prehistoric Art of Zimbabwe*. Modus Publications.

Garland, and Phyl. 1971. *The Sound of Soul: The Story of Black Music*. Pocket Books.

Garrison, William Lloyd. Jan. 8, 1831. "Editorial in the Liberator." In *Chronicles of Protest*, edited by Bradford Chambers, 1968. Mentor Books.

Garvey, Amy Jacques. "Quoted in Bennet Jr. Lerone." *The Ghost of Marcus Garvey: Interviews with the Crusader's Two Wives*. Ebony. 1960.

———. 1987b. *The Philosophy and Opinions of Marcus Garvey: Or, Africa for the Africans*. The Majority Press.

Gates, Henry Louis Jr. 2000. "Foreword." In Constantine-Simms. *Delroy. The Greatest Taboo: Homosexuality in the Black Community*. Alyson Books.

Gaye, Pape Amadou. 1980. *Practical Course in Wolof/Cours Pratique de Wolof: An Audio-Aural Approach, Student's Manuel* edited by United States Peace Corps. Regional Training Resources Office.

Genovese, Eugene D., and Jordan Roll. 1999. *Roll: The World the Slaves Made*. Random House, Nelson. *Hip Hop America*. New York: Penguin Books.

"Early." 1993. In *Lure and Loathing: Essays on Race, Identity and the Ambivalence of Assimilation*, edited by Gerald. Penguin.

Gerima, Haile. 1993. *Sankofa*. Mypheduh Films.

Gibson, Ashton, with Lewis, Charles. 1985. *A Light in the Dark Tunnel: Ten Years of West Indian Concern and Caribbean House*. Centre for Caribbean Studies.

Gilman, Sander L. 2000. *Smart Jews: The Construction of the Image of Jewish Intelligence*. Lincoln University of Nebraska Press. *Between Camps: Nations, Cultures, and the Allure of Race*. Penguin Books.

Ginsburg, Ralph. 1988. *100 Years of Lynching*. Black Classic Press.

Gioseffi, Daniela. 1997. "Is There a Renaissance in Italian American Literature?" In Reed. *Ismael. Multicultural America:Essays on Cultural Wars and Cultural Peace*. Penguin.

Gisselquist, David, John J. Potterat, Stuart Brody, and Francois Vachon. 2003. "Let It Be Sexual: How Health Care Transmission of Aids in Africa Was Ignored." *International Journal of STD & AIDS* 14 (3): 148–61. https://doi.org/10.1258/095646203762869151.

Gladwell, Malcolm. 2000. *The Tipping Point: How Little Things Can Make a Big Difference*. Little, Brown & Company.

Glissant, Edouard. 1992. *Caribbean Discourse: Selected Essays*, translated by Michael J. Dash. University Press of Virginia.

Gobineau, De, and J. Arthur. 2002. "Inequality of the Human Races." In *Black Canadians: History, Experiences, Social Conditions*, edited by Joseph Mensah. Fernwood Publishing.

Godfrey, Dave. 1971. "Friday Afternoon at the Iowa City Airport." In *Power Corrupted: The October Crisis and the Repression of Quebec*, edited by Abraham Rothstein. New Press.

Goffman, Irving. 1959. *The Presentation of Self in Everyday Life*. Doubleday Anchor Books.

Goldenberg, Tia. Dec. 10 2003. *National Post*.

Gopnik, Alison et al. 1999. *The Scientist in the Crib: Minds, Brains and How Children Learn*. William Morrow and Company.

Gordon, Albert F., and Leonard Kahan. 1976. *The Tribal Bead: A Handbook of African Trade Beads*. Tribal Arts Gallery.

Gordon, Beverly. 1994. "African-American Cultural Knowledge and Liberatory Education: Dilemmas, Problems, and Potentials in a Postmodern American Society." In *Too Much Schooling, Too Little Education: A Paradox of Black Life in White Societies*, edited by Mwalimu J. Shujaa. Africa World Press.

Gosine, Mahin. 1986. *East Indians and Black Power in the Caribbean: TheCase of Trinidad*. Africana Research Publications.

Gottlieb, Karla. 2000. *The Mother of Us All: A History of Queen Nanny, Leader of the Winward Jamaican Maroons*. Africa World Press.

Gould, Stephen Jay. 1981. *Mismeasure of Man*. W.W. Norton & Company.

Government of Ontario. 1994. *Racism Behind Bars: The Treatment of Black and Other Racial Minority Prisoners in Ontario Prisons*. Queen's Printer.

Grégoire, Henri. 1996. *On the Cultural Achievement of Negroes*, translated by Cassirer and Jean-Francois Brière. University of Massachusetts Press.

Grimal, Nicholas. 1994. *A History of Ancient Egypt*, translated by Ian Shaw. Blackwell Publishing.

Grovogui, Siba. "N'Zatioula." *Sovereigns, Quasi Sovereigns and Africans: Race and Self-Determination in International Law*. Vol. 3, Borderlines. University of Minnesota Press. 1996.

Gubar, Susan. 1997. *Race Changes: White Skin, Black Face in American Culture*. Oxford University Press.

Guillermoprieto, Alma. 1991. *Samba*. Random House.

Gunst, Laurie. "Born Fi." *Dead: A Journey Through the Jamaican Posse Underworld*. Henry Holt and Company. 1995.

Gunther, Hans F. K. 1992. *The Racial Elements of European History*, translated by G. C. Wheeler. Methuen and Company.

Gunther, John. Apr. 1959. *The Drums of History: Africa Past, Present, Prophecy*. Holiday, Magazine.

Gurdjieff. Cited in Moore, James. 1991. *Gurdjieff: A Biography*. Element Books.

Gwaltney, John Langston. 1980. *Drylongso: A Self-Portrait of Black America*. Random House.

H

Habtu, Alem, and Agbeyegbe. "Yemi." *Africa Before the White Man*. Queens College of The City University of New York. 1971.

Hacker, Andrew. 1992. *Two Nations: Black and White, Separate, Hostile, Unequal*. Macmillan.

Hafkin, Nancy J., and Edna G. Bay, eds. 1976. *Women in Africa: Studies in Social and Economic Change*. Stanford University Press.

Hall, David. 1995. "Living in Hell: America the Unprincipled Place." In *Living in Hell: The Dilemma of African-American Survival*, edited by Mose Pleasure Jr. and Fred C. Lofton. Zondervan Publishing Hose.

Hall, James. 1994. *Sangoma: My Odyssey into the Spirit World of Africa*. G. P. Putnam's Sons.

Hall-Alleyne, Beverley. 1984. "Creole Languages." *ACIJ. Research Reviews*. African-Caribbean Institute of Jamaica 1.

Hansberry, Lorraine. 1964. *The Movement: Documentary of a Struggle for Equality*. Simon & Schuster.

———. "To Be Young, Gifted and Black." *Adapted by Robert Nemiroff*. New American Library. 1970a.

Harding, Vincent. 1969. "Religion and Resistance Among Ante Bellum Negroes." In *The Making of Black America – The Origins of Black Americans*. Vol. 1. TE: Kingsport Press, edited by August Meier and Elliot Rudwick.

Hare, Nathan. 1991. *The Black Anglo-Saxons*. Third World Press.

"Champions of the Human Rights Struggle: Gil Noble and una Mulzac – Third Annual Grass-Roots Tribute." *Harlem*. New Afrikan People's Organization. 1987.

Harper, Philip Brian. "Are We Not Men?." *Masculine Anxiety & the Problem of African-American Identity.* Oxford University Press. 1996.

Harris, Robert, Nyota, and Grandassa, eds. 1992. *Carlos Cooks and Black Nationalism: From Garvey to Malcolm.* The Majority Press.

Harris, Joseph E., ed. 1982. *Global Dimensions of the African Diaspora.* Howard University Press.

———. 1987. *Africans and Their History.* Penguin Books.

Harris, Judith Rich. 1998. *The Nurture Assumption: Why Children Turn Out the Way They Do.* The Free Press.

Harris, Rendel. 1927. *More About Egypt and Its Colonies.* W. Heffer & Sons.

———. 1927. *Traces of Ancient Egypt in the Mediterranean.* W. Heffer & Sons.

Hashim, Muhammad Hammad Jalal. "Ahmad." *To Be or Not to Be: Sudan at Crossroads.* Beacon Press House. 2004.

Haskins, James. 1987. *Black Dance in America: A History Through Its People.* HarperCollins Publishers.

Haskins, James, and Kathleen Benson. 1999. *Bound for America: The Forced Migration of Africans to the New World.* Morrow Junior Books.

Haskins, Jim. 1977. *The Cotton Club: A Pictorial and Social History of the Most Famous Symbol of the Jazz Era.* Random House.

Hawthorne, Peter. Jan. 8 2000. "The Trouble with Sorry." *Time Europe Magazine.*

Hedges, Warren. 1997. "If Uncle Tom Is White, Should We Call Him 'Auntie': Race and Sexuality in Postbellum U.S. Fiction." In *Whiteness: A Critical Reader*, edited by Mike Hill. New York University Press.

Heinrich, Jeff. Mar. 21 2004. "Racial Slurs: Words People Use to Hurt." *Therapeutic Gazette*, Sunday.

Henry, Annette. 1998. *Taking Back Control: African Canadian Women Teachers' Lives and Practice.* State University of New York Press.

Herbert, Eugenia W. 1993. *Iron, Gender and Power: Rituals of Transformation in African Societies.* Indiana University Press.

Hernton, Calvin C. 1987. *The Sexual Mountain and Black Women Writers: Adventures in Sex, Literature, and Real Life.* Doubleday Publishing.

Herrnstein, Richard, and Charles Murray. 1994. *The Bell Curve: Intelligence and Class Structure in American Life.* The Free Press.

Higgins, Chester Jr. "In the Spirit of Abraham." *Common Quest: The Magazine of Black Jewish Relations.* 1998.

Higgins, Godrey Esq. "Anacalypsis: An Attempt to Draw Aside the Veil of Saitic Isis or an Inquiry into the Origin of Languages Nations and Religions." *Brooklyn, NY: A & B Publishers.* 1992.

High, Joe. 1988. "Quoted." In *Bullwhip Days: The Slaves Remember-An Oral History*, edited by James Mellon. Avon Books.

Hill, Daniel G. "The Freedom-Seekers: Blacks in Early Canada." *Agincourt: The Book Society of Canada*. 1981.

Hill, Lawrence. 2001a. *Black Berry, Sweet Juice: On Being Black and White in Canada*. Harper Flamingo.

Hill, Mike, ed. 1997. *Whiteness: A Critical Reader*. New York University Press.

Hill, Robert A. 2001b. *Dread History: Leonard P. Howell and Millenarian Visions in the Early Rastafarian Religion*. Research Associates School Times Publications.

———. 1991d. "Waset, the Eye of Ra and the Abode of Maat: The Pinnacle of Black Leadership in the Ancient World." In *Egypt Revisited*, edited by Ivan Van Sertima. Transaction Publishers.

Hilliard, Asa G., 3rd. 1995. *The Maroon Within Us: Selected Essays on African American Community Socialization*. Black Classic Press.

Hinsbruner, Jay. 1996. *Not of Pure Blood: The Free People of Color and Racial Prejudice in Nineteenth-Century Puerto Rico*. Duke University Press.

Hobson, Christine. 2000. *The World of the Pharoahs: A Complete Guide to Ancient Egypt*. Thames & Hudson Incorporated.

Hochschild, Adam. 1998. *King Leopold's Ghost*. Houghton Mifflin.

Hoffman, Donald D. 1998. "Visual Intelligence: How We Create What We." *Southeastern Europe*. W. W. Norton Company.

Hoffman, Stanley. 1963. "In Search of a Thread: The U.N. In the Congo Labyrinth." In *Africa and World Order*, edited by Norman J. Padelford and Rupert Emerson. Praeger.

Hogben, L., and Frederick Bodmer. 1944. *The Loom of Language*. W.W. Norton & Company.

———. 1995d. *Art on My Mind: Visual Politics*. The New Press.

———. 1995e. *Killing Rage: Ending Racism*. Henry Holt and Company.

———. 1996. *Reel to Real: Race, Sex, and Class at the Movies*. Routledge.

———. 1997. *The African Heritage of American English*. Indiana University Press.

———. 2003a. *Rock My Soul: Black People and Self-Esteem*. Atria Books.

———. 2003b. *Teaching Community: A Pedagogy of Hope*. Routledge.

Hooper, Edward. 2000. *The River: A Journey to the Source of Hiv and Aids*. Little, Brown and Company.

Hornblum, Allen M. 1998. *Acres of Skin: Human Experiments at Holmesburg Prison – A True Story of Abuse and Exploitation in the Name of Medical Science*. Routledge.

Horne, Gerald. 2001. *From the Barrel of a Gun: The United States and the War Against Zimbabwe, 1965–1980*. University of North Carolina Press.

Horowitz, Leonard G. 1997. *Emerging Viruses: Aids and Ebola: Nature, Accident or Intentional?* Tetrahedron Publishing Group.

Houghton Mifflin. 1992. *The American Heritage Dictionary of the English Language.* Third Edition.

Howard, Jeffrey, and Ray Hammond. 1985. *Rumors of Inferiority.* New Republic.

Huet, Jean-Christophe. 1994. *Villages Perchés des Dogon du Mali: Habitat, Espace et Société.* L'Harmattan.

Hughes, Langston. 1974. *Selected Poems Langston Hughes.* Random House.

Hughes, William. 1992. *Critical Thinking: An Introduction to the Basic Skills.* Broadview Press.

Hurmence, Belinda, ed. 1990. *Before Freedom, When I Just Can Remember: Twenty-Seven Oral Histories of Former South Carolina Slaves.* John F. Blair.

Hutchinson, Earl Ofari. 2000. "My Gay Problem, Your Black Problem." In *The Greatest Taboo: Homosexuality in the Black Community,* edited by Delroy Constantine-Simms. Alyson Books.

Hutchinson, George. 1997. *The Harlem Renaissance in Black and White.* Harvard University Press.

I

IDAF (International Defence and Aid Fund.) *Apartheid: The Facts. London: Canon Collins House.* 1983.

IFC (International Festival Committee), and *FESTAC.* 1977. *chapters 77. London: Africa Journal Limited.*

Ignatiev, Noel. 1995. *How the Irish Became White.* Routledge.

Ingham, Kenneth. 1967. *A History of East Africa.* rev. ed. Praeger Publishers.

Ipam, Edicef. 1970. *Histoire: Le Monde, Due 17e Siècle au Début du 19e Siècle.*

Iroko, A. Félix. 1994. *Une Histoire des Hommes et des Moustiques en Afrique.* Editions Harmattan.

J

Jackson, George. 1990. *Soledad Brother: The Prison Letters of George Jackson.* Bantam Press.

———. 1990b. *Blood in My Eye.* Black Classic Press.

———. 1970. *Introduction to African Civilizations.* Citadel Press.

Jacobs, Harriet J. 2000. "Quoted." In *Incidents in the Life of a Slave Girl, Written by Herself*, edited by Maria Child. Harvard University Press.

Jacobson, Matthew Frye. 2000. *Whiteness of a Different Color: European Immigrants and the Alchemy of Race*. Harvard University Press.

———. 1983. *Walter Rodney and the Question of Power*. Race Today Publications.

———. 1989. *The Black Jacobins: Toussaint L'Ouverture and the San Domingo Revolution*. Random House.

——— et al. 1980. *Fighting Racism in World War II: Coverage on the Black Struggle from the Socialist Workers Party, 1939–1945*. Monad Press.

———. 1995. *Seeing Ourselves: Exploring Race, Ethnicity and Culture*. Thompson Educational Publishing.

James, Etta, and David Ritz. 1995. *Rage to Survive*. Villard Books.

James, Joy, and T. Denean Sharpley-Whiting. 2000. *The Black Feminist Reader*. Blackwell Publishing.

Jennings, Christian. "Across the Red River": Rwanda. *Burundi & the Heart of Darkness*. Orion Books. 2000.

Jibunoh, Elizabeth [Personal Communication]. 1990.

Jim, Bailey. 1988. "Letting the Genie out of the Bottle." In *Thirty Years of Drum: Extracts and Images – As Told by Drum's Publisher, Editors, Contributors and Photographers, The Beat of Drum: The Story of a Magazine That Documented the Rise of Africa*, edited by Angela Caccia. Drum Magazine.

Johnson, Charles S. 1969. *Shadow of the Plantation*. University of Chicago Press.

Johnson, Howard. 1991. *The Bahamas in Slavery and Freedom*. Ian Randle Publishers.

Johnson, John William, Thomas A. Hale, and Stephen Belcher, eds. 1997. *Oral Epics from Africa: Vibrant Voices from a Vast Continent*. Indiana University Press. https://doi.org/10.2979/2535.0.

Johnson, Ken [Personal Communication]. Dec. 10 2003.

Johnson, Leola, and David Roediger. 1997. "Hertz Don't It? Becoming Colorless and Staying Black in the Crossover of O. J. Simpson." In *Birth of a Nation'hood: Gaze, Script, and Spectacle in the O. J. Simpson Case*, edited by Toni Morrison and Claudia Brodsky. Pantheon Books.

Jones, James H. 1982. *Bad Blood: The Tuskegee Syphilis Experiment – A Tragedy of Race and Medicine*. Collier-Macmillan.

Jones, Leroi. 1963. *Blues People: The Negro Experience in White America and the Music That Developed from It*. Morrow Quill Paperbacks.

Jourdan, Rober. 1997. *Music, the Brain and Ecstasy: How Music Captures Our Imagination*. Avon Books.

K

Kabou, Axelle. 1991. *Et Si l'Afrique Refusait le Développement?* Editions Harmattan.

Kane, Boubacar, and Rama Carrie-Sembène. "Manuel De Conversation / Handbook." *Wolof/Français/Anglais.* Librairie Sankoré. 1978.

Kashmeri, Zuhair. 1991. *The Gulf Within: Canadian Arabs, Racism and the Gulf War.* Lorimer and Co.

Katz, Wlliam Loren, ed. 1995. *Eyewitness: A Living Documentary of the African American Contribution to American History.* Simon & Schuster.

Kecskési, Maria. 1987. *African Masterpieces and Selected Works from Munich: The Staatliches Museum Fur Volkerkunde.* The Center for African Art.

Kelman, Suanne. 1993. *All in the Family: A Cultural History of Family Life.* Penguin, 1998.

Kennedy, Paul. *Preparing for the Twenty-First Century.* Random House.

Kenyatta, Jomo. 1965. *Facing Mt. Kenya.* Random House.

Kesteloot, Lilyan. 1991. *Black Writers in French: A Literary History of Negritude*, translated by Ellen Conroy Kennedy. Howard University Press.

Key, Wilson Bryan. 1981. *Subliminal Seduction: Ad Media's Manipulation of a Not so Innocent America.* Signet Books.

———. 2001a. *Jakaranda Time: An Investigator's View of South Africa's Truth and Reconciliation Commission.* Garib Communications.

———. "Interrogating the Truth: From the Destruction of Khoisan Culture to Apartheid." *Oral Presentation.* Senate Chambers, York University. 2003.

———. *Beyond the Truth Commission: Interrogating South Africa's Original Sin.*" presentation made at York University and World Social Forum. Mar. 22, 2003c.

King, Martin Luther Jr. 1964. *Stride Toward Freedom: The Montgomery Story – Birth of Successful Non-Violent Resistance.* Harper & Row.

King, Norman, ed. 1987. *Oprah: Her Remarkable Life Story, an Unauthorized Biography.* William Morrow.

King, Richard. 2001. *Melanin: A Key to Freedom.* Lushena Books.

Kinsbruner, Jay. 1996. *Not of Pure Blood: The Free People of Colour and Racial Prejudice in Nineteenth Century Puerto Rico.* Duke University Press.

———, ed. 1988. *The African Exchange: Toward a Biological History of Black People.* Duke University Press.

———, ed. 1999. *Plague, Pox & Pestilence: Disease in History.* Orion Publishing Group.

Kishtainy, Khalid. 1982. *The Prostitute in Progressive Literature*. Alison and Busby.

Kiteme, Kamuti. 1992. *We, the Panafrikans: Essays on the Global Black Experience*. Edward W. Blyden Press.

Kitwana, Bakari. 2002. *The Hip Hop Generation: Young Blacks and the Crisis in African-American Culture*. Basic Civitas Books.

Kivel, Paul. 1996. *Uprooting Racism: How White People Can Work for Racial Justice*. New Society Publishers.

Ki-Zerbo, J. 1967. In Commager. *General History of Africa*. abridged 1st ed.: *Methodology and African Prehistory*. UNESCO, Paris, edited by Henry Steele. *The Struggle for Racial Equality: A Documentary Record*. New York: Harper and Row. Baobab Books, Martin Luther. "The Reverend Dr. Martin Luther King Jr. Writes a Letter from the Birmingham Jail."

Klein, Michael. 1991. *The Real Story of the Rev. Al Sharpton: The Man Behind the Sound Bite*. Castillo International.

Kleinman, Sherryl, and Martha Copp. 1993. *Emotions and Fieldwork*. Sage Publications. https://doi.org/10.4135/9781412984041.

Kofsky, Frank. 1970. *Black Nationalism and the Revolution in Music*. Pathfinder Press.

Komisar, Lucy. "The New Feminism." *New York: Warner*. 1972.

Kotey, Paul H. 1998. *Twi: Twi-English, English-Twi*. Hippocene Books.

Kuhn, Thomas S. 1970. *The Structure of Scientific Revolutions*. 2nd ed. enlarged ed. University of Chicago Press.

Kunene, Mazizi. Cited in "An Interview with Mazizi Kunene on African Philosophy". 1977. *Ufahamu*, edited by Chipasa Luchembe. African Activist Association VII, *no. 2, African Philosophical Thoughts*.

Kunz, George Frederick. 1971. *The Curious Lore of Precious Stones*. Dover Publications.

L

La Guma, Alex, ed. 1978. *Apartheid: A Collection of Writings on South African Racism by South Afrikans*. International Publishers.

Laing, R. D. 1970. *The Politics of Experience and the Bird of Paradise*. Penguin Books.

Landeck, Beatrice. 1971. *Echoes of Africa in Folk Songs of the Americas*. Van Rees Press.

Landsdowne, Dolly. 1986. "When Land Is an Instrument: Tracing the Connections Between Land and the Oppression of Indigenous Peoples." *First Nations a Global Dialogue* 17 (4).

LaRocca, Nick. "Quoted in Bergreen, Laurence." *Louis Armstrong: An Extravagant Life*. Doubleday Publishing. 1997.

Latimer Associates. 1991. *The Secret Relationship Between Blacks and Jews*. Vol. 1. Nation of Islam.

Le Vine, Victor T., and Timothy W. Luke. 1979. *The Arab-African Connection: Political and Economic Realities*. Westview Press.

———. 1985a. *Letters to Marcia: A Teacher's Guide to Antiracist Education*. Cross Cultural Communications Centre.

———. 1993a. *Making Diversity Work, the Training Manual: Career Equity for Youth*. Guidance Centre Ontario Institute for Education.

———. 2002a. "Antiracist Education: Pulling Together to Close the Gaps." In *Beyond Heroes and Holidays: A Practical Guide to K-12 Anti-racist, Multicultural Education and Staff Development*, edited by Enid Lee et al. Teaching for Change.

——— [Personal Communication]. Jun. 2003.

———, Clem Marshall. 1993. "Kaleidoscope of Health: A Training Manual for Race and Ethnocultural Equity in the Ontario Health Care System." *Association*. Ontario Hospital.

——— et al. 1983. *Black Studies: A Resource Guide for Teachers*. Intermediate Division Ontario Ministry of Education.

Lee, Martin A., and Norman Solomon. 1991. *Unreliable Sources: A Guide to Detecting Bias in News Media*. Carol Publishing.

Lees, Sue. 1996. *Carnal Knowledge: Rape on Trial*. Penguin Books.

Leid, Utrice C. "Something Smells-And It's Just-Us." *The City Sun*, Oct. 19–25 and October 26-November 1 1988.

———. 1968b. *To Be a Slave*. Scholastic Incorporated.

———. "Look Out Whitey! Black Power's Gon." *Get Your Mama!* Grove Press. 1969.

Lewis, Rupert. 1988. *Marcus Garvey: Anticolonial Champion*. Africa World Press.

Leyton, Elliot. 1986. *Hunting Humans*. McLelland & Stewart.

Lincoln, C. Eric. 1974. *The Black Church Since Frazier*. Schocken Books.

Lindqvist, Sven. 1996. *Exterminate All the Brutes*, translated by Joan Tate. The New Press.

Litwack, Leon F. 1979. *Been in the Storm so Long: The Aftermath of Slavery*. Alfred A. Knoph.

Liverpool, Horace. 2001. *'Chalkdust.' Rituals of Power and Rebellion: The Carnival Tradition in Trinidad and Tobago 1763–1962. Chicago: Research Associates School Times Publishing*. Frontline Publishing Distribution Int'l Inc.

Logan, Rayford W. 1965. *The Betrayal of the Negro: From Rutherford B. Hayes to Woodrow Wilson*. Collier Books.

Lorenz, Konrad. 1971. *On Aggression*, translated by Marjorie Kerr Wilson. Bantam Books.

Lugard, Flora S. 1997. *A Tropical Dependency: An Outline of the Ancient History of Western Sudan with an Account of the Modern Settlement of Northern Nigeria*. Black Classic Press.

Lukacs, John. 1998. *The Hitler of History*. Alfred A. Knopf.

Lundy, Benjamin. Apr. 1830. "The Genius of Universal Emancipation" [Editorial]. In edited by Bradford Chambers *Chronicles of Protest*. Mentor Books: 1968.

Lynch, Hollis R. 1969. "Pan-negro Nationalism in the New World, Before 1862." In *The Making of Black America*. Vol. 1 - *The Origins of Black Americans*. TE: Kingsport Press, edited by August Meier and Elliot Rudwick.

M

Mack, Douglas R. A. 1999. *From Babylon to Rastafari: Origin and History of the Rastafarian Movement*. Research Associates School Times Publications.

Mackie, Richard. Aug. 8 2003. "Black Politicians Attack Runciman Comments." *Globe & Mail*, Friday.

Maduno, Chukwudi Okeke. *White Magic: The Origins and Ideas of Black Mental and Cultural Colonialism*. Inc. 1994. Hampton: U.B. & U.S. Communications Systems.

Maggiore, Christine. "What If Everything You Thought You Knew About Aids Was Wrong?." *Studio City, CA*. American Foundation for AIDS Alternatives. 2004.

Magubane, Bernard. 1982. *The Politics of History in South Africa*. United Nations Centre Against Apartheid.

Mahoney, Florence. 1995. *Stories of Senegambia*. Ministry of Education.

———. 1978a. *Primitive Government: A Study of Traditional Political Systems in Eastern Africa*. Penguin Books.

———. 1979. *African Societies*. Cambridge University Press.

Major, Clarence, ed. 1994. *Juba to Jive: A Dictionary of African-American Slang*. Penguin Books.

Makeba, Miriam, with Hall, James. 1987. *Makeba: My Story*. Penguin Books.

———. "As Told to Alex Haley." *The Playboy Interview Playboy Magazine*. May 1963.

———. 1981b. *Black Revolution in Two Speeches*. Pathfinder Press.

———. "As Told to Alex Haley." *The Autobiography of Malcolm. X*. Ballantine Books. 1990.

Malherbe, Michel, and Cheikh Sall. 1989. *Parlons Wolof: Langue et Culture*. L'Harmattan.

Malio, Nouhou. 1996. "Edited Hale." In *The Epic of Askia Mohammed*, edited by A. Thomas. Indiana University Press.

Mallan, Caroline. Aug. 9 2003. "Runciman Attempts to Mend Fences: Makes Phone Calls to Lincoln Alexander but Minister Won't Apologize for Remarks on Blacks." Toronto Star." *Saturday.*

Mandaza, Ibbo. 1999. *Reflections on the Crisis in the Democratic Republic of the Congo.* SAPES Books.

Mandela, Nelson. *Citizens of a Single Rainbow Nation.* Cited in Turner, Robin L. 1997. "Emerging Conceptions of Citizenship in South Africa: An Examination of Curriculum 2005." Presented at a Conference on Multicultural Citizenship in the "new" South Africa.

Mandela, Winnie. "Quoted in Matatu, Godwin." *Carnage in Soweto.* Africa, Magazine. Jul. 1976.

———. 1985b. *Part of My Soul Went with Him.* Penguin Books.

Mandella, Ademola. 2002. *Authentic Hair.* Cosmic Nubian Enterprises.

Mangru, Basdeo. 1993. *Indenture and Abolition: Sacrifice and Survival on Guyanese Sugar Plantations.* TSAR Publications.

Mansingh, Laxmi. 2002. "India in the Making of Caribbean Culture." In The 2nd Conference On Caribbean Culture. University of the West Indies.

Maquet, Jacques. 1981. *Les Civilisations Noires.* Marabout.

Marable, Manning. 1984. *Race, Reform and Rebellion: The Second Reconstruction in Black America 1945–1982.* Macmillan Press.

Marchessault, Janine, ed. 1995. *Mirror Machine: Video and Identity.* YYZ Books.

Marchetti, Victor, and John D. Marks. 1975. *The CIA and the Cult of Intelligence.* Dell Publishing.

Markovitz, Irving Leonard. 1977. *Power and Class in Africa.* Prentice Hall.

Markowitz, Gerald, and David Rosner. 2000. *Children, Race, and Power.* Routledge.

Marsalis, Wynton. "Quoted in Wiley, Ralph." *Dark Witness: When Black People Should Be Sacrificed (Again).* Random House. 1996.

Marsh, Joss. 1998. *Word Crimes: Blasphemy, Culture, and Literature in Nineteenth-Century England.* University of Chicago Press.

Marshall, Clem. 1993. *All Eyes on Africa.* MangaCom Inc.

———. 1993b. "Understanding Racism: Prisms in the Stream." In Lee. *Enid. Making Diversity Work, the Training Manual: Career Equity for Youth.* Office of International Science and Engineering.

———. Oct. 23 1997. "At What Price Dignity?" *Share.*

———. Oct. 12 2000b. "No Use of N-Word Acceptable." *Share.*

———. Oct. 25 2001b. "Winnie Madikizela-Mandela a Priceless Gift." *Share.*

———. "CBC Forum Ignored Reality." *Share.* Jun. 20 2002b.

———. 2002c. "When the Frame Becomes the Picture." In *Beyond Heroes and Holidays: A*

Practical Guide to K-12 Anti-racist, Multicultural Education and Staff Development, edited by Enid Lee et al. Teaching for Change.

———. Aug. 14 2003d. "End the Violence: Just Play Fair." *Share.*

———. Sept. 11 2003e. "How Black Folks Turned the ROM Around." *Share.*

———. *Email to Canadian Broadcasting Corporation.* Personal Communication on Bias of Newscast Coverage of Current Events in Haiti." March. 2004b.

———. 2004c. *Personal Collection of Original Poems.* Toronto.

Martin, Tony. 1985. *The Pan-African Connection: From Slavery to Garvey and Beyond.* The Majority Press.

———. 1992b. *Early Writings.* Penguin Books.

———. *Capital: A New Abridgement.* 1999. Oxford University Press.

Masolo, D. A. 1994. *African Philosophy in Search of Identity.* Indiana University Press. https://doi.org/10.2979/1037.0.

Maspero, Sir G. 1990. *Popular Stories of Ancient Egypt.* G. P. Putnam's Sons.

Masse, Martin. Jan. 9 1999. "Pierre Vallières Défenseur de la Liberté." *Québécois Libre.*

Mastalia, Francesco, and Alfonse Pagano. 1999. *Dreads.* Workman Publishing Company.

Matatu, Godwin. Jul. 1976. *Carnage in Soweto.* Africa, Magazine.

Mather, Cotton. Cited in McCrum, Robert, Cran William, and Robert MacNeil. 1987. *The Story of English.* Faber & Faber.

Matthiessen, Peter. 1983. *The Tree Where Man Was Born.* E. P. Dutton.

Mauer, Marc, and Meda Chesney-Lind. 2002. *Invisible Punishment: The Collateral Consequences of Mass Imprisonment.* The New Press.

May, Samuel J. 1969. "Quoted in Pease, William H & Jane H. "Antislavery Ambivalence: Immediatism", Expediencey, Race." In *The Making of Black America.* Vol. 1 – *the Origins of Black Americans.* TE: Kingsport Press, edited by August Meir and Elliot Rudwick.

———. 1986. *The Africans: A Triple Heritage.* Little, Brown & Company.

———. "Quoted in Anderson, S.E." *The Black Holocaust for Beginners.* Writers and Readers Publishing Inc. 1995.

Mbeki, Govan. 1964. *South Africa: The Peasants' Revolt.* Penguin Books.

Mbiti, John. 1970. *African Religions and Philosophy.* Doubleday Publishing.

McCall, Nathan. 1995. *Makes Me Wanna Holler: A Young Black Man in America.* Random House.

McCray, Walter Arthur Rev. 1992. *The Black Presence in the Bible: Discovering the Black and African Identity of Biblical Persons and Nations.* Black Light Fellowship.

McCrum, Robert, Cran William, and Robert MacNeil. 1987. *The Story of English*. Faber & Faber.

McEvedy, Colin. 1982. *Atlas of African History*. Facts on File.

McGovern, Ann. 1965. "The True Story of Harriet Tubman." *Wanted Dead or Alive Toronto: Scholastic Book Services*.

McIntosh, James C. 1997. "That Which Cannot Be Destroyed: 7 Articles About Dr. Abdulalim Shabazz the World's Foremost Mathematics Educator." *Publications*. CEMOTAP.

———. 1998a. *State Rape: The Tawana Brawley War*. CEMOTAP Publications.

McIntyre, Charsee C. L. 1993. *Criminalizing a Race: Free Blacks During Slavery*. Kayode Publications.

McKague, Ormond, ed. 1991. *Racism in Canada*. Fifth House.

McLuhan, Marshall. 1981. "Media Ad-Vice: An Introduction." In *Subliminal Seduction: Ad Media's Manipulation of a Not so Innocent America*, edited by Wilson Bryan Key. Signet Books.

———, Quentin Fiore. 1968. *War and Peace in the Global Village*. Bantam Books.

———. 1971. *Touch the Earth*. Simon & Schuster.

McMullin, Dan Taulapapa. 1998. "American Samoa." In *Resistance in Paradise: Rethinking 100 Years of U.S. Involvement in the Caribbean and the Pacific*, edited by Deborah Wei and Rachael Kamel. American Friends Service Committee.

McNally, Rand. 1968. *World Atlas*. Rand McNally and Company.

Means, Sterling M. 1978. *Black, Egypt and Her Negro Pharoahs*. Black Classic Press.

Meier, August, and Elliot Rudwick, eds. "The Making of Black America" Vol. 1. *The Origins of Black Americans*. TE: Kingsport Press. 1969.

Melching, Molly. "Ndank-Ndank: An Introduction to Wolof Culture." *Gorée, Senegal: Corps de la Paix américain/American Peace Corps*. 1981.

Mellon, James, ed. 1988. *Bullwhip Days: The Slaves Remember – An Oral History*. Avon Books.

Melvern, L. R. 2000. *A People Betrayed: The Role of the West in Rwanda's Genocide*. Zed Books.

Mensah, Joseph. 2002. *Black Canadians: History, Experiences, Social Conditions*. Fernwood Publishing.

———. 1966c. *Red Land, Black Land*. Dodd, Mead and Company.

———. 1978. "The Pleasures of Life." In *Ancient Egypt: Discovering Its Splendours*, edited by Jules B. Billard. National Geographic Society.

"Feelings, Tom." *The Middle Passage*. Penguin. 1995.

Mies, Maria, V. Bennholdt-Thomson, and Claudia Von Werlhof. 1991. *Women: The Last Colony*. Zed Books.

Miles, Angela. 1996. *Integrative Feminisms: Building Global Visions 1960s- 1990s*. Routledge.

Miller, John. May 1 1997. "Don't Count Race at All." *USA Today*.

Millette, Robert, and Gosine Mahin. 1985. *The Grenada Revolution: Why It Failed*. Africana Research Publications.

Millington, Porter. "'Whitefolks are How Folks and Blackfolks are What Folks.' Interview Quoted in, Gwaltney, John Langston." *Drylongso: A Self-Portrait of Black America*. Random House. 1980.

Mokonyane, Dan. 1994. *The Big Sellout by the Communist Party of South Africa And the African National Congress: Recent Developments in South Africa and the Eclipse of the Revolutionary Perspective*. Nakong Ya Rena.

Monmonier, Mark. 2002. *Spying with Maps*. University of Chicago Press.

Montag, Warren. 1997. "The Universalization of Whiteness: Racism and Enlightenment." In *Whiteness: A Critical Reader*, edited by Mike Hill. New York University Press.

Montréal, P. Q., ed. 1979. *CSN, 150 Ans de Lutte: Histoire du Mouvement Ouvrier au Québéc (1825–1976)*.

Moon, Bucklin, ed. 1945. *Primer for White Folks*. Doubleday Publishing, Doran and Co.

Moore, Deborah Lela. 1991. *The Pineal Gland and Melatonin: Their Relationship to Blacks*. Professional Education Services.

Moore, Michael. 2001. *Stupid White Men: And Other Sorry Excuses for the State of the Nation*. HarperCollins.

Moore, Richard B. 1992. *The Name 'Negro' Its Origin and Evil Use*. Black Classic Press.

Moore, Robert. 2002. "Racism in the English Language." In *Beyond Heroes and Holidays: A Practical Guide to K-12 Anti-racist, Multicultural Education and Staff Development*, edited by Enid Lee et al. Teaching for Change.

Morgan, Joan. "Quoted in Beatty, Paul." *The White Boy Shuffle*. Henry Holt. 1996.

———. 1999. *When Chickenheads Come Home to Roost: My Life as a Hip Hop Feminist*. Simon & Schuster.

Morris, D. Aldon. 1984. *The Origins of the Civil Rights Movement: Black Communities Organizing for Change*. Macmillan.

Morrison, Silbourn. 1992a. "Mosiah". *Rastafari the Conscious Embrace: The Idea. The Dream. Philosophy*. Itality Publishing House, ECA Associates.

Morrison, Toni. 1992b. *Race-ing, Justice, Engendering Power: Essays on Anita Hill, Clarence Thomas, and the Construction of Social Reality*. Pantheon Books.

———. 1993c. "Time Magazine Interview." In *Multicultural America: Essays on Cultural Wars and Cultural Peace*, edited by Ismael Reed. Penguin.

———, Claudia Brodsky Lacour, ed. 1997. *Birth of a Nation'hood: Gaze, Script, and Spectacle in the O. J. Simpson Case*. Pantheon Books.

Moses, Wilson Jeremiah. 1998. *Afrotopia: The Roots of African American Popular History.* Cambridge University Press. https://doi.org/10.1017/CBO9780511582837.

Mosley, Walter, Taylor, and Clyde, eds. 1999. *Black Genius: African American Solutions to African American Problems.* W. W. Norton and Company.

Motlana, Nthatho. "Quoted in Mandela, Winnie." *Part of My Soul.* Penguin Books. 1985.

Mudenge, S. I. G. 1986. *Christian Education at the Mutapa Court: A Portuguese Strategy to Influence Events in the Empire of Munhumutapa.* Zimbabwe Publishing House.

Mudimbe, V. Y. 1988. *The Invention of Africa: Gnosis, Philosophy, and the Order of Knowledge.* Indiana University Press. https://doi.org/10.2979/2080.0.

Mukherjee, Rudrangshu. 1993. *The Penguin Ghandi Reader.* Penguin.

Mulder, Kenneth W. 1991. *Seminoles: Days of Long Ago.* Mulder Enterprises.

Mun Wah, Lee. 1994. *Color of Fear.* Stir Fry Productions.

Munro, J. Forbes. 1976. *Africa and the International Economy 1800–1960.* Rowman & Littlefield Publishing Group.

Mutunhu, Tendai. "Nehanda of Zimbabwe (Rhodesia) the Story of a Woman Liberation Leader and Fighter." *Ufahamu* VII (1). In *Memoriam, Henry B. Masauko Chipembere 1930-1975: Tributes and Articles by Mtewa & Phillips.* 1976. African Activist Association.

Myers, Linda James. 1988. *Understanding an Afrocentric World View: Introduction to an Optimal Psychology.* Kendal/Hunt Publishing.

Myrdal, Gunnar. "An American Dilemma": Vol. 1. *The Negro in a White Nation.* Mc-Graw-Hill. 1964.

———. "An American Dilemma": Vol. 1i. *The Negro Social Structure.* McGraw-Hill. 1964.

N

Nadel, S. F. 1971. *Byzance Noire: Le Royaume des Nupe du Nigeria.* Maspéro.

Naficy, Hamid, and Teshome H. Gabriel. 1993. *Otherness and the Media: The Ethnography of the Imagined and the Imaged.* Harwood Academic Publishers.

Naidoo, G. R. 1988. "The Durban Gang." In *Thirty Years of Drum: Extracts and Images in the Beat of Drum: The Story of a Magazine That Documented the Rise of Africa – As Told by Drum's Publisher, Editors, Contributors and Photographers,* edited by Angela Caccia.

Nakanishi, Don T., and Tina Yamano Nishida. 1995. *The Asian American Educational Experience: A Source Book for Teachers and Students.* Routledge.

Nangoli, Chief Musamaali. 1988. *No More Lies About Africa: Here Is the Truth from an African.* African Heritage Publishers.

Nantulya, Paul, and Stephen Othieno Jr. 1999. "Blood Brothers." *Pan Afrikanist* 1 (2).

Neal, Mark Anthony. 2002. *Soul Babies: Black Popular Culture and the Post- Soul Aesthetic*. Routledge.

Nehusi, Kimani S. K., and Ian Isodore Smart, eds. 2000. *Ah Come Back Home: Perspectives on the Trinidad and Tobago Carnival*. Original World Press.

Nelson, Jill, ed. 2000. *Police Brutality: An Anthology*. W. W. Norton and Company.

Nelson, Thomas, ed. "The Holy Bible: New King James Version." *Nashville, TE*. National Publishing Co. 1985.

Neto, Antonio. 1988. "Quoted in 'Angola's New Boss Antonio Neto: Poet President.'." In *Thirty Years of Drum: Extracts and Images in the Beat of Drum: The Story of a Magazine That Documented the Rise of Africa – As Told by Drum's Publisher, Editors, Contributors and Photographers*, Drum Magazine, edited by Angela Caccia. Nairobi, Kenya.

New York State Special Commission on Attica, ed. 1972. *The Official Report of New York State Special Commission on Attica*. Bantam Books.

Newkirk, Pamela. 2000. *Within the Veil: Black Journalists, White Media*. New York University Press.

Newman, Shirlee P. 2000. *The African Slave Trade*. Grolier Publishing.

News Broadcast: "Racism in the Ontario Provincial Police." CBC Radio. 2004.

Newton, Edmund. Febr. 8 1975. "Eugene Genovese." *New York Post*.

Nhubu, Francis, and Gadzikwa. 2001. *Madzimbabwe Which Way?* Gadzikwa Publications.

Niane, Djibril T. "Sundiata: An Epic of Old Mali." *Longman*. Présence africaine. 1965.

Nichols, Bill. 1981. *Ideology and the Image*. Indiana University Press. https://doi.org/10.2979/1985.0.

Nketia, J. H. Kwabena. 1977. "La Musique dans la Culture africaine." In International Festival Committee. *FESTAC 1977*, edited by Africa Journal Limited.

———. 1962. *I Speak of Freedom: A Statement of African Ideology*. Frederick A. Praeger.

"Mani Kongo". "Personal Letter to King Manoel of Portgual." 1969. In *Challenge of the Congo*, edited by Kwame Nkrumah. Panaf Books.

———. 1969a. *Challenge of the Congo*. Panaf Books.

———. 1970b. *Consciencism: Philosophy and Ideology for De-colonisation*. Panaf Books.

———. 1985. *Africa Must Unite*. Panaf Books.

Null, Gary. 1975. *Black Hollywood: The Black Performer in Motion Pictures*. Citadel Press.

Nyaba, Peter Adwok. 2002. "'The Afro-Arab Conflict in the 21st Century: The Racial and Religious Dimensions of the Sudanese Conflict and Its Possible Ramifications in East, Central and Southern Africa in the Next Millennium.' *Tinabantu*." *Journal of African National Affairs* 1 (1).

Nyere, Julius. 2001. "Leaders Must Not Be Masters." In *African Philosophy: An Anthology*, edited by Eze Chukwudi. Blackwell Publishing.

O

Oates, James, ed. 1983. *The Ruling Race: A History of American Slaveholders*. Vintage Books.

Obadele, Imari Abubakari. 1991. *America the Nation-State: The Politics of the United States from a State-Building Perspective*. rev. ed. House of Songhay.

Obeng, Ernest E. 1988. *Ancient Ashanti Chieftaincy*. Ghana Publishing Corporation.

Obiechina, Emmanuel. 1972. "Franz Fanon: The Man and His Works." *Ufahamu*. African Activist Association VIII, *no. 2, Walter Rodney On Problems Of Third World Development*.

Okoye, Mogwuko. 1977. "Franchir les Océans." In International Festival Committee. *FESTAC 1977*, edited by Africa Journal Limited.

Olderogge, Dmitry, and Werner Forman, eds. 1969. *The Art of Africa: Negro Art*. Hamlyn Publishing.

Oliver, Melvin L., and Thomas M. Shapiro. 1997. *Black Wealth/White Wealth: A New Perspective on Racial Inequality*. Routledge.

Oliver, Roland. 1999. *The African Experience: From Olduvai Gorge to the 21st Century*. Phoenix Press.

O'Neill, John. 1971. "Violence, Language and the Body Politic." In *Power Corrupted: The October Crisis and the Repression of Quebec*, edited by Abraham Rothstein. New Press.

Onyewuenyi, Innocent C. 1994. *The African Origin of Greek Philosophy: An Exercise in Afrocentrism*. University of Nigeria Press.

———. Cited in Reznikov, Andrei. 2001. *George Orwell's Theory of Language*. Writers Club Press.

Orwell, George. Cited. 2002. "Collins, John & Glover, Ross." In *Collateral Language: A User's Guide to America's New War*. New York University Press.

Osahon, Naiwu. 1993. *God Is Black*. Heritage Books.

Osei, G. K. "The African Concept of Life and Death." *London: The African Publication Society*. 1981.

Ouspensky, P. D. 1977. In *Search of the Miraculous: Fragments of an Unknown Teaching*. Harcourt Brace Jovanovich.

Owens, Joseph. 1976. *Dread: The Rastafarians of Jamaica*. Kingston Press: Sangster's Book Stores.

Paddock, Charley. "Quoted in Edwards, Harry." *The Revolt of the Black Athlete*. The Free Press. 1969.

Padelford, Norman J., and Rupert Emerson, eds. 1963. *Africa and World Order*. Praeger.

Pakenham, Thomas. 1991. *The Scramble for Africa: White Man's Conquest of the Dark Continent from 1876 to 1912*. Avon Books.

Palast, Greg. 2004. *'Counting on Democracy.' 74 Minutes*. Global Vision Inc.

Pan, Lynn. 1991. *Sons of the Yellow Emperor: The Story of the Overseas Chinese*, Mandarin. Reed International Books.

Panassié, Hugues. 1944. *The Real Jazz*, translated by Anne Sorelle Williams. Smith & Durrell.

Parham, Thomas A., ed. 2002. *Understanding Personality and How to Measure It in Counselling Persons of African Descent: Raising the Bar of Practitioner Competence*. Sage Publications.

Park, Mungo. 1945. "Quoted in Dubois, W.E.B. 'African Culture.'." In Primer for White Folks, edited by Bucklin Moon. Doubleday Publishing, Doran and Co.

Parker, Robert, with Rashke, Richard. 1986. Capitol Hill in Black and White. Dodd, Mead and Company.

Passevant, Christiane, and Portis Larry, eds. Dictionnaire Black: Cinéma. Littérature. Social. Musiques. Sport. Arts. Science. Paris: Jacques Grancher, 1995.

Patterson, Orlando. 1991. Freedom in the Making of Western Culture. Vol. 1. HarperCollins.

Patterson, William L. 1971. We Charge Genocide: The Crime of Government Against the Negro People. International Publishers.

Paul, Daniel N. We. 2000. Were Not the Savages. Fernwood Publishing.

Payer, Cheryl. 1974. The Debt Trap: The IMF and the Third World. Penguin Books.

Pedicelli, Gabriella. "When Police Kill: Police Use of Force in Montreal and Toronto." Montreal, P.Q. Véhicule Press. 1998.

Pelligrino, Charles. 1994. Return to Sodom and Gomorrah. Avon Books.

Pennington, James, and W. C. 1970. "The Fugitive Blacksmith." In Afro-American History: Primary Sources, edited by Thomas R. Frazier. Harcourt, Brace & World.

Pérez, Louis A., ed. 1992. Slaves, Sugar, & Colonial Society: Travel Accounts of Cuba, 1801–1899. Scholarly Resources Incorporated.

Perry, Theresa et al. 2003. Young Gifted and Black: Promoting High Achievement Among African-American Students. Beacon Press.

Pieterse, Jan Nedeerveen. 1992. White on Black: Images of Africa and Blacks in Western Popular Culture. Yale University Press.

CLEM MARSHALL

Pinckard, G. "Letters from Guiana, 1796–97." Daily Chronicle. Guiana Edition No. 5. Georgetown. 1942. Quoted in Daly, Vere T. 1993. A Short History of the Guyanese People. Macmillan Press.

Pinkney, Alphonso. 1994. Lest We Forget: White Hate Crimes, Howard Beach and Other Racial Atrocities. Third World Press.

Pollard, Velma. 2000. Dread Talk: The Language of Rastafari. rev. ed. ed. McGill-Queen's University Press.

Pongweni, Alec J. C. 1982. Songs That Won the Liberation War. The College Press.

Porter, Michael. 1997. Kill Them Before They Grow: Misdiagnosis of African American Boys in American Classrooms. African American Images.

Powell, Adam Clayton Jr. 1994. Adam by Adam: The Autobiography of Adam Clayton Powell Jr. Carol Publishing Co.

Powell, Rev, and P. Raphael. 1979. The Invisible Image Uprooted: A Mystery Revealed. Philemon Co.

Prabhupada, Bhaktivedanta Swami. 1981. A.C. Bhavagad-Gita as It Is. Bhaktivedanta Book Trust.

Prah, Kwesi Kwaa. 1997. Beyond the Colour Line: Pan-Africanist Disputations. Vivlia Publishers, RSA.

———. "The Post-colonial Elite and African Language Policies. Unpublished Paper Given On: "Language Policies in Sub-Saharan Africa: Issues", Constraints and Possibilities." Cape Town. RSA: World Congress of Comparative Education. 1998b.

———. "'Letter to Ali Mazrui.' in Unpublished Letter by the Founder of the Centre for the Advanced Study of African Society." Personal Correspondence with Bankie, directed by F. Bankie of CASAS. RSA. 2002d.

———. 2002e. "Looking Backwards and Then Forwards: Africans and the 21st Century, Tinabantu." Journal of African National Affairs 1 (1).

Premdas, Ralph R., ed., ed. 1993. The Enigma of Ethnicity: Race in the Caribbean and the World. University of the West Indies.

Pride, J. B., and Janet Holmes, eds. 1984. Sociolinguistics. Penguin Books.

Q

Quaison-Sackey, Alex. 1966. Africa Unbound: Reflections of an African Statesman. Praeger.

Quamina, Odida T. 1987. Mineworkers of Guyana: The Making of a Working Class. Zed Books.

Quattrocchio, P. Giuseppe. Kikuyu. Nairobi, Kenya: Text Book Centre. 1989.

Quayson, Ato. 2000. Postcolonialism: Theory, Practice or Process? Polity Press.

Quigg, Philip W., ed. 1964. *Africa: A Foreign Affairs Reader.* Frederick A. Praeger.

Quirk, Robert E. 1993. *Fidel Castro.* W. W. Norton and Company.

Quoniam, Pierre, ed. 1977. *Le Louvre*, translated by C. De Chabannes. Editions des Musées Nationaux.

R

Ra, Ankh Mi. 1995. "Let the Ancestors Speak – Removing the Veil of Mysticism from Medu Netcher: A Guide to the Grammar of the Language of Kemet." In *Temple*. JOM International Inc.

Radi, Lamia. Sept. 22 1999. "Famous Belly Dancer Borrowed Name and Style from the Samba, Agence France Presse."" *National Post.*

Rainwater, Lee, and William L. Yancey, eds. 1967. *The Moynihan Report and the Politics of Controversy.* M.I.T. Press.

Rajshekar, V. T. 1987. *Dalit: The Black Untouchables of India.* Clarity Press.

Rake, Alan. 1988. "Grass Roots in East Africa." In *Thirty Years of Drum: Extracts and Images in the Beat of Drum: The Story of a Magazine That Documented the Rise of Africa – As Told by Drum's Publisher, Editors, Contributors and Photographers*, edited by Angela Caccia. Drum Magazine.

Ransford, Oliver. "The Great Trek." *London, GB.* Sphere Books. 1974.

Raper, Arthur F. 1970. *The Tragedy of Lynching.* General Publishing Co.

Rashad, Adib. 1991. *The History of Islam and Black Nationalism in the Americas.* Writers Inc.

Rashidi, Runoko. 1999. *African Presence in Early Asia.* Transaction Publishers.

Rawlings, J. J. 1987. *The New Direction and Purpose: Selected Speeches, January 1, 1986 – December 31, 1986.* Ghana Information Services.

Reade, Winwood. 1994. *'Savage Africa.'* Quoted in Blyden, Edward W. *Christianity, Islam and the Negro Race.* Black Classic Press.

Reagon, Bernice Johnson. 1992. *We'll Understand It Better by and by: Pioneering African American Gospel Composers.* Smithsonian Institution Press.

Reed, Ismael, ed. 1997. *Multicultural America: Essays on Cultural Wars and Cultural Peace.* Penguin.

Regis, Louis. "The Political Calypso: True Opposition in Trinidad and Tobago 1962–1987." *The University Press of the West Indies.* 1999.

Reich, Wilhelm. 1991. *The Mass Psychology of Fascism*, translated by Vincent R. Carfagno. HarperCollins Canada Limited.

Repo, Satu, ed. 1998. *Making Schools Matter: Good Teachers at Work.* James Publishing Lorimer & Co.

"New York Times with Wicker, Tom." 1968. *Report of the National Advisory Commission on Civil Disorders*. E.P. Dutton and Company.

Reznikov, Andrei. 2001. *George Orwell's Theory of Language*. Writers Club Press.

Rich, Adrienne. 1978. *Disloyal to Civilization: Feminism, Racism and Gynephobia*. Chrysalis.

Richard, Little. "Quoted in 'Foreword' to Turner, Ike with Nigel Cawthorne." *Taking Back My Name: The Confessions of Ike Turner*. Virgin Books. 1999.

Ripley, C. Peter et al., eds. "The Black Abolitionist Papers" Volume II. *Canada*. 1830–65. Vol. 2. University of North Carolina Press, 1986.

Rivelli, Pauline, and Robert Levin. 1979. *Giants of Black Music*. Da Capo Press.

Roberts, Dorothy. 1997. *Killing the Black Body: Race, Reproduction and the Meaning of Liberty*. Pantheon Books.

Robeson, Susan. 1981. *The Whole World in His Hands: A Pictorial Biography of Paul Robeson*. Citadel Press.

Robinson, Randall. 2000. *The Debt: What America Owes to Blacks*. Dutton.

———. 1970c. *A History of the Upper Guinea Coast 1545–1800*. Clarendon Press.

———. 1971. *The Groundings with My Brothers* [London: Bogle l'Ouverture Publications].

———, ed. 1979. *Guyanese Sugar Plantations in the Nineteenth Century: A Contemporary Description from the 'Argosy'*. Release Publishers.

———. 1982b. *A History of the Guyanese Working People. 1881–1905*. Johns Hopkins University Press.

———, How Europe Underveloped Africa. 1982. *Washington, DC: Howard U Press*.

———, Walter Rodney Speaks. 1990. *The Making of an African Intellectual*. Africa World Press.

Rogin, Michael. 1998. *Blackface, White Noise: Jewish Immigrants in the Hollywood Melting Pot*. University of California Press.

Root, Deborah. 1996. *Cannibal Culture: Art, Appropriation and the Commodification of Difference*. Westview Press.

Rose, Tricia. 1994. *Black Noise, Rap Music and Black Culture in Contemporary America*. Wesleyan University Press.

Ross, and Ian. 1997. *fareWel*. Scirocco Drama.

Rotberg, Robert I., ed. 1973. *Africa and Its Explorers: Motives, Methods, and Impact*. Oxford University Press.

Rothstein, Abraham, ed. 1971. *Power Corrupted: The October Crisis and the Repression of Quebec*. New Press.

Rowan, Carl T. Oct. 1957. "Has Paul Robeson Betrayed the Negro?" *Ebony*.

Rubin, William, ed. 'Primitivism'. 1984. In *20th Century Art: Affinity of the Tribal and the Modern*. The Museum of Modern Art.

Russell, Dick, ed. 1999. *Black Genius and the American Experience*. Carroll & Graf Publishers.

Russman, Edna. 1978. "Change in a Changeless Land." In *Ancient Egypt: Discovering Its Splendours*, edited by Jules B. Billard. National Geographic Society.

Ryan, Selwyn. 1992. "The Rise and Fall of Black Entrepreneurship in Post Emancipation Trinidad." In *Sharks and Sardines: Blacks in Business in Trinidad and Tobago*, edited by Selwyn Ryan, Lou Anne Barclay and St. Augustine. University of the West Indies Press.

S

Sabo, Don et al., eds. 2001. *Prison Masculinities*. Temple University Press.

———. 2001. "System to the Supermax Prison." In *Prison Masculinities*. Temple University Press.

———, Ruchell Magee. 1971. *The Soledad Brothers & Other Political Prisoners, If They Come in the Morning: Voices of Resistance*. Signet Books.

Sagarin, Mary. 1970. *John Brown Russwurm: The Story of Freedom's Journal, Freedom's Journey*. Lothrop, Lee, Shepard & Co.

Sagay, Esi. 1983. *African Hairstyles: Styles of Yesterday and Today*. Heinemann.

Samb, Amar. 1983. *Initiation À la Grammaire Wolof*. IFAN.

Samb, Babacar. 1990. "Les Routes Transsahariennes et le Trafic des Esclavigistes à Travers Le Sahara: Le Problématique de Sa Légitimité (XIVe-XVe Sièle)." In Sow. *Dépendance et Liberté: L'Afrique et le Monde Méditerranéen dans l'Antiquité*, edited by Mame Sokhna. Terebi.

Sankara, Thomas. 1988. "The Bourkina Faso Revolution 1983–1987." In *Thomas Sankara Speaks*. Pathfinder Press.

Sapa. 2003. *I Am Agent RS 452B*. Business Day.

Sargant, William. 1997. "Battle for the Mind." *Tavistock's Imperial Brainwashing Project: EIR Special Report*. In edited by L. Wolfe. EIR News Service.

———. 1971b. *The Sacred Stools of the Akan*. Ghana Publishing Corporation.

———. 1974. *Ghana in Retrospect: Some Aspects of Ghanaian Culture*. Ghana Publishing Corporation.

———. 1977. *Girls' Nubility Rites in Ashanti*. Ghana Publishing Corporation.

Sartre, Jean-Paul. 1976. *Black Orpheus*. Présence africaine.

Scammell, W. M. 1975. *International Monetary Policy: Bretton Woods and After*. Macmillan Press.

Schatzberg, Rufus, and Robert J. Kelly. 1997. *African American Organized Crime: A Social History*. Rutgers University Press.

Schmidt, Hans. 1971. *The United States Occupation of Haiti, 1915–1934*. Rutgers University Press.

Schneider, Vimala. "The Healing Power of Color." *Yoga Journal*. Boulder, CO. 1987.

Schuyler, George S. 1966. *Black and Conservative: The Autobiography of George S. Schuyler*. Arlington House Publishers.

Schwarz-Bart, Simone. 2001. In *Praise of Black Women: Ancient African Queens*, translated by Rose-Myriam Rejouis and Val Vinokurov. University of Wisconsin Press.

Scobie, Edward. 1972. *Black Britannia: A History of Blacks in Britain*. Johnson Publishing.

Scott, Jill. "Quoted in Neal, Mark Anthony." *Soul Babies: Black Popular Culture & the Post-Soul Aesthetic*. Routledge. 2002.

Searle, Chris. 1984. *Words Unchained*. Zed Books.

Seecharan, Clem. 1993. *India and the Shaping of the Indo-Guyanese Imagination 1890s-1920s*. Peepal Tree Press.

Segal, Ronald. 2001. *Islam's Black Slaves: The Other Black Diaspora*. Farrar, Straus & Giroux.

Segy, Ladislas. 1985. *African Sculpture Speaks*. Da Capo Press.

Seidman, G., D. Martin, and P. Johnson, eds. 1985. *Zimbabwe: A New History*. Zimbabwe Publishing House.

Serpico, Frank. Mar. 14 2000. "Amadou's Ghost: Diallo Speaks to Serpico." *The Village. Voice.*

Service des communications de la centrale de l'enseignement du Québéc,

Shakur, Afeni. 1995. "We Will Win: Letter from Prison." In *The Black Panthers Speak*, edited by Philip S. Foner. Da Capo Press.

Shakur, Assata. 1987. *Assata: An Autobiography*. Lawrence Hill and Company.

Shamuyarira, Nathan M. et al. 1995. *Mugabe's Reflections: Zimbabwe and the Contemporary World*. Har-Anand Publications.

Shapiro, Herbert, ed. "White Violence and Black Response: From Reconstruction to Montgomery." *Amherst: University of Assachusetts Press*. 1988.

Sharawy, Helmi. "Arab Culture and African Culture: Ambiguous Relations." *Alesco, the Dialogue Between the Arab Culture & Other Cultures*. Arab League, Educational, Cultural and Scientific Organisation. 1999.

Shays, Ruth. "'When You Don't Know When You Have Been Spit on, It Does Not Matter Too Much What Else You Think You Know.' Interview in, Gwaltney, John Langston." *Drylongso: A Self-Portrait of Black America*. Random House. 1980.

Sheik-Abdi, Abdi. 1993. *Divine Madness: Mohammed Abdulle Hassan (1856–1920)*. Zeb Books.

Sheldrake, Rupert. 2003. *The Sense of Being Stared At*. Crown Publishing Group Publishers.

———. "Quoted in Kofsky, Frank." *Black Nationalism & the Revolution in Music*. Pathfinder Press. 1970d.

———. 1979. "Quoted in Hentoff, Nat". "Archie Shepp: The Way Ahead." In *Giants of Black Music*, edited by Pauline Revelli and Robert Levin. Da Capo Press.

———. "Quoted in Sidran, Ben." *Black Talk: How the Music of Black America Created a Radical Alternative to the Values of Western Literary Tradition*. Da Capo Press. 1981c.

Shields, Carol, and Marjorie Anderson. 2001. *Dropped Threads: What We Aren't Told*. Random House.

Shipman, and PAT. 2002. *The Evolution of Racism: Human Differences and the Uses and Abuses of Racism*. Harvard University Press.

Shiveley, Charley. 1983. "Beyond the Binary: Race and Sex." In *Black Men/White Men*, edited by Michael J. Smith. Gay Sunshine Press.

Shoat, Ella, and Robert Stam, eds. 1997. *Unthinking Eurocentrism: Multiculturalism and the Media*. Routledge.

Shroff, Farah. 1997. "All Petals in the Flower: Celebrating the Diversity of Ontario's Birthing Women Within First Year Midwifery Curriculum." In *The New Midwifery*, edited by Farah Shroff. Women's Press.

Shujaa, Mwalimu J., ed. 1994. *Too Much Schooling, Too Little Education: A Paradox of Black Life in White Societies*. Africa World Press.

Siefert, Charles. 1938. *The Negro's or Ethiopian's Contribution to Art*. Black Classic Press.

Sifford, Charlie. 1996. "Just Let Me Play." In *Brotherman: The Odyssey of Black Men in America: An Anthology*, edited by Herb Boyd and Robert L. Allen. Ballantine Books.

Silverstein, Ken. Nov. 2000. "Making the Case for Racial Reparations." *Harper's Magazine*.

Simpson, O. J. I. 1995. *Want to Tell You: My Response to Your Letters, Your Messages, Your Questions*. Little, Brown and Company.

———. 1978b. "The Gift of Writing." In *Ancient Egypt: Discovering Its Splendours*, edited by Jules B. Billard. National Geographic Society.

———. 1998. *The Art and Architecture or Ancient Egypt*. Yale University Press.

Singh, Amritjit. 1997. "The Possibilities of Radical Consciousness: African Americans and New Immigrants." In *Multicultural America: Essays on Cultural Wars and Cultural Peace*, edited by Ismael Reed. Penguin.

Slater, Rodney. 2002. "Quoted in 'Bill Clinton Named to Black Hall of Fame: Honoured for His Work Fighting Aids in the Caribbean.'" *Caribbean Camera, Toronto*.

Smith, Dorothy E. 1999. *Writing the Social: Critique, Theory, and Investigations*. University of T Press. https://doi.org/10.3138/9781442683747.

Smith, Elbert B. 1967. *The Death of Slavery: The United States, 1837–65*. University of Chicago Press.

Smith, Elliot G. "The Influence of Ancient Egyptian Civilization in the East and in America." *London: The African Publication Society*. 1983a.

Smith, Frank. 1983b. *Essays into Literacy*. Heinemann Educational Books.

Smith, Lillian. 1945. "Addressed to White Liberals." In *Primer for White Folks*, edited by Bucklin Moon. Doubleday Publishing, Doran and Co.

Smith, M. G. 1993. "Race and Ethnicity." In *The Enigma of Ethnicity: Race in the Caribbean and the World*, edited by Ralph R. Premdas. University of the West Indies.

Smith, Michael J., ed. 1983. *Black Men/White Men*. Gay Sunshine Press.

Smith, Venture. 1970. "'A Narrative of the Life and Adventures of Venture, a Native of Africa but Resident about Sixty Years in the United States of America.' Quoted." In *Afro-American History: Primary Sources*, edited by Thomas R. Frazier. Harcourt, Brace & World.

Smith, W. Stevenson. 1998. *The Art and Architecture of Ancient Egypt*. Yale University Press.

Sobel, Lester A. 1967. *Civil Rights 1960–66*. Facts on File.

"Social Democrat" [Editorial]. 1897. London.

Somé, Malidoma. 1995. *Of Water and the Spirit: Ritual, Magic and Initiation in the Life of an African Shaman*. Penguin.

Somerville, Keith. "Winnie: 'Africa's Evita'." *BBC News*. 2003.

Sonko-Godwin, Patience. 1995. *Leaders of the Senegambia Region: Reactions to European Infiltration 19th–20th Century*. SunRise Publishers.

Sorel, Georges. 1967. *Reflections on Violence*, translated by T. E. Hulme. Collier Books.

Sormani, Giuseppe, ed. 1967. *The Illustrated Library of the World and Its Peoples: Africa North and East*. Vol. 2. Greystone Press.

Southern, Eileen. 1997. *The Music of Black Americans: A History*. 3rd ed. WW Orton & Co.

Sow, Mame Sokhna, ed. 1990. *Dépendance et Liberté: L'Afrique et le Monde Méditeraneén dans l'Antiquité*. Terebi.

Sowell, Thomas. 1996. *Migrations and Cultures: A World View*. HarperCollins.

Spencer-Strachan, Louise. 1992. *Confronting the Color Crisis in the African Diaspora: Emphasis Jamaica*. Afrikan World Infosystems.

Spender, Stephen. 2001. *World Within World: The Autobiography of Stephen Spender*. Random House.

Spingarn, Joel. 1993. "Editorial on Spying, NAACP." In *Commercial Appeal*. Memphis, TN.

Stagliano, Julie. "Senegal: A General Historical and Cultural Survey." *Dakar, Senegal: American Embassy*. 1984.

Stamp, Kenneth M. 1956. *The Peculiar Institution: Slavery in the Antebellum South*. Random House.

Staples, Brent. 1994. *Parallel Time: Growing up in Black and White*. Avon Books.

Staples, Robert. 1993. "The Illusion of Racial Equality: The Black American Dilemma." In *Lure and Loathing: Essays on Race, Identity and the Ambivalence of Assimilation*, edited by Gerald Early. Penguin.

Steele, Claude. 2003. "Stereotype, Threat and African-American Student Achievement." In *Young Gifted and Black: Promoting High Achievement Among African-American Students*, edited by Theresa Perry et al. Beacon Press.

Stengel, Richard. Jan. 30 1995. *South African Marxist Joe Slovo*. New Republic.

Steumpfle, Stephen. 1995. *The Steel-Band Movement: The Forging of a National Art in Trinidad and Tobago*. The Press University of West Indies.

Stevens, Frank. 1984. *Alternative Publishing Co- Operative Limited*. Black.

Stocking Jr., George W. 1968. *Race, Culture, and Evolution: Essays in the History of Anthropology*. Collier-Macmillan Canada.

Stowell, Jay S. "Adventures in Methodist Education." *New York: The Methodist Book Concern*. 1922.

"Kisch, John & Map, Edward." *A Separate Cinema: Fifty Years of Black- Cast Posters*. New York: Farrar, Strauss, and Gerioux. 1992.

Strauss, Anselm, and Juliet Corbin. 1990. *Basics of Qualitative Research: Grounded Theory Procedures and Techniques*. Sage Publications.

Strauss, Leo, ed. 1997. *Jewish Philosophy and the Crisis of Modernity: Essays and Lectures in Modern Jewish Thought*. SUNY Press. https://doi.org/10.1353/book21440.

Stringfellow, William. "My People Is the Enemy: An Autobiographical Polemic." *New York: Doubleday & C0*. 1966.

Strom, Margot Stern, and William S. Parsons, eds. 1982. *Facing History and Ourselves: Holocaust and Human Behavior*. Intentional Educations.

Stuckey, Sterling. 1984. "'I Want to Be African': Paul Robeson and the Ends of Nationalist Practice and Theory 1919–1945." *Massachusetts Review* 6.

Sunahara, Ann Gomer. 1981. *The Politics of Racism: The Uprooting of Japanese Canadians During the Second World War*. James Publishing Lorimer & Co.

Suso, Lamin [Personal Communication]. May 1993.

Suzar. 1996. *Blacked Out Through Whitewash*. Vol. 1. Aldor Productions.

Syme, Ronald. 1971. *Toussaint the Black Liberator*. William Morris & Co.

CLEM MARSHALL

T

Tabata, I. B. 1974. *Imperialist Conspiracy in Africa*. Prometheus Book Company Company.

Tafari, Ikael. 2001. *Rastafari in Transition: The Politics of Cultural Confrontation in Africa and the Caribbean (1966–1988)*. Chicago, IL: Times Publications. Frontline Publishing Distribution Int'l Inc. and Miguel Lorne Publishers.

Takaki, Ron, ed. 1993. *A Different Mirror: A History of Multicultural America*. Little, Brown and Company.

Tani, E., and Kaé Sera. 1985. *False Nationalism False Internationalism: Class Contradictions in the Armed Struggle*. Seeds Beneath The Snow.

Tannenbaum, Frank. 1946. *Slave & Citizen: The Negro in the Americas*. Random House.

Tatum, Beverly Daniel. 1997. *Why Are All the Black Kids Sitting Together in the Cafeteria: And Other Conversations About Race?* HarperCollins.

Taylor, Arthur. 1993. *Notes and Tones: Musician-to-Musician Interviews*. Da Capo Press.

Terkel, Studs. 1992. *Race: How Blacks & Whites Think & Feel About the American Obsession*. Doubleday Publishing.

Thiong'o, Ngugi wa. 1983. *Barrel of a Pen: Resistance to Repression in Neo- Colonial Kenya*. Africa World Press.

Thomas, Alexander, and Samuel Sillen. 1993. *Racism and Psychiatry*. Carol Publishing.

Thomas, J. J. 1993. *The Theory and Practice of Creole Grammar*. London: New. Beacon Books, with Margaret Cezair Thompson. *From Kingston to Kenya: The Making of a Pan-Africanist Lawyer*. Dover, MA: The Majority Press.

Thompson, Robert Farris. 1984. *Flash of the Spirit: African & Afro-American Art & Philosophy*. Random House.

Tilahun, Wondimneh. 1979. *Egypt's Imperial Aspirations over Lake Tana and the Blue Nile*. Addis Ababa University.

Tillman, Senator. 1964. "The Congressional Record." In *White America: From Slave Ship to Ghetto Riots – What It Has Meant, for Two Centuries, to Be Black*, edited by Martin Duberman. In Signet.

Tompkins, Peter. 1978. *Secrets of the Great Pyramid*. Fitzhenry & Whiteside Limited.

Torgovnick, Marianna. 1990. *Gone Primitive: Savage Intellects, Modern Lives*. University of Chicago Press.

Tosh, Peter. 2000. "Davies, Omar." In *Reggae and Our National Identity: The Forgotten Contribution of Peter Tosh*. Pear Tree Press.

Touré, Sekou. 1978. *Sekou Touré. Panaf Great Lives*. Panaf Books. Serequeberhan, Tsenay. 1994. *The Hermeneutics of African Phiosophy:Horizon and Discourse*. Routledge.

Trachtenberg, Marvin, and Isabelle Hyman. 1986. *Architecture: From Prehistory to Post-modernism / the Western Tradition*. Harry N. Abrams.

TRC, and R. S. A. 1998. *Report of the Truth and Reconciliation Commission*. Hugh. *The Rise of Christian Europe*. GB: Thames Hudson, 1966.

Truth, Sojourner, and Nell In Irvin, eds. 1998. *Narrative of Sojourner Truth; a Bondswoman of Olden Time, with a History of Her Labors and Correspondence Drawn from Her 'Book of Life'- Also, A Memorial Chapter*. Penguin Books.

Tsomondo, Micah S. 1976. "The Zionist and the Apostlic Prophetic Churches in Zimbabwe: A Critical Conceptualization of Cultural Nationalism". *UFAHAMU. Journal of Religion in Africa*. African Activist Association VI, *no. 3*.

Turner. "Ike with Nigel Cawthorne." *Taking Back My Name: The Confessions of Ike Turner*. Virgin Books. 1999.

———. 1993. "Introduction." In Walker, David, edited by David Walker's *Appeal to the Colored Citizens of the World but in Particular, and Very Expressly to Those of the United States of America*. Black Classic Press.

Turner, Robin L. 1997. *Emerging Conceptions of Citizenship in South Africa: An Examination of Curriculum 2005*. IDASA.

———. 1992. *Richard B. Moore, Caribbean Militant in Harlem*, edited by Burghardt and Joyce Moore. Indiana University Press. https://doi.org/10.2979/2828.0.

Tutu, Desmond. 1982. *Crying in the Wilderness: The Struggle for Justice in South Africa*. William B. Eerdman's Publishing Company.

———. 1994b. *The Rainbow People of God: The Making of a Peaceful Revolution*. Doubleday Publishing.

Tyson, Timothy B. 1999. *Radio Free Dixie: Robert F. Williams and the Roots of Black Power*. University of North Carolina Press.

V

Vambe, M. T., ed. 2001. *Orality and Cultural Identities in Zimbabwe*. Mambo Press.

Van Dantzig, Albert. 1980. *Forts and Castles of Ghana*. Sedco Publishing Limited.

———, ed. 1985b. *Blacks in Science: Ancient and Modern*. Transaction Books.

———, ed. 1991. *Egypt Revisited*. Transaction Publishers.

———, ed. 1992. *African Presence in Early America*. Transaction Publishers.

Varley, Helen, ed. 1980. *Color*. Leon Amiel Publisher.

Vaziri, Mostafa. 1992. *The Emergence of Islam: Prophecy, Imamate, & Messianism in Perspective*. Paragon House.

Veal, Micheal E. 2000. *Fela: The Life and Times of an African Musical Icon*. Temple University Press.

Veecock, June [Personal Communication]. 1994.

Villarosa, Linda, ed. 1994. *Body & Soul: The Black Woman's Guide to Physical Health and Emotional Well-Being*. HarperCollins.

Vogel, Susan Mullin, and Mario Carrieri. 1986. *The Aesthetics of African Art*. The Center for African Art.

Von Trotha, General. "Quoted in Hochschild, Adam." *King Leopold's Ghost*. Houghton Mifflin. 1998.

W

Wade, Peter. 1995. *Blackness and Race Mixture: The Dynamics of Racial Identity in Colombia*. Johns Hopkins University Press.

Wadinasi, Sedeka, and Alhamisi. 1972. "Black Music: A Degenerating Art Form." *Ufahamu*. L.A.: African Activist Association *VII, no. 3, The Interdisciplinary Issue*.

Walcott, Rinaldo. 2003. *Black Like Who? Writing. Black. Canada*. Insomniac Press.

Walker, David. 1993. *David Walker's Appeal to the Colored Citizens of the World but in Particular, and Very Expressly to Those of the United States of America*. Black Classic Press.

Walker, James St. G. 1980. *A History of Blacks in Canada: A Study Guide for Teachers and Students*. Minister of State for Multiculturalism.

Walvin, James. 1993. *Black Ivory: A History of British Slavery*. HarperCollins.

Wangoola, Paulo [Personal Communication]. fall 2002.

Ward, Geoffrey, and Ken Burns. 2000. *Jazz: A History of America's Music*. Alfred A. Knopf.

Warner-Lewis, Maureen. 1996. *African Continuities in the Linguistic Heritage of Jamaica*. African Caribbean Institute of Jamaica.

Warren, Wini. 1999. *Black Women Scientists in the United States*. Indiana University Press.

Washington, Elsie B. 1996. *Uncivil War: The Struggle Between Black Men and Women*. Noble Publishing Incorporated.

Waters, Mary C. 1999. *Black Identities: West Indian Immigrant Dreams and American Realities*. Harvard University Press.

Weinberg, Eli. 1981. *Portrait of a People: A Personal Photographic Record of the South African Liberation Struggle*. International Defence and Aid Fund for Southern Africa.

Weisbord, Robert G., and Arthur Stein. 1972. *Bittersweet Encounter: The Afro-American and the American Jew*. Schocken Books.

Wells, Ida B., and Alfreda M. Duster. 1970. *Crusade for Justice*. University of Chicago Press. https://doi.org/10.7208/chicago/9780226189185.001.0001.

Wessels, Anton. 1990. *Images of Jesus: How Jesus Is Perceived and Portrayed in Non-European Cultures*, translated by John Vriend. William B. Eerdman's Publishing Company.

West, Cornel. 1993. *Race Matters*. Beacon Press.

"Indus Kush Khamit." *What They Never Told You in History Class*. Luxor Publications. 1983.

Wheeler, B. Gordon. *Black California*. 1993. *The History of African-Americans in the Golden State*. Hippocrene Books.

White, Garth. "The Development of Jamaican Popular Music." Pt. 2: Urbanization of the Folk: The Merger of the Traditional and the Popular in Jamaican Music. In *ACIJ (African-Caribbean Institute of Jamaica)*. *ACIJ Research Review*, (1). 1984.

Wiesel, Elie. 1986. *Night*, translated by Stella Rodway. Bantam Press.

———. 1995. *All Rivers Run to the Sea: Memoirs*. Schocken Books.

Wilcox, Roger Clark, ed. 1971. *The Psychological Consequences of Being a Black American: A Collection of Research by Black Psychologists*. John Wiley & Sons.

Wiley, Ralph. 1996. *Dark Witness: When Black People Should Be Sacrificed (Again)*. Random House.

Williams, Chancellor. 1976. *The Destruction of Black Civilization: Great Issues of a Race from 4500 B.C. to 2000 A.D.* Third World Press.

———. 1984. *From Columbus to Castro: The History of the Caribbean*. Random House.

———. 1994. *British Historians and the West Indies*. A&B Books Publishers.

———. 1994c. *Capitalism and Slavery*. University of North Carolina Press.

———. 1999. *Hebrewisms of West Africa*. Imprint Editions.

Williams, Patricia J. "The Alchemy of Race and Rights: Diary of a Law Professor." Harvard University Press, edited by Deborah *Picturing US: African European Identity in Photography*. New York: The New Press. 1994.

———. 1991e. *Black-On-Black Violence: The Psychodynamics of Black Self-Annihilation in Service of White Domination*. Afrikan World Infosystems.

———. 1992c. *Understanding Black Adolescent Male Violence: Its Remediation and Prevention*. Afrikan World InfoSystems.

———. 1993d. *Awakening the Natural Genius of Black Children*. Afrikan World Infosystems.

———. 1993e. *The Falsification of Afrikan Consciousness: Eurocentric History, Psychiatry and the Politics of White Supremacy*. Afrikan World InfoSystems.

———. 1998. *A Moral Political and Economic Imperative for the Twenty-First Century*. New York: Afrikan World InfoSystems. Blueprint Publishers for Black.

Wilson, Harriet E. 1983. *Our Nig; or, Sketches from the Life of a Free Black*. Random House.

Winfrey, Oprah. 1987. "Quoted." In *Oprah: Her Remarkable Life Story, an Unauthorized Biography*, edited by Norman King. William Morrow.

Wingerson, Lois. 1991. *Mapping Our Genes: The Genome Project and the Future of Medicine*. Penguin Books.

Winks, Robin. 1972. *The Blacks in Canada: A History*. McGill-Queen's University Press.

Wolfenstein, Eugene Victor. 1993. *The Victims of Democracy: Malcolm X and the Black Revolution*. Guilford Press.

Wong, Milton. 2000. "Chancellor of Simon Fraser University." *Chinese World Magazine* 1 (2).

Wood, Joe, ed. "Malcolm X in Our Own Image." *New*. St. Martin's Press. 1992, Bobby. "Let's Talk 'Indian': A Status Indian Suggests That the Vocabulary We Use to Describe Indians Only Serves to Oppress Them." *First Nations, A Global Dialogue* 17, no. 4 (1986).

———. 1969b. *The Miseducation of the Negro*. Associated Publishers.

———. "The Education of the Negro Prior to 1861." *Brooklyn, NY: A & B Books Publishers*. ca. 1995.

Woodward, C. Vann. 1966. *The Strange Career of Jim Crow*. Oxford University Press.

Woolson, Gayle. 1977. *Divine Symphony*. Baha'i Publishing Trust.

World Federalist Association. "The Campaign to End Holocaust and Genocide." *Jamaican Xpress*, Febr. 20 to March 20 2004.

Wright, Marguerite A. 2000. *I'm Chocolate, You're Vanilla: Raising Healthy Black and Biracial Children in a Race-Conscious World – A Guide for Parents and Teachers*. Jossey-Bass.

Y

Yankah, Kojo. 1987. *The Trial of J. J. Rawlings: Echoes of the 31st December Revolution*. Ghana Publishing Corporation.

———. 2001d. "Exodus: Rastafari, Repatriation, and the African Renaissance." In *A United States of Africa?* Pretoria, edited by Eddy Maloka. Africa Institute of South Africa.

———. 2002. *'Marshalling Memory in Self-Defence against Anti- African Racism: The Rastafari Colon, Panama-Kimberley, South Africa Connection.' Presentation for Black Ethnicity Month*. Panamá, Colon.

Yeboah, Samuel Kennedy. "The Ideology of Racism." *Hansib Publishing: GB*. 1988.

Yette, Sam. 1971. *The Choice: The Issue of Black Survival in America*. Cottage Books.

Z

Ziorklui, Emmanuel Doe. 1988. *Ghana: Nkrumah to Rawlings – A Historical Sketch of Some Major Political Events in Ghana from 1957–81*. Em-Zed Books Centre.

Zoeller, Fuzzy. Apr. 13 1997. "Finally, Woods, Zoeller Meet Face to Face." *Abilene Reporter-News*.

www.ingramcontent.com/pod-product-compliance
Lightning Source LLC
Chambersburg PA
CBHW040827300326
41914CB00058B/1231